I never hurt nobody but myself
and that's nobody's business
but my own.

BILLIE HOLIDAY

*It rankles me when somebody
tries to force somebody
to do something.*

JOHN WAYNE

Ain't Nobody's Business If You Do

The Absurdity of Consensual Crimes in a Free Society

Peter McWilliams

Prelude Press
8159 Santa Monica Boulevard
Los Angeles, California 90046
1-800-LIFE-101

ISBN: 0-931580-53-6

Editor: Jean Sedillos
Research, general manager, and savior: Chris GeRue
Typography, desktop publishing: Victoria Marine
Production: Paurvi Trivedi
Copy editing: Debbie Sidell
Desktop publishing: Leesa Chatlos, Pamela Duell,
Stephanie Horsley, Janet Stoakley, Carol Taylor
Proofreading: Lorraine Harrell, Kevin Martin
Computers: Perry Segal
State-by-state chart: Scott Ford, David Goldman
Author photograph: Christopher McMullen
Book and cover design: Peter McWilliams

A portion of this book was originally published in *Playboy*.

*Everything used in this book
is from public sources.
The stuff that's available publicly
is far more frightening
than a lot of people realize.*

TOM CLANCY

Contents

Part I. On Freedom

Part II. Why Laws against Consensual Activities Are Not a Good Idea

Part III. How Did Consensual Crimes Become Crimes?

Part IV. Consensual Crimes and the Bible

Part V. The Consensual Crimes—A Closer Look

Part VI. Questions Answered, Answers Questioned

Random thoughts on consensual crimes: essays on various aspects
of consensual crimes and personal freedom

Part VII. What to Do?

I was in prison
and you came
to visit me.

JESUS OF NAZARETH
Matthew 25:36

This book is dedicated, with love, to my favorite co-author, John-Roger, who has forgotten more than I'll ever know about freedom.

⚖ ⚖ ⚖

And to the more than 350,000 people in jail for "crimes" that did not physically harm the person or property of another.

Perhaps the sentiments
contained in the following pages,
are not yet sufficiently fashionable
to procure them general favor;
a long habit of
not thinking a thing wrong,
gives it a superficial appearance
of being right,
and raises at first
a formidable outcry
in defence of custom.
But the tumult soon subsides.

THOMAS PAINE
Common Sense
January 1776

Ain't Nobody's Business If You Do

The Absurdity
of Consensual Crimes
in a Free Society

Introduction

> *Why doesn't everybody leave everybody else the hell alone?*
>
> JIMMY DURANTE

THIS IS A BOOK ABOUT FREEDOM—the freedom to discover who we are and what we want, the freedom to live our own lives.

The one idea behind the book is this: *You should be allowed to do whatever you want with your own person and property, as long as you don't physically harm the person or property of another.*

Simple. Seemingly guaranteed to us by that remarkable document known as the Bill of Rights. And yet, and yet—it's not the way things are in our time.

Roughly *half* of the arrests and court cases in the United States each year involve consensual crimes—actions that are against the law, but directly harm no one's person or property except, possibly, the "criminal's."

More than 350,000 people are in jail *right now* because of something they did, something that did *not* physically harm the person or property of another. In addition, more than 1,500,000 people are on parole or probation for consensual crimes. Further, more than 4,000,000 people are arrested *each year* for doing something that hurts no one but, potentially, themselves.

The injustice doesn't end there, of course. Throwing people in jail is the extreme. If you can throw people in jail for something, you can fire them for the same reason. You can evict them from their apartments. You can deny them credit. You can expel them from schools. You can strip away their civil rights, confiscate their property, and destroy their lives—just because they're different.

As members of a society, we must draw a hard, firm line as to what *is* and what *is not* acceptable behavior, what *is* and *is not* moral. At what point does behavior become *so* unacceptable and *so* immoral that we tell our government to lock people up?

The answer, as explored in this book: We lock people up *only* when they

> *No loss by flood and lightning,*
> *no destruction of cities and temples*
> *by hostile forces of nature,*
> *has deprived man*
> *of so many noble lives and impulses*
> *as those which his intolerance*
> *has destroyed.*
>
> HELEN KELLER

physically harm the person or property of another.* Anything less than that is insufficient grounds for tossing someone in jail.

Contained in this answer is an important assumption: After a certain age, our persons and property belong to *us*. No one should be able to put us in jail no matter *what* we do to ourselves or our property—even physically harming them—as long as we do not physically harm the person or property of another.

Yes, if we harm ourselves, it may *emotionally* harm others. That's unfortunate, but not grounds for putting us in jail. If it were, every time we stopped dating person A in order to date person B, we would run the risk of going to jail for hurting person A. If person B were hurt by our being put in jail, person A could be put in jail for causing person B hurt. This would, of course, hurt person A's mother, who would see to it that person B would go to jail. Eventually, we'd *all* end up in jail. As silly as that situation sounds, it is precisely the logic used by some to protect the idea of consensual crimes.

If you look into the arguments in favor of laws against any consensual crime, they are usually variations of "It's not *moral!*" And where does the objector's sense of morality come from? His or her religion. Some claim "community values" as the basis of morality, but where does this set of community values come from? The sharing of a similar religion.**

To a large degree, we have created a legal system that is, to quote Alan Watts, "clergymen with billy clubs." Says Watts:

> The police have enough work to keep them busy regulating automobile traffic, preventing robberies and crimes of violence and helping lost children and little old ladies find their way home. As long as the police confine themselves to such activities they are respected friends of the public. But as soon as they begin inquiring into people's private morals, they become nothing more than armed clergymen.

Please don't think I'm against religion. I'm not. *Individual* morality based on religious or spiritual beliefs is wonderful. It can be an excellent guide for living *one's own life*. It is, however, a terrible foundation for deciding who does and does not go to jail.

---

*The finer points of this definition, and most of the "what about if . . ." questions are discussed in the chapter, "What Are Consensual Crimes?" While all rules have exceptions, please consider *not physically harming the person or property of nonconsenting others* as the basic definition of activities which should *not* be crimes.

**For those laws that are primarily based on the rules of society and not the rules of religion, please see the chapter, "Separation of Society and State."

If people physically harm your person or your property, they go to jail. If not, they don't. Every other behavior we would *like* them to follow must be accomplished through education or persuasion—not force of law.

In exchange for extending this tolerance to others, we know that unless we physically harm another's person or property, we will not be put in jail. This assurance gives us the boundaries within which we can live our lives. It allows us to explore, to take risks and—as long as we risk only our own person and property—we know that at least we won't be taking the risk of going to jail.

> *That which we call sin in others
> is experiment for us.*
>
> RALPH WALDO EMERSON

With freedom, of course, comes responsibility. As we take risks, bad things will probably happen—that's why they're called "risks." At that point, we must learn to shrug and say, "That's life," not, "Why isn't there a law against this? Why isn't the government protecting me from every possible negative occurrence?" When we consent to do something—unless there is clear deception or fraud—we become responsible for the outcome.

We must become involved, educated, aware consumers—and teach our children to be the same. Just because some activity is *available,* and just because we won't be thrown in jail for doing it, doesn't mean it is necessarily *harmless.*

If it's not the government's job to protect us from our own actions (and whoever said the government was equipped to do that when the government can't seem to buy a toilet seat for less than $600?), then the job returns to where it always has been: with us.

⚖ ⚖ ⚖

Consensual crimes are sometimes known as *victimless crimes,* because it's hard to find a clear-cut victim. The term *victimless crimes,* however, has been so thoroughly misused in recent years that, as a description, it has become almost useless. One criminal after another has claimed that his or hers was a victimless crime, while one public moralist after another has claimed that truly victimless crimes do, indeed, have victims. It seems easier to use the lesser-known phrase *consensual crimes* than to rehabilitate the better-known phrase *victimless crimes.*

What are the consensual crimes? Before listing the most popular ones, I want to point out that the regulators of our morality have spent a lot of money making them all sound *just terrible.* The propaganda against consensual crimes has tainted the very words, so that even reading them can make one uncomfortable.

On the other hand, the consensual crimes themselves have had nothing but word-of-mouth to get their message across. Considering the vast PR campaign against them, they've done pretty well: each of them seems to be flourishing.

> *It has been my experience that folks who have no vices have very few virtues.*
>
> ABRAHAM LINCOLN

Please keep in mind that I am not advocating *any* of the consensual crimes. Some of them are harmful to the person doing them. Others are only potentially harmful to the doer. Still others are simply life-style choices.

No matter how harmful doing them may be, however, it simply makes no sense to *put people in jail* for doing things that do not physically harm the person or property of another. Further, the government has no *right* to put people in jail unless they *do* harm the person or property of another. The United States Constitution and its Bill of Rights prohibit it.*

We all have the right to be different. The laws against consensual activities take that right away. Even if you don't want to take part in any of the consensual crimes, a culture that puts people in jail for consensual offenses is also a culture that will disapprove—forcefully, clearly, and oppressively—about something "different" you may want to do.

If we let *anyone* lose his or her freedom without just cause, we have *all* lost our freedom.

With this thought in mind, here are the most popular consensual crimes: gambling, recreational drug use, religious drug use, prostitution, pornography and obscenity, violations of marriage (adultery, fornication, oral sex, anal sex, bigamy, polygamy, cohabitation), homosexuality, regenerative drug use and unorthodox medical practices ("Quacks!"), unconventional religious practices ("Cults!"), unpopular political views ("Commies!"), transvestism, not using safety devices (such as motorcycle helmets and seat belts), public drunkenness, jaywalking, loitering, and vagrancy (as long as they don't become trespassing or disturbing the peace).

Even if you *don't* want to take part in any of the consensual crimes, working to remove the consensual crimes from the books has a trickle-down effect of tolerance, acceptance, and freedom for the things you *do* want to do. (This may be one trickle-down theory that actually *works*.)

While exploring the extremes of social prejudice, we can explore our personal prejudices as well. For example, when you read the list of consensual crimes, did you put them into categories? "Yes, these should be legal," or "No, these should not be legal"?** I suggest that, to the degree we want to put people in jail for what they

---

*If you are a citizen of a country other than the United States, this book still applies. The odds are that your country is a signatory of the United Nations Declaration of Human Rights, which also guarantees the freedom of individual expression.

**People often use the word *legal* too loosely. They fail to give sufficient thought as to what *legal* and *illegal* really mean. When we say about a given activity that it should be illegal, what we're saying is that, if someone takes part in that activity, we should *put that person in jail*. When it comes

do to their own person or property, to that degree we have some work to do on ourselves.

But this isn't just *my* idea. Here's how another person—a carpenter by training—put it: "Why do you look at the speck of sawdust in your brother's eye and pay no attention to the plank in your own eye? How can you say to your brother, 'Brother, let me take the speck out of your eye,' when you yourself fail to see the plank in your own eye? You hypocrite, first take the plank out of your eye, and then you will see clearly to remove the speck from your brother's eye."

> *My definition of a free society is a society where it is safe to be unpopular.*
>
> ADLAI E. STEVENSON

That, of course, was said by Jesus of Nazareth, that dear man most people use as the authority to "lock the bastards up."*

The fact that his idea would be so controversial 2,000 years later, and more than 200 years after we formed a government based on "life, liberty and the pursuit of happiness," shows how much work we have to do.

⚖️ ⚖️ ⚖️

Here's the condensed list of reasons why having laws against consensual activities is not a good idea (each point has a chapter of its own later in the book):

It's Un-American! America is based on personal freedom and the strength of diversity, not on unnecessary limitation and slavish conformity. The American dream is that we are all free to live our lives as we see fit, providing we do not physically harm the person or property of another.

It's Unconstitutional. The United States Constitution and its Bill of Rights *clearly* give us the right to pursue our lives without the forced intervention of moralists, do-gooders, and busybodies.

Laws against consensual activities violate the separation of church and state. The Constitution guarantees us that not only can we freely practice the religion of our choice, but also that the government will not impose religion upon us. Almost all the arguments in favor of maintaining laws against consensual activities have a religious foundation. (The prohibitions against drugs, for example, grew directly from the evangelical revivals of the 1820s and 1830s. These same revivals gave us Prohibition in the 1920s.) The government is then asked to enforce these religious beliefs by arresting the nonbelievers and putting them in jail. As I

to consensual crimes, when people say, "It should be illegal," what they usually mean is, "That's not right," "That's not a good idea," or "That's immoral." When using the word *illegal*, it's important to remember how *forceful* the force of law truly is. We are all entitled, of course, to our *opinions* about certain activities, but do we *really* want to lock people up who don't go along with our opinions?

*Those who have their Bibles handy can read all about it in Matthew 7:3–5 and Luke 6:41–42. Much more on people's misrepresentation of Jesus in Part IV, "Consensual Crimes and the Bible."

already mentioned, as good as religious beliefs may be for running one's *personal* life, they are a very bad basis for deciding who should and should not be put in prison.

Laws against consensual activities are opposed to the principles of private property, free enterprise, capitalism, and the open market. If everything thus far has sounded hopelessly liberal, here's a nice conservative argument: Our economic system is based on the sanctity of private property. What you own is your own business; you can give it away, trade it, or sell it—none of which is the government's business. Whether you make or lose money on the transaction is not the government's business (until it's time to collect taxes). This is the system known as capitalism. We recently fought (and won) a forty-five-year cold-and-hot war against communism to maintain it. For the government to say that certain things cannot be owned, bought, given away, traded, or sold is a direct violation of both the sanctity of private property and the fundamental principles of capitalism. ("Get the *National Review* on the phone! Tell them to stop the presses!")

It's expensive. We're spending more than fifty *billion* dollars *per year* catching and jailing consensual "criminals." In addition, we're losing at least an additional $150 billion in potential tax revenues. In other words, each man, woman and child in this country is paying $800 per year to destroy the lives of 5,000,000 fellow citizens. If we did *nothing else* but declare consensual crimes legal, the $200,000,000,000 we'd save each year could wipe out the national debt in twenty years, or we could reduce personal income tax by one-third, or we could buy President Clinton 100,502,513,000 Big Macs. Another economic high point: moving the underground economy of consensual crimes aboveground would create 6,000,000 tax-paying jobs.

Lives are destroyed. Yes, by taking part in consensual crimes, people *may* destroy their own lives. This is unfortunate, but it is their choice. The problem with making consensual activities *crimes,* however, is that the government moves in and *by force* destroys the life of the consensual "criminal." A single arrest and conviction, even without a jail sentence, can permanently affect one's ability to get a job, housing, credit, education, and insurance. In addition, there is the emotional, financial, and physical trauma of arrest, trial, and conviction. If any significant amount of jail time is added to this society-approved torture, an individual's life is almost certainly ruined.

Consensual crimes encourage *real* crimes. Because consensual crimes are against the law, taking part in them costs significantly more money than is necessary. In order to pay these artificially inflated prices, some of those who take part in consensual crimes go out and commit *real* crimes: mugging, robbery, burglary,

> *The government of the*
> *United States*
> *is not, in any sense,*
> *founded on the Christian religion.*
>
> GEORGE WASHINGTON
> 1796

forgery, embezzlement, and fraud. If the consensual activities were cheap, real crimes would decrease significantly. In addition, to someone who is regularly breaking a consensual law, *all* laws start to seem unimportant.

> *If we've learned anything in the past quarter century, it is that we cannot federalize virtue.*
>
> PRESIDENT GEORGE BUSH
> 1991

Consensual crimes corrupt law enforcement. Asking the police to enforce a crime that does not have a clear-cut victim makes a travesty of law enforcement. The law enforcement system is based on a *perpetrator* and a *victim*. In consensual crimes, perpetrator and victim are one and the same. Whom are the police supposed to protect? Theoretically, they arrest the perpetrator to protect the victim. With a consensual crime, when the perpetrator goes to jail, the victim goes too. It's a sham that demoralizes police, promotes disrespect for the law, and makes arresting real criminals more difficult. It's sad that the enforcement of laws against consensual crimes has turned one of the true heroes of our society, the honest cop, into an endangered species.

The cops can't catch 'em; the courts can't handle 'em; the prisons can't hold 'em. As it is, the police are catching less than 20% of the *real* criminals—those who *do* harm the person or property of others. There is simply no way that the police can even make a *dent* in the practice of consensual crimes. (Because consensual crimes have no victims, they are seldom reported to the police.) Even if the police *could* catch all the consensual criminals, the courts couldn't possibly process them. The courts, already swamped with consensual crime cases, simply can't handle any more. *Real* criminals walk free every day to rape, rob, and murder because the courts are so busy finding consensual criminals guilty of hurting no one but themselves. Even if the courts *could* process them, the prisons are already full; most are operating at more than 100% capacity. To free cells for consensual criminals, real criminals are put on the street every day.

Consensual crimes promote organized crime. Organized crime grew directly out of an earlier unsuccessful attempt to legislate morality: Prohibition. Whenever something is desired by tens of millions of people each day, there will be an organization to meet that desire. If fulfilling that desire is a crime, that organization will be organized crime. Operating outside the law as organized criminals do, they don't differentiate much between crimes with victims and crimes without victims. Further, the enormous amount of money at their disposal allows them to purchase the best police, prosecutors, witnesses, judges, juries, and politicians money can buy. And guess who finances some of those let's-get-tough-on-consensual-crime campaigns? You guessed it. Once consensual crimes are no longer crimes, organized crime is out of business. (The other major financiers of the crack-down-on-consensual-crime campaigns are the religious right, which finds it easier to raise money from its followers

> *We are so concerned to flatter*
> *the majority that we lose sight*
> *of how very often it is necessary,*
> *in order to preserve freedom*
> *for the minority,*
> *let alone for the individual,*
> *to face that majority down.*
>
> WILLIAM F. BUCKLEY, JR.

with fear and hate than with love. Organized crime and the religious right. Strange bedfellows.)

Consensual crimes corrupt the freedom of the press. Reporting on consensual crimes has turned a good portion of the media into gossips, busybodies, and tattletales. With so much *important* investigation and reporting to be done concerning issues directly affecting the lives of individuals, the nation, and the world, should we really be asking one of our most powerful assets—the free press—to report who's doing what, when, where, how, and how often with other consenting whom's?

Laws against consensual activities teach irresponsibility. If we maintain that it is the government's job to keep illegal anything that might do us harm, it implies that anything *not* illegal is harmless. Clearly, this is not the case. Cigarettes, for example, are perfectly legal and yet cause more problems, pain, and death than all the consensual and nonconsensual crimes *combined*. Either people must be taught that what is legal is not necessarily harmless, or our prohibitions must extend *at least* to cigarettes. The current hypocrisy practiced in our society is unjust, misleading, and deadly.

Laws against consensual activities are too randomly enforced to be either a deterrent or fair. If your chances of being caught at something are only one in ten million, that's hardly a deterrent. That's roughly the ratio between consensual crime participation and arrests. The fact is, the laws against consensual crimes provide almost no deterrent whatsoever. In fact, their very illegality sometimes makes consensual crimes fascinating, irresistible, and glamorous. The one person in ten million who gets caught, however, is not really a criminal, but a martyr—a victim of a society that refuses to face the fact that personal morality cannot be legislated.

Laws against consensual activities discriminate against the poor and minorities. In selecting which consensual activities should and should not be crimes, the views of the poor and minorities are seldom considered. Therefore, many consensual activities that the mostly white, male, heterosexual, affluent, Christian lawmakers have deemed illegal do not necessarily reflect the preferences or experiences of minority groups. Further, the laws against consensual activities are not uniformly enforced—the poor and minorities, for a variety of reasons, tend to get the brief end of the stick.

Problems sometimes associated with consensual activities cannot be solved while they're crimes. Some people take part in consensual crimes as a symptom of, or escape from, deeper problems. These problems are not easily addressed until we dispense with the irrational, illogical, and transparently inaccurate societal myth that *all* participation in illegal consensual activities is *always* wrong. It wasn't until after Prohibition, for example, that those who had real drinking problems could see, admit to, and do something about them. Maintaining the fallacy that participation in illegal consensual activities is *always* wrong keeps those for whom it *is* wrong from doing something constructive about it.

We have more important things to worry about. The short list of national and global problems more deserving of our precious resources includes: *real* crime (robbery, rape, murder—the chances are one in four that you or someone in your household will be "touched," as they say, by a violent crime

> *All men are frauds.*
> *The only difference*
> *between them is that*
> *some admit it.*
> *I myself deny it.*
>
> H. L. MENCKEN

this year), abducted children (more than 400,000 abducted children each year), insurance fraud (a $100 billion per-year problem that adds from 10% to 30% to all insurance premiums), illiteracy (one in seven American adults is functionally illiterate; one in twenty cannot fill out a job application), poverty (14.2% of the population—35.7 million people—live below the poverty level; a good number of these are children), pollution (all the pending environmental disasters cannot be summed up in a single parenthesis), our addiction to foreign oil (the Gulf War should have been called the Gulf-Standard-Mobil War), terrorism (the bombing of the World Trade Center was, in reality, a terrorist warning: the next time it might be an *atomic* bomb), AIDS (by the year 2000, the largest number of HIV-infected people will be heterosexual women), supposedly government-regulated but not-really-regulated industries (the $500 billion savings and loan bailout is an obvious example) and last, but certainly not least, the national debt ($4 trillion, and growing faster than almost anything in this country other than religious intolerance).

It's hypocritical. Cigarettes do more damage and cause more deaths than all of the consensual crimes *combined*. Each year, 300,000 people die as a direct result of smoking. And yet, cigarettes are perfectly legal, available everywhere, are heavily advertised, and cigarette companies are free to use their influence on both politicians and the media (and, boy, do they). How can we tolerate such hypocrisy in this country? We are, as Thomas Wolfe pointed out, "making the world safe for hypocrisy."

Laws against consensual activities create a society of fear, hatred, bigotry, oppression, and conformity; a culture opposed to personal expression, diversity, freedom, choice, and growth. The prosecution of consensual crimes "trickles down" into ostracizing, humiliating, and scorning people who do things that are not *quite* against the law—but probably "should" be. "They're *different;* therefore they're *bad*" seems to be the motto for a large segment of our society. We are addicted to normalcy; we seem to have a cultural obsession to "fit in"; even if it means we must lop off significant portions of ourselves, we must conform.

⚖️ ⚖️ ⚖️

> *The first thing to learn in intercourse with others is non-interference with their own particular ways of being happy, provided those ways do not assume to interfere by violence with ours.*
>
> WILLIAM JAMES

There's no need to accept the validity of *all* these arguments; the validity of any *one* is sufficient grounds to wipe away all the laws against consensual activities.

In this book, we will explore each of the consensual crimes, asking not, "Is it good?" but, "Is it worth throwing someone in jail for?" We'll explore the prejudice about consensual crimes—the very prejudices we have been conditioned to believe. You'll find that the number of lies within lies within lies is amazing.

Allow me to share a few horrifying facts:

- More people are in federal prison now for drug violations than the *total* federal prison population when Reagan first declared war on drugs in 1982.

- In fighting the war on certain consensual crimes—most particularly drugs and prostitution—we have lost one of our most precious rights: due process. In the past, the only way your possessions could be taken from you was if a court said so, after you had a chance to present evidence and tell your side of the story. This is no longer the case. Now, police, sheriffs, and federal law enforcement authorities can *at their discretion* take your house, car, other possessions, and money (including all you have in the bank, savings, and investments) if *they* determine that you used these assets for an "illegal act." In order to get your possessions back, you must go to court and prove that they were *not* used for breaking the law. (The money gained from these property seizures goes directly to the law enforcement agencies seizing the property. Hmmm.)

- In 1992, thirty-two officers from eight different government organizations stormed a house and killed a sixty-one-year-old man in front of his wife on his own property. According to the district attorney of Ventura County, California, the government was after his property. The government claimed that he was growing marijuana, but no marijuana was found. His property was worth more than $5 million, and in a briefing before the raid, documents were distributed to the officers showing not only the appraisal of the property they were about to attack, but the recent selling price of a nearby property. The organizations were the Los Angeles County Sheriff's Department, the Los Angeles Police Department, the Federal Drug Enforcement Agency, the California State Bureau of Narcotic Enforcement, the U.S. Forest

Service, the Jet Propulsion Labora-
tory(!), the National Guard, and the
National Park Service—which owned
the land surrounding the victim's
property and admits to wanting the
land.

- If people want to "get" you, they
merely have to call one of those toll-
free numbers and say that you're dealing drugs. If they *really* want to get you,
all they have to do is say that you're
dealing drugs to *children*. If they really,

> **PRESIDENT BUSH:**
> *If we speed up that turnaround
> on the asset forfeiture thing—
> well, I don't want to interrupt.*
>
> MAYOR OF BOISE, IDAHO:
> *Mr. President, you do
> whatever you wish.*

really want to get you, they'll say you're part of a cult that sells drugs
to children. If the police find *any* drugs—even prescription drugs not
in their proper containers or marijuana growing wild on your property—they can take your house, car, all assets, and take *you* to jail.
Try getting out of jail without a lawyer, and try getting a lawyer
without money.

- Also threatened is our protection against double jeopardy (being
tried twice for the same crime). In 1985, a fifty-year-old Florida man was
caught growing marijuana. He was convicted in a state court, served
a year in a state prison, and was released. In 1991, federal authorities
came in and tried him for a *federal* drug law, *using exactly the same
evidence* as had convicted him in the state court. He is currently serving life imprisonment in a federal prison without possibility of parole.

- In Michigan, more than 135 people are currently serving life sentences without possibility of parole for possession of drugs. In 1991,
the United States Supreme Court upheld one case in which a man
was serving a life sentence without the possibility of parole for having 1.4 pounds of cocaine in a shaving kit in the trunk of his car. (He
was stopped for a traffic violation.) The court ruled that, yes, it was
cruel, but not *unusual* punishment, and let the sentence stand.

- In Connecticut, if you sell someone drugs and he or she dies as a
result of using those drugs, you can be put to death. (HELPFUL HINT
TO DRUG DEALERS: Do not sell drugs in Connecticut to anyone who
looks even *remotely* suicidal.)

- In Georgia, a man committing sodomy (in this case, oral intercourse)
in the privacy of his own bedroom was arrested and sentenced to life
imprisonment. In 1986, the United States Supreme Court upheld this
sentence.

> Truth resides in every human heart,
> and one has to search for it there,
> and to be guided by truth
> as one sees it.
> But no one has a right
> to coerce others to act according
> to his own view of truth.
>
> MOHANDAS K. GANDHI

Responsibility is the price of freedom. So is tolerance. We may not *like* what others do with their person and property, but as long as they are not harming the person or property of nonconsenting others, we must permit them to do as they please. In this way, we guarantee ourselves the freedom to do as *we* choose, even though others may not like it, as long as we don't harm the person or property of another.

⚖ ⚖ ⚖

In the time it took you to read this introduction, 342 persons were arrested for consensual crimes in the United States.

Police attempt to arrest U.S. veterans during a political protest in Washington, D.C., July 28, 1932. When the police failed, General Douglas MacArthur used infantry, cavalry, tanks, and tear gas to drive the protesters out of Washington.

Resort to military force is a first sure sign
that we are giving up the struggle
for the democratic way of life,
and that the Old World has conquered
morally as well as geographically—
succeeding in imposing upon us
its ideals and methods.

JOHN DEWEY
1939

Author's Notes

> *Nobody can be
> so amusingly arrogant
> as a young man
> who has just discovered
> an old idea
> and thinks it is his own.*
>
> SYDNEY J. HARRIS

I'VE BEEN WAITING *years* for someone to write this book. If someone had, I wouldn't have had to. Since no one has, I did.

I have never worked longer or harder on a book.

Why did I do it? Why has Peter gone political?

Back at Allen Park High School, back in the wonder years of the sixties, I was—with astonishing regularity—suspended for things I had written (mostly harmless satires on the teachers). Wasn't this censorship? Yes. Was there no one to defend my rights? Yes. There was no one. (One thing they *didn't* teach us about in high school was the ACLU.)*

When I was eighteen, and again when I was nineteen, I was arrested for a consensual crime. No one likes getting caught, of course, and most people who get caught claim (a) they're innocent, (b) the law is unfair, or (c) both.

I stuck to (b): With all the *real* crime going on (Allen Park is a suburb of Detroit), didn't the police have better things to worry about than what I was doing alone or with consenting others?

In my middle-teens I had been caught shoplifting, and I felt just that: *caught*—I had done something wrong. I knew it was wrong; I did it anyway; and I got caught. I didn't like it, but it never occurred to me that laws against shoplifting

---

*In 1985, my alma mater called. It was inducting me into the Allen Park High School Hall of Fame. Could I *please* address the graduating class? The plaque read, in part, "in recognition of your outstanding contribution in [sic] the field of literature." I flew back to Michigan, and when I arrived they told me I had two minutes for my address. "That's not an address," I said, "that's a zip code." In my allotted two minutes of inspiration, I advised the students of the graduating class to do with a passion whatever it was they had gotten suspended for—in eighteen years, I told them, they might get into the Hall of Fame.

> *It is time for a new generation*
> *of leadership,*
> *to cope with new problems*
> *and new opportunities.*
> *For there is a new world*
> *to be won.*
>
> JOHN F. KENNEDY
> July 4, 1960

were unfair. Even though my victim was a big company, and even though there was no violence involved, I knew that some people, somewhere, owned the company, and my crime hurt them. But I *didn't* understand why activities that hurt no one but, potentially, myself should be illegal. I also didn't understand why, with shoplifting, I was never even arrested (just lectured and released), and with the consensual crime* I was not only arrested, but tried, convicted, and sentenced to two years probation. It seemed as though, if anything, it should have been the other way around.

From the mid-sixties to the early-eighties, although the subject of consensual crimes (mostly referred to as "victimless crimes") was occasionally discussed and a number of scholarly tomes were published (some of them quite good), a comprehensive view of the subject for "just folks" like me never appeared. (At least I haven't seen it.)

Once the "War on Drugs" was declared, however, *all* discussion stopped. One might as well have tried saying something good about Emperor Hirohito in 1942. ("Nice uniform!") Throughout the eighties, the media reported the drug busts and showed the stacked bodies of cocaine plantation workers. Nowhere did I hear anyone ask, "Who did these people hurt?" "Why are they being arrested?" or "Why are we so proud that these people are dead?" The wartime rhetoric against drugs reflected negatively on all consensual crimes. Intolerance escalated as quickly as "the war."

In 1988, when I co-wrote with John-Roger *You Can't Afford the Luxury of a Negative Thought: A Book for People with Any Life-Threatening Illness—Including Life*, I discovered that some people—including people that the medical establishment had given up for dead—could be put in jail for trying certain alternative therapies. Why? "Unapproved therapies might prove harmful." These are people *given up for dead* by the very people who do the approving!

I also learned that some people in advanced stages of life-threatening illnesses suffered needlessly because certain painkilling drugs were not available by prescription. Why? "Someone other than the patients might get a hold of the drugs and use them for recreational purposes." And what happens if the people in agony—or their loved ones—try to get these drugs on their own? Jail.

When I co-wrote *DO IT! Let's Get Off Our Buts*, I realized that by suggesting people fulfill their hearts' desires, I might also be suggesting that they break the law. For example, the millions of gay people in the United States have heart's

---

*I'm not being coy about what the crime was. I discuss it on page 226. For now, pick any one: the example works no matter which consensual "crime" I committed.

desires that—in many states—lie on the other side of the law.

The more I discovered, the more I was reminded of Rémy de Gourmont's comment, "The terrible thing about the quest for truth is that you find it."

I wondered: What should I do? Should I advocate letting people die because they can't get alternative treatment, or letting them die in agony because they can't get certain painkilling drugs? Should I advocate that people *not* fulfill their dream if it's against the law—even if fulfilling that dream physically harms no one else? These questions, and others like them, led to some serious thinking on my part.

> *Ye shall know the truth,*
> *and the truth*
> *shall make you mad.*
>
> ALDOUS HUXLEY

This book is a result of that thinking. It is also an unflinching look at how far the bigots of this world have gone, how much religious-based intolerance has become an accepted part of our lives, and what we can do about it.

This book is bound to be controversial. It asks simple questions, such as, "Shouldn't we, as adults, be allowed to do as we please, as long as we don't physically harm the person or property of another?" "If they're not hurting anyone, why don't we just leave them alone?" and "Don't we have more important things to worry about than regulating the personal morality of consenting adults?"

It's the sort of controversy that might have been caused by asking in 1773, "Why don't we break from England and start our own country?" or, in 1833, "Aren't slaves human beings and therefore entitled to their freedom?" or, in 1963, "Shouldn't Vietnam have the right to determine its own form of government?"

They're all variations of "The emperor wears no clothes."

As Bertrand Russell observed, "*Change* is scientific, *progress* is ethical; change is indubitable, whereas progress is a matter of controversy." To progress! "You say what you think needs to be said;" wrote Herb Lock, "if it needs to be said, there are going to be a lot of people who will disagree with it or it wouldn't need to be said."

One of the fears about discussing consensual activities is that if you defend a certain practice, you're often accused of *being* or *doing* that. Well, if you're wondering about me, why not assume that I *do it all?* Yes, just presume that I am a drug-selling homosexual prostitute gambler who drunkenly loiters all day with my six wives and four husbands, making and watching pornography while being treated by strange medical practices and running a cult on the side.

You can also assume my motives to be the darkest, most selfish, and pernicious you can imagine. No matter how many times I say that I'm not advocating *any* of the consensual crimes, someone will, of course, accuse me of "recruiting" for them *all*.*

---

*It's a classic example of projection: the religions that believe most in vigorous proselytizing are the

> *I don't make jokes—*
> *I just watch the government*
> *and report the facts.*
>
> WILL ROGERS

Although the subject is serious, this book is occasionally funny. My only defense for this is the explanation given by other prejudiced people throughout the ages: "That's just the way I am." Yes, I'm a prejudiced person. I am intolerant of intolerance. I have a bias against hypocrisy and a weakness for absurdity. I know if I lose my sense of humor about a subject for any period of time, I am truly lost.

Take Reverend Jimmy Swaggart,* for example. Every time he slammed his Bible on the pulpit, I knew ten thousand more consensual "criminals" were going to prison. When he was caught with a prostitute, he insisted it was the devil's work and asked his congregation to forgive him. Pretty standard Christian-preacher-hand-in-the-cookie-jar response. Not much reaction to that. When he was caught a *second* time, however, he told his congregation, "The Lord told me it's flat none of your business!" Now *there's* a funny statement. Amen, Brother Swaggart! I look forward to the day when I can be similarly amused by Pat Robertson and Jerry Falwell.

Call it a quirk in my personality. Call it a defense mechanism. But in my mind, things seem to go from bad to worse to absurd to funny. Then they start all over again. This, for example, is from the *1993 World Almanac and Book of Facts:*

> Dorothy Ries filed a $40 million lawsuit against Texas evangelist Robert Tilton, saying he continues to send solicitation letters to her dead husband, promising that God will restore his health.

If one could only remind Reverend Swaggart of Hyman Rickover's advice, "If you are going to sin, sin against God, not the bureaucracy. God will forgive you but the bureaucracy won't."

That's the trouble, of course: we have taken sins out of God's domain, where they can be forgiven, and put them in the domain of law, where they can only be plea-bargained.

Not only do we attempt to drag personal morality into the public arena; we put it into the hands of the least efficient organization on earth: government bureaucracy. "The only thing that saves us from the bureaucracy is inefficiency," Eugene McCarthy pointed out. "An efficient bureaucracy is the greatest threat to liberty." How inefficient is the bureaucracy? Well, in sunny California, my adopted home, the government spent four years and $600,000 to produce twenty-five drafts of a "wellness guide." What are some bureaucratic suggestions for

---

same ones that accuse others of recruiting. What they call "witnessing" and "testifying"—hence God's work—becomes "recruitment" and "brainwashing" when used by others, hence the work of the devil.

*As Henny Youngman might add, "Please!"

AIN'T NOBODY'S BUSINESS IF YOU DO

wellness? "Don't buy something you can't afford" and "Don't beat, starve, or lock up your kids." Or this letter, sent from the South Carolina Department of Social Services:

> "Your food stamps will be stopped effective March, 1992, because we received notice that you passed away. May God bless you. You may reapply if there is a change in your circumstances."

> *When we start deceiving ourselves into thinking not that we want something or need something, not that it is a pragmatic necessity for us to have it, but that it is a moral imperative that we have it, then is when we join the fashionable madmen.*
>
> JOAN DIDION

Increasingly, in utter desperation of a war lost, the enforcement of laws against consensual activities is being turned over to the military. You may recall then–Air Force Chief of Staff Curtis LeMay's 1965 comment:

> My solution to the problem would be to tell [the North Vietnamese Communists] they've got to draw in their horns and stop their aggression or we're going to bomb them into the Stone Age.

The first problem with this is that the military is not just a bureaucracy; it's a *heavily armed* bureaucracy. The lighter side of the dilemma is illustrated by this news item:

> When the army tested a new air-defense gun called the Sergeant York, which was designed to home in on the whirling blades of helicopters and propeller-driven aircraft, it ignored the chopper targets. Instead, the weapon demolished a ventilating fan on a nearby latrine.

The second—and more important—problem is the fact that in war, the first fatality is the truth. The second fatality is the civil rights of all "dissidents." How much farther can my jaw drop than it did as I listened to then–Los Angeles Police Chief Daryl Gates testify before Congress that casual drug users should not be arrested, but taken out and shot? His reasoning? The country is at war, and all who use drugs are traitors. A good number of people agreed with Chief Gates. It wasn't his drug comments; it was the Rodney King beating that brought him down.

This is a book about our loss of freedom.

It will probably be uncomfortable to read about. It's uncomfortable to write about. Alas, I know of no other road to freedom.

The price of freedom is eternal—and internal—vigilance.

And an occasional laugh.

Peter McWilliams

PART I

ON FREEDOM

What Are Consensual Crimes?

> *A wise and frugal Government,*
> *which shall restrain men*
> *from injuring one another,*
> *shall leave them otherwise free*
> *to regulate their own pursuits*
> *of industry and improvement.*
>
> THOMAS JEFFERSON
> *First Inaugural address*
> 1801

A CONSENSUAL CRIME IS any activity—currently illegal—in which we, as adults, choose to participate that does not physically harm the person or property of another.

The difference between consensual crime and *real* crime is that real crime physically harms the person or property of a nonconsenting other.

Does this mean that consensual crimes are without risk? No. Nothing in life is without risk. The sad or happy fact—depending on how you feel about life—is that we're all going to die. We don't like to face that reality in this country; it's one of our primary cultural taboos. We like to think that, *if only* we can keep ourselves and our loved ones *safe enough,* none of us will ever die. Obviously, this is not the case.

Life is a sexually transmitted terminal disease.

Consensual crimes are sometimes referred to as "victimless crimes." Every scoundrel committing a *real* crime has declared it a victimless crime, attempting to argue that a crime without physical *violence* is also a crime without a victim. Everyone who has been robbed with a fountain pen—or computer terminal—rather than a gun knows that's not true. Another group claiming protection under the victimless crime umbrella are those, such as drunk drivers, who recklessly endanger innocent (nonconsenting) others. Just because they didn't actually *hit* someone, it was OK that they were going 70 the wrong way on a one-way street. Not so. Meanwhile, all the intolerance mongers, attacking a *consensual crime,* maintained the crime *did so* have a victim. ("We're *all* victims!" is one of their favorite phrases.) Besides, it's hard to find *any* activity in life that does not, potentially, have a victim.

People who live in Florida may become victims of hurricanes; drivers of cars

> *Freedom is the right to choose:*
> *the right to create for oneself*
> *the alternatives of choice.*
> *Without the possibility of choice*
> *and the exercise of choice*
> *a man is not a man*
> *but a member, an instrument,*
> *a thing.*
>
> ARCHIBALD MACLEISH

may become victims of traffic accidents; and each time we fall in love we may become the victim of someone tearing the still-beating heart from our chest and stomping it into the dust of indifference at their feet. (Sorry, it's been a hard month.) Does this mean that we should outlaw Florida, automobiles, or falling in love? Of course not. It's not whether or not we are *victims* that puts such activities outside the realm of criminal law enforcement, but that we, as adults, knowing the risks, *consented* to take part in them. "Please know that I am aware of the hazards," Amelia Earhart wrote to her husband before her last flight, "I want to do it because I want to do it."

Consent is one of the most precious rights we have. It is central to self-determination. It allows us to enter into agreements and contracts. It gives us the ability to choose. Being an adult, in fact, can be defined as having reached the age of consent. It is upon reaching the age of consent that we become responsible for our choices, our actions, our behaviors. (*Nothing* in this book, by the way, refers to children. Children have not yet reached the age of consent. This book discusses *only* activities between consenting adults.)

A primary aspect of responsibility is *learning*. When facing a new opportunity, we ask, "What are the risks? What are the rewards?" After educating ourselves, we evaluate. Then we choose.

Sometimes we land on the sunny side of risk, and get the reward. Sometimes we land on the dark side of risk, and get the consequences. Either way, as responsible adults, we accept the results (sometimes kicking and screaming, but we accept them nonetheless).

Our society has decided, however, that some activities are just *too* risky, and that people who consent to take part in them should be put in jail. The laws against such activities create *consensual crimes*. Ironically, many activities far more risky than the officially forbidden activities are not crimes. Why should cocaine be illegal and Drano not? Whether snorted, swallowed, or injected, Drano is far more harmful to the body than cocaine. And yet Drano is available in every supermarket. *Children* can buy Drano. (To avoid suspicion, they might have to buy a few things with it—such as a dozen condoms—but no one asks, "What are you doing with this Drano? You're not going to *snort it*, are you?") There is also no "Drano law," which prohibits us from ingesting Drano. Nor is there an Omnibus Drano Act designed to reduce the international use and trafficking of Drano.*

---

*If you think this is some sort of far-out example, pushed beyond the point of absurdity just to make a point, allow me to quote Colin Campbell in the March 10, 1993, edition of the *Atlanta Journal and*

All the consensual activities that the government makes illegal must have *some* upside. People don't bother with things that have only a down-side. (In this way, consensual crimes are the government's way of writing a handbook for rebels, saying, in effect, "This is the latest thing we think should be illegal. Try it next.")

Another way of defining consensual crimes is this one from Hugo Adam Bedau:

> Government should allow persons to engage in whatever conduct they want to, no matter how deviant or abnormal it may be, so long as (a) they know what they are doing, (b) they consent to it, and (c) no one—at least no one other than the participants—is harmed by it.

> *A civilized society is one which tolerates eccentricity to the point of doubtful sanity.*
>
> ROBERT FROST

⚖️ ⚖️ ⚖️

Adults commit some consensual crimes on their own; others require at least one other consenting adult. Some consensual crimes go both ways. (Isn't that *just like* a consensual crime?)

- Gambling requires at least one other consenting adult. Gambling with yourself is legal, but not much fun.

- The recreational use of drugs can be done either alone or with consenting others; both are illegal.

- Using certain drugs for healing or regeneration without a prescription is usually done alone, but one sometimes needs a health practitioner ("quacks," as the government fondly refers to them) to recommend the substances.

- The religious use of drugs can be done alone, with others, and, by definition, probably requires God's consent too.

- Prostitution always involves another. (Paying yourself to have sex is a perfectly legal thrill.)

- Pornography has traditionally been enjoyed alone and, with the advent of the VCR, is becoming increasingly so. (Pee-Wee Herman, take note.) Nonetheless, with pornography, some consenting adults

Constitution: "Plaza Drugs never closes. But I was disturbed to hear how some of the homeless veterans who live in the jungle not far away buy Lysol there so they can cut it and ingest it in ways that make them very high and radically unhealthy." Lysol! My God! When Lenny Bruce appeared on "The Steve Allen Show" in the late 1950s and did a routine about children sniffing airplane glue, the audience's response was, "What an exaggerated concept, but we'll go along with it so we can enjoy the routine." What Lenny said about glue was true. I can only pray that I'm wrong about Drano.

> *Liberty exists in proportion to*
> *wholesome restraint;*
> *the more restraint on others*
> *to keep off from us,*
> *the more liberty we have.*
>
> DANIEL WEBSTER
> 1847

had to make it, other consenting adults had to manufacture it, and still other consenting adults had to sell it. (Since child pornography, by definition, involves children, and children, by definition, have not yet reached the age of consent, child pornography is a real crime, not a consensual crime.)

- Since the homosexual acts that are forbidden in half the states of this union—oral copulation and other forms of "sodomy"*—are exceedingly difficult to do alone (not that I've ever tried, you understand), we would have to put homosexual sex in the category that requires at least one other consenting adult. (For the most part, masturbation is not an illegal act. I wonder if the homophobic people of the world have considered the fact that *every* time a person masturbates alone, it is, by definition, a homosexual act.)

- Bigamy and polygamy (illegal everywhere), as well as adultery and fornication (selectively illegal—check your local listings), always require another.

- Unconventional religious practices often require other "cult members," not to mention the notorious "charismatic cult leader." If you want to be *truly* unconventional, you can make up your *own* religion, and practice it *all by yourself.* Again, seeking God's consent would seem to be in order. (Unless you decide that *you* are God. Ooooh. Kinky.)

- Similarly, unpopular political views are often held with other "radical, commie, pinko" comrades, all of whom consent to follow "the party line." Others study the issues on their own and create their own politics. (Dangerous!)

- The violation of helmet laws and seat belt laws are pretty much solo activities, but some "criminals" conspire to do it together.

- Transvestism, public drunkenness, loitering, jaywalking, and vagrancy all can be done alone or with others.

Why are these consensual activities considered crimes while other consensual

---

*Many people consider *sodomy* as only "anal intercourse." Not so. In most states that have sodomy statutes, sodomy includes oral intercourse too. If you've ever taken part in oral intercourse—actively or passively, with a member of your own sex or the opposite sex—many states consider you a *sodomite.* Welcome to the club.

activities are not? We'll explore that question in detail in Part III, "How Did Consensual Crimes Become Crimes?" but the answer in brief is *religious beliefs*. Almost all of the consensual crimes find the basis of their restrictions and prohibitions in religion. Even the idea that one *should* take good care of oneself has a religious base. ("The body is the temple of the soul.")*

> *Heterosexuals don't practice sodomy.*
>
> SENATOR STROM THURMOND
> May 8, 1993

Taking part in the consensual crimes, however, is not necessarily anti-God or even anti-religion. The prohibitions against certain consensual activities grew from a *misinterpretation* and *misapplication* of biblical teachings. (This thought is discussed in detail in Part IV, "Consensual Crimes and the Bible.") The fact is, however, that religious beliefs (or misbeliefs) are what most people use when choosing what is right or what is wrong *for themselves*. This is fine. It's when they try to bestow that system of right and wrong upon others—by force—that consensual *crimes* are born.

The argument that society prohibits consensual crimes to protect itself is almost instantly transparent. Any number of things that are far more damaging both to individuals and to society are perfectly legal. (These are discussed in detail in the chapter, "Putting the 'Problem' in Perspective.") Besides, society can protect itself: it doesn't need the government's help. (Please see the chapter, "The Separation of Society and State.")

Others argue that the "victims" of consensual crimes are those who love the consensual criminals, who watch with pain and horror as their loved ones take a toboggan ride to hell (with jet engines flaring). Here we return to the risk factor and the question of who, ultimately, is responsible. Falling in love is a risk. Lovers may become drug addicts, may gamble away all their money, or may join a cult. They may also leave you for someone else, leave you *not* for someone else, or just leave and not tell you whether there's someone else or not. (If they own a house, or have a long-term lease on an apartment, this indicates that they are more stable. They probably will not leave you. They will probably throw you out.) As the song goes, "there's a broken heart for every light on Broadway." There's also a broken heart for every romantic greeting card in the Hallmark store. Show me a heart, and I'll show you a scar.

Using the argument that having laws against consensual activities protects romantic relationships (sometimes known as "the family") perpetuates the illusion that, if it weren't for these consensual activities, we'd all fall in love once and live

---

*As Paul put it, "Do you not know that your body is a temple of the Holy Spirit, who is in you, whom you have received from God? You are not your own; you were bought at a price. Therefore honor God with your body" (1 Corinthians 6:19–20).

> *What do you get when you play country music backwards?*
>
> *You get your girl back,*
> *your dog back,*
> *your pick-up back,*
> *and you stop drinking.*
>
> LOUIS SAABERDRA

happily ever after. Like our denial of death, we deny the reality that, as stated by Lily Tomlin: "We're all in this alone."

But this book is not intended to bring you the shocking news that none of us is going to last forever, and that love is not even going to last as long as we do. It's to get consensual crimes off the books and into the arena of other low-, medium-, and high-risk activities that comprise the crazy-quilt of activities we call life.

Let us assume, however, just for a moment, that it *is* the job of the government to protect people from themselves and to protect innocent wives and husbands from being emotionally hurt by the self-destructive behavior of their spouses. Let's assume we *are* our brothers' keeper—whether our brothers like it or not. Is the best way to protect a wayward brother by seizing all his property and putting him in jail? Is this helping either the "criminal" or the people who love him? Would a wife *really* feel more secure knowing that her husband is safe in jail* and not running around with gamblers? Would a husband *truly* be happier living on the street, penniless, because the state accused his wife of selling marijuana, and tossed her in jail while seizing the house, car, and all their joint** assets?

"But what about the children?" some lament, "The children are the victims!" Children are too young to give their knowing consent; that, by definition, is why they are children. If children are genuinely being harmed, it is the job of the government to remove them from the harmful environment.

Children belong to themselves; they are not "owned" by parents. Parents or guardians are the *caretakers* of children until the children reach the age of consent. At that point, children become adults, and what they do with their person and property is their own business. Until that time, parents are legally responsible for the actions of their children. This does not, however, give parents the right to "do whatever they like" with their children in the same way that these parents, as adults, can do whatever they like with their possessions, property, or bodies. Parents are like the custodians of a large estate: eventually they must turn it over to its rightful owner and, until that time, they are bound to be good stewards. So, although parents may do with their own person and property whatever they choose, they do *not* have the same right when it comes to the persons and property of their children.

Certainly parents who continuously physically abuse their children should be kept away from those children. That *is* the law's business. It is not, however, the

---

*"Safe in jail." Now *there's* a contradiction in terms.

**No pun intended.

business of this book to define or even explore what is and is not a violation of children and childhood. As I mentioned before, this book deals with activities between consenting adults *only*.*

To put parents in jail, however, for things that they consent to do with other consenting adults, activities that do *not* directly involve children—their own or others—is counterproductive. Is a parent's possible "bad example" worse for the children than throwing the parents in jail, confiscating their money and property, and making the children wards of the state?

> *The United States ranks 13th on the Human Freedom Index. Twelve other countries are freer than the United States.*
>
> UNITED NATIONS

Children are one of our most precious resources. The environment some parents provide for their children is appalling; but it is ignorance, not consensual crimes, that causes bad parenting. Prenatal care in this country is a national shame; twenty-two other countries have lower infant mortality rates than the United States.** Every day, children *in this country* die of malnutrition and preventable diseases. These are enormous problems. The abuse and neglect of children, however, is a multileveled problem that will yield only to multilevel solutions. Pretending that the enforcement of consensual crimes is making that problem any better, when it is only making it worse, is short-sighted.

⚖ ⚖ ⚖

No matter how many adults consent to do something, this group of "consenting adults" does not have the right to harm the person or property of even *one* nonconsenting human being. Recognizing this fact avoids such tortured arguments as, "The two of us are adults and we consented to take this car, so that makes car theft a consensual crime." Unless they have the consent of the *owner* of the car, taking it is *not* a consensual crime, but a *real* crime.

Just because it's difficult to tell who the specific victim is or might be in a given activity does not necessarily make an activity a consensual crime. Shooting a bullet into the air in the middle of a city is not a consensual crime; it is a real

*Whenever people bring children into the argument of consensual crime between adults, I know that these people have exhausted all logical arguments and are reduced to emotional pleas. As George M. Cohan once said, "Many a bum show has been saved by waving the flag." Many a bum argument has been won by appealing to a person's natural tendency to protect the young. In discussing what consenting adults do that does not directly involve children, the argument is a cheap shot.

**Those who may try to argue that more children die due to America's "drug problem" might take note of the fact that the Netherlands has almost no drug restrictions and it has a higher percentage of children who live to be one year old than the United States. In fact, the punishment for drug crimes is more severe in the United States than in *any* of the twenty-two countries that have a lower infant mortality rate than the U.S.

> *Do what's right for you,*
> *as long as it don't hurt no one.*
>
> ELVIS PRESLEY

crime. The bullet *may* fall to earth and cause no damage. Nonetheless, it is still so *potentially* harmful to the person or property of nonconsenting others that it is still a crime. Not many people shoot bullets into the air, but many do hurtle 3,000-pound "bullets" down streets and highways while intoxicated. Just because one "gets away with it" and arrives at one's destination without physically harming the person or property of another does not make the very *act* of driving under the influence any less criminal.

Then there are the crimes that have so many victims the effect is hardly felt by any one of them. These include such real crimes as insurance fraud, pollution, and (gulp) tax evasion.

Just because certain acts do not involve *violence*, does not make them legal. As Woody Guthrie pointed out, "Some men rob you with a six-gun and some men rob you with a fountain pen." Whether the crime is committed with a gun or a fountain pen, if it is done without the consent of those being robbed, it's still a crime.

To avoid committing crimes, then, all we need to remember is what we were probably told when we were five: "If it's not yours, leave it alone." To which we might add, "If it *is* yours, you can do what you like with it, as long as you don't harm the person or property of another."

In all this discussion of crimes and victims is the matter of *innocence*. Here I mean *innocence* in the sense of "not consenting" rather than "not guilty."

If you are walking down the street and get hit by a baseball that someone intentionally dropped from a tall building, you are innocent. The person who dropped the ball is guilty of a crime and is responsible for all damage. He or she may not have *intended* to hit you, but the intentional dropping of a baseball from a tall building includes the possibility (in fact, the high probability) that the ball will physically harm the person or property of another. If you are playing second base, however, and get hit by a baseball, *you* are responsible, not the batter. When you consent to play second base, contained within that consent is accepting the possibility that you will be hit by a baseball. It comes with the territory.

Batters do not hit balls with the intention of striking players. In fact, batters try to hit balls as far *away* from opposing team members as possible. Although being hit by a baseball while playing second base is unfortunate, you are at best (worst?) only a victim of Newton's First Law of Physics: "If a body is moving at a constant speed in a straight line, it will keep moving in a straight line at a constant speed unless . . . *ouch!*" The batter may feel very bad about it, but the batter has committed no crime.

Although the physical harm done to you may be the same with either a dropped ball or a batted ball, in one situation you were innocent and another person was guilty of a crime; in the other situation, you were responsible because *you gave your consent*. (No, you didn't give the batter consent to hit you, but you consented to the risks of baseball.)

It *is* the law's job to protect innocent people from likely harm to their person or property. It is *not* the law's job to protect adults from the risks of their own consensual activities.

> *In framing a government, which is to be administered by men over men, the great difficulty lies in this: you must first enable the government to control the governed, and in the next place, oblige it to control itself.*
>
> JAMES MADISON

It is the law's job, for example, to reasonably insure that the food and drugs we purchase are pure and that the measurements are accurate. It is *not* the law's job to tell us when, where, how, why, or how much of this food or drug we should or should not consume. It is the law's job to see that the gambling it regulates—from casinos to the stock market—is fair, that all players have an equal chance. It is not the law's job to determine how much we can bet, how skilled we are, or how much we can afford to lose. The law should regulate *where* prostitution can take place, but not *that* it can take place.

As Arthur Hoppe wrote in the *San Francisco Chronicle,* September 2, 1992:

> In a series of dramatic raids last week, police rounded up a number of hardened jaywalkers. They will undoubtedly claim they've broken the back of San Francisco's notorious jaywalking ring. . . .
>
> Just as you might suspect. It's another case of creeping government paternalism. Even we most notorious jaywalkers endanger no one but ourselves. Once again, the government is out to protect me from me.
>
> This isn't the function of government. The government is a fictitious entity created by us individuals to protect ourselves from each other. I agree not to murder them in return for their agreeing not to murder me. Fair enough. But if I want to kill myself, that's my business.
>
> Unfortunately, this fictitious entity we created more and more takes on a life of its own. It pokes its nose into everything. . . . It tells me I'm too stupid to wear a seat belt and too careless to wear a motorcycle helmet. If I don't, it says, wagging its finger, I will be sent to bed without any supper. . . .
>
> The function of government is to protect me from others. It's up to me, thank you, to protect me from me.

(It might be good to note here that when jaywalking becomes *obstructing traffic,* then it becomes a crime. Until then, it's not.)

It may seem that if people were running around doing what they wanted, society would run amuck. Wouldn't this lead to all sorts of immorality? No. The need to be social, to interact, to be part of a *society* takes care of that. Let's explore the difference between personal and social morality.

> *Liberty is the only thing*
> *you cannot have*
> *unless you are willing*
> *to give it to others.*
>
> WILLIAM ALLEN WHITE

Personal Morality
Versus
Social Morality

> *Whether or not legislation is truly moral is often a question of who has the power to define morality.*
>
> JEROME H. SKOLNICK

SOME PEOPLE BELIEVE that consensual crimes should remain crimes because they are "immoral." It's too easy to respond, "No, they're not immoral!" To the people who find them immoral, they are and may always be immoral. That is their *personal* morality. But there is another kind of morality, *social* morality. Let's explore the differences between these two (or, as they used to tell us in school, "compare and contrast personal and social morality"). Here's my essay:

Personal morality is all those things that we *personally believe* will make us happier, safer, healthier, more productive, and all-around better human beings. It includes all the personal "rights" and "wrongs" we choose to believe. It is everything that we think will help us in our individual process of "life, liberty, and the pursuit of happiness." In a free society, we should be free to explore, experiment with, discard, or adopt *any* belief or activity that might enhance our lives, *unless* we violate social morality.

Social morality is not physically harming the person or property of another.

Our personal morality comes from many sources—religion, philosophy, good advice, family, culture, society, ancient wisdom, modern scientific thought, and many others. From the many beliefs about how to live, we *choose* the ones that apply to *our* lives.

Sometimes we choose consciously—we read a book, like one of its ideas, try it, find that it works, and choose to make it part of our lives. Other times, we choose by default. Our family (church, club, or whatever) has always done a thing a certain way and we continue doing it that way without any further exploration, investigation, or thought.

Our culture conditions us to be "good," and we either go along with that pro-

> *In a free society, standards*
> *of public morality can be measured*
> *only by whether*
> *physical coercion—*
> *violence against persons or*
> *property—occurs.*
> *There is no right*
> *not to be offended*
> *by words, actions or symbols.*
>
> RICHARD E. SINCERE, JR.

gramming or we challenge it and adopt other behavior that we personally find "more good." This collection of beliefs and practices forms our morality—our *personal* morality.

When a group of individuals comes together to form a society, however, there must be a way of deciding how personal morality fits into the social morality—what is considered "right" and "wrong" within that society. The framework of that society is determined by *how* this right and wrong is established.

In a *dictatorship* or *monarchy,* the dictator, king, or queen decides what's what. The ruler's personal morality *becomes* the social morality. Hitler didn't like the Jews? Get rid of them. King Henry VIII didn't like the way the pope was treating him? Then ban Catholicism and form the Church of England.

In a *totalitarian state,* a committee or ruling body of some kind decides what's best for everybody. (The populace seldom, if ever, has a chance to decide who is part of that committee.) The collective personal moralities of the committee members become the social morality. The result is very much like a dictatorship, except blander. ("A committee is a group of individuals who all put in a perfectly good color," Alan Sherman pointed out, "and it comes out gray.") In a totalitarian state, there is no one to blame—it was all done "by committee." Even the people *on* the committee can criticize committee actions. To whom can one complain? Oh, there's probably a form to fill out somewhere, a line to stand in, or a government building to write to. Totalitarianism can become tyranny by bureaucracy.

Some societies are based on religious or spiritual beliefs. The person or group whom the society deems to be most in touch with God, spirit, nature (or whatever represents the highest collective belief of the society) is put in charge. Moses consulted only with God before laying down the laws. Jesus did not take a vote among his disciples over points of theology or practicality. He simply told them the way it was, and the ones who didn't like it, left.*

In a *democracy* each person has one vote to cast and, hence, an equal say in the way things are run. In the Declaration of Independence, however, there is a catch to this democratic process: each person is endowed with certain "unalienable Rights, that among these are Life, Liberty, and the pursuit of Happiness." In other words, the right to life, liberty, and the pursuit of happiness cannot be taken away from an individual *even* by the democratic process. So, if 250,000,000 people agree that chartreuse is not the "right" color for hair, our form of democracy, nonetheless, guarantees the one individual who chooses chartreuse hair the free-

---

*See John 6:53–69, including this at 6:66: "From this time many of his disciples turned back and no longer followed him."

dom to go green. In this way, the collective personal moralities of even a majority of the people cannot dictate the personal moralities of the minority of people.

But where are the limits? If we say, "We were hungry and we stole food because we are entitled to life," or "Hitting innocent people with a stick is an expression of our liberty to wave a stick around," or "Joy riding in other people's cars makes us happy," then we obviously have a conflict. Where does our right to life, liberty, and the pursuit of happiness end?

> *Moral indignation is*
> *in most cases*
> *2% moral,*
> *48% indignation*
> *and 50% envy.*
>
> VITTORIO DE SICA

As the old saying goes, "Your freedom to swing your fist ends where my nose begins."

Another basic element of our government is the right to private property. Under *communism*, everything is communally owned. Under *socialism*, certain things are owned by the government and other things are not. Under *capitalism*, you own what you own until you sell it or give it away, at which point it is owned by someone else.

Our property, then, becomes an extension of ourselves. Property represents a certain amount of energy we invested in something, or a certain degree of good fortune we may have had. The energy is ours and the good fortune is ours, and the symbol of that energy or good fortune is our property.

So, to paraphrase the above maxim, your right to swing your fist ends where my window (television, model airplane collection, etc.) begins.

Something else we own is our *person*, that is, our body and all the things associated with it. One of the major precepts of our form of government is that, after a certain age, your body becomes your own. Yes, your parents created it, fed it, clothed it, and educated it, but, after a certain age, you are not *legally* bound by the wishes of your parents. This idea is radically different from the beliefs of those cultures which once held that children were the permanent property of their parents.

So, we own our bodies (after the age of consent) and we own our property, and what we do with them is our own business, as long as we don't physically harm the person or property of another. In exchange, we allow others the freedom to do with their person and property whatever they like, as long as they do not physically harm our person or property. This is the fundamental agreement under which everyone is guaranteed maximum freedom and maximum protection.

To ask if something is moral or not on a social level, we need only ask, "Is it physically harming the person or property of another?" If the answer is no, it's moral. If the answer is yes, it's immoral.

On the *personal* level, however, we must ask an even more intimate and funda-

> Without doubt the greatest injury of
> all was done
> by basing morals on myth.
> For, sooner or later, myth is recognized
> for what it is,
> and disappears.
> Then morality loses the foundation
> on which it has been built.
>
> LORD HERBERT LOUIS SAMUEL

mental question: "Will this action I want to take harm *my own* person or property?" Answering that question in all situations—and then attempting to act accordingly—should keep us so busy that we don't have time to worry about what other people (especially strangers) are doing with and about their own personal morality.

At times we may *seem* to be physically harming ourselves. We know, in fact, that we are simply sacrificing momentary happiness for future gain. People jogging, for example, usually appear to be in pain. A compassionate person, not familiar with the jogger's greater goal, might stop and offer the jogger a ride. (And a couple of aspirin.) A person seeing a jogger for the first time might report to friends, "I saw this poor person running down the road wearing only shorts. There must have been some terrible accident."

Some caring souls, with the sincere goal of putting an end to pain, might suggest that jogging be outlawed. This group might show pictures of Jimmy Carter and George Bush looking *extremely* unhappy jogging and compare them to pictures of Eisenhower riding a golf cart or Reagan riding a horse looking extremely happy. As seemingly conclusive proof, the Anti-Jogging League could point out that the man who started it all, Jim Fixx, author of *The Complete Book of Running,* died at fifty-two while running. Jogging, obviously, is immoral.

Joggers, however, know that jogging, for them, is perfectly moral. They know that they are sacrificing a momentary pain for a greater gain. While they may never convince the nonjoggers of jogging's benefits (although, God knows, they try, they try), they're glad to live in a free country where their idiosyncrasy is tolerated. Although their scantily clad bodies and expensively shod feet may be considered an annoyance to some, they take their freedom and allow others the freedom to sit in doughnut shops and consume their daily dozen.

The problem of postponing immediate pleasure to attain eventual satisfaction becomes even more pronounced when we enter the world of religion. People may routinely and systematically deny themselves earthly pleasures in order to gain eternal paradise. If this is the belief of certain people, should the government step in and *insist* that they enjoy themselves more often? Conversely, if the believers become popular enough or powerful enough, should they be able to, by law, prohibit everyone from doing whatever the believers consider *too* pleasurable? The answer to both these questions—to preserve the rights of both the heathen and the holy—must be, "No."

The First Amendment of the Constitution guarantees us both freedom *of* religion and freedom *from* religion. This means that no one can stop you from practicing your religious beliefs and, in exchange, you allow others the freedom to practice theirs. The limitation? As usual, it is when another's person or property is physically harmed.

Religion can be an excellent basis for shaping one's *personal* morality, but in society we must exercise *social morality.*

That's the joy of a free society. Personal moralities that are diametrically opposed can co-exist, side by side, when each respects the social morality of not physically harming the person or property of another.

I'm not asking that any new system of government be adopted; I'm merely suggesting that we try the system we already have. As United States Supreme Court Justice Robert H. Jackson explained:

> *Give me chastity*
> *and self-restraint,*
> *but do not give it yet.*
>
> SAINT AUGUSTINE

> The very purpose of a Bill of Rights was to withdraw certain subjects from the vicissitudes of political controversy, to place them beyond the reach of majorities and officials and to establish them as legal principles to be applied by the courts. One's right to life, liberty, and property, to free speech, a free press, freedom of worship and assembly, and other fundamental rights may not be submitted to vote; they depend on the outcome of no elections.

What, then, is the relationship between society and the state? The same as the relationship between the church and state: separation.*

---

*Please see the chapter "Separation of Society and State."

The Enlightenment
or
We Were So Much Older Then;
We're Younger Than That Now

> *My people and I*
> *have come to an agreement*
> *which satisfies us both.*
> *They are to say*
> *what they please,*
> *and I am to do*
> *what I please.*
>
> FREDERICK THE GREAT
> (1712–1786)

IT WAS KNOWN AS the Enlightenment. Remarkable human beings shined the light of reason on areas of human endeavor that, for centuries, were kept in the darkness of dogma, indifference, and prejudice. Philosophy, anatomy, medicine, astronomy, music, physics, and even the most taboo subjects of all—religion and government—were explored anew. It was the time of Bacon, Locke, Descartes, Spinoza, Voltaire, Rousseau, Franklin, Jefferson, Swift, Kant, Sir Isaac Newton, Mozart and Beethoven.* The death of Beethoven—punctuated by lightning—marked the end of the Enlightenment.

Nothing would ever be the same again.

One of the great experiments of the Age of Enlightenment—an experiment that continues to this day—is the government of the United States. No less than Voltaire's *Candide* or Beethoven's symphonies, the Declaration of Independence and the United States Constitution with its Bill of Rights are masterpieces of the Enlightenment.

Helping to lay the foundation of the Enlightenment (also known as the Age of Reason) was John Locke (1632–1704). Locke was an Englishman who, due to his "treasonous" thoughts, spent a good deal of time outside England. When he began to explore government, he—like all good thinkers—started at the beginning. He asked: "Why should there be a government? What is the purpose of government?" These questions, *in themselves,* were considered treasonous. At that time, everyone *knew* that there was a government because God wanted it that

---

*Also of this period are Francois Boucher and Jacques-Louis David, who, respectively, created the paintings used on the front *(The Toilet of Venus)* and back *(The Death of Socrates)* covers of this book.

> *It is not only vain, but wicked,*
> *in a legislator to frame laws*
> *in opposition to*
> *the laws of nature,*
> *and to arm them*
> *with the terrors of death.*
> *This is truly creating crimes*
> *in order to punish them.*
>
> THOMAS JEFFERSON
> 1779

way. If God didn't want it that way, there wouldn't be a government. Since there was a government, that's the way God wanted it. Anyone who questioned further was guilty not only of treason, but heresy. The church and the state ruled together, by Divine Will. Anyone who questioned this arrangement questioned the authority of God. For such blasphemy, the law declared, one should be put to death. Many were. Nonetheless, John Locke asked his question, "What is the purpose of government?"

That he had the audacity to ask the question displeased the powers that were. The answers he discovered displeased them even more.

First, Locke concluded that all human beings are endowed with what he called *natural rights.* Human beings, individually, belonged to themselves. This notion directly countered the belief that one's body belonged to the state and that one's soul belonged to the church. One could be granted *privileges* from the state and purchase *indulgences* from the church, but the "rights of man," both here and hereafter, belonged to the state and the church.

Locke did not accept this. He argued that human beings had rights that were inherent in being human: If one were a human, one had these rights. Among many inherent qualities, humans had a head, limbs, the ability to breathe, to digest food, and, as Thomas Jefferson—deeply influenced by Locke—wrote a hundred years later, the right to "life, liberty, and the pursuit of happiness."

The idea that humans owned their own lives and had certain freedoms simply because they *were* was central to the Enlightenment. Locke's ideas were as radical as, oh, suggesting today that drugs and prostitution be legalized. The powers that were in Locke's day had a good thing going and had successfully convinced just about everyone that things were just the way they ought to be; anyone with any other ideas was a traitor, a heretic, and in league with the devil. The light of reason, however, penetrated this darkness, and a handful of great minds saw the logic and the fundamental *rightness* of individual liberty and natural rights.

If we are free, then, and if we have natural rights, why should we give some of these rights over to a government? The only reason for doing so, Locke explained in his *Two Treatises of Government* (1690), was that humans get more from the government by surrendering some rights than they would get by keeping them. Individuals enter into societies and form communities because *it serves the individual.* When society is entered into, one gives up certain rights with the understanding that one will receive as much or more in other benefits.

For example, a community of people might agree that, if bandits come, everyone will join together and fight off the bandits. Even if only *one* person in the community is attacked by bandits, the entire community agrees to rise up and protect that one member. In this way, each member of the community is giving away a natural right (the right not to risk your life to save someone else) for a benefit (protection from invaders).

Another example: Within the community, everyone might agree that what one grows or makes is one's own and cannot be taken away without one's permission. Being part of this community, then, means giving up a certain right (taking all you can) in exchange for a benefit (keeping what you've got). You agree not to take things from people weaker than yourself in exchange for knowing that you will not have your things taken by people stronger than you. For Locke, government was

> *Every tyrant who has lived has believed in freedom—for himself.*
>
> ELBERT HUBBARD

> for the regulating and preserving of property and of employing the force of the community in the execution of such laws, and in the defense of the commonwealth from foreign injury, and all this only for the public good.

Noticeably absent from this plan is religion. Prior to Locke, religion was used—sometimes for good and sometimes for ill—as the fundamental moral principle behind government. Protecting the country from outside invaders and protecting the person and property of the individual were often less important than the beliefs of the monarch's religion. During the 1600s, the regular alternation of Catholic and Protestant monarchs on the throne of England led to enormous suffering and waste. Locke saw firsthand the unfairness, impracticality, and downright unreasonableness of the state based on the ruler's religion. In his "A Letter Concerning Toleration," Locke began the process of separating church and state. A trained physician, he knew this would be a delicate, but necessary, operation. The letter was first published in 1689 and revised by him several times prior to his death in 1704.

Locke, who also trained for the clergy, did not attack religion. He used the arguments *of* religion to show that both church and state would, in fact, be better off apart. The state has its job; the church has its job; and, when both are left to do their jobs, everything is fine. It's when the government tries to do the church's job and the church tries to do the government's job that all sorts of mischief arise and freedoms are lost.

Just as he argued in *Two Treatises on Government* that an individual's body and property belong to the individual, in "A Letter Concerning Toleration" he argued that the individual's soul belongs to the individual, not the church. "The care, therefore, of every man's soul belongs unto himself and is to be left unto himself." Thus the basis for freedom of religion was established.

But what if a person is clearly off the path and headed for unhappiness in this lifetime and hellfire in the next? Shouldn't we do something to help that person? No, argues Locke, if we are compelled to help another, that help must be limited to *persuasion*. "It is one thing to persuade, another to command," wrote Locke; "one thing to press with arguments, another with penalties." If these wayward souls fail to heed our arguments and continue to harm themselves, placing their afterlife in danger, should we not physically alter their course? Absolutely not, Locke maintains.

> If any man err from the right way, it is his own misfortune, no injury to thee; nor therefore art thou to punish him in the things of this life because thou supposest he will be miserable in that which is to come.

The government, Locke explains, must have the power of physical force to protect people and their property from the physical violations of others. Using the government's physical power, however, to enforce a religious belief is thoroughly inappropriate.

> Let them not supply their want of reasons with the instruments of force, which belong to another jurisdiction and do ill become a Churchman's hands.

If we can't win people over to our belief in God by reason, we shouldn't ask the government to back up our inability to reason with physical force. This is unseemly, Locke maintains, both in the eyes of reason and in the eyes of God.

But what if we don't insist that people do things to save their souls? What if we only ask them to do things which are good for them in this lifetime? Don't we have the right to make people take good care of themselves in this world? No, says Locke. "No man can be forced to be rich or healthful whether he will or no." To which Locke makes a significant addition: "Nay, God Himself will not save men against their wills." Obviously, God *can* keep people from doing things that harm themselves in this life but, for whatever reason, does not do so. How dare we, as humans, presume to know more than God? By what arrogance do we interfere with other people's lives by force, when God chooses not to do so? In other words, far from *helping* God's work by using the force of government to enforce "His laws," our interference may be *hindering* that work.

Locke's thoughts on the separation of church and state and the purpose of government influenced the great minds that shaped the government of the United States. In 1825, while creating the University of Virginia, Jefferson acknowledged the authors who most influenced the American experiment:

> . . . that as to the general principles of liberty and the rights of man, in nature and in society, the doctrines of Locke in his essay concerning the true

original extent and end of civil government and of Sydney in his discourses on government may be considered as those generally approved by our fellow citizens of Virginia and the United States.

We'll explore in later chapters what Jefferson and the founding fathers did with Locke's enlightened work when we take a look at the Virginia Statute on Religious Freedom, the Declaration of Independence, and the Constitution. For now, as a preview, let's have one of the United States Constitution's Greatest Hits, the First Amendment, which hit number one on the charts in 1791:

> *Republic.*
> *I like the sound of the word.*
> *It means people can live free,*
> *talk free, go or come,*
> *buy or sell, be drunk or sober,*
> *however they choose.*
>
> JOHN WAYNE

> Congress shall make no law respecting an establishment of religion, or prohibiting the free exercise thereof; or abridging the freedom of speech, or of the press; or the right of the people peaceably to assemble, and to petition the government for a redress of grievances.

Isn't that beautiful? It's played a lot, but it's seldom heard. If it were, this book wouldn't be necessary.

⚖️ ⚖️ ⚖️

Enough 1791 nostalgia; let's fast-forward to some 1859 nostalgia.

What can one say about 1859 with respect to consensual crimes? "It was the best of times, it was the worst of times." That fits. Charles Dickens first published that in 1859, the opening line of his book *A Tale of Two Cities*. (He forgot to complete the line, however: It is the best of times and the worst of times, *all* the time.) Among 1859's "worst of times," the Supreme Court upheld the Fugitive Slave Act, which said that slaves who escaped to free states had to be returned to their "owners." (In 1857, the Supreme Court declared that slaves were property and not human beings.) Georgia passed a law in 1859 stating that slaves freed in wills were not free, and that freed slaves who went into debt would be sold again to satisfy the debt. Nevertheless, the hit song of the year was "I Wish I Was in Dixie's Land." (Away! Away!) Fundamentalists were infuriated by the publication of Charles Darwin's *On the Origin of Species*, but were comforted by the publication of "Nearer My God to Thee."

In England, the House of Commons finally seated its first Jewish member, Lionel Rothschild. Although elected two years before, he had been unable to take his seat because the oath of office insisted he proclaim his "true faith of a Christian." In 1859, Parliament reluctantly altered the oath. In Manchester, England, some were outraged at the opening of the world's first playground. Swings and horizontal bars,

> *We are all tolerant enough*
> *of those who do not agree with us,*
> *provided only*
> *they are sufficiently miserable.*
>
> DAVID GRAYSON

they determined, were far too dangerous for children, and should not be permitted. On the drug front, cocaine was first isolated from cocoa leaves, and the Great American Tea Company began selling extra-potent Chinese and Japanese tea at one-third the going rate. The latter venture was such a success, it became the Great Atlantic and Pacific Tea Company, and later simply the A&P. Fortunately, no one attempted to protect circus performers from themselves. Gravelet successfully crossed Niagara Falls on a tightrope, and, in Paris, Jules Lèotard demonstrated his discovery: the trapeze act. The song, "The Man on the Flying Trapeze" was written about him, and the shockingly tight tights he wore were named after him. The fact that women came to see more than his act shocked even Paris.

So, in 1859, while the United States was about to be "engaged in a great civil war, testing whether that nation, or any nation so conceived [in Liberty] and so dedicated [to the proposition that all men are created equal], can long endure," a major event in the history of personal freedom took place in England: John Stuart Mill published "On Liberty."

"On Liberty" was the first major writing since the Bill of Rights (almost seventy years before) to clearly delineate the relationship between the individual and the enormous powers of the state. Unlike Locke, Mill lived in an England where he could speak his mind freely without fear of treason. As long as he didn't, oh, call Queen Victoria "fat," he was fairly safe.

John Stuart Mill (1806–1873) was concerned. "That so few now dare to be eccentric," he wrote, "marks the chief danger of the time." It wasn't that people were being put in jail for consensual crimes that most concerned Mill; it was that the population as a whole carried these prisons around with them. People's fear of punishment for consensual crimes stifled personal growth, thus stifling the advancement of the culture.

> It is not by wearing down into uniformity all that is individual in themselves, but by cultivating it, and calling it forth, within the limits imposed by the rights and interests of others, that human beings become a noble and beautiful object of contemplation. . . .
>
> Where, not the person's own character, but the traditions or customs of other people are the rule of conduct, there is wanting one of the principal ingredients of human happiness, and quite the chief ingredient of individual and social progress. . . .
>
> In proportion to the development of his individuality, each person becomes more valuable to himself, and is therefore capable of being more valuable to others. . . .

The worth of a State, in the long run, is the worth of the individuals composing it. . . . A State which dwarfs its men, in order that they may be more docile instruments in its hands even for beneficial purposes—will find that with small men no great thing can really be accomplished.

Mill argues, then, that the real victims of repressive laws are not just the people caught and punished for violating those laws, but *everyone*—individually and collectively.

> *The policy of*
> *the American government*
> *is to leave their citizens free,*
> *neither restraining*
> *nor aiding them*
> *in their pursuits.*
>
> THOMAS JEFFERSON

The peculiar evil of silencing the expression of an opinion is, that it is robbing the human race; posterity as well as the existing generation. . . . If the opinion is right, they are deprived of the opportunity of exchanging error for truth: if wrong, they lose, what is almost as great a benefit, the clearer perception and livelier impression of truth, produced by its collision with error.

The solution? Discover your "own character"; become involved in "cultivating" and the "development" of your "individuality": follow your desires, as long as you do not physically harm the person or property of another.

Liberty consists in doing what one desires. . . .

So long as we do not harm others we should be free to think, speak, act, and live as we see fit, without molestation from individuals, law, or government. . . .

The only freedom which deserves the name, is that of pursuing our own good in our own way, so long as we do not attempt to deprive others of theirs, or impede their efforts to obtain it.

Is society responsible for the moral good of an individual? No, says Mill. "Each is the proper guardian of his own health, whether bodily, or mental and spiritual." Mill writes that one's independence over anything that "merely concerns himself," is "absolute. Over himself, over his own body and mind, the individual is sovereign." Mill writes, "Neither one person, nor any number of persons, is warranted in saying to another human creature of ripe years, that he shall not do with his life for his own benefit what he chooses to do with it."

What are the limits to all this free expression? "The liberty of the individual must be thus far limited; he must not make himself a nuisance to other people." Is this the loophole through which society can determine that any number of consensual activities are crimes? No, says Mill; there must be genuine "harm," "injury to others."

That the only purpose for which power can be rightfully exercised over any member of a civilized community against his will is to prevent harm to others. His own good, either physical or moral, is not a sufficient warrant. . . .

There should be different experiments of living, that free scope should be given to varieties of character, short of injury to others; and that the worth of different modes of life should be proved practically, when any one thinks fit to try them.

> *For why should*
> *my freedom*
> *be judged*
> *by another's conscience?*
>
> PAUL
> 1 Corinthians 10:29

What can society do to individuals who practice behaviors that society finds distasteful, but do not physically harm the person or property of another? "Advice, instruction, persuasion, and avoidance by other people if thought necessary by them for their own good, are the only measures by which society can justifiably express its dislike or disapprobation of his conduct." And what should be the individual's response to excessive advice, instruction, persuasion, dislike, and disapprobation? Mill suggests that "intrusively pious members of society" be told "to mind their own business." And he adds, "This is precisely what should be said to every government and every public, who have the pretension that no person shall enjoy any pleasure which they think wrong."

> There is a limit to the legitimate interference of collective opinion with individual independence: and to find that limit, and maintain it against encroachment, is as indispensable to a good condition of human affairs, as protection against political despotism. . . .

> If all mankind minus one were of one opinion, and only one person were of the contrary opinion, mankind would be no more justified in silencing that one person, than he, if he had the power, would be justified in silencing mankind.

Most-people-don't-like-it is, thus, insufficient ground for stifling unpopular thought or behavior. Protecting the minority's freedom is the purpose of government, not oppressing the minority for the comfort of the majority.

> The will of the people, moreover, practically means the will of the most numerous or the most active *part* of the people; the majority, or those who succeed in making themselves accepted as the majority; the people, consequently may desire to oppress a part of their number; and precautions are as much needed against this as against any other abuse of power.

As examples of the majority using force to control an unpopular minority, Mill cites no less than the lives of Socrates and Jesus.

> Mankind can hardly be too often reminded that there was once a man named Socrates, between whom and the legal authorities and public opinion of his time there took place a memorable collision. . . . This acknowledged master . . . was put to death by his countrymen, after a judicial

conviction, for impiety and immorality.

As to Jesus being sentenced to death for "blasphemy," and the men who took such an action, Mill says:

> The high-priest who rent his garments when the words were pronounced, which, according to all the ideas of his country constituted the blackest guilt, was in all probability quite as sincere in his horror and indignation as the generality of respectable and pious men now are in the religious and moral sentiments they profess.

> *In a civilized society,*
> *all crimes are likely to be sins,*
> *but most sins are not and*
> *ought not to be treated*
> *as crimes.*
> *Man's ultimate responsibility*
> *is to God alone.*
>
> GEOFFREY FISHER
> ARCHBISHOP OF CANTERBURY

For the pious who are unwilling to change their mind and who dismiss Mill's examples as ones that could not possibly apply to themselves, Mill makes this comment:

> Orthodox Christians who are tempted to think that those who stoned to death the first martyrs must have been worse men than they themselves are, ought to remember that one of those persecutors was Saint Paul.*

Mill rejects the idea that individual expression will lead to uncontrolled atheism, hedonism, and other ism's. Those who want us to be other than ourselves are the same people who think that "trees are a much finer thing when clipped . . . into the figures of animals than as nature made them." To the contrary, Mill claims that it is only by following our inner nature—the desires and instincts that God gave us—that we discover ourselves and truly begin to fulfill our divine purpose.

> If it be any part of religion to believe that man was made by a good Being, it is more consistent with that faith to believe that this Being gave all human faculties that they might be cultivated and unfolded, not rooted out and consumed, and that he takes delight in every nearer approach made by his creatures to the ideal conception embodied in them, every increase in any of their capabilities of comprehension, of action, or of enjoyment.

Amen.

---

*Mill knew his Bible. Paul, before his conversion, was a Jewish Pharisee and Roman citizen named Saul who persecuted the early Christians with the same zeal he later used to spread Christianity. Paul never met Jesus while he lived on earth. Much more on this in Part IV, "Consensual Crimes and the Bible."

Relationship

*Because of the diverse
conditions of humans,
it happens that some acts are virtuous
to some people,
as appropriate and suitable to them,
while the same acts are
immoral for others,
as inappropriate to them.*

SAINT THOMAS AQUINAS

WHEN WE USE the word *relationship*, we generally use it to describe how we relate to other people. When we want to *really* single someone out as special, we say, "We are in a relationship." That's the one that usually starts with "Some Enchanted Evening," and too often ends, "Another One Bites the Dust."

I'd like, however, to use the word *relationship* in the broadest possible sense: how we *relate* to everyone and everything—either mentally, emotionally, or physically.

Unless we are physically attacked, how we relate to something—our relationship to it—can cause more difficulties than the thing itself. With some things, we have good relationships; with others, we have bad relationships. When most of our relationships are going well, we say life is good; when most of our relationships are going poorly, we say life is bad. Things are neither good nor bad *in themselves*, but get a reputation for being good or bad based on how most human beings relate to them. Individually, we can have a good relationship with "dreadful" things, and we can have a bad relationship with "wonderful" things.

Iodine, for example, is neither good nor bad in itself. Taken in small quantities, iodine is an essential nutrient. Taken in larger quantities, iodine is a lethal poison. One could say people were in a good relationship with iodine if they had just enough but not too much; and one could say people were in a bad relationship with iodine if they had so little they had an iodine deficiency, or so much they had iodine poisoning. (Being dead from iodine would be a *very* bad relationship with iodine.)

We could have bad relationships with things that almost everyone agrees are good. Food, for example. Food is not only good, it's *necessary*. Some people are in a good relationship with food: they eat enough to keep alive, but not so much

> *I like white trash cooking.*
> *Cheeseburgers.*
> *The greasier the better.*
> *Mashed potatoes served in a scoop,*
> *a little dent in the top for the gravy.*
> *Drake's Devil Dogs for dessert.*
> *Pure pleasure;*
> *no known nutrient.*
>
> ORSON BEAN

that it endangers their health. Other people have a bad relationship with food: they eat so little, so much, or so much of the wrong foods, that it negatively affects their lives. Some health food advocates have a good relationship with their *own* food, but a bad relationship with *other people's* food. "Yuck! How can they eat such *garbage?*" they mutter, while munching raw carrots. For health-food addicts, it's not the food they eat, but their attitude toward other people's food that eventually eats at them.

Our lives are made up of both good and bad relationships: we may have a good relationship with our dog, a bad relationship with money, a good relationship with our health, a bad relationship with programming our VCR, and so on. There may be some things you have a good relationship with that most people have a bad relationship with (speaking in public, the IRS, airline food); and you may have a bad relationship with things that most people have a good relationship with (movies edited for television, lite beer, NutraSweet).

The idea behind laws against consensual activities is that if some people are in a bad relationship with something, then that thing should be banned. The problem with *that* solution is that it doesn't solve anything: the problem doesn't lie with the thing itself, but with some people's relationship to it.

Yes, there are some things with which it is easier to be in a bad relationship than others. Cigarettes practically *beg* for a bad relationship. But then, they were *designed* that way. For the several centuries prior to the Civil War, tobacco's use was primarily recreational: people would inhale it, choke, get dizzy, fall on the floor, roll around—typical Saturday night yuks. For the most part, people used tobacco (a botanical relative of deadly nightshade, by the way) once or twice a week, and that was it.

After the Civil War, the South needed a cash crop less labor intensive than cotton. A special strain of tobacco was developed that allowed people to inhale deeply without coughing. This let people smoke almost continuously, if they liked. It also resulted in almost immediate addiction.*

Almost everyone who smokes is addicted to tobacco. While there are many "social drinkers," there is almost no such thing as the "social smoker." Smokers begin smoking from the time they wake up in the morning and continue smoking regularly throughout the day until they go to sleep. The inability to "take it or leave it" is a clear sign of addiction.

---

*This is why Americans spend more each year on tobacco than they do on shoes, furniture, household appliances, prescription drugs, dentists, health insurance, higher education, air travel, or car insurance, and more than four times as much as they spend on flowers, funerals, or books.

AIN'T NOBODY'S BUSINESS IF YOU DO

Addiction is a sure sign of a bad relationship. At first, the addictive substance (or activity) makes us "high." After a while, however, the body builds up an immunity to the substance (or activity), and more and more is needed to achieve the same euphoric effect. Unfortunately, the toxic effects of the substance (or activity) eventually counteract the elation. At that point, we take the substance (or partake in the activity) more to get by than to get high.

> *I have every sympathy*
> *with the American*
> *who was so horrified*
> *by what he had read*
> *of the effects of smoking*
> *that he gave up reading.*
>
> LORD CONESFORD

A perfect example is caffeine. At first, caffeine produces extra energy, alertness, and a sense of well-being. The body, however, becomes immune to caffeine faster than almost any substance. Soon people are drinking coffee or Coca-Cola or eating chocolate (an eight-ounce bar of chocolate has as much caffeine as a half a cup of coffee) to get them back to "normal." ("You *know* I'm not myself until I've had my morning coffee.") Many marijuana smokers report that, regardless of the amount consumed, the highs of today don't seem to match the highs of yesterdays. ("I haven't had any good weed in *years.*") In fact, the body has become immune to the intoxicating effects of THC—marijuana's psychoactive substance. Once that happens, one just gets "stoned," not "high."

People can become addicted to (that is, form bad relationships with) many of the things we usually think of as "good." Some people become addicted to romance—not love or loving, but the initial rush of "falling in love." So many people become addicted to otherwise productive work that psychologists have coined a term for them: *workaholics.* Even the highest forms of attainment and attunement are not immune to the dangers of addiction, as Father Leo Booth explains in his book, *When God Becomes a Drug.*

> When, in the name of God, people hold black-and-white beliefs that cut them off from other human beings; when, in the name of God, they give up their own sense of right and wrong; when, in the name of God, they suffer financial deprivation; then, they are suffering from religious addiction.

No matter how good something is, it can become bad through a bad relationship. Conversely, no matter how bad most people think something is, some people can have a good relationship with it—without physically harming the person or property of others.

Many people would be surprised to learn that some prostitutes actually *enjoy* their work, consider the service they provide as valuable as that of any other professional, and are physically and emotionally healthier than some of those who claim, "All prostitutes are *sick* and spend their time spreading their sickness to others."

Cocaine (especially in its smokeable form, crack) is considered by many to be

> *Fanaticism consists
> in redoubling your effort
> when you have
> forgotten your aim.*
>
> GEORGE SANTAYANA

instantly and irreparably demoralizing, demeaning, and destructive. And yet, there are thousands upon thousands of people who have used cocaine regularly*—albeit recreationally—for years (in some cases, decades) and have managed to create great art, business empires, and, yes, even grow healthy children. Most people think heroin is the most addictive and destructive of drugs. It *is* addictive (although, according to former Surgeon General C. Everett Koop, not as addictive as cigarettes) and bad relationships with heroin *have* destroyed lives, but a good relationship with heroin or its less potent brother, morphine, is not impossible. Dr. William Stewart Halsted, one of the four doctors who founded the Johns Hopkins Medical Center and known as the father of modern surgery—a responsible, productive, well-respected physician and educator—took morphine daily for almost his entire professional life. Forty-seven years after he died, his secret came out. The only thing that made his relationship with morphine potentially unhealthy was the fact he had to keep it so hidden. This is not a rare story in the medical community.

And adultery is always wrong, right? Certainly no one in a position of social or political leadership—the one who sets an example for an entire people—should commit adultery. Right? Well, if history is anything to go on, that's not necessarily true. Accusations have been made, and some well documented by noted historians, that every United States president since FDR—with the possible exceptions of Harry S. Truman, Jimmy Carter, Richard Nixon, and Gerald Ford—have strayed from the sanctity of their marriage vows. Of the exceptions, Carter was doing it in his heart, Nixon was doing it to the country, and Truman was too busy playing either piano or poker.** (Ford was happy to be driven around in the Lincoln.)

Kennedy's pre- and in-office escapades must be some kind of record. He had more skeletons in the closet than the gay catacombs. According to FBI files, in 1942

---

*What is regular for one person is not regular for another; again, it depends on one's relationship to the drug. As with indulging in anything—exercise, sex, television, prayer—the time between indulgences is just as important to a healthy relationship as the indulgences themselves.

**In his autobiography, Clark Clifford revealed that one of his jobs in the Truman White House was arranging regular poker games. They included top government officials as well as visiting heads of state. One game was with Churchill. Truman ordered that he lose, but not lose big. Churchill lost $250. That's the equivalent of about $2,000 today. Truman considered that "not losing big." This gives you an idea of the stakes at these poker games. Although discussed in the book in a wink-wink those-were-the-good-old-days manner, the president of the United States regularly committed felonies with the heads of our own and of foreign governments. Can you imagine the president, the prime minister of England, and five other top-ranking government officials all arrested and jailed for gambling? Nonetheless, gambling arrests were common in the United States in those days, and they continue to be to this day.

he had a torrid affair with a woman generally believed to be a Nazi spy, Inga Arvad. The FBI bugging of their trysts revealed no spying, but a good deal of "sexual intercourse." (That's one of those technical FBI terms.) FBI files also reveal that Kennedy was married briefly when he was twenty-two, and his father, Joseph P. Kennedy, put pressure on two successive New Jersey governors (the state in which the wedding had taken place) to have the marriage removed from the records.* He was successful. Cardinal Spellman, a family friend, arranged for an annulment in 1952. The following year, he officiated at the wedding ceremony of Kennedy to Jacqueline Bouvier. Over the years, Kennedy was linked (so to speak) with Gene Tierney, Angie Dickenson, Jayne Mansfield (I am *not* making this up) and, of course, Marilyn Monroe. As Edie Adams wrote in her autobiography, *Sing a Pretty Song*, "I may be the only shapely, blonde female then between the ages of fifteen and forty-five who said no to JFK, but it wasn't because I wasn't asked." The story about Kennedy's affair with Marilyn Monroe while he was in the White House is now famous. When she became too demanding and threatened to become a political liability, Kennedy, like all good presidents, turned the "matter" over to his attorney general, Robert Kennedy, who filled his brother's, um, who took his brother's place. The stories of JFK's infidelities became such common knowledge that Bette Midler said in her act, "Guess what? *I* slept with Jack Kennedy! Guess what else?" she would ask, gesturing to her back-up singers, the Harlettes, "*They* slept with Jack Kennedy." Few people in the audience needed to have the joke explained. It is rumored that Kennedy was visited in the White House by Dr. Max Jacobson, who was later labeled by the tabloids "Dr. Feelgood" due to his propensity for giving his patients injections of amphetamines and other mood-elevating substances to cure anything from a cold to an impending divorce. After an investigation, he lost his medical license.** Who knows how many of Kennedy's staff were also "treated" by Dr. Jacobson while at the White House. Can you imagine? For three years, the fate of the world might have been in the trembling hand of an intravenous speed-freak that hovered over the great nuclear Button.

President Clinton had not one, but two scandals revealed during his campaign, but he was elected anyway. This demonstrates either the maturing of the American electorate or the country's utter frustration with Bush. (I like to think the

> *If we cannot end our differences, at least we can help make the world safe for diversity.*
>
> JOHN F. KENNEDY

*Kennedy senior once cabled his son on the election trail, "Spend as much as you need to, but don't get carried away. I'll be damned if I'll buy you a landslide!"

**Dr. Jacobson told Alan Jay Lerner about the Kennedy White House visits. Perhaps it is ironic—or perhaps not—that Alan Jay Lerner wrote the lyrics to the song most often associated with the Kennedy years, "Camelot," while speeding along under Dr. Jacobson's care.

former, but I fear it's the latter.) It turned out that Clinton smoked marijuana and may have had an affair with a woman named Gennifer Flowers (not necessarily, but not necessarily *not* at the same time). People, for the most part, shrugged and repeated the phrase from the 1960s, "So what if he's smoking flowers?" Happily, the electorate decided that Clinton's behavior in the State House was more important than his behavior in his own house, and he was elected by a broad margin.

The wave of "tell all" biographies (and autobiographies), so popular in the last two decades, has clearly shown that *everybody's* got a bad relationship with *something*. No matter how great, accomplished, successful, or magnificent a person may be in one area of life, there always seems to be that little dark corner he or she tries so desperately to keep hidden.

At first, these revelations about the heroes of our time seem as though they were written by editors of supermarket tabloids. "LORD LAURENCE OLIVIER AND DANNY KAYE WERE LOVERS!" After the initial shock and laughter die down, a surprisingly large number of these revelations turn out to be true. In his meticulously researched biography, *Laurence Olivier,* Donald Spoto revealed what Hollywood insiders had known for years: that for the entire decade of the 1950s, Kaye provided the nurturing, encouragement, and emotional support Olivier was no longer receiving from Vivien Leigh. (Scarlett O'Hara had become Blanche du Bois.) Did their indulgence in this "crime"* negatively affect their careers? No. All indications are that their careers were mutually enhanced by it.

What if their "crime" had become public knowledge? *That* would have destroyed their careers—and just about every other part of their lives. Danny Kaye would never have had his TV series, which ran for four years in the early 1960s after the affair had ended, nor would his exemplary work with the United Nations Children's Fund have been permitted. ("A *homosexual* with our *children?!*") Olivier's brilliant work in the last three decades of his life probably never would have happened; he never would have been made director of the National Theater, thus, it probably never would have gotten off the ground; he certainly wouldn't have been elected to the House of Lords. (Although there are certainly homosexuals in that august body, when the more-open-about-his-sexuality Sir John Gielgud was suggested for lordship, one person commented, "England already *has* a queen.") Spoto's book portrays Kaye as a deeply devoted admirer of Olivier and Olivier as, well, an *actor.* Like most performers, Lord Olivier's weakness was *praise,*

---

*At that time, homosexual acts between consenting adults—even between consenting *actors*—were illegal in all the places where the affair took place: England, New York, and California.

which just happened to be Kaye's strength.

Even the silly books, where rumor is reported as fact (Kitty Kelly with her "Kitty Litter" being the reigning queen of that genre), also lead to a giant "So what?" and a bit of tolerance for the variety of relationships of which human beings are capable. So what if Ron and Nancy smoked pot in the governor's mansion? Did Sinatra do it "his way" with Nancy in the White House? If so, so what? If so, the two of them should be the poster boy and poster girl for the Geriatric Sex Foundation.

> *I am an actor.*
> *Of _course_*
> *I can play a heterosexual!*
>
> SIR JOHN GIELGUD

The point being that people can have a bad relationship with some parts of their life (marital fidelity, for example) and still have a good relationship with other parts of their life (career, public service, and so on).

William F. Buckley, Jr., has taken daily, for thirty years, a psychoactive prescription drug known as Ritalin. Ritalin is prescribed to hyperactive children and lethargic adults. (It seems to calm kids down and pick adults up.) Mr. Buckley apparently has a good relationship with this drug. Anyone who knows him will tell you he has never, *ever,* experienced either of Ritalin's most common side effects: weight loss and irritability. Mr. Buckley, in his usual candor, freely admitted to his decades of daily usage. As Ritalin has for some people amphetamine-like effects, rumor got out that Buckley "took speed" every day. This is, of course, an exaggeration and oversimplification. When I asked him about this, Buckley wrote me:

> I hope you will have a chance to mention that what the doc said, after I had fainted (first and last time) was that my blood pressure is so low that I should either take a quarter pound of chocolate in mid afternoon, or a Ritalin. Big deal! I doubt, by the way, that a doctor would nowadays say that because some people are affected adversely by Ritalin. But after 30 years, nobody has detected any change in me, haahahahhhhhaaaaaaa, eeeeeeee, ooooooooooo-ooooooooooooooooooooooo oooooo! Now I'm feeling uiqte [*sic*] fine, as you can see.

Good relationships with drugs are possible without a doctor's prescription, and—as any doctor will tell you—bad relationships with drugs are possible even *with* a doctor's prescription. The point again: it is not the substance, but the *relationship to the substance* that causes problems. Attempting to control the substance in no way helps control the problem—in fact, it only makes the problem worse.

Bad relationships do not come from the *substance* being badly related to; they come from the *person* doing the relating. If someone is in a bad relationship with a substance, and you take the substance away, the person will find a new substance and enter into a bad relationship with it. There seems to be something in people who are in a bad relationship that requires—nay, *demands*—a bad relationship. The

> *Our relations with a good joke are direct and even divine relations.*
>
> G. K. CHESTERTON

substance is secondary—almost incidental—to the desire for the relationship. This transference of addiction can occur even when a substance is given up by choice. People who stop smoking, for example, will sometimes put on weight. They simply transfer their bad relationship with tobacco to a bad relationship with food. If you eliminate people's bookies, they'll take up with stockbrokers. Deprive people of coffee, and they'll turn to diet Coke.

People with *addictive personalities* use certain substances to manifest their addiction. In other words, addictive people are giving some innocent substances (and activities) a bad name.

Most people who condemn currently illegal consensual activities know little or nothing about them. All they know are the sensationalized media accounts designed not to educate, but *titillate*. Unless they take part in the activities themselves—or have close friends who do—most people have bad relationships with these consensual activities. The primary emotions seem to be revulsion and fear, which are born of ignorance. Revulsion and fear keep one from investigating and learning that there is nothing much to be repulsed by or afraid of. It is a closed loop of ignorance (ignore-ance). Bad relationships promote worse relationships. Worse relationships promote impossible relationships. Impossible relationships promote laws against consensual activities.

The unwillingness to see that "It is my judgment, based upon my ignorance, that is causing the problem" *is* the problem.

Most people, of course, do not *intentionally* set out to create a bad relationship. Most relationships initially start out good, and gradually—often imperceptibly—become bad. If, however, a formerly good relationship has turned bad and we don't realize it yet, no one has the right to throw us in jail for our lack of perception. If we do realize the relationship has become bad, and we choose to continue with it for whatever reason, no one has the right to arrest us for our poor choices. As long as our relationships don't physically harm the person or property of another, we are free to choose the things we relate to and how we relate to them.

ᘓ ᘓ ᘓ

People use all kinds of things for their corruption, but nothing corrupts everybody. Successful change takes place by changing the individual, not prohibiting activities or substances.

Prohibition: A Lesson
in the Futility (and Danger)
of Prohibiting

> *Prohibition is a great*
> *social and economic experiment—*
> *noble in motive and*
> *far-reaching in purpose.*
>
> HERBERT HOOVER

PROHIBITION (1920–1933 R.I.P.) was known as The Noble Experiment. The results of the experiment are clear: innocent people suffered; organized crime grew into an empire; the police, courts, and politicians became corrupt; disrespect for the law grew; and the per capita consumption of the prohibited substance—alcohol—increased dramatically, year by year, for the thirteen years of this Noble Experiment, never to return to the pre-1920 levels.

You would think that an experiment with such clear results would not need to be repeated; but the experiment is being repeated; it's going on today. Only the prohibited substances have changed. The results remain the same. They are clearer now than they were then.

Let's take a look to that not-too-distant-mirror of not-too-long-ago.

Prohibition did not strike suddenly; *zap*—one day you could get a drink and the next day you could not. It settled on the country gradually, county by county, state by state, for the better part of a century. National Prohibition in 1920 was simply the final turn of the spigot.

Alcohol was consumed in all the colonial settlements in America. No one was particularly against drinking—even the Puritans enjoyed it. What they frowned on was drinking to excess: drunkenness. This was of practical concern in the smaller communities: there were crops to plant, fish to catch, animals to trap, and a wilderness to be tamed. If one's excessive drinking got in the way of these activities, the community as a whole might suffer; thus, it was frowned upon and this frowning found its way into some early laws.

The first of them, in Virginia in 1619, through New Hampshire's law of 1719 were against *drunkenness,* not against *drinking.* The first law with a religious base was passed in New York in 1697; it ordered that all public drinking establishments

> *There are more
> old drunkards
> than old doctors.*
>
> BENJAMIN FRANKLIN

be closed on Sunday because, on the Lord's day, some rascals spent more time worshiping the bottle than the Bible. In 1735, the religious had a prohibition law enacted for the entire state of Georgia. The law was a complete failure and was abandoned in 1742.

For the most part, however, during the 1700s and early 1800s, those opposing liquor on religious grounds used preaching and persuasion rather than politics and laws to make their point. These efforts were known as the Temperance Movement, and its goal was to voluntarily temper use of spirits.

By 1820, complete abstinence from all alcoholic beverages was a basic rule of most evangelical churches. The intense revivalism of the 1820s and 1830s preached that alcohol was a tool of the devil and that Satan himself was in every drop. Moral campaigns to spread the truth about "demon rum" and other Lucifer Liquids to the poor, ignorant sinners raised huge amounts of money.

Never mind that Jesus' first miracle was turning water into wine at the wedding feast at Cana. Never mind that Jesus and his apostles drank wine at the Last Supper. Never mind that Jesus promised to drink again with his disciples in Paradise.* For anyone who had the impertinence to actually *read* the New Testament and question why wine (which was obviously not condemned by Jesus) should suddenly become such a wicked, evil thing, the preachers explained that the word for *wine* in the language Jesus spoke could also mean "grape juice" or "grape jelly." Jesus trafficked only in these, the preachers would say, not in wine. Those who doubted that Jesus turned water into grape juice at the wedding feast or that grape jelly was served at the Last Supper were considered infidels, heathens, and condemned to the fires of eternal perdition.

The rhetoric about drinking heated and became increasingly sentimental in the 1840s as former drunkards "saw the light," telling in pamphlet and speech the harm alcohol did to themselves and to the innocent members of their families. Booklets such as *The Reformed Drunkard's Daughter* told the heart-rending (or perhaps, more accurately, heart-*rendering)* story of a man who had not seen a sober moment in fifteen years. He suddenly woke up when, one cold, wintry day, his little daughter Hannah pleaded, "Papa, please don't send me for whiskey today." Yes, drinking was a crime, not just a crime against God and a crime against decency, but a crime

---

*Matthew, who was present at the Last Supper, quotes Jesus as saying (in chapter 26, verse 29): "But I say unto you, I will not drink henceforth of this fruit of the vine, until that day when I drink it new with you in my Father's kingdom." (That was the King James translation, which was used by the evangelicals in the early 1800s. The New International Version, favored by many evangelicals today, says essentially the same thing.) Both Mark (14:25) and Luke (22:18) also quote Jesus as saying this.

AIN'T NOBODY'S BUSINESS IF YOU DO

against innocent wives and children.

By the late 1840s, everyone who was going to be convinced by persuasion or fear of hell had already signed a temperance pledge. Some fanatics decided that this was not enough: *everyone* had to be sober *all the time* for their *own good* and the good of *all*. Temperance turned to prohibition and prohibition meant politics.

For some, alcohol *was* a problem. Some found the solution to their drinking through God, others through reason, others through

> *I once shook hands with Pat Boone and my whole right side sobered up.*
>
> DEAN MARTIN
>
> *There's something about me that makes a lot of people want to throw up.*
>
> PAT BOONE

medicine (Dr. Benjamin Rush, the Surgeon General of Washington's Continental Army, prescribed complete abstinence). But how to keep alcohol away from the rest? The answer: make it illegal to all. Put the full force of law behind it. Those who did not have a problem with drink, who could take it or leave it, were asked to leave it—permanently—for the glory of God and the greater good of all.

Maine went completely dry in 1851 and, by 1855, so had New Hampshire, Vermont, Delaware, Michigan, Indiana, Iowa, Minnesota, Nebraska, Connecticut, Rhode Island, Massachusetts, and New York. In some states, prohibition was declared unconstitutional; in others, it went virtually unenforced, but the primary setback to prohibition after 1855 was the Civil War.*

Then there was the aspect of alcohol that, due to its later abuses, we usually laugh about today: its "medicinal" value. At the time of the Civil War, however, alcohol was one of the most frequently prescribed—and the most effective—medicines known to doctors. (The Native Americans had some useful herbal concoctions, but they were not consulted.) No one quite knew *why* whiskey worked; they just knew it did. It was poured on external wounds to help them heal. It cured any number of internal maladies, including one that swept throughout the Northern troops dubbed "the Tennessee Quick Step" (later called "Montezuma's Revenge" by visitors to Mexico and "the Pharaoh's Curse" by visitors to Egypt). The germ theory would eventually scientifically explain the antibacterial, antiviral and antiparasitic nature of alcohol.

During the Civil War, the use of anesthesia was in its infancy. At makeshift battlefield hospitals, ether and chloroform were in short supply. Alcohol was not. Many an operation was performed—and a life saved—with the patient heavily "under the influence." Then there was the basic, overall good feeling produced by spirits, and the healing effect they could have on what we now call psychosomatic illness. If

---

*It's hard to keep alcohol away from troops in time of war. Thanks to the prohibitionists, whiskey in the U.S. Army was eliminated in 1830, but field commanders, at their discretion, could issue a "ration" of whiskey to each man—about four ounces. Private purchase and consumption of alcohol by military personnel, even in dry states, was condoned, and only drinking while on guard duty, on maneuvers, or just prior to battle was punished.

nothing else, alcohol eased the pain while nature did the healing.

Soldiers returning from the Civil War, many of whom were exposed to alcohol either recreationally or medicinally for the first time during the Civil War, wanted none of this talk about temperance. They had lived through hell and didn't want some "Bible thumper" telling them what they could and could not drink. There were also far more important issues to deal with in both the North and the South than who drank what where. Prohibition was put on the back burner.

> *My dad was the town drunk.*
> *Usually that's not so bad,*
> *but New York City?*
>
> HENNY YOUNGMAN

The cause came back to life in the 1880s. Women joined the fight, becoming politically active for the first time. A broad range of social reforms was demanded—banning tobacco, closing all theaters, labor laws, women's suffrage, and even socialism—but the only one that caught on was the proposal to close the saloons.

Saloons were seen as hotbeds of corruption, contagion, and vice. These male-only (except for "dance-hall girls") establishments were positive hell holes. Drinking, gambling, prostitution, political corruption, tobacco smoking, tobacco chewing (and its natural by-product, spitting), dancing, card playing, and criminal activity of all kinds were all traced to the saloon. Saloons were irresistible temptations to the otherwise righteous and virtuous men of the community. Invited there for a social drink by the "recruiters of Satan," the young men of the community found themselves hopelessly caught in a spider's web of immorality, lust, and depravity. Alcohol (a.k.a. the devil) was the spider at its very center. The Anti-Saloon League was formed, "an army of the Lord to wipe away the curse of drink."

One of the anti-saloon monthly magazines—very popular with evangelical churches—offered the following:

> "Come in and take a drop." The first drop led to other drops. He dropped his
> position; he dropped his respectability; he dropped his fortune; he dropped
> his friends; he dropped finally all prospects in this life, and his hopes for eter-
> nity; and then came the last drop on the gallows. BEWARE OF THE FIRST DROP.

If people were not afraid for their own life and the eternal damnation of their immortal soul, they should at least fear for the children. "In this age of cities, temptations about our youth increase, such as foul pictures, corrupt literature, leperous shows, gambling, slot machines, saloons, and Sabbath breaking. *We are trying to raise saints in hell.*" To these bulwarks of Prohibition ("Satan is drink" and "save the children"), the evangelical reformers added two familiar fears: racism and fear of "foreigners."

Stories of newly freed slaves drinking their first alcohol and raping white women were repeated again and again. Prohibitionists exploited the fear and hatred of the immigrants felt by many "Americans." The millions of "wretched refuse" and "huddled masses yearning to breathe free" brought with them the drinking habits of their homelands. Irish loved whiskey; Germans loved beer; Italians loved wine. That they were primarily Catholics in this primarily Protestant country only made the prejudice worse. If one could just get the bottle (or the beer stein or the wine glass) out of their hands, the immigrants would have a spiritual awakening, see God's true purpose for them, become Protestants and, *ipso facto*, good citizens.

> *Although man is already ninety per cent water, the Prohibitionists are not yet satisfied.*
>
> JOHN KENDRICK BANGS

As Paul Sann pointed out in his book, *The Lawless Decade*, "The Drys invariably found a way, however slick, to air the view that it was the immigrant much more than the 100% American who needed the splendid discipline of Prohibition."

By the 1890s, prohibitionists were prominent on school boards. Anti-alcohol material flooded the school house. Young children were asked to memorize this pledge:

> I promise not to buy, sell, or give
> Alcoholic liquors while I live;
> From all tobacco I'll abstain
> And never take God's name in vain.

High school biology books showed the physiological ruin a single drink caused the human body. Most of these children grew into staunch Prohibitionists. A few needed a drink.

By the turn of the century, more than half the state legislatures—dominated by rural Protestants—had declared their states "dry." The wet people within the dry states did not complain too much, however—there were loopholes. The primary loophole was this: since interstate commerce was regulated by the federal government and not by the individual states, one could order liquor by mail. As state after state became dry, the parcel post wagon jingled, jangled, clinked, and sloshed with increasing wetness.

This infuriated the Drys and, in 1913, the Interstate Liquor Act, which prohibited the shipment of alcohol into dry states, passed over President Taft's veto. This was a major coup for the Drys. Still not content, they used the anti-German feelings surrounding World War I and the association of Germans with beer ("the Kaiser's mightiest ally") to press for all-out national prohibition. In 1917, the Eighteenth Amendment to the Constitution was proposed.

The Prohibitionists got an unexpected boost from a strange quarter: disease. The influenza epidemic of 1918 killed 20 million people worldwide. This was more than twice the number of people killed worldwide during the four years of World War I; 548,000 died in the United States, the equivalent today of 1,500,000

> *Prohibition only
> drives drunkenness
> behind doors and
> into dark places
> and does not cure
> or even diminish it.*
>
> MARK TWAIN

people dying in a single year. Guess what the preachers blamed for this disaster? Sin, of course. God was punishing a wicked nation for straying from the path of righteousness. Only a great *moral crusade* could save the nation. Alcohol, as usual, was high on the hit list.

If the evangelicals had simply tempered their intemperance, they might have, over time, gotten more of what they wanted. By 1920, thirty-three states covering 63% of the population of the United States had already voted themselves dry. The Prohibitionists could have probably closed every saloon outside big cities and, by continuing to control the curriculum in the schools, might have created generation upon generation of teetotalers and moderate drinkers. If they had allowed people their mail-order hooch, beer, and wine, the Prohibitionists would have come closer to controlling alcohol use. But they got greedy.

As with all reformers who are aiming for "the perfection of mankind," one success is only the foundation for another campaign designed to perfect humans even further. That success leads to yet another campaign, and a series of unbroken successes leads inevitably to excess. Prohibition was one such excess. The Eighteenth Amendment was ratified by the necessary number of states on January 29, 1919; and, on January 29, 1920, Prohibition became the law of the land. The final turn of the screw came with the Volstead Act.

The Eighteenth Amendment only prohibited "manufacture, sale, or transportation of intoxicating liquors . . . for beverage purposes." Although this was the "supreme law of the land," it still required an Act of Congress to make it enforceable. Enter the super-dry, ultra-religious congressman from Minnesota, Andrew J. Volstead.

Many who supported the Eighteenth Amendment took the term "intoxicating liquors" to mean, well, *liquor:* whiskey, rum, and other distilled spirits. Most liquors were at least 40% alcohol ("eighty proof"); some, particularly of the "greased lightning" variety, were as much as 90%. Surely beer, with its 3–7% alcohol content, and wine, with its less-than-fifteen percent alcohol content, would be permitted—with certain restrictions and regulations, of course.

Much to people's surprise, Volstead, backed by the triumphant evangelicals, defined "intoxicating liquors" as any beverage containing more than *one-half of one percent* alcohol. Using the momentum of the anti-German, anti-beer bias, Volstead was able to pass his National Prohibition Act over President Wilson's veto. Understandably, many supporters of the Eighteenth Amendment felt betrayed.

Also feeling betrayed were many of the veterans returning home from World War I. Like the Civil War veterans, they had fought a brutal and bloody war. In

Europe, particularly in France, they had seen that moderate daily alcohol consumption and ordinary life could co-exist. Many learned that what they had been taught about the inherent dangers of alcohol was simply not true. Although expressed light-heartedly in songs such as "How Ya Gonna Keep 'Em Down on the Farm after They've Seen Paree," the disillusionment over what they had been taught versus what they had experienced ran deep. Coming home to find that the evangelicals, reformers, prudes, and blue noses had won a total victory embittered the veterans even more.

> *They can never repeal it.*
>
> SENATOR ANDREW J. VOLSTEAD

Oblivious to the discontent of many (or simply chalking it up to "the devil's last grumblings" on the issue), the Drys celebrated. "Hell will be forever for rent," declared evangelist Billy Sunday, who looked forward to an America "so dry, she can't spit." The Anti-Saloon League claimed, "Now for an era of clear thinking and clean living." A Long Island church leaflet crowed, "An enemy has been overthrown and victory crowns the forces of righteousness."

A religious belief had become the law of the land. Never mind that if Jesus tried turning water into wine in the United States, he could have been arrested for boot-legging, or that the Last Supper might have been raided by federal Prohibition agents. In exchange for giving up one of their basic freedoms, the people of the United States were promised great things by the reformers. The great things never came. As Herbert Asbury described in his book, *The Great Illusion:*

> The American people had expected to be greeted, when the great day came, by a covey of angels bearing gifts of peace, happiness, prosperity and salvation, which they had been assured would be theirs when the rum demon had been scotched. Instead they were met by a hoard of bootleggers, moonshiners, rum-runners, hijackers, gangsters, racketeers, triggermen, venal judges, corrupt police, crooked politicians, and speakeasy operators, all bearing the twin symbols of the eighteenth amendment—the Tommy gun and the poisoned cup.

⚖ ⚖ ⚖

Prohibition began easily enough: the people who drank stocked up on liquor before it was illegal; those who planned to give up drinking treated January 28, 1920 as though it were New Year's Eve, and the following day their New Year's resolutions began. The poor, who couldn't afford to stock up, were catered to by saloon keepers who, rather than closing voluntarily, stayed open until they were shut down. They moved their bottles from behind the bar to under the bar and continued with business as usual. It would take months to close them all down, and, after they were closed, many bought new booze and opened again. In an attempt to keep them from reopening, the federal authorities began destroying not just the liquor, but bars, fixtures and furnishings.

After a year or so, the reserves (and resolves) were depleted, and people got thirsty again—including some people who had never been thirsty before. The fact that alcohol was now *prohibited* made it somehow *irresistible*. There's always something tantalizing about forbidden fruit—in this case, the fruit of the vine.

> *I'm only a beer teetotaler, not a champagne teetotaler; I don't like beer.*
>
> GEORGE BERNARD SHAW

Once people wanted to drink, nothing could stop them. Good old American ingenuity came to the fore. By 1923, finding ways to "beat the feds" had surpassed even baseball as the national pastime.

- The saloons went underground and became speakeasies. There were lots of them. The 16,000 saloons in New York City, for example, became (depending upon whose estimate you believe) from 32,000 to more than 100,000 "speaks." Unlike the saloons, which were men-only institutions, the speakeasies welcomed women, and the women came.

- Supplying the speakeasies with the necessary beer, wine, and liquor required great organization. It was also a crime. Hence, the birth of organized crime. Paying off the local, state, and federal authorities required some organization too—and no small amount of money. Due to the outrageously inflated alcohol prices caused by Prohibition, money was no problem. In one year, Al Capone made $60 million (the equivalent of about $2 billion today) in liquor sales alone—plenty to go around, and it did.

- Mexico was wet, and Canada was far from dry. The border towns, both north and south, were well supplied with Canadian Club and José Cuervo.

- Anchored just outside the three-mile limit, lining both the Atlantic and Pacific coasts, were ships laden with spirits from other lands. (In all history, the only country to ever even *try* complete prohibition was the United States.) Some of these boats catered only to the professional bootlegger, but many would sell liquor by the case to the amateur rumrunners who either owned or rented boats. The rental of pleasure boats increased sharply during Prohibition.

- Beer brewing, wine making, and distilling became common practices in the home. An enterprising home brewer could make enough liquid refreshment to give as gifts or even sell. (When selling, of course, one had to be careful: one did not want to be caught by the feds or, worse, by the mob.)

- Grain alcohol was legal when sold for "industrial use only." With the right alterations, however, it became safe to drink and, with the right recipe, occasionally palatable. One could mix up a batch of this in the bathroom; hence, *bathtub gin.*

- The California grape growers, no longer permitted to make wine, produced a grape juice product known as Vine-Glo. The Vine-Glo literature carefully instructed buyers what *not* to do, because, if they did those things, they would have wine in sixty days. The demand for grape juice grew dramatically during Prohibition. (No doubt religious people, discovering that Jesus drank only grape juice, decided to follow in his footsteps.) In 1919, 97,000 acres were devoted to growing grapes for "juice." By 1926, it was 681,000 acres. In 1929, the U.S. government loaned the grape growers money to expand even further.

- Beer with an alcohol content of less than one-half-of-one percent (named "near beer," although many claimed that those who gave it that name were lacking in depth perception) was legal. In order to make it, however, one had to make regular beer and then boil off the alcohol. Every so often, somebody forgot to take that last step and real beer accidentally wound up for sale in speakeasies. (Oops!)

- All you had to do to stay entirely within the law was get sick. The Eighteenth Amendment only prohibited alcohol for "beverage purposes." Medicinal alcohol was perfectly legal and, for some unknown reason, doctors began prescribing more and more of it during the 1920s. In addition, various elixirs, tonics, and other patent medicines available over-the-counter without prescriptions relied heavily upon the medicinal qualities of alcohol. (Very heavily.)

⚖️ ⚖️ ⚖️

In a little more than a decade, the holy war called Prohibition was lost. In 1920, John F. Kramer, the first commissioner charged with enforcing Prohibition, somberly stated, "The law says that liquor to be used as a beverage must not be manufactured. We shall see it is not manufactured, nor sold, nor given away, nor

> *When I sell liquor,*
> *it's bootlegging.*
> *When my patrons serve it*
> *on a silver tray*
> *on Lakeshore Drive,*
> *it's hospitality.*
>
> AL CAPONE

hauled in anything on the surface of the earth or under the earth or in the air."

By 1931, it was all but over. A presidential committee reported the obvious: Prohibition was not working. Al Capone, the nation's premier bootlegger, was sentenced to eleven years in prison for the only crime they could prove he committed—tax evasion. By 1932, both presidential candidates, Franklin D. Roosevelt and Herbert Hoover, favored repeal.

Realizing that repeal was inevitable but would take awhile, Roosevelt had Congress amend the Volstead Act to permit beer with a 3.2% alcohol content. On December 5, 1933, the Twenty-first Amendment to the Constitution officially repealed the Eighteenth Amendment—the only time in the history of the United States that an amendment has been repealed—and Prohibition was history.*

It may have been history, but the effects of Prohibition lived on; some of them are still with us today. Here are the results of our country's "great social and economic experiment":

1. **It created a disrespect for the law.** Never before had so many otherwise law-abiding citizens broken the law—and had so much fun doing it.** If this law was so enjoyable to break, what other laws might be worth disregarding too? Many also concluded that *all* laws regarding alcohol must be worthless. "Who said I shouldn't drive when I'm drunk? I think I drive *better* after a few drinks. And who set these repressive speed limits anyway?" That was the sort of dangerous thinking fostered by Prohibition.

2. **It eroded respect for religion.** God and the Bible were used to justify Prohibition and, as Prohibition failed, it seemed to some as though the failure was God's. Some accurately concluded that it was the *misinterpretation* of the Bible by a handful of self-appointed interpreters of God's word that caused all the trouble, but many believed that the *interpretation* was correct and that *God* had failed. Did the evangelicals who caused the suffering and chaos admit that they had made a mistake? No. Prohibition's failure was simply a sign that "Satan never sleeps," and they were off prohibiting other things—drugs, prostitution, and "isn't it time we did something

---

*The Twenty-first Amendment allowed the states to choose for themselves whether or not they would be dry. Kansas chose to stay dry until 1948, Oklahoma until 1957, and Mississippi until 1966.

**The violations were astonishing. The flouting of the law had an auspicious beginning in 1920 with a still found on the farm of Senator Morris Sheppard. It was producing 130 gallons of whiskey a day. Senator Sheppard was the author of the Eighteenth Amendment. By the end of Prohibition, a San Francisco jury drank the evidence and declared the defendant not guilty. Midway through the experiment, federal law enforcement officers set up their own speakeasy in midtown Manhattan. It took them nine months to get caught, and when they did, they simply claimed that they were "investigating."

about these scandalous motion pictures? Have you seen the latest Mae West? Disgusting!"

3. It created organized crime. Prior to Prohibition, organized crime was nothing to speak of. Prohibition made the gangster not just well paid, but well liked. These aren't *real* bandits, the public thought, these are Robin Hood–like characters—blockade runners—who flout the law to bring us what we want. They were given cute nicknames like "Pretty Boy," "Legs," and "Scar

> *When a friend warned him that alcohol was slow poison, Robert Benchley replied, "So who's in a hurry?"*

Face." By 1927, Al Capone controlled not only all illicit commerce in Illinois—from alcohol to gambling to prostitution—but also the majority of the politicians, including most police commissioners, the mayor of Chicago, and the governor. By the end of the decade, organized crime was *so* organized that they had a national convention in Atlantic City. Who could forget Dutch Schultz from New York? Solly Weissman from Kansas City? The Purple Gang from Detroit? Even when the chairman of the board, Mr. Capone, took an enforced vacation in 1931 and Prohibition ended in 1933, the "company" did not go out of business. They simply found new merchandise and services to market.

The syndicate did not differentiate between crimes with and crimes without innocent victims. Once outside the law, their stock in trade became doing anything illegal—for a price. The "protection" racket preyed on honest, independent business people. When the mob was asked to "enforce" a contract (people in the underground seldom have access to the court system and, when they do, seldom have patience for, as Shakespeare called it, "the law's delay"), the "enforcers" rarely investigated to see whether or not the "claim" was fair. They took their money and made their "hit," which could be anything from a threat to a murder.*

Some organized crime went legitimate, but its sales techniques were not necessarily those of which Dale Carnegie would approve. After Prohibition, the mobsters had a lot of unused trucks and warehouses. Some got into trucking and warehousing. Try as they might to stay legitimate, once one is used to strong-arm tactics to sell one's products, settle disputes, or wipe out—er, be successful in overcoming the challenges of—the competition, it can be difficult.

Even when organized crime does take over a consensual crime, such as drugs, it does so *without* the controls or restraints that keep it free of innocent

---

*Henry Ford hired hundreds of mobsters to pose as workers, infiltrate his plants, and spy on other workers, some of whom were attempting to organize a trade union. It was an open secret that the fellow worker you were talking to on the assembly line might be a syndicate member working directly for Henry Ford. This scare tactic worked for some time and, when the fear wore off and union organizing continued, organized crime was ready, willing, and able to express Mr. Ford's displeasure of organized labor in a more *persuasive* way.

victims. The scene from the movie *The Godfather* in which the heads of the five families gather to discuss the future of drug distribution (One of them says, "I want it regulated! I don't want it sold near schools or playgrounds.") is, well, fiction. Organized crime is famous for its *democratic* approach to money: all dollars are created equal and such niceties as the age of the person bringing the dollars are only the concern of "legitimate" businesses.

> *The country couldn't run*
> *without Prohibition.*
> *That is the industrial fact.*
>
> HENRY FORD

In short, Prohibition created an organized criminal class which is with us to this day.

4. Prohibition permanently corrupted law enforcement, the court system, and politics. During Prohibition, organized crime had on its payroll police, judges, prosecutors, and politicians. If mobsters couldn't buy or successfully threaten someone in a powerful position, they either "wiped him out" or, following more democratic principles, ran a candidate against the incumbent in the next election. They put money behind their candidate, stuffed the ballot box, or leaked some scandal about the incumbent just before the election (or all three). It didn't much matter. The important thing was *winning,* and more often than not, someone beholden to organized crime rose to the position of power.

After more twelve years of purchases, threats, and elections, organized crime had "in its pocket" the political and governmental power structure of most medium-to-large cities, and several states.

After Prohibition, some organized crime bosses made a fortune wielding this power. As good capitalists, they sold police protection, court intervention, and political favors to the highest bidder. Some of these bidders, it turns out, were guilty of crimes that had innocent victims or received government approval for schemes that victimized many. The police, courts, and politicians didn't differentiate between crimes with or without innocent victims any more than organized crime did—and if an official had a sudden fit of morality, it was too late: after years of corruption, the syndicate added blackmail to its list of persuasive techniques.

A great many famous men—names we recognize and respect today—were said to have "underworld connections." Those men sometimes used organized crime and its connections to obtain certain political favors: favors to help their businesses, conceal family indiscretions, or—spoiled as rich people often are—simply "get their way." In addition to those directly under the thumb of organized crime, Prohibition created a class of police, judges, prosecutors, and politicians who were, in a word, *buyable.* When Al Capone "went away" in 1931, some of his corrupt officials sold their services to the highest bidder. There were, of course, plenty of bidders and, due to Capone's thoroughness, plenty of sellers.

Not only were honest citizens unprotected from schemes the government was supposed to protect them from, but dealing with a dishonest city government—from getting a permit to an unbiased day in court—often required a payoff. In some cities, corruption went from top to bottom, and it was the citizenry who suffered. There were plenty of corrupt politicians before Prohibition, just as there were criminals, but the sheer *volume* of money (and, consequently, corruption) that Prohibition brought with it created what might be called *organized* corruption on local and state levels. The new police, judges, prosecutors, and politicians were "strongly requested" to look the other way as the graft passed by, and some succumbed to the easy money they saw being made all around them.

> *How do you look when I'm sober?*
>
> RING LARDNER

The $30,000-a-year politician whose net worth approaches half a million dollars after only four years in office is such a common story that it has become a joke. ("How did you make your money?" "Good investments.") Unfortunately, what politicians "invested in" often hurt every member of the community they were sworn to serve. Some popular beliefs (and, in some cases, truths) about law enforcement, politics, and government in general ("You can't fight City Hall." "The rich get away with murder." "You can't change the system.") were not necessarily created by Prohibition's political corruption, but it certainly supported them in people's minds.

Prohibition forced a number of citizens to decide that government cannot be trusted—an unfortunate point of view with unfortunate consequences.

5. Prohibition overburdened the police, the courts, and the penal system. Even with only token enforcement, Prohibition violations overburdened the police, clogged the court system, and filled the jails. The honest police, judges, and prosecutors found it impossible to do their jobs; there wasn't enough time, personnel, or money. On March 3, 1923, *Time* reported that "44% of the work of the United States District Attorneys is confined to Prohibition cases." By 1928, there were more than 75,000 arrests per year. In 1932, there were 80,000 Prohibition convictions (not just arrests, but *convictions*).

6. People were harmed financially, emotionally, and morally. The basic *unfairness* of Prohibition was astounding. Prohibition caused a direct hardship on hundreds of thousands, perhaps millions of people. First, there were those who, in 1919, were legitimately involved in the production, distribution, and sale of alcohol. They either lost their jobs or were forced to become criminals. (If what you've been doing your entire professional life becomes illegal and you keep doing it, you become a criminal.) Brewing, distilling, and wine making are arts—professions that have been practiced and refined over thousands of years. What

> *All I ever did was*
> *supply a demand*
> *that was pretty popular.*
>
> AL CAPONE

are people to do when their profession, honored and respectable, suddenly becomes a crime? With few options, some turned from brewmaster to bootlegger overnight. Others couldn't stand the idea of being a criminal and took far lower paying and less fulfilling jobs.

And what about the people who owned the breweries, distilleries, and wineries? Many had invested their lives and savings in equipment, research, and good will. Overnight, through no fault of their own, their businesses were destroyed and investments wiped out. If it was a publicly held company, the stockholders, (many of whom were small investors) found their stock suddenly worthless (a harbinger of what would happen to millions of Americans a decade later when the stock market crashed).

Then there were the tens of thousands of workers employed in honest jobs—or who came back from the war looking to be rehired at their jobs—making, bottling, packaging, distributing, selling, delivering, serving, and growing the raw materials for alcoholic beverages. Imagine if the industry in which you worked was declared "immoral" by a powerful religious faction and it suddenly became illegal. What would you do? The negative propaganda—much of it grossly exaggerated or downright dishonest—disseminated by the evangelicals tainted the entire alcoholic beverage industry and everyone who worked in it. It was hard for these people to find jobs in other industries. Saying, "I worked in a brewery" or "I worked in a liquor store" had a tinge of disrespectability. Many of these people, out of economic necessity, were forced into a life of crime, doing precisely what they did before it became a crime.

Then there were the tens of thousands of people who worked in bars, restaurants, beer gardens, hotels, resorts, and related businesses that went out of business as a direct result of Prohibition. Yes, the speakeasies could hire some of these people—if they became criminals. Others, in order to keep their jobs, had to look the other way. Although hotels, for example, had sternly worded signs warning that drinking alcohol in hotel rooms was a federal crime and that violators would be prosecuted, the sight of a bellman carrying a tray with nothing but glasses, ice, and a bottle or two of ginger ale was common. The bellman in this instance, in order to keep his job, had to become an accessory to a federal crime. Such difficult choices corrupted the morals of millions.*

---

*In Geroge Bernard Shaw's *Pygmalion*, Henry Higgins asks Alfred P. Doolittle, "Have you no morals, man?" to which Doolitle calmly replies, "Can't afford 'em." A lot of people, some of whom may have favored Prohibition, found themselves in similar situations: the farmer selling grain to a known bootlegger, the landlord renting a basement knowing it might become a speakeasy, the entertainer or musician offered a job playing in a speakeasy.

AIN'T NOBODY'S BUSINESS IF YOU DO

7. Prohibition caused physical harm.
When "safe" alcoholic beverages were no longer available (that is, beverages in which the purity and alcoholic content were regulated by law), people began assembling all sorts of concoctions, either for their own use or for sale. Some worked; some didn't. Some killed. Alcohol made from fruits, vegetables, or grains—either fermented or distilled—tends to be safe. Alcohol distilled from wood products ("wood alcohol") is not. Wood alcohol, nonetheless, smells like alcohol, tastes like alcohol, and gets you high.

> *I have taken more out of alcohol than alcohol has taken out of me.*
>
> SIR WINSTON CHURCHILL

Some desperate people tried to find ways of making wood alcohol safe to drink; some despicable people repackaged it and sold it as "the real thing." Some used inexpensive wood alcohol to cut the more expensive grain alcohol to make it go further. During the Noble Experiment, more than 10,000 people died from wood-alcohol poisoning, 1,565 in 1928 alone. With "cutting" becoming a common practice in bootlegging and tens of millions of people drinking each day, the only reason that this figure wasn't higher was because of a peculiar characteristic of wood alcohol: before you died from it, you would go blind—permanently, irreversibly, blind (hence, the term *blind drunk*). While drinking, if one's vision began to go, the drill was clear: stop drinking and upchuck as much as you could, as fast as you could. If people acted quickly enough, sometimes they would not end up with complete blindness, but with only a case of impaired vision—plus permanent kidney, liver, and brain damage.

Rather than having a little "Christian charity" for these people who, if alcohol had been legal, would have had nothing more than a hangover, the evangelicals proclaimed that they "had it coming" for breaking both God's law and the law of the land.

In addition, there were the various beatings, stabbings, shootings, and killings between the bootleggers and the feds, the feds and the bootleggers, and the bootleggers amongst themselves. Along the way, any number of innocent people were caught in the crossfire, saw something they shouldn't have seen and were eliminated, or were rubbed out due to "mistaken identity."

8. Prohibition changed the drinking habits of a country—for the worse.
Prior to Prohibition, almost all drinking took place outside the home. Some—mostly recent immigrants—had beer or wine with meals; some of the rich had a little brandy or port after dinner; but, for the most part, alcohol consumption in the home was "for medicinal purposes only." Because the public drinking places closed, people (especially the poor: speakeasies tended to be expensive) began drinking at home more and more. With liquor now conveniently stored at home, people could drink more more often.

> *There should be asylums*
> *for habitual teetotalers,*
> *but they would probably*
> *relapse into teetotalism*
> *as soon as they got out.*
>
> SAMUEL BUTLER

Another phenomenon was drinking to get drunk. Prior to Prohibition, alcohol consumption was secondary to eating or socializing. With Prohibition, people gathered with the primary intention of getting drunk. ("I got a new bottle, just off the boat. Come over tonight and we'll drink it.") Although some speakeasies served food, people didn't go to the speakeasies to eat; they went to drink.

Prohibition also forced people to drink more than they usually would: if caught with a bottle, one could be arrested, so, before traveling, one tended to finish it. This got people into the habit of drinking more. If it was illegal to carry a bottle with you and you weren't sure there would be liquid refreshment at your destination, you might drink enough for the entire evening prior to leaving home. This got Americans in the habit of driving drunk.

The open and increasingly fashionable flouting of Prohibition caused drinking to become a public occurrence. The hip flask became a symbol of rebellion. It was used everywhere: football games, theaters, at work. People carried booze in hollow canes, hot water bottles, even garden hoses wrapped around their waists.

Prior to Prohibition, women drank very little and almost never distilled spirits. Some women had a little elderberry wine, some a little sherry. That immigrant women drank beer or wine was considered an outrage to the guardians of (Protestant) morality, and keeping this evil habit from spreading to the pure womanhood of (Protestant) America was one of the Prohibitionists' most persuasive arguments. Prohibition, in fact, had just the opposite effect. Saloons, which were all-male preserves (except for bar maids, entertainers, and ladies of the evening), gave way to the speakeasies, which were decidedly co-educational. Outside the speakeasy, the passing of the flask included women as well as men. At home, men included their wives (and sometimes wives included themselves) in imbibing. Now that alcohol had to be stored at home—an uncommon practice prior to Prohibition—women decided to take a taste and find out what all the fuss was about. They found out.

Another necessary invention of Prohibition made alcohol far more popular: the cocktail. People turned to hard liquors during Prohibition because, drink for drink, it was cheaper to produce and easier to transport than beer or wine. In the same amount of space it took to transport eight ounces of beer, one could transport eight ounces of alcohol, which became the basis for eight drinks. In addition, the quality of unaged distilled alcohol was, to say the least, harsh. ("Sippin' whiskey," brandies, and other liquors designed for direct consumption are aged for years to mellow the flavor and take the edge off.)

The solution? Simple. The cocktail. Prior to Prohibition there were few mixed drinks. Gin and tonic began as a medicinal preparation during the British colonization of India. To protect against malaria, the British consumed a small amount of quinine mixed in water each day and, to take the bitterness from the quinine, they would add some sugar. To this, gin was added, initially for medicinal purposes. Long after returning to England, and with malaria no longer a concern, the Englishman continued consuming gin and tonics on a more recreational basis. Scotch mixed with a little soda or water was an acceptable, but not terribly popular, mix. And that was about it. The

> *In a generation,*
> *those who are now children*
> *will have lost*
> *their taste for alcohol.*
>
> JOHN FULLER
> 1925

mixing of alcohol with every known sugar-water combination, soft drink, and fruit juice grew directly out of Prohibition's attempt to make bootleg liquor more palatable. Millions of people who didn't like the taste of beer, wine, or hard liquors found cocktails irresistible.

9. Prohibition made cigarette smoking a national habit. High on the evangelicals' hit list, second only to alcohol as a substance that *had to* be prohibited, was tobacco. In 1921, cigarettes were illegal in fourteen states, and anti-cigarette bills were pending in twenty-eight others. The prohibition of cigarettes, promoted by the very people who gave us the prohibition of alcohol, made cigarette smoking almost irresistible. As the experiment of Prohibition failed, the anti-cigarette laws fell. By 1930, they were legal almost everywhere; the consumption had nearly tripled. Hollywood used cigarettes to indicate independence, sophistication, and glamour.

10. Prohibition prevented the treatment of drinking problems. It was stylish, fashionable, trendy, and daring to be drunk. No one had a drinking problem. ("I drink; I get drunk; I fall down. Where's the problem?") With alcohol illegal, there were no social norms for reasonable, moderate alcohol consumption against which to compare one's own drinking. The official social sanction (enforced by law) was complete sobriety. Anything less, from one drink per week to ten per day, made one a Wet. Anyone who suggested to a friend, "You may have a little problem here," sounded like one of the preachy blue noses whose moralizing started the trouble in the first place.

With the clearly immoderate act of Prohibition, all moderation was destroyed. The only "therapy" recommended by the Drys was jail and prayer. And how could people go for pastoral counseling for a possible drinking problem? People were thrown out of congregations for drinking only once. Imagine what might happen if one admitted to drinking enough times to cause a problem. Alcoholism, unrecognized and untreated, became an epidemic during Prohibition *due* to Prohibition. (Within a few years after Prohibition, some people began to realize that they had personal problems that involved drinking and, by the end of the 1930s, Alcoholics Anonymous was formed—the first of many organizations to point out that drink-

> *Robert Benchley's list of infallible symptoms of intoxication in drivers:* • *When the driver is sitting with his back against the instrument panel and his feet on the driver's seat.* • *When the people in the back seat are crouched down on the floor with their arms over their heads.* • *When the driver goes into the rest-room and doesn't come out.*

ing for some people is the symptom of an illness, an illness that could be successfully treated.)

11. Prohibition caused "immorality." Far from Prohibition leading to Great Moments in Morality, as the evangelicals had hoped, it, in fact, led directly to an unparalleled explosion of immorality—as immorality was defined by them. As speakeasies were unregulated, outlawed, underground, and co-educational, they tended to breed unregulated, outlawed, underground, and co-educational activities. Because the sexes mingled freely, the sexes tended to mingle freely. A great deal of the marked increase in sexual promiscuity during the 1920s can be directly linked to the potent combination of alcohol and an atmosphere of illicit activity and abandon.

Prostitution also flourished—although professionals complained that some of these newly liberated women were destroying the business by giving it away. Drugs other than alcohol were used by people who never would have come into contact with them were it not for the permissive atmosphere of the speakeasies.

College, traditionally a center for higher learning, became, for some, the center for learning how to get higher. Alcohol paved the way for seeking "kicks" in other formerly forbidden activities. "Anything goes" became the slogan of an entire generation.

All these developments, of course, were soundly denounced in lurid terms by the keepers of morality—but then, those were the things they said about alcohol, too.

12. Prohibition was phenomenally expensive. The exact cost of this thirteen-year experiment is difficult to estimate. Between law enforcement, courts, the operation of jails, and all the rest, some estimates top a billion dollars (and this is a billion dollars when a Ford factory worker—among the highest paid unskilled laborers—made only $5 a day*). In addition to this cost, let's not forget the taxes on alcohol the government lost because of Prohibition, and the profit denied honest business people, diverted into the pockets of organized crime. The artificially increased price of alcohol hit the poor and working classes hardest of all. In all, it was a very expensive experiment.

⚖ ⚖ ⚖

Prohibition had a handful of good effects: Fewer people listened to the ranting of self-appointed moralists; women took an important (albeit wobbly) step towards

---

*Some Ford workers made more. Henry Ford, for example, made $264,000 per day in 1921, about $8.4 million in today's dollars.

personal freedom; and lawmakers became *slightly more hesitant to prohibit things.*

The effects were, however, mostly negative. For good or for ill, there's hardly an American alive today whose life was not touched by Prohibition.*

George Santayana's comment, "Those who cannot remember the past are condemned to repeat it," has been repeated so often that it has become a cliché. If only we would remember the past as often as we remember to quote Santayana.

> *We learn from history that we do not learn from history.*
>
> HEGEL

Alas, we have forgotten our recent past and are repeating it even now.

---

*My father—under the influence, as they say—got into a fight during Prohibition and was forced to leave his native Alabama. He fled to Detriot, where he much later met my mother and had me. Also during Prohibition, in Detroit, my grandmother (my mother's mother) lost her first love in a bootlegging accident. (Her fiancé was overcome by fumes, collapsed, and drowned in five inches of mash.) My grandmother's father insisted that she marry; she chose my grandfather and had my mother who, much later, met my father, and etc. Without Prohibition there would be no me—and I'm still not sure whether to add that to the list of advantages or disadvantages.

Putting the "Problem" in Perspective

EVER SINCE the United States declared war on drugs (poor drugs), "the drug problem" has scored in opinion polls as one of the top five concerns of the American public. During the decade preceding the official declaration of war in 1982, however, America's concern about drug use hovered around #20.* Interestingly, it was not that public concern grew, and a war was declared; rather, a war was declared, wartime propaganda grew (at an alarming rate), and the concern rose. It's like Charles Foster Kane's reply to the photographer who cabled, "NO WAR IN CUBA." Kane cabled back, "GIVE ME THE PICTURES; I'LL GIVE YOU THE WAR." It's as though someone looked at the deterioration of Soviet communism (a perennial top-five concern) and said, "We need a new war here; let's find a problem." In fact, many of the anti-drug warriors are the same people who were, just a decade ago, fervent anti-communists. They attack drugs with *precisely* the same rhetoric as they attacked communism. (Please see the chapter, "Unpopular Political Views.")

On another front, gays have served in the United States military ever since General Von Steuben arrived at Valley Forge in February 1778. He was recommended to General Washington by Benjamin Franklin. Von Steuben turned the rag-tag troops into a fighting army by spring; as Burke Davis pointed out in his book, *George Washington and the American Revolution*, General Von Steuben "transformed the army, and the value of his service could hardly be overestimated."

*For example, in 1974, Dr. Peter Bourne, who later became President Carter's drug policy advisor, called cocaine "the most benign of illicit drugs currently in widespread use." Today it is widely believed that if you come within even a *block* of cocaine, it will do such immediate and irreparable harm to your mental functioning that you will become one of those people who actually believes that those little buttons you push to change the light at a crosswalk are actually *connected* to something.

> *AIDS is not just
> God's punishment
> for homosexuals;
> it is God's punishment
> for the society that
> <u>tolerates</u> homosexuals.*
>
> REVEREND JERRY FALWELL
> 1993

Von Steuben was gay. More than two hundred years later, President Clinton took office and, of all the problems facing the country and its new president, what got most press (and, therefore, seemed most pressing)? Would Clinton honor his campaign pledge to stop throwing people out of the military simply for being gay? You would think he was trying to give Maine to Canada—oh, the furor, the furor.

And so it continues down the list of consensual crimes: Los Angeles seems more concerned about fighting prostitution than pollution; the Bureau of Alcohol, Tobacco, and Firearms ignores the 22,000 alcohol-related traffic deaths, the 300,000 cigarette-related deaths, and the 10,000 handgun deaths in 1993, and instead waged war on 100 Branch Davidians in Waco, Texas; authorized medical practitioners overbill insurance companies to the tune of $80 billion per year while the Food and Drug Administration (the federal agency assigned to watch over the medical community) sees to it that dying people cannot have the most effective painkilling medications, launches armed raids on healers doing anything "unorthodox," and wants to require a prescription for doses of vitamin C larger than 60 milligrams.

We have lost our perspective.

Some of the reasons for this loss of perspective are detailed in later chapters. This chapter is a laundry list of, well, our dirty laundry. We have a lot more pressing concerns than putting people in jail for activities that do not physically harm the person or property of another.

This chapter is not designed to support the predictions of doomsday theorists; it is merely intended to put things into perspective. It also does not purport to offer *solutions* to any of these problems—this book offers a solution to only one problem, the "problem" of consensual crimes. Solving the problems in this chapter is going to take commitment, creativity, money, and a lot of work—precisely the resources currently squandered in the futile attempt to regulate individual morality.

In this chapter, we will use two words that have become increasingly popular in recent years, *billion* and *trillion*. Because *million, billion,* and *trillion* rhyme, we often think of them as roughly the same amount of money: "Oh, a billion is more than a million, but not a whole lot more."

A billion is a *whole lot more.*

- A million dollars in hundred dollar bills forms a single stack approximately three feet high.

- A billion dollars is a single stack twice as high as the Empire State Building.

- A trillion dollars is a single stack 570 *miles* high. It reaches the threshold of outer space.

- If a million dollars in hundred dollar bills were laid end to end,* they would stretch approximately 97 miles— roughly the distance from New York to Philadelphia.

- One billion dollars laid end to end would circle the globe at the equator nearly four times; alternatively, they could go two-fifths of the distance to the moon.

JON WINOKUR:

How did you react to winning a Pulitzer?

DAVE BARRY:

I figured it was just one more indication of the nation's drug problem.

- One trillion dollars in one hundred dollar bills, laid end to end, would circle the equator 3,900 times. Or, if you don't want to go around the world that many times, one trillion dollars in hundred dollar bills, laid end to end, would extend from the earth to the sun, and, once there, you would still have $41 billion to burn.

- One last example: if you had a million dollars, and spent $1,000 per day, you would, like Donald Trump, run out of money in two years and nine months.

- If, however, you had a billion dollars and spent $1,000 per day, it would take you 2,737 years, 10 months and 1 week to run out of money. (That last week would probably be fairly stressful.)

- If you had a trillion dollars and spent $1,000 a day, you would be destitute in 2,739,726 years (and some change, but, as with the national debt, who's counting?).

Speaking of trillion and the national debt, let's begin our list** with the national debt.

The National Debt. Forty-five years of fighting the Cold War had devastating economic effects on both the Soviet Union and the United States; the only difference is, the United States had better credit than the Soviet Union—the Soviet Union is bankrupt; the United States is merely in receivership. As a nation, we (as

---

*Every time I hear these end-to-end analogies, I think of Dorothy Parker's remark, "If all the debutantes in New York were laid end to end, I wouldn't be surprised." Or, as Will Durst asked, "Did you know that if you took all the veins and arteries out of a man's body and laid them end to end, that man would die?" More to the point of this book, Arthur Baer said, "If you laid all our laws end to end, there would be no end."

**This list is in no particular order. In my view, any *one* of the items is more deserving of our time, money, and attention than *all* the "wars" against consensual activities.

of 1993) owe more than $4 trillion ($4,000,000,000,000.00); that's $16,000 for *each* man, woman and child in the United States. The average American family owes more to "the company store" than they do on their house. (The share of the national debt for a family of five is $80,000. If they have a cat, it's $82,000. If they have a dog, it's $83,000. If they have a *large* dog, it's $85,000.) The interest alone on the national debt is somewhere between $199 billion and $296 billion per year (depending upon whom you listen to—the government [$199 billion] or balanced-budget advocates [$296 billion]). More than 40% of personal income taxes go just to pay the *interest* on the national debt. As the national debt is an embarrassment to both Democrats and Republicans, it took an independent, Ross Perot, to bring the problem to national attention.*

It's too bad that we didn't take Cicero's advice given around 63 B.C.:

> The budget should be balanced, the Treasury should be refilled, public
> debt should be reduced, the arrogance of officialdom should be tempered
> and controlled . . . lest Rome become bankrupt.

We also didn't take the suggestion of Thomas Jefferson in 1789 when he warned the electorate: "The principle of spending money to be paid by posterity, under the name of funding, is but swindling futurity on a large scale." Well, futurity, do you feel swindled? *(Futurity.* Sounds like one of those prototype automobiles from the 1950s. "Drive into the '60s with the new Ford Futurity.") As Sid Taylor, research director for the National Taxpayers Union, put it, "Deficit spending is bankruptcy pending." But not all world leaders believed that a large national debt was a bad thing. One of the most famous national leaders in this century said, "No country has ever been ruined on account of its debts." The year was 1940. The economic expert: Adolf Hitler.

The Savings and Loan Debacle. It's going to cost the federal government (that is, *us)* more than half a *trillion* dollars to bail out the savings and loans. That's an amount equal to all federal, state, and local government spending on education for the next four years. Dave Barry calls the S&L bailout the "964.3 hillion jillion bazillion dollar" scandal. Where were the regulatory agencies? Rather than regulating private lives, shouldn't the government spend its time regulating the public institutions it is charged to regulate? As Linda Winer pointed

---

*Although I said I wouldn't offer any solutions, here's a fairly obvious one: between the money we spend every year prosecuting consensual crimes and the revenue lost by not taxing consensual activities, if we did nothing else, the elimination of consensual crimes would wipe out the national debt in twenty years. As it is, our current policy on consensual crimes will add a trillion dollars to the national debt in the next five years.

out in New York *Newsday*, August 9, 1991,

Texans have the U.S. Justice Department task force on obscenity to thank for its 18-month sting operation, which included setting up cloak-and-dagger agents in a phony video business called "Good Vibrations," reportedly with the intention of making an example of the porno devils. Nice work. We certainly could have used some of that federal enterprise when the S & L executives were stealing the country away.

> *While Congress was snoozing, the American taxpayers were losing.*
>
> SENATOR BOB DOLE

And where are the crooks who committed the *real* crime of "misappropriating" all that money (an average of $2,000 for every man, woman, and child in the United States)? We go to Panama to drag "drug lords" to "justice"; where are the indictments against the "S&L lords"? As Senator Richard C. Shelby complained, "The taxpayers are on the hook for hundreds of billions of dollars, and yet, criminals are still playing golf at the country club."

Other Supposedly Regulated Delights. The same federal regulatory agencies that let the S&Ls get away with financial murder apparently let another *endearing* financial organization get away with *genuine* murder. I am referring to that billionaires' social club, the Bank of Credit and Commerce International, or BCCI. This multinational "bank" was, in reality, a clearing house for crooks. Here's an excerpt from Senator John D. Kerry's congressional testimony on August 8, 1991:

You need a Mirage jet to go to Saddam Hussein? BCCI could facilitate it. If you wanted weapons in the Mideast, and possibly even atomic weapons? Who do you call? BCCI. You want drug money to move from cartel to safe haven? BCCI. It gave new meaning to the term *full service bank*. . . .

What strikes me particularly is the degree to which this bank thought it could steamroll any obstacles that lay in its path. Certain laws and standards were no barrier. Why? Because BCCI thought it could buy everything. Buy lawyers, buy accountants, buy regulators, buy access, buy loyalty, buy governments, buy safety, buy protection, and even buy silence. . . .

With purchased endorsements from more elected officials than you could wave a laundered checkbook at, BCCI was able to illegally take over several American banks with hardly an investigation. What about murder? It is said that murder (under the more corporately acceptable title, *assassination*) was part of BCCI's stock in trade. Whereas most banks have departments such as Trust, Savings, Money Orders, New Accounts, Safety Deposit Boxes, and Loans, BCCI had Assassinations, *Coups d'État*, Money Laundering, Arms Trafficking, Nuclear Weapons, and Political Destabilization. The BCCI. Lovely people to be in business with; and, while the federal regulators were out regulating consensual crimes, it made American banks part of its empire.* And what is the next scandal in a supposedly government-regulated industry? I nominate . . .

Health Care Fraud. Insurance fraud is the biggest white-collar crime in the nation, second only to income-tax evasion. Each year, $80 billion is stolen from health insurance companies, Medicaid, and Medicare by the medical establishment. It uses cute terms like "overbilling," but it's really stealing. And much of it is done by *doctors* and *hospitals,* the very people and institutions we trust with our *lives.* Overbilling also jacks up medical insurance premiums so that millions of people who otherwise would have health insurance, can't afford it. The average American's share of this *real* crime last year: $320. However, according to the House Subcommittee on Human Resources, "In some jurisdictions, federal prosecutors may not accept criminal health-care cases involving less than $100,000 because of limited resources. . . . Prosecutorial and judicial resources are limited, necessarily restricting the number of cases that can be legally pursued." With well over half the prosecutor case load made up of drug offenses, it's not hard to guess what's limiting those resources. (From 1982 to 1990, drug-related cases in federal courts increased by almost 400%.) The congressional report goes on to say, "The deterrent and financial benefits of pursuing fraud must be weighed against the considerable legal and administrative costs of doing so." If only the government would use the logic it applies to the real crime of fraud on consensual crimes.

Automobile Insurance Fraud. More than $17.5 billion a year is paid in inflated auto insurance claims. Who pays? Everyone who buys auto insurance—and everyone who can't afford to. Car insurance fraud adds 10% to 30% to every car insurance bill. And what is the government doing to end this crime? Not much. According to a journal of the insurance industry, *Insurance Review,*

> With law enforcement officials mired in murder and drug cases,** and

---

*This scandal involved *so* many people in Washington, and was such a *truly* bipartisan effort, that we don't hear much about it anymore. When Washington as a whole wants to cover up something, they usually (a) find a scapegoat and (b) step up the "war" on some consensual activity (now that we don't have Russia to kick around anymore). The scapegoat was Clark Clifford, who arranged poker games for Truman and Vietnam for Johnson. For his influence peddling, his law firm—over an 18-month period—received $33 million from BCCI. Congress (mostly lawyers) can only respond with horror—and envy. Meanwhile, the American public knew more about David Koresh's cult of 100 than how (and who in) the federal government looked the other way while BCCI illegally bought up American banks. Nice spin control!

**While I certainly don't think that law enforcement time should be taken away from murder

industry investigators focused on costlier and more sophisticated scams, the odds that an otherwise law-abiding citizen will be caught, much less prosecuted, for his misdeeds are minuscule. The Florida study concluded that as long as policy holders are knowledgeable, and not too greedy, they can "commit fraud with impunity."

Real Crime. In addition to paying more than you need to for insurance due to fraud, or watching your tax money (which you *must* pay) bail out savings and loan mismanagement and embezzlement, there are other *real* crimes to worry about. On the average, every four years you or someone in your household will be robbed, raped, or physically assaulted. (That once-every-four-years statistic does *not* include murder, manslaughter by drunk drivers, kidnaping, child abuse, or other violent crimes.) Five out of six people living in the United States will be the victims of violent crimes during their lifetimes. For every 133 people you meet, one of them will be murdered. (If you live in a household of five, the chances are 1 in 27 that one of you will be murdered.) Then there are embezzlers, shoplifters, and other "white-collar criminals" who add to the price of everything we buy; a dramatic increase in "hate crimes" (that is, violent crimes against people just because they happen to belong to an ethnic, national, religious, or sexual minority); and so many others. And where are the police? Crimes with real victims (us) are out of control, yet roughly half the law enforcement time is spent investigating consensual crimes. Eliminating consensual crimes would effectively double law enforcement personnel and easily halve the number of real crimes almost overnight. (There I go again: offering solutions.)

Abducted Children. According to the United States Department of Justice, 400,000 children are abducted every year. There are currently 1.4 million missing children in this country. Of the 1.4 million, some of them are runaways, some were abducted by family members, some are simply "missing" (the "lost, injured, or otherwise missing" category lists 440,000). Some children are kidnaped—primarily for rape, and torture. When they are no longer young enough to be interesting, they are killed.

Although there is a central clearing house to report all missing children, there

> **LARRY KING:**
> *Don't you think it would be better to legalize victimless crimes like drugs and prostitution and divert the resources to more important things like the rapes and assaults and things like that?*
>
> **SENATOR TOM HARKIN:**
> *No, I don't agree with that at all.*
>
> "LARRY KING LIVE"
> CNN, 1992

investigations to track down insurance fraud, more law enforcement time is spent on drugs than murders—a frightening thought in itself. Here's one example of the ratio between "murder" and "drug cases" in the United States: In 1991, there were fewer than 25,000 arrests for murder and more than 1,000,000 arrests for drug violations. Of these more-than-1,000,000 arrests, 672,666 were for simple possession. Here's an even more frightening statistic: In 1990, the average sentence at U.S. District Courts for first-degree murder was 12.8 years; for "other drug-related statutes," 20.4 years. Might I make it even more appalling? The drug terms are usually *mandatory*; by law they *must* be served. Murderers, on the other hand, can be paroled at any time.

is no federal law instructing local law enforcement personnel to send information to this clearing house. Many law enforcement officials don't even know the National Center for Missing and Exploited Children exists. The FBI does not get involved in kidnapings unless a ransom is demanded (which almost never happens anymore) or unless the parents can prove that, after abduction, the child was transported across a state line (good luck proving that). When Project Alert was formed in 1992 to help locate missing children, it had a whopping initial budget of $200,000. This is .0015% of the federal drug enforcement budget, or .0004% of what is spent prosecuting consensual crimes in this country each year.

Those who say that consensual crimes really *do* have victims—that consensual crimes are a bad influence on children—might want to consider whether the time, money, and effort spent keeping children safe from "bad examples" might be better spent reuniting abducted children with their parents and putting some of the worst imaginable criminals—people who abduct small children for rape, torture, and murder—behind bars. Perhaps the people who want to make the entire world as wholesome as Disneyland should consider the anguish of hundreds of thousands of parents who are not only physically separated from their children, but are also tortured by thoughts of the horrors their children are being subjected to.

Meanwhile, Project Alert is doing what it can to recruit volunteers, especially among retired law enforcement personnel. These saints are known as *travelers*, and "travel they do," said Senator Alfonse D'Amato;* "they live by the waysides and bysides of America, and attempt to track down [abducted children]."

God bless the travelers.

Terrorism. We don't hear much about terrorism in this country because if we

---

*Ironically, as supportive as Senator D'Amato is in fighting the real and genuinely pernicious crime of child abduction, he is also one of the hardest of the hard-liners when it comes to drugs. In 1993, when I wrote him giving my views on consensual crimes, Senator D'Amato wrote back, "In 1988, my legislation authorizing the death penalty for drug-related killings became law. . . . I have also introduced the Drug Kingpin Death Penalty Act, providing for the death penalty for major drug dealers, even if there is no killing." He then points out that "the drug traffickers are killing our kids." No, Senator: *drug dealers* aren't killing our kids, *child abductors* are killing our kids. Let's stiffen the federal penalties against *them*. Child abduction is not even a federal crime unless the abductor crosses a state line. As it is now, in some states, a child abductor can be found guilty, sentenced, paroled, and back on the street within a few years—even if the abduction involved multiple rape and murder. But Senator D'Amato does not say he has proposed legislation to stiffen penalties for child abduction. He ends his letter stating, "It is time for [drug dealers] to face the punishment they deserve, and that punishment is the death penalty."

really knew what was going on, we'd all be, well, *terrorized*. The car bomb (or, more accurately, the mini-van bomb) explosion at the base of the World Trade Center in March 1993 was not only an act of terrorism—it was a warning. "Imagine if this were a nuclear device . . ." was the terrorists' *real* message. If it *had been* a nuclear bomb, there would be no more Manhattan (an irony, since the code name for the scientists who invented the atom bomb was the Manhattan Project). With Manhattan goes the financial center of the world, the communications center of the United States, and the corporate headquarters of more major U.S. companies than you can rattle off in the time it takes a physics professor to explain $E = mc^2$. One atom bomb in Los Angeles would wipe out the movie industry and what was left of the television industry (much of which went with Manhattan). It could also create enough seismic vibrations to set off The Big One. Another atom bomb in Washington, D.C., would wipe out the federal government. And one in Chicago would eliminate the idea that the Midwest was somehow immune to attack. Four atom bombs, and the United States as we know it would cease to be. (I haven't even discussed the lasting effects of radiation, especially if they happen to be "dirty" bombs—which terrorists' bombs almost certainly would be.) We would, however, still have 24-hour news coverage of the death of the United States: CNN is located in Atlanta.

> *It's time to stop living with the paranoia of "what if" and start facing the reality of "what is." "What is" is a real crisis in education, in health care, in the economy. "What is" the real national security, is the need for a nation to feel secure.*
>
> BARBRA STREISAND

The international underground originally set up to sell drugs has decided—with typical big-business logic—to sell *anything* the customer wants to buy. One of these organizations, the previously mentioned BCCI, has come to light. Many have not. Underground organizations are perfectly willing to sell the parts necessary to make atomic bombs. As Senator John D. Kerry reported during a Senate investigation of the Bank of Credit and Commerce International,

> The spread of nuclear weapons, needless to say, creates even greater risks for confrontation and of destruction. When a bank like BCCI moves drug money and big-dollar weapons money and helps terrorists acquire the material to make nuclear bombs . . . while political leaders who are supposed to be protecting them move aside, then governments themselves wind up becoming partners in the enterprise of those criminals.

The only thing Russia had that, for example, Sadaam Hussein or the Ayatollah Khomeini did not was a delivery system for their atom bombs. Russia had missiles. With the World Trade Center bombing, however, terrorists proved that, although they don't have missiles, they *can* rent Avis mini-vans.

Meanwhile, what are the FBI, CIA, and United States Customs—our only realistic defense against terrorism—up to? You guessed it: defending us against consensual

> *The current environment is*
> *so polluted with hysteria that*
> *nothing rational can happen*
> *to solve the drug problem.*
> *Until we're able to get*
> *the facts into perspective and*
> *debunk the myths, we're just*
> *not going to make progress and*
> *effectively deal with these issues.*
>
> GEORGETTE BENNETT

crimes. Drugs, of course, head the list. Within the United States intelligence agencies, the War on Communism has now become the War on Drugs. The war on terrorism is a footnote. To see that drugs and our intelligence agencies are intimately linked, one need only look at the classification they receive within the U.S. Senate: the subcommittee of the Senate Foreign Relations Committee responsible for studying these problems is the Terrorism, Narcotics, and International Operations Subcommittee. This subcommittee courageously explores international terrorism, but is bogged down by the War on Drugs.

And what are customs officials trained to find? Drugs, of course. Do you think one in a thousand customs officials knows what the components of a nuclear bomb look like? But how many know what cocaine looks like or how marijuana smells? And then there are all those drug-sniffing dogs. How about a few *pluto-nium*-sniffing dogs? (Some 9,600 pounds of plutonium and highly enriched uranium are missing from U.S. inventories. It takes only 15 pounds of plutonium to make an atomic bomb.)

And where are J. Edgar's best? After an investigation that lasted several years, on June 30, 1992, more than 1,000 FBI agents *simultaneously* swooped down on doctors and pharmacies in fifty cities, making arrests and confiscating everything in sight, in an attempt to stop prescription drugs from ending up "on the black market." It was called Operation Gold Pill. The FBI, however, does not just protect us from purloined prescription drugs. On June 23, 1991, after extensive investigation, 150 FBI agents invaded the bankrupt mining town of Wallace, Idaho, and confiscated every video poker machine from every bar in town. It wasn't that these video poker machines accepted bets, like the Las Vegas versions, but they were *used for betting.* (People would bet each other and sometimes the bar owner on who could get more points. Horrors!) According to a *New York Times* article on August 20, 1991,

> Federal lawyers are moving in court to take control of the places that were raided, a move that would make the Government owner of every bar in Wallace.
>
> To a community that considers itself on its knees, racked by a series of economic and environmental calamities, the raid has provoked protests and stirred old animosities.
>
> In an age when banking scandals have cost the nation's taxpayers billions of dollars, many residents here say the Government has spent far too much time and money on video poker machines in a crippled mining town.

Meanwhile, on September 28, 1992, the Office of the Attorney General and the Office of the Drug Enforcement Administration revealed "a truly unique joint effort involving the participation of law enforcement agencies on three continents." Was this "truly unique" international effort designed to track down and uncover terrorism? No. It was a two-year operation known as Operation Green Ice. Its purpose was not to find terrorists, but to terrorize drug dealers. "Operation Green Ice has a message for drug dealers everywhere: the world is mobilized against you. U.S. law enforcement will continue with our colleagues around the world to defeat these purveyors of human misery." Couldn't all of this intelligence be used more intelligently? Let's start by making sure the terrorists don't have the tools for their terrorism.

> *I am concerned about the national debt. I am concerned about international terrorism. But, I'm scared to death about drugs.*
>
> WILLIAM VON RAAB
> *Commissioner*
> *U.S. Customs Service*

Environmental Disasters. One might expect the flashing electronic billboard above L.A.'s trendy Hard Rock Cafe to provide information about either music or food. Instead, it has two rows of numbers. One is labeled POPULATION OF THE WORLD and the other, ACRES OF RAIN FOREST REMAINING. At a rate of roughly one-per-second, the population number grows, while the rain forest number shrinks. It's a graphic illustration of the collision course we are on: both population growth and the destruction of the rain forest are out of control. The population of the world swiftly approaches six billion. By early in the next century, it will double. Overpopulation is the basis of all environmental problems. The rain forests are not only the lungs of the earth—creating oxygen and removing impurities*—they are also the medicine chest. Eighty percent of all pharmaceutical drugs come from plant products. Less than three percent of the plants in the rain forest have been identified. Whole species of plants that might contain the cure for current and future diseases are being destroyed forever. Yet, instead of tying U.S. foreign aid to reasonable population growth or preservation of the rain forests, to what do we tie it? The elimination of drug production and trafficking. We are far more concerned about destroying poppy fields in Thailand or cocaine farms in Colombia than preserving the rain forests in Brazil.

Then there's the ozone. In his 1993 Pulitzer Prize–winning play, *Angels in America,* Tony Kushner describes the ozone layer:

> When you look at the ozone layer, from outside, from a spaceship, it looks like a pale blue halo, a gentle, shimmering aureole encircling the atmosphere encircling the earth. Thirty miles above our heads, a thin layer of three-atom oxygen molecules. . . . It's a kind of gift, from God, the crown-

---

*More than 40% of the earth's oxygen is produced by the Amazonian rain forests. Each year, an area of rain forest the size of Ohio is destroyed. Eighty percent of Amazonian deforestation has taken place since 1980.

> We shall never understand
> the natural environment
> until we see it
> as a living organism.
> Land can be healthy or sick,
> fertile or barren, rich or poor,
> lovingly nurtured or bled white.
>
> PAUL BROOKS

ing touch to the creation of the world: guardian angels, hands linked, make a spherical net, a blue-green nesting orb, a shell of safety for life itself.

A poetic description of a natural phenomenon that is, well, poetic. The ozone layer filters out the harmful rays of the sun. If the ozone layer ceased to be, so would we. (My attempt at poetry.) We are destroying the ozone layer. And, in one of those bureaucratic ironies, the government agency designated to study the ozone, NASA, is also helping to destroy it. According to Helen Caldicott, the doctor who blew the whistle the loudest and longest on the absurdity of nuclear armaments, each time the space shuttle goes up, .25% of the ozone layer is destroyed. That means with four hundred space shuttle launchings, bye-bye ozone. It means there *cannot be* a space station (it would require too many space shuttle flights), and that we should consider piercing the ozone with rockets about as carefully as we submit to surgery: it had better be important. So, NASA sends up a space shuttle to study the ozone, destroying the ozone in the process.

A few random environmental disasters: ¶ During the summer of 1992, 2,000 U.S. beaches were closed due to toxic levels of water pollution. ¶ In the fifteen major urban metropolitan areas, from 1987 to 1990, there were 1,484 "unhealthy" air days (more than half of them were in Los Angeles). ¶ Acid rain—precipitation containing sulfuric and nitric acids—continues to reign, destroying lakes, forests, and crops. ¶ Global warming—caused, in part, by burning fossil fuels—may melt the ice caps, raising ocean levels and flooding coastal areas. More than 53% of the U.S. population live in coastal areas. ¶ Ten percent of all species are endangered. In the world at large, the cheetah, jaguar, leopard, giant panda, rhinoceros, tiger, several whale species, the African chimpanzee, gorilla, orangutan, and many monkey species are officially considered endangered.* In the United States, the endangered species list includes the woodland caribou, the Columbian white-tailed deer, the California condor, the whooping crane, the peregrine falcon, the wood stork, the American crocodile, the crayfish, several species of butterfly, and, the symbol of America itself, the bald eagle. Our planet loses three species per day. By the year 2000, 20% of all species could be lost forever. ¶ Wetlands act as natural flood and water control systems, filter impurities from the water, serve as spawning grounds and nurseries for between 60% and 90% of U.S. commercial fisheries (thus vital to the nation's $10 billion per year fishing harvest), and provide a natural habitat for a wide variety of species. One-third of the nation's endangered or threatened species live in or depend on wetlands. And yet, as a percentage of

*The latter are *primates*, folks—the animal species closest to humans.

land area, wetlands have declined from 12% to 5% in the last two hundred years. Twenty-two states have lost more than 50% of their wetlands, and ten states have lost at least 70%. While Bush was fighting his War on Drugs, he also declared a war on wetlands. In 1991, the Bush administration asked for legislation that would redefine wetlands, making available 33% of the currently established wetlands for development. ¶ An Environmental Protection Agency review of the 1,000 worst hazardous waste dumps revealed that 80% were leaking toxins into ground water. ¶ Due to lead plumbing, one in six Americans drinks water with excessive amounts of lead. ¶ We are running out of landfills. The average American disposes of four pounds of solid waste per day. In a lifetime, the average American will produce 600 times his or her adult body weight in garbage. In 1988, Americans disposed of 14 million tons of plastic, 31.6 million tons of yard wastes, and 180 million tons of other wastes. There are also tons and tons of nuclear waste, which remains deadly for centuries. How do we dispose of this? Where do we put it? What kind of containers can we store it in? These questions have not been adequately answered, and yet we continue to produce nuclear waste.

> *The United States spends half again as much on the drug war as it does on the Environmental Protection Agency.*
>
> DAN BAUM
> *The Nation*
> 1992

The United States is the pollution capital of the world. We are 6% of the world's population, but consume 70% of the world's resources. We also produce far more than our share of the pollutants. The world is not happy with us about this.* Alan Watts once said that, from the earth's point of view, the human race could be considered nothing more than a bad case of lice. If that's an accurate analogy, the United States is the breeding ground. There is simply *no way* the entire world can support the lifestyle of even an impoverished American. If every family in China wanted nothing more than a refrigerator, the escaping fluorocarbons just to *manufacture* them would destroy the ozone. The American dream, infinitely exported, would be a nightmare. Our 6% of the world's population pollutes more than the other 94% *put together.* Americans, for the most part, are benignly unaware of this, but the rest of the world is not. In the world view, the Ugly American of the 1960s has been replaced by the Arrogant American of the 1990s. Future wars and terrorist attacks are more likely to be protesting our pollution than our politics.

Oil Addiction. America is, quite simply, addicted to foreign oil. Although Nixon, while president, declared that the United States should be energy independent by the end of the decade (which decade *was* the Nixon decade?), and

---

*This is an understatement comparable to that of the NASA spokesman who referred to the Challenger explosion as, "Obviously a major malfunction."

> *German soldiers were
> victims of the Nazis
> just as surely as the victims
> in the concentration camps.*
>
> PRESIDENT RONALD REAGAN
> 1985

although Carter gave an executive order stating that the average fuel efficiency of automobiles sold in 1990 should be 40 mpg, Reagan—succumbing to the pressures of the petroleum and automobile lobbies—progressively reduced that minimum standard each year he was in office. Today we have, on average, 27.5 mpg cars. If we had gotten to 40 mpg in 1990, there would be no need to import oil. We could, in fact, become an oil-*exporting* nation. The direct result of Reagan's policy came to visit his successor, Bush; it was called, appropriately, the Gulf War. Although Bush was properly outraged when he spoke of one small sovereign nation being overrun by an imperialist, nasty, larger nation, everyone knew the war was about oil. In the words of tell-it-like-it-is Perot: "Does he *really* want us to believe that we're going in to defend a nation [Kuwait] whose leader has a Minister of Sex, whose job it is to get him a new virgin to deflower each Thursday night?" Although the Gulf War cost us "only" 390 American lives, it could have been far worse; and the anxiety suffered by the troops and their families in the early days of deployment, with rumors of poisonous gases and prolonged desert fighting, was torture enough. Unnecessary torture.

Our dependence on foreign oil and the hundreds of billions of dollars paid to the Middle East has given enormous power to a group of people who are—to put it mildly—politically unstable. If it wasn't for our dependence on foreign oil, could an Ayatollah afford to casually put a $2 million price tag on the head of Salman Rushdie? Would Israel need $3 billion of U.S. foreign aid per year in order to play keep-up-with-the-Joneses-in-military-equipment with its neighbors? We are also *burning* a limited resource—petroleum—which we would be better off using to make certain plastics, synthetics, lubricants, and solvents that are derived best or exclusively from oil. The irony is that America is rich in energy resources—both natural in the form of wind, water, and sunlight, and renewable through plant-based ethanol, methane, and diesel-grade vegetable oils. (See the chapter, "Hemp for Victory.") Our oil addiction is unnecessary.

Illiteracy. What on *earth* is going on in our schools? More than 100,000 high school students take guns to class every day; 5% of the population cannot fill out a job application; 13% are considered "illiterate"; 20% are considered "functionally incompetent"; 34% are considered "marginally competent"; and 80% cannot look at a bus schedule and determine what time the next bus arrives. (I must admit, based on some of the bus schedules I've seen, I may be in that 80%.) Even if people *are* taught to read and write, they're not taught much about *life*. As John-Roger and I pointed out in our book *LIFE 101: Everything We Wish We Had Learned About Life In School—But Didn't,*

By the time we graduate from high school, most of us have spent more than 14,500 hours in the classroom. Along the way, we learned (and promptly forgot) several million facts.

But in all that time did we learn—or even explore—the meaning of life? Did we learn how to love ourselves? Did we learn the importance of forgiving ourselves and others? Did we learn about worthiness (and how to get it), the power of thoughts (and how to use them), or the value of mistakes? We know who wrote, "To be or not to be, that is the question," but we don't know the answer.

According to a 1993 survey, 39% of high school seniors did not know what the Holocaust referred to.

TIME MAGAZINE

That our educational system is not designed to teach us the "secrets of life" is no secret. In school, we learn how to do everything—except how to live.

On far less esoteric levels, any number of *practical* things aren't directly taught in twelve years of schooling: how to sew on a button, how to diagnose basic automobile problems, how to set goals and achieve them, how to budget money, how to budget time, what the police will and will not do to protect you, how to file a case in small claims court, how to find an apartment, how to fill out a credit application, how to do one's personal income tax. Junior high school and high school are designed to prepare one for *college*—which is good for those going on to college; but those who aren't would benefit more by learning a trade. If we taught kids what they *wanted* to know rather than what some removed academicians think everyone *should* know, school might become a place children want to attend, instead of the current detention centers they *must* attend. The school system's inability to teach the basics of life and how to make a livelihood leads directly to . . .

Poverty. Not only is it a cliché to say that it's a sin people starve to death in this richest country on earth; even *saying* that it's a cliché has become a cliché. We have somehow numbed ourselves to one of the greatest tragedies in our midst. There are 35.7 million people living below the poverty level in the United States. That's 14.2% of the total population. From 1978 to 1990, 20% more Americans fell below the poverty level. (I guess trickle-down economics just didn't trickle down far enough.) Meanwhile, the ratio of the average CEO's salary to that of a blue collar worker in 1980 was 25 to 1; in 1992, it was 91 to 1.

AIDS. There is a myth that AIDS is limited to homosexuals, intravenous drug users, and prostitutes. This myth may end up killing millions of heterosexual, drug-free men and women who wouldn't dream of visiting or becoming a prostitute. The fact is, world-wide, there are more heterosexually transmitted cases of

On May 31, 1987,
President Ronald Reagan
made his first speech on AIDS
after a six-year public silence
on the issue.

TONY KUSHNER

AIDS than all other cases combined. The World Health Organization estimates that, by the year 2000, more heterosexual women will be newly infected with the AIDS virus than any other group. The Center for Disease Control reports that, in the United States, "the percentage of AIDS cases attributed to heterosexual contact has increased 21% from 1990 to 1991." And yet many continue to believe that, if they avoid sex with homosexuals, intravenous drug users, and prostitutes, they will be safe. The spread of this disease into the heterosexual world in the United States is a direct result of the centuries-old prejudices held against homosexuals, drug users, and prostitutes. It will be a sad irony to watch this prejudice turn, bite, and perhaps devour its keepers. But that's just what's happening. Funding and research has lagged for AIDS because, after all, it only affects "fags, junkies, and whores. So what if they all get a terrible disease and die?" An all-out effort made a decade ago might have wiped out the disease before it reached the heterosexual community. Now it is too late. The disease is being spread through the heterosexual world due to the belief, "it can't happen here." Heterosexuals still seem to think that the simple advice, "Use a condom when you have intercourse," only applies to "them." This them/us attitude, promoted by centuries of irrational hatred and fear, is coming home to roost. It looks surprisingly like a vulture—a vulture crossed with the creature from *Alien*.

Other Problems. In case you're interested, the Union of International Associations has published a 2,133-page book entitled *Encyclopedia of World Problems*. In eight million words—enough for 80 to 100 normal-sized books—the *Encyclopedia* describes 13,167 problems. This is up from 10,233 problems in 1986 and a considerable jump from the 2,560 problems listed in 1976. This may be the beginning of a new science—*problemology*.

⚖ ⚖ ⚖

It should be clear that we have far more pressing demands upon us than regulating what consenting adults do by themselves or with other consenting adults. Surely we have better things to do with our precious resources than protect the delicate sensibilities of some self-appointed moralists.

EARLE LIEDERMAN
The Acme of Physical Perfection

Author of "Muscle Building," "Science of Wrestling," "Secrets of Strength," "Here's Health," "Endurance," etc.

If You Were Dying To-Night

and I offered something that would give you ten years more to live, would you take it? You'd grab it. Well, fellows, I've got it, but don't wait till you're dying or it won't do you a bit of good. It will then be too late. Right now is the time. To-morrow or any day, some disease will get you and if you have not equipped yourself to fight it off, you're gone. I don't claim to cure disease. I am not a medical doctor, but I'll put you in such condition that the doctor will starve to death waiting for you to take sick. Can you imagine a mosquito trying to bite a brick wall? A fine chance.

A RE-BUILT MAN

I like to get the weak ones. I delight in getting hold of a man who has been turned down as hopeless by others. It's easy enough to finish a task that's more than half done. But give me the weak, sickly chap and watch him grow stronger. That's what I like. It's fun to me because I know I can do it and I like to give the other fellow the laugh. I don't just give you a veneer of muscle that looks good to others. I work on you both inside and out. I not only put big, massive arms and legs on you, but I build up those inner muscles that surround your vital organs. The kind that give you real pep and energy—the kind that fire you with ambition and the courage to tackle anything set before you.

A REAL MAN

When I'm through with you you're a real man. The kind that can prove it. You will be able to do things you had thought impossible. And the beauty of it is you keep on going. Your deep full chest breathes in rich, pure air, stimulating your blood and making you just bubble over with vim and vitality. Your huge square shoulders and your massive muscular arms have that craving for the exercise of a regular he man. You have the flash to your eye and the pep to your step that will make you admired and sought after in both the business and social world.

This is no idle prattle, fellows. If you doubt me, make me prove it. Go ahead, I like it. I have already done this for thousands of others and my records are unchallenged. What I have done for them, I will do for you. Come then, for time flies and every day counts. Let this very day be the beginning of new life to you.

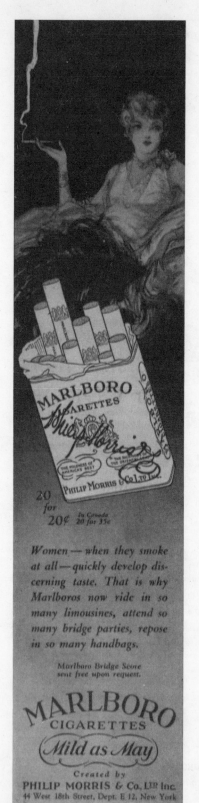

Women — when they smoke at all — quickly develop discerning taste. That is why Marlboros now ride in so many limousines, attend so many bridge parties, repose in so many handbags.

Marlboro Bridge Score sent free upon request.

MARLBORO
CIGARETTES
Mild as May

Created by
PHILIP MORRIS & Co. Ltd Inc.
44 West 18th Street, Dept. E 12, New York

In 1927, Marlboro Country was
hardly a hang-out for he-men.
Welcome to Marlboro Country!
"Mild as May."

You Hypocrites!*

> *Hypocrisy—*
> *prejudice with a halo.*
>
> AMBROSE BIERCE

WHEN WE SAY we're going to do something, and we don't do it, that's lying. Most would agree that is not very nice behavior. But there is behavior even more un-nice: *espousing* a philosophy and establishing a policy while, at the same time, *practicing* something entirely different. That's hypocrisy. There is so much deceit, deception, and falsehood within hypocrisy that lies are no longer *events;* they are part of a *continuum.*

Throughout history, few things have been condemned more often and more soundly than hypocrisy. Almost 3,000 years ago, Homer wrote, "I detest that man, who hides one thing in the depths of his heart, and speaks forth another." In the sixth century B.C., Lao-tzu said, "To pretend to know when you do not know is a disease." In the fifth century B.C., Confucius say, "Hold faithfulness and sincerity as first principles," and "[The superior man] speaks according to his actions." In the fourth century B.C., Plato observed, "False words are not only evil in themselves, but they infect the soul with evil."

There seems to be little Jesus of Nazareth hated more than hypocrisy; he condemned it more than anything else. "Hypocrite" was his favorite swear word. (Jesus Christ was severely limited when it came to swear words. When really upset, what could he say? "Me!" or "Me damn it!"? His favorite seemed to be, "Hypocrite!") Jesus condemns hypocrisy at least twenty times by name in the New Testament (Matthew 6:2, 6:5, 6:16, 7:5, 15:7, 22:18, 23:13, 23:15, 23:23, 23:25, 23:27, 23:28, 23:29, 24:51, Mark 7:6, 12:15, Luke 6:42, 12:1, 12:56, 13:15) and condemns the idea of hypocrisy many more.

*Please don't get upset: I'm just quoting Jesus (Matthew 15:7, 22:18, 23:13, 23:15, 23:23, 23:25, 23:27, 23:29, Mark 7:6, Luke 13:15).

> *The only vice
> that can not be forgiven
> is hypocrisy.*
>
> WILLIAM HAZLITT

Here's one sample:

> Woe to you, teachers of the law and Pharisees, you hypocrites! You shut the kingdom of heaven in men's faces. You yourselves do not enter, nor will you let those enter who are trying to (Matthew 23:13).

Jesus also claims that hypocrites "have neglected the more important matters of the law—justice, mercy and faithfulness" (Matthew 23:23). Peter advised, "Therefore, rid yourselves of all malice and all deceit, hypocrisy, envy, and slander of every kind" (1 Peter 2:1). (More about Jesus and hypocrisy in the chapter, "His Master's Voice?")

In the fourteenth century, Geoffrey Chaucer called a hypocrite, "The smyler with the knife under the cloke." Shakespeare, of course, had something to say about hypocrisy (he had something to say about *everything*): "With devotion's visage and pious action we do sugar o'er the devil himself." Molière noticed an interesting consequence of hypocrisy, which is as true today as it was then: "Hypocrisy is a fashionable vice, and all fashionable vices pass for virtue."

During the Revolutionary War, Thomas Jefferson gave some insight into the underpinnings and history of hypocrisy:

> Is uniformity attainable? Millions of innocent men, women, and children, since the introduction of Christianity, have been burnt, tortured, fined, imprisoned; yet we have not advanced one inch towards uniformity. What has been the effect of coercion? To make one half the world fools, and the other half hypocrites.

Less than a hundred years later, Abraham Lincoln wrote:

> Our progress in degeneracy appears to me to be pretty rapid. As a nation we began by declaring that "all men are created equal." When the Know-Nothings get control, it will read "all men are created equal, except Negroes and foreigners and Catholics." When it comes to this, I shall prefer emigrating to some country where they make no pretense of loving liberty—to Russia, for instance, where despotism can be taken pure, and without the base alloy hypocrisy.

Leo Tolstoy (one of the people Lincoln could have met had he gone to Russia) observes that seeing things with a child's eyes often reveals hypocrisy more readily than does analysis:

> Hypocrisy is anything whatever may deceive the cleverest and most penetrating man, but the least wide-awake of children recognizes it, and is revolted by it, however ingeniously it may be disguised.

One of the most perceptive revealers of hypocrisy in our country, Mark

Twain, was once told by a blustering tycoon, "Before I die, I mean to make a pilgrimage to the top of Mt. Sinai in the Holy Land and read the Ten Commandments aloud." "Why don't you stay right home in Boston," suggested Twain, "and keep them?"

This brings up a problem observed by André Gide, "The true hypocrite is the one who ceases to perceive his deception, the one who lies with sincerity." People actually start to *believe* they are not being hypocritical; they say one thing and do another with impunity—with pride, in fact. They have told themselves so many rational lies about their self-deception, they deceive themselves. Those who have lost track of their hypocrisy—especially those who begin to consider it virtuous—are the most dangerous hypocrites of all. Unfortunately, they're the most prevalent form.

> *The prohibition law,*
> *written for weaklings and derelicts,*
> *has divided the nation,*
> *like Gaul, into three parts—*
> *wets, drys, and hypocrites.*
>
> FLORENCE SABIN
> 1931

We need not look far, however, to find hypocrisy. Alas, hypocrisy begins at home. As Don Marquis pointed out, "A hypocrite is a person who—but who isn't?"

⚖ ⚖ ⚖

With respect to consensual crimes, *hypocrisy* is spelled C-I-G-A-R-E-T-T-E-S.

More than 300,000 deaths *each year* in the United States are related to cigarette smoking. According to the American Council on Science and Health, cigarette smoking is the #1 cause of preventable death in the United States. Four of the five leading causes of death are related to cigarette smoking. One in six deaths in this country, 87% of all lung cancer deaths, and 30% of all other cancer deaths are tobacco related. Cigarettes are the #1 cause of heart disease, and heart disease is the #1 cause of death in the United States. Out of 100 regular smokers in the United States, one will be murdered, two will die in traffic accidents, and 25 will be killed by tobacco use.

And yet, not only are cigarettes perfectly legal and available everywhere; tobacco growers are subsidized by the federal government,* and cigarettes are

---

*One of the most virulent supporters of consensual crime prosecution, Senator Jesse Helms of North Carolina, is also one of the most outspoken supporters of the tobacco industry and the federal government's tobacco grower subsidies. He is violently opposed to restrictions of any kind on tobacco. This comes as no shock: North Carolina is the #1 tobacco-producing state in the nation. With towns such as Winston-Salem and Raleigh, who's surprised? In fact, North Carolina produces nearly 40% of the tobacco grown in this country. In his book, *Merchants of Death*, Larry C. White tells about a 1986 incident involving government subsidies to tobacco growers in which "it is only the taxpayers who are being shortchanged—for about $1 billion. . . . Jesse Helms is responsible for this boondoggle." It should be pointed out that Helms is firmly on the side of the tobacco *companies* and *large* growers, not on the side of the independent "family" tobacco farms. Has anyone explained to Senator Helms how much more his state could make growing hemp? (See "Hemp for Victory.")

> *While the collateral consequences*
> *of drugs such as cocaine*
> *are indisputably severe,*
> *they are not unlike those*
> *which flow from the misuse*
> *of other, legal, substances.*
>
> U.S. SUPREME COURT JUSTICE
> BYRON R. WHITE

advertised using beautiful young people and with such words as *enjoy, refresh,* and that perennial favorite, *satisfaction.*

Cigarettes are our country's most serious drug problem. Three thousand teen-agers start smoking each day—more than 1,000,000 each year. "A teenager who smokes more than one cigarette," says Andrew Weil, M.D., "has only a 15% chance of remaining a non-smoker." More than 50% of all smokers start before they are eighteen. According to the American Cancer Society, "The pharmacologic and behavioral processes that determine addiction [to tobacco] are similar to those that determine addiction to drugs such as heroin and cocaine."

If you're wondering whether tobacco harms truly innocent victims, the answer is "YES!" (And how.) More than 53,000 deaths each year are attributed to secondhand cigarette smoke—the smoke breathed by people in the same room as a smoker. Secondhand (or environmental) cigarette smoke is far more cancerous than even primary cigarette smoke. A study of nonsmoking women whose husbands smoked a pack or more a day found that these women were *twice* as likely to develop lung cancer as women who were married to nonsmokers. Death from environmental tobacco smoke is the #3 preventable cause of death in the United States (just behind regular smoking and alcohol).

"Well, she can leave the room when he smokes. She's still responsible," some might argue. All right. What about children? This from the American Cancer Society:

> Environmental tobacco smoke (ETS) poses additional health hazards for unborn and young children. Children exposed to secondhand smoke have increased risks of respiratory illnesses and infections, impaired development of lung function, and middle ear infections. If a woman smokes while she's pregnant, her baby may be born with low birth weight, birth defects, chronic breathing difficulties and learning disabilities. Women who smoke a pack or more a day suffer about a 50% greater risk of infant mortality. Infants born to women who smoked during pregnancy are more likely to die from Sudden Infant Death syndrome.

According to the American Academy of Pediatrics, more than 9,000,000 children under the age of *five* are exposed daily to environmental tobacco smoke. Those people who justify enforcing laws against consensual activities because they may "set a bad example" for children need to look no further than this *actual physical* harm to which parents expose their children—unborn and born—everyday. The relative handful of crack-addicted babies, while certainly a concern, don't hold a candle to 9,000,000 environmental smoke–inflicted babies. (At least drug addicts don't keep giving their babies drugs after they're born.)

And then there's the *cost*. Cigarettes cost the economy *$65 billion* annually. That's $2.17 *per pack* of cigarettes to treat smoking-related diseases and in lost productivity.

Meanwhile, we are exporting this death. Cigarette exports have increased 200% since 1985. (Exports to Japan have increased 700% in that same period.) The world wants to visit Marlboro Country. Have we bothered to warn them that Marlboro Country is Boot Hill? Worldwide, cigarettes kill 2,500,000 each year.*

> It is now clear that disease risk
> due to inhalation of tobacco smoke
> is not limited
> to the individual who is smoking.
>
> FORMER U.S. SURGEON GENERAL
> C. EVERETT KOOP

In addition to *causing* cancer, the cigarette industry itself *is* a cancer. Cigarettes are extremely profitable (drug dealing usually is). Cigarette companies take in about $28 billion in cigarette sales each year, and on that make a profit of more than $6 billion. That's a profit margin of 23%. Most companies are *thrilled* with a profit margin of 10%. (The national corporate average in 1991 was 6.9%.) *Forbes* magazine commented, "Only the Mint makes money more easily than cigarette companies." Ironically, it's *because* cigarettes are deadly that competition is low: other companies simply don't want to be involved in peddling death. (Addictions they don't mind; death, they do. Call them old-fashioned.) Six tobacco giants make practically every brand of cigarette sold in the United States. How do they avoid anti-trust or price-fixing proceedings? They simply argue that the more cigarettes cost, the better: fewer people will buy them; therefore, fewer people will smoke. As hypocrites often do, they play both sides of every coin—and they have a lot of coins. Once people are hooked, they're hooked, and they'll pay whatever is necessary for their next fix.

With this money, the cigarette industry keeps the simple fact that tobacco is the most addictive substance in the world, and that cigarettes kill, away from the American public. Cigarette companies spend a fortune each year on advertising, and they use that clout to eliminate or soften media stories that might be hazardous to the health of the tobacco industry. In the past, only the media accepting cigarette advertisements were vulnerable to this pressure. Now, the cigarette companies have bought just about every wholesome brand in America.** Now they

*Senator Jesse Helms is the senior Republican on the *Terrorism, Narcotics*, and International Operations Subcommittee (a subcommittee of the Senate Foreign Relations Committee). Guess which of these—terrorism or narcotics—Senator Helms finds to be the greatest threat to Western Civilization? For Senator Helms, an act of international terrorism is when foreign countries threaten to increase their import tariffs on American cigarettes.

**Nabisco, General Foods, Oreo Cookies, Jell-o, Ritz Crackers, Planters Peanuts, Triscuits, Miller Beer, Jim Beam Bourbon, Kool-Aid, Log Cabin Syrup, Oscar Mayer Wieners, Maxwell House Coffee, Entenmann's Cakes, Post Grape-Nuts (Euell Gibbons is rolling in his grave), Fleischmann's Margarine, Kraft (yes, something as American as Kraft Macaroni & Cheese is owned by a tobacco company), Carefree Sugarless Gum, Lifesavers, Fig Newtons, Animal Crackers, Cool-Whip,

> *This very night*
> *I am going to leave off tobacco!*
> *Surely there must be*
> *some other world*
> *in which this*
> *unconquerable purpose*
> *shall be realized.*
>
> CHARLES LAMB
> 1815

can use their advertising clout to control almost all media—even television, where cigarette ads have been banned for years.* The fear of losing ad revenue dictates many editorial and business decisions. The *Reader's Digest*, for example, has always refused cigarette ads and has published some scathing articles about cigarettes and the tobacco industry. In 1986, however, even the *Reader's Digest* turned down a *paid* advertisement about the dangers of smoking from the American Heart Association. (To *Reader's Digest's* credit, it continues to run articles on the dangers of smoking.)

But the cigarette companies don't control just elected officials (Jesse Helms is but one of many politicians in the tobacco industry's pocket—or pouch) and much of the media. In early 1984 (that ominous year), Greg Louganis, a former smoker, was asked by the American Cancer Society to be national chairman of its annual Great American Smokeout. Louganis—one of the finest Olympic athletes of all time—was excited. He had smoked from junior high until he was twenty-three. He quit because he saw a twelve-year-old smoking, asked the boy why, and

Velveeta, Pinkerton Guards, and Franklin (Ben is rolling in *his* grave) Life Insurance (a company that gives lower rates to nonsmokers). This list is subject to change. Cigarette companies buy and sell other businesses as easily as you or I might pick up a box of Triscuits, a six-pack of Miller Genuine Draft, or a roll of Lifesavers—they just throw them in their shopping cart and head for the check-out counter (the stock market). At one time, they owned Colonel Sanders and Seven-Up; they weren't profitable enough—or didn't give them the clout they wanted—so out they went.

*When cigarette advertising was allowed on television, the cigarette companies put enormous pressure on all shows to include smoking as one of the "good guy" activities and eliminate smoking as a "bad guy" activity. In other words, they wanted the heroes to smoke and the villains to do something else—playing pool was okay, taking other drugs was fine, driving expensive cars was okay. Gene Roddenberry told me an amusing story which, when it happened, was far from amusing. While he was creating "Star Trek," the network (NBC) and the production company (Paramount) put enormous pressure on Roddenberry to include cigarettes on board the starship *Enterprise*. Roddenberry pointed out that, considering the health risks known about cigarettes even in 1966, no one would be smoking by stardate 1513.1 (circa A.D. 2264) (except, perhaps, for those who "cling on" to the idea that tobacco addiction is a good thing). The network and studio executives used both pressure and persuasion. They tried to get Roddenberry enthused about how cigarettes would look in the twenty-third century. Maybe they would be *square* instead of *round;* perhaps they would come in *colors;* perhaps cigarettes would even *light themselves!* Roddenberry's creative juices were not stimulated. Finally, the executives gave him an ultimatum: either the starship *Enterprise* would officially be declared a Smoking Zone, or Roddenberry's other radical idea—to have a woman as an officer of the Star Trek crew—would have to be abandoned. The executives were clever in offering this choice: Roddenberry's wife was already cast to play the female officer. After quite a bit of soul-searching, Roddenberry came to the only conclusion he could: both cigarettes and his wife did not get an intergalactic boarding pass. The irony was that, in later years, when smoking was less fashionable, Paramount pointed with pride to "Star Trek" as one of the few shows in syndication that had none of those "distasteful" cigarettes.

AIN'T NOBODY'S BUSINESS IF YOU DO

was told, "I want to be just like you!" Louganis stopped cold. He later said, "After I
quit, I wanted to tell every twelve-year-old
that I had quit." His story, told at the peak
of his Olympic fame, could have inspired
tens of thousands to quit smoking. Alas, it
was not to be.

Louganis trained in California at the
Mission Viejo pool. His coach, the best in
the world, was employed by Mission Viejo.
Philip Morris owns the entire town of Mission Viejo. Philip Morris made it clear: if

> *In Europe, when tobacco*
> *was first introduced,*
> *it was immediately banned.*
> *In Turkey, if you*
> *got caught with tobacco,*
> *you had your nose slit.*
> *China and Russia imposed*
> *the death penalty*
> *for possession of tobacco.*
>
> ANDREW WEIL, M.D.

Louganis became chairman of the Great American Smokeout, he would lose his
pool and his coach. Philip Morris also threatened to fire other Mission Viejo
employees close to Louganis. Louganis had no choice. He declined the American
Cancer Society's invitation, without comment. As Larry C. White pointed out in
The Merchants of Death, "The threat of Louganis's being sent away from Mission
Viejo, away from his coach, was the sports world's equivalent of saying, 'I'll kill
your mother.'" The California Department of Health said it best: "Smokers are
addicts. Cigarette companies are pushers."

Is all this an argument for banning cigarettes? No. It's *education*, not *prohibition*
that makes constructive change. Remember when cigarettes were considered
glamorous, sophisticated, and even healthy? No one believes that now. Through
education alone, more than 40,000,000 Americans have quit smoking. This chapter simply shows that we have a deeply ingrained hypocrisy in our culture. It
allows cigarette companies to knowingly kill 300,000 people each year and make a
profit on it, while we insist that our government arrest consensual "criminals"
whose harm, either to themselves or to others, if combined, doesn't even *begin* to
approach the damage done by cigarettes.

In terms of addiction, prescription and over-the-counter drugs run a close
second (and some say, first) to cigarettes. Tens of millions of Americans can't get
through the day without (that is, they are addicted to) tranquilizers and amphetamines, or can't make it through the night without sleeping pills. Each year
125,000 deaths are linked to prescription drugs. In 1989, Tom Kelly, then–Deputy
Administrator of the Drug Enforcement Administration, said on C-SPAN (where
else?),

> I think it's very obvious that, on the legitimate side of drug use, we have be-
> come a totally drug dependent society in this country. That's strictly on the
> legitimate side. That's what we teach our children in this country today.
> How bad is it? . . . We have about 30 million people who are regular users of
> stimulants. We have about 20 million who are regular users of
> depressants—excuse me, of sedatives. And we have about 8 million who are
> chronic users of tranquilizers. And that's all on the legitimate side. Thinking

> *If you are young*
> *and you drink a great deal*
> *it will spoil your health,*
> *slow your mind,*
> *make you fat—*
> *in other words,*
> *turn you into an adult.*
>
> P. J. O'ROURKE

of those numbers, are we not drug-dependent on the legitimate side?

And let's not forget America's Favorite Drug, *caffeine*. According to a research report published, in the *Archives of General Psychiatry* in 1992:

> Our results indicate that some coffee drinkers exhibit common signs of drug dependence, i.e., they self-administer coffee for the effects of caffeine, have withdrawal symptoms on cessation of caffeine and experience adverse effects from caffeine intake.

The most widely used recreational drug in this country, of course, is alcohol. A 1990 study by the U.S. Department of Health asked participants which drugs they had used in the past thirty days. It was found that 51% had used alcohol, while only 5% had used marijuana, and less than 1% had used cocaine. A 1991 U.S. Department of Health study asked young people, ages eighteen to thirty, the same question. Almost 71% had used alcohol within the past thirty days; 28% had used cigarettes; 13% had used marijuana; 2% had used cocaine; less that 2% had used stimulants; about 1% had used tranquilizers; and less than 1% had used LSD, inhalants, and steroids. None of the study participants had used heroin and only 0.5% had used other opiates. Of high school students, 2% said they currently used cocaine, 14% said they currently used marijuana, while 59% said they currently used alcohol. (It was found that 28% of the high school seniors smoked cigarettes.)

Alcohol is also the recreational drug most likely to be *abused*: 43% of college students, 35% of high school seniors, and 26% of eighth grade students (thirteen-year-olds!) said that they had had five or more drinks *in a row* at some point during the last two weeks. In 1990, more than half the fatal car accidents in this country were related to alcohol—killing 22,083 people.* This is the equivalent of a fully

---

*The old saying, "Statistics don't lie, but liars use statistics" describes perfectly the people and organizations trying to overestimate the "drug problem" in this country. I have seen this figure of 22,083 listed as "drug and alcohol-related traffic fatalities." They were, almost entirely, alcohol-related. Another of my favorites is the statistic officially labeled, "Drug Abuse–Related Emergency Room Episodes." It says that 371,208 people were admitted to emergency rooms in 1990 for drug abuse–related reasons. I have seen this figure bandied about as proof that drugs are not safe, and are a horrendous problem ("Almost 400,000 people wind up in emergency rooms every year due to the drug epidemic!" people shriek). Further examination, however, shows that 172,815 of the cases—46%—were attempted suicides. To call attempted suicide a "drug abuse–related" occurrence is absurd. Drugs were the *method*, not the problem. Just because 1,000 people commit suicide by jumping off tall buildings, does not make tall buildings dangerous. Only 29,817 of the 371,208 total emergency room episodes resulted from "recreational use" of drugs (that's only 8% of the total) and 74% of those patients were treated and released without being admitted to the hospital. (The figure 29,817 certainly indicates a problem, but compare it with the 300,000 smoking *deaths*. There are approximately 6,000 "illicit" drug deaths each year—2% of the tobacco deaths.)

loaded 747 crashing. Three times a week. Fifty-two weeks a year. An additional 469,000 nonfatal car crashes involved alcohol. *Half* of all teenage fatalities are alcohol-related. In a confidential survey of high school seniors who had received a traffic ticket in the last twelve months, 10% of them admitted being under the influence of alcohol at the time they received the ticket. Only 3% were under the influence of marijuana or hashish, and 1% under the influence of all other drugs. Alcohol is involved in 80% of fire deaths, 77% of falls, 65% of drownings, 65% of murders, 60% of child abuse cases, 35% of rapes, and 55% of all arrests. More than 11 million Americans have seen a family member killed or seriously injured by a drunk driver in the last nine years. Society's loss in wages, productivity, medical and legal costs caused by death and injuries in drunk-driving crashes exceeds $24 billion each year. On an average Friday or Saturday night, one out of every ten drivers on the road is drunk. In 1991, 13% of all male arrests were for drunk driving. According to a 1992 study by the National Center for Health Statistics, "10,500,000 Americans are alcoholics; 76,000,000 more are affected by alcohol abuse, having been married to an alcoholic or problem drinker or having grown up with one."

> *Laws do not persuade just because they threaten.*
>
> SENECA
> A.D. 65

Is this a call for a new Prohibition? No. As with cigarettes, the key to helping people from hurting themselves is education. (More on this in the chapter "Education, Not Legislation.") There is, however, a great deal more we could do to protect *innocent*, nonconsenting victims of alcohol abuse such as sober drivers and pedestrians. (Please see the chapter, "Fail-Safe Safety Devices.")

⚖ ⚖ ⚖

There are only two possible things we, as a nation, can do to remove this hypocrisy: ban cigarettes, alcohol, caffeine, and have *all drugs*—including those currently sold over-the-counter—require a prescription from at least *two* doctors, *or* we can remove the laws against consensual activities. We can no longer afford to maintain the pretense that we really *care* whether or not people harm their own person and property. If we really cared, we'd outlaw tobacco, alcohol, caffeine, and over-the-counter medicines. We are obviously *not* going to do this.

Does removing laws against consensual activities and keeping tobacco, alcohol, caffeine, and over-the-counter medicines legal make us an uncaring nation? Not at all. It makes us a *mature* nation; one that realizes you cannot legislate morality, prevent people from hurting themselves, or protect people from the consequences of behavior they *choose* to take part in. If we accept this mature stance (which is already the supreme law of the land: the Constitution), then we must remove all legal restrictions on consensual activities. There is no other way.

PART II

WHY LAWS AGAINST CONSENSUAL ACTIVITIES ARE NOT A GOOD IDEA

THE NEXT SEVERAL CHAPTERS elaborate in some detail why consensual crimes are not a good idea. Please keep in mind as you read these chapters that you don't have to agree with *all* of the points or all of the objections—any one is sufficient reason to stop putting people in jail for activities that do not harm the person or property of nonconsenting others.

OUR RIGHTS AND OUR LIBERTIES.

L. JOHNSON & Co.

397

It's Un-American!

THE UNITED STATES is the most diverse country on earth. Nowhere else in the world do so many people with differing ethnic, religious, racial, and cultural backgrounds live side by side in relative peace and harmony. The "melting pot" did not melt us into one, uniform people, but melted away the intolerence, prejudice, and the notion that one group or another "shouldn't be here."

This didn't happen right away, of course—there was nothing magical about this soil. It happened over time. The prejudice of one generation became the toleration of the next generation became the fascination of the next generation became the norm of the next.

Drawn by the concept of a "new world" and, later, "the land of the free," settlers eventually realized that, in order to get the freedom they sought, they would have to give others freedom as well. This realization sometimes came through rational thought, but was more often a compromise in settling bloody disputes.

The Europeans who first came to America fell roughly into three categories: (1) those seeking religious freedom, (2) those seeking fame and fortune, and (3) criminals.* These three elements were already at odds, and within each element there was discord.

---

*England did not have prisons as we know them for its common classes—only the aristocracy got to spend years "in The Tower." For the average British citizen, punishments for small crimes included fines, flogging, or some other torture. Sentences for greater crimes were served on prison ships or by exile for a number of years, often for life. The prisoner was thus "transported" to the foreign land, America being the favorite choice from the mid-1600s through 1776. In that year, the offspring of formerly transported criminals became *terribly* uncooperative. From 1776 on, Australia picked up the slack.

> *It gives me great pleasure indeed
> to see the stubbornness
> of an incorrigible nonconformist
> warmly acclaimed.*
>
> ALBERT EINSTEIN

On the religious front, the Catholics and the Protestants hated each other, and both hated the Jews. Protestants divided along the lines of those who were happy with the Church of England (the Anglicans) and those who wanted major reforms (the Puritans).

Those seeking fame and fortune vied for land claims, trading rights, transport routes, reserved parking places, and the dozens of other things entrepreneurs squabble over.

The criminals were anything from political dissidents and recalcitrant serfs to thieves and murderers. They had little in common except that they had broken England's common law.

The religious, ambitious, and malicious Europeans, all hating each other, made up of splinter groups that didn't get along, also had to contend with the Native Americans (and vice versa). When the Europeans arrived, there were as many as 4,000,000 Native Americans on the land now known as the United States. The natives who were, at first, friendly, or, at worst, had a live-and-let-live attitude toward the immigrants, eventually turned hostile. Spain, starting with Christopher Columbus's shipping natives back to Spain as slaves, had created a policy (by then over a century old and, therefore, a *tradition*) of enslaving, exploiting, and abusing the natives. The natives in the more tropical climes might have put up with this, but the native North Americans would have none of it. Here began the most dramatic—and the most tragic—failure of the melting pot to melt. As many differences as the European settlers had among themselves, they had more in common with each other than they did with "the redskins." The Native Americans were never officially included in the melting pot—even those who converted to Christianity, learned English, and attempted to fit into the white man's ways.

Within the colonies, the changes started when some of the children of the Puritans turned out to be not quite as religious as their parents. Conversely, the children of some of the criminals were more religious.* In both cases, the older generation shook their heads and moaned, "What's the younger generation coming to?" When the slightly less religious children of the Puritans and the slightly more religious children of the criminals married, the Puritan parents and the criminal parents discovered they had something in common after all: children who were *positively out of their minds!* Some children married Native Americans; others married the new immigrants. They all had children, and the first generation of true Americans was born.

Soon, another group was added: slaves from Africa. They, as the Constitution

---

*The entrepreneurial settlers were too busy taking meetings and shuttling to and from England on the red-eye to have children.

euphemistically puts it, "migrated" to America—but much against their will. They weren't even *included* in the melting pot until after the 1860s, and significant melting did not take place until the 1960s. (One prays that the melting will be completed some time before the 2060s.)

After the Revolutionary War and the formation of "a new nation conceived in liberty and dedicated to the proposition that all men are created equal," people seeking freedom of all kinds began flocking to America. The French, who were our allies in the Revolutionary War, were welcome, but "spoke funny." The Chinese, who were imported as cheap labor to build the railroads, were despised, abused, but eventually accepted. The Irish, who came to escape the devastation of the potato famine and the tyranny of England, arrived at roughly the same time as the Italians. These two took an instant dislike to one another. It was nearly a century before this animosity dissolved. The Jews came from many countries, primarily Russia and eastern Europe, where one pogrom after another encouraged them to try the religious freedom promised in the Constitution. They did not find it. Strong anti-Semitism and "restricted" hotels, clubs, restaurants, and whole neighborhoods caused the sort of ghettoizing the Jews had unfortunately become accustomed to in their native lands. This discrimination would not decrease until after World War II, when Hitler demonstrated to the world the ultimate result of religious intolerance. America finally woke up in the late 1940s and began to refer proudly to its "Judeo-Christian" heritage.

The underlying philosophy that made the melting pot work was a belief that was both high-mindedly enlightened and street-wise practical: "You allow me my diversity and I'll allow you yours." It's an ongoing process: ever changing, ever growing, ever looking for the balance between the extremes.

> *Those who won our independence believed that the final end of the state was to make men free to develop their faculties. They valued liberty both as an end and as a means. They believed liberty to be the secret of happiness and courage to be the secret of liberty.*
>
> JUSTICE LOUIS BRANDEIS

⚖ ⚖ ⚖

The status quo has always tried to keep the status, well, quo. "The way it is is the way it's meant to be, the way God wants it to be, and if you don't like it here, you can go back where you came from." Recently, for example, we have seen an influx of immigrants from "non-Christian nations" (India, other parts of Asia, and the Middle East) which has struck fear into the hearts of those who protect "traditional American values" (that is, *their* values). That these Hindus, Buddhists, and Muslims are turning out to be perfectly good citizens is even *more* disturbing. ("They must be up to something.")

So, a movement is afoot to declare the United States a "Christian nation," so that, when all naturalized citizens swear allegiance to the flag, they will also swear

> *The ugliness of bigotry*
> *stands in direct contradiction*
> *to the very meaning of America.*
>
> HUBERT H. HUMPHREY

allegiance to the particular interpretation of Christianity popularized by, among others, St. Pat Robertson and St. Jerry Falwell. The new immigrants will have to abandon their native religion just as they chose to abandon allegiance to the country of their birth. If God is on our side, however, our hard-won freedom *of* religion and freedom *from* religion will not be so easily usurped.

Ruling by religion was tried in this country and it failed—miserably. Here, for example, is an early colonial law:

> If any man have a stubborn or rebellious Son, of sufficient understanding and years, *viz. fifteen years of age*, which will not obey the voice of his Father, or the voice of his Mother, and that when they have chastened him, will not hearken unto them; then shall his Father or Mother, being his natural Parents, lay hold on him, and bring him to the Magistrates assembled in Court, and testifie unto them, that their Son is Stubborn and Rebellious, and will not obey their voice and chastisement, but lives in sundry notorious Crimes, such a son shall be put to death.

The law then states the specific biblical chapter and verse on which the law was based (Deuteronomy 21:18–21 KJV).

> If a man have a stubborn and rebellious son, which will not obey the voice of his father, or the voice of his mother, and *that,* when they have chastened him, will not hearken unto them: Then shall his father and his mother lay hold on him, and bring him out unto the elders of his city, and unto the gate of his place; And they shall say unto the elders of his city, This our son *is* stubborn and rebellious, he will not obey our voice; *he is* a glutton,* and a drunkard. And all the men of his city shall stone him with stones, that he die.

How many of us would be alive today if that law were still on the books?**

---

*Far be it from *me* to cast the first stone, but . . . have you seen Jerry Falwell lately? Hasn't anyone told him that gluttony is one of the Seven Deadly Sins? Hasn't anyone warned him what would happen to him if his cry for "God's law to become man's law" should include Deuteronomy 21:18–21, or Proverbs 23:2 ("put a knife to your throat if you are given to gluttony")? Proverbs 28:7 says that Jerry shames his whole congregation (and their fathers) ("a companion of gluttons disgraces his father"). And Titus 1:12–13 gives us *all* the authority to call Rev. Falwell to task ("'Cretans are always liars, evil brutes, lazy gluttons.' This testimony is true. Therefore, rebuke them sharply"). I'll let Jerry be rebuked by one who knew overindulgence well, but who never lost his sense of humor about it, Orson Welles: "Gluttony is not a secret vice." Frankly, I don't care if Jerry consumes more than several third-world nations combined. I just wish he wouldn't do it in public where it frightens the children. (THIS JUST IN: Rush Limbaugh has agreed to be Jerry Falwell's personal trainer. Film at eleven.)

**I know I wouldn't. (But then, neither would my father.)

The founding fathers realized ruling by religion wouldn't work, and, wisely, prevented it. The United States opted for a *free* nation, not one bound by any person's or group's interpretation of any religious text. (More on this in the chapter, "Laws against Consensual Activities Violate the Separation of Church and State, Threatening the Freedom of and from Religion.")

Diversity, not conformity, is the true strength of America.

⚖ ⚖ ⚖

> *Restriction of free thought*
> *and free speech*
> *is the most dangerous*
> *of all subversions.*
> *It is the one un-American act*
> *that could most easily defeat us.*
>
> JUSTICE WILLIAM O. DOUGLAS

In nature, purebreds can excel in certain characteristics at the expense of others: they may be beautiful, but stupid; gentle, but sickly; ferocious, but unpredictable. It's the crossbreds that have the strength, flexibility, and multileveled instincts not only to survive, but to *thrive* in a broad range of conditions.

The United States is not just a crossbred; it's a mongrel—the most mongrel nation on earth. It's what gives us our strength, sensitivity, tenacity, flexibility, common sense, and spunk. ("You have spunk, don't you?" Lou Grant asked Mary Richards at their first meeting. Mary nodded proudly. Lou glared at her: "I *hate* spunk.")

Many citizens of the United States have stopped even trying to trace their national roots. When asked, "What nationality are you?" they respond, "American." And rightly so.

I have flowing in my veins Irish, Italian, a little Cherokee, and God knows what-all. I'm an American. The struggle between the Irish and the Italians came to an end with me and tens of thousands like me. How could the Italians hate me? I'm part Italian. How could the Irish hate me? I'm part Irish. How can I side with the settlers? I'm part Native American. How can I side with the Native Americans? I'm mostly settler. I can understand many points of view. I have compassion for many sides. And I am one of millions who has the blood of many nations flowing through our veins: the wealth of many cultures, the wisdom of many generations—and many, many ways to love God.

As Bishop Fulton J. Sheen explained it,

> Democracy cannot survive where there is such uniformity that everyone wears exactly the same intellectual uniform or point of view. Democracy implies diversity of outlook, a variety of points of view on politics, economics, and world affairs.

> Hence the educational ideal is not uniformity but unity, for unity allows diversity of points of view regarding the good means to a good end.

"If there is any fixed star in our constitutional constellation," said Supreme

> *That at any rate is the theory
> of our Constitution.
> It is an experiment,
> as all life is an experiment.*
>
> JUSTICE
> OLIVER WENDELL HOLMES, JR.

Court Justice Robert H. Jackson, "It is that no official, high or petty, can prescribe what shall be orthodox in politics, nationalism, religion, or other matters of opinion or force citizens to confess by word or act their faith therein."

America is a bold, dynamic, audacious, enthralling, ongoing experiment. There have been many risks, many embarrassments (Richard Speck, John Hinckley, Jeffrey Dahmer) and many glories (Luther Burbank, Helen Keller, Thomas Edison,* Liberace**).

Where else but in America could we read this news item?

A De Kalb County, Georgia, Superior court ruled that Gary Eugene Duda, 35, could change his first name to "Zippidy." Duda said that he had already been called "Zippidy" by friends for most of his life.

The American experiment has seen its tragedies (the execution of Sacco, Vanzenti, and the Rosenbergs, the imprisonment of 100,000 Japanese Americans during World War II, the nuclear arms race) and its triumphs (Lindbergh's flight to Paris, putting a man on the moon, word processors).

The experiment continues.

There are some who want to call the experiment off, who want to roll back America to those happy, carefree, God-fearing pre-Constitutional times. Then, *their* God would rule. By force of law.

Let's not let them.

---

*Imagine: one man invented the electric light, the phonograph, the motion picture, the ticker tape, and the improved telephone. This is a man who knew the value of experimentation.

**Another man who knew the value of experimentation. What other culture could create Liberace? Flamboyance and eccentricity are certainly a part of our national character—essential and valued parts. And who was more flamboyantly, eccentrically himself than Liberace? When told by a concerned fan, "You wouldn't smile so much, Mr. Liberace, if you heard the things people said about you," Liberace smiled, "I heard 'em. You know what else?" Liberace smiled broader, "I started 'em."

Laws against Consensual Activities
Are Unconstitutional

ALTHOUGH THE DECLARATION of Independence is not, like the Constitution, the "law of the land," it is certainly the *spirit* of the land. In the words of Abraham Lincoln,

I have never had a feeling, politically, that did not spring from the sentiments embodied in the Declaration of Independence . . . which gave liberty not alone to the people of this country, but hope to all the world, for all future time. It was that which gave promise that in due time the weights would be lifted from the shoulders of all men, and that all should have an equal chance. This is the sentiment embodied in the Declaration of Independence. . . . I would rather be assassinated on this spot than surrender it.

The Declaration of Independence was not about just independence from England or even Europe—it was a declaration of independence from ignorance, religious intolerance, and political tyranny.

There is, by the way, no signed Declaration of Independence from July 4, 1776. The Declaration of Independence was approved by voice vote on July 2, 1776, and the parchment copy was signed by the first delegates on August 2, 1776. Other signatures rolled in throughout the year. (Thomas McKean did not sign until 1781.) (What we call the "Declaration of Independence" is officially "The Unanimous Declaration of the Thirteen United States of America.") The only reason we celebrate the Fourth of July is that both Thomas Jefferson and John Adams remembered it as the date of the signing. There is, however, no congressional record of a signing taking place on that date. Were it not for Adams and Jefferson remembering it being on the Fourth, the Fourth of July would either be the Second of July or the Second of August.

> *For most Americans
> the Constitution had become
> a hazy document,
> cited like the Bible
> on ceremonial occasions
> but forgotten in the
> daily transactions of life.*
>
> ARTHUR M. SCHLESINGER, JR.

That both men—first comrades, then political enemies, and finally friends—should misremember the day is the basis of one of those truth-is-stranger-than-fiction stories. In July 1826, Thomas Jefferson awoke, asked, "Is it the Fourth yet?" Told that it was, he quietly died. Five hours later, John Adams, not knowing of Jefferson's demise, said, "Thomas Jefferson still survives!" and died.

July 4, 1826 marked the fiftieth anniversary of July 4, 1776.

In his last letter, written ten days before his death, Jefferson gave his final thoughts on the Declaration of Independence:

> May it be to the world, what I believe it will be (to some parts sooner, to others later, but finally to all), the signal of arousing men to burst the chains under which monkish ignorance and superstition had persuaded them to bind themselves, and to assume the blessings and security of self-government. That form which we have substituted, restores the free right to the unbounded exercise of reason and freedom of opinion. All eyes are opened, or opening, to the rights of man.
>
> The general spread of the light of science has already laid open to every view the palpable truth, that the mass of mankind has not been born with saddles on their backs, nor a favored few booted and spurred, ready to ride them legitimately, by the grace of God. These are grounds of hope for others. For ourselves, let the annual return of this day forever refresh our recollections of these rights, and an undiminished devotion to them.

Jefferson wrote into the Declaration of Independence one of the most brilliant definitions of freedom in history:

> We hold these truths to be self-evident, that all men are created equal, that they are endowed by their Creator with certain unalienable Rights, that among these are Life, Liberty, and the pursuit of Happiness.

We don't use the terms *inalienable* or *unalienable** much today, but in the eighteenth century the terms were well known and often used.

Alienable is a form of the word *alienate:* to take away from, to separate. If someone is accused of "alienation of affection," he or she is charged with taking

---

*There is no real difference between *unalienable* and *inalienable*. The best guess as to how *inalienable* became *unalienable* is that the "u" replacing the "i" was simply what we would call today a typographical error. It was probably not changed because the founding fathers were in a hurry. This Declaration was a hot document. The Declaration of Independence called for the *violent overthrow* of the British government in what was then known as British America. This was high treason and punishable by death. The signers of the Declaration of Independence were not exaggerating when they said, "For the support of this Declaration . . . we mutually pledge to each other our Lives, our Fortunes, and our sacred Honour." It's little wonder, then, that the difference between *inalienable* and *unalienable* would not be challenged.

(alienating) the love of someone away from someone else. An alienable right, then, is a right that can be taken from you or a right that you can transfer to another.

For example, owning a car is an alienable right. Selling the car and transferring the title to another *alienates* your right to own and drive that car—you have alienated yourself from the possession and use of the car. If you have an alienable right to something, the government can—with just cause—take it from you. In time of war, or building a new freeway, the government can take your house, for which you are theoretically paid the fair market value.

> *One of the things that really bothers me is that Americans don't have any sense of history. The majority of Americans don't have any idea of where we've come from, so they naturally succumb to the kind of cliché version that Ronald Reagan represented.*
>
> ROBERT MASSIE
> *Pulitzer Prize–winning historian*

Inalienable rights, on the other hand, are rights that can not be taken from you or transferred to another *no matter what*. These are the basic rights guaranteed to every citizen of the republic. What did our founding fathers consider to be our basic inalienable rights? "Among these are Life, Liberty, and the pursuit of Happiness."

Wrote Samuel Eliot Morison in *The Oxford History of the American People* (1965),

> These words are more revolutionary than anything written by Robespierre, Marx, or Lenin, more explosive than the atom, a continual challenge to ourselves as well as an inspiration to the oppressed of all the world.

Life, liberty, and the pursuit of happiness. Note that inalienable rights are not *limited* to life, liberty, and the pursuit of happiness: "*among these* are Life, Liberty, and the pursuit of Happiness" (emphasis added). Life, liberty, and the pursuit of happiness cannot be taken from us; they are inalienable.

Life, liberty, and the pursuit of happiness—probably the most famous phrase in American literature. *Life* is obvious; it is our physical life. *Liberty* is the freedom to live that life the way we choose. The phrase *the pursuit of happiness* is so vague, so broad, and so far-reaching that it is, well, *revolutionary*. Even today. It, of course, does not *guarantee* us happiness; but it does give us the right to *pursue* happiness—whatever we think that may be, in whatever way we think will get us there.

Naturally, there are limits. *My* pursuit of happiness might include *your* new car. Does that mean that I, as a citizen, have a right to take your car? Of course not. Where should the limitation be? As you already know, I propose the limits are the physical harming of another's person or property. As I'll attempt to show here and in other chapters, this is precisely the same limitation that the founding fathers had in mind when they created our government.

⚖ ⚖ ⚖

Before forming the government, however, there was a little business of a revolutionary war. King George III of England did not, after reading the Declaration of Independence, say, "Oh, they'd like their independence; I hope they enjoy it." No. England is not famous for letting her people go. Only Princess Di got away from the British monarchy without a fight.

Soon after the Declaration of Independence the thirteen colonies of British America gathered together under the loosely stated Articles of Confederation—a document designed to last the length of the war. All the power was put in the hands of a Continental Congress. The Continental Congress had the dual disadvantage of being (a) a committee, and (b) unable to tax. They had the power to "request" money from the various state legislatures, but, as you can imagine, such requests often went unheeded.* Two important lessons were learned from the Continental Congress "experiment": (a) committees do not govern well, and (b) a government is no government without the power of taxation.

After the war, in the summer of 1787, a group of elected representatives was given the task of adapting the Articles of Confederation into a permanent document outlining an ongoing government for the Confederated States of America. This group of fifty-five delegates took to their task with rare enthusiasm. Some historians say they ignored their mandate entirely. Jefferson, who was in France at the time, expressed concern that they "met in secret session." The delegates threw out the Articles of Confederation and began work on a new document, the Constitution of the United States of America. From that point on, the gathering of those fifty-five delegates was known as the Constitutional Convention.

Although Jefferson was absent, many great men were there. Jefferson acknowledged them as an "assembly of demi-gods."** Benjamin Franklin arrived each morning, carried in a sedan chair by convicts through the streets of Philadelphia—he was 81 and suffered gout. Also present were future presidents John Adams and James Madison. Alexander Hamilton was there; he, along with

*It got so bad at one point that the standing army—who had not been paid in months—marched on the Continental Congress. The army asked George Washington to lead them and become the first king of America. Washington turned down the idea and severely rebuked the troops for their actions. The troops, nonetheless, got paid. (We came very close to trading in England's King George III for our own King George I.)

**Thomas Jefferson would later regret this endorsement of Alexander Hamilton. Hamilton and Jefferson, who both served in George Washington's first presidential cabinet, were such bitter enemies and political rivals, yet each so powerful and persuasive, that they began the two-party system. The parties they started—Democratic-Republican for Jefferson and Federalist for Hamilton—have little to do with today's Democratic and Republican parties, but it's how the two-party system was born.

Madison, later "sold" the Constitution—and the concept of a strong federal government*—to the citizenry in a series of eighty-five newspaper articles known as *The Federalist*. George Washington prepared for his role as the nation's first president by presiding over the convention.

The major question facing the convention—and American politics at large—was how much power would remain at the state level, and how much would go to the federal government.

> *The minute you read something that you can't understand, you can almost be sure it was drawn up by a lawyer.*
>
> WILL ROGERS

The federalists believed that a strong federal—that is, national—government was essential. Without a strong federal government, they argued, the thirteen colonies would become like the countries of Europe—eternally caught in the political dance of alliances, betrayals, intrigues, and hostilities that had marked the history of Europe for more than a thousand years. Federalists argued further that each state would be ripe for individual plucking by the aggressively imperial powers of France, Spain, and Russia, or by a return engagement from Great Britain. Moreover, the federalists observed that all the people of the colonies had pulled together and won a rousing victory for life, liberty, and the pursuit of happiness. These courageous and victorious souls were now one people. They were members of one country, a country that—united—defeated the strongest military power on earth. These people of one nation did not want to return to being citizens of individual states, states that—if history were any indicator—would be at each other's throats within a matter of years over borders, territorial rights, and tariffs. And if one state went to war against another, did one really want to fight brother against brother?**

The anti-federalists held that states' rights were sovereign. Each state already had a constitution—or was busy working on one—and that was to be the supreme law of the people within that state. Why couldn't the Confederated States get along as well as, say, the Nordic countries, which were independently sovereign, lived together in peace, and banded together for protection in time of war? This was what the Articles of Confederation were intended to do: form an alliance against Great Britain and nothing more. Once victorious, the states would return immediately to the status quo. Oh, it might be nice, the anti-federalists acknowledged, to have some

*The concept for a federal government was taken from the confederation of five Native American tribes—the Mohawk, Oneida, Onondaga, Cayuga, and Seneca—known collectively as the Iroquois Federation. Hiawatha, paddling between the tribes in his white canoe, persuaded them to form a *confederation*, from which the word *federalist* comes. The Iroquois Federation had a common council (congress) to which each tribe had a fixed number of delegates.

**Precisely this scenario took place over the struggle between states' rights and federal rights less than seventy-five years later—the American Civil War.

> *The Constitution is not neutral.*
> *It was designed*
> *to take the government*
> *off the backs of people.*
>
> JUSTICE WILLIAM O. DOUGLAS

sort of central government, but it should be more a meeting place, a forum in which the various sovereign states could meet and discuss treaties, national defense, trade, and the like. In this, the anti-federalists wanted something more along the lines of the current United Nations than the United States.

As in all politics, the final document became a compromise.

The federalists, such as Monroe and Hamilton, demanded a strong chief executive with sweeping powers. He (women were not allowed to *vote,* much less run for office) would be something of an emperor, but one chosen by the people in regular, but widely spaced, elections.

The anti-federalists thought that a simple amendment to the Articles of Confederation—something along the lines of "Resolved, that this document is null and void"—was all that was necessary. ("And can't we go home now? Who wants to be in Philadelphia in the summer, anyway?")

The compromise was that there *would* be a strong federal government, but that the power would be held jointly between three equal branches—the executive, the legislative, and the judicial. The Constitution, however, would be "the supreme law of the land," superseding all state constitutions and laws on certain specific points, but leaving the states free to legislate on all matters not given to the federal government.

Overall, the Constitution of the United States is a federalist document. The federalist nature is evident in the first line. The original draft read, "We the people of the states of . . ." and then proceeded to list each state. The revised document, the one that we know today, begins simply, "We the People of the United States. . . ."

One people, one nation. One supreme law.

⚖️ ⚖️ ⚖️

Allow me to highlight certain portions of the Constitution that apply most directly to our discussion of consensual crimes.

The Constitution begins with the famous preamble giving the purpose of the Constitution:

> We the People of the United States, in Order to form a more perfect Union, establish Justice, insure domestic Tranquility, provide for the common defense, promote the general Welfare, and secure the Blessings of Liberty to ourselves and our Posterity, do ordain and establish this Constitution for the United States of America.

The preamble is heavy with phrases and ideas, seemingly designed to make the average complacent, king-loving, God-fearing colonial American uncomfortable, nay, *miserable.*

We the People . . . Here, it's we the people; not we the Protestants, we the Catholics, we the atheists, but we the *people—all* the people.*

Compare this simple, direct, all-inclusive opening with the typical formal governmental document of the days of monarchy. The documents were always in the name of the *monarch* who ruled by the grace of *God,* and were usually granting a *privilege* to some Special Class of Human Beings, or

> *It was we, the people;*
> *not we, the white male citizens;*
> *nor yet we, the male citizens;*
> *but we, the whole people,*
> *who formed the Union.*
>
> SUSAN B. ANTHONY

taking some right away from one Special Class of Human Beings and giving it to an Even More Special Class of Human Beings. Take, for example, the opening of the Magna Carta:

> John, by the grace of God, King of England, Lord of Ireland, Duke of Normandy and Acquitaine, and Count of Anjou, to the archbishops, bishops, abbots, earls, barons, justiciars, foresters, sheriffs, provosts, officers, and all his bailiffs and faithful people, Greeting. Know that by the inspiration of God and for the salvation of our soul and those of all our ancestors and successors, to the honor of God and the exaltation of the Holy Church, and the improvement of our kingdom . . .

Note the delineation of power—the pecking order, if you will. We knew who was on first (God), who was on second (the king), who was on third (the archbishops). Somehow you knew that in a disagreement between, say, an archbishop and one of the "faithful people" (far, far down the list), the archbishop would win.

None of this nonsense opens the Constitution. In a government document at that time, it was radical not to mention the ruling monarch and downright *revolutionary* not to mention God. Even the individual states don't get special recognition. From the outset, it was a document without classes of people, with no highs, no lows, no one better or worse than another; it is a document of "We the People."

In Order to form a more perfect Union . . . The intent was to form a union (a government) "more perfect" than had ever existed before. The imperfections (injustices) of other governments were well known and documented. The most obvious example of an *imperfect* union was the Inquisition.** The Inquisition had been alternately smoldering and flaring since the late 1400s. Not only were heretics tortured and burned alive, but, when taken over by the government (as it

---

*As we shall discuss in the chapter, "How Did Consensual Crimes Become Crimes?", this did not include women, Native Americans, or blacks. Subsequent amendments did include them. The Constitution, as it stands today—and as it has stood since 1920—excludes no individual or group of United States citizens from the phrase "We the People."

**Like the Spanish Flu, the Inquisition was certainly not limited to Spain.

soon was), the Inquisition was a tool of terror and oppression against anyone's actions, values, or ideas that made the rulers uncomfortable. (They still did all this, of course, in the name of God.)

Galileo, for example, was summoned before the Inquisition in 1633 at the age of sixty-nine and forced to publicly admit he was wrong and apologize for any confusion he may have caused by claiming that the Earth was *not* the center of the universe and that the Earth revolved around the sun. (The apocryphal story has him saying under his breath as he listened to the pronouncement of the Inquisition, "It moves just the same.") Because he recanted, he was spared being burned alive and was instead placed under house arrest for the last nine years of his life.

The great thinkers of the Enlightenment—who adored scientific advancement—found the persecution of Galileo appalling. They used it again and again as an example of what governments should *not* do.

The "more perfect Union of the United States," then, would be one not based on intolerance, injustice, prejudice, religious beliefs, or the whims of the ruling class—be that a group or an individual. It was based on "Life, Liberty, and the pursuit of Happiness."

Establish Justice . . . Justice—basic fairness in the government's interactions with its people—was notably lacking in 1787. Throughout the world, one was generally presumed guilty when accused and had a few frantic moments in which to prove one's innocence while one's method of punishment was being prepared. Those afforded a trial of any kind—a luxury in itself—were often given such treatment as "trial by fire," in which the accused carried a red-hot bar of iron up three stairs and then dropped it (if you had blisters on your hands three days later, you were guilty), or "trial by water," in which you were thrown into a body of water and, if you sank and didn't re-surface (something human bodies seldom do when thrown into water), you were presumed innocent and were set free (providing, of course, you didn't drown before they fished you out). For the common person, trial before a jury of one's peers was nearly unheard of. Generally, it was before a magistrate or bailiff who was policeman, judge, jury, and executioner all in one.

The idea that there would be justice—just laws justly applied to all—was again revolutionary. The vast, *vast* majority of injustices discussed by the great writers of the Enlightenment consisted of punishing "crimes" that had no innocent victims. No one complained when a highwayman was hung; it was the hanging of heretics (after torturing them so that "the spirit of the devil" would leave their bodies) that incensed these writers. If one was killed while physically attacking a king, well, *c'est la politique.* What infuriated the thinkers of the Enlightenment was that people were condemned for high treason and beheaded because they, oh, refused to acknowledge the monarch's right to dump his current wife and marry anyone he chose. (This was the fate of Sir Thomas More, who never actually criticized the marriage of King Henry VIII and Anne Boleyn, but committed the capital offense— *so* offensive to the king—of keeping silent about it. If this was the treatment received by the chancellor of England, second in power only to the king, imagine the injustices heaped upon less lofty subjects.)

> *The illegal we do immediately.*
> *The unconstitutional*
> *takes a little longer.*
>
> HENRY KISSINGER

To the framers of the Constitution, such excesses of the ruler's power and of religion's power were *not* justice. Each citizen was entitled to justice *without* being aligned to one or both of the ruling powers.

It was the government's job to *guarantee* justice to *any* citizen whose liberty was being threatened. This meant, for example, that the government could not arrest and punish an individual because his or her views upset the members of either a ruler or a religion. This is what the founding fathers meant by "establish Justice."

Ensure domestic Tranquility . . . It's hard to imagine that the domestic tranquility which our founding fathers wanted to preserve was the tranquility of the self-righteous. On the contrary, they seemed to enjoy tweaking the righteousness of the mighty, promoting anything but tranquility in the domiciles of authority. The sort of don't-rock-the-boat-let's-not-upset-the-apple-cart-leave-well-enough-alone complacency ("If we legalize all the consensual crimes, think of all the *trouble* it will cause") was decidedly not the domestic tranquility the founding fathers intended to promote. They advocated—and succeeded at—a violent revolution against a government (Great Britain's) that did little more than impose minor taxation without representation. How much less the American colonists under Great Britain suffered than the "perpetrators" of consensual crimes have suffered under the United States. No, "domestic Tranquility" meant freedom—however upsetting the results might be to some—not conformity for the sake of "smoothing things over."

Promote the general Welfare . . . It's hard to believe that the framers of the Constitution—as a way of promoting the general welfare—would have considered jailing (at great cost) a group of people who were not hurting anyone else. The general welfare they were trying to promote was a government in which all people had sufficient individual freedom to explore ideas, themselves, and life itself, and to do with that life what they thought best. The general welfare was a government of freedom of thought and action for which our forebears fought and, in some cases, died.

> *Fear of serious injury cannot*
> *alone justify suppression*
> *of free speech and assembly.*
> *Men feared witches*
> *and burned women.*
> *It is the function of speech*
> *to free men from the bondage*
> *of irrational fears.*
>
> JUSTICE LOUIS D. BRANDEIS

Secure the Blessings of Liberty to our-selves and our Posterity . . . That's us: Posterity.

⚖ ⚖ ⚖

Article I of the Constitution discusses the various qualifications for holding office. The only requirements are age, citizenship, and residency. It's more important to note what qualifications are *not* given. There was no need to espouse religious, political, or moral beliefs, sexual preference, or anything else in order to be elected. If you were elected, you could serve. As we will discuss in the next chapter on separation of church and state, some states at that time had any number of religious restrictions—belief in the Christian religion, a belief in the Trinity, to be a practicing Protestant—for those holding office. These restrictions were swept aside by the Constitution.

As we shall see when we discuss the Tenth Amendment, what the Constitution *doesn't* say is equally as important as what it *does* say. Essentially, all rights not taken by the Constitution for the federal government remain those of the states or the people. But just so there would be absolutely no doubt about the framers' intent, Article VI of the Constitution reiterates,

> . . . no religious Test shall ever be required as a Qualification to any Office or public Trust under the United States.*

Article I, Section 8 lists what the Congress—and, hence, the government of the United States—has the power to do. This section is known as the *Enumeration of Powers*. It deals with functions such as collecting taxes, borrowing money, regulating commerce, standardizing bankruptcy laws, coining money, punishing counterfeiters, establishing a post office, assigning patents and copyrights, setting up courts, punishing pirates, declaring wars, raising armies, maintaining navies—the practical running of government.

Nowhere in the Enumeration of Powers is there anything remotely resembling "regulation of personal or public morality," "making sure no citizens hurt themselves by experimental, reckless, or even downright foolish behavior," "maintaining the purity of the nuclear family," or "locking up any person who does something considered 'sinful' by any religion that has a lot of lobbying power, and is equally vocal about what is Right and what is Wrong." No. The Enumeration of Powers gives the government the power to *run the government,* not the personal or religious lives of the people.

---

*Although eleven of the thirteen colonies had some religious test of office, this article was unanimously passed by the Constitutional Convention. It would be used as ammunition by those who opposed the Constitution, claiming it was a Godless document, worthy only of a Godless people.

The last paragraph of Article II, Section 1 begins,

> Before [the president] enter on the Execution of his Office, he shall take the following Oath or Affirmation:—"I do solemnly swear (or affirm) . . ."

The use of the words *affirmation* and *affirm* here is significant. In the eighteenth century it was clearly understood that an *oath* was something taken before God; an *affirmation* was something taken on one's own personal integrity. One would either be "sworn

in" before God, or one would make an affirmation, personally affirming to tell the truth, uphold the office, or whatever one was about to do.

In England at the time, you could *only* take an oath; you could not make an affirmation. Before giving testimony in a court of law, one had to claim allegiance to the Christian faith and then swear, by God, to tell the truth. If one failed to do this, one could not provide testimony. The ramifications of the law were far reaching. If, for example, someone robbed you, and, if only the two of you were present, it was not your word against his: if the robber agreed to take an oath and you did not, only the *robber's* evidence would be admissible in court. This put all non-Christians at a great disadvantage. The courts of law (as well as the magistrates, bailiffs, and other officials of the law) were, for the most part, unavailable to them. The same was true if one were accused of a crime: unless one claimed allegiance to the Christian religion, one could not testify in one's own defense. This law remained in effect in England until 1879. (As already mentioned, it wasn't until 1859 that the "Christian" portion of the oath of office was eliminated, and England seated its first Jewish member of Parliament.)

To add the words *affirmation* and *affirm* (and to repeat them in Article VI) is a clear and intentional separation of church and state. The existence of this separation, when discussing consensual crimes, is critical, and will be explored in detail in the upcoming chapter, "Laws against Consensual Activities Violate the Separation of Church and State, Threatening the Freedom of and from Religion"* and all of Part IV, "Consensual Crimes and the Bible."

Article III, Section 3 states the limitation of what would be determined as treason:

---

*Here are two small indicators of how far away we've come from the concept of separation of church and state: (a) It is *always* referred to as the president's "Oath of Office," never the "Affirmation of Office," and (b) the last phrase, "so help me God," which seems to be a standard part of the inauguration, is *not* part of the Constitution nor any of its amendments. All that the president swears or affirms is that he or she will "faithfully execute the Office of the President of the United States, and will to the best of my Ability, preserve, protect and defend the Constitution of the United States."

> *In a democracy, the opposition
> is not only tolerated
> as constitutional,
> but must be maintained
> because it is indispensable.*
>
> WALTER LIPPMANN

Treason against the United States, shall consist only in levying War against them, or in adhering to their Enemies, giving them Aid and Comfort. No Person shall be convicted of Treason unless on the Testimony of two Witnesses to the same overt Act, or on Confession in open Court."

This is a major statement affirming freedom of expression. For us, living in an age when the royal family of England has more tabloid coverage than Cher, Madonna, and aliens from outer space combined, it's hard to imagine what a significant statement this was.

In eighteenth-century England—and in most of the world, for that matter—saying, for example, "The king is a tyrant," would probably have gotten you beheaded. Further, if someone *said* that you said the king was a tyrant, that would probably have been enough to ensure your execution. Shortly after King Henry VIII had Sir Thomas More beheaded for high treason because More refused to acknowledge the king's marriage to Anne Boleyn, he also had Anne beheaded for high treason. The grounds? Infidelity. All it took was one person to admit—under torture—that he "loved" Boleyn, and Boleyn lost her life. Can you imagine the blood bath in the royal family if the same rules applied today? One wouldn't have to consider whether or not England should remain a monarchy—there'd be no monarchs left.

Back then it was high treason merely to say something that the monarch did not like. The preferences of the monarch, from religion to fashion, were well known—sometimes laws—and to flout convention might upset the monarch, which was treason. (Actually, upsetting a duke, earl, or baron was *treason;* upsetting the king was *high* treason.) "That the king can do no wrong," wrote Sir William Blackstone in 1769, "is a necessary and fundamental principle of the English constitution."

The founding fathers basically said, "Enough of this!" To insult, affront, or even seriously disturb the monarch was a consensual crime. Making the king uncomfortable, the founding fathers determined, was no longer grounds for punishment.

The founding fathers asked themselves, "What is the purpose of laws against treason," just as they asked themselves, "What is the purpose of all law?" The purpose of laws against treason was to defend the United States against acts of physical violence—"levying War against" it, or giving "Aid and Comfort" to those who were physically warring against the United States. Here, the principle that every crime needs a victim is again established. In defending this principle, the founding fathers opened themselves to all sorts of discomfort. Some of them knew they would serve in some public capacity and, by making war the only basis for treason, they were giving the people and the press free reign to attack them in any way other than physically.

The second point, involving "two Witnesses to the same overt* "Act" or "Confession in open Court," prohibited people from manipulating others by threatening to accuse them of treason. Just as today threats of exposing or prosecuting consensual crimes are often used to blackmail and to extort information and behavior from an unwilling party, so, too, the treason laws were used for underhanded manipulation. ("If you don't do this for us, we will testify

> *If there is any fixed star in our constitutional constellation, it is that no official, high or petty, can prescribe what shall be orthodox in politics, nationalism, religion, or other matters of opinion or force citizens to confess by word or act their faith therein.*
>
> JUSTICE ROBERT H. JACKSON

that you spoke badly about the king and you will be executed." "If you don't do what we want, we'll say we saw you with a prostitute [or selling drugs, or et cetera] and you will be put in jail.") Requiring that there be *two witnesses* to an *overt* act makes it much more difficult to falsify charges for the manipulation of others.**

Article IV, Section 2 begins, "The Citizens of each State shall be entitled to all Privileges and Immunities of Citizens in the several States." This, once again, affirms that the Constitution is the supreme law of the land and that no state can take away the "Privileges" or "Immunities" (protections) given by the Constitution and the federal government. (This protection would be strengthened and deepened by the Fourteenth Amendment.)

At the close of the main body of the Constitution—desperate to find God in there somewhere—some people will point to the words "the Seventeenth Day of September in the Year of our Lord one thousand seven hundred and Eighty seven." They say, "You see, they claim that Jesus is their Lord."

"The Year of our Lord" is, of course, a technical legal term commonly used in the eighteenth century. It no more acknowledges that Jesus is Lord than writing, "It happened in 436 B.C." acknowledges that Jesus was the Christ. It's an agreed-upon way that happened to be invented by some monks to count the days. The Gregorian Calendar—the one that's been in use since 1582—required the papal decree of Pope Gregory XIII for its adoption. (Science did not determine things then; the pope did.) Although the current calendar is a "religious document," issued by a papal bull, to say that each time we refer to the calendar it is an act of Catholicism, Christianity, or religion of any kind is absurd. Besides, at least three

---

*Note the use of the word *overt*. One can't just be *thinking* about doing something; one actually has to *do* it. This, again, supports the notion that it is an act of *physical* harm (in this case, war) that constitutes a crime.

**If all crimes have clear-cut victims, it's much more difficult to falsify testimony. For example, "He offered to sell me drugs," is much easier to falsify than, "He threw a brick through my window." To prove the latter, one would need to provide a brick and a shattered window. To prove the former, one would simply need a good imagination.

signers of the Constitution—George Washington, John Adams, and Benjamin Franklin—were not Christians at all. They were Deists. (More on this in the next chapter.)*

The Bill of Rights

Once it was decided that there would be a strong, central (federal) government, many people—most notably, Thomas Jefferson and James Madison—wanted to make sure that the power of that government was severely limited. They wanted to be certain that the government did what it needed to do, and nothing more. Other than defending the borders, establishing treaties, settling disputes, and the other essential functions, they wanted to make sure the government left the people blessedly alone for "Life, Liberty and the pursuit of Happiness." "I am for a government rigorously frugal and simple," wrote Jefferson. "Were we directed from Washington when to sow, when to reap, we should soon want bread."

Jefferson and the others called for a Bill of Rights, a series of amendments to the Constitution which clearly delineated what the government could and, more importantly, could *not* do in terms of regulating individual thought and behavior.

Those who favored the Constitution without a Bill of Rights argued that such guarantees were not necessary—that they already *were* contained within the main body of the Constitution. The Enumeration of Powers, they claimed, limited the government to basic functions. None of these enumerated powers infringed on the individual unless that individual harmed the person or property of another. The government could not take on additional powers—such as regulating speech, religion, the press, or anything else—without adding a constitutional amendment. In other words, if the Constitution didn't say that the government specifically *could* do something, it couldn't. As Alexander Hamilton explained,

> For why declare that things shall not be done which there is no power to
> do? Why, for instance, should it be said that the liberty of the press shall

---

What's the Constitution between friends?

TIMOTHY J. CAMPBELL
*Response to President Cleveland,
who refused to support a bill
because it was unconstitutional*

---

*If you think I'm getting a little paranoid here in thinking that anyone in his or her right mind would use the single phrase, "in The Year of our Lord," to ignore all the constitutional guarantees of the separation of church and state, allow me to quote the once (and probably future) presidential hopeful, founder and chairman of the Christian Broadcasting Network, described by his publisher as "America's best known and most listened to Christian leader" (Jerry Falwell, eat your heart out), Pat Robertson, from his book *The New Millennium*: "When George Washington signed our Constitution, he dated it 'In the year of our Lord, 1787.' There was only one Lord whose birthday dated back 1787 years: Jesus Christ. The founding document of the United States of America acknowledges the Lordship of Jesus Christ, because we were a Christian nation." Mr. Robertson conveniently fails to report that George Washington was *not* a Christian.

not be restrained, when no power is given by which restrictions may be imposed?

"No," said those in favor of a Bill of Rights, *"we* all understand that the intent of the government is not to restrict freedom, but we don't know what some nefarious people twenty, thirty, fifty years from now might attempt to do with the Constitution. The Constitution is a contract between the government and the people. It is important to spell out clearly not only what the government can do, but what it cannot do."*

> *A bill of rights is what the people are entitled to against every government on earth, general or particular and what no just government should refuse to rest on inference.*
>
> THOMAS JEFFERSON
> *Letter to James Madison*
> December 20, 1787

"But," argued those against a Bill of Rights, "if we specifically say that the federal government *cannot* do certain things, then the implication will be that it *can* do everything else. The list of what it can't do could go on forever. And what about those things it can't do that haven't been invented yet?"

Those in favor of a Bill of Rights responded, "We will make the limitation general enough to cover large areas of freedoms, but specific enough to give a clear indication of what we mean. The basic form of government in the world today is tyrannical and opposed to individual freedoms. We want the people of the United States, all the world, and all of posterity to see clearly—without having to read between the lines—the freedoms the government simply cannot take away."

The pro–Bill of Rights argument won the day. So those in favor of the Constitution as it was said, "Let's pass the Constitution as it is, and we'll immediately begin working on a Bill of Rights." It was this promise of a Bill of Rights that got the Constitution enough support to become the supreme law of the land. The basic Constitution was submitted to the states for ratification in 1787, and was ratified by 1788; in 1789 at the first session of Congress, the Bill of Rights was proposed, and its adoption was certified on December 15, 1791. (The three states that failed to ratify the Bill of Rights—Massachusetts, Georgia, and Connecticut—eventually did so. In 1939.)

Let's look at the Bill of Rights in reverse order—the way David Letterman reads his "top ten" lists. From a popular point of view, the First Amendment—guaranteeing freedom of religion, speech, the press, assembly, and petition—seems the most important. From a legal point of view—and many of the founding fathers were lawyers, and the judges in the courts that interpret the Constitution are *all* lawyers—number ten is the most significant.

The Tenth Amendment reads,

---

*"In questions of power," Thomas Jefferson wrote, "let no more be heard of confidence in man, but bind him down from mischief by the chains of the constitution."

> [The Bill of Rights is] designed to
> protect individuals and minorities
> against the tyranny
> of the majority,
> but it's also designed to protect
> the people against bureaucracy,
> against the government.
>
> JUDGE LAWRENCE TRIBE

The powers not delegated to the United States by the Constitution, nor prohibited by it to the States, are reserved to the States respectively, or to the people.

This affirms what the founding fathers all agreed to at the time—that if the Constitution didn't *specifically* take a power (that is, a right or a freedom) away from the people, the people kept it. This settled, once and for all, the fundamental question, "Does the government inherently have all the power and then dole out specific rights to the people, or do the people inherently have all the power and—in exchange for certain benefits—surrender specific powers to the government?" Concerning the government of the United States, the answer is clear: the people inherently have the power, and turn specific powers over to the government.

These powers were detailed in the Constitution (the Enumeration of Powers), and all other powers belonged to the people. In exchange for these powers, the federal government agreed to do certain things—including protect its citizens from attack by a foreign country, the violence of another individual, and even from attempts by the individual states to interfere with the free exercise of their inherent rights.

The Ninth Amendment says,

> The enumeration in the Constitution, of certain rights, shall not be construed to deny or disparage others retained by the people.

Just because the Constitution says you have certain rights does not mean that you don't also have *other* rights which the Constitution didn't bother to enumerate. This amendment was designed to counter the argument, "If we list certain rights, then it might be supposed that those are the *only* rights the people have." As in the Tenth Amendment, the people clearly hold all the rights, and just because *some* of those basic rights are listed in the Constitution does not in any way mean to limit the rights not mentioned. Just because the Constitution does not, for example, specifically guarantee the right to eat whatever we choose, does not give the federal government the authority to dictate The Official Diet of the United States and compel us by law to eat certain things and not to eat other things.

The Eighth Amendment reads,

> Excessive bail shall not be required, nor excessive fines imposed, nor cruel and unusual punishments inflicted.

To me it seems both cruel and unusual to punish people for doing something that potentially could hurt only themselves. This is especially true when the punishment is often worse than the damage they might do to themselves. Such punishment is, however, *so* usual we've become numb to its cruelty. Anyone who has ever suffered the indignity of an arrest knows that the arrest in and of itself is a punishment. At the very least, it's unusual. Then you have to find an attorney; that's where the *real* cruelty starts. Even if you serve no jail time, the arrest will always be part of your permanent record and could prevent you from being hired (or could cause you to be fired from your current job), could mean being turned down for a loan application, housing, and so much else. One arrest—even without a conviction—can significantly and permanently reduce the quality of your life. In the later chapter, "Enforcing Laws against Consensual Activities Destroys People's Lives," we'll explore this further. If it's true—as the moralists claim—that certain consensual activities are *so harmful* to the individual taking part in them that they should be illegal, isn't taking part in them punishment enough? Adding arrest, trial, and conviction seems cruel and unusual.

> *Can any of you seriously say the Bill of Rights could get through Congress today? It wouldn't even get out of committee.*
>
> F. LEE BAILEY

The Seventh Amendment guarantees a jury in civil matters. While the government is there to protect us from harm, it cannot protect us from all possible harm, nor can it lock up everyone whom we feel has harmed us. The government can, however, guarantee a fair system by which disputes between individuals (civil matters) can be settled. This system is a trial by jury.

We can't make everything a *criminal* matter, the Constitution is saying; we can't lock up every citizen who displeases another citizen. Citizens do, however, harm each other in ways not prohibited by criminal law, and there should be a system for rectifying the harm.

If, for example, I borrow ten dollars from you and do not pay it back when promised, I have physically harmed you (by not returning your property). I have not, however, *stolen* from you in a criminal way: you did, after all, consent to loan it to me. Nonetheless, the ten dollars is rightfully yours. While you cannot put me in jail, you can take me to court, and the government's job is to (a) make sure the rules of the court are fair and equally applied to us both, and (b) use force, if necessary, to carry out the judgment of the court. If the court finds in your favor and orders me to pay the money but I refuse to pay it (never loan money to a writer), the court can send law enforcement agencies to seize my property, sell it, and pay you your ten dollars from the proceeds (plus your costs in taking me to court). It cannot, however, throw me in jail until I pay up.

This amendment acknowledges that not every physical harm one person does another is a criminal offense. How much *less* a criminal offense it must be, then, when people only potentially harm *themselves*. Not only does the Constitution have no *authority* to regulate personal morality; it also has no system by which to do so.

> *The privilege against self-incrimination is one of the great landmarks in man's struggle to make himself civilized. . . . The Fifth is a lone sure rock in time of storm . . . a symbol of the ultimate moral sense of the community, upholding the best in us.*
>
> ERWIN GRISWOLD
> *former dean of Harvard Law School*

This amendment also gives moralists a system by which they can protect themselves without using the full force of the criminal justice system. The moral groups can take those who offend them to civil court. Let a jury decide. (Environmental and consumer protection groups have had great success in this area.) The reason most moral groups don't do this is (a) most of their cases would be thrown out of court for lack of sufficient grounds and (b) most cases that went before a jury would lose.

Instead, moral groups threaten legislators, badger police, and frighten the public into using the *criminal* arm of the law to punish the very same actions they could not control in civil court. For example, if there were no laws against drug use, can you imagine Pat Robertson taking me to civil court and getting a court order prohibiting me from smoking pot in my own home? Jerry Falwell believes drinking alcohol is a sin. Can you imagine how few liquor stores he could close by taking them to court? (His ancestors, however, closed down *all* the liquor stores during Prohibition by making possession of liquor a criminal offense.)

The Constitution made provisions for civil disputes so that the government could use the criminal enforcement branch of the government for only the most clearly criminal acts. The civil acts—even many that *do* cause physical harm to others—the Constitution left to the civil courts.

The Sixth Amendment deals with criminal prosecution which, alas, brings us to consensual crimes. This amendment guarantees "the right to a speedy and public trial, by an impartial jury." One of the requirements for this jury trial in criminal prosecutions is for the accused "to be confronted with the witnesses against him." In a trial for a consensual crime, who are the witnesses *against* the person accused? In a genuine crime (except murder, of course) the innocent victim can come forth and testify against the accused. If someone pushes you down and takes your money, you can go into court and testify against the accused. If there is no clear-cut victim, however, who says *anyone* should testify "against" you? That the government should be against *any* consensual crimes is certainly not part of the Constitution, the Declaration of Independence, the Bill of Rights, or any of the other documents on which our system of government is based. So where does all this againstness come from? We'll explore this more fully in Part III, "How Did Consensual Crimes Become Crimes?" They do *not* come from the Constitution.

The *Fifth Amendment* is most famous for the provision that one does not have to testify against oneself in a criminal case. This is what it means to "take the Fifth." This amendment, too, offers protection against consensual crimes: since the only clear-cut victim in a consensual crime is the person involved in the crime, and the person involved in the crime is the one who would be accused, the Fifth Amendment says that you can't be forced to testify against yourself. If you *were* made to testify against yourself, you would often be torn between self-incrimination and perjury. Hence, a lot of consensual crimes have—thanks to the Constitution—not been prosecuted as vigorously as they might. Courts can prove *possession* of drugs, but not necessarily drug *use;* prostitutes can be convicted for *soliciting,* but not necessarily *having sex;*

> *The 4th Amendment and the personal rights it secures have a long history. At the very core stands the right of a man to retreat into his own home and there be free from unreasonable governmental intrusion.*
>
> JUSTICE POTTER STEWART

gamblers can be convicted for *being in a place* where gambling is taking place, but not actually *gambling.*

Another important guarantee of the Fifth Amendment reads, "Nor shall private property be taken for public use without just compensation." This affirms the sanctity of private property. The government does not own or control our property; we do. If the government takes it "for public use," the government must provide "just compensation." In other words, even if the public—the *people*—has a pressing need for your private property, they can't have it unless they justly compensate you. This is a clear statement that the government will protect the individual against the majority and even protect the individual against the government itself. As we will explore more fully in the chapter, "Laws against Consensual Activities Are Opposed to the Principles of Private Property, Free Enterprise, Capitalism, and the Open Market," the idea of *private* property encompasses the idea that we can do with our property as we see fit—use it, sell it, trade it, give it, and, yes, even destroy it. As long as it doesn't infringe on the person or property of another, it ain't the government's business if we do.

The Fourth Amendment begins,

> The right of the people to be secure in their persons, houses, papers, and effects, against unreasonable searches and seizures, shall not be violated . . .

Again, we have a clear directive that the government should stay out of our *private property,* unless it has a very specific search warrant (described in the rest of the amendment). The idea that the government should punish people for doing something that could potentially hurt only themselves is fundamentally unreasonable. Hence, any searches and seizures of "persons, houses, papers, and effects" for the purpose of discovering that people might be harming themselves (and, therefore, should be imprisoned) are unreasonable.*

---

*Consensual crimes have been used to make such "unreasonable" search and seizure seem more reasonable. For example, a car is considered an extension of one's person, house, papers, and effects, and a police officer cannot search a car without a warrant. The courts have added, however, that if

The Third Amendment reads,

> This provision speaks for itself. Its plain object is to secure the perfect enjoyment of that great right of the common law, that a man's house shall be his own castle, privileged against all civil and military intrusion.
>
> JUSTICE JOSEPH STORY
> 1833

No Soldier shall, in time of peace be quartered in any house, without the consent of the Owner, nor in time of war, but in a manner to be prescribed by law.

Once again, the Constitution affirms the absolute sanctity of private property. Even a *soldier*—who may someday risk his or her very *life* to defend your life and property—cannot spend the night in your house without your permission. Second, the amendment shows that, in time of war, things change. In time of war, it is understood that certain sacrifices must be made,* but *even then* a soldier can't stay in a private house unless a law is passed allowing him or her to do so. In other words, the legislature must become involved. This is one of many safeguards in the Constitution against a police state, against a military body that decides its needs are more important than those of a citizen and takes what it wants by force. In order for this to happen, according to the Constitution, the Congress must first declare war and then, in addition to declaring war, pass a law stating that, for the duration of the war, soldiers may stay in private houses without the owners' permission and (going back to the Fifth Amendment) stating what sort of compensation the owners of the houses shall receive.

The Second Amendment affirms "the right of the people to keep and bear Arms." This is the amendment—interpreted literally—that the National Rifle Association uses to keep all kinds of firearms—including 200,000,000 handguns—completely legal in this country, even though no other civilized nation has such a lack of restrictions and no other civilized nation has such an astonishingly high rate of murder by handgun. (The United States had 11,411 handgun murders in 1991; Canada had 136. Other countries have so few handgun murders that they don't even separate the statistics out from general firearms murders; for instance,

---

police officers can easily sense "probable cause" to believe a crime has been committed, they have the right to search the car on the spot without a warrant. (An example of probable cause might be a large amount of what appears to be fresh blood on the back seat.) If, in their "probable cause" search for one thing, they find another (or if they merely destroy the car in the process), it is acceptable. If, when stopping a car, the police claim to "smell marijuana," many courts have upheld this as probable cause. Obviously, certain less-than-ethical police officers can claim to "smell marijuana" to justify overriding the United States Constitution whenever they wish.

*That the American people rise to the occasion of war is well known and used by those who want to manipulate us. Thus, the War on Drugs, War on Pornography, War on Immorality, Defense against the Attack on Our Families, and so forth. If I were that kind of manipulative person, I would probably declare War on Consensual Crimes, but, frankly, I don't want to spend that much time being *against* anything. I would rather be *for* life, liberty, and the pursuit of happiness than *against* pettiness, paternalism, and paranoia.

Australia had 76 murders by all types of firearms.) The NRA *insists* that it is our *constitutional right* to "keep and bear Arms."

The intent behind this amendment, however, comes clear when the amendment is read in its entirety. The full text reads,

> A well regulated Militia, being necessary to the security of a free State, the right of the people to keep and bear Arms, shall not be infringed.

This amendment dealt with keeping a militia armed. A militia was made up of people who—when a need arose—grabbed their muskets and protected the home front. At that time, most people were hunters and, hence, pretty good shots. Today, the National Guard fulfills that need: civilians trained in weaponry and warfare who can be called up at a moment's notice. Even when mobilized, however, National Guard troops are not asked to bring their own guns; these are supplied to them. I doubt if many non–National Guard gun-owning civilians really expect to be called into the service of their country—midnight specials in hand.

I went on like this, not to attack the National Rifle Association's stand on handgun ownership, but merely to point out that just because a portion of the Constitution may be antiquated does not make it obsolete. So, if anyone argues against the contention that crimes without clear-cut victims are unconstitutional* by saying, "What the Constitution *says* and what it *means* are two different things. Things are different now," just remember the NRA and the right to bear arms.

⚖ ⚖ ⚖

In this space between the Second and the First Amendments, permit me an aside to briefly discuss liberalism and conservatism. It is in this space between the Second and the First Amendments that liberals and conservatives have their greatest split: liberals love the First Amendment, conservatives love the Second. This is also the space where liberals and conservatives show their greatest similarities: each uses the same reasoning in attempting to deny the other rights guaranteed by the Constitution.

"Yes, it's in the Constitution, *but . . .*" and then follow a variety of reasons why the supreme law of the land should be suspended in this particular case. The arguments for banning guns sound perfectly reasonable to liberals, and the arguments for banning pornography (for example) sound perfectly reasonable to conservatives. To the celebration and consternation of both sides, the Constitution guarantees both the right to bear arms and to bare arms (and anything else one

*And chances are that he or she will be a member of the National Rifle Association.

> *If drugs are criminal,*
> *only criminals*
> *will have drugs.*

chooses to bare).

Like it or not, the Constitution is the rules of the game. The rules cannot be changed by argument. The only way the Constitution can be changed is through *amendment*.

Many will consider this book a liberal tome. It's not. It may *seem* that way only because the conservatives have been more successful in keeping the constitutional rights most important to them intact: as much as liberals might like it to be, gun ownership is not a crime. The conservatives are to be congratulated for this. If the conservatives hadn't done as good a job, and gun ownership was illegal, it would be on the list of consensual crimes. As the NRA puts it, "Guns don't kill people. People kill people." Amen. *Owning* something should not be illegal, but rather *using* something to physically harm the person or property of another.

The liberal agenda to ban private ownership of guns is as much a constitutional violation as the conservative agenda to continue the ban on prostitution, gambling, or other currently illegal consensual activities. (The War on Drugs now cuts across conservative/liberal lines, although it started out as a conservative notion.) Rather than take away the conservative constitutional guarantees with the same logic that the conservatives use to keep the laws against certain consensual activities on the books ("It *hurts* people!"), the liberals might be better off using some of the conservative tactics in pursuing their own not-fully-realized constitutional rights. (The NRA is powerful, but the ACLU is no slouch.)

To continue to live together under the Constitution, liberals must learn to give the conservatives their constitutional "favorites," (gun ownership, private property, strong militia), and conservatives must learn to give the liberals their favorites (freedom of press, freedom of and from religion, personal privacy). Until the Second Amendment is repealed, people have a right to own guns. Until the First Amendment is repealed, people have the right to free speech, press, and religious choice. That's politics. That's tolerance. That's compromise. That's co-operation. That's the Constitution. That's life.

ᠪᠠ ᠪᠠ ᠪᠠ

There. Now that I've got *everybody* mad, let's move on to the greatest friend of the currently illegal consensual activities, the First Amendment.

The *First Amendment.* Ah, the best for last. The First Amendment, forty-five words that spell "freedom." Here it is in its full glory:

> Congress shall make no law respecting an establishment of religion, or prohibiting the free exercise thereof; or abridging the freedom of speech,

or of the press; or the right of the people peaceably to assemble, and to petition the Government for a redress of grievances.

Allow me to emphasize one portion of the First Amendment: "Congress shall make *no law*—" allow me to emphasize that again:

> *I am for the First Amendment
> from the first word to the last.
> I believe it means what it says.*
>
> JUSTICE HUGO BLACK

NO
LAW

allow me to emphasize that once again:

NO

LAW

> *The First Amendment*
> *makes confidence*
> *in the common sense*
> *of our people and*
> *in the maturity of their judgment*
> *the great postulate*
> *of our democracy.*
>
> JUSTICE WILLIAM O. DOUGLAS

—"respecting an establishment of religion, or prohibiting the free exercise thereof; or abridging the freedom of speech, or of the press; or the right of the people peaceably to assemble, and to petition the Government for a redress of grievances." (Emphasis added.)

By what authority does Congress *dare* make laws based on limiting assembly, speech, and, especially, religion? The Enumeration of Powers, as we have seen, does not give it this authority. The freedom of religion is guaranteed to us twice: the freedom *from* religion and the freedom *of* religion. Most laws against consensual activities—as we will explore in detail later—are based on religious beliefs.

With the implementation of the Constitution, the United States government broke from almost every other government in the world by not establishing an official state religion ("Congress shall make no law respecting an establishment of religion . . ."). In the 1700s, Virginia (the home state of Thomas Jefferson and George Washington) used tax dollars to support the Anglican church. Both Jefferson and Washington saw firsthand how un-free, unfair, and downright unworkable that was. In the next chapter on separation of church and state we'll explore the restriction of freedom, not just by the established state religion, but by the battles fought over *which* religion would become The One.

The second clause prohibits Congress from making any law "prohibiting the free exercise" of religion. *If the Constitution guaranteed no other freedom than this, it would be enough to immediately abolish all consensual crimes.* Who is to say the practice of my religion should not include any activity currently on the list of consensual crimes? But, more on this in the next chapter.

Congress shall also make no law "abridging the freedom of speech, or of the press." Well, there go all the censorship arguments. Period. "No law" is *no law.* I don't know how anything could be any clearer than that—and yet, and yet . . .

As Frank Zappa explained,

> Asked random questions about the First Amendment and how they would like to have it applied, if you believe in polls at all, the average American wants no part of it. But if you ask, "What if we threw the Constitution away tomorrow?" the answer is "No, that would be bad!" But living under the Constitution is another story altogether.

Also guaranteed in the First Amendment is "the right of the people peaceably to assemble." This constitutional guarantee is often set aside in the hysteria over consensual crimes. All the law enforcement agencies have to do is claim that the people peaceably assembling are primarily homosexuals (or prostitutes, or drug dealers, or bookies, or indigents), declare the assembly to be "loitering," and the assembly could be disassembled. Even private gatherings have a long history of being "raided." This clearly goes against the freedom of peaceable assembly clause, but it's been going on for so long that people forget to notice.

The final guarantee of the First Amendment is the right of the people to "petition the government for a redress of grievances." Have I suggested yet that you write a letter to all of your elected representatives suggesting the elimination of all laws against consensual activities? No? I'll get around to it.

> *When we lose*
> *the right to be different,*
> *we lose*
> *the privilege to be free.*
>
> CHARLES EVANS HUGHES

⚖ ⚖ ⚖

Over the years, other amendments have been added to the Constitution which either directly or indirectly affect consensual crimes. None of them gives the federal government the right to control crimes without clear-cut victims—except for the Eighteenth Amendment, which, as we have seen, was so blatantly unsuccessful that it was repealed by the Twenty-first Amendment thirteen years later. Even Prohibition proved that, if you want to regulate some activity that does not have a clear victim, it takes a constitutional amendment to do so. No state or federal law has the power to override the individual freedoms guaranteed in the Constitution and the Bill of Rights.

Let's look at a few of the amendments which have passed since the Bill of Rights.

The Thirteenth Amendment, passed just after the Civil War, outlawed slavery and involuntary servitude except "as a punishment for crime whereof the party shall have been duly convicted." Here again is the question: What is a crime? I maintain that the Constitution says a crime requires a nonconsenting victim. Hence, all the people currently spending time in prisons for consensual crimes are being held in involuntary servitude against the precepts of the Constitution.

The Fourteenth Amendment—hard won by the Civil War—guaranteed that a state could not take away the freedoms granted by the Constitution.

> . . . No State shall make or enforce any law which shall abridge the privileges or immunities of citizens of the United States; nor shall any State deprive any person of life, liberty, or property, without due process of law; nor deny to any person within its jurisdiction the equal protection of the laws. . . .

This amendment affirmed once again that the Constitution and the Bill of Rights were the *supreme* law of the land and the rights guaranteed by the Constitution could not be taken away by any state under the guise of, oh, "state's rights."

> *The layman's constitutional view
> is that what he likes
> is constitutional
> and that which he doesn't like
> is unconstitutional.*
>
> JUSTICE HUGO BLACK

It also guarantees that a state cannot "deprive any person of life, liberty, or property, without due process of law." This affirms, once again, that we are innocent until proven guilty in a court of law, and that no group—even a majority—has the right to deprive "any person" of his or her "life, liberty, or property" just because the majority doesn't like the way that person is living. The Fourteenth Amendment is our greatest protection against a police state and against rule by the iron whim of either the majority or a highly vocal minority.

The Sixteenth Amendment, passed in 1913, gives the federal government the authority to "collect taxes on income." This reaffirms that the Constitution can only be changed *by amendment.* Although taxing people's incomes removes a great deal of power from the people, there is something that removes even more power from them: putting them in jail. How we can put people in jail for a consensual activity *without* a constitutional amendment is beyond me.

The Eighteenth Amendment. The day this amendment was ratified was a dark day in the history of freedom. One has to give the Prohibitionists credit, however, for at least *doing it right.* If the government is going to take away basic freedoms, the only *way* it can do that is through a constitutional amendment. All lesser laws must fall before the "supreme law of the land" and the supreme law of the land strongly sides with individual freedom.

The Nineteenth Amendment gave women the right to vote. It's hard to believe that in this country women did not have the right to vote until 1920. The outrageousness of this is another issue. From the point of view of this book and consensual crimes, however, the fact that an amendment needed to be passed in order to give women the right to vote is significant. The Constitution *could* have been re-interpreted to include women, but it was not. A change—in this case giving rights rather than taking them away—required a constitutional amendment.

Section 1 of the *Twenty-first Amendment,* ratified in 1933, repealed the Eighteenth Amendment. When discussing consensual crimes, however, Section 2 of the Twenty-first Amendment is far more interesting:

> The transportation or importation into any State, territory, or possession
> of the United States for delivery or use therein of intoxicating liquors, in
> violation of the laws thereof, is hereby prohibited.

This was a compromise tossed to the Prohibitionists (still powerful in 1933) which allowed individual states to continue Prohibition if they so chose. Note that the control of "intoxicating liquors" had to be *constitutionally given* from the federal government to the state governments. The implication here is that other consensual activities— such as the use of drugs other than alcohol—are *not* within the province of the state to enforce. If people feel so strongly about the War on Drugs (or warring on any other consensual activities), why don't they do the right thing by America, freedom, and the Constitution and propose an amendment?

> *I believe in only one thing: liberty;*
> *but I do not believe in liberty*
> *enough to want*
> *to force it upon anyone.*
>
> H. L. MENCKEN

The Twenty-seventh Amendment is mentioned here primarily for its entertainment value. It limits the number of pay raises Congress can vote itself. (Not the *amount* of the raise; just the *number* of raises.) Proposed in 1789 by James Madison, it was finally ratified in 1992. It only took Congress 203 years to put even token fiscal limitations on itself. Too bad it didn't act as slowly in passing laws against consensual activities.

⚖ ⚖ ⚖

So what happened? If the Constitution is so clear about our personal freedoms— as it obviously is—how did we lose them?

The fact is, we never had them.

As Professor Robert Allen Rutland explained,

> For almost 150 years, in fact, the Bill of Rights was paid lip service in patriotic orations and ignored in the marketplace. It wasn't until after World War I that the Supreme Court began the process of giving real meaning to the Bill of Rights.

After the Bill of Rights was passed, it was pretty much forgotten. In a July 1818 letter to Thomas Jefferson, John Adams wrote,

> When people talk of the freedom of writing, speaking, or thinking, I cannot choose but laugh. No such thing ever existed. No such thing now exists; but I hope it will exist. But it must be hundreds of years after you and I shall write and speak no more.

When it came to guaranteeing personal freedoms (known today most often as *civil rights*) the federal government was lackluster at best. When it came to using the Constitution to raise money or wage war, however, the government was in top form. (Ah, echoes of today.)

The first major challenge between federal rights and states' rights took place in 1794. In 1791, Secretary of the Treasury Alexander Hamilton passed a tax on, among other things, liquor, to help pay off the Revolutionary War debt (which

> *[The South] has too much*
> *common sense and good temper*
> *to break up [the Union].*
>
> ABRAHAM LINCOLN
> August 1860

was, in relative terms, greater than our current national debt). A group of Pennsylvania farmers decided they shouldn't have to pay a tax on their homemade whiskey, but the federal revenue collectors (the "revenuers") did not agree. The federal authorities applied pressure and the chief revenuer's house was torched by the rebellious farmers. President George Washington led thirteen thousand troops to quell what the revenuers told him was an organized mass rebellion. The troops found no rebellion. Several arrests were made, there were two convictions (later pardoned by Washington), and the Whiskey Rebellion was over.

Many, including Thomas Jefferson, expressed great concern that the federal government should violently overreact. The reaction was also very expensive. The point, nonetheless, had been made: Don't mess with the federal government when it comes to paying your federal taxes.

The Sedition Act of 1798 made it a crime to criticize the president, the government, or Congress. It was passed mostly to suppress Jefferson and his followers who were not happy with, among other things, the lack of government action on behalf of personal freedoms. The government's response? Get rid of the problem by silencing the criticism. It made Jefferson—who, at this time, only wanted to retire to his library and do some writing—angry enough to run for president. He won, and his opposition saw to it that the Sedition Act was withdrawn just before he took office. Jefferson, much to his credit (and, no doubt, his personal discomfort), did not have the act reinstated. "I tolerate with the utmost latitude," he wrote, "the right of others to differ from me in opinion."

Because his political opposition was strong, Jefferson was unable to make many of the social reforms he sought. He did, however, do something very strange: He *bought* land from France (the Louisiana Purchase). "We have an army; France isn't going to fight hard for it; why don't we just *take* it?" said the loyal opposition. "It will cost less than buying it." Jefferson didn't see things this way— France did have legal claim to it, after all, and buying is far more civilized and rights-respecting than war. (Unfortunately, the civil rights of the Native Americans in this "French-owned" territory were not given much sway.)

Jefferson was so unsatisfied with his inability to implement more of the Bill of Rights during his term that he did not even mention his presidency in his epitaph:

> Here was buried Thomas Jefferson author of the Declaration of American
> Independence of the Statute of Virginia for Religious Freedom and the
> father of University of Virginia.

From the passage of the Bill of Rights in 1791 until the Civil War, states were generally allowed to violate civil rights at will, as long as the federal government got its taxes and its troops in time of war.

The Civil War was not, as most people think, fought for the civil rights of the slaves. It was, in fact, an extension of the Whiskey Rebellion. The federal government said, "You do it our way," and the southern states said, "No, we're going to do it *our* way." Slavery was only one of the ways in which North and South disagreed—and not one of the major ones. The main disagreements were over (1) money, and (2) men and equipment for war (a variation of [1]).

The judicial view of slavery was made clear in 1857 with the Dred Scott Decision. It stated that slaves were not human beings, but "articles of merchandise," that slaves "had no rights which the white man was bound to respect," and that slaves were never entitled to become citizens of the United States. (If you ever question the fallibility of the Supreme Court, look no further than this decision.)

When he was elected to office in 1860, Abraham Lincoln said he did not like slavery personally, but he was willing to endure it for the sake of peace and national unity. Lincoln firmly proclaimed, however, that he *would* have a Union; he would do whatever was necessary to preserve that Union.

Shortly after his inauguration in 1861, seven southern states decided to rebel against what they viewed as a too-paternal attitude and seceded from the Union. Had Lincoln acknowledged their right to secede from the Union, there probably would have been no war. Instead, Lincoln blockaded the southern seaports (essential for trade), the Confederates fired on Fort Sumpter, and the war was on. In 1862, Simon Cameron, U.S. Secretary of War, wrote,

> President Lincoln desires the right to hold slaves to be fully recognized.
> The war is prosecuted for the Union, hence no question concerning
> slavery will arise.

It wasn't until 1863 that Lincoln issued the Emancipation Proclamation—a political move more than anything else—to get the Northern Abolitionists on his side after two years of bloody fighting and few victories. What was later portrayed as a holy war for civil rights was, in fact, the federal government putting down its foot firmly and finally: *it* was the government, and the United States Constitution (not any state constitution) was the supreme law of the land.

Shortly after the North won the Civil War, the Thirteenth Amendment officially abolished slavery "within the United States, or any place subject to their jurisdiction." Although the slaves were technically free, they were not recognized as citizens. Denied all civil liberties, many of them continued working only for

> *It's easy for people to assume*
> *that the Bill of Rights will be,*
> *as somebody once called*
> *the Constitution,*
> *a machine that runs itself.*
> *I disagree.*
> *I think eternal vigilance*
> *is the price*
> *of keeping it in working order.*
>
> LAWRENCE TRIBE

food and shelter, or what became known as "slave wages."

The Fourteenth Amendment, ratified in 1868, said, "Enough of that," gave full and equal citizenship to all slaves and equal vote to all black men over the age of twenty-one, applied the personal freedoms guaranteed in the federal Constitution to the citizens of all states, and prohibited states from making laws restricting any of these rights.

And then everything was quiet again.

In 1896, the Supreme Court ruled that "separate but equal" facilities for blacks and whites were constitutional. This decision officially institutionalized the "loophole" to personal freedoms which kept blacks and whites separate and "equal" in principle, but not equal in practice. (Separate-But-Equal remained in effect until the 1954 Supreme Court decision in which the Supreme Court essentially overturned itself.)

It was not until 1925, in fact, that the Supreme Court ruled the Fourteenth Amendment (1868) *did* apply the Bill of Rights (1791) to *all* citizens of *all* states. U.S. Supreme Court Justice Edward T. Sanford wrote for the majority in 1925,

> Freedom of speech and of the press, which are protected by the First Amendment from abridgment by Congress—are among the fundamental personal rights and "liberties" protected by the due process clause of the Fourteenth Amendment from impairment by the States.

Gradually, gradually, over time, the Supreme Court—and even occasionally Congress and the president—have "given" us the rights the Bill of Rights declared for all citizens more than two hundred years ago.

As I said, it's not that the freedoms guaranteed by the Constitution were taken from us—we never had them. Why haven't we had them? Because we never took them. No one is ever given freedom. Power is never given away freely—either by a tyrant, a bureaucracy, or any combination thereof. Rights—even *inalienable* rights—*must be claimed.*

In 1912, Woodrow Wilson set the stage for a century of people demanding their natural and constitutional rights:

> Liberty has never come from the government. Liberty has always come from the subjects of government. The history of liberty is the history of resistance. The history of liberty is a history of the limitation of governmental power, not the increase of it.

That's what this book is about: getting a few of the rights we've had available to us since 1791, but that we never took the time or trouble to claim.

Freedom, anyone?

Laws against Consensual Activities Violate the Separation of Church and State, Threatening the Freedom of and from Religion

> The government of the
> United States
> is not, in any sense,
> founded on the Christian religion.
>
> GEORGE WASHINGTON
> 1796

IN 1982, ON THE CELEBRATION OF his ninetieth birthday, Dumas Malone, noted historian and Thomas Jefferson biographer, was asked, "What is the most fortunate aspect of American history?" Malone replied,

The fact that we became a nation and immediately separated church and state —it has saved us from all the misery that has beset mankind with inquisitions, internecine and civil wars, and other assorted ills.

In the 1700s, the separation of church and state was a radical idea—almost as radical as it is today.

There is little doubt, however, that America was founded on the passionate pursuit of The Almighty: Almighty God and the Almighty Dollar.

Less than seven weeks after arriving in the New World, Columbus wrote in his journal,

And I say that Your Highnesses ought not to consent that any foreigner does business or sets foot here, except Christian Catholics, since this was the end and the beginning of the enterprise, that it should be for the enhancement and glory of the Christian religion, nor should anyone who is not a good Christian come to these parts.

It's hard to tell, though, whether this line was written by Columbus the Believer, Columbus the Diplomat, or Columbus the Frightened.

Columbus the Believer. He *may* have been a devout Roman Catholic (although his mother was probably Jewish), and Roman Catholics at that time believed it was their divinely ordained duty to make sure *everyone* was a practicing Roman Catholic *no matter what*. If persuasion failed, "no matter what" included exclusion, coercion, fear, economic deprivation, torture and—for the good of your immortal

> *What a pity,*
> *when Christopher Columbus*
> *discovered America,*
> *that he ever mentioned it.*
>
> MARGOT ASQUITH

soul (and to set an example for other slackers)—death. As a good Catholic, Columbus would not want non-Catholics sharing in this little piece of heaven he called the New World.

Columbus the Diplomat. Making such a statement would make him *seem* like a devout Catholic, which, for the reasons just listed, had its positive effects. Similarly, *not* appearing to be a good Catholic would have detrimental effects on the man who was now the governor of the New World and was about to be—or so he thought—one of the richest men in the world. (Columbus's deal with the Spanish crown included a 10% commission on all wealth produced in or imported from the New World.)

Columbus the Frightened. The Spanish Inquisition was, after all, in full bloom and was being used more and more for personal and political purposes. Any of the Spanish nobles (some of whom were helping the church run the Inquisition) might be envious of Columbus's new-found fame, power, and, let's not forget, *wealth.* He would be especially vulnerable if one of his parents were Jewish—the people whom the church officially blamed for every calamity to Christians since, and certainly including, the Crucifixion. As they say in Spain, Columbus had to watch his *nalgas.*

A little over a hundred years later, those who worshiped at that universal seat of religion, the Almighty Dollar (or, as it was back then in England, the Almighty Pound), arrived in the New World. Virginia was settled by Sir Walter Raleigh (although he never set foot in the colony himself) more for his personal gain and financial enhancement than for the glory of God. The original settlers of the colony had the idea that the Indians would do all the work and the white man had only to provide ideas and direction. But somehow the native tribes in Virginia—those savages!—failed to cooperate. The intrinsic intellectual superiority of the white man somehow escaped these Native Americans. Eventually, the colonists were asked by their leaders to *work.* Each man, woman, and child in the settlement was given a military rank. The duties of each rank were spelled out to the smallest detail. Penalties were harsh—whipping for a second offense and a year on a British prison ship for a third offense. Complaining was not permitted, and there was no going back to England—this is your life, Virginia.*

All of this oppression was done, of course, in the name of God. What God

---

*The descendants of this group eventually got all the "servants" they could use. By 1670, there were 2,000 African slaves in Virginia; by 1715, there were 23,000; and in the glorious year of independence—for the white American males, at least—1776, there were 150,000 slaves, some of them owned by George Washington and Thomas Jefferson. By that time, the Native Americans had been, uh, displaced.

AIN'T NOBODY'S BUSINESS IF YOU DO

wanted—and was kind enough to communicate to the settlers by way of the British crown and its many emissaries—was tobacco. A powerful strain of Virginia tobacco was popular in Great Britain. God wanted the people of England to have their tobacco (making the first cash crop from America a drug, by the way). In addition, God wanted the investors in the Virginia Company to turn a profit on their investments and, by God, if it took a police state to bring about God's will, so be it.

> *Perhaps, after all,*
> *America never*
> *has been discovered.*
> *I myself would say that*
> *it had merely been detected.*
>
> OSCAR WILDE

சு சு சு

IN The Name of God, Amen . . . Having undertaken for the Glory of God, and Advancement of the Christian Faith, and the honour of our King and Country, a voyage to plant the first colony in the northern parts of Virginia. . . .

So began the Mayflower Compact of 1620. No secular voyage this. A group of people on board the *Mayflower* were called "pilgrims" because they were on a religious quest. They were journeying to the New World to found the City on the Hill, the New Jerusalem. It was to be a shining beacon for the entire world; proof not only that Christianity was the One True Way, but that their specific *interpretation* of Christianity was the One True Interpretation.

Besides, England had had enough of them. They were known as the Puritans, and, oh my goodness, were they *pure*. Protestants protested against Catholicism and Puritans protested against Protestantism. Even though the Protestants had overthrown the Catholic church in England—a monumental undertaking—the Puritans wanted to "purify" Protestantism even further. By the early 1600s, England had been through *decades* of religious wars and was tired of it all.

In 1534, King Henry VIII separated from the Catholic church ("the Church of Rome") and established Protestantism as the official state religion—the Church of England. Although this was a major advance for Protestantism, the Puritans were not pleased. It was, they thought, the same Catholic hierarchy and form of worship under a new name. When Queen Mary ascended the throne in 1553, Roman Catholicism returned to England; a great many Protestants—especially Puritans—were executed or exiled. In 1558, with the ascension of Elizabeth I, Protestantism returned. Although Protestant, Elizabeth still wasn't pure enough for the Puritans. They continued to protest against the Protestants and, not surprisingly, were repressed. The Puritans spent the next forty-five years being pure anyway. Like the Pharisees of old, they established elaborate customs to separate themselves—the chosen elite—from the heathen, condemned-to-perdition, mainstream Protestants and the completely-lost-from-all-hope-of-salvation Roman Catholics. Almost every aspect of Puritan life was set, regulated, and ordered. The smallest detail of life style became a religious function which either glorified God or condemned one to hellfire.

In 1603, the Puritans had their last, best hope—King James IV of Scotland became James I of England. King James was a Calvinist and the Puritans thought of themselves as Calvinists. (The Puritans' form of Calvinism, however, had become far more severe since the death of John Calvin in 1564.) They presented their many grievances to King James I in 1604, but, as the Puritans were not part of the power structure, they were dismissed. "No bishop, no king," James told them. So, the Puritans set their sights on the New World.

The Puritans were well-educated, hard-working (the "Puritan work ethic" lives today—in name, at least), and had amassed great influence in the educational and business communities of England. They decided to demonstrate to the world how Puritanism (which, of course, they thought of as the *true* Christianity) could flourish when not repressed by Catholics and quasi-Catholics (Protestants). It would be a community of such spiritual integrity, moral purity, and economic productivity that the people of the world would unanimously herald it a success—the scales would fall from their eyes, they would drop their chains of religious oppression, and the world would be safe for Puritan Calvinistic Christianity for ever and ever. Amen.

By 1620 they were ready to go. They sailed for the New World with no small burden: the spiritual destiny of humankind rested on their shoulders. Their goal was Virginia, but God apparently had other plans—more northerly plans. The ship was blown off course. They landed in Massachusetts. Hmmm. This meant they were no longer bound by the agreements they had made with the Virginia Company. While still on the Mayflower, they made their own Compact. They were now free—to freeze to death. It was colder than anyone expected. (Massachusetts is like that.) As Ulysses S. Grant later explained, "The Pilgrim Fathers fell upon an ungenial climate, where there were nine months of winter and three months of cold weather."

Due almost entirely to the compassion, openness, and generosity of the Native Americans (whose behavior was downright *Christian),* more than half of the Puritans survived their first winter in what is now Plymouth, Massachusetts. (They first spent some time at Provincetown, which began a New England tradition of dropping by P-town for a little R&R.) The Native Americans taught the pilgrims how to hunt, fish, and grow crops; showed them which plants were nutritional, which were medicinal, and which were purely recreational.

The pilgrims learned quickly, applied what they learned with diligence, and made a success of things. Everything went along fine until the next generation grew up. Those pesky youngsters! The pilgrims soon learned what a brief study of history could have taught them—that religious belief is not hereditary.

Those who toed the line of Puritan orthodoxy were part of a group, a community, an extended family where life was congenial, and everyone helped one another. Those who strayed from the fold (by being either less devout or, in rare cases, more devout than the elders considered proper) were punished. If that didn't bring them into line, they were banished. Connecticut and Rhode Island were founded by "impure" Puritans.*

> *My ancestors were Puritans from England.*
> *They arrived here in 1648 in the hope of finding greater restrictions than were permissible under English law at that time.*
>
> GARRISON KEILLOR

And then there were the French. Good God, the French! Some of them had no religion at all, and those who did were what only could be called Bastard Catholics. They weren't after religious freedom; they were after beaver pelts. And stories were circulating—these stories were told *only* to indicate what immoral heathens these French really were—that the trappers were having more than social intercourse with the Indians!**

The Puritan adventure was but one example of religion motivating migration. Lord Baltimore settled Maryland in the hope of establishing a haven for Roman Catholics. Although most of the settlers were Protestants, the land was owned by Catholics. (Not unlike New York City today.) The fastest way to advancement in the colony was to "see the light" and convert to Catholicism. When William and Mary ascended the throne and re-established Protestant rule in England, however, the descendants of Lord Baltimore were relieved of their land and power. When

---

*Rhode Island was founded by Roger Williams, who had such radical thoughts as opening the church membership to anyone who wanted to join, and separating the Puritans entirely from the Church of England (rather than trying to purify it from within). His *most* unpopular thought was that it wasn't a Christian act to occupy Indian land without paying the Indians. Well, what can you do with such an uncooperative radical as this? Such anti-God thinking had to be x'ed out. This meant either execution, excommunication, or exile. The Puritans chose excommunication and exile. The executions would come later.

**This was quite true. Some members of the Native American tribes admired the white man and offered their women to him; the offspring were raised within the tribe. News of this flexible, casual, experimental quality of the Native Americans was brought back to Europe by the French trappers. This influenced the French philosophers—particularly Rousseau—who found it a perfect example of man living in nature, enjoying his inherent natural rights. This philosophy was brought back across the Atlantic in the works of Rousseau, Voltaire, and John Locke. It inspired Franklin, Jefferson, Paine, and others in shaping their political philosophies.

> *I'm really
> a timid person—
> I was beaten up
> by Quakers.*
>
> WOODY ALLEN

Lord Baltimore's offspring "saw the light," however (again), and became Protestants, their land was returned to them.

The Dutch settled New Netherlands for purely economic purposes. Peter Stuyvesant took what he learned about authoritarianism, control, and domination from his Calvinist minister father and applied it to the practice of making money for the Dutch West India Company. *Naturally,* God was on his side. When the English captured the colony in 1664, it became New York, named after the Duke of York. When the Duke of York became King of England in 1685, New York became an official crown colony.

The Carolinas, it was thought, would be ideal places to produce silk. They were not. Georgia was settled as a method for the populace of Britain's overcrowded debtors' prisons to start a new life. The restrictions were harsh and the limitations were economic, not religious.

William Penn knew well the dangers of following an unpopular religion. In England, he was fined and ultimately dismissed from Oxford for refusing to attend chapel. He was imprisoned four times for writing or speaking his religious beliefs.* Penn was a member of the Society of Friends or, as they are better known, the Quakers. He intended his *Penn-sylvania* (the woodlands of Penn) to be a haven for all religious minorities, not just Quakers. Most of his time was spent persuading the British government to allow his "holy experiment" to continue. This kept him in England and, consequently, Penn only spent two two-year periods in the colony that bore his name. It was because Penn not only tolerated but welcomed diversity that Pennsylvania became the most diverse, dynamic, and prosperous of the original thirteen colonies. This provided fertile ground for free and, later, radical, and later still, revolutionary thinking.** By 1776, Philadelphia was the largest city in the thirteen colonies, with a population of 40,000. This was larger than Boston and New York combined (24,000).

⚖ ⚖ ⚖

By 1770, the British American Colonies had become a billion-pound enterprise, importing more than £1 billion of goods from England and exporting nearly £2 billion. (Remember the days when *other countries* had to worry about a

---

*What *can* one *do* with a man who says things like, "It is a reproach to religion and government to suffer so much poverty and excess," or "The public must and will be served." Heavens!

**Benjamin Franklin, at twenty, chose Philadelphia as his permanent home over New York and his native Boston. (His relocation may have had something to do with his meeting his wife-to-be on his first day in Philadelphia.) Many years later, Franklin, a rich man and well-respected in England, risked losing it all—and his life—by signing the Declaration of Independence.

trade deficit with the United States?) The effects of religion were still felt—even the centers of higher learning (Harvard, Yale, Princeton) began as religious institutions. For the most part, however, by the early 1770s, currency was king in the colonies.

God—or, more accurately, those who appointed themselves the representatives of God—was not about to give in without a fight to the devil-inspired influences of materialism and the preoccupation with worldliness.

> *The legitimate powers of government extend to such acts only as are injurious to others. But it does me no injury for my neighbor to say there are twenty gods, or no God. It neither picks my pocket nor breaks my leg.*
>
> THOMAS JEFFERSON

Churches that once had rigid restrictions on membership opened their doors to all. "Harvests," they were called. God, not man, chose who would and would not *directly* experience salvation. With some good ol' hellfire and brimstone preaching, the fear of damnation, and the knowledge that only God could save them from the eternal flaming pit, the congregants had direct spiritual experiences that we would now call "born again." It was known as the Great Awakening. While still high on the ecstasy of deliverance, the new converts were convinced that the rules and regulations of that particular variation of Christianity were what God *really* desired—in fact, demanded—if one wanted to be truly and permanently saved. The ecstasy of the Awakening was just a taste of what one could look forward to in paradise—provided one followed God's laws here on earth without deviation or question. The alternative? An eternal afterlife of bubbling sulfur.

On the other—cooler—end of the spectrum, were the great thinkers of the Enlightenment. Deism was the religion of the age of Enlightenment. If *reason* could be applied to government, science, and philosophy, surely (they reasoned), it could also be applied to religion. That there was a God, in the form of a creator, was reasonable; *something* had to create this incredible universe—the wonders of which were, through telescope and microscope, being revealed daily—and *something* had to account for the miracle of life itself.

"An overruling Providence," Jefferson called it, "which by all its dispensations proves that it delights in the happiness of man here and his greater happiness hereafter." Jefferson also referred to the creator as "that Infinite Power which rules the destinies of the universe." Neither of these, by the way, was secretly written by Jefferson and communicated to an "in" group of friends; both came from his first inaugural address.

In Washington's first inaugural address, he referred to this creative energy as "the Great Arbiter of the Universe." Deists called this power "God" or "the Creator."

The Deists were *not* Christians. This comes as something of a shock to the religious right, who decorate their homes in Early American furniture, or the

> *A substantial portion of Deist literature was devoted to the description of the noxious practices of all religions in all times. For many religious Deists the teachings of Christ were not essentially novel but were, in reality, as old as creation.*
>
> ENCYCLOPEDIA BRITANNICA

conservative Daughters of the American Revolution* who make almost religious pilgrimages to Mount Vernon and Monticello. It is, nonetheless, true that the first three presidents—Washington, Adams, and Jefferson—(as well as Benjamin Franklin) were Deists, not Christians.**

The Deists admired, even loved, Jesus as teacher and as an example ("Imitate Jesus," Franklin reminded himself), but they had little use for the portion of the New Testament that did not deal directly with the life and sayings of Jesus. They did not believe in "the revealed word"—Peter, Paul, John, the Prophets, Moses, it didn't matter. If God wants to reveal something to me, a Deist reasons, He certainly has the power to reveal it to me Himself. What Jesus did and actually said while on earth was studied and deeply appreciated. Studied too, according to Samuel Adams, were "Confucius, Zoroaster, Socrates, Mahomet [sic]" and many other teachers and sources of wisdom. It was not so much *who* said a truth that mattered, but whether or not it rang the bell of truth *within the reader.* This indicator of truth within the reader, it was believed, was put there by the Divine as a way of *divining* truth from falsehood. Whatever they would read—be it a Bible, book, or almanac—they would always listen for the bell.

Deists found, however, something of value to take from *any* religious practice: for example, the Quaker custom of sitting quietly and listening for revelations was much admired.

Deists did not believe in hell. They believed that God only wanted what was good for mankind, and hell did not seem like a reasonable idea to be coming from one who wanted only good. Deists believed in repentance: if they wronged another person, they made it up *to that person.* God, being God, did not have feelings that could be hurt, therefore, did not need to be apologized to.

And where was God in the daily working of things? Deists believed that God, like all good creators, after creating Creation went off to create something else. One can see, admire, and even stand in awe of Michelangelo's David and not expect to see Michelangelo nearby answering questions, much less fulfilling re-

---

*My forefather, Patrick McWilliams, arrived on these shores in 1774, which I suppose makes me a Daughter of the American Revolution—or at least half a Daughter of the American Revolution. On my mother's side of the family, I am a Son of Ellis Island. My mother's father came over on the boat from Sicily—probably shipmates with Vito Corleone. I am told that, on my father's side, my great, great grandmother was a Cherokee princess. (As Will Rogers, who had more Native American blood than I, wrote, "My forefathers didn't come over on the Mayflower, but they met the boat.") In my atypicalness, I am about as typical as they come. Daughter, son, princess—I am proud of them all.

**The fourth president of the United States, James Madison, was almost certainly a Deist as well.

quests. Nietzsche's idea that "God is dead" seemed in 1890 to be the height of blasphemy, heresy, and bad taste. The Deists, however, would have no trouble with this concept. They might be momentarily saddened to hear of Michelangelo's passing, but it would not interfere for very long with their enjoyment of Michelangelo's creations.

In accordance with this view of God, Deists did not pray. They may have given praise, as in "Lord, what a beautiful morning," the same way one may say, "Lord, what a beautiful painting," but they did not pray to ask for things. They believed that, as part of the creation, God created logically discoverable methods by which needs, desires, and wants could be fulfilled; and, by discovering and practicing the techniques of desire fulfillment, one could fulfill one's desires. God may have set up the system, but was not necessary for the delivery of the goods any more than Benjamin Franklin, who created the postal system, needed to deliver every letter personally.

> *Voltaire gloried in the name Deist. The Catholic Church in 18th-century France did not recognize fine distinctions among heretics, and Deist and atheist works were burned in the same bonfires.*
>
> ENCYCLOPEDIA BRITANNICA

"I simply haven't the nerve to imagine a being, a force, a cause which keeps the planets revolving in their orbits," said Quentin Crisp (who would have made a fine Deist), "and then suddenly stops in order to give me a bicycle with three speeds." If you wanted a bicycle with three speeds, the Deists believed, you did what was necessary to get the money and then went to where the bicycles were sold and bought one. Knowledge, planning, and work were required, not prayer.

Because Deists didn't believe in the sole divinity of Jesus (They took seriously Jesus' prediction, "Anyone who has faith in me will do what I have been doing. He will do even greater things than these" [John 14:12]), or in hell or eternal damnation, most Christians were down on Deists. Christians denounced the Deists as heretics who were too cowardly to say what they *really* were: *atheists.* Deists did not suffer the restrictions of Christians gladly. Deists accused Christians of turning God into a tyrant for their own selfish ends. It was an unfriendly stalemate at best. This from the Encyclopedia Britannica,

> The Deists were particularly vehement against any manifestation of religious fanaticism and enthusiasm. . . . Any description of God that depicted his impending vengeance, vindictiveness, jealousy, and destructive cruelty was blasphemous. . . . The Deist God, ever gentle, loving, and benevolent, intended men to behave toward one another in the same kindly and tolerant fashion.

As Deism became increasingly refined, it eventually evaporated by the mid-1800s, a victim of its own refinement. It was a little too cool for those who wanted to *know* that they were saved—that took a religion with *history* such as Roman Catholicism with popes going back to St. Peter, and, hence, Christ; or one of the evangelical religions in which one *experienced*—even if only for a moment—the bliss of salvation.

♉ ♉ ♉

There is little doubt that the separation of church and state was a major theme of the American Revolution.

The resolution of the first Continental Congress issued in October 1774 listed among the "infringements and violations of the rights of the colonists" the fact that the British Parliament had established as the official state religion the "Roman Catholic religion in the province of Quebec" which, the Continental Congress claimed, had the effect of "erecting a tyranny there to the great danger . . . of the neighboring British colonies." The members of the first Continental Congress were not specifically anti-Catholic (although it's certainly true that most of them were either Protestants or Deists, and also true that Protestants and Catholics were not on the best of terms back then) but were complaining of the "tyranny" of *any* state-authorized religion.

In January 1776, Thomas Paine published *Common Sense.* This pamphlet, more than anything else, moved popular opinion from merely *protesting* against British rule to openly *rebelling* against it. Without *Common Sense* paving the way, it is doubtful that the Declaration of Independence would have been issued in July of that year—if at all. Here are some common sense ideas Thomas Paine had about the freedom of religion:

> This new world hath been the asylum for the persecuted lovers of civil and religious liberty from every Part of Europe. Hither have they fled, not from the tender embraces of the mother, but from the cruelty of the monster. . . .

> As to religion, I hold it to be the indispensable duty of all government, to protect all conscientious professors thereof, and I know of no other business which government hath to do therewith. . . .

> For myself I fully and conscientiously believe, that it is the will of the Almighty, that there should be a diversity of religious opinions among us. . . .

Paine argued that "above all things the free exercise of religion" was essential to freedom.

Declaring independence from the king of England in 1776 was the first taste of religious freedom that most Americans had. Calling the king a tyrant and breaking all ties with him may seem today like a purely political move, but it was not viewed that way in 1776. The king, it was believed, was the direct representative of God on earth, personally crowned by the highest church authority. Just as people owed God

allegiance, so too, and in the same proportion, they owed the king allegiance. Obeying
the king was the same as obeying God; disobeying the king was the same as disobeying
God.

Whenever the revolutionary war was
not going well, many people moaned, "This
is what we get for offending the king. God
is not on our side." When the war was
finally won, however, in 1781, Americans
finally started believing that life without a
king was possible. They also started think-
ing that, perhaps, life with God but *without* a state-chosen religion was possible as
well.

> *I consider the government of the
> U.S. as interdicted by the Constitu-
> tion from intermeddling with relig-
> ious institutions, their doctrines,
> discipline, or exercises . . .civil
> powers alone have been given to the
> President of the U.S. and no
> authority to direct the religious
> exercises of his constituents.*
>
> THOMAS JEFFERSON

In Virginia, a state rich in religious tradition, Thomas Jefferson tried for more
than a decade to have the principles of religious freedom incorporated as part of
Virginia's bylaws. In January of 1786, with the help of James Madison, he finally
succeeded. It was a testament not only to Jefferson's persuasive ability and determination, but also to the gradual awakening of the American public. His Virginia
Statute of Religious Liberty stands as a lighthouse of religious freedom and
would probably have as much trouble passing through any legislative body today
as it did back in the late 1700s.

The Virginia Statute of Religious Liberty begins by stating that "Almighty God
hath created the mind free," and attempts to influence others in religious matters by
using the force of government "tend only to beget habits of hypocrisy and meanness." Further, claimed Jefferson, laws based on religious beliefs are not just a civil
injustice, but "a departure from the plan of the Holy author of our religion." After
all, if God wanted to physically punish people for not obeying the precepts of a
certain religion, He could, because it "was in his Almighty power to do."

> Our civil rights have no dependence on our religious opinions, any more
> than our opinions in physics or geometry.

Jefferson went on to point out that whenever one asks "the civil magistrate to
intrude his powers into the field of opinion" and stop the spread of one thought
or another "on the supposition of their ill tendency," the government is caught in
"a dangerous fallacy, which at once destroys all religious liberty" because the
magistrate will simply "approve or condemn the sentiments of others only as
they shall square with or differ from his own."

Jefferson maintains that the civil government has plenty to do; there is barely
"time enough for the rightful purposes of civil government," and the government
should only instruct "its officers to interfere when principles break out into overt
acts against peace and good order." Jefferson continues, stating that "truth is great
and will prevail if left to herself." Truth "has nothing to fear from the conflict"

unless truth, by human intervention, is "disarmed of her natural weapons, free argument and debate."

All men shall be free to profess, and by argument to maintain their opinion in matters of religion, and that the same shall in no wise diminish, enlarge or affect their civil capacities.

As we are free to declare, and do declare, that the rights hereby asserted are the natural rights of mankind, and that if any act shall hereafter be passed to repeal the present, or to narrow its operations, such act will be an infringement of natural right.

> *The day that this country ceases to be free for irreligion, it will cease to be free for religion.*
>
> JUSTICE ROBERT H. JACKSON

When our founding fathers gathered in 1787 to write a Constitution, the thirteen colonies were a crazy quilt (or, if you prefer, a cornucopia) of religious beliefs, philosophies, and practices. Eleven of the thirteen colonies had religious requirements in order for men to serve in the state legislature. Some of the state constitutions embraced the church; others kept the church at arm's length. Some gave preference to one religious denomination or another.

The range of attitudes written into state constitutions and laws was quite remarkable. Massachusetts and Virginia represented two extremes.

Massachusetts, inspired by the Puritans and the total intermingling of church and state, thought that church and state should not only embrace each other, but should lie down together—after a proper marriage, of course. Here is an excerpt from its constitution, passed in 1780:

> As the happiness of a people, and the good order and preservation of a civil government, essentially depend upon piety, religion, and morality; and as these cannot be generally diffused through a community, but by the institution of the public worship of GOD, and of public instructions in piety, religion, and morality; Therefore, to promote their happiness and to secure the good order and preservation of their government, the people of this Commonwealth have a right to invest their legislature with power to authorize and require . . . the institution of the public worship of GOD, and for the support and maintenance of public Protestant teachers of piety, religion and morality.

Virginia, on the other hand, inspired by the works of Thomas Jefferson, James Madison, George Washington, and a truly unhappy experience with state mandated and supported religions, made a clear separation of church and state in its constitution passed in 1776:

> No man shall be compelled to frequent or support any religious worship, place or ministry whatsoever; nor shall any man be forced, restrained, molested or burdened in his body or goods, or otherwise suffer, on

account of his religious opinions or belief; but all men shall be free to profess, and by argument to maintain, their opinions in matters of religion, and the same shall in no wise affect, diminish, or enlarge their civil capacities. And the legislature shall not prescribe any religious test whatever; nor confer any particular privileges or advantages on any one sect or denomination; nor pass any law requiring or authorizing any religious society, or the people of any district within this commonwealth, to levy on themselves or others any tax for the erection or repair of any house for public worship, or for the support of any church or ministry; but it shall be left free to every person to select his religious instructor, and make for his support such private contract as he shall please.

> *It is much to be lamented that a man of Dr. Franklin's general good character and great influence, should have been an unbeliever in Christianity, and also have done so much as he did to make others unbelievers.*
>
> DR. JOSEPH PRIESTLEY

In some states, as it had been in Virginia, a single church was established. Others restricted public office to Protestants. Some required belief in specific doctrines of the Christian religion, such as the divinity of Jesus, the Trinity, and immortality. The constitution of North Carolina is an example:

No person who shall deny the being of God, or the truth of the Christian religion, or the divine authority of the Old or New Testament, or who shall hold religious principles incompatible with the freedom or safety of the state, shall be capable of holding any office or place of trust in the civil department within this state.

Then the Americans looked at the world outside the thirteen colonies and they looked at history. Here, church and state—religion and politics—were so permanently, continuously, and unabashedly intermingled that the study of one automatically included the study of the other. Senator Sam J. Ervin, Jr., offers this account of two millennia of religious belief influencing government policy, or unscrupulous government officials using religion to achieve their own ends:

The ugliest chapters in history are those that recount the religious intolerance of the civil and ecclesiastical rulers of the Old World and their puppets during the generations preceding the framing and ratifying of the First Amendment.

These chapters of history reveal the casting of the Christians to the lions in the Colosseum at Rome; the bloody Crusades of the Christians against the Saracens for the possession of the shrines hallowed by the footsteps of the Prince of Peace; the use by the papacy of the dungeon and the rack to coerce conformity and of the fiery faggot to exterminate heresy; the unspeakable cruelties of the Spanish Inquisition; the slaughter of the Waldenses in Alpine Italy; the jailing and hanging by Protestant kings of English Catholics

> *We must respect*
> *the other fellow's religion,*
> *but only in the sense*
> *and to the extent that*
> *we respect his theory*
> *that his wife is beautiful*
> *and his children smart.*
>
> H. L. MENCKEN

for abiding with the faith of their fathers; the jailing and hanging by a Catholic queen of English Protestants for reading English Scriptures and praying Protestant prayers; the hunting down and slaying of the Covenanters upon the crags and moors of Scotland for worshiping God according to the dictates of their own consciences; the decimating of the people of the German states in the Thirty Years War between Catholics and Protestants; the massacre of the Huguenots in France; the pogroms and persecutions of the Jews in many lands; the banishing of Baptists and other dissenters by Puritan Massachusetts; the persecution and imprisonment of Quakers by England for refusing to pay tithes to the established church and to take the oaths of supremacy and allegiance; the banishing, branding, imprisoning, and whipping of Quakers, and the hanging of the alleged witches at Salem by Puritan Massachusetts; and the hundreds of other atrocities perpetrated in the name of religion.

It is not surprising that Blaise Pascal, the French mathematician and philosopher, was moved more than three hundred years ago to proclaim this tragic truth: "Men never do evil so completely and cheerfully as when they do it from religious conviction."

What Senator Ervin fails to mention, however, is that religious intolerance involving Christians began with Christ himself who, although put to death by Rome, was charged with "blasphemy" by the ruling religious body of the day, the Sanhedrin.

The idea that the church and the state should be separate was far more revolutionary than the frequently used proposal that the people should take arms against a tyrannical ruler. From the pharaohs of ancient Egypt to the republics of ancient Greece and Rome, up to and including King George III and King Louis XVI (and, of course, his queen, Marie Antoinette), the rulers of the people either *were* gods or held their positions through the *direct mandate* of God, and wielded power by Divine Right.

Just as we today generally think that a rich person (especially a self-made rich person) must know *something* that the rest of us don't, so too it was assumed that people with political power had *some* kind of connection to God that the average person did not. God was the giver of life; God was the giver of power; and God obviously gave more power to a king than to a serf.

For every ruler whose belief in God made him or her just, compassionate, caring, and giving, there was a ruler who used the name of God to suppress, exploit, terrorize, and intimidate. Usually it was the tyrants who had their names writ large in history, but there were as many rulers who sincerely believed in the more benevolent aspects of religion and sincerely (and, in some cases, successfully) administered a state with the kindness, encouragement, and fairness of a good parent.

In any system of government there has to be some influence to keep the ruler in check. It's human nature to grow accustomed to what we have, become bored by it, and want more. After we have more for a little while, that becomes the norm, we become bored with *it,* and want even more. What, then, is there to keep the ruler from increasing power, opulence, and luxury almost indefinitely—and always at the expense of the people? The answer in most political systems was, simply, God. God—in the form of the church (as an external authority) or the ruler's religious belief (as an internal authority)—was the system of checks and balances that would keep a ruler from becoming a yardstick.* One ruler could be devout and giving. The next could be a tyrant. When the checks and balances worked, they worked; when they didn't, they didn't. There seemed to be no rhyme or reason for their working or not working.

Lord, there's danger in this land. You get witch-hunts and wars when church and state hold hands.

JONI MITCHELL

What bothered the founding fathers about the intermingling of church and state was not that it *never* worked, but that it worked *intermittently.* Like good monarchs and bad monarchs, the good and bad were too random, too illogical, too *unreasonable* a system on which to base an ongoing government.

So, even if there *had been* a single religion happily practiced by all the citizens of the thirteen colonies (which there was not), a religion that divinely inspired a leader who was a true servant of God and the people, the intermingling of church and state would *still* have been unacceptable because no one knew how severely future despots might distort or manipulate that religion to their own selfish use.

The solution, then, was to *separate* church and state, build a "wall of separation" between them, as Jefferson wrote:

> Believing with you that religion is a matter which lies solely between man and his God, I contemplate with solemn reverence that act of the whole American people which declared that their legislature should "make no law respecting an establishment of religion or prohibiting the free exercise thereof" thus building a wall of separation between Church and State.

Although it was highly experimental and relatively untried, the concept of separation fit perfectly with the founding fathers' needs and intentions:

*The yard, as a form of measurement, came from the circumference of the king's waist—a testament to the opulence (and corpulence) of kings.

> *The First Amendment has erected*
> *a wall between church and state.*
> *That wall must be kept*
> *high and impregnable.*
> *We could not approve*
> *the slightest breach.*
>
> JUSTICE HUGO BLACK

1. The separation of church and state allowed the founding fathers to avoid the debate on which of the many diverse—and sometimes contradictory—religious beliefs then practiced in the thirteen colonies should be the official state religion. This debate almost certainly would have destroyed the Constitutional Convention, and the states might never have united.

2. Although the separation of church and state may not have allowed for those elevated periods of spiritual benevolence that took place when government and grace combined, it would also protect against the extravagantly wasteful and downright terrifying religious-political endeavors such as the Great Crusades, Spanish Inquisition, and the home-grown Salem Witch Hunts.

3. Being able to choose and practice one's own religion without government intervention, pressure, or control was completely harmonious with the concept that all rights *naturally* belonged to the individual who voluntarily surrendered specific rights in exchange for the benefits and protection of government. Taking a fresh look at it, why *should* people give up their natural right to choose and practice a religion? And why *should* the government, as part of its service to the people, choose, support, and enforce by law one particular religious belief over all others? The answer to these questions leaned overwhelmingly in the direction of leaving religious freedom where, uh, God originally put it—in the hands of the individual.

As James Madison wrote,

> We hold it for a fundamental and undeniable truth, that religion, or the duty we owe our Creator and the manner of discharging it, can be directed only by reason and conviction, not by force or violence. The religion then of every man must be left to the conviction and conscience of every man; and it is the right of every man to exercise it as these may dictate. This right is in its nature an unalienable right.

And so the Constitution of the United States of America was written without a single mention or reference to God—something almost unheard of in political documents of that time.* If the various indicators of separation of church and state in the main body of the Constitution—discussed in the previous chapter—were not enough, the freedom *from* state-imposed religion and the freedom *of* religious practice were both guaranteed by the First Amendment. (If *this* were not enough, the

---

*The Declaration of Independence mentioned a Deistic form of God, which is not surprising considering that Jefferson and the two other members of the committee to draft the Declaration of Independence were Deists. These references are "the separate and equal station to which the Laws of Nature and of Nature's God entitle them," "Creator," "the Supreme Judge of the World," and "Divine Providence."

Fourteenth Amendment made sure each state paid attention to the First Amendment.)

⚖️ ⚖️ ⚖️

And so there it was, and is, a shining example—clear, bright, and unambiguous—as to the religious rights retained by all citizens of the United States of America:

> Congress shall make no law respecting an establishment of religion, or prohibiting the free exercise thereof. . . .

No qualifications. No excuses. No exceptions. No apologies.

The first part, "Congress shall make no law respecting an establishment of religion . . ." means that the government cannot dictate a religious belief to be practiced by all people. Further, it means that the individual beliefs of certain religions cannot be written into law simply because a number of people—even a majority of people—believe them to be so.

This application of the First Amendment is central to the discussion of consensual crimes. In listening to the reasons why laws against consensual activities are enacted, or why laws against consensual activities should not be eliminated, one begins to peel away the layers of an onion, and at the core of that onion is almost invariably a religious belief. The progression usually goes something like this:

"It's not right."

"Why is it not right?"

"Because it's not moral."

"Why is it not moral?"

"Because God says so."

And this is usually followed by some reference—sometimes specific, but usually vague—to the Bible,* a sermon, a televangelist, or a story remembered from Sunday School (or was it Cecil B. de Mille?).

Knowing about that pesky separation of church and state rule (honored as much in the breach, it seems, as the observance), some politicians and commentators do the best they can to cloud the fact that criminalizing consensual activities is a religious issue. "The people of this country don't want this. The people of this country think it's wrong." Nine times out of ten, the people believe what they believe based on what they heard in church, through televangelism, or by simply accepting the opinion of other highly convinced people who got their opinions through church or televangelism.

---

*The Bible has been used so often, by so many people to support laws against consensual activities, that we will explore it in detail in Part IV, "Consensual Crimes and the Bible."

If all the religious-based laws against consensual activities were removed from the books, most of the books would be much thinner.

If, however, the first half of the First Amendment's religious guarantees were not there, the second half would be enough to *actively permit* all consensual activities:

. . . or prohibiting the free exercise thereof . . .

"Thereof" refers, of course, to religion. Congress, then, can make no law prohibiting the free exercise of religion. There go the laws against consensual activities.

All one must do is claim that the practice of a consensual crime is a "sacrament" in one's "church" and *any* of the consensual crimes can then be practiced under the protection of the law. There, of course, must be *some* restrictions—not harming the person or property of another immediately springs to mind.

When it comes to civil rights, however, saying, "It's my religion; therefore I'm protected by the First Amendment," is not a sufficient argument. It's an *accurate* argument, and even a *workable* argument, but it potentially adds a layer of pretense and hypocrisy to an individual's life, freedom, *and* religion. One should be able to participate in consensual activities without having to explain: "I do this because it's part of my religion." One should only have to say, "I'm entitled to do this because it does not physically harm the person or property of another."

There should be no need for prostitutes (the Rahabites) to hearken back to Rahab, the prostitute whom God saved when Jericho fell; for gays (the Beloveds) to use scripture to prove that Jesus and his disciples were all lovers; for drug users (the Learyans) to say they're using chemicals for mystical and religious experiences, the wine at the last supper and the changing of water to wine at the wedding feast at Cana being just two scriptural examples of consciousness-altering spiritual activities; for gamblers (the Holy Rollers or Vegasites) to point out that the apostles cast lots to choose a replacement for Judas; for pornographers (the Lovelacians) to claim that God created Adam and Eve without clothing, and that we each came into this world without clothing, therefore, lack of clothing is what God wants; and on and on.

We should be entitled to do what we do, providing we don't physically harm the person or property of another, simply because we want to do it.

What we have today is a contemporary Inquisition in which 4,000,000 people are arrested each year and 350,000 people are currently in prison for "crimes" that offend the spiritual sensibility of highly vocal "religious" people. This situation directly violates the separation of church and state and the religious freedoms guaranteed by the United States Constitution.

The people who want to maintain laws based upon their religious beliefs are taking their constitutionally guaranteed right of religious freedom too far—they are physically harming the persons and property of others and using the peace officers of this country to enforce their excessive exercise of a sacred constitutional right.

Being an Episcopalian interferes neither with my business nor my religion.

JOHN KENDRICK BANGS
1862

Laws against Consensual Activities
Are Opposed to the Principles of
Private Property, Free Enterprise, Capitalism,
and the Open Market

> *Don't get the idea that*
> *I'm one of these*
> *goddamn radicals.*
> *Don't get the idea that I'm*
> *knocking the American system.*
>
> AL CAPONE

THERE ARE FEW certainties in American history, even recent American history—Did FDR know about Pearl Harbor in advance? Who killed JFK? What brand of hair dye did Reagan use?

What we firmly believe is true, later turns out to be false. In the war against Iraq, we prided ourselves on the precision of the missiles and the "pinpoint" bombing. Later, we found out that more than half the missiles and bombs did not hit their targets.

Things change, or, as Arthur Miller so eloquently put it, time bends.

There is one fact of American history, however, that no one doubts: Our founding fathers believed deeply in the principle of private property. As Adam Smith (the original) wrote in his *Wealth of Nations,* published in 1776,

> Every man, as long as he does not violate the laws of justice, is left perfectly free to pursue his own interest his own way, and to bring both his industry and capital into competition with those of any other man or order of men.

Among other qualities, the founding fathers were, in a word, *rich.*

One of the signers of the Declaration of Independence, Robert Morris, was rich enough to *become* the treasury during the revolutionary war: his personal credit line saved the United States from bankruptcy. Benjamin Franklin made a fortune from his inventions and publications. Thomas Jefferson was born well-off and, upon his marriage, assumed control of his wife's considerable land and fortune, making him (them?) truly wealthy. And, at the time of the Constitutional Convention, George Washington was, quite simply, the richest man in America.

It wasn't that poor people were *excluded* from the Continental Congress,

> *The United States is*
> *a great country and rich in itself—*
> *capable and promising to be*
> *as prosperous and as happy as any.*
>
> GEORGE WASHINGTON

where the Declaration of Independence was drafted, or from the Constitutional Convention, where the Articles of Confederation became the United States Constitution; it was just that who *but* an independently wealthy person could volunteer to go to Philadelphia, unpaid, at the height of the growing season, for an indefinite period of time?

Not that they all came for purely selfless, patriotic reasons; each had his own agenda, often financial. The complaints against the British crown that caused the Revolution were mostly monetary: taxes on tea, import duties, interference of trade, and the like. The British soldiers were not raping the women, selling the men into slavery, or randomly plundering the countryside. No. The colonists were *furious* when a law was passed saying that, if no other accommodations were available, British soldiers were allowed to be temporarily quartered in the colonists' *barns*. (It upset the livestock.) In the history of occupation and imperial domination, the North American colonies received benign, almost deferential treatment from the British Crown.

America, for the British, was an economic enterprise. It was a market for British goods; a supplier of its needs; and a good place to send its religious fanatics, political dissidents, and criminals. (As we discussed, to be "transported for life" to the colonies was a common punishment.) This kept England both thriving and tidy. England liked the fact that the British Americas were flourishing and only wanted to "wet its beak" a little.

It wanted its beak a little too wet, according to the founding fathers. Even though the taxes England levied on the English were fifty times greater than the taxes it levied on the colonists, the colonists protested. It was an economic hardship up with which they would not put.* The taxes were not so much levied against the consumers as against the merchants—the importers and the exporters of goods. The taxes cut into their profits and they didn't like it.

But it was more than just the taxes; it was the way in which England was meddling with the commerce of the country in general.** Any sort of change required endless dealings with the bureaucracy that was England, and the American

---

*Someone once wrote Sir Winston Churchill, complaining that he had ended a sentence with a preposition. He wrote back agreeing that such unforgivable grammatical errors were among the things up with which he would not put.

**For example, the Proclamation of 1763 ordered that all Anglo-Americans remain east of the Allegheny Mountains and that any dealing with the Native Americans, for either lands or goods, must take place through London-appointed commissioners. The Native Americans no more respected the authority of these commissioners than did the colonists. But the commissioners were, by law, in the middle of every trade, treaty, or barter between the Native and the Anglo-Americans.

entrepreneurs were tired of it. The freedom they wanted was freedom to develop the country's resources without the meddling, red tape, and second-guessing of British bureaucrats.

And so the colonists had a revolution, and, by making economic alliances with France and Spain, the second and third greatest military powers of the day, the colonists won.

By 1786 the United States was in an economic mess. Its primary trading partner, Britain, wanted nothing to do with the rebellious upstarts; France and Spain were helping themselves to the portions of North America they wanted; and the war had plunged the country $60 million into debt—an amount, relatively speaking, larger and more burdensome than our current $4 trillion deficit.

The gathering in Philadelphia in the summer of 1787 was more an economic conference than a political one, although the two, then as now, were intimately connected. Politically, various founding fathers wanted everything from a monarchy to a strong federal government, from no state governments to powerful state governments. Economically, no one even *thought* of proposing a system other than individual ownership of private property. The only questions were (a) how do I most effectively trade my private property with others? and (b) how do I get more of it? Harking back to John Locke, "Government has no other end than the preservation of property."

What the founding fathers wanted—and what they empowered Congress to do in the Constitution—was to provide a safe place for commerce to thrive and trading to prosper. *Every one* of the seventeen enumerated powers given to Congress by the Constitution provided for a safe and fertile soil in which to do business: secure borders by developing and regulating armed forces (six of the powers relate to this), borrow money, regulate commerce, control immigration and establish uniform laws for bankruptcy, establish a common legal tender and coin money, punish counterfeiters, establish post offices, build post (toll) roads, issue patents and copyrights, settle disputes, and keep the sea lanes free of pirates. Powers #1 and #17—to collect taxes and to govern the nation's capital—gave the federal government the means to carry out powers #2–16. In addition, the Constitution prohibited the individual states from doing most of these things so that the United States would have one single, strong, central, economic environment.

All of the individual rights in the Constitution and the Bill of Rights were added not just because they were the "sacred rights of man" and made for good government; they also made for good *business*. To have the government involved in regulating religion, morality, and personal behavior was not only costly; it would distract the government from its primary task: keeping the world safe for commerce.

> *Next to the right of liberty, the right of property is the most important individual right guaranteed by the Constitution and the one which, united with that of personal liberty, has contributed more to the growth of civilization than any other institution established by the human race.*
>
> PRESIDENT WILLIAM H. TAFT

⚖ ⚖ ⚖

The essence of private property is that what's yours is yours; and it remains yours until you give it, trade it, or sell it. While it is yours, the government will protect—by force if necessary—your right to keep and use ("enjoy") it. Once you give it, trade it, or sell it to another, however, you have lost all title to it, and the government will now protect whomever you gave, traded, or sold it to.

What you do with property while it is yours is entirely your business. If you abuse it, misuse it, or even destroy it, the government cannot step in and stop you. If you have a table and put it under a leak in the roof, the government cannot step in and insist that you either move the table or fix the roof. It's your table, your roof, your leak, and your life.*

The limit of doing what you want with your property, of course, is when you begin to interfere with the property of others. Just because you own a hammer, it doesn't mean that you get to hit anything you want with it—just the things you own or have the owner's consent to hit.

You have the freedom to give, trade, or sell your private property. You can either make or lose money on a transaction and it's not the government's business, except where taxation comes in. As long as the government gets its due, however, you can do what you want. The government will not prevent you from being a foolish businessperson and it will not reward you for being a fantastic one. As long as there is a free-will exchange without undue coercion or fraud, all interactions and exchanges of private property are the private concerns of the people involved.

This right of private property certainly extends to our bodies. Whether I choose to be fit or fat, have a Cover Girl complexion or put tattoos on every square inch of my body, shave my head or let my hair grow long, work for $1 a year with one organization or $100,000 a year with another, is simply not the government's business.

I'm not going to argue the pros and cons of private ownership, free enterprise, capitalism, and the free market system. That's another discussion. What is indisputably true is that *this is the economic system we have;* it is the economic system we

---

*This principle has been sorely contested at times. When the Japanese businessman who spent more than $100 million on two Van Goghs said he wanted to be buried with the paintings, it didn't cause much stir because it was naturally assumed that the family would, sooner or later, dig him up and reclaim the paintings. When it was discovered, however, that he wanted to be *cremated* with the paintings, it caused an international furor that made even the front page of the *Wall Street Journal.* The debate over the extent and absoluteness of private property was cut short by the businessman's announcement that he would not, after all, take the Van Goghs with him. Why? The controversy was beginning to hurt his business.

AIN'T NOBODY'S BUSINESS IF YOU DO

have had since the ratification of the Constitution in 1789. It is precisely the system that the anti-Communists have worked so hard for so long to keep firmly in place. They have succeeded. Firmly in place it is.

ふ ふ ふ

Our economic system is one of the best arguments against consensual crimes.

Laws against consensual activities are a restriction of trade. If I want to buy a farm, grow grapes, and make wine—as long as I meet all permit and licensing requirements—I am free to make such decisions as whom to hire to help me make the wine, how much to charge per bottle, or whether to use plastic corks or cork corks. If the enterprise is successful, I become an honored taxpayer, employer, wine maker, and citizen.

If, on the other hand, I choose to buy a farm and grow marijuana with the intent of selling it for profit, I would be a felon, a criminal, a drug lord, and a disgrace.

If a photograph I had taken pleased you, and in exchange for the hour I would have to spend in the darkroom to produce a print you were willing to pay money, you would be a patron of the arts; the person selling the photograph to you would be an agent; and I would be an artist.

If, however, you found my body attractive and wanted to pay money to spend an hour with it in a dark room,* you would be a john; the arranger of our meeting would be a pimp; I would be a whore; and, in all but seven counties of these United States, we would all be criminals.

If I announced that I was giving myself in marriage to a wonderful person, friends would send presents and distant relatives would send congratulations.

If I announced I was giving myself in marriage to a wonderful person who was already married, or was a man (or both), I would receive psychiatric gift certificates from friends, and a visit from the constable compliments of distant relatives.

Going through a list of consensual crimes, it's easy to see that our right to give, trade, or sell our person or property to another is severely hampered.

Of course, people *are* making money—and lots of it—from the false scarcity created by making consensual activities crimes. To coin a new bumper sticker: WHEN DOING BUSINESS IS A CRIME, ONLY CRIMINALS ARE IN BUSINESS. As we have seen, organized crime in this country is directly traceable to Prohibition. When Prohibition went away, organized crime did not—it switched products and kept selling. That's because the government kept prohibiting things people wanted to

> *Private property was the original source of freedom. It still is its main bulwark.*
>
> WALTER LIPPMANN

---

*With this example, we are skating on the far edge of hypothetical—nay, *apocryphal*.

buy.

When the government *pretends* that certain businesses are not going on (after all, they *are* against the law, so *of course* no one would take part in them), all the government regulations, inspections, and licensing that keep products uniform and safe are impossible. When we drink a beer or a glass of wine, we know the approximate alcohol content and can regulate our intake and activities accordingly. We know the alcohol content because it is established and regulated by law. When we take an illegal drug, we have no idea of its strength, and consequently are unable to regulate either our dosage or behavior.

Pope offers qualified praise of capitalism
CHICAGO TRIBUNE, May 3

Pope assails capitalist evils
CHICAGO SUN-TIMES, May 3

Free market gets Pope's blessing
WASHINGTON TIMES, May 3

Pope warns against godless capitalism
THE WASHINGTON POST, May 3

Healthcare workers—and even restaurant employees—have certain required procedures and practices to guarantee their own and their clients' health and safety. No such restrictions apply, for example, to prostitution—and the lack of same is killing people.

When business is open and aboveboard, both businesses and consumers can be protected against *real* crime such as fraud, violence, and theft. As it is now, when indulging in any of the consensual crimes, it's the law of the Old West— and sometimes the law of the jungle.

Another legitimate aspect of regulation—impossible as long as the government holds certain transactions illegal—is keeping minors from patronizing certain businesses. No liquor store in its right mind would knowingly sell to a minor. Do you think the same is true of drug dealers? The artificially high prices created by the criminalization of certain activities make opening new territories—such as schoolyards—profitable. One hears about drug dealers giving out samples of certain substances to school children. Have you ever heard of a liquor manufacturer, distributor, or retailer handing out samples of alcohol on the playground? ("Hey, kid! Over here. Just got a new shipment of Stoli. One hundred proof. Check it out.") If drugs were available at a fair market price (plus, of course, an exorbitant tax) and sold in licensed and regulated retail outlets, the "marketing" to minors would dramatically decrease. This is true for all consensual crimes in which minors are currently encouraged to take part.

Which brings us to another far-from-insignificant point: taxation. Yes, taxes; everyone's favorite five-letter four-letter word. All those billions and billions and *billions* of dollars that change hands annually through the businesses created by consensual crimes are completely untaxed. No income tax. No sales tax. No capital gains. *Nothing.* We'll explore the financial ramifications of that in the next chapter. In this chapter, however, I'll only note that having massive industries— the consensual crimes—completely untaxed puts the businesses that *are* taxed under an enormous burden. All the tax money that goes toward maintaining a healthy business environment, enjoyed by both licit and illicit businesses, is paid entirely by the "legal" business world.

The consensual crime business is also unfair to legitimate businesses in that the "honest" businessperson is competing against "crooks" for consumer dollars. Aboveground businesspersons must abide by certain rules, restrictions, and professional standards designed to create fairness in the marketplace. Illicit businesspeople have no such rules, regulations, or standards for professional con-

> *Don't I have the right*
> *to do what I want*
> *with my own money?*
>
> MATTHEW 20:15

duct. They can do whatever they get away with—which, obviously, is quite a lot.

The artificially inflated prices caused by criminalizing certain acts of commerce take a large amount of money out of the "legitimate" loop of business and place it in the underworld. Protection money, pay-offs, kick-backs, bribes, legal fees, and all the other expensive but necessary costs of doing business in the consensual crime trade consume huge amounts of money that might otherwise go to aboveground businesses.

Let's say an honest, hardworking citizen has $50 set aside each week under the general category of "recreation." Let's say that $40 of this goes for recreational chemicals that, were they not against the law, would cost, even with an exorbitant tax, $4. This extra $36 per week—72% of this person's total recreational budget—goes directly into the hands of criminals. With this $36, our citizen might have chosen to go out and do something else, thus spreading money into the general aboveground economy, rather than stay home and watch television. When reading about the billions and billions of dollars spent each year by consumers taking part in consensual crimes, please keep in mind that (a) those dollar amounts are outrageously inflated only because these activities have been deemed illegal, and (b) all that money is being taken directly from the general aboveground economy and put in an underground economy where it is neither regulated, controlled, nor taxed. (And a good deal of it ends up abroad.) Imagine what an incredible boost to the U.S. economy the reintroduction of these lost billions would be.

As Jeff Riggenbach wrote in *USA Today,*

> As long as no children are involved, these "crimes" are merely what Harvard philosopher Robert Nozick calls "capitalist acts between consenting adults." In a free society, capitalist acts between consenting adults are not illegal, regardless of how many bluenoses might disapprove of them.

ᛞ ᛞ ᛞ

Setting aside all thoughts of commerce, business, and exchange, however, there still is the question of personal property. Are we allowed to own whatever we want, providing it does not physically harm the person or property of another? The Con-

> *Freedom
> and the power to choose
> should not be the privilege of
> wealth.
> They are the birthright
> of every American.*
>
> PRESIDENT GEORGE BUSH

stitution both implies and clearly states, yes. So, what are all these laws about *possession?* If you are caught possessing (not using, not selling) a certain amount of drugs, you could spend the rest of your life in prison, or—if one of the truly insane War-on-Drug laws is enacted—you could be *put to death.* This is the extreme, but lesser penalties apply for possessing the products or paraphernalia associated with certain consensual crimes.

How the mere *possession* of something— be it drugs, medical equipment, or gambling paraphernalia—harms *anyone, anywhere, any time,* including the person possessing it, is completely beyond me. Even in cases of treason—the crime which the government should be most concerned about from the standpoint of self-preservation— mere *thoughts* about treason or even *discussions* about treason are not enough. The Constitution says one must commit an "overt Act" of treason to be convicted of this crime. Surely, then, an *act* must be necessary before arresting and jailing people for consensual crimes as well. It's not. Criminalizing possession is an example of how far from the Constitution—and all logic and reason—the matter of consensual crimes has gone. You can be arrested for possessing something that, even if you used it, would not physically harm the person or property of a nonconsenting other.

⚖ ⚖ ⚖

The Nobel Prize–winning economist Milton Friedman is the ultimate guru of the free-market system. As Professor Friedman wrote in his 1962 book *Capitalism and Freedom,*

> Freedom in economic arrangements is itself a component of freedom broadly understood, so economic freedom is an end in itself. . . . Economic freedom is also an indispensable means toward the achievement of political freedom.

In 1986, as rhetoric was fanning the fires of the War on Drugs into an inferno, Professor Friedman (then one of Reagan's economic advisors) calmly stated his views:

> I'm in favor of legalizing drugs. According to my value system, if people want to kill themselves, they have every right to do so. Most of the harm that comes from drugs is because they are illegal.

If only Reagan had had his hearing aid turned up.

⚖️ ⚖️ ⚖️

A PRIMER OF AMERICAN SELF-GOVERNMENT

1. Understand, honor and preserve the Constitution of the United States.

2. Keep forever separate and distinct the legislative,
executive and judicial functions of government.

3. Remember that government belongs to the people,
is inherently inefficient,
and that its activities should be limited
to those which government alone can perform.

4. Be vigilant for freedom of speech,
freedom of worship, and freedom of action.

5. Cherish the system of Free Enterprise
which made America great.

6. Respect thrift and economy, and beware of debt.

7. Above all, let us be scrupulous
in keeping our word and in
respecting the rights of others.

PHILIP D. REED

Enforcing Laws against Consensual Activities
Is *Very* Expensive

> *We don't seem to be able
> to check crime,
> so why not legalize it
> and then
> tax it out of business?*
>
> WILL ROGERS

THIS IS A CHAPTER about *money*—what it costs us to enforce laws against consensual activities in good old Yankee dollars. We will not be exploring the cost in human suffering, the cost to our civil rights, the cost of our religious freedom, the cost to our moral character, or the cost to our human resources. This is a chapter about dollars and lack of sense.

We will explore not only what we *spend* each year enforcing laws against consensual activities, but also what we might *gain* if we brought the underground economy of consensual activities aboveground.*

Let's start with what we spend on consensual crimes, and let's start with the easy figures. Because there's a war going on, we get wartime reporting (that is, *lots* of reporting) on drugs. Tens of millions of dollars are spent each year, gathering, compiling, analyzing, and publishing drug statistics. The Department of Justice even has a toll-free number (1-800-666-3332); at taxpayers' expense, you can have all your questions answered about drug busts, drug laws, and the War on Drugs' battle plan. What we are spending on the consensual crime of drug use is easy to discover—sort of.

The obvious figures are: each year we spend $13 billion** at the federal level and $16 billion at the state and local levels to catch and incarcerate (and, to a far

---

*Except where noted, all the statistics in this chapter come from one branch or another of the United States government—the Bureau of Justice Statistics; Drug Enforcement Administration; Bureau of Census; Bureau of Customs; Coast Guard; Bureau of Alcohol, Tobacco and Firearms; Border Patrol; Internal Revenue Service—or from "experts" who have testified before congressional subcommittees.

**Please remember that a million dollars is a stack of $100 bills three feet high; a billion dollars is a stack of $100 bills twice as high as the Empire State Building; and a trillion dollars is a stack of $100 bills 570 miles high.

> *In October 1990, the Nation's civil and criminal justice system employed 1.7 million persons, with a total October payroll of almost $4.3 billion.*
>
> U.S. DEPARTMENT OF JUSTICE

smaller degree, educate) drug possessors, users, manufacturers, and traffickers. That comes to $29 billion a year.*

Although this is a staggering sum of money, it is only the amount spent by the Justice Department, law enforcement, courts, and correctional institutions—the nail 'em and jail 'em people. What about the other governmental divisions? Here the figures get murkier. Government bureaucrats don't like taxpayers calling up and asking bothersome questions such as, "Where does the money go?" Even though they're all *proud* to be doing their part to end the evils of drug abuse, they don't want to set a precedent. "If we tell them how much we spend fighting drugs, the next thing they'll want to know is how much we spend on *lunches.*" That would be too much. Getting information, then, has not been easy. They either don't have it; don't know who has it; don't know where I can get it; and why do you want it, anyway?

Some of our public servants just lied. This is especially true when we went beyond questions about the War on Drugs and asked, for example, about the War on Cults. During the Waco, Texas, incident, a spokesperson for the Bureau of Alcohol, Tobacco, and Firearms (ATF) told me it was spending "only" $500,000 per *week* in Waco, Texas, and that was all money that would be spent anyway: if all those ATF agents weren't in Texas, they'd be someplace else, and the $500,000 a week covered their salaries and basic expenses; however, during the House Judiciary Committee meetings on the incident, the figure "a million dollars a day" was bandied about freely. No one denied this amount, although the people from the ATF had little trouble denying everything else. The difference between $7 million a week and $500,000 a week is substantial. There were a lot of those differences. There are probably any number of differences I never discovered.

For example, how much of the $21 billion we spend each year on foreign aid, international financial programs, and diplomacy is used to "persuade" other countries to stop growing, manufacturing, and exporting nasty drugs to the United States? Hint: almost all foreign aid to countries that even *might* produce drugs is tied directly to those countries' pledges to eradicate the drug menace within their borders. Of the $21 billion, shall we conservatively say $3 billion?

---

*I hope you don't mind if I round off some of these numbers to the nearest billion. *(If only* I could make that statement when discussing my personal income tax with my accountant.) I also hope you don't mind that, in this chapter, I avoid such modifiers as *approximately, more than, almost, nearly,* and so on. So if I say, "State and local governments spent $16 billion in 1991 on drug enforcement," know that I've rounded it off. If I say, "State and local governments spent $15,888,665 on drug enforcement," you'll know that I'm being precise. Assume that if you don't see lots of digits, I've rounded them off.

AIN'T NOBODY'S BUSINESS IF YOU DO

How much of the $4 billion Coast Guard budget is spent on intercepting drug-running boats? The Coast Guard claims about one quarter of that. Shall we take their word for it? Okay. Here's another $1 billion.

And then we have that great Black Hole of money, information, and proportion: the Defense Department. How much do the Army, Navy, Air Force, and Marines spend keeping America drug free? We know they're going to spend $300 billion this year on *something*, but how much of it will be

> *The blame for [the national debt] lies with the Congress and the President, with Democrats and Republicans alike, most all of whom have been unwilling to make the hard choices or to explain to the American people that there is no such thing as a free lunch.*
>
> SENATOR WARREN RUDMAN

fighting the War on Drugs? The word *war*, of course, makes them salivate. Before it was the Department of Defense, it was the Department of War. How much military personnel, resources, and equipment will it spend locating and eradicating poppy, cocaine, and marijuana fields worldwide?

A clue comes from the 1993 Department of Justice publication *Drugs, Crime, and the Justice System:*

> The Posse Comitatus Act of 1876, which prohibited military involvement in law enforcement, was amended in 1982 to allow State and local law enforcement officials to draw on military assistance for training, intelligence gathering, and investigation of drug violations. The amendment provided for the use of military equipment by civilian agencies to enforce drug laws.

> In 1989, Congress enacted a law designating the Department of Defense as the lead agency for detecting and monitoring aerial and maritime transit of illegal drugs.

In Thailand, for example, the U.S. military supplies the Thai government with planes, reconnaissance equipment (for the airplanes), computers (to analyze the reconnaissance), and training (how to operate the computers that analyze the reconnaissance gathered from the equipment flown in the airplanes). What are they looking for? Poppy fields, the source of opium, the source of heroin.* This scenario is repeated in country after country.

In the United States, military helicopters are engaged in low-flying surveillance looking for the "killer weed growing in backyards," so that ground-based law enforcement personnel can kill it. (And arrest the owner, and confiscate the

---

*Remember in *The Wizard of Oz* when the witch wanted to keep Dorothy, Scarecrow, Tinman, and Lion from reaching the Emerald City? She placed a field of poppies between them and the city gates. "Poppies, poppies," she murmured as she caressed her crystal ball, "poppies will put them to sleep." And what does Glinda, the good witch, send to wake them up? Snow—a popular slang term for amphetamines—particularly cocaine. The screenwriters, *of course*, had *no* knowledge of drugs, and these two occurrences are *absolutely coincidental*. (And "Lucy in the Sky with Diamonds" had nothing to do with LSD.)

> *State prison construction budgets are up 73% since fiscal year 1987. 44 states are building new prisons or expanding existing ones.*
>
> CORRECTIONS COMPENDIUM
> 1992

owner's property, and practice the now-standard scorched-earth policy.)

And then there's the military's War on Drugs *within* the military. If they spent half a billion dollars from 1980 to 1990 ferreting out homosexuals in the military (and we can add *that* $500,000,000 to the cost of consensual crime enforcement), imagine how much they spend eradicating the far more prevalent consensual activity of drug use. (The Defense Department's budget for military police, courts, and jails is separate from the Bureau of Justice's expenditures.)

So what portion of this $300 billion does the Defense Department spend fighting the War on Drugs? Let's say a *very* conservative $7 billion.

The War on Drugs alone, then, is costing $40 billion per year. What about the rest of the consensual crimes? Here the statistics are not so readily available.

In some cases, information is *simply not available.* In the arrest statistics for consensual crimes, for example, only drug abuse, gambling, prostitution, drunkenness, disorderly conduct, and vagrancy are separated out. Homosexuality, adultery, bigamy, and polygamy are put into a category called "sex offenses" which includes arrests for any number of nonconsensual sexual activities. Further, consensual crimes are often hidden in other categories. For example, when two people agree to perform a consensual activity, they are sometimes charged with "conspiracy to commit a felony." By charging people with conspiracy, the police don't have to prove the people actually *did* something, only that they *conspired* to do it. The word *conspiracy* has some fairly evil connotations. It simply means, however, agreeing to do something. So, if you simply *agree* with another person to engage in an act* of drug use, prostitution, sodomy, adultery, gambling, or anything else illegal, you can be arrested for conspiracy. You can also be arrested for conspiring to blow up a building, murder someone, or kidnap a four-year-old. It all goes under the general category of "conspiracy to commit a felony." There are other terms that hide consensual crimes. *Pandering* and *racketeering* are two favorites.

Then there's the category called "All Other Offenses." Dumped into this category are 3,240,000 arrests—22% of the total arrests in 1991. What's in *that* category? Nobody knows. It's a catch-all where violations of all local, state, and federal ordinances that don't fit into clear-cut categories are put. How many of those are consensual crimes is anybody's guess.

⚖ ⚖ ⚖

---

*Police love saying, "engage in the act."

AIN'T NOBODY'S BUSINESS IF YOU DO

So, of the arrests for consensual crimes we can separate out, here is our list for 1991:

Prostitution..............................98,900
Drug abuse violations............1,010,000
Gambling................................16,600
Drunkenness...........................881,100
Disorderly conduct...................757,700
Vagrancy.................................38,500

That's 2,802,800 arrests. We know it costs the federal and state governments $29 billion for the 1,010,000 drug arrests, so we can deduct those from the total. That leaves 1,792,800 arrests. If we know the government spent $29 billion prosecuting 1,010,000 drug offenders, we can conservatively estimate that it spent at least another $10 billion prosecuting the other 1,792,800 known consensual crime arrests, plus the probably several million more hidden in categories that also contain nonconsensual crimes.

Adding the $3 billion of foreign aid and the $8.5 billion spent by the Coast Guard and the military on consensual crimes, it's fair to say that we spend $50 billion a year prosecuting consensual crimes. In fact, it's something of an understatement.

There are innumerable financial costs I'm not including in that $50 billion. Each year, for example, $10 billion in personal property is stolen and never recovered. As we shall see in the chapter, "Consensual Crimes Encourage *Real* Crime," most of these thefts are committed by addicts to pay for the artificially inflated price of their drugs. Many of these thefts involve violence. According to the American Association for Public Health, violence in this country "costs nearly $500 billion in medical care and lost productivity." Why do we have a War on Drugs? Why don't we declare a War on *Violence*?

⚖ ⚖ ⚖

"There are two kinds of statistics," wrote Rex Stout, "the kind you look up and the kind you make up." When we want to explore how much money the American economy loses each year by keeping the traffic of consensual crimes underground, you can make up as many statistics as I—or any "expert"—can invent. Surveys asking people to admit to criminal activity are notoriously inaccurate, and "statistics" given about some future event aren't statistics at all, but projections, guesstimates, crystal-ball gazing, and blue-skying. Whether you see "Blue Skies" or "Stormy Weather," it's still a weather forecast and, as Gordy, the weatherman on "The Mary Tyler Moore Show," defensively asked, "What do you think I can do? Predict the future?"

Determining how much money is lost to the U.S. economy due to laws against consensual activities requires knowing two things: (a) How big is the underground of consensual crimes, and (b) How much bigger or smaller would this economy become if it were legalized?

Determining the size of the underground economy depends on law enforcement estimates and surveys. This is a problem. Law enforcement estimates go up and down depending on what law enforcement wants the estimates to show. When law enforcement wants more money, it gives estimates of crime so severe it would seem that, for the protection of all citizens, leaving one's house should be illegal. On the other hand, when law enforcement wants to show what a stellar job it is doing, the crime wave of April becomes the sunny beach of May.

The other way to determine the level of consensual crime activity is through surveys conducted either over the phone, in writing, or in person. However, even when surveys are conducted "anonymously," the person being surveyed hardly feels anonymous. An organization, after all, had to call or write you. It has your phone number or address. When you go in person to take part in an "anonymous" survey, you can hardly walk into the interview wearing a ski mask. (As these surveys sometimes take place in federal buildings, you had better *not* walk in wearing a ski mask—unless it's in Minneapolis in the dead of winter; then *not* wearing a ski mask would look strange.) Whether taking the survey by phone, by mail, or in person, the participant has every reason to believe that his or her identity is not entirely secret. Therefore, when one's responses could have criminal consequences, one tends to revert to self-protection and, quite simply, lie. Studies that asked for recent drug usage, for example, backed up by urine samples, revealed that only about half the people who had taken drugs (as revealed in the urine samples) admitted in the survey to having taken them.

What does this mean? It means we don't know how big the underground economy in consensual crime is. Looking at the number of studies I've seen, one begins to get an idea of at least a *range* of underground commerce. I cannot, however, in good conscience say, "Because of this statistic, this study, this report, and this expert's opinion, we know the underground economy is . . ." and then give a reliable figure. How can one make a prediction without accurate data? And how can we predict the future when we still disagree about the past?

For example, although most historians agree that alcohol consumption increased during Prohibition, there is a school of thought that says alcohol consumption *decreased* during Prohibition, and took quite some time after Prohibition to build up to pre-Prohibition levels. Therefore, to people who believe this claim, Prohibition was a success. This reconstruction of history seems to have been circulated by William Bennett while he was drug czar, as justification for (a) the drug war and (b) his czarship.* Others who find it too inconvenient, uncomfortable, or time-consuming to re-evaluate their stance on drugs also bandy about the Prohibition-as-a-success argument.

This view of history relies on official government statistics on the consumption of alcohol before, during, and after Prohibition. These figures, for the most part, did not track home brewing, bootlegging, al-

> *Stop wasting jail space on prostitutes, drug users and other victimless criminals. Even if we find it morally acceptable to imprison these people for choices they make regarding their bodies, we must realize that we simply cannot afford to continue clogging the court system and the prison system with these harmless "criminals."*
>
> EDWARD B. WAGNER

lowing grape juice to ferment into wine *("Bad, grape juice, bad!")*, using industrial alcohol for personal consumption, and "importing" alcohol from Canada, Mexico, and beyond the three-mile limit. About the only alcohol the government officially tracked during Prohibition was alcohol produced for medicinal purposes. While this was used for recreational purposes as well, it certainly did not reflect alcohol's complete recreational use. Prohibition ended as America was in the depths of Depression. Many people couldn't afford food, so it's not surprising they couldn't afford alcohol. The depression led directly to World War II, where sacrifices and shortages were commonplace, and a good deal of the drinking population (the young men) were shipped overseas where they did their drinking (or at least wanted to). Declaring that Prohibition "worked" is an example of using official—but drastically incomplete—figures to support a convenient point of view.**

So, guess along with me as we try to determine what the underground economy in consensual crimes might currently be, what it might become if it were allowed to rise aboveground, and how much we can tax it (without driving it back underground again).

We know more about the size of the underground of drugs than any other consensual crime. Experts testifying before congressional committees say that

---

*Now *there's* a TV show: "The Czarship Enterprise." Each week we look at the pressures and pleasures of the world's only czar: the Drug Czar of the United States. On this week's show, the Drug Czar gives a speech to the Washington Press Club, pointing out that it was the communists who overthrew the czar in Russia; therefore, the only people who oppose the czar in the United States must be communists too. Sponsored by Budweiser and Coca-Cola.

**It's interesting to note that none of the people who claim Prohibition was successful is calling for a return of Prohibition. If it was so successful, why not bring it back? The answer is obvious: it would cause a hue and cry in this country that has seldom been huen or cried. Prohibition didn't work then for the same reasons it wouldn't work now, and anyone who seriously threatens its return will hear a chorus of, "We're mad as hell, and we're not going to take it anymore," that would drown out even the "Anvil Chorus." (Or, if you're a listener to classic rock radio, would drown out the drum solo in "In-A-Gadda-Da-Vida." And, if you're not a listener to classic rock radio, you're younger or older than I.)

$1 trillion in drug money is laundered each year. It is estimated that 40%, or $400 billion, of this is laundered in the United States. The remaining $600 billion is laundered outside of the United States, but much of that $600 billion either could have originated in the United States, or could have been used by a middleman to purchase drugs bound for the United States. (The U.S. is the #1 drug market in the world.)

That's just the amount _laundered._ It doesn't have to be laundered until some of the big guys want to spend money in big ways on big things. Smaller amounts of "dirty" money pass between smaller players all the time. All these cash transactions don't fit into that $1 trillion figure of laundered money.

Another indication of the plenitude of drugs and the volume of sales is that each time one law enforcement agency or another announces a new record drug bust, in which tons and tons of some illicit substance worth billions of dollars were seized—usually with a comment such as, "At least this poison won't find its way into the schoolyards of America"—the street price for that particular drug does not alter _one cent._*

Another way to estimate the size of the underground drug market would be to look at the value per pound of drugs seized and multiply that by the amount of drugs most experts claim is never detected. We would still get an astronomical figure.

We can't pretend, however, that this would be the figure for drug sales if drugs were legal. The only thing that keeps drug prices high is that drugs are illegal. When legal, the marketplace will soon dictate the proper price. That people have been willing to pay outrageously inflated prices for drugs indicates they would also be willing to pay outrageously inflated taxes on drugs. Yes, some people will abuse drugs (as they already do), and drug abuse will have its costs to society (as it already does). Drugs, however, unlike cigarettes, will be able to pay their way— _and_ create a significant amount of government revenue.** What pot smoker, for example, would not pay $5.00 for a pack of ten neatly rolled joints, even if $2.50 of that went for taxes?

*Which makes one question the ruthlessness—or at least business sense—of drug dealers. They easily could raise their prices by, oh, 10%, explaining, "You read about that big bust in the paper, didn't you? Goods are scarce." The oil companies did it during the oil shortage in the 1970s. The price of gasoline went up during the shortage. It must have been one hell of a shortage, because the prices haven't come back down.

**For cigarettes to pay their way, they would have to be taxed at $2.17 per pack—the amount lost to cigarette-related disease and death. State and federal taxes combined—even in the highest taxing states—are less than $1.00 per pack. For each pack sold, then, society loses at least $1.17.

Currently, legalized gambling is a $300 billion industry. In terms of *illegal* gambling, the amount gambled on sports *alone* is estimated at more than $300 billion—$5 billion just on the Super Bowl. One can imagine the increase in aboveground gambling if there were casinos in all major cities, slot machines in bars, and video poker games at 7-Elevens. If gambling were legal, placing a bet on almost anything you wanted could be done over the phone, using your VISA or MasterCard. In New York, right now, you can make a phone call and bet on the horses using the charge card of your choice. (I don't think they take Bloomingdale's. Yet.)

> *I'll tell you, it's Big Business.*
> *If there is one word*
> *to describe Atlantic City,*
> *it's Big Business.*
> *Or two words—Big Business.*
>
> DONALD TRUMP

As gambling winnings traditionally go unreported, therefore not taxed, allow me to propose placing a tax on gambling winnings. When one wins, taxes are automatically collected. The amount of the bet would be deducted from the winnings first, so one would be taxed on pure winnings. For example, if you bet $5 and won $25, you would only be taxed on the $20. Honest people who win private wagers can remain in the good graces of their government by sending in a small donation from time to time.* If this tax is lower than the tax people must pay on profits they make on the stock market, it may, finally, bring the stock market around to admitting that it is, after all, an enormous gambling institution.

Prostitution. Hmmmm. That's an interesting one. No one seems to even *guess* at the number of prostitutes. The only state in the United States in which prostitution is even partially legal, Nevada,** is very closed-mouthed about how much money prostitution takes in. It has a Brothel Association, and the man who is the head of it will talk to you (nice fellow), but how much the bordellos take in and how much they pay in taxes is treated as some sort of state secret. (Which,

---

*Okay. It's late. I'm hallucinating. However, by law, if you live in New York City and purchase something outside New York City, but bring it into New York City for use there, you must pay the New York City sales tax. So, if you buy a VCR in New Jersey and bring it into New York City, you owe New York City that sales tax. There is a form to fill out which should accompany your check for this sales tax. Twenty-five of these forms were printed in 1953 when the law was passed. Twenty of these forms still remain. One form was used by a member of a religious group who believes avoiding tax is a sin. (One of those weird cults.) One form was used by someone who mistakenly thought you had to fill it out if you were marrying someone who lived in New Jersey. Another was taken by a collector who owns one of every form the government has printed since 1924. (His collection is stored in the airplane hangar that formerly housed the *Spruce Goose*.) One was used by a clerk in the forms department to write down a phone number when no other paper was readily available. And one form is unaccounted for because, after all, the forms have been in the hands of a bureaucracy for forty years.

**Prostitution is legal in the unincorporated areas of seven counties in Nevada, plus seven towns in those counties.

> *What it comes down to is this:*
> *the grocer, the butcher, the baker,*
> *the merchant, the landlord,*
> *the druggist, the liquor dealer,*
> *the policeman, the doctor,*
> *the city father and the politician—*
> *these are the people who make*
> *money out of prostitution.*
>
> POLLY ADLER
> *A House is Not a Home*

apparently, it is.) To determine the national prostitution economy, we could take the number of arrests and multiply it by the number of clients the average prostitute sees between arrests, and multiply that figure by the average amount the average client contributes (financially, that is) and that would give us a figure. The problem is, most prostitutes I've talked with don't get arrested even *once* in a given year—most haven't been arrested at all. The number of clients between arrests, then, would be difficult to determine.

So what I thought I'd do is compare prostitution to an already aboveground industry that is most similar to prostitution. Instantly, of course, I thought of the legal profession. And instantly, of course, I thought of adding, "No, that's not fair to prostitutes." But then I thought both the comparison and the joke were far too obvious for a subtle book aimed at social change such as this. (I'll save them for another book.) We need an industry that projects a friendly image, satisfies a real need at a fair price, is conveniently located, and is designed for rapid turnover. The obvious answer: fast food.* McDonalds alone pulls in $21 billion a year; Burger King, $6.4 billion. Even the slogans fit: "We do it all for you" and "Have it your way." Then there's Wendy's (sounds like a bordello, doesn't it?) and Jack-in-the-Box. (I'm not saying a *word*. I'm not even going to *mention* In-N-Out Burger.) Some innovative bordellos might, like the burger chains, offer drive-through service: pick what you want from a large illustrated menu, pay at window #1, pick up your order at window #2.

Of course, not everyone wants fast food. So, there are dining places from Denny's to Lutece that could be the inspiration for more substantial bordellos. There could even be a theme park, Bordelloland. (Disney's theme parks rake in $3.3 billion per year.) Also known as the Magic Fingers Kingdom, it could feature such attractions as Wenches of the Caribbean, The Haunted Whore House, the Gay Nineties Dance Hall, Chip and Dale's Chippendale Review, and the Mayflower Madam River Cruise. (I bet you thought this was gonna be some boring chapter full of numbers and statistics. I was going to do a whole thing here on Mickey and his dog Pimpo and Minnie Madam, but I think we've had enough silly puns for this chapter. Let's get on with it.**)

Unlike drug prices, prostitution rates will probably not lower significantly

---

*I certainly hope the prostitutes of America don't mind being compared with an industry that raises environmentally inefficient animals, kills them, grinds them up and serves them with a smile. If any do, I apologize.

**"Let's Get on with It" is a ride at Magic Mountains, Bordelloland's chief competitor.

with legalization. Illegality does not significantly increase the price of prostitution—just the risk to both prostitute and client. Also, if prostitution ever became acceptable, the amount spent on flowers, candy, and greeting cards would probably drop. The loss to these industries would have to be deducted from the increase to the aboveground economy caused by legalizing prostitution. Nevertheless, the economy, overall, would be ahead.

> *For seven and a half years*
> *I've worked alongside*
> *President Reagan.*
> *We've had triumphs.*
> *Made some mistakes.*
> *We've had some*
> *sex . . . uh . . . setbacks.*
>
> GEORGE BUSH

Drugs, gambling, and prostitution are the Big Three underground "moneymakers" in consensual crime. There would be, however, significant boosts to the economy if the stigma attached to the other consensual crimes were eliminated through legalization.

Removing the laws and, over time, the stigma of homosexuality would cause more and more gays to come out—come out and *spend their money.** Cities with large gay populations such as New York, San Francisco, and Los Angeles don't just have gay bars, but gay restaurants, gay bookstores, gay mini-malls, gay clothing stores (which carry clothing that looks very much like the clothing the GAP will be selling six months later), gay gyms, gay coffee shops, gay video stores, gay supermarkets, and just about every other gathering place you can name. West Hollywood, California, with a 30% gay population, has a gay hardware store and a gay Mrs. Field's Cookies. Not that gays don't buy their basics in Idaho, but, with the potential of seeing old friends and meeting new friends, they might be coaxed out more often and into buying a few nonessentials.

If bigamy and polygamy took off, look at the boon to the wedding industry! Already a $32 billion industry, imagine how much more it would rake in if it didn't have to wait for people to get divorced before they got married again. And again. And again.

If we legalize—even encourage—transvestism, some people would be buying an entire second wardrobe. What a shot in the arm for the clothing industry. And *shoes.* Let's not forget *shoes.* Somewhere out there in America are any number of men, who, deep in their heart, want to be Imelda Marcos. And who knows how many women have Donald Trump's taste in suits? (His suits may not *look* very good, but they're *very* expensive.)

And so on down the list of consensual crimes.

⚖ ⚖ ⚖

Another great advantage of moving an underground economy aboveground is that for every $50,000 you move aboveground, you create a new aboveground

---

*This is a *mercenary* chapter.

job (or move someone who is currently working in a non–tax-paying underground job into a tax-paying aboveground job). Removing the laws against consensual activities would create at least 6,000,000 new jobs (or turn 6,000,000 underground employees into tax-paying citizens).

෪ ෪ ෪

In all (with high taxes on drugs, the spur to the economy, the 6,000,000 more taxpayers, and all the other factors discussed), my "expert" conclusion is that legalizing consensual crimes would add $150 billion in tax revenue to the government treasury. When we eliminate the $50 billion we are currently spending to enforce the laws against consensual activities, we're looking at $200 billion per year in increased revenue.

That amount could be used in any of the following ways:

- Pay off the national debt in twenty years.

- Reduce personal income taxes by one-third.

- Allow the Pentagon to purchase 23 wrenches, 16 office chairs, and 243 paper clips.

- Send every man, woman, and child in the United States a check for $800 each year.

- Pay for *three rounds of congressional pay raises.*

- Pay everyone's doctor and dentist bills.

- Send a check for $87,000 to every high school graduate for furthering his or her education or for starting real life.

- Pay for the gasoline and repair of every car in the United States.

- Quadruple the amount of money spent on education.

- Pay all utility and phone bills in the United States.

- Send every person over 85 years old a check for $66,000 with a note saying, "Hey, congratulations!"

Rather than spinning our wheels asking what we can do to stop consensual crimes, why not direct all that creative energy toward how we can best spend that $200 billion?

Enforcing Laws against Consensual Activities Destroys People's Lives

WHAT THE ENFORCEMENT of laws against consensual activities does to individuals is nothing short of criminal. The government is destroying the very lives of the people it is supposedly helping and saving.

A single arrest, even without a conviction, is, in many cases, enough to ruin a life; a conviction and a year in jail are almost guaranteed to. All this, of course, is "for their own good." As the Horace of Spain (1559–1619) wrote, "No pain equals that of an injury inflicted under the pretense of a just punishment."

Let's take a look at the process of arrest, trial, conviction, and jail. Please don't think of this as something happening to some "criminal" who "deserves it." Think of it as something happening to you or one of your friends or relatives. If you have *ever* taken part in *any* consensual crime, it was luck alone that kept at least some of these things from happening to you.

As the song goes: there, but for fortune, go you or I.

The scenario given in this chapter may or may not apply to a first offense for a consensual crime. You may get a suspended sentence, or probation. The second offense becomes more serious, and with a third offense you're almost certainly looking at jail time. The offenses, of course, do not have to be in the same category of consensual crimes for their collective harm to accumulate.

When you are arrested, you are thrown into a world of violent criminals handled by individuals (a.k.a. the police) who are well-trained in treating people like violent criminals. Don't expect that you will be treated any differently. (A friend of our family used to regale us with both horror and laughter at the treatment he received during an arrest. After recounting an indignity or personal violation, he would lift his hands to heaven and say, "Who was I supposed to call?

> The right
> to be let alone
> is indeed
> the beginning of
> all freedom.
>
> JUSTICE WILLIAM O. DOUGLAS

The police? They were already there!")

Prior to—or simultaneously with—the arrest, comes the search.

You can be home one evening watching TV or sitting home one Saturday afternoon reading a book, when a knock comes at the door. "Who's there?" you ask, having seen some nicely uniformed police officer in a documentary on crime prevention recommend that you never open your door without knowing who is on the other side.

"Open the door. It's the police. We have a warrant* to search your premises." This is likely to be the only warning you get before your door is broken down, because the police automatically assume that you are (a) guilty and (b) hurriedly destroying the evidence: flushing drugs, pornography, and prostitutes down the toilet. The door, is opened (by you or by them) and, without a moment's hesitation, three or four or five or ten uniformed and/or ununiformed police begin going through everything you own.

Here, the first truly frightening question may cross your mind: how do you know whether or not these are really police? Answer: you don't. Even if they flash a badge, everyone knows that fake badges are readily available. If you have the presence of mind to ask to use the telephone to call the station house to confirm that this is an authorized search, the request will almost certainly be denied; the police assume you are a criminal with lots of underworld connections and have no desire for you to call your "friends" for help. Also, during a search, they don't want any unnecessary witnesses around, and they *certainly* don't want any busybody lawyers challenging some aspect of the search while it's actually going on.

So there you are, surrounded by a group of armed authority figures who are going through everything you own, putting "suspicious" articles into boxes or plastic bags, and you can only *hope* it's really the police and not some enterprising band of criminals. (On the other hand, maybe one should hope it is *only* a band of criminals—stuff can be replaced; time in prison cannot.)

---

*The Constitution guarantees that there will be no "unreasonable searches and seizures" and that a warrant must be issued by a judge only "upon probable cause." Unfortunately, the word "probable" has degenerated into "possible," also known as "Let's have a look." In the overheated passion of war, such as the War on Drugs, constitutional guarantees are somehow less important than "winning the battle." So, sometimes search warrants are issued on anonymous tips, or on the word of a police officer who received an anonymous tip. Sometimes police officers ask for and judges issue warrants that they know, if the case were taken to a high enough court, would be thrown out on constitutional grounds ("unconstitutional search and seizure"). The warrant is issued anyway because, chances are, some contraband will be found and the person will plea bargain by confessing guilt to a lesser crime. "Justice" will be served and the Constitution, once again, will be dishonored. Even without an arrest or conviction, the trauma of a search itself is sometimes used by law enforcement agencies as a "warning."

At about this point, you are "Mirandized." Amidst the hub-bub of your fish tank being drained (who knows what you're hiding under the sand), your toilet being dismantled (lots of room for contraband behind, in, or "down there"), and every container in your kitchen being emptied onto the counter ("This oregano smells a lot like marijuana"), being read your constitutional rights sounds something like this: *"Mumble mumble* you have the right to remain silent *mumble mumble* right to an attorney *mumble mumble* can

> *Once the law starts asking questions, there's no stopping them.*
>
> WILLIAM S. BURROUGHS

and will be used against you *mumble mumble* do you understand?" And then, amidst this atmosphere of physical, emotional, and psychological terror, the questioning begins. By this time, often, you will be handcuffed.

You are asked about people, incidents, and things going back as far as seven years (the statute of limitation on most felonies). You are asked to remember where you were, who you were with and what you were doing at a particular time, on a particular date. If you're like most people, you don't remember what you had for dinner two weeks ago, much less what you did two years ago, but "not remembering" is treated as a clear indication of "withholding evidence," "interfering with justice," and being "uncooperative." If you happen to remember something, anything, these comments will be carefully recorded, and, if you happen to remember something different later, it will be taken as a sign that "you truly don't have an accurate memory of the situation," that you "lied to the police," and, therefore, must be guilty (as we knew all along).

Once they're armed with a search warrant, anything the police recover of an "illegal nature" or even a "suspicious nature" is fair game. They can dismantle and destroy anything that might hold any illegal substance—and, considering how compact certain drugs are, this means that they can dismantle and destroy anything. They can take with them any "suspicious substances" for laboratory testing. This could include all vitamins and the entire contents of your medicine cabinet, kitchen pantry, and garage. Anything that might be used to "document" your criminal activity can be confiscated. This means all files, correspondence, notes, diaries, address books, phone bills and other telephone records, video tapes, audio tapes, and even your computer. If you do business from your home, a police search can put you out of business immediately. Getting back your possessions can take weeks, months, and, in some cases, years. You may find yourself trying to reconstruct your personal and business records from scratch at a time when you need them most—while gathering evidence for your defense. Meanwhile, the police could well be calling all the people in your phone book or professional database, asking if they know you and, when they respond yes, asking them such questions as, "Do you know anything about this person's involvement with drugs (prostitution, homosexuality, gambling, etc.)?" (This humiliation could become a national event if the film crew from "COPS!" or one of the other voyeuristic TV shows accompanies the police.)

Anything that might indicate what "kind of person" you are can also be seized, even if it's not directly related to any crime. This includes books on certain subjects, the magazines to which you subscribe, the newspapers you read, even what station your radio was tuned to (which means, of course, confiscating your radio)—anything that might make you look unusual, peculiar, unconventional, or make a jury of twelve "normal" people think you're pretty weird overall and probably deserve to go to jail for either the crime you are being charged with or the many crimes you've gotten away with.

You may not be arrested yet, but you could be taken to the police station for "questioning" or upon "suspicion." Your property that hasn't either been destroyed by the police or taken with them ("seized") is pretty much up for grabs. If the police broke down your door, they don't exactly call a carpenter and locksmith to make sure that everything is secure before they head off for their next round of searching and seizing. They may put some tape across the outside of your door, saying "POLICE LINES. DO NOT CROSS," which, to any burglar, means "LOOT INSIDE. OWNER SAFELY IN JAIL. WELCOME." There is the story of one person who had been searched and seized, telling another who had gone through a similar experience, "After the police left, burglars came, ransacked my apartment and took everything of value," to which the other victim replied, "How could you tell?"

Sometimes you can't tell. If you're carted off before the police are finished searching and seizing, you may come home and not know the difference between vandalism and the work of professional law enforcement. If you can't get bail together quickly, you may never see any of your property again. If the police suspect that you were using your home, car, or any other possessions for drug selling, they too will be immediately seized, and you may never see them again either.* But, we're getting slightly ahead of our story.

---

*If you are suspected of using a car, your house, your property, or anything else in the sale of drugs, that car, house, or property can be taken from you immediately and you must prove that it was not used for the sale of drugs. In other words, it is not up to the government to prove that you did use it to sell drugs. In order to get back your car, house, property, etc., the burden of proof is on you. This is a complete reversal of the fundamental tenet of law, "innocent until proven guilty," but, then, there's a War going on out there, and war is hell. So, in addition to proving your own innocence and keeping your body out of jail, you must also prove the innocence of your car, house, property, etc., in order to get them back. Good luck.

When you are taken downtown ("downtown" does seem to be the favorite euphemism for a police station; even if you live downtown, you will still be taken downtown), you will probably be put in some sort of holding cell (or, as they call it, a holding tank) for an indefinite period of time. (The Supreme Court says that you can be held for forty-eight hours without being charged.) If you are lucky, you will be alone in such a cell. Most likely, however, what with jails at 101% capacity thanks to the rigorous enforcement of laws against consensual activities, you will probably find yourself in a much larger cell with some *real* criminals who have also been recently arrested—some yelling, some moaning, some covered in blood (their own or others'), some vomiting, and some with little or no control of other orifices. Once there, you are a criminal. There is no distinction made between criminals whose crimes have innocent victims and criminals whose crimes do not. Even if you are not harassed, molested, abused, exposed to a contagious illness, or raped, the sights, smells, and sounds are hideous enough. The odor of one person vomiting, for example, can cause a chain reaction of retching to which few are immune.

> *The [Supreme] Court during the past decade let police obtain search warrants on the strength of anonymous tips. It did away with the need for warrants when police want to search luggage, trash cans, car interiors, bus passengers, fenced private property and barns.*
>
> DAN BAUM

Seldom do holding tanks have anything soft in them, such as mattresses, pillows or blankets. Concrete, wooden, or metal slabs are the most that one can hope for, and here—due to overcrowding—there is seldom room to actually lie down. If you are not physically strong enough to stake out your own territory, in fact, you may end up sitting on the floor or standing until the police get around to questioning you, which might not be until some time the next day, or the next. (Suspects are sometimes put in the worst holding cells to intentionally "soften them up" for questioning.)

Then there is the questioning. Questioning is *designed* to be traumatic. Whether they use subtle psychological manipulation, or hellfire and brimstone histrionics, or a combination of the two in the classic "good cop, bad cop" approach, questioning is designed to make you feel guilty about *everything* so that you'll confess your guilt about *something*. You'll be asked to explain pieces of your life pulled from the search and taken out of context: Polaroid pictures, journal entries, personal letters.

Somewhere, you will be faced with yet another major choice. If you had to—with one or two phone calls—contact a good, competent, honest criminal attorney, could you do it? Remember, you wouldn't have your address book— that's being gone through by some rookie detective, looking for "evidence." The fact is, very few people would know how to contact a criminal attorney because so few people—including those who occasionally take part in consensual crimes—think of themselves as criminals (and rightly so, but that's the argument

> *Criminal lawyer.*
> *Or is that redundant?*
>
> WILL DURST

of this whole book, isn't it?). Eventually, the first wave of a very dark ocean known as The Truth About Lawyers reaches your beach (cell). Criminal lawyers want *retainers* that is, money up front of anywhere from $5,000 to $25,000. Although, technically, a retainer is given against fees and if the fees are not used the retainer will be refunded, in reality, retainers are seldom refunded, especially in criminal cases. This is just the tip of the legal iceberg which frequently runs into hundreds of thousands, and can run into millions of dollars.

If you are arrested for a consensual crime involving drugs, it will be harder for you to obtain the services of an attorney than if you had been arrested for a less serious charge such as, say, murder. If an attorney takes your case for a drug charge and you are found guilty, the attorney may be forced by the courts to give the law enforcement agencies making your arrest all the money you've paid to the attorney. It's part of the assets forfeiture law. The courts have ruled that not only are your house, car, money, land, investments, bank accounts, and other tangible assets forfeitable, but everything you've paid your attorney as well. Consequently, criminal attorneys are hesitant to take on drug cases. Therefore, murderers, rapists, and robbers are getting better legal representation than druggies.

Many attorneys (un)scrupulously investigate the client's net worth and, lo, when the case is over, the final bill comes to within a few thousand dollars of this amount. If they can't justify charging all this money themselves, they call in any number of attorneys as "specialists" or "consultants." These same attorneys call *your* attorney in *their* cases to act as a "specialist" or "consultant."

The only alternative is to declare yourself too poor to hire an attorney, in which case you will be assigned a public defender who is overworked, underpaid, and sometimes not very good (which may be why he or she got a job as a public defender in the first place), or you can wait to be assigned to a private attorney doing *pro bono* (that is, free) work.* Attorneys do this so that they can say, "Yes, I charge $300 an hour, but I also do a good deal of pro bono work." (This is a good deal like corporations saying, "Yes, we pollute the air terribly, but we donate to

---

*Some say that pro bono comes from the Latin term pro bono publico, which means "for the public good." Others claim it was named after Edward de Bono, the British writer who said, "A myth is a fixed way of looking at the world which cannot be destroyed because, looked at through the myth, all evidence supports that myth." The myth that the lawyers are trying to perpetuate, of course, is that something they do is for the public good. Pro bono may have something to do with Cicero's question, Cui bono? which means "To whose advantage?" When applied to law, pro bono has little to do with being in favor of the lead singer of U2 or preferring Sonny over Cher, although it has quite a lot to do with "I got you, babe."

the American Lung Association.") In pro
bono work your case immediately goes to
the bottom of the pile under all the cash
cases, and you would most likely get better
representation from the law firm's recep-
tionist, who is probably the only person you
will ever talk to about the case except on
the days when you see your attorney in
court.

Judge:
a law student
who marks his own papers.

H. L. MENCKEN

After you are arrested, questioned, and
charged, you are arraigned. Basically, this is
going before a judge who will set bail. Ah,
bail. Let's say that your bail is set at a nice, low, reasonable $50,000. Can *you* put
your hands on $50,000—in cash? From inside a jail? Can anyone you know—who
would do it for you—immediately come up with $50,000 in cash? If the answer to
these questions is "no," your choice is either (a) stay in jail until your trial or (b)
visit the bail bondsman. Bail bondsmen take 10% of the bail in cash (they are kind
enough, however, to take Visa, MasterCard, and American Express). To put up a
$50,000 bond, they take $5,000. Even if the case is dropped *the next day,* they keep
the $5,000. Still, if you can post bail in any form, you're one of the lucky ones:
51% of all inmates being held in jails in 1991 were prisoners awaiting their trial. If
you're fortunate enough to have—or to have friends who will help you put up—
the $5,000, you are then free to return to whatever is left of your house or
apartment, providing your house, car, or other property was not confiscated under the assets forfeiture laws.

You're also free to return to work. Ah, work. What, with the detention, questioning, arresting, arraigning, and gathering of bail money, you may have been in
jail for several days, or even several weeks. What do you tell your boss? In all
likelihood, your boss already knows. The friendly detectives from the police department have probably already visited your boss, asking if you had behaved in
any "unusual" ways which might indicate that you were involved in drugs (prostitution, gambling, sodomy, etc.).

In all likelihood, you will be fired. If you argue (quite correctly) that you
haven't been convicted of anything, and that one is, in our country, innocent until
proven guilty, the boss will probably vaguely refer to something such as, "Where
there's smoke, there's fire," or "At our company, we can't even risk the *hint* of
impropriety."

Finding another job will not be easy. An arrest, even if it ends in a dismissal or
an acquittal in court, remains on your record. Many companies check for arrest
records as a standard part of screening applicants. Banks, credit card companies,
lending institutions, rental agencies, and others use it as an indication of credit
worthiness. Even though it is blatantly unfair, and directly violates the tenet that
you are innocent until proven guilty, many companies use a "record of arrests" as

> *Government is like fire.*
> *If it is kept within bounds and*
> *under the control of the people,*
> *it contributes to the welfare of all.*
> *But if it gets out of place, if it*
> *gets too big and out of control,*
> *it destroys the happiness and*
> *even the lives of the people.*
>
> HAROLD E. STASSEN

a reason not to hire you, rent you an apartment, or extend credit.

Ironically, the presupposition of guilt for consensual crimes is even higher than for violent crimes. If you are accused of, say, holding up a bank at gunpoint, even your boss would probably say, "Oh, I doubt it." If, however, you are accused of propositioning a hooker by moonlight or smoking a joint by candlelight, most people conclude, "Yeah, he probably did it." "Why was she dumb enough to get caught?"

It is here that you go through the traumatic experience of finding out who your real friends are. Some might rally 'round with love, support, and material assistance. Others you will find to practice that ancient wisdom, "A friend in need is a friend to be avoided."

Now too, is the time when that church or religious group you've been supporting for so many years shows its true colors. If your alleged crime is one of the consensual crimes, chances are, your church considers it a sin. Some clergy advise accepting the punishment for a consensual crime as an extension of God's punishment for having sinned and as a lesson not to do such an evil, horrible, despicable-in-the-eyes-of-the-Lord thing again.

And, of course, consensual crimes put an incredible strain on the family. If a spouse doesn't know about his or her partner's forays into consensual crimes, an arrest is a shocking way to find out. If the spouse does know and, perhaps, even takes part in the consensual crime with his or her significant other, there is still lots of room for incrimination. "I *told* you not to bring that stuff in the house!"

An arrest could cause a divorced husband or wife to permanently lose custody of the children.* And what about the children and their schoolmates' taunts that their mother or father is a "jail bird"?

If you're engaged or dating someone, how will he or she take it? We all like to think that our beloved will stand firmly by our side. Yes, that's what we all like to think.

And what if it was one of your children, or your brothers or sisters, or even one of your parents who was arrested? How much of your time, energy, and, most importantly, financial resources could you commit to keeping him or her out of jail? Successfully defending a criminal prosecution can easily cost hundreds of thousands

---

*In Oregon, for example, if you are arrested with even less than an ounce of marijuana, you can be charged with endangerment; your children can be taken from you and placed in the state's foster care system. Statistically, your child has while in that foster care system a 20% chance of being either physically or sexually abused. The children will also be exposed to kids who are, themselves, criminals. What innocent children might be exposed to could destroy their entire lives. This practice, of course, protects children from parents who might occasionally smoke marijuana.

AIN'T NOBODY'S BUSINESS IF YOU DO

of dollars. Where would you have to draw the line? Your savings? Your home? Your credit limit? It's traumatic having to put a dollar amount on the people we love, but when they're accused of a consensual crime, that is, like it or not, what we must do.

It's little wonder, then, that, at this point, most people accused of consensual crimes seriously contemplate suicide. Not only is one's own life in shambles—the loss of possessions, living space, savings, reputation, job, friends, future—but the fear of be-

> *Under a government which*
> *imprisons any unjustly,*
> *the true place for a just man*
> *is also a prison . . .*
> *the only house in a slave State*
> *in which a free man*
> *can abide with honor.*
>
> THOREAU

ing a burden on the friends and family who are willing to help is a pressure some people simply cannot bear. All this despair, combined with the fear of prison, can make suicide seem not only the most logical, but the *only* solution. At the very least, one finds oneself in an ever-deepening and seemingly bottomless depression. (If this chapter is becoming too depressing, please remember that, unlike the consequences of being arrested for a consensual crime, this chapter *does* have an end.)

If you choose to live (which, by the way, I *do* recommend), now starts the seemingly endless round of hearings, motions, further questionings, preparation of defense and waiting, waiting, waiting. One thing you will not have to wait for are your attorney's bills. These will come on time, and you will be expected to pay them on time.

Somewhere along the line, the plea bargaining begins. Anyone who says that gambling is illegal in the United States needs only look at plea bargaining to know this is not the case. In plea bargaining, you are asked to gamble the rest of your money or the rest of your life on the verdict of your trial. Rather than go for an all-or-nothing, guilty-or-not-guilty, on the charge for which you are accused, you agree to plead guilty to a lesser charge with a preset lesser sentence. If you accept the "bargain," you will have a permanent criminal record—not just an arrest, but a conviction—and you may spend some time in prison, but less time than if you were found guilty of the original charge. The good news, however, is that the legal bills stop; the interminable waiting is over; and you can get on with what's left of your life. If you want to bet on The Trial, however, it means that the legal bills begin to escalate, and, if found guilty, you will almost certainly get a worse punishment than you would have had if you pled guilty to the lesser charge. (Prosecutors and some judges don't seem to like pushy people cluttering up the court systems looking for justice.)

A plea bargain may be the only economic alternative. It's hard to get a job when an employer discovers you are awaiting trial and may have to "go away" for, oh, five years at some point in the indefinite future.

Once the credit card companies find out about your arrest, they'll probably

> *They call it
> the Halls of Justice
> because the only place
> you get justice is
> in the halls.*
>
> LENNY BRUCE

start canceling your cards. (If you use a credit card with the bail bondsman to get out of jail, that's a red flag to the credit card companies.) People awaiting trial, you see, have this nasty habit of going bankrupt. Can you imagine why? Lawyers know this too, which is why they work very hard to be paid on a regular basis. (Bankruptcy attorneys want the full amount before they even *touch* a case.)

If you go to trial, you usually have the choice between a jury trial or a trial before a judge (a "bench trial"). When charged with a consensual crime, you are dealing not just with the facts of guilt or innocence; you are also dealing with individual prejudices. On hearing what you're accused of doing, will the prejudice of the jury be such that your guilt will be presumed and the trial merely a formality? Judges tend to be a bit more sophisticated, having dealt with *real* criminals who go around raping, robbing, and murdering, but judges have their prejudices too. They also have political pressure. During a "crackdown" or "war" on this or that consensual crime, a judge is more likely to find guilt and sentence heavily. Economics enter the picture once again: jury trials tend to last longer than bench trials, and legal fees during criminal trials often run $2,000 to $5,000 per day, per attorney. (If they don't have all your money yet, your attorneys will strongly recommend that you have at least two attorneys representing you at the trial.

Prosecutors hate to lose; so, if the trial looks as if it's going in your favor, you will be offered better and better plea-bargains. Your attorney doesn't want to lose either (it's very difficult to collect a final bill from a client who is in prison); so, if the case seems to be going against you, your attorney will recommend accepting poorer and poorer bargains.

Meanwhile, everyone is involved in the psychological guessing game of "reading the jury." Who's on our side? Who's not on our side? Who's for us? Who's against us? Who loves us? Who hates us? This process begins with the selection of the jury and continues throughout the trial. If you have *a lot* of money, your attorney can hire a professional who will, during the selection process, do on-the-spot instant psychological profiles of each potential juror along with a recommendation as to whether or not the juror would be favorable or unfavorable to your case. Once the juror is selected, investigative companies can give overnight reports as to the net worth, politics, religion, marital status, sexual preference, and spending habits of each juror. This overnight profile costs, oh, $5,000 to $15,000 per jury, and the attorney will claim it's "an invaluable tool" in helping to shape your defense.

A lot of invaluable tools are available, and the more valuable you are, the more invaluable they become. There is, for example, the expert witness. The expert witness is a professional who is paid an exorbitant amount of money to give the "expert opinion" that you are right and the state is wrong. A popular expert witness in consensual crime trials is the psychiatrist. For, $3,000 to $10,000 each (you'll want at least two), the psychiatrist will "examine" you and claim that you're not a criminal, you're just *sick;* you don't need *jail,* you need *treatment.* Why, with a year or two of therapy you could once again be a productive member of society. (The only thing that made you an *un*productive member of society, of course, was being ar-

> *A jury consists of twelve persons chosen to decide who has the better lawyer.*
>
> ROBERT FROST

rested, but it's best not to mention that at this point in the trial.) Yes, if you were sentenced, that is, if the court referred you to five psychiatric sessions per week for a year, that would be much better for you and all of society than that same year in the Big House. And, if the court takes this suggestion, that's only another $25,000 to $50,000.

When the case finally goes to the jury, the highest-pressure waiting begins. Juries can deliberate for several minutes or several days. The plea bargaining can still continue. Until the jury actually announces its verdict, it isn't a verdict, and, if a bargain is struck, the judge can call in the jury, thank them for their efforts, and send them on their way.

If the verdict comes back not guilty, you do not get back your legal fees, the arrest remains on your record, you probably won't get back your job, and you probably wouldn't want the friends, family, or fiancées who didn't stand by you. You will get back the evidence that was seized during the initial search (it will have been gone through, categorized, labeled, disassembled, with much of it missing—but you'll get it back). Even if you *are* found innocent, however, you must still go to court again to get back your house, car, money, and other property seized under asset forfeiture laws. (Believe it or not.)

If you are found guilty, the next wait begins: the wait for sentencing. During this time, you can choose whether or not to appeal your case. "An appeal," explained Finley Peter Dunne, "is when you ask one court to show its contempt for another court." If you thought the first round of legal fees was expensive, when you move into the world of appellate courts, legal fees go into hyperdrive.

One exciting thing to appeal for is a mistrial. Here, you are asking the appellate court to declare your original trial invalid because of a technical legal error made by the judge, jury, or prosecution. If you are successful in winning this appeal, your trial will be declared null and void—but you have to start all over again: another trial, another jury, another set of legal fees.

You can also appeal on constitutional grounds. Your lawyer can claim—using some of the brilliant arguments given in the chapters, "Laws against Consensual Activities Are Unconstitutional" and "Laws against Consensual Activities Violate

> JUDGE: *Are you trying to show contempt for this court?*
>
> MAE WEST: *I was doin' my best to hide it.*

the Separation of Church and State, Threatening the Freedom of and from Religion"—that the very law violates your constitutional rights and that the court should overturn the law. Here, you are looking at cases going to state supreme courts and, perhaps, even the federal Supreme Court, and you are looking at legal fees, not in the hundreds of thousands, but in the millions.

While the case is on appeal, if you don't want to spend time in jail, there is a little matter of additional bail. You are now, in the eyes of the court, a convicted criminal; thus the bail will probably be higher than the first time around. Not everyone can meet bail, of course. Chances are, you won't be able to afford anything other than accepting your sentence and doing your time.

Let's talk about doing time.*

If you've never visited a penitentiary, you might want to do so. The worst ones, however, are rarely, if ever, open to the public. For the most part, the keepers of prisoners don't want the public to know about prisons. The average citizen would be reluctant to send even a *real* criminal, much less a hooker or a pot smoker, to such a fiendishly hideous place.

Here's what Jimmy Hoffa—who visited and served time in many prisons had to say:

> I can tell you this on a stack of Bibles: prisons are archaic, brutal, unregenerative, overcrowded hell holes where the inmates are treated like animals with absolutely not one humane thought given to what they are going to do once they are released. You're an animal in a cage and you're treated like one.

Thanks entirely to the crackdown on various consensual crimes, prisons—never designed for comfort in the first place—are overcrowded. In 1991 they were filled to 101% of capacity, and they've gotten worse since then. Cells designed for two inmates are holding three, sometimes four.

The first two things you'll notice on entering a penitentiary** are the noise

---

*There is a distinction between jails and prisons. Jails are run by cities, municipalities, and counties and are for housing prisoners either awaiting trial or serving less than a one-year sentence. Prisons (penitentiaries) are run by the state or federal government and are usually for housing prisoners serving a sentence of a year or longer. Due to the overcrowding of prisons, however, a small percentage of prisoners sentenced to more than a year are serving their time in county jails. The descriptions given here of the prison system are equally true of county jails; the only difference is that county jails are often worse.

**Well, the first thing you'll probably notice is what it took Big Mike on "Your Show of Shows" a little while to find out: BIG MIKE: "While I was in solitary, I spent a lotta time thinkin'. I did a lot of

AIN'T NOBODY'S BUSINESS IF YOU DO

and the smell. The smell is body odor, cigarette smoke, the scent of unflushed or backing up toilets, a hint of diarrhea, a touch of
vomit, and wafting through it all is the
strange but clearly unpleasant aroma of the
mysterious substances the prisoners are fed.
The noise is a cacophony of televisions, ra-
dios—all tuned to different stations—boom
boxes, and voices. Some of the voices are
shouting. Some of the voices are babbling
because their owners have gone 'round the
bend. Some of the voices are singing, chant-

> *If England treats her criminals*
> *the way she has*
> *treated me,*
> *she doesn't deserve to have any.*
>
> OSCAR WILDE

ing, or praying. Some of the voices are just communicating, but because the
person they are communicating with could be several cells away, to the untrained
ear, the conversation sounds like the rest of the yelling. (Sometimes twenty or
thirty of these conversations are going on simultaneously.)

There is absolutely no privacy. A toilet (with no toilet seat) is bolted to the
wall of each cell. It is usually only inches from the bottom bunk. If it becomes
clogged and will not flush, it may take several days to get fixed, but the prisoners
have to use it anyway.

There is usually no ventilation. This keeps the smells and any airborne bacte-
ria or viruses carefully contained. Air conditioning? Hardly. It's sweltering in the
summer and usually over- or under-heated in the winter. It is a textbook breeding
ground for misery and disease.

There are few telephones. Needless to say, it's collect calls only. Visitation days
are once a week (in some prisons, once a month) and you usually see your friends or
loved ones (those who are willing to travel the hundreds, sometimes thousands of
miles) through a thick, plastic partition. No touching is permitted. In some prisons,
you talk by telephone as the separation between the two of you is not only bullet-
proof, but sound-proof. These conversations may be monitored and recorded.

In most prisons, reading is limited to what's in the prison library, which could
not, even by an elaborate stretch of the imagination, be called extensive. In many
prisons, reading material must be sent directly from the publisher. Books, magazines, or newspapers sent by individuals are returned or destroyed. That means, if
you want to read a book that's out of print (which most books are) or is printed
by a publisher that does not do direct mail order, you are out of luck.*

thinkin'. I thought about the walls . . . the bars . . . the guards with the guns. You know what I figured out?" OTHER CON: "What?" BIG MIKE: "We're in prison."

*Meanwhile, those convicted of the so-called white collar crimes such as embezzlement, fraud,
stock swindles, perjury, graft (crimes that clearly do have innocent victims) are frequently serving
their sentences in what are known as country-club prisons. These are often converted motels, hotels, and even resorts with very low security. They permit long in-person visits from friends and
family; conjugal visits from spouses and, in some cases, "fiancées"; televisions; VCRs; telephones;

> *Imprisonment,*
> *as it exists today,*
> *is a worse crime than*
> *any of those*
> *committed by its victims.*
>
> GEORGE BERNARD SHAW

Then there's a matter of money. Except for the absolute necessities, you must pay for everything you get: books, stationery, postage, cigarettes, cassette tapes, everything. You can make this money at a prison job that pays approximately twenty cents per hour. If you are transferred from one prison to another—which can happen at any time and as often as the penal authorities dictate—you must leave all but the basic necessities behind and start over.

If you are either marginally young, marginally attractive, or white (and heaven help you if you're all three), your chance of being raped is about as good as your chance of getting a cold or the flu: that is, *very good*. Even if you go to a prison that makes an attempt to separate "likely targets" from the rest of the prison population, rape doesn't take long—and who is to say rape is not going to take place within that separated population?

Rape in prison is something of a sport, like hunting. Devout heterosexuals, who would just as soon kill (and may have killed) a male who approached them with a sexual proposition, seem to become sexually ravenous as soon as the prison door slams behind them. Rape, of course, in any situation is not a sexual act; it is an act of violence, domination, control. The macho sport in prison is who-you-can-get-how-often-and-when. The only way to keep from becoming an open target and susceptible to gang rapes and individual hits at every possible opportunity is to become the "punk" of the most powerful hunter you can. He will then protect you from all the rest—although he may occasionally trade you or give you as a gift to one of the other dominant hunters.*

By the way, if you report any of this to the authorities, you will be killed. It's

and any sort of reading material. Some even have swimming pools and tennis courts. The food is considerably better than in a standard prison and, if you don't like what's on the menu, you can often order out from one of the area restaurants that deliver. For those who have been used to living a high life on the money they have stolen from others, the lifestyle of a minimum security prison is, of course, torturous—but they did commit a crime, other people suffered for it, and they do have to pay. But how much more do persons condemned to regular prisons have to pay for crimes they committed that have no victims other than, potentially, themselves?

*This obviously depicts the scene in a male prison. A parallel form of violent and psychological dominance, although not as sexually charged, takes place in women's prisons. The ratio of men to women behind bars is 18:1. Only 5.8% of the prison population in 1991 was women. There is evidence, however, that women are more often mistreated by prison personnel. This from the New York Times, January 8, 1992: "Since female prisoners are routinely mistreated in Florida's jails and prisons, it is hard not to conclude that there is a double standard for violence: One for men and quite a different one for women. According to the 1990 Report of the Florida Supreme Court Gender Bias Study Commission, 'Women are treated more harshly than similarly situated male offenders.' In the U.S., men commit 90% of all violent crimes, women 10%. Nearly half of the women are battered and kill in self-defense."

that simple. Turning in a "fellow" prisoner will mark you, both in and out of prison, for the remainder of your life (which will not be a long one).

Although rape is excruciatingly painful, humiliating, and degrading, if you don't die of hemorrhaging, you survive; that is, you would have until AIDS came along. Due to the high incidence of intravenous drug use, both in and out of prison, and completely unprotected sexual activity inside of prison, AIDS has reached epidemic proportion

> *Do you think someone who is about to rape you is going to stop and think about a condom?*
>
> ELI ADORNO
> quoted in the *New York Times*

within the prison system. In 1991, 15% of all deaths in prison were AIDS-related. Condoms, of course, are not provided by most prisons. Prisoners are not *supposed* to be having sex; therefore, they're *not*; therefore, they don't need condoms. Even when condoms are available, rapists tend not to use them even to potentially save their own lives—it just isn't very macho.

As a perpetrator of a consensual crime, you will probably end up at the bottom of the prison pecking order. Everyone seems to know, even before you arrive, exactly what you're in for. There is prejudice against consensual criminals in prison, too—but in the reverse. Consensual crimes are thought of as somewhat wimpy things, and since your crime did not involve violence against another person or another person's property, it will be assumed that you won't fight back. You will be taken advantage of at every opportunity. Your pillow, blanket, and even mattress may be "borrowed" by another cellmate. Your clean towel will be exchanged for a dirty one. Any "food" that is even marginally edible will be consumed by others. ("You don't want this, do you?") Your hunter, by the way, will not protect you from all this; he is only there to protect you from sexual advances. If you do want additional protection, you will have to provide additional favors: money, cigarettes, running errands—little tokens of your appreciation.*

Of course, all prison life is not fun and games. There is some serious learning to be done. When you are sentenced to prison, you are enrolled in the Institute of Higher Criminal Learning, the world's finest university of crime. Here, you make contacts and learn a new trade. It's obvious that, if you are unable to get a job while awaiting trial, you certainly aren't going to get one as an ex-con. At least not

---

*All of this, of course, refers to American prisons, which are veritable summer camps compared to foreign prisons. As of this writing, there are approximately 2,500 American citizens being held in foreign jails. Approximately half are being held on drug charges. Most countries have enacted strict anti-drug laws at the urging of the United States government. The more than 800 American citizens currently being held in Jamaican and Mexican prisons, for example, would probably be released tomorrow if America set an example of freedom and declared consensual crimes no longer crimes, and encouraged other countries to do the same—certainly with regard to American citizens visiting that country.

> *Pretty soon,*
> *there will not be any*
> *debate in this city*
> *about overcrowded prisons.*
> *AIDS will take care of that.*
>
> DISTRICT ATTORNEY
> MARIO MEROLA

in the pristine nine-to-five world of American business. To make a living when you get out, then, you have two choices: become a professional writer or become a professional criminal. The professional writing game seems to be pretty full, what with Stephen King turning out a new book every three weeks and Norman Mailer no longer sponsoring former prisoners with literary aspirations. With writing unavailable, that leaves the alternative form of crime: crime.

As with the prison pecking order, having a conviction for *only* a consensual crime does not look very good on your criminal résumé (or is it dossier?). Fortunately, in prison you will have many opportunities to prove yourself worthy of recommendation to one of the outside criminal organizations. You could show your daring, for example, by distributing drugs within the prison. Doing this, you might even put a few dollars aside over and above your weekly protection payment. Smuggling weapons, either into or around the prison, is always popular—and will get you high points for courage. Even if you don't want to be a part of some of the more serious crimes for which those weapons are used, being a lookout while those crimes take place can get you high points for low risk.

What do they give you on release, on what can you start a new life? It varies from state to state, but it's usually $100 and a new suit.

Meanwhile, whatever remnants of a life you had on the outside are now almost entirely gone. Loves find other loves. Friends find other friends. Apartments get rented to other tenants. People change and, more importantly, so do you.

Prison is a crash course in the darker side of life. Few survive it without becoming a different person: more cynical, jaded, fearful, angry. It's hard to trust again, hard to believe, easy to hate a system that destroyed your life behind the pompous pretense of "saving you from yourself," "for your own good."

⚖ ⚖ ⚖

Some may consider this a hopelessly bleeding-heart-liberal argument. "These people knew that what they were doing was against the law; they did it anyway; they got caught; and they're responsible for their actions. If they don't like the law, they can work to *change* it, not break it. When you break the law, you take a risk, and getting caught and paying the price is part of that risk." To people who make this argument, I would say this: Consider the ramifications not just to that *individual*, but to the society and the economy as a whole. Almost every person who goes through the criminal justice system and is incarcerated for, say, a year, becomes a permanent *negative economic unit*. Most people in society are positive economic units—that is, they produce more in goods, services, or ideas than they consume. Negative economic units, however, are a drain on society and the economy. An ex-con is essentially unemployable—especially during times of high unemployment. This forces the ex-con—in order to physically survive—to go on welfare, turn to crime, or both. Crime and welfare are a drain on the economy and on society. Eventually, enough of these negative economic units become a great economic black hole

> *[The prison guards are] capable of committing daily atrocities and obscenities, smiling the smile of the angels all the while.*
>
> JEAN HARRIS

that, unseen, sucks the energy from even the most productive economy. By turning ordinary consenting adults, who are out looking for a little fun, into criminals, we are creating millions of vampires, ready to suck the life-blood out of the economy and the society.

We must be *very careful* that we do not *unnecessarily* create negative economic units. There will always be the criminals—those who go about physically harming the person and property of others—and they will need to be put away. It's the cost of doing business in a free society. Each life destroyed, however, by the arrest, trial, and incarceration of a consensual "criminal" is an unnecessary *permanent liability* on our society and our economy. These people simply don't believe in the American dream anymore, that the American system is fair, or that it works. And why should they? Each time, as a child or an adult, they pledge allegiance to the flag, they are promised "liberty and justice for all." They used that liberty, and what did they get? Injustice. So much for the republic for which it stands. This psychic drain can be even more destructive than the economic drain, destroying the optimism, enthusiasm, and well-being of a nation.

The laws need to be *fair*: that is, not based on the system of rights and wrongs personally held by those in power. The only reasonable, objective criterion is: "If you physically harm the person or property of another, we will take you away from innocent people and property for a period of time so you won't be able to harm them. When we let you out, if you keep harming, we will keep you away from other people and their property permanently." Although the vast majority of Americans and their leaders find some action or activity personally abhorrent, if it's not physically harming the person or property of another, there is no reason to put people away for engaging in that activity. The majority should take this "liberal" (although I prefer the word *tolerant*) view *for their own protection*. It is better to have positive—or at least neutral—economic units who occasionally offend than have permanent negative economic units silently sucking away the resources and psychic energy of a nation.

The laws against consensual activities, then, "hurt us all." Each life destroyed due to the enforcement of these laws is like a piranha. Alone, piranhas are relatively harmless. When enough of them combine, however, they can turn a live cow into a skeleton within two minutes. Imagine what they can do to the goose that laid the American Golden Egg.

ᘒ ᘒ ᘒ

Even without police intervention, the laws against certain consensual activities make them far more dangerous than they need to be. Activities involving consensual crimes are completely unregulated—either by governmental or private consumer groups. It's not the law of the marketplace, but the law of the jungle that prevails. The list of these unnecessary risks is long indeed. Here are some obvious examples:

- The purity, dosage, and even type of drug are completely unregulated. The government reports that the purity of heroin sold ranges from 32% to 90%. This is quite a range. It proves fatal thousands of times each year. Of the slightly more than 6,000 drug overdoses each year, the majority of them could be prevented if drug users simply knew the dosage of the drug they were using.

- Low-grade marijuana is sometimes laced with the drug PCP to make the pot seem to be a higher grade. It's hard for users to know whether or not they've gotten great pot or PCP pot. Alas, PCP is far more damaging than even the most potent marijuana. Similarly, LSD is "enhanced" (without the buyer's knowledge) with strychnine, a lethal poison.

- When dosages are unknown, it is difficult for the user to moderate consumption. If marijuana were legal, for example, the THC (the psychoactive element in marijuana) level could be printed on each package. People could then intelligently moderate their usage. As it is, one joint could have twenty times more THC than another, and the user—short of trial and error—has no way of knowing. This becomes particularly dangerous when it comes to driving, operating machinery, or even cooking. With alcohol, one can moderate intake. The same is not true of uncontrolled substances.

- Because they come into close physical contact with customers, prostitutes can spread STDs (Sexually Transmitted Diseases), including AIDS. If prostitutes were licensed professionals, a licensing requirement could include regular medical testing for STDs, and the results of these tests could be made available to potential clients.*

- Gay bars, coffee houses, and bookstores are often forced into the less-than-savory parts of town. The higher crime of these areas is visited upon the gay visitors, and makes the prevention of hate crimes such as gay-bashing more difficult.

- The *real* crime (violence, robbery, extortion) often associated with consensual crimes often takes place only because the consensual crimes *are* crimes. A customer robbing a prostitute or a prostitute robbing a customer would be far less likely to happen, for example, if both prostitutes and bordellos were licensed, and if either party could call the police when a nonconsensual crime took place.

- If gambling were legal, credit could be extended to gamblers based on the prevailing credit policies of the aboveground marketplace. ("Sorry, a $100 bet takes you over your VISA credit limit. Do you want to put part of this on your MasterCard?") As it is, credit is extended in a haphazard fashion and collection techniques are more intrusive and violent than even those practiced by DiscoverCard Services (although I know that's hard to believe). Having gambling illegal also exposes a number of "innocent" civilians who simply want to gamble to organized criminals they may not quite be ready for, or deserving of.

⚖ ⚖ ⚖

By now, however, we are veering into the chapter, "Consensual Crimes Encourage *Real* Crimes." (This chapter is about ruining lives. Having your arm broken by the Mafia would probably not ruin your life. It may play havoc with your penmanship for a while, but your life would go on.)

At any rate, I'm tired. Do you need a break? I do. Thinking about people being sent to prison for consensual crimes is exhausting. "It's all so solemn," Pauline Kael observed, "like Joan Crawford when she's thinking."

> *Don't do drugs because if you do drugs you'll go to prison, and drugs are really expensive in prison.*
>
> JOHN HARDWICK

***Even a clean bill of health, however, is no excuse for unsafe sex. The only sane approach to sex these days—whether purchased, persuaded, or complimentary—is to assume everyone is HIV positive and protect oneself accordingly.

Intermission
to Part II

THIS SECTION of the book is starting to get a bit heavy. First the Constitution, then religious rights, then all that talk about money, and then that depressing information about arrests, trials, and jails.

If we *must* punish people for consensual crimes, I suggest an alternate method. It's not my idea, so I cannot claim a Nobel for it, but I certainly expect a Pulitzer for my journalistic brilliance in bringing it to a wide segment of the American population.

Here's the idea, as reported in the 1993 edition of the *World Almanac and Book of Facts:*

> Chicago teacher Bruce Janu deals with kids who are late to his class or talk out of turn by sentencing them to the Frank Sinatra Detention Club. Students are forced to listen to tapes of "My Way," "Love and Marriage," and other Sinatra classics. There is no talking and no homework.

> The students "just hate it," Janu says. "I get a grimace, like, 'I can't believe I'm listening to this, something my parents and grandparents listened to.' I get a lot of rolls of the eyes." Janu says the kids can sing along, but no one has.

> A senior got two "Franks" in a day—60 whole minutes of Sinatra. "I just got to where I couldn't stand it," he said.

And now, on to crime.

Consensual Crimes
Encourage *Real* Crimes

> [When a victimless criminal] is
> treated as an enemy of society, he
> almost necessarily becomes one.
> Forced into criminal acts,
> immersed in underworld-related
> supply networks, and ever conscious
> of the need to evade the police, his
> outlooks as well as behavior
> become more and more anti-social.
>
> EDWIN M. SCHUR
> *Victimless Crimes*

WE LIVE IN A SOCIETY of *agreements;* in fact, if these agreements (or, if you prefer, *contracts)* were not in place and kept by most of the people most of the time, voluntarily, society as we know it would be impossible.

We agree, for example, to drive on the right side of the road. Why the right side of the road rather than the left side of the road is a fairly arbitrary decision—half the world drives on the left side of the road. We, however, drive on the right side of the road. Even though no one *asked* our opinion as to which side of the road we would *prefer* to drive on (it was a decision made long before any of us was born), we still follow that agreement almost unthinkingly.

Can you imagine what driving would be like if even a sizable minority of people refused to voluntarily honor that agreement? What if some people *chose* to drive on the left side of the road at every possible opportunity? Can you imagine the chaos? Can you imagine the number of police it would take to, *by force,* keep all cars on the right side of the road?

During the 1992 Los Angeles riots, television showed us what happens when this tightly knit fabric of agreements begins to unravel. There was simply no way law enforcement could stop people from looting. The video images of this were astonishing: people would be seen carrying televisions, dishwashers, and VCRs out of electronics stores; a police car would pull up; people would set down whatever they were carrying, walk two feet away from it, stand there; the police car would drive away; people would pick up their loot and head off.

Watching an entire store picked clean in less than thirty minutes by an unorganized group of people struck fear in the hearts of Los Angeles residents: "What would happen if these people came to my house? What would stop them

> *Thieves respect property.*
> *They merely wish the property*
> *to become their property*
> *that they may*
> *more perfectly respect it.*
>
> G. K. CHESTERTON

from coming into my apartment and taking everything in a matter of minutes?"

Answer: nothing.

Then something interesting happened. On television, a bit of video was played over and over. At first, it was humorous, but, with repeated viewings, it grew increasingly disturbing. On the video, someone had a looted television in the back of his pick-up truck. While he was caught in the traffic jam caused by other drive-in looters, two pedestrian looters picked up the television from the back of his pick-up truck and walked away with it. The man had a choice: his pick-up truck or the television. He chose his pick-up truck—and also to avoid the confrontation of the probably superior force of two-against-one.

This image was disturbing because even the people watching the scene on a freshly looted television set began to realize that anyone with superior force could come in and take the television at any time. The police were not going to protect them any more than the police protected the store owner who owned the television set only hours before.

It wasn't the curfew or calling out the National Guard or a "show of strength" that brought the riots to an end. It was people voluntarily returning to the social contract of not harming other people's person or property. They did it out of fear—not fear of jail, but fear that, if most people did not keep that contract most of the time, one's own possessions could never be considered secure, ever, no matter what. People, as they say, "returned to their senses," and the sense they returned to was common sense.

It is not police protection, it turns out, that keeps us safe. It is the social agreement not to harm each other's person and property. The police are there only for that small fraction of a percentage of people who choose not to honor the agreement.

The agreements of our society are written in the form of *laws*. For the most part, the laws existed before we were born and the laws will exist after we're gone. Some of them are absolute ("Thou shalt not steal") and some of them are arbitrary ("Drive with your headlights on, not your parking lights").* In Rome, for example, people drive at night with their parking lights on, but their headlights off. It works just as well and gives a quieter, softer glow to the city.**

Most people are willing to cooperate with both the absolute and the arbitrary agreements of the society into which they were born, providing (a) that the

---

*What on earth are parking lights used for anyway?

**Maybe parking lights are included so that when in Rome, if we take our cars with us, we can do as the Romans do.

majority of other people follow them, and (b) that those agreements are fair: that they somehow make sense. "Don't harm another's person or property and he or she will not harm your person or property" (a modern restating of "Do unto others as you would have them do unto you") makes sense. We will make personal allowances knowing that other people are also making personal allowances for us; the result being that our person and property are kept safe from the "looting" of others.

> *Members of society must obey the law because they personally believe that its commands are justified.*
>
> JUDGE DAVID BAZELON
> *Questioning Authority*

For those who don't choose to obey the agreements—the laws of society—there are police, courts, jails, and, in some states, even death.

When laws are arbitrary, however, people are less likely to personally sacrifice in order to obey them. A law against an activity which potentially can only hurt the person or property of the person committing the "crime" is far less likely to be honored than a law against an activity that does physical harm to the person or property of another.

Far, far, *far* more consensual crimes take place than crimes with innocent victims. We hear more about crimes with innocent victims than we do about consensual crimes because crimes with innocent victims tend to get reported. The victim calls the police and says, "Hey, there's been a crime here." With the consensual crime, who's going to call the police? Except for some busybodies, do-gooders, and police entrappers, no one's going to report the consensual crime.

People take part in consensual crimes because they are appealing, available, and because "Everybody's doing them." A person discovers that he or she has broken the law, had a good time doing it, and reaped few, if any, negative consequences. This positive reinforcement makes it easy to commit the consensual crime again. And again. And again. Other consensual crimes are tried and found "not bad." Although not yet officially caught, the person is, nonetheless, living outside the law (an outlaw) and a criminal many times over.

Meanwhile, the leaders of society—the keepers of the rules—are going on and on about how bad drug use, homosexuality, prostitution, etc., are. Our leaders certainly seem more concerned about these than, say, shoplifting, insurance fraud, stealing from work, or other crimes with genuine victims. This society certainly seems to be more concerned with combating "cults," homosexuals, and drugs than it is with combating sexism, racism, and air pollution.

The transition, then—thanks to the "moral structure" dictated by society—from committing consensual crimes to committing crimes with innocent victims can be an easy one.

Once the fabric of obeying the rules of society is torn, it is very difficult to mend. The distinction between right and wrong becomes blurred; the criterion

> *It is not the business of the law*
> *to make anyone*
> *good or reverent or moral*
> *or clean or upright.*
>
> MURRAY ROTHBARD

for choosing to perform a certain action is no longer "Is this right?" but "Will I get caught?" The person becomes an outcast in a world in which the police are the enemy and not the protector, in which everyone who appears to follow the rules of society is fair game, and in which one looks out for number one, no matter what the cost to others.

ᔔ ᔔ ᔔ

Declaring certain activities "criminal" has caused artificially inflated prices of consensual crimes, thus guaranteeing real crime. If drugs were legalized and regulated, no drug user, even the most severely addicted, would have to spend more than $5 per day on drugs. As it is now, some people have $200, $300, $400 *per day* habits. To get two hundred dollars' worth of drugs a day, one must be either (a) rich, (b) a doctor, (c) a thief, or (d) a drug dealer. Most end up, by default, at (c) and (d). In order to clear $200 a day, one must steal $2,000 a day in goods (fences pay approximately ten cents on the dollar) or directly rob at least one person per day (although it's usually more than one, as few people carry that much cash with them).

According to Mark Moore of Harvard University, as reported by the National Institute of Justice,

> Very large proportions of those arrested for street crimes such as robbery, burglary, and larceny are drug users. The addict's need for money to finance his habit and the mechanisms of addiction establish a link between drugs and crime. Insofar as drug use itself is illegal, society has linked drugs to crime directly. Any possession or use is, by definition, criminal conduct.

The result: each addicted drug user becomes a mini–crime wave. It's not the drug that causes the crime; it's the *prohibition* of the drug. Having to come up with $200 per day might turn any of us into criminals. Five dollars a day: that's easy. A drug user could get that by panhandling. He or she might even get a part-time job.*

Some drug users make the money to pay the artificially inflated prices by selling drugs—in fairly large quantities. As I have pointed out before, these people are not too particular whom they sell to: they can't afford to be. They'll sell to children, if

---

*Contrary to the popular stereotype, a great many regular drug users—including heroin addicts—live relatively normal, productive lives. Most of the dangers from heroin come from the fact that it is illegal. Even the National Institute on Drug Abuse admits, "Most medical problems are caused by the uncertain dosage level, use of unsterile needles and other paraphernalia, contamination of the drug, or combination of a narcotic with other drugs, rather than by the effects of heroin (or another narcotic) itself."

they have the money. Because the drug underworld cannot depend on police protection
or take disputes to civil courts, disagreements
tend to be handled in an unpleasantly messy,
and highly criminal fashion.*

Consensual crimes tend to dehumanize
the people who take part in them, not just
in the eyes of society, but in the eyes of the
participants themselves. This attitude is not
based on any evil intrinsic to consensual
crime, but simply the conditioning of society, backed up by police, courts, and pris-

> *Petty laws*
> *breed great crimes.*
>
> OUIDA
> 1880

ons. A client, for example, may look on a prostitute as "just a hooker" and the
prostitute, in turn, might look on the client as "just a trick." In this atmosphere of
mutual disrespect, the true crimes of violence and thievery in either direction are
more likely.

When the society teaches its members to hate a group of people, such as gays,
simply because they *are*, the sort of thievery, blackmail, and recreational violence
("fag-bashing") perpetrated against gays by real criminals is predictable. Gays,
fearing scandal, or even being arrested themselves, often don't report such crimes.
Young criminals have found that, even when caught red-handed robbing or maim-
ing, all they have to do is accuse their victim of "putting the make" on them
and—regardless of the sexual orientation of their victim—their chances of getting off without so much as even being arrested significantly increase. The homophobia of certain law enforcement officers puts the burden of proof on the
victim. And many a victim, even those who are blatantly heterosexual, will back
down from pressing charges because they are afraid of being accused in court or
in the press of being homosexual.

Consensual crimes also encourage real crime by eroding public confidence in
law enforcement. People are afraid to cooperate with police because it may
allow the police to discover some little, hidden, private secret that would be best
for the police not to know.

Consider the following example: The police are chasing a real criminal, a

---

*In the early 1970s I was staying with a friend in San Francisco. She was a model and, in order to
make ends meet, she sold ounces of marijuana on the side. She never was very good with money
and failed to realize that, when you're dealing with certain underworld types, you had *better* be
good at dealing with money—at least *their* money. One morning I left early to fight an unfair traffic
ticket. I returned to find my friend face down in a pool of blood, cut 38 times with a paring knife. It
was clearly not a robbery; nothing was taken; and it made a very good news story: BEAUTIFUL
MODEL MYSTERIOUSLY MURDERED. That such a beautiful woman was murdered in a such a messy
way was not only meant to punish her; it was also meant to be an example from organized crime to
all the other mini-dealers who didn't pay their bills on time. Some say, "If she hadn't been involved
in selling drugs, she would be alive today." I say, "If marijuana were legal, she would have had no
motivation for selling the drug and she would be alive today."

> *Wherever a Knave is not*
> *punished,*
> *an honest Man*
> *is laugh'd at.*
>
> GEORGE SAVILE
> (1633–1695)

murderer, say, and he disappears into a twelve-unit apartment building. The police know that the criminal is in one of the apartments. But which one? A quick search of each apartment will, by process of elimination, quickly reveal the criminal.

The police knock at apartment #1. Inside, an alumnus of the Haight-Ashbury scene, now 63, is at work on his third doctoral thesis (*Jack Kerouac, John Steinbeck, and Harvey Lembeck: A Triple Biography*). He's about to open the door, but when he hears that it's the police, he remembers a box in the closet containing his antique drug collection (featuring a microdot of genuine Owsley Purple Haze), which he has been saving for the Recreational Pharmaceutical Museum he plans to open just as soon as drugs are legalized. He decides that the police might not appreciate the rich heritage contained in that box, so he doesn't open the door.

In apartment #2, the twice-monthly meeting of the Free Love Society is well under way and, when they hear that it's the police, they don't even *consider* opening the door.

The occupant of apartment #3 is engaged in her twice-nightly meeting of the Paid Love Society and wouldn't dream of voluntarily opening the door to the police, either.

In apartment #4, a group of heterosexual men are watching a Judy Garland movie. When they hear it is the police, there is a frantic dash to find the video tape of Super Bowl XXVII highlights. "It's too late," one says; "they already heard her singing." "They'll never believe we're straight," says another. "What shall we do?" "Let's call Ron Reagan, Jr. He'll know how to get out of this." They decide not to answer the door and wait until the police go away so Judy can go on singing.

In apartment #5 is a poker game. No answer.

In apartment #6 live five polygamists and their twelve children (who make up for the lack of family values in all the other apartments). Afraid that the children will not be able to accurately identify a single mama and a single papa (this is *truly* the household of the mamas and the papas), the polygamists ignore the police. In addition, the children have learned an important lesson on how to treat the police.

In apartment #7 is the weekly meeting of the First Church of Obi-Wan Kenobi. After deciphering the real meaning of *Obi-Wan Kenobi* ("Oh, be one. Know. Be."), the members gather together to worship various *Star Wars* characters. They would no more let the police into their worship than Luke would ask emissaries of the Empire to join in a sacred Jedi ceremony.

In apartment #8, Dr. Quackenbush is experimenting with some new healing paraphernalia which he has just imported from Switzerland (or from the set of the *Bride of Frankenstein*—it is hard to tell). Two years ago, just before he was about to discover the secret of immortality (he had already discovered the secret of immorality, and what good is one without the other?), the police had come in under the authority of the FDA and seized his equipment. He was not about to let it happen again. He does not open the door.

> *As a heterosexual ballet dancer, you develop a thick skin.*
>
> RONALD REAGAN, JR.

The occupant of apartment #9 has the most extensive pornography collection in, well, the entire building. As a woman once pointed out, "everything that is not socks in a man's sock drawer is pornography." The occupant of #9 has *a lot* of sock drawers—and only one pair of socks (black). Like the Metropolitan Museum of Art, he has room to display only a small part of his collection at a time. What is currently displayed, however, is sufficient cause for the occupant of #9 to quickly evaluate whether or not to open the door to the police; he glances at the poster of Candy Barr, and decides, "No."

Mrs. Elvira Shootlemeyer, a widow, lives in apartment #10. Mrs. Shootlemeyer has a truly unusual and remarkably unpopular political view: she wants to see Richard Nixon re-elected president of the United States. Her walls are covered with posters she carefully hand-lettered: "Ford pardoned him. Jesus forgave him. Why can't you?" "He wouldn't *dare* do anything now," "Re-elect Nixon—just for the hell of it" and "Nixon-Bush in '96." Her political organization (CREEPA: Committee to Re-Elect the President Again) has seven members, Mrs. Shootlemeyer and her six cats. When she hears it is the police at her door, Mrs. Shootlemeyer recalls that it was the police who caught the Watergate burglars and started all the trouble in the first place. She refuses to open the door.

In apartment #11 lives Bertha D. Nation, a former NBA basketball center who is now a transvestite of transformational proportions. When wearing her/his five-inch stiletto heels (the ones custom-made by Frederick's of Hollywood in consultation with the Army Corps of Engineers), she/he is over seven feet tall. She/he has learned to stay away from the police and low-hanging chandeliers.

Meanwhile, in apartment #12, the sought-after criminal is listening to Schubert while burning the clothes he wore and systematically destroying any other evidence that could possibly link him to the murder.

Time was when people cooperated with the police fully, openly, immediately. If the police inquired about a friend or relative, it was assumed that the friend or relative was the innocent victim of a crime and the police were trying to help. Now there is the fear that the friend or relative might be involved in a consensual crime. Our frank and immediate cooperation with the authorities might just help

> *The most efficacious method*
> *of dealing with deviancy*
> *is to ignore,*
> *to the furthest point*
> *of our tolerance,*
> *those items*
> *which we find offensive.*
>
> GILBERT GEIS

put a friend or a relative in jail. Even though we may not personally approve of our friends' or relatives' extracurricular activities, and, in fact, may think it best that they didn't take part in them, we don't want them to go to jail, and we *certainly* don't want to help put them there. Having a friend or relative in jail is hard enough; having inadvertently helped put him or her there can be intolerable.*

As most people at one time or another have taken part in one consensual crime or another, the respect given law enforcement officers has seriously eroded. A Robin Hood mentality has people identifying more with the criminals than with the police—who seem to be acting increasingly like the Sheriff of Nottingham.

Consensual crimes simply overburden an already groaning criminal justice system. With one *real* crime (murder, negligent manslaughter, forcible rape, robbery, aggravated assault, burglary, theft, motor vehicle theft, arson) happening every two seconds in the United States, do we really want the precious time of law enforcement officials spent regulating the private lives of individuals? Stories such as this, from the June 13, 1991 edition of the *New York Times,* are increasingly common:

> The man charged with stabbing a former Rockette to death was indicted yesterday as prosecutors remained under pressure to explain their handling of an earlier case against the defendant.
>
> The Manhattan District Attorney's office has been criticized for allowing the defendant to plea bargain 15 months ago to a trespass charge after hav-

---

*In the summer of 1968, I was living in Michigan. Rumor had it that pot was growing wild in neighboring Indiana. This was a fairly wild concept, but it was a wild time and there were many wild rumors. Some of them were accurate (there was a drug called speed that sped everything up) and some were not (smoking the inside of a banana peel will not get you high). We drove down to Indiana and, lo, there was marijuana growing by the side of the road. We picked some, took it home, and, as we were instructed to do by a book on marijuana cultivation, hung it upside down to dry. I was living in the basement of my parents' home. I used the downstairs bathroom for my curing shed. My father *never* went downstairs—except, of course, that week. (The bathroom upstairs had stopped working and my father went downstairs.) He opened the door to find a hanging garden of earthly delights. He was not amused. At that time, the general belief was that, if you smoked pot, you would die of heroin addiction within six months. It was common knowledge. Not wanting this fate for his son, he went to talk to his good friend and drinking buddy, who happened to be a police detective. My father only wanted the stuff taken away and for the detective to have a little talk with me. The detective got carried away, took the stuff away, *and* took me away. I was charged with possession of narcotics (a felony) and my father was subpoenaed to testify against me. My father, a deeply honest man, was forced to testify against his eldest son. For first offenses, at that time, people were getting from two to five years in prison. I'm sure that it was one of the most painful days of his life. Watching him on the stand in agony made it one of my most painful days, too. (I plea bargained and was given two years' probation.)

ing been charged with attacking a woman with an ice pick. The defendant received a 45-day sentence and served 30 days. . . .

Mr. McKiever had been arrested three other times: in 1982 for trespassing, in 1982 for petty larceny and in 1978 for grand larceny. . . .

At a news conference announcing the indictment in the slaying, Robert M. Morgenthau, the District Attorney, defended his office's action last year. . . . "I don't blame the public for being upset. This is a tragedy, and I wish it could have been averted. There are a lot of potentially dangerous people running around on the streets, and we'd like to lock up every one of them, but we can't do it. . . ."

Some lawyers say Mr. Morgenthau and his prosecutors are often forced into difficult decisions by a system that is overburdened by too many criminals and not enough judges.

"People blame Mr. Morgenthau, but what really can he do?" said William E. Hellerstein, a professor at Brooklyn Law School. . . . "There is still a lot of time being devoted to victimless crimes, . . ." he said. "But meanwhile there are large chunks of activity, violent activity, that as a practical matter has become decriminalized because the system cannot cope."

> *What I'd like to see police do is deal with important issues and not these sorts of victimless crimes when society is riddled with problems.*
>
> ALDERMAN RODNEY BARKER

Here's how overworked law enforcement is in the United States: Only 21% of the people who commit murder and negligent manslaughter, forcible rape, robbery, aggravated assault, burglary, theft, motor vehicle theft, or arson are ever arrested; 79% of them—almost four out of five—get off scot-free.

The state of law enforcement is, in fact, worse than that. By the time the real criminals go through the court system, very few of them spend any time in jail. According to the National Center for Policy Analysis,

> Only 17% of all murders lead to a prison sentence; only 5% of all rapes lead to a prison sentence; and a convicted felon goes to prison less than 3% of the time in cases of robbery, assault, burglary, and auto theft.

The deterrent law enforcement is supposed to provide against real crime is, then, almost nonexistent. Why should a criminal even pause before committing a crime? The answer is, obviously, not the fear of going to jail.

⚖ ⚖ ⚖

With people literally getting away with murder (one in six), only 5% of the forcible rapes leading to prison, and nearly eight out of ten burglars getting off without so much as an arrest, is it sane, rational, or practical to ask law enforcement officials to enforce "morality"?

Consensual Crimes
Corrupt Law Enforcement

> *Only in a police state*
> *is the job of a policeman easy.*
>
> ORSON WELLES

MOST PEOPLE IN law enforcement do not consider consensual crimes as crimes. Each year since 1930, the United States Department of Justice and the Federal Bureau of Investigation have published a telephone book–sized document known as the *Uniform Crime Reports*. Their advisory board includes the International Association of Chiefs of Police and the National Sheriffs Association. And what crime statistic do the U.S. Department of Justice, the Federal Bureau of Investigation, the International Association of Chiefs of Police, and the National Sheriffs Association think most important? They have two categories: *violent crime* and *property crime*. Under violent crime are murder and negligent manslaughter, forcible rape, robbery, and aggravated assault. Under property crime are burglary, larceny-theft, motor vehicle theft, and arson. The report says that these crimes, known collectively as the "Crime Index," are used "for gauging fluctuations in the overall volume and rate of crime."

According to the report, in the 1980s "law enforcement called for a thorough evaluative study that would modernize the UCR (Uniform Crime Reporting) program." After years of study, what was added to the report? Hate crime statistics and law enforcement officers killed and assaulted.

Not a *single* consensual crime in the lot.

Law enforcement is based on a very simple premise: there is a *perpetrator* and a *victim*. The police catch the perpetrator and put him or her in jail. The courts then decide the guilt or innocence of the perpetrator and an appropriate punishment if guilty. This protects the victim and others from further victimization and keeps the perpetrator from further perpetrations.

A serious problem arises when the perpetrator and the victim are one and the same. Such is the case with consensual crimes. If the perpetrator and the victim

> *The police*
> *are not here*
> *to create disorder.*
> *The police are here*
> *to preserve disorder.*
>
> MAYOR RICHARD DALEY

are one, and the police put the perpetrator in jail, they are putting the victim in jail too. How, then, can the police protect the victim? The answer is, they can't. Law enforcement, thus perverted, begins to deteriorate.

With a real crime, the innocent victim goes to the police and reports it. The police then set about to catch the criminal. With consensual crime, who is there to report the crime? Obviously, no one directly involved with it. Everyone consented to it, so they're not going to be complaining to the police. The police, then, must become spies, busybodies, and entrappers in order to catch consensual criminals victimizing themselves. You can imagine how demoralizing and corrupting this entire procedure can be to both police and society.

As Jackson Eli Reynolds reported in *The Washington Post,*

> Drug offenses . . . may be regarded as the prototypes of non-victim crimes today. The private nature of the sale and use of these drugs has led the police to resort to methods of detection and surveillance that intrude upon our privacy, including illegal search, eavesdropping, and entrapment.

> Indeed, the successful prosecution of such cases often requires police infringement of the constitutional protections that safeguard the privacy of individuals.

Why, then, don't law enforcement officials speak out against consensual crimes? Some do, but their voices are often not heard. They dare not speak out too loudly because, after all, it's not a popular position—not with the general public, not with religious leaders, not with organized crime, not with politicians (who use crackdown-on-consensual-crime rhetoric to get easy votes), and not with some law enforcement officials.

Law enforcement officials who are against the legalization of consensual crimes tend to fall into three categories: the conservative, the concerned, and the corrupt.

The Conservative. These are the ones who, due to their personal convictions (usually religious), do not like one, some, or all of the consensual crimes. These officials usually discuss "morality," "the family," and "the values of decent Americans."

There's not much to say, other than that these law enforcement officials are sincerely misguided. They are in a better position than most to know that personal morality cannot be regulated by force. They are faced daily with innocent victims of preventable crimes, whose suffering could have been avoided if there were more police to patrol certain areas. These officials watch violent criminals, who they *know* are guilty, go free because there aren't enough detectives to gather the evidence necessary for conviction. And yet, because these officials believe personally that consensual crimes are wrong, they believe that consensual "criminals" should be punished.

The Concerned. These law enforcement officials know that the pursuit of consensual crimes is (a) hopeless, (b) a waste of time, and (c) counterproductive. Yet, when they consider the consequences of legalization, they become concerned. For example, drunk drivers kill more than 22,000 people

> *Stan Guffey,*
> *a high school basketball referee,*
> *was working a game*
> *in Oklahoma City*
> *when a policeman came*
> *onto the court and arrested him*
> *for not calling enough fouls*
> *during the game.*
>
> 1993 WORLD ALMANAC AND
> BOOK OF FACTS

each year. If drugs were legalized, wouldn't this rate be increased by "stoned" drivers? One doesn't need to see too many traffic accidents to realize that whatever we need to do to prevent even *one more* of these should be done. These officials are concerned, too, that a useful tool for investigating and gaining confessions to *genuine* crimes might be taken away. (In order to have a consensual crime charge dropped, some suspected persons "talk" and provide valuable information about real crimes.)

As to these people's concerns, I pray that a thoughtful reading of this book will ease many of them. We'll explore the genuine crime of operating a motor vehicle while incapacitated (for whatever reason) in the chapter, "Fail-Safe Safety Devices." As to using consensual crimes as a tool for gathering information on genuine crimes, I can only suggest that loyal law enforcement officers were probably concerned when physical torture was officially removed from their arsenal of interrogation. As effective as using consensual crime violations to reveal information about real crimes may be, its potential for abuses far outweighs its advantages. For example, in order to get off, a suspect might give false evidence against someone, helping to convict an innocent person. As much as law enforcement officials want crimes solved, only corrupt law enforcement officials want those crimes "cleared" by the conviction of innocent parties. Which brings us to . . .

The Corrupt. These are the law enforcement officials who are getting something personally by consensual crimes remaining crimes. At the lower levels of corruption, are police officers looking for easy *collars*. A collar is a police term meaning "arrest." Many police departments require a minimum number of collars by each officer per month. As the month nears its end, police officers actively seek arrests to fulfill their quotas. What do you suppose are the easy collars to make? People committing some of the consensual crimes, of course. What could be easier than going where drug dealers and prostitutes ply their trades, or where gays and gamblers hang out, and, well, hanging out until something "illegal" is either offered or observed? Not only are these easy arrests; they also tend to be relatively risk-free. Consensual "criminals" (other than higher-level drug dealers) are not famous for carrying weapons or even, for that matter, resisting arrest.

> *Few men have virtue*
> *to withstand the highest bidder.*
>
> GEORGE WASHINGTON

At the next level of corruption are the officers who get "free samples" from drug dealers, prostitutes, and such.

At the next level up (down?) are the ones who get financial kickbacks for looking the other way. Then there are those who get the collars *and* the cash. The famous "suitcases full of money" are very real, especially in drug dealing (prostitutes don't tend to carry suitcases full of money). How much money is in a suitcase full of cash? From the time of the bust until the suitcase gets checked into evidence, the contents could be down by, oh, $50,000 to $100,000. With the outrageously inflated prices caused by the illegalization of drugs, $50,000 or $100,000's worth of cocaine or heroin could get sidetracked on the trip downtown, and nobody would notice. If somebody did notice, well, an arrangement could be made.

Sometimes otherwise honest cops go wrong simply because the amounts of money involved in consensual crimes are entirely too tempting. These are cops, for heaven's sake, not saints.

This "easy money" corruption goes right to the top. One example: When an accused consensual criminal's land, property, or money is seized under federal assets forfeiture laws, the income is split between federal and local law enforcement. According to an article in the *Los Angeles Times* (April 13, 1993), however, the Los Angeles Sheriff's Department failed (shall we say) to turn over $60 million to the feds. A former sheriff's department sergeant was quoted as saying the sheriff's department "stole $60 million" from the feds in 1988 and 1989 drug busts, and the *Times* added, "he is convinced such practices continue."*

In addition to the opportunity for pilfering cash and drugs seized in raids, organized crime offers police large sums of money in exchange for information, participation, or cooperation. In multimillion dollar drug deals, a sizable amount is set aside for "security." If consensual crimes go, all the law enforcement personnel on the take wouldn't have very much left to take.

There's not much to say about corrupt law enforcement officials. Even though their graft may have begun innocently enough—perhaps even accidentally—over time they become spoiled, complacent, and lazy. If you're getting $200,000 a year for simply looking the other way, why would you want to go back to $38,000 a year looking for criminals? This laziness extends even into the milder forms of corruption, such as padding the collar quota with consensual crimes. Those who have been on the easy "vice" details—entrapping prostitutes and gays or rounding

---

*This doesn't surprise me; but I do have a procedural question: Whom do the feds call when the criminal is the Los Angeles County Sheriff's Department? The LAPD? The National Guard? The governor? ("Oh, governor: the Sheriff's Department has been naughty again!") Is this one of those things that has to go before the U.N.? Inquiring minds want to know.

up pornographers and gamblers—are not going to be pleased at the prospect of returning to the real world of cops and robbers where the robbers make their living using *weapons* on victims and police alike.

And, in case you think the judicial system is keeping a watchful eye on police corruption, this news item should soothe:

> In Michigan, Alger County Circuit Court Judge Charles Stark sentenced convicted rapist David Caballero to pay $975 in court costs and $200 compensation to the victim and serve three years' probation, after which the conviction would be removed from his record. Stark explained he gave Caballero the lenient sentence because a conviction would have prevented the twenty-one-year-old college student, a criminal justice major, from achieving his goal of becoming a police officer.

> *If my business could be made legal and women like me could make a big contribution to what Mayor Lindsay calls "Fun City," and the city and state could derive the money in taxes and licensing fees that I pay off to crooked cops and political figures.*
>
> XAVIERA HOLLANDER
> *The Happy Hooker*

The percentage of crooked cops? Of course, no one knows. In my kinder, gentler moments, I like to think it's small, very small. That's what I like to think. I also like to think that, like all addictions, greed and easy money can be successfully treated and overcome. In my kinder, gentler moments, I also like to think that the rehabilitation rate can be high, very high.

⚖ ⚖ ⚖

It's time we returned to respect and admiration for law enforcement, and made law enforcement, once again, a respectable and admirable profession. With the mixed feelings that many people have about police, some who are naturally drawn to the field of law enforcement have mixed feelings about becoming police. This reluctance is unfortunate.

When we, as a society, stop forcing the police to be, as Alan Watts put it, "clergymen with billy clubs,"* we will naturally appreciate them for the service they provide each day.

No one has mixed feelings about firefighters, for example. Firefighters are there when we need them and, when we don't, they are happy to play cards, watch television, and give lectures on fire prevention and disaster preparedness. If, however, we gave the firefighters the added responsibility of making sure that there were no inappropriate *sexual* fires blazing in the community, then we would probably start to look at firefighters with a wary eye.

As absurd as this situation sounds, this is *precisely* the job we've given the police. It's an impossible job that invites corruption and dissipates respect. The

---

*Alan Watts was British; in the United States, it's clergymen with .38 caliber revolvers, magnums, machine guns, helicopters, tanks, and sophisticated surveillance systems.

> *When you're a lawman*
> *and you're dealing with people,*
> *you do a whole lot better*
> *if you go not so much by the book*
> *but by the heart.*
>
> ANDY TAYLOR
> *"The Andy Griffith Show"*

police have been burdened with this job for far too long. It's time to free the police to do their real job, which is catching real criminals—people who physically harm the person or property of others. Period.

As Norval Morris and Gordon Hawkins explained in their book, *The Honest Politician's Guide to Crime Control,*

> The prime function of the criminal law is to protect our persons and our property; these purposes are now engulfed in a mass of other distracting, inefficiently performed, legislative duties. When the criminal law invades the spheres of private morality and social welfare, it exceeds its proper limits at the cost of neglecting its primary tasks. This unwarranted extension is expensive, ineffective, and criminogenic.

Personally, I have great respect for the police, not only because they have the courage to face muggers and murderers, but also because they have the courage to face all that *paperwork*. As P. J. O'Rourke pointed out,

> A modern arrest requires a stack of forms as thick as a Sunday *New York Times* "Arts and Leisure" section, and filling them out is as complicated as buying something at Bloomingdale's with an out-of-state check. A modern conviction requires just as much effort and tedium in court. The average D.C. cop, for example, spends twenty days of his month testifying or waiting to do so.

Most of the police I've met are genuinely dedicated to peace, in the broadest sense of the term. They want people to feel safe in their homes, in their cars, in their businesses, walking down the street. If they can keep in check that small percentage of the population who wants to violate that peace, they consider their job well done.

I wholeheartedly support that job, and if we removed the futile enforcement of laws against consensual activities from their job descriptions, policemen, policewomen, sheriffs, constables, G-men, G-women, and all the rest would once again be something they haven't been called in some time: peace officers.

AIN'T NOBODY'S BUSINESS IF YOU DO

The Cops Can't Catch 'Em;
the Courts Can't Handle 'Em;
the Prisons Can't Hold 'Em

> *Efforts to combat this tidal wave*
> *of [violent] crime*
> *are continually frustrated*
> *by a criminal justice system*
> *that is little more*
> *than a revolving door.*
>
> SENATOR ALFONSE D'AMATO

THE MORE THAN 4,000,000 arrests made each year for consensual crimes are not even the tip of the iceberg of consensual crimes committed; they're more like the *ice cube* of the iceberg. When you consider the number of times that drugs are possessed, used, or sold; prostitutes paid; bets made; illicit sex bade; loiterers in the shade; vagrants on parade; and transvestites in masquerade; it's easy to see that the cops can't catch 'em, the courts can't handle 'em, and the prisons can't hold 'em. To give one obvious example: In 1991, fewer than 15 million people were arrested for *all* crimes in the United States. In that same year, according to the Department of Health and Human Services, almost 26 million people illegally used drugs. The criminal justice system was burdened beyond capacity with the 15 million arrests (one million of which were drug arrests). Can you imagine what would have happened if they had added 25 million more? And that's just drugs.

When it comes to consensual crimes, the term *criminal justice* is something of an oxymoron, like jumbo shrimp or military intelligence. There's no *justice* because they're not really *criminals*. As we explored in the chapter, "Enforcing Laws against Consensual Activities Destroys People's Lives," putting people who, at worst, don't respect *their own* person or property into a system designed for people who don't respect *other people's* person or property has a good many detrimental effects on the former.

It also has detrimental effects on the system itself. Avowed to treating all criminals alike (the woman holding the scales of justice is blindfolded), the courts, when they become overcrowded, treat *all criminals* a little bit easier, including the ones who go around physically harming another's person or property.

> *George Bush has increased*
> *our prison capacity*
> *by 118 percent in three years.*
> *The Department of Justice's budget*
> *has gone up 70 percent*
> *in three years.*
> *It's one of the fastest growing*
> *agencies in government.*
>
> ATTORNEY GENERAL BARR
> February 24, 1992

The scales of justice are a delicate balance. We may be able to add more jail cells by spending more money, but a properly balanced court takes more than just an additional wing on the courthouse. Good judges take decades of seasoning. Around each judge must be gathered a support system of court clerks, legal researchers, court reporters, bailiffs, and other individuals who are not so much assembled as they are *grown*.

In our courts we seek the highest wisdom. We seek the guidance of intelligence and maturity. Overcrowding the court system with consensual noncriminals keeps the bad judges in place, encourages incompetent lawyers to become judges, and prevents the truly good judges from doing their best.

As *Legal Times* accurately predicted in 1989,

> Before long the judiciary could become just another bureaucracy, with thousands of judges and magistrates processing dreary caseloads likely to attract only hacks and drones to the bench.

The courts can be corrupted at any of four levels: prosecutors, judges, juries, or witnesses. The techniques of corruption include threats of violence, blackmail, and bribery.

The life of a prosecuting attorney is not an easy one. Working through the district attorney's office, prosecuting attorneys receive a set salary and no bonuses for winning cases. The defense attorney hired by the defendant in a criminal case can make more money in a week than the prosecuting attorney makes in a year. The budget constraints and the overcrowded judicial system have made the prosecutors' workload nearly unbearable. A defense attorney may be able spend months working on a case; a prosecuting attorney, weeks, sometimes days. In addition, prosecuting attorneys are subject to political and public pressures generally not suffered by attorneys in private practice. ("The newspapers are tearing us apart and the governor is furious. We need more drug convictions!")

Those who end up in the prosecutor's office instead of private practice usually do so for one of three reasons. First, there are those who really care. They are the true public servants and have a mission to clean up crime. They know that for the criminal justice system to work, the state needs attorneys who are as good as the defense. This balancing of attorney capability (known as the adversary system) leads most often to justice. These prosecutors would rather have satisfaction in their job than a second BMW in their garage. Second, some people use the DA's office as a stepping stone for either higher political office or their own career advancement. A couple of years' experience as a prosecuting attorney looks good on the résumé of someone who aspires to hold political office or a position in a

AIN'T NOBODY'S BUSINESS IF YOU DO

criminal justice law firm. The district attorney's office is a crash course in criminal law as it *really* happens, and some people take this course before moving on to personally bigger and better things. Third, some attorneys just can't get a job with a law firm, are too timid to go into private practice, and end up working at the district attorney's office in the same way that many civil service employees throughout the government bureaucracy get their jobs: because they studied enough and passed all the tests. It doesn't

> *Concepts of justice must have hands and feet or they remain sterile abstractions. The hands and feet we need are efficient means and methods to carry out justice in every case in the shortest possible time and at the lowest possible cost.*
>
> JUSTICE WARREN E. BURGER

mean that they can actually do the work with any noticeable degree of effectiveness, but they have passed all the tests. They may not rise quickly up the ladder, but at least the job is secure and there's a regular paycheck.

The prosecutors' likelihood of corruptibility obviously goes in 3-2-1 order. That is, the relatively inept civil servant prosecutor with not much personal motivation or future ambitions would be most likely to accept a payoff in exchange for either botching up the prosecution or providing the defense with some essential information. As not much is expected from prosecutors at this level anyway, they can get away with throwing a case here or there for years.

Prosecutors at the second level may not be so susceptible to bribery, but they are to blackmail. These attorneys with higher aspirations, who are only using the DA's office for a stepping stone, don't want any scandal. If someone likes to take part in one consensual crime or another on his or her own time and the "opposition" finds out, it can be used as ammunition. This creates a Catch-22 situation in which, because consensual crimes are illegal, people who commit them are corruptible. The only reason they are corruptible, of course, is that they are prone to blackmail, and the only reason they are prone to blackmail is that they commit crimes that have no victims, but are nonetheless illegal. Once these people commit the real crime of tampering with the legal system, they are in the pocket of the criminal or crime organization that initially blackmailed them, whether they go on to become prosecutor, judge, representative, senator, or governor. The seed of ongoing real crime is, once again, the laws against consensual activities.

In the first level are the true public servants who are fairly noncorruptible, as long as they maintain their true mission, which, heaven willing, will continue throughout their lives. (Unless they're open to blackmail for taking part in a consensual crime. See above.)

The sophisticated will, of course, remember this exchange from "The Addams Family":

> GOMEZ ADDAMS: I've gone through the city ordinances, the Bill of Rights, and the seventeen volumes of assorted jurisprudence—and I've come to a conclusion.

> *Judges . . . rule on the basis of law,*
> *not public opinion,*
> *and they should be totally*
> *indifferent to pressures*
> *of the times.*
>
> JUSTICE WARREN E. BURGER

MORTICIA ADDAMS: What?

GOMEZ: That we haven't got a leg to stand on.

UNCLE FESTER: Not even if we bribe the judge?

Judges fall into roughly the same categories as prosecutors in terms of motivation and degrees of corruptibility. Like district attorneys, some judges have to concern themselves with either election or re-election. To get on or stay on the bench, some make the devil's bargain with organized crime: in exchange for money, connections, or the suppression of certain potentially embarrassing information by organized crime (which is primarily financed by the artificially inflated prices of the consensual crime commodities), the judges will make favorable rulings whenever members of that syndicate or its dear friends come before the bench. These cases sometimes involve consensual crimes and sometimes they don't. Living and working outside the law, organized crime has no recourse to the legal system, so certain internal enforcement measures which *do* involve victims are sometimes detected by the police. The judges are expected, nonetheless, to rule in favor of mob members whether the charge is marijuana or murder.

The jury is as susceptible as its twelve members. With enough investigation money (and the perpetrators of organized consensual crimes have plenty of that), the defense can know by the first day of the trial almost everything there is to know about each of the jurors. Which would be most susceptible to a threat, a bribe, or a little blackmail? Except in rare cases, the jurors go home after court adjourns and can easily be contacted by telephone. One or two highly motivated jury members can often bring up enough reasonable doubts (and juries in criminal cases are instructed to reach their conclusion of guilt beyond a reasonable doubt) in the minds of the other jurors to bring about a verdict of not guilty. At worst, it only takes one member of a jury to withhold his or her guilty vote for there to be a hung jury.* After a hung jury, the prosecutor is usually more than willing to enter into passionate plea bargaining: the concept of retrying the same case from scratch (which is what must happen with a hung jury) is, at best, disheartening. After a second or third hung jury, the case might be dropped entirely. Making "arrangements" with jurors is such a common practice that it's known by the relatively trivial phrase *jury tampering*, which in no way conveys the seriousness or the significance of the crime.

---

*In the Old West, an entire jury accused of taking a bribe was taken out and hung from the nearest tree. This may be the origin of the term *hung jury*. The term may have already been in use—perhaps coming from the use of the word *hanging* as in "just hanging there, not doing anything"—and the outraged townspeople may have found the visual pun "hung jury" too much to resist.

AIN'T NOBODY'S BUSINESS IF YOU DO

Finally, there are witnesses. Far from the melodramatic courtroom myth, the last-minute inclusion of a "secret witness" almost never happens. (In courtroom dramas, whenever a surprise witness is introduced, the judge invariably proclaims, "This is highly irregular!") By law, the witnesses each side plans to call to the stand must be presented to the other side some time before the trial. Thus witnesses, like jurors, judges, and prosecutors, are open to pretrial persuasion. Many trials are never brought to court because someone "gets to" the main witness for the prosecution, who "suddenly remembers" a different set of facts.

> ALEX REIGER: *Louie, when you walk into that hearing room, you're going to be under oath. You know what that means?*
>
> LOUIE DE PALMA: *Yeah. It means they gotta believe you. I love this country.*
>
> "TAXI"

And then there are witnesses who are paid specifically to bear false witness. Their payment may be in the form of money, drugs, or favors; or they may simply be blackmailed. These people will claim that the defendant couldn't *possibly* have been at the scene of the crime because they were all spending the weekend together in Wyoming, fishing by day and reading the Bible aloud at night. False witnesses can also be used to impugn the credibility of otherwise credible witnesses for the prosecution.

When you combine the delicate balance in the criminal justice system with the large amounts of money made by the peddlers of consensual crimes (especially drugs and gambling), the potential for corruption is high and, like most potentials in human nature, it eventually has been realized. The big players with the big money tend to get off, while the little players tend to get scrupulous prosecutions and big sentences. In this way, defenders of the criminal justice system can say, "See, we're doing *so much* about drugs (or whatever the consensual crime may be). Our conviction rate is up and the sentences are stiffer."

In courts that aren't corrupt, just the massive overloading caused by the burden of processing consensual criminals as though they were real criminals causes, at best, a system with enough loopholes for plenty of real criminals (especially the ones who can afford the best lawyers) to go free.

This from the *Los Angeles Times*, April 25, 1993,

> Two more senior federal judges recently joined a growing list of their colleagues nationwide in refusing to preside over drug cases as a protest to the extreme and counter-productive sentences they are required to impose in these cases. We are sympathetic with their distress. Tough, inflexible federal sentencing rules, once considered "the answer" to rising drug use and crime, threaten to make a mockery of our federal criminal justice system. . . .
>
> A young offender convicted of first-time possession of $50 worth of drugs might be sentenced to a 20-year prison term or even a life term without the possibility of parole. . . .

> *There are not enough jails,*
> *not enough policemen,*
> *not enough courts to enforce a law*
> *not supported by the people.*
>
> HUBERT H. HUMPHREY

Nearly 60% of all federal prisoners are now drug felons. Average prison terms for federal drug offenders have shot up 22% since 1986—while those of violent criminals fell by 30%. . . .

Congress has been unwilling to amend the Draconian sentencing law for fear of seeming "soft on crime." But the protests of these respected judges, along with the private rumblings of hundreds more across the country, must signal Congress that the law is unfair and unworkable.

The solution? Obviously, stop pretending that consensual activities are crimes. This would stop most organized crime and its threats, blackmail, and bribery overnight, and would immediately cut the workload of the criminal justice system by about half. This would give the courts time to decide the guilt or innocence of people accused of real crimes such as murder, rape, robbery, aggravated assault, burglary, larceny, theft, motor vehicle theft, arson, hate crimes, forgery, counterfeiting, fraud, embezzlement, buying and selling stolen property, vandalism, carrying concealed weapons, child molestation, and driving under the influence of alcohol or other intoxicating substances.

⚖️ ⚖️ ⚖️

Prisons, as previously noted, are filled to capacity and beyond. In most areas an early-release program has been instituted which, of course, fails to differentiate between prisoners whose crimes had innocent victims and prisoners whose crimes did not. This puts truly dangerous criminals out on the street sooner, giving them extra months, and in some cases years, to rape, rob, and plunder.

We've already discussed what inhumane and deplorable institutions prisons have become. Due to overcrowding caused by the War on Drugs, prisons (not enjoyable places under the best of conditions) have become intolerable. Some of them violate the constitutional guarantee against "cruel and unusual punishment." With the overcrowding, any hope of rehabilitation, job placement, counseling, therapy, or achieving any other high-minded goals is completely derailed. The entire penal system is working overtime to simply "keep 'em fed and find 'em a bed."

In between the prisons and the courts lies the probationary system. Here (theoretically), the prisoner's past and current conduct is thoroughly examined by a parole officer who then recommends to the judge or the parole authorities whether or not the prisoner can safely be reintroduced into society. In the old days, parole officers actually had a little time to do this; today they do not. Parole officers could sometimes separate otherwise decent people who simply had a few bad breaks from professional criminals who had been lucky enough to only have a few arrests. A parole officer could also investigate and gauge the amount of progress a prisoner made towards rehabilitation. Once a prisoner was released, a parole officer had the time to follow up and sometimes even help the parolee find housing and a job.

Alas, no such luxury of time exists anymore for these activities. Due to the overcrowding caused by a society that seems intent on punishing "immoral" people, the modern-day parole officer barely has enough time to scan a file, make a few perfunctory phone calls, spend a few minutes talking to a prisoner, and make a hastily formed recommendation before moving on to the next case. The punishment of consensual crimes has turned the well-intended parole system into a method for murderers, thieves, and rapists to get out in a few years and continue their lives of crime, much to the detriment of us all.

Of all the tasks of government, the most basic is to protect its citizens from violence.

JOHN FOSTER DULLES

⚖ ⚖ ⚖

With the overcrowding and corruption of the parole, penal, and criminal justice systems, even Solomon, in all his wisdom, would be hard pressed to dispense justice with a fair and even hand.

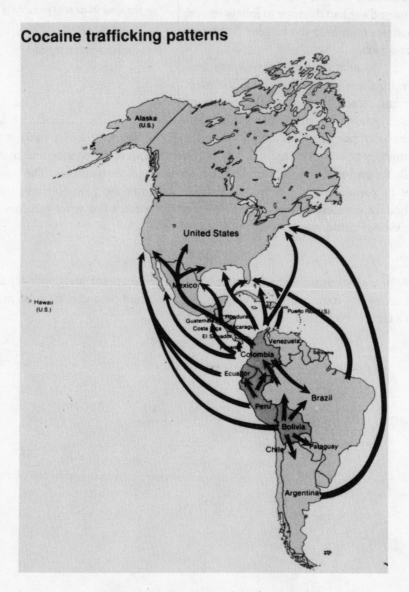

Cocaine trafficking patterns

Map courtesy U.S. Department of Justice—
or the U.S. Weather Service—the files got confused.

Consensual Crimes
Promote Organized Crime

> *You can imagine my embarrassment when I killed the wrong guy.*
>
> JOE VALACHI

MOST CRIMES with innocent victims are individual enterprises, small businesses at best. Murder, rape, robbery, assault, burglary, theft, arson, hate crimes, forgery, counterfeiting, fraud, embezzlement, buying and selling stolen property, vandalism, carrying concealed weapons, child molestation, and driving under the influence of alcohol or narcotics can usually be done by one, two, or, at the most, three people.

Supplying the needs of people who engage in consensual crimes, on the other hand, is Big Business. Drugs are the best example. Getting all that marijuana, hashish, cocaine, heroin, and other chemicals to those millions of eager users (many of whom receive home delivery) every day is a task of great planning, preparation, personnel, coordination—in short, *organization*. Because the moralists of our society have chosen to label the distribution of these obviously desired substances *crimes*, these various Big Businesses are known as *organized crime*.

The big-business, international quality of organized crime today is evident even in the name it chooses to call itself. In the early days, the various crime organizations were called *families* because they were, in many cases, extended family units. As organized crime grew into a business in which anyone could play, it became known as the *syndicate*. Today it's known as the *cartel*, a word of international scope (the Germans spell it *Kartell*, the French *cartel*, and the Italians *cartello*).

As we have seen, organized crime was first organized around a consensual crime during Prohibition. Making and distributing alcohol required breweries, distilleries, bottling plants, truck drivers, places to sell it (speakeasies), waiters, cooks, jazz musicians to entertain—it was a regular empire. When Prohibition ended in 1933, the empire was firmly in place and, with a little retooling, the empire turned to distribution of other consensual crimes: prostitution, gambling,

> *I hate this "crime doesn't pay" stuff. Crime in the U.S. is perhaps one of the biggest businesses in the world today.*
>
> PAUL KIRK
> *Wall Street Journal*

and drugs. The United Underworld Bank (loansharking), which grew into one of the largest financial institutions in America during Prohibition, continued.

The organized crime of today is nothing like the organized crime of yesterday—it's much better; therefore, it's much worse for the rest of us). Organized crime is more professional, more protected, better financed, better run, and more, well, *organized*. Organized crime competes with IBM, GM, and Sears, for law school and MBA graduates. (Based on results, IBM, GM, and Sears have not gotten the cream of the crop.) Organized crime's boats outrun the Coast Guard, their planes out fly the Air Force, their soldiers out shoot the Army, and their intelligence is smarter than the CIA's.

As Franklin D. Roosevelt observed,

> A man who has never gone to school may steal from a freight car, but if he has a university education he may steal the whole railroad.

In addition to police, judges, prosecutors, and politicians, organized crime also has on the payroll doctors, scientists, and journalists in all media whose job it is to predict and report how terrible life would be if consensual crimes were legalized. (Organized crime's very existence depends on consensual crimes remaining illegal: it remembers all the ground its forefathers lost after Prohibition was repealed.) The media people on the payroll are also to report that organized crime is on the decrease, that its influence is minimal, and that the government is doing an absolutely crackerjack job of rounding up the few minor hoodlums that remain. (*"No one* is beyond the reach of the federal authorities. Well, just look at Noriega.")

Unlike the old days, organized crime is hardly homegrown. Consensual crimes (especially drugs) have international investors. Most of the ill-gotten gains leave our shores, never to return. (Well, they *sometimes* return—when the investors buy a bank, high-rise office building, or other legitimate business.)

The heavy-handed tactics and enforcement by violence continue, of course. Some things are, well, *traditional*. Organized crime doesn't differentiate between crimes with innocent victims and crimes without. The well-oiled, well-run, well-connected machine runs just as well whether promoting a crooked investment scheme (bilking widows out of their retirement money) or importing cocaine (for obviously willing, nay, *eager* consumers). The criterion is never "Is it right?" only "Is it profitable?" The reason organized crime has stayed primarily with

PROMOTE ORGANIZED CRIME

consensual crimes is that, due to the artificially inflated prices, consensual crimes are
the most profitable.*

The flow of money, thanks to the consensual crimes, goes something like this: To
pay the outrageously inflated price of their
addiction, people steal things—from you
and me. If what was stolen is not money,
the item is taken to a fence, who pays about
ten cents on the dollar (if the item is in new
condition). The underworld resells the item
at a profit. For every $100 of merchandise

> *You can get much farther
> with a kind word and a gun
> than you can
> with a kind word alone.*
>
> AL CAPONE

stolen, perhaps $30 goes into the syndicate coffers. Then there are people who
steal money. When people steal money to buy drugs, *all of it* goes into the underworld coffers (with the exception of a few snack foods picked up at 7-Eleven). The
drug money is then laundered by a trillion-dollar international scheme of money
scrubbing, and the newly legitimized dollars are stored in Swiss bank accounts,
off-shore banks, and other places outside the United States where they cannot be
traced—or taxed.

And here is another way that organized crime hurts us: no taxation. All this
money made is, for the most part, tax free. Organized crime learned well the
lesson taught by Al Capone, who, as we mentioned earlier, was sent away for
eleven years, not for racketeering, bootlegging, or murder, but for tax evasion.
The lesson organized crime learned was not to pay *more* taxes, but to be a lot
more careful when it came to bookkeeping.

Upon the legalization of consensual crimes, some of the underground will
wallow around looking for new and better crimes to commit. Many—like the
speakeasy operators who overnight became owners of successful nightclubs
when Prohibition was repealed—will move aboveground (some by choice, some
out of necessity) and continue business as usual. For the first time in a long time,
they will be able to focus on business and not on the business of protecting
themselves from the police. The police will be able to find real criminals. The
press will be able to report on this, and we could all celebrate the cycle of economic increase and criminal decrease.

Well, I can dream, can't I?

---

*Next to drugs, the highest profitable activity of organized crime is loansharking, in which money is
loaned without collateral. If you don't pay, however, you get a visitation from Big Louie, who will
persuade you in no uncertain terms that borrowing money and not paying it back is a violation of
the Eighth Commandment. Most loan shark customers, of course, borrow money to pay the artificially inflated prices of consensual crimes. If consensual crimes were made legal, most of the demand for loansharking would dry up.

Consensual Crimes Corrupt
the Freedom of the Press

> *Whenever people are well-informed*
> *they can be trusted*
> *with their own government.*
>
> THOMAS JEFFERSON

A FREE PRESS, which leads to an informed populace, is central and essential to freedom. As Thomas Jefferson quite rightly put it, "The basis of our government being the opinion of the people, the very first object should be to keep that right; and were it left to me to decide whether we should have a government without newspapers, or newspapers without a government, I should not hesitate for a moment to prefer the latter" (January 16, 1787).

"The press" is an extremely broad term and includes all systems that make information available to people: newspapers, television, radio, books, lectures, movies, art, dance, telephone, cassettes, CDs, video discs, magazines, electronic bulletin boards, computer networks, billboards, video tapes, you name it. It's generally known as "the press" in our country because, when the founding fathers wrote freedom of the press into the Bill of Rights, the printing press was the most popular form of mass communication. Today we call it "the media."*

All of the world's major religions, philosophies, schools of political thought, and systems of government were spread through writing. In fact, the spread of civilization, religion, and the written word occurred simultaneously, each dependent on the other. The written word inspired, and the inspiration was spread to others through the written word. All of the great religions are based on a great "book"—that is, a collection of writings—even before there *were* books. The Egyptians had the Book of the Dead; the Hindus had the Upanishads; the Jews had the Torah, which included the Ten Commandments (written on *stone* by *God*,

---

*Because there is so much *talking* going on in the media these days, freedom of the press and freedom of speech have overlapped. Fortunately, both are guaranteed in the First Amendment.

> *A man has only to murder*
> *a series of wives in a new way*
> *to become known*
> *to millions of people*
> *who have never heard of Homer.*
>
> ROBERT LYND

for heaven's sake); Homer's *Iliad* and *Odyssey* told of the Greek gods; and the writings of Zoroaster, Lao-Tse, Confucius, Buddha, the Jewish prophets, and the Greek poets made the sixth century B.C. a remarkable century indeed. Without writing and the ability to circulate this writing (a "free press"), these traditions would have influenced very few and would probably be entirely forgotten today.

Christianity first spread due to a freedom-of-speech tradition in the Jewish synagogues: any adult Jewish male was free to have his say. Jesus (and, later, his various disciples) used this freedom to spread his teachings.* Although Jesus never wrote a word,** selections of what he said were written down and circulated on scrolls. These "sayings" scrolls were very popular and, considering that there was no printing back then and each had to be copied by hand, they were what we would now call "bestsellers"—sort of a *Lord's Little Instruction Book*.

After the death of Jesus, the "quote books" continued to be popular and the letters (epistles) from various church fathers were copied, widely circulated, and studied. The surviving letters of Paul make up the majority of the New Testament. Thirty years or so after the death of Jesus, the sayings books were expanded by Matthew, Mark, Luke, and, later, John into the story of Jesus that we now know as the first four books of the New Testament. Four hundred years after the time of Christ, the Bible as we know it was gathered together.

The Bible was to become the most banned book in the world. For centuries, reading the Bible was forbidden—it was said that the ordinary person could not handle the power conveyed by direct contact with God's holy word. In fact, banning the book allowed unscrupulous religious and political leaders to manipulate the populace into submission, threatening eternal damnation for disobedience.

Gutenberg's decision to use the Bible in 1455 as the first book printed on his new press is portrayed by many as an act of great faith—such a man of God to print a holy book instead of a romance novel. It was, in fact, an act of rebellion—a major statement for freedom of the press.

*There were certain risks involved in this, however. If others found what you were saying blasphemous, you could be stoned (which happened to Stephen), or, at the very least, run out of town (which happened to Jesus when he taught at the synagogue in his hometown, Nazareth).

**The only mention of Jesus writing was while figuring out how to save the adulteress from being stoned—and figuring out how to save himself as well: "They were using this question as a trap, in order to have a basis for accusing him. But Jesus bent down and started to write on the ground with his finger. When they kept on questioning him, he straightened up and said to them, 'If any one of you is without sin, let him be the first to throw a stone at her.' Again he stooped down and wrote on the ground" (John 8:6–8). What he wrote, alas, is not recorded. I like to think it was some variation of "Ain't nobody's business if she do."

Prior to Gutenberg, all Bibles were copied by hand by monks in monasteries. The Catholic church had a monopoly on the production and distribution of Bibles. Not only were they very expensive, but their distribution was carefully controlled. Buying a Bible was part of a package deal: you usually had to build a chapel to house it and hire a priest (one who could read and write) to interpret it. Like buying a computer in the 1950s, it was a major commitment.

Gutenberg changed that. His Bible was relatively cheap (by Bible standards of the day), and available to anyone who had the price. For the first time, the word of God could be read and studied without the permission or interpretation of the holy mother church. Some say that this one act of freedom of the press was the greatest single factor behind the Reformation. The Bible, religion, Christianity, and the world would never be the same.

The ink of a scholar is more sacred than the blood of the martyr.

MOHAMMED

In our own country, one book, more than anything else, was responsible for the revolutionary war: *Common Sense* by Tom Paine. This book (more a pamphlet, actually) was published in January 1776. Then, the mood in the British colonies was to continue negotiations with the mother country. A war against king and crown—the direct representatives of God on earth—was still, for many, unthinkable. *Common Sense* changed that. It sold more than 500,000 copies within a few months. That's one copy for every eight people living in the colonies.* Certainly everyone who could read back then read it. It changed people's attitudes from placation to rebellion almost overnight.

In July of 1776, no sooner had the Declaration of Independence been approved by the Continental Congress than it was "off to the press." Copies were printed and reprinted throughout the colonies, and a good number of the colonists had read and studied it by the time the official signing took place in early August. The document was widely circulated throughout Europe, where the mere possession of it in some countries was an act of treason, punishable by death. The Declaration fulfilled its intended purpose, and a nation prepared for war.

After the United States Constitution was written in 1787, it had to be "sold" to the electorate. This was done through a series of eighty-five articles—written primarily by James Madison and Alexander Hamilton—printed in newspapers throughout the land. The articles are now collectively known as *The Federalist*. Without these, it is doubtful that the radical experiment known as the United States ever would have happened. Clearly seeing the power of the press, the founding fathers

---

*This is the equivalent of a book selling more than 31,000,000 copies today. The biggest bestsellers sell fewer than two million copies in the first few months. Madonna's book, *Sex*, is considered a publishing phenomenon, yet initially sold fewer than a million copies.

> *The literature of a people must so ring from the sense of its nationality; and nationality is impossible without self-respect, and self-respect is impossible without liberty.*
>
> HARRIET BEECHER STOWE

guaranteed its complete freedom in the very first amendment they added to that Constitution.

Probably the most influential book of the entire 1800s was a novel, Harriet Beecher Stowe's *Uncle Tom's Cabin*. (The alternate title was *Life Among the Lowly*.) Published in 1852, it portrayed slaves, not as chattel or animals, but as human beings, and (gasp!) portrayed their white owner, Simon Legree, as the villain. Talk about your book burnings in the South! Of the 300,000 copies sold during the first year, who knows how many were purchased in the South *specifically* for burning. The book and its 1853 follow-up collection of factual documents, *The Key to Uncle Tom's Cabin*, did more than anything else to sway popular opinion in the North toward the abolition of slavery. Without these books, anti-slavery might never have been a major theme of the Civil War.

In 1906, a book by Upton Sinclair, *The Jungle*, took a look at the meat packing industry in the United States. A novel that was filled with many frightening and disturbing facts, *The Jungle* single-handedly changed the way all food products were processed and packaged in the United States, and made major strides toward the enactment of worker protection, specifically child-labor laws.

Radio found its stride in the 1930s, and some say that Franklin Delano Roosevelt literally talked the nation out of its depression. By the late 1930s, as storm clouds gathered over Europe (as the more dramatic histories of the day like to put it), the mood of the American people was fiercely isolationist. "No more European wars!" was the battle cry. And yet, in the late 1930s, Americans were gently prodded into taking sides by what they heard on the radio. The major protagonists in the "European War" were England and Germany. What we heard from Germany were the unintelligible sounds of a ranting lunatic followed by the lock-step masses shouting, *"Sieg heil! Sieg heil! Sieg heil!"* England, on the other hand, had the warm, gentle, sometimes roaring voice of Winston Churchill. Not only could most Americans understand what he was saying, he had a sense of humor. Surely it would be okay to lend this nice man a few boats and lease him a few airplanes. And so, lend-lease was born, and the United States was no longer officially neutral.

Edward R. Murrow, on CBS Radio, reported firsthand the devastation of German bombings on London during the blitz, which further tilted American sympathies toward the underdog, England. His voice did more to fight Hitler than probably any other. In 1954, he was to use television to take on yet another monster, Senator Joseph McCarthy and his witch hunt. "We must not confuse dissent with disloyalty," said Murrow on that historic telecast. "We will not be driven by fear into an age of unreason if we remember that we are not descended from fearful men, not from men who feared to write, to speak, to associate and to defend causes which were, for the moment, unpopular." In both instances, he risked his life; in both instances, he won. (He lost the battle with cigarettes, however, dying of lung cancer in 1965.)

In our own time (well, I suppose that depends on when you were born, doesn't it?— in *my* own time, at any rate), we saw a president toppled by a couple of reporters, Woodward and Bernstein, who inspired thousands of young people to take up investigative journalism. Then, after Woodward and Bernstein were portrayed in the movies by Dustin Hoffman and Robert Redford, *tens* of thousands swelled the enrollment of journalism schools.

> *I am entirely persuaded that the American public is more reasonable, restrained and mature than most of the broadcast industry's planners believe. Their fear of controversy is not warranted by the evidence.*
>
> EDWARD R. MURROW

⚖️ ⚖️ ⚖️

Through the media we learn about our world, our life, medical breakthroughs, scientific advances, toppling regimes, the truth about history, useful news, trivial news, useful trivial news, good news, bad news—*news.*

We rely on it, depend on it for accuracy, and, if it turns out to be inaccurate, we expect some other news organization to do an exposé of the exposé.* Freedom of the press is a fundamental right, up there with freedom of speech and freedom of and from religion. A free press is not a luxury; it's a necessity.

How do consensual crimes corrupt our free press? Several ways.

First, since committing a consensual crime is breaking the law and since breaking the law is news, reporters are often sent out looking for video on drug busts or stories on who is sleeping with whom and whether they're married to someone else and whether they're paying or getting paid for it. In the end, none of this has much to do with our lives (certainly not in the way that murderers, rapists, robbers, polluters, price-fixers, and bribe-takers do). So, like the police, courts, and prisons, the reporters' time and the media's space are filled with fluff. And not very interesting fluff at that. (You've seen one drug bust on television, you've seen 'em all.)** There's plenty of international tension, domestic issues, real crime, corruption, and consumer activism to keep every reporter and his or her place of reporting busy, productive, and of service to the community. There *might* even be a little time to dig up some *good* news.

*So, when an overanxious producer at NBC News is filming the test crash of a GM truck and gives the crash a little "extra added realism" by planting a remote-controlled exploding device, one expects the other media to blow the whistle on NBC—especially if GM wins a lawsuit about it. GM did, and the other media did. Ah, a free press.

**"From the American newspapers," Lady Astor wrote, "you'd think America was populated solely by naked women and cinema stars."

Secondly, since consensual crimes are not based on hurting others, but on religious interpretations by a handful of moralists, a good many journalists have been turned (some willingly, some not) into professional gossips and busybodies. Gossip is fine, gossip is entertaining, but it belongs more on "Entertainment Tonight" and bestseller lists than it does on any of the network evening newscasts. "The things most people want to know about," wrote George Bernard Shaw, "are usually none of their business." Did Gary Hart *really* deserve to lose all of his political credibility because he took a boat ride with a young beauty? Mr. Hart's wife did not object; his ocean-going companion did not object; one must assume Mr. Hart himself did not object. To quote a television commercial of roughly that same time frame: "Where's the beef?"* Was this one seagoing sexual misadventure really sufficient grounds to completely ignore everything *political* about him, everything this man stood for, spent a lifetime building, and was doing a fairly good job at bringing to the arena of public discussion? Gary Hart was sacrificed to a group of yapping moralists who claim that "an adulterer" is not fit to run for president. The yapping was served up by a "free" press bound by the chains of delivering late-breaking scandals with photos, video, and sound bites if at all possible. And what did the American people get? A truly dull campaign: Dukakis versus Reagan. Yawn. As Jay Leno observed, *"Dukakis is Greek for Mondale."*

Third, just as when cops need some easy collars and round up some consensual criminals, so, too, reporters—when there's dead air to fill or an article to file—go out and round up some consensual crime stories. Need some quick video? Take a female reporter, put her in some fishnet stockings and a dress cut low enough to reveal her journalistic integrity, have her walk the streets with the streetwalkers, and follow her with a hidden camera. (The camera could even be hidden in a van marked ACTION NEWS and you'll still get good video—men are terribly unobservant when their testosterone is raging.) If you *really* want ratings, put a male reporter in the same costume and situation. Want to turn that chapter in your novel or that scene in your screenplay about the evils of drug addiction into a Pulitzer—or at least a story you'll get paid for? Just quote a few government statistics and preface all your fictional quotes with such comments as "well-placed sources say . . ." "a well-known dealer who refused to be identified by name . . ." or "anonymous undercover

---

*I *think* that commercial happened at about the same time as Gary Hart's quickly aborted presidential campaign. I cannot be sure. History for me is broken into four phases: (1) before I was born, (2) from the time of my birth until now, (3) now, and (4) has it happened yet? I do know that both Gary Hart's being caught in adultery—not quite in the act, but at least in the yacht—and that dear lady asking "Where's the beef?" happened some time during Phase 2.

sources claim . . ." and *voilá:* unbelievable fiction becomes believable "nonfiction."

Finally, as with police, journalists should regain the respect they are entitled to. Reporting a lot of "trash for cash" has tarnished the good name of reportage. Remember when Walter Cronkite, as the anchor of an evening newscast, was considered "the most trusted man in America"? Why not return to those thrilling days of yesteryear? It wasn't just Walter Cronkite; Huntley and Brinkley were well respected.

> *A free press*
> *is not a privilege*
> *but an organic necessity*
> *in a great society.*
>
> WALTER LIPPMANN

Brinkley's still at it, saying wonderfully honest things, such as "The one function that TV news performs very well is that when there is no news we give it to you with the same emphasis as if there were." There are, of course, other contemporary examples: Hugh Downs, Larry King, John Chancellor, and Bill Moyers.

The press not only cheapens itself by playing tattletale and reporting the consensual exploits of others; it also "eats its young" by reporting on the consensual activities of its own. An absurd example of the latter involves an attractive female "reporter" who invited Larry King up to her hotel room, which just happened to have more hidden cameras than Allen Funt's bathroom. Well, the tape went on and on *and on,* and Mr. King made nary an improper move. But, dull as it was, they showed the tape anyway. After all, Larry King is a star; there's air time to fill; and, even if he didn't do anything, it will make a great teaser: "Larry King follows our reporter up to her hotel room! What happens then? Tune in tonight and find out!" (Although I don't remember the name of the show, why do I have the sneaking suspicion it was on Fox?* "All the networks are struggling now with their desire to put on live executions, if they could, to get the ratings," said Gary David Goldberg; "I think the difference is that Fox would put on naked live executions.")

We're entitled to a free press, and the press is entitled to be free from rumor-mongering and reporting on the latest scandal from Gossip Central.

Later, in the chapter, "Pornography, Obscenity, Etc.," we'll explore how censorship even more directly corrupts the freedom of the press.

---

*I checked. It was Fox.

Laws against Consensual Activities
Teach Irresponsibility

> *If you want a Big Brother,*
> *you get all*
> *that comes with it.*
>
> ERIC FROMM
> *Escape From Freedom*

IRRESPONSIBILITY IS as old as mankind—literally. When God asked Adam, "Have you eaten from the tree that I commanded you not to eat from?" Adam answered, "The woman you put here with me—she gave me some fruit from the tree, and I ate it." Note the dual layer of irresponsibility: Adam blames not only *Eve;* he also blames *God* for putting her with him.

Irresponsibility is as old as womankind, too. After God heard Adam's rational lies, he turned to Eve and asked, "What is this you have done?" And Eve responded, "The serpent deceived me, and I ate." (Modern translation: "The devil made me do it!") It seems that the buck never stops in Eden. It's amazing that the serpent didn't blame its upbringing, claim it was high on drugs, or simply plead insanity. At the very least, it could have argued that it was only following its religious beliefs. But responsible or not, God punished them all, and so here we all are today.

One wonders how the world might be different if Adam and Eve had the personal responsibility of, say, Janet Reno. Attorney General Reno, although she had far more legitimate-sounding excuses than Adam and Eve ("I've only been in this job a month," "This was all going on before I got here," "This was all done by conservative Republicans to discredit the new administration," or, "The FBI made me do it"), took full responsibility for the Waco, Texas, tragedy. What if it had been Janet Reno who ate of the forbidden fruit?

GOD: Have you eaten from the tree that I commanded you not to eat from?
RENO: Yes.
GOD: Did anyone put you up to it?
RENO: I am entirely responsible for eating the forbidden fruit.
GOD: Why did you do this?

> *The real freedom of any individual*
> *can always be measured*
> *by the amount of responsibility*
> *which he must assume*
> *for his own welfare and security.*
>
> ROBERT WELCH

RENO: I was acting on the best information I had available at the time.

GOD: What information was that?

RENO: I understood that my eyes would be opened and then I would be like God. I admire you so much, naturally I wanted to be like you.

GOD: Are you trying to flatter me?

RENO: Yes, I am responsible for that action. The statement is, nonetheless, true. I'm sorry that I disobeyed you. In retrospect, I can see it was a mistake. I will do everything within my power to see to it that a similar mistake does not happen again.

GOD: Well, all right. I see you've learned a lesson, and I guess that's what life's about. You can stay in the garden, but don't let it happen again.

RENO: I'll do my best. Thank you, sir.

Did you ever notice how *disarming* it is when people take full responsibility and how *irritating* it is when they blame? If people spent half as much mental energy finding a way to keep an unfortunate occurrence from happening again as they spend on finding reasons why (a) what happened wasn't so bad, or (b) "I had nothing to do with it," the world would be a lot better off.

Responsibility is often confused with *blame*. When someone asks, "Who's responsible for this?" people often hear, "Who's to blame for this? Who can we punish?" More accurately, responsibility means that we are willing to accept the *consequences* for the choices we make. The unwillingness—and for some it appears to be a congenital inability—to accept the consequences for choices is the definition of childishness and immaturity.

When children make a bet and lose, they get out of it by saying, "I had my fingers crossed!" So many of the explanations adults give to justify their behavior sound just as silly.

No sooner was the term *victimless crime* coined than every scalawag, rascal, and down-and-dirty crook used it out of context to justify his or her genuinely criminal behavior. Michael Milken, for example, paid a public relations agency $150,000 *per month* to transform him from criminal to victim. The goal, as James Stewart explains in his book, *Den of Thieves*, "was to turn public opinion from outrage to neutrality to acceptance, and finally to admiration." How did the PR people do this? By claiming Milken's legion of crimes, which caused plenty of innocent people to suffer, were victimless crimes. Because he didn't use a gun or a lead pipe, the PR firm did its best to convince the public that a crime without physical *violence* is also a crime without innocent *victims*. This, of course, is nonsense, but with $150,000 a month and a few gullible journalists, you can fool some of the people some of the time. After the concept that Milken's transgressions were victimless crimes was swallowed by enough of the press and public, the PR agency made it look as though *he* were the victim. (No wonder some people hate the term *victimless crime.*) "The campaign was remarkably effective," reported Stewart, and the *Christian Science Monitor* lamented, "This episode demonstrates once more how modern public relations can manipulate public opinion. Some of the press, sadly, was sucked in by the blather."*

Responsibility also means the *ability* to *respond:* no matter what happens to us, there's always some response we can make. The response is sometimes external, some-

> *We have not passed that subtle line*
> *between childhood and adulthood*
> *until we move*
> *from the passive voice to*
> *the active voice—that is,*
> *until we have stopped saying,*
> *"It got lost,"*
> *and say, "I lost it."*
>
> SYDNEY J. HARRIS

times internal, often both. Even when one's external options are severely limited, one can choose to respond to them internally in productive and even uplifting ways. In his book, *Man's Search for Meaning,* Viktor Frankl recounts his experiences in a Nazi concentration camp. Subjected to physical horrors beyond imagining, Frankl learned that although he was not responsible for where he was or what was happening around him, he *was* responsible for his *reaction* to the events around him. He discovered this was a personal freedom the Nazis could not take away.

> The last of the human freedoms—to choose one's attitude in any given set
> of circumstances, to choose one's own way.

But in our society, these courageous examples of responsibility and personal freedom are seldom discussed. We always seem to be on the lookout for *who's to blame?* Somehow, we think, if we can prove it's someone else's *fault,* it will make everything "all better." Somehow we believe that Life will comfort us in its arms, like a nurturing parent; if we can only prove we had nothing to do with our injury, we will receive extra strokes. "The tree made me fall out of it."

"Did the tree make you fall? Did it push you out?"

"Yes. It pushed me!"

"Oh you poor thing. That bad tree. Shall we chop it down?"

"Yes! Let's chop down that bad tree!"

We seem to be seeking from life a giant parental "Oh, you poor thing." Although such comments may be momentarily comforting, they do very little to teach us to climb trees better.

In eternally looking for someone or something outside ourselves to blame, *we turn*

---

*This from *Den of Thieves:* "The securities laws were implemented to help protect that process [of rewarding merit, enterprise, innovation, hard work, and intelligence], to guard the integrity of the markets and to encourage capital formation, by providing a level playing field on which everyone might pursue their fortunes. Violations of the securities laws are not victimless crimes. When insider traders gain windfall stock profits because they have bribed someone to leak confidential business secrets, when prices are manipulated and blocks of stock secretly accumulated, our confidence in the underlying fairness of the market is shattered."

> *A man must pay the fiddler.*
> *In my case it so happened that*
> *a whole symphony orchestra*
> *often had to be subsidized.*
>
> JOHN BARRYMORE

ourselves into victims. We begin to believe that we are powerless, ineffective, and helpless. "There was nothing I could do," people whine, as an affirmation of their powerlessness, rather than, "What could I have done?" This self-victimization erodes our character, our self-esteem, and our personal integrity. We begin to believe that we cannot do—are not able to respond. Irresponsibility makes us increasingly irresponsible.

⚖ ⚖ ⚖

The idea that certain consensual activities should be crimes supports and helps to create irresponsibility. The idea behind consensual crimes is that the government—like a great, caring parent—will protect us from the bogeyman, the wicked witch, and inhospitable trees. "We have thoroughly investigated everything," the government assures us, "and you will be safe as long as you don't do these things." To make *sure* we don't do those things, the government locks up everyone who attempts to lead us into temptation and, as an example, puts a few bad boys and girls away. (A multi-year version of "Go to your room!")

If we accept the view that government is the Great Protector, then it logically follows that whatever the government does *not* prohibit is, therefore, okay. If the government is so concerned about our safety that it will put people in jail for doing certain things, all the things that the government will *not* put people in jail for must be safe. If the government doesn't think an activity is harmful enough to make a law against, then it must be relatively harmless. As we have seen, this is not the case.

Each of us is unique. We have our own set of needs, wants, tolerances, reactions, strengths, weaknesses, abilities, strong points, and weak spots. Some people are deathly allergic to wheat, while others can chew double-edged razor blades. (I saw it on a newsreel once. Eeeeee!) Few people fit within the "norm" on absolutely everything. To be *perfectly* normal is abnormal.

Government-set standards for personal behavior are based on the average, what's true for most people. By making the norm the law, the government encourages us not to explore our own strengths and limitations, but to adapt and fit in as best we can to the norm. The strength and power of the diversity within us are never fully explored. Our depths are never plumbed and our heights are never scaled. We are not taught to learn from our mistakes, only to blame others for them. We don't discover what *responses* we are able to make, therefore, we never become truly responsible.

This limitation creates a double danger: We may avoid the currently illegal consensual activities that may be, for us, a component of our health, happiness, and well-being. On the other hand, we may blithely indulge in perfectly legal consensual activities that cause us great harm. At the very least, this double jeopardy is unsatisfying. At worst, it's deadly.

Once we realize things aren't going so well, we either wake up and start exploring our response options (which is difficult, because there's little in our cultural programming to support such action), or we decide we aren't playing society's game fully enough and begin looking "out there" for the solution to our dissatisfaction with even more vigor.

> *You can get Dozie Doodles without a prescription. They can't do you any harm.*
>
> LAURA PETRIE
> *"The Dick Van Dyke Show"*

We look for ways in which the world is "doing it to us," and, boy, do we find them. As Jimmy Carter was kind enough to point out, "Life is not fair," and, if we look for unfairness, unfairness will be found. The harder we look, the more we find.

Some people become professional victims. They complain and sue their way to riches. "I saw a little lawyer on the tube," sings Joni Mitchell, "He said, 'It's so easy now, anyone can sue. Let me show you how your petty aggravations can profit you.'" In Framingham, Massachusetts, a man stole a car from a parking lot and was killed in a subsequent traffic accident. His estate sued the parking lot owner, claiming he should have done more to keep cars from being stolen. Does one smell a RAT (Reasonable Attorney Transaction)?

If people leave your house drunk and become involved in an accident, you can be held responsible, even if they *insisted* upon leaving. If people are drunk and leaving your house, what are you supposed to do? Tackle them? Mace them and grab their keys? Shoot them, for their own protection and the protection of others?

In his book, *A Nation of Victims*, Charles J. Sykes gives more examples:

> An FBI agent embezzles two thousand dollars from the government and then loses all of it in an afternoon of gambling in Atlantic City. He is fired but wins reinstatement after a court rules that his affinity for gambling with other people's money is a "handicap" and thus protected under federal law.

> Fired for consistently showing up late at work, a former school district employee sues his former employers, arguing that he is a victim of what his lawyer calls, "chronic lateness syndrome."

On the other extreme, another group of people use their well-honed victim-finding mechanism to help other (often unwilling) people discover how they are screwing up their lives. "The busybodies have begun to infect American society with a nasty intolerance—a zeal to police the private lives of others and hammer them into standard forms," wrote Lance Morrow in his *Time* essay, "A Nation of Finger Pointers." He continues,

> Zealotry of either kind—the puritan's need to regiment others or the victim's passion for blaming everyone except himself—tends to produce a de-

pressing civic stupidity. Each trait has about it the immobility of addiction. Victims become addicted to being victims: they derive identity, innocence and a kind of devious power from sheer, defaulting helplessness. On the other side, the candlesnuffers of behavioral and political correctness enact their paradox, accomplishing intolerance in the name of tolerance, regimentation in the name of betterment.

The irony is not lost on our British brethren across the sea, from whom, two-hundred-and-some years ago, we broke in the name of liberty. "[There is] a decadent puritanism within America:" the *Economist* reports, "an odd combination of ducking responsibility and telling everyone else what to do." Britain—that suppressor of liberty—is, ironically, far freer with regard to consensual activities than the we're-going-to-have-a-revolution-for-freedom United States.

⚖ ⚖ ⚖

Two of the basic common-sense rules of personal behavior are: (1) Make sufficient investigation before taking part in anything and (2) If you consent to do something, you are responsible for the outcome. Laws against consensual activities undermine both rules of responsibility.

The situation is unfortunate but, hey, let's be responsible about it. We can't spend too much time blaming consensual crimes for irresponsible attitudes. "I'd be a responsible person if it weren't for consensual crimes!" That's irresponsible.* Whatever degree of irresponsibility we may have, let's be responsible for it.

The existence of consensual crimes is a problem to which we are *able* to respond. Let's work to change the laws, and, until then, in the words of Sergeant Esterhaus of "Hill Street Blues," "Let's be careful out there."

---

*How about a new TV show: "That's Irresponsible!" Each week people appear and tell their victim stories. The most irresponsible victim is named the winner (by some genuinely unfair process) and gets to choose from among three prizes. Whichever prize is chosen, the contestant gets a different one. The prize, of course, is shipped so that it arrives broken. And then, after the contestants tell all their friends to watch, the show never airs.

Laws against Consensual Activities
Are Too Randomly Enforced
to Be Either a Deterrent or Fair

> *We simply do not catch*
> *a high enough percentage of users*
> *to make the law a real threat,*
> *although we do catch enough*
> *to seriously overburden*
> *our legal system.*
>
> JACKSON ELI REYNOLDS
> *The Washington Post*

THE PERFECT LAW is one which, when broken, is followed by immediate punishment. This punishment follows in all cases, in all situations, every time the law is broken, no matter what.

A perfect example of such a law is the law of gravity. Each time we violate the law of gravity, the consequences are immediate and consistent. If you drop something, it falls—every time. The law is not suspended for your birthday, religious holidays, or because you have friends in high places. What do we do when a law is so absolute and ruthless? We obey it and we forget about it.

Learning to obey the law of gravity is not easy. Observe the struggle children have learning to walk and to hold things without dropping them. Once these skills are learned, we forget about the struggle and, in fact, we forget about the law. If you slip and fall, what do you blame? The crack in the sidewalk? The ice? The banana peel? People who have learned to be more responsible don't blame things outside themselves. They say, "I wasn't looking where I was going," "I wasn't careful enough," or "I lost my balance." The truth is that, when you slip and fall, the thing that made you fall was *gravity*. When a plane crashes or an expensive vase hits the ground, the cause is gravity. And yet, we never read a headline that says, "GRAVITY KILLS 137 IN AIRLINE CRASH."

Nature is full of such laws: keep breathing; stop bleeding; if you're in King Kong's hand and he's halfway up the Empire State Building, don't do anything to upset him. Violating these laws has immediate negative consequences, and the violator is increasingly encouraged to return to the fold of abiding by the law.

An example of a human law might be "when you're in your car, drive on the roads." When driving a car on something other than the roads, one soon discovers

> *The growth of drug-related crime is a far greater evil to society as a whole than drug taking. Even so, because we have been seduced by the idea that governments should legislate for our own good, very few people can see how dangerously absurd the present policy is.*
>
> JOHN CASEY

impassable terrain, impenetrable barriers, and angry gardeners, making further forward movement impossible.

And so it is with crime. The more likely one is to get caught, the less likely one is to commit a crime.

There is, for example, a greater chance of being arrested and convicted for robbing a bank than for robbing a retail establishment, and a greater chance of being caught robbing a retail establishment than robbing a home. Criminals know this, which is why more homes are robbed than retail establishments, and more retail establishments are robbed than banks. But even house burglaries are kept in check because every burglary has an innocent victim—the owner of the house—and the crime usually gets reported to the police.

Consensual crimes, however, by definition, have no innocent victims. If you smoke a joint or visit a prostitute or place a bet with a bookie, neither you nor the prostitute nor the bookie is going to call the police to report the "crime." Each time a person takes part in a consensual crime, there is only a *miniscule* chance that person will be caught—or that the crime will even be reported to the police. Thus, the deterrent factor in consensual crime is almost entirely missing.

For every consensual crime arrest, there are millions of undetected, unreported, and unpunished occurrences. Some say the answer is to beef up law enforcement, make more arrests, and put 'em all "behind bars where they belong." It's just such statements—bristling with ignorance and arrogance—that have gotten us into the mess we're in now. If *every* person who *ever* committed a consensual crime were put behind bars, there would be more people behind bars than in front of them.

"Make the punishments more severe! Set an example!" That doesn't work either. Even historically, when consensual crimes were punished more severely than now—by flogging, dismemberment, burning at the stake—the incidence of consensual crimes was not abated, nor did harsh punishment "set an example" for the youth. It sometimes made the consensual crime all but irresistible. "If people risk *torture* for it," many concluded, "it must be pretty terrific."

Each time you get in the car, there is a statistical chance you will be injured, disabled, or killed. If you *knew* that one of these was going to happen on a particular day, the chances are good you wouldn't drive that day. Not knowing on what day it *might* occur, however, you get in your car and drive off, thinking about where you're going and what to listen to along the way, not about death on the highway. Each time someone takes part in a consensual crime, there is chance—a statistically slim chance, but a chance—that he or she will be arrested, tried, and sentenced to prison. It is a such a small chance, however, most people don't even think about it.

If the chance of punishment is so slim, why even write this book? One of the reasons (the one being discussed in this chapter) is fairness to those who are unlucky enough to be in the wrong place at the wrong time.* Most traffic accidents happen in the same way: someone was in the wrong place at the wrong time.

The pain and suffering heaped upon this minuscule, random sampling, the few unfortunates who happen to be caught partaking in a consensual crime, *can* be eliminated overnight through legislation. We need only repeal the laws that put them in jail in the first place and grant a general amnesty for those who fell on the short side of the odds.

> *The ultimate result*
> *of shielding men*
> *from the effects of folly*
> *is to fill the world with fools.*
>
> HERBERT SPENCER

---

*Another reason is to draw the line against the watchdogs (perhaps I should say, pit bulls) of everyone else's morality.

Laws against Consensual Activities
Discriminate against
the Poor, Minorities, and Women

> *Bear in mind this sacred principle,*
> *that though the will of the*
> *majority is in all cases to prevail,*
> *that will to be rightful must be*
> *reasonable; that the minority*
> *possess their equal rights, which*
> *equal law must protect,*
> *and to violate would be oppression.*
>
> THOMAS JEFFERSON
> 1801

IF YOU HAVE LOTS OF MONEY, you can pretty much take part in consensual crimes with impunity. A middle-class person runs more risk than a rich person, and a poor person runs the greatest risk of all.

Rich people have drugs delivered by a reputable dealer who supplies "pure" drugs of uniform strength. Middle-class people go to fairly reputable dealers who usually sell, out of their apartments, drugs of varying degrees of purity and potency. Poor people go to crack houses where a purchase is made through a slit in a door; the dealer is completely unknown; the impurity and impotence of the drug is almost guaranteed; and customers are lucky to get out of there alive. In addition, crack houses established for more than a week are well known to both police and crooks. The crooks know that everybody going to the house has money; the police know that everyone leaving has drugs. On the way in, the crooks ask for a small donation (oh, 100%) of your drug money (and, if you have it on you, your rent money, food money, and season-tickets-to-the-Philharmonic money). On the way out, the police arrest you.*

As it is with drugs, so it is with all the consensual crimes. With prostitution, the rich can afford expensive, exclusive escorts; the middle class deal with relatively safe call girls; and the poor with hookers on the streets. For legal gambling, the rich can fly to Atlantic City, or Las Vegas. The middle class enjoy poker clubs or Las Vegas Nights at the local church; and the poor are stuck with buying

---

*Police, in quest of their monthly quota of collars, have been known to wait outside crack houses and arrest, one after another, the customers as they exit. Like an anteater outside the main opening of an anthill, they arrest their fill. Some police districts intentionally allow popular crack houses to remain in business because the customers are such easy pickings for officers in need of meeting their collar quota.

> *He didn't know the right people.*
> *That's all a police record means*
> *in this rotten crime-ridden country.*
>
> RAYMOND CHANDLER

lottery tickets at the supermarket (which, as we shall see in the chapter on gambling, have worse odds than even the most crooked gambling casino).

Across the entire spectrum of consensual crimes, the poor have less selection, lower quality, more arrests, and a far higher danger of being the innocent victims of genuine crimes.

As we explored in the last chapter, consensual crimes are sporadically enforced. This type of arrest pattern invites a law enforcement officer to act on his or her personal prejudices, especially cultural stereotypes. The prosecutor, judge, and jury will—sometimes subconsciously—go along. "Blacks and Hispanics use drugs." "Provocatively dressed women are prostitutes." "Effeminate men are homosexuals." And on and on.

All of this accounts for the outrageously disproportionate arrest rates between rich and poor and between whites and blacks. According to the 1991 Uniform Crime Reports, 58% of the drug arrests were of whites versus 41% for blacks; 45% white arrests for gambling, and 47% black arrests for gambling. For prostitution, 60% white, 38% black. Vagrancy, 51% white, 47% black. This sounds evenly distributed until you consider that, in 1991, blacks composed only 12% of the U.S. population. Does this mean that blacks are more crime prone than whites? No. For a crime where there really is an innocent victim, driving under the influence of drugs or alcohol, 89% of those arrested were white, only 9% black. Other liquor law violations show whites on top: 87% versus 10%. Public drunkenness was 81% white, 16% black. This means that on a per capita basis, roughly the same number of blacks as whites were arrested for driving under the influence of alcohol or narcotics or other liquor violations. On the other hand, also on a per capita basis, three times as many blacks were arrested for drug abuse than whites.

This uneven enforcement tends to support the belief held by the poor and nonwhites that the police are there to protect the rich and the white at the expense of the poor and nonwhite. The uneven enforcement increases distrust and even contempt among the poor and nonwhites for all law enforcement. In these racially troubled times, it is a rift that we can ill afford.

Edwin M. Schur observed in his book, *Victimless Crimes,*

> The uneven impact of actual enforcement measures tends to mirror and reinforce more general patterns of discrimination (along socioeconomic, racial and ethnic, sexual, and perhaps generational lines) within the society. As a consequence, such enforcement (ineffective as it may be in producing conformity) almost certainly reinforces feelings of alienation already prevalent within major segments of the population.

Alcohol is used by 17% more whites than blacks (all these figures are on a per capita basis), and alcohol, society says, is fine (and legal). Marijuana is used once a week or more by twice as many blacks as whites, and marijuana, we're told, is bad. Cocaine is used by almost three times as many blacks, and we're told cocaine is just terrible. Blacks use heroin four times more often than whites and, well, heroin is so bad (we've been told), we don't even consider it.

On the other hand, hallucinogens are used by three times more whites than blacks, and we don't worry much about hallucino-

> *Because law enforcement resources have been concentrated on the street drug trade in minority communities, drug arrests of minorities increased at 10 times the rate of increase for whites.*
>
> LOS ANGELES TIMES

gens at all. How many peyote busts have you seen on "COPS!"? Who was the last politician who promised to "Get tough on mushrooms"? When was the last time you were warned that LSD would ruin your chromosomes? Whites use nonprescribed (illegal) tranquilizers 50% more often and stimulants twice as often as blacks, and we hear very little about these "dangers."

Wouldn't it be better for all classes of society—economic, ethnic, racial, sexual, and religious—to agree that physically harming the person or property of another is simply wrong, immoral, and will not be tolerated by rich, poor, black, white, or anyone else? Isn't this the basis of a saner, freer, more solid society?

Due to consensual crimes, we are raising a generation that believes anything is right as long as you get away with it. This philosophy is as foolish and unthinking as Hemingway's "What's moral is what you feel good after," and far more dangerous. We need to establish an agreed-upon foundation for our social morality. As I'm sure you've guessed, my nomination is: "Do what you will, just don't physically harm the person or property of another."

Those who wish to sit smugly by, expecting police to ram the "proper" moral values down the throat of every "heathen, infidel, and low life," may find that the heathens, infidels, and low lifes are, to quote Paddy Chayefsky, as mad as hell and not going to take it any more. If for no other reason than to protect their own person and property, those currently in power should allow others to do whatever they please with *their* person and property.

If the arrests for consensual crimes were proportionately spread among the middle class and the rich, they wouldn't be crimes for long. The outrage one feels and the action one is liable to take when an injustice strikes oneself, close friends, or family (especially one's *mother*), is much more likely to become action of repeal than when one simply reads a cold statistic in a book about consensual crimes.

Women

Although there are more women than men in this country (women make up more than 51% of the population), women account for only 23% of the arrests made, and, of all people currently in prison, less than 6% are women.

At best, this means that women are more honest, peaceful, and law-abiding than men. At worst, it means that women are too smart to get caught. Whatever the reason, it's clear that men are, unquestionably, the criminal element in this country.

The crimes for which women *are* arrested, however, are more likely to be consensual crimes.

Of all the crimes in the federal government's Crime Index (murder, manslaughter, rape, robbery, aggravated assault, burglary, larceny-theft, motor vehicle theft, and arson) the one women are most likely to take part in is larceny-theft. For the most part, it does not involve stealing from individuals, and, except for purse-snatching, does not involve violence.* Women are three times more likely to commit larceny-theft than all the other crimes in the Crime Index combined (although men still commit more than twice as many larceny-thefts as women). Factoring out this one crime, women commit less than 11% of the Crime Index crimes reported.

By comparison, 17% of drug arrests are of women, and almost 34% of the women in jail are there for drug offenses (compared with 22% of the men). In fact, there were more drug arrests of women than arrests of women for murder, manslaughter, rape, robbery, aggravated assault, burglary, motor vehicle theft, and arson combined. More than 20% of the arrests for that catch-all consensual crime, "disorderly conduct," are women. And, not surprisingly, more than twice as many women are arrested for prostitution than men (the only crime in which women outnumber the men.)**

Women not only commit fewer crimes; the crimes they commit tend to be crimes without innocent victims or, at worst, crimes without *individual* victims. Women seem to have an intuitive sense about crime that harms others and crime that does not. Consequently, enforcement of laws against consensual activities strikes more heavily against women than against men. Perhaps this is why the song, "T'aint Nobody's Biz-ness If I Do," seems to be recorded more often by women than men.

---

*This does not mean to excuse these crimes, or to pretend that they are consensual crimes—they are not. It does, however, indicate that when women turn to crime (often as a method of paying artificially inflated drug prices) they choose crimes with the *least* amount of physical harm; crimes that spread the financial loss among the largest number of victims.

**Although prostitution is obviously an activity that requires two people—a buyer and a seller—and although, technically, both are considered equally wrong in the eyes of the law, when the female seller is arrested, the male buyer is often let go. Another reason more women than men are arrested is that most prostitution arrests are often made by male undercover vice cops, who arrest but are not arrested themselves.

Meanwhile, women are more likely to be the innocent victims of *real* crime (rape, obviously, and crimes such as purse-snatching, for which there is no male equivalent), than are men, and the police—diverted to catching consensual criminals—leave women unnecessarily unprotected.

If plainclothes police officers went to high-crime areas and protected women rather than high-vice areas and arrested women, we'd *all* be a lot better off.

If we accept and acquiesce in the face of discrimination, we accept the responsibility ourselves. We should, therefore, protest openly everything . . . that smacks of discrimination or slander.

MARY McLEOD BETHUNE

Problems Sometimes Associated with Consensual Activities Cannot Be Solved While They Are Crimes

NO ONE WILL DENY that the reason some people take part in consensual crimes is personal problems. No one will deny that taking part in consensual crimes can also create or exacerbate problems.

As long as certain consensual activities remain illegal, it is difficult for people who take part in those activities to know whether or not they have a problem (a bad relationship) with that activity.

It wasn't until after Prohibition was repealed, for example, that people began to face up to their drinking problems. Those for whom drinking was a problem were—then as now—a small percentage of the people who drank; had Prohibition continued, most of them probably would never have faced their problems. Complete abolition automatically creates its opposite: complete abandon. When both were removed from the subject of alcohol, people could see clearly where they fell on the spectrum of "normal" alcohol consumption. Prohibition ended in 1933; the first chapter of Alcoholics Anonymous was founded a few years later. Had the cultural stereotype that everyone who drinks is a hopeless drunk, and the counter-cultural hero (the more you drink in one sitting, the better person you are), not been eliminated by Prohibition's repeal, it's doubtful that Alcoholics Anonymous would have gotten off the ground.

As long as drugs, for example, are illegal, it's hard to say to a friend, "You might have a problem here," without sounding like a bad drug-education commercial. People taking drugs have become immune to criticism: there's so much criticism, and so much of it is nonsense. (Please see the chapter, "Education, Not Legislation.") "Drug education" seems to be developed by people who know nothing about drugs. It's propaganda and justifications, not education. People taking drugs simply stop listening—even to their friends. This is not the case with, say, alcohol. Yes,

> *When we remember*
> *we are all mad,*
> *the mysteries disappear*
> *and life stands explained.*
>
> MARK TWAIN

alcoholics tend to deny they have a problem (denial is a symptom of addiction), but alcoholics cannot wrap themselves in the garb of the social martyr: "*My* only problem is that drugs are *illegal.*"

Among social groups where most drugs are equally available and equally acceptable, some people have been able to see that they have a problem. This has led to the growth o f Cocaine Anonymous, Drugs Anonymous, Potsmokers Anonymous, Narcotics Anonymous, the Betty Ford Clinic, and the many drug treatment centers.

Some people don't know why they take part in illegal consensual activities, other than they're not going to let any damn busybodies tell them what to do. As St. Augustine wrote in his *Confessions* (circa A.D. 398),

> Near our vineyard there was a pear tree laden with fruit that was not attractive in either flavor or form. One night, when I [at the age of sixteen] had played until dark on the sandlot with some other juvenile delinquents, we went to shake that tree and carry off its fruit. From it we carried off huge loads, not to feast on, but to throw to the pigs, although we did eat a few ourselves. We did it just because it was forbidden.

If the "forbidden fruit" temptation were removed, people could choose to take part in a consensual activity or not—as they do now with alcohol—based on risks and merits of the activity itself. When consensual activities are illegal, it's hard to tell if the motivating factor is (a) simple rebellion, (b) the need for recreation, or (c) a deep-seated difficulty.

Problems are caused when the balance is off, when the relationship with something (often ourselves) is not good. When activities are prohibited, it's difficult to look at that balance; it's hard to explore the relationship. The laws against consensual activities hide the potential problems from the people who need to know about them most: the people who take part in the activities.

If one doesn't realize he or she has a problem, one cannot get effective treatment. (Being "sentenced" to a treatment center does very little good except, possibly, to keep someone out of jail.) Solving a problem takes personal commitment, and that commitment comes through recognition. Keeping consensual crimes crimes, blocks that recognition.

In the words of Shakespeare, ". . . all are punish'd."

Laws against Consensual Activities Create a Society of Fear, Hatred, Bigotry, Oppression, and Conformity; a Culture Opposed to Personal Expression, Diversity, Freedom, Choice, and Growth

> *The soft-minded man always fears change. He feels security in the status quo, and he has an almost morbid fear of the new. For him, the greatest pain is the pain of a new idea.*
>
> MARTIN LUTHER KING, JR.

MOST HUMAN BEINGS fear change. Dislike of the new, the different, the out-of-the-ordinary seems to be instinctual. This makes sense: prehistoric humans found that a new animal might try to eat them, a strange vegetable might poison them, or a differently dressed human might try to kill them. Safety lay in sameness, predictability, the status quo.

This view of safety naturally led to the demand for conformity within the group. It started with children who—for their own survival—were taught to eat certain foods and to avoid others, play with certain animals but stay away from others, walk in certain areas but avoid others. As children grew, they learned the cultural taboos: what to wear and what not to wear, what to say and what not to say, what to do and what not to do.

In some cases, the tribal taboos were practical—avoiding certain wild animals, for example. In other cases, they were not. A watering hole may have been off limits simply because an elder saw a wild beast there many generations before and declared it taboo. This taboo continued even though the wild beast hadn't been there in years. An important source of water was lost to the entire tribe just because a wise elder once suggested one day, "Stay away from that watering hole."

Enter the nonconformists. There have always been a small percentage of humans who found sameness, predictability, and the status quo *boring*. They balked at conformity. They wanted newness, difference, risk. What most of the tribe called danger, they called adventure. What most saw as fearful, they saw as exciting. They were the explorers, the experimenters, the eccentrics.

These nonconformists had a mixed reputation in the tribe. Some discovered new territories, techniques, and modes of behavior beneficial to the entire tribe.

> *Idiot, n. A member of a large*
> *and powerful tribe*
> *whose influence in human affairs*
> *has always been*
> *dominant and controlling.*
>
> AMBROSE BIERCE

Others put the entire tribe in danger by their stubborn refusal to coöperate. The former became the heroes; the latter became the villains. Before the heroes became heroes, however, they went through a phase of *seeming to be* villains: they took part in—and later advocated—change, and (as the majority would say) we all know *instinctively* that change is not a good thing.

And so the minority favoring change has led the majority, kicking and screaming, into the future.

And this is as it should be. Society needs the majority of people to maintain the status quo; consistency is necessary to grow things, build things, and raise children. An adventurer might plow a field and plant a seed, then become hopelessly impatient a week later when that seed fails to bring forth fruit. So the adventurer is off to a new field, planting a new seed. The conformist who stays by the planted seed for a season has the benefit of the harvest. Will and Ariel Durant, in their *History of Civilization*, say that history is like a fast-moving river, ever changing, bringing along the new, moment by moment. Civilization, however, happens on the banks of the river where the vast majority of humanity live, watching the river go by, building their houses, planting their crops, raising their children.

A healthy society needs a balance between the new and the old, between change and keeping things the same, between trying something different and maintaining tradition. If change happens too quickly, there's no time to see if the *previous* change is working. If change doesn't happen quickly enough, a society stagnates and begins persecuting the very adventurers who could have led it to a new and better place.

A perfect example of too much change too soon was the aftermath of the French Revolution. From 1793 until 1800, France was ruled by *government du jour.* As Peter Weiss described it, "Years of peace, years of war, each one different than the year before." That was the trouble: no new form of government had a chance to work. It was toppled, its leaders beheaded, and a whole new form of government was put in its place. After a dozen or so attempts at "democracy," the French welcomed the dictator Napoleon with open arms. He brought what France desperately needed: law, order, and a sense of continuity.

An example of not changing quickly enough is the story of Jesus. He brought to an embittered people—burdened by a tradition of killing and a thirst for vengeance—precisely the thing they needed most: the concept of forgiveness. *Forgive* in Aramaic (the language Jesus spoke) is *shaw.* It means, "to untie." Jesus was asking these people to untie themselves from the beliefs, traditions, and practices that, although they worked in the past, were no longer serving them. He also brought them the good news that the kingdom of God—for which they had so patiently waited—was *at hand;* there was no need to wait any more. Where was this kingdom of God? Not "out there" or "up there." The "kingdom of God is within," he told them.* Well, all of this was entirely too radical, so they killed him. (We'll explore this further in Part IV, "Consensual Crimes and the Bible.")

ϟϟ ϟϟ ϟϟ

> *The doctrine of
> the Kingdom of Heaven,
> which was the
> main teaching of Jesus,
> is certainly one of the
> most revolutionary doctrines
> that ever stirred and
> changed human thought.*
>
> H. G. WELLS

How can we tell, as a society, which side of the balance point we are on, whether we're permitting too much or persecuting too much, whether we've gone too far in the direction of change or gone too far in the direction of conformity?

An excellent indicator is a society's attitude toward consensual crimes. Let's take a look at two proposals, both considered "different" based on our current cultural norms. One is "The best way to receive is to take—by force if necessary"; the other, "The best way to receive is to give—even if it means giving everything you own." Neither of these positions will have the majority of our society flocking to them. Most Americans would not voluntarily practice either. And yet, in a healthy society, the practice of one of these philosophies should be illegal and the practice of the other should not.

Let's say that each philosophy has a particularly charismatic leader. Two new groups find their way on to the American scene: the Takers and the Givers. The adherents of each group believe what they believe with fanatical, almost religious devotion. *Time* and *Newsweek* do cover stories, and "60 Minutes" does a special two-hour episode ("120 Minutes"). The leader of the Takers says that Americans have gotten too soft, that the basic natural principle of survival of the fittest has been eliminated. Our gene pool is polluted. We will die as a society if we don't do something soon. We must put survival of the fittest back into our daily lives. The solution? If you want something, take it. If the people who own it can successfully defend it, they get to keep it. If the people taking it successfully take it, it's theirs—until they are defeated by another Taker. This would get the fat off of humanity *fast.* We would become strong, lean, and powerful once again.

The leader of the Givers maintains that energy is a flow, and the more you give, the more can flow back to you. If you feel you don't have enough, it's not because you need to *take;* it's because you need to *give.* Humanity is in trouble because we have not accepted the natural principal of giving practiced by the sun which gives us light, the trees which give us fruit, and all the other plants which

*Luke 17:21.

> *We are all full of weakness
> and errors,
> let us mutually pardon
> each other our follies—
> it is the first law of nature.*
>
> VOLTAIRE

give us oxygen. We have taken too much; it's time to give. And the more we want, the more we should give. If we want it all, we should give all that we have away.

As an example, the leader of the Takers takes a car, takes over a house ("If you can't defend your own house, you don't deserve to live there"), and takes—against their will—two or three attractive women as "his own." ("If their husbands want them, they can come and get them.")

The leader of the Givers, by way of example, gives away everything he owns and, whenever he is given something, immediately gives that away too. Even when given food, he eats only a few bites and gives the rest away.

From the point of view of society, who should be put in jail? One? Both? Neither? Acting purely to protect society, it's the leader of the Takers whose behavior should be restrained: his actions are physically harming others.

The actions of the Givers' leader are potentially only harming himself. He may give everything away, his philosophy may be flawed, and he may get little or nothing in return. His followers who likewise give everything away are also potentially hurting no one but themselves. If the philosophy fails, there will be sufficient examples that reveal it as a failure, and the vast majority of society will not follow suit.

The Takers, however, can do a great deal of harm to others before their philosophy is proven unworkable. Long before people learn it's awfully inconvenient and very expensive to go to the grocery store in a tank (and to make sure that your tank is bigger than everyone else's tank), society has a right to defend itself from a minority of people involved in an experiment that hurts unwilling others.

Two radical points of view, and yet it's appropriate for society to move in and stop, by force, one, and, conversely, to practice tolerance of the other. What's the difference? One has innocent victims, the other does not. Both involve change. Both may be uncomfortable to observe. But in one case, the change physically harms unwilling others, and in the other, the change only potentially harms those who voluntarily take part in it. Society has the right to defend itself from theft, rape, and violence; society does not have the right to defend itself from mental or emotional discomfort.

From an enforcement point of view, it's very easy to tell when the Takers have crossed the line: when they take without the owner's permission. How does one set laws, however, against the Givers? Pass a law saying that no one is allowed to give anything anymore? That you cannot give away more than 25% of your net worth? That before you give anything away you must prove to an official of the state that giving it away will not negatively affect your well-being? (These suggestions may sound absurd, but take a look at the wording of some of the consensual crime laws.)

Further still, without an innocent victim, who's going to complain? "She gave me five dollars, officer! Put her in jail!" Without a victim, it's highly unlikely that most of the "crimes" committed by Givers would ever be brought to justice. In order to catch them, the police would have to go undercover, pretending to be people in need, waiting for some gullible Giver to give something away. Then the whole question of entrapment arises. Is a Giver guilty of a crime only when the Giver gives unsolicited, or is the Giver also guilty when the receiver has asked? These are fine legal points—precisely the ones that come up in the apprehension and trial of consensual criminals every day.

> *Let us forget such words,*
> *and all they mean,*
> *as Hatred, Bitterness and Rancor,*
> *Greed, Intolerance, Bigotry.*
> *Let us renew our faith*
> *and pledge to Man,*
> *his right to be Himself,*
> *and free.*
>
> EDNA ST. VINCENT MILLAY

Meanwhile, all those Takers out there are taking, and the police are so busy entrapping the Givers that there is no time to arrest very many Takers. The police, then, are so busy protecting the Givers "from themselves" and from setting a "bad example" for the rest of society, that the innocent victims of the Takers, who are *genuine victims,* get taken.

⚖️ ⚖️ ⚖️

When society protects itself from change too enthusiastically, it robs itself of the new information, ideas, and behaviors that might make for a healthier, more productive, happier society. When most people's natural fear of the new is supported by law, the law justifies the fear, thus institutionalizing prejudice against anything different. ("It's against the law; it must be wrong; my fear is right.") When religious leaders rummage about the Bible for "scriptural proof" that the prejudice is justified (and, as we shall see, you can prove *anything* by selectively quoting the Bible), then the prejudice is enshrined in holiness. "The law says it's bad; God says it's bad; I feel that it's bad; therefore, it's bad."

An attitude such as this *demands* conformity. "How dare you go against what the law, God, and I know to be *true?*" In our culture, we've been asked to walk an increasingly narrow line which shows us what we can and cannot put in our bodies, whom we can and cannot love, what kind of sex we can and cannot have, how we can and cannot heal ourselves, the recreational activities we can and cannot take part in, what version of God we can and cannot worship, and how we can and cannot worship.

The message clearly is, "Morality, our way, *or else!*"

We create a culture in which people are incapable of free choice because the culture doesn't allow one to gather enough information to make a choice. Experiments in and discovery of viable lifestyle alternatives are replaced by a list of should's, must's, have-to's, you'd-better's, and don't-you-dare's. Some people have the feeling their choices in life are as limited as that of a child being asked, "Do you want to go to bed now, or five minutes from now?" Sure, there's a choice, but it's an awfully narrow one.

☙ ☙ ☙

We are not permitted to grow up. America has become a Never-Never Land in which the citizens are promising to be good little boys and girls in exchange for the government, like good parents, protecting them from every evil, fulfilling every need, and making every major decision for them. And the government-authorized religious beliefs (authorized by the laws the government chooses to enact) tell us what to do while we're here and how to insure a happily ever hereafter.

The repression created by suppressing consensual activities has a "trickle down" effect: "If these activities can get us put in jail, what about this much longer list of behaviors that are also disapproved of by the people who hold the jail keys?" We have become a nation of individuals afraid to explore, afraid to try new things, afraid to be different. Consequently, we never fully discover, much less fulfill, our individual dreams, our hearts' desires. Our individual strengths, talents, and abilities are never developed; we sacrifice the better part of ourselves in order to be the way we "should" be, and both we and society as a whole suffer because of it.

We deprive ourselves of the best political leaders because we maintain this pretense that our leaders should somehow be "perfect"—perfect as defined by the keepers of conformity. Thank heavens that this narrow-mindedness is loosening up. Kennedy was a Catholic; Carter had "lust in his heart"; Reagan was divorced; and Clinton smoked pot.* Yes, the times, they are a-changing. If it had been Kennedy who admitted to smoking pot—even being in the same *room* as pot—in 1960, Nixon would have been "the one" to have had the affair with Marilyn Monroe.

Alas, the times (that is, *we*) are not changing quickly enough. The fishbowl world, in which *everything* a candidate *ever* did is fully exposed, has run ahead of our acceptance for things people do that do not physically harm the person or property of another. The press's ability to tell us "what's so" has outstripped the

---

*Shortly after the famous "I smoked pot but I didn't inhale" statement, Clinton admitted that he was "as dumb as a mule-post" to make such a foolish remark. Yes, he inhaled. Dave Barry parodied this in *his* run for president on Larry King's show: "Yes, I injected the needle into my vein, but I never pushed the plunger!" Paul Krassner remarked in *The Realist,* that the official presidential song could become "Inhale to the Chief."

American public's ability to respond, "So what?"

Gary Hart had a tryst on a boat called *Monkey Business*, apparently with his wife's permission. So what? Jimmy Swaggart enjoys entertaining prostitutes (or vice versa) in cheap motel rooms. So what? Jerry Brown practices eastern religions and is rumored to practice bisexuality as well. So what? Jim Bakker seemed to like dallying with both sexes (as though his sexual ambiguity was not clear from his choice of wife). So what?

> James Bryce wrote his classic study
> of the United States,
> _The American Commonwealth,_
> in the 1880s.
> One of the chapters is titled,
> "The Best Men Do Not
> Go Into Politics."
>
> JOHN CHANCELLOR

Of the above list, it was only Jim Bakker's misappropriation of church funds that made him an unworthy leader—that was a crime with many innocent victims. All the rest are consensual crimes (including Bakker's multi-gender escapades) and don't affect their leadership abilities one bit.

We have, then, people who are afraid to take leadership positions because some incidents from their pasts are sure to be judged by the moralists. Or we get leaders who are so dull—or so good at covering their tracks—that no taint of nonconformity is possible; example: George Bush. We may be getting the leaders we deserve, but not the best available.

⚖ ⚖ ⚖

Ironically, our society's insistence on conformity hurts the very institutions which it is designed to protect. When we attempt to force everyone into a certain set of behaviors, beliefs, or activities, those very behaviors, beliefs, and activities become eroded and diluted by the people who don't truly want to behave, believe, or act in that way, but are merely doing so out of fear that doing otherwise would "cost them."

Take marriage, for example. Most consider this a highly desirable institution, one in which they look forward to spending the majority of their lives. Some, however, go along with Mae West, who agreed that it was a great institution, but added, "I'm not ready for an institution yet." To force people into marriage who do not want to get married hurts the individual being forced to marry, his or her spouse, any children they may have, and the institution of marriage itself.

If a man is gay and is strongly encouraged to marry because marriage will "cure" him, not only is he harmed, but, because he is not providing the love and support one who spontaneously desires to marry would have, his wife and children are harmed too. The same is true of a heterosexual man or woman whose primary passion in life is his or her career. Our culture attempts to force *everyone* into marriage, like it or not ("You'll learn to like it"). That's why half the marriages end in divorce within five years; it's not a breakdown in morality: it's the

> *This may sound terribly selfish,*
> *but I love the freedom that I have.*
> *I don't have to worry*
> *about a man's wardrobe,*
> *or his relatives,*
> *or his schedule,*
> *or his menu,*
> *or his allergies.*
> *I would not be married again.*
>
> ANN LANDERS

attempt to *force* a particular morality upon everyone. If only the people who naturally wanted marriage married each other, and the people who wanted to do other things felt free to do them, then everyone—and the institution of marriage—would be much better off.* This is true of just about every area of human endeavor—education, personal growth, and even (perhaps especially) religion.

If people do not freely choose to take part in something based on an inner need, desire, or, at the very least, curiosity, the power of the institution is diluted, its purpose diffused, and its future in question. *For the good of the institutions we want to preserve*, we must stop forcing people into them by social pressure, coercion, and—especially—force of law.

⚖ ⚖ ⚖

A society that punishes people simply for being different, for exploring the rich diversity of human experience, for experimenting with alternate lifestyles—as long as that being, exploration, and experimentation does not physically harm the person or property of another—is a society condemned to pettiness, vindictiveness, crushing conformity, oppression, decay, and ultimately death. A society that tolerates or, preferably, *celebrates* diversity, exploration, and experimentation—again, keeping in mind the limitation of not physically harming the person or property of another—is strong; its citizenry is mature, responsible, able to make rational choices; it is a society that is dynamic, creative, and alive.

---

*This "everyone must be married and have children" nonsense hits women particularly hard. Programmed by society to believe that they aren't "truly women" until they are married and have successfully reproduced, those who choose to pursue a career other than motherhood can go through some difficult emotional times. Men can biologically postpone the decision to breed until much later in life. In their early thirties, women hear the biological timeclock ticking (which, due to the pressures of society, sometimes sounds like a biological timebomb). Men don't even *start* to hear the ticking until they're well into middle age (which men have convinced themselves is somewhere around fifty-five, which is hardly middle age—how many 110-year-olds do you know?). Well, at least (thank heavens) the term *old maid* has dropped from the vocabulary.

AIN'T NOBODY'S BUSINESS IF YOU DO

PART III

HOW DID
CONSENSUAL CRIMES
BECOME CRIMES?

How Did Consensual Crimes Become Crimes?

> *The trouble with most folks*
> *isn't so much their ignorance,*
> *as knowing so many things*
> *that ain't so.*
>
> JOSH BILLINGS

THE LAWS AGAINST CONSENSUAL activities—intrinsically unfair—are rooted in the darker side of human nature. Fear, anger, paranoia, prejudice, power-seeking, paternalism, infantilism, pettiness, vindictiveness and self-righteousness are seldom counted among the highest forms of human expression.

This chapter is not the history of consensual crime; it is a review of the underlying causes of consensual crimes, and of the primary forces that keep the laws against consensual activities firmly in place.

Religion

Ironically, the very institution that should, in theory, inspire human beings toward higher levels of experience and expression—religion—too often panders to humanity's baser instincts in order to have *its* laws become *everyone's* laws. Misguided religions—nearly all of them Christian denominations—have created a situation in which we, as a society, can destroy the lives of four million people each year—not just with impunity, but with a sense of righteous enthusiasm. It's the Crusades, the Inquisition, and the Salem Witch Hunts not just *again*, but *still*.

In condemning those who misuse "Christianity," I want to make it very clear that I am *not* condemning Jesus Christ. He did not teach hatred, suppression, or hypocrisy. In fact, he spoke out against them at every opportunity. Jesus taught love, healing, and tolerance. This is Christianity. Some Christian *religions*, on the other hand, too often preach intolerance, forced conformity, and hatred. (As promised, we will explore this phenomenon in detail in the next section of the book, "Consensual Crimes and the Bible.")

I am not saying that religion is *only* a dark force in our country. Far from it.

> *Nobody can deny but religion*
> *is a comfort to the distressed,*
> *a cordial to the sick,*
> *and sometimes a*
> *restraint on the wicked.*
>
> LADY MARY WORTLEY MONTAGU
> (1689–1762)

Religion can and does inspire both individuals and the nation to greater expressions of love, compassion, and generosity. Ministers signed both the Declaration of Independence and the Constitution. Religion was a major force behind the abolition of slavery. Since the formation of our nation, religious groups have fed the poor, cared for the sick, and condemned injustice. In our own time—from Baptist minister the Reverend Dr. Martin Luther King, Jr., to Catholic nun Mother Teresa—men and women of faith have been beacons of caring, giving, and positive (albeit uncomfortable) social change. Like human nature, religion has its light side and its dark side. The darker side of religion is primarily responsible for laws against consensual activities, and it is the dark side I condemn. If I had the eloquence of Shakespeare, I might say to those religions, "Throw away the worser part of it, And live the purer with the other half."

Nor am I saying that religion is the *primary* dark force in this country; *greed,* in my estimation, is the winner of that award. Greed is the motivation behind most *non*consensual crimes. But this is a book about consensual crimes, and when it comes to legislating morality, the strongest voices are found emanating from religion, religious people, or ideas of limitation that originated in religion.

The darker side of human nature is contained in the human *animal* more than it is in the human *being* or the human *spirit.* Please keep the following facts about animals in mind:

Animals can be trained. Dogs do not naturally stand on their hind legs wearing tutus, howling on pitch to a recording of the Mormon Tabernacle Choir singing "The Battle Hymn of the Republic." David Letterman has made a fortune bringing such Stupid Pet Tricks to the American public. At first they seemed strange, even cruel, but, in time, we grew to like them. We're trainable.

Animals can be tricked. Think of the donkey after the carrot, the hamster on the wheel, and the press believing in 1962 that it wouldn't have Nixon to kick around anymore.

Animals are easily intimidated. Animals in the wild seem to be afraid of nearly everything—and rightly so: each animal is part of some other animal's all-you-can-eat smorgasbord.

Animals are easily infuriated. If an animal can't escape, it will attack. Some animals attack even if they *can* escape. This is not only how they get their jollies; it's also how they get their dinner.

Animals are reflexive. Animals are not known for *thought;* they are known for *instinct.* The primary instincts of animals are (a) to eat, (b) to avoid being eaten, and (c) to mate. The higher animals also instinctively protect their young. (When they're no longer young, however, they become just other competitors for [a] and [c].)

Animals have short memories. "I have the attention span of a hummingbird," wrote novelist Christopher McMullen. Most animals have enough trouble remembering the basics of food-finding, not being found as food, finding a mate, and protecting their young to remember much else. Even in these four basic areas, animals are remarkably forgetful. A squirrel, for example, forgets where it buries most of its nuts.

> *The shepherd always tries to persuade the sheep that their interests and his own are the same.*
>
> STENDHAL

These qualities of the animal kingdom are well known and well used by the manipulators of the world. Madison Avenue may have made manipulation a science, but religion—long before there was Madison Avenue, Madison, or even science—made manipulation an art. "How can we more effectively manipulate souls to God?" seems to be the primary question religious leaders discuss when they get together and talk shop. Not that manipulation—in the form of persuasion—is a bad thing; it's when manipulation becomes *legislation* that the trouble begins.

Getting individuals to do good (as good is defined by religion) for getting to heaven, for knowing God, or for goodness sake, is a perfectly legitimate use of persuasion. It's when people are told to do good (again, as defined by religion) *or else* (and the government has within its power a great deal of *or-elseness*), that persuasion becomes perverted. The law is perverted, society is perverted—and religion itself is perverted.

Fear and Anger

As humans, we are—like it or not—stuck in animal bodies which had to survive and evolve, as animals, for millions of years. Anything remotely resembling culture has only been around for the past few thousand years. What we might call the "higher functions"—the thought and behavior that separate humans from the rest of the animal kingdom—take place, for the most part, in the portion of the brain that, evolutionarily, developed last.

Most of us don't have to go back too many generations to find ancestors who had to fight or flee *for their lives* on a regular basis. The ones who fought and/or fled most successfully lived to fight and/or flee another day. More importantly (in terms of *us*), they lived to reproduce another night. In the scheme of natural selection, the fight or flight response—being necessary for survival—survived.

This *fight or flight response* (as scientists call it) survives—nay, thrives—in us today. It is an automatic, inborn response. When we perceive danger, or even

> *Few people can be happy unless they hate some other person, nation, or creed.*
>
> BERTRAND RUSSELL

potential danger, the body prepares itself to either *fight* or *flee* for its *life*. The senses scan the environment, looking for what might be wrong; the brain focuses only on the potentially bad or harmful; adrenalin pours into the blood; blood rushes to the skeletal muscles; we become tense, alert, and *ready*.

The two primary emotions of the fight or flight response are *anger* (fight) and *fear* (flight). In the days of our ancestors, these emotions were necessary for survival. Today, they are the most limiting emotions we have.*

We call anger by a lot of names—ire, dudgeon, wrath, temper, rage, fury, offense, indignation, umbrage, pique, huff, tiff, fume, bitterness, resentment, hostility, exacerbation, hard feelings, spleen, gall, bile, bad humor, enmity, animosity, ill will, bad blood, virulence, acrimony, acerbity, exasperation, irritation, annoyance, vexation, aggravation, displeasure, dissatisfaction, discontentment, disapproval, disapprobation; being pissed, steamed, and ticked off.

Fear also has a lot of aliases—anxiety, shyness, nervousness, dread, fright, terror, horror, panic, alarm, dismay, consternation, trepidation, apprehension, misgiving, uncertainty, mistrust, distrust, qualm, worry, concern, cowardice, timidity, hesitation, cold feet, second thoughts, phobia, foreboding, solicitude, and the creeps.

Feeling fear goes back to childhood programming; for children it was quite appropriate. Young children don't know the difference between drinking milk and drinking poison, between playing on the playground and playing in the street, or between playing with the nice neighbor's poodle and the nasty neighbor's pit bull. Parents, in all loving, teach their children not to do anything new. The feeling of excitement that arises whenever we're about to try something new we are trained to call fear, and we are trained not to do the new thing.

Naturally, being inquisitive children, we do a lot of the new things anyway. When we are caught, we are punished. Then we experience *guilt*. Guilt is the anger we feel at ourselves for having done what we know we shouldn't have done. These are the two feelings that make us so resistant to change—fear before the change and guilt after.

---

*Fear is, in fact, the energy to do our best in a new situation—but that is not how we are programmed to treat it. We are programmed to treat fear as a reason *not* to do anything new. Anger is simply the extra energy necessary to make physical change in the external world. Unfortunately, we have been programmed to use this energy merely to "sit and seethe." We can, of course, reprogram ourselves, but it takes a lot of work. For some suggestions on doing this, please see two of the books I co-authored with John-Roger, *You Can't Afford the Luxury of a Negative Thought* and *DO IT! Let's Get Off Our Buts*.

Unfortunately, when we're old enough to distinguish between what is genuinely harmful and what is merely new and exciting, no one draws us aside and says, "Fear is really the energy to do your best in a new situation. It's energy for action. After you've established that something is not going to be physically harmful, then use the energy to *do*, not as a reason for not doing."

So, we go through our lives not doing the things that we really want to do—we are adults, following programming appropriate for children. Because of fear, we often don't pursue the careers we want, the relationships we desire, the social changes we'd like to see, or the spiritual goals we seek.

People feel fear about many of the consensual activities that are now crimes because participating—or even accepting someone else's participation—in them represents a change in lifestyle or attitude. Many people believe that if they're afraid of something, there should be a law against it. When fear becomes truly profound, it's called *paranoia*.

> *Everybody comes from*
> *the same source.*
> *If you hate*
> *another human being,*
> *you're hating part of yourself.*
>
> ELVIS PRESLEY

Paranoia

Paranoia is not only fear of what *is*, but of what's *not*. Here, I'm not referring to paranoia in the clinical sense, as in paranoid schizophrenic, but to the paranoia we all feel from time to time.

An aspect of paranoia, fundamental to its existence, is known as *delusions of grandeur*. If I fear that an entire group of people is out to get me, I've made the underlying assumption that *I'm worth getting*. The self-importance that underlies paranoia, in reality, is just as illusionary as the imagined threat itself. People huddle in little groups (sometimes tens of millions strong) proclaiming that "our way of life is being threatened" by one or another of the consensual crimes. This implies, on one hand, that their "way of life" is important enough for a group to organize against it, and, on the other, that their "way of life" is in desperate need of defending. This is the nature of paranoia—delusions of persecution built upon delusions of grandeur; the key word, of course, is *delusions*.

Paranoia often slithers through our brain in sentences beginning, "What if?" ("What if I go to the party and don't meet anybody? What if I meet four people and can't make up my mind who to talk to? What if the one I like best doesn't like me? What if I get a flat tire on the way home?" "What if, while I'm waiting for AAA, a band of thieves robs me of everything, including my self-respect?" With enough what-ifs, we conclude, "I don't think I'll go to the party after all.")

> We must never forget that
> if the war in Vietnam is lost
> the right of free speech
> will be extinguished
> throughout the world.
>
> RICHARD M. NIXON
> October 27, 1965

We tend to repeat some variation of this monologue whenever we contemplate anything *new.* Anytime *change* is in the wind, fear begins flapping its wings. As humans, we seem to like change—to a degree. Then we call fear, *excitement.* When the change is more than we're comfortable with, we call it fear. When fed by the what-ifs our mind produces in seemingly endless profusion, fear can grow to a full-fledged attack of paranoia. People then usually decide to "keep things the way they are."

When it comes to consensual crimes, it's easy to see how paranoia puts these crimes on the books and keeps them there. In sifting through the various "truths" reported about consensual crimes, I found that the vast majority are nothing more than paranoid delusions repeated often enough to become generally believed. John Kenneth Galbraith explained the process as it happens, in miniature, in our nation's capital:

> Washington politicians, after talking things over with each other, relay misinformation to Washington journalists, who, after intramural discussion, print it where it is thoughtfully read by the same politicians, who generally believe it. It is the only successful closed system for the recycling of garbage that has ever been devised.

As the child fears a shadow on the wall, thinking it's a spider, society holds on to its cultural fears supporting the laws against consensual activities even though these fears are simply not supported by fact.*

These mutually-agreed-upon, handed-down-from-generation-to-generation, inaccurate-but-nonetheless-believed fears have another name—*prejudice.*

Prejudice

Prejudice means to pre-judge something. Unlike paranoid fears, which we are fully capable of creating for ourselves, prejudice is usually learned. It is added to one's own paranoia, then taught to others.

Prejudice relies heavily on stereotypes and generalities. *All* people in a certain group do a certain thing, and that thing—*as we all know*—is wrong. Therefore, all the people in that group deserve to be avoided, set apart, disliked, despised, feared, closely watched, mistrusted, abused, repressed, suppressed, persecuted, and prosecuted.

Prejudicial beliefs are supported by such vague and sweeping arguments as "it's common knowledge that . . .," "everybody knows that . . .," "we all agree that . . .,"

---

*Fear is a disease which *can* be spread by telephone, newspapers, television, radio, books, political speeches, church pulpits, etc.

"all right-thinking people agree that . . .," "it's been known for generations that . . .," and so on.

Many people invite God in at this point and begin quoting the Bible out of context, or quoting the conclusions of others who have quoted the Bible out of context. They declare that something is wrong, bad, evil, and wicked because "God doesn't like it, and, if God doesn't like it, then all good people should work hard to get rid of it." At this point, they say, it becomes not only one's moral duty, but also one's *spiritual* duty, to avoid, condemn, repress, and punish.*

> *I don't like principles.*
> *I prefer prejudices.*
>
> OSCAR WILDE

As we all know—and it has even been scientifically proven—all prejudiced people are heartless, cold, calculating, cruel, hypocritical, reprehensible bigots. They deserve to be drummed out of our society just as they have driven out of their society everyone *they* didn't like. Turnabout, after all, is fair play. What goes around comes around. God wants us to love one another, so let's get rid of all these hateful people so that we can love one another without interference.

See? I'm doing it: trying to teach you to be prejudiced against prejudiced people. Then, of course, a more enlightened group may come along and teach us to be prejudiced against people who are prejudiced against prejudiced people. The cycle never ends. In fact, many prejudiced people are very good people. They have just been miseducated, ill taught, or, to use a more technological term, improperly programmed. The ignorance passed down from generation to generation was never challenged.

Another important aspect of prejudice is that it tends to become a self-fulfilling prophecy. If it is believed that a certain group of people are dishonest, then no one will hire them, and, without jobs, they are forced to turn to dishonest activities in order to make a living. Then the statistics are rolled out that *prove* this group of people is, indeed, more dishonest than another group (who are able to get jobs, because they are believed to be honest).

⚖ ⚖ ⚖

"The first Law of Journalism:" wrote journalist Alexander Cockburn, "to confirm existing prejudice, rather than contradict it." Journalists, talk radio hosts, and television reporters—knowing that pandering to prejudice sells—quote statistics out of context ("Statistics don't lie, but liars use statistics.") and play on emotional

---

*Few people who quote the Bible as a justification for their prejudices have actually read the Bible, much less studied various books of the Bible in their historical and cultural context. When the Bible is used in this way, what one believes the Bible says is nothing more than another prejudice.

heartstrings in an illogical, but, alas, convincing way.

They will, for example, show a mother—a child on each knee and one in her arms—tearfully describing how the man she married was an ideal husband and father until drugs (or gambling, or prostitutes, or another man) came along, and now she hasn't heard from him in three months, and her babies need shoes because winter is coming. This is intercut with scenes of the finance company evicting the mother and her three children from their house, the eldest daughter being refused entry to kindergarten because she couldn't afford crayons, and the mother standing in line at a federally funded bulk cheese distribution center. At this, the television reporter, microphone held high, looks directly into the camera, and says, "Drug use (or gambling, prostitution, homosexuality): a consensual crime? I think not!" The reporters who like to think of themselves as *balanced* end the piece with: "Drug use (or gambling, prostitution, homosexuality): a consensual crime? *You decide.*" Presented with that steaming pile of prejudicial "facts," what *can* one decide? The "thoughtful viewer" concludes, "I came to the decision *on my own* that drug use (or gambling, or prostitution, or homosexuality) is *not* a consensual crime."

No one ever asks the logical questions: If this husband had left his family because he was bored, should we ban boredom? If he had run off with his neighbor's wife, should we then ban heterosexuality? Neighbors? Neighbor's wives? If he went off to become a missionary spreading God's holy word to a spiritually impoverished area such as Beverly Hills, should we then ban religion? In fact, people leave people all the time, and those left behind often suffer. When husbands march off to war, we praise them. When they run off with a whore, we blame them. (*And* blame the whore for "leading the man into temptation.")

Rare is the journalist who will take the risk and attack the ignorance *behind* the prejudice. For the most part, when someone has the courage to say, "The emperor wears no clothes," he or she is more often ridiculed than rewarded.

⚖️ ⚖️ ⚖️

Inherent within all prejudices are smaller prejudices that keep the larger ones in place. One of the greatest of these sub-prejudices is "Anyone who attacks the prejudice is just as bad as—if not worse than—the object of the prejudice." A close variant of this is, "Whoever defends the thing I'm prejudiced against must *be* one!" If you are, for example, a drug user, publicly defending drug use is an invitation to surveillance and arrest—an invitation few law enforcement agencies can refuse. If you are *not* a drug user, why go through all the trouble of being thought of as one?

It's no wonder that popular prejudices stay so *popular.*

After a while, prejudices take on the patina of time. They become *traditional.* They become the *values* of a culture. When challenging age-old popular prejudices, one appears to be challenging *traditional values.* This is potentially life-threatening work; few people take part in it.

Few have the clarity of vision, sense of purpose, and unbridled courage of, say, Martin Luther King, Jr. On the night before

> *Any frontal attack on ignorance*
> *is bound to fail*
> *because the masses are always*
> *ready to defend their most*
> *precious possession*
> *—their ignorance.*
>
> HENDRIK VAN LOON

he was assassinated for challenging the "traditional values" of racism and segregation, he said,

> I just want to do God's will. And He's allowed me to go to the mountain. And I've looked over, and I've seen the promised land. So I'm happy tonight. I'm not worried about anything. I'm not fearing any man.

Power

People who persecute consensual criminals out of prejudices are, in a certain sense, innocent. They do it because they *genuinely believe* the persecution is right. (They are *not* innocent, of course, in that they fail to take the time to personally investigate the facts behind the prejudices and form their own conclusions.)

There is a more nefarious group of people, however, who knows—to one degree or another—that the prejudices are not based on fact, and yet continue to wave them about anyway in order to protect or enhance their power or the power of their group.

It's hard to believe, for example, that all the televangelists who quote the Bible haven't read the passages immediately preceding and following the portions they quote to justify suppression of consensual activities. Reading these passages in context renders most of the televangelists' "proof" illogical and absurd. And yet, they quote out of context anyway.

Most politicians know that there are far more serious problems facing this country than consensual crimes. They know, however, that—in certain areas, in front of certain groups—they will get more votes by dragging out the popular prejudices to which people respond with knee-jerk hatred and fear.

Here, fear and anger are used at their manipulative best. Televangelists get more contributions, politicians get more votes, newspapers get more readers, radio gets more listeners, and television gets more viewers when they can whoop up the fear and hatred of the populace. Everyone in the public eye knows this technique, and many shamelessly pursue it.

Power is one of the most addictive drugs around. No one wants to give it up. Even if they *do* want to give it up, they don't because they—or the people who have power over *them*—are already hooked.

Paternalism

The benign use of power is *paternalism*. Power seeks for greedy, self-serving ends. Paternalism seeks to be an all-pervasive parent, protecting its children from any possible danger, foolishness, and even discomfort.

> *Many people never grow up.*
> *They stay all their lives*
> *with a passionate need for*
> *external authority and guidance,*
> *pretending not to trust*
> *their own judgment.*
>
> ALAN WATTS

Frankly, paternalism scares me more than raw power-grabbing. People on power trips know what they want and, when it becomes increasingly difficult for them to get it, they tend to back off. There's always another day and another way. They're pragmatic. It's only business.

People who think of themselves as the all-loving parents of helpless children are *expected* to make self-sacrifices. They don't stop in their "persecution of evil" when the going gets rough—in fact, rough-going often inspires them to greater, more desperate acts. Outer resistance is a sign that progress is being made; it is also a rallying call for that great Universal Paternal Energy (provided by Mother Nature and available to all Good Parents in time of need).

Paternalism says, "I know what's good for you better than you do and I will use force, if necessary, to get you to do some things and not do others." The first part of that statement, "I know what's good for you better than you do," may or may not be true. The person assuming the role of parent may or may not know what is or is not best for the "child."

When paternalists are trying to control other adults, this I-know-what's-good-for-you-in-all-situations attitude is a form of arrogance. The *actual* experience of parenthood generally leads parents to conclude, "I don't know *what* the hell's going on." Children seem to grow into whatever they grow into—like plants. Having a child is like planting a seed—except that you don't know what kind of seed you've planted. You water it; green things start coming out of the ground; you help the plant grow up healthy by continuing to water it (supply its needs) and give it sunlight (love), but you can't determine what kind of fruit it will bear. If it's a radish, it's a radish; trying to turn it into a tomato plant won't work—even if you firmly believe that tomatoes are better than radishes. Treating it like a tomato plant isn't going to help. No matter what you do to a radish plant, you'll never get it to grow tomatoes. And, if you're too obsessed with tomatoes to care for the plant as it truly is, you might not get radishes either.

There is no way you're going to get a football player out of a child destined to be Barry Manilow's biographer. One can imagine Ronald Reagan's consternation when his only son, Ronald, Jr., told him he wanted to be a ballet dancer. In time, however, Papa Reagan attended, with pride, his son's premiere performance. This is what tends to happen—children who go their own way, regardless of parental disapproval, produce something of which the parents are eventually proud. ("Look! My son wrote the *definitive* biography of Barry Manilow.") Or, children listen to the disapproval, don't allow themselves to grow in the direction they want, and in later years the parents wonder, "Why doesn't my child *produce* something—*anything?*" One of the most perceptive observations about child-rearing was made by none other than Harry S. Truman. "I have found the best way to give advice to your children," he said, "is to find out what they want and then advise them to do it."

> *The trouble with the world*
> *is that the stupid are cocksure*
> *and the intelligent*
> *are full of doubt.*
>
> BERTRAND RUSSELL

If a parent can't reasonably decide what's best for a child—an individual whom the parent knows intimately—how can one presume to be a parent on a national scale to 250 million individuals whom one doesn't know at all? The answer, obviously: It can't be done. And yet, that's what any number of people—with all the best intentions—try to do.

This is especially true of the "parents" who have had some personal negative experiences in one area or another. "I know all about _____. I spent twenty years as _____. It almost ruined my life!" And so, with all the intensity of a parent saving his or her child from the pirates, this "parent" charges off to see that _____ is banned so that no other poor, innocent creature suffers the same twenty-year fate.

Let us suppose that somewhere out there *is* the Perfect Parent. Let's suppose that this Perfect Parent knows what is Precisely Right for us in every situation. I doubt *very much* that the response of the Perfect Parent to a disobedient child is to turn the child over to the police and the criminal justice system. To be arrested and investigated (much less tried, convicted, and punished) goes far beyond whatever discipline the loving parent may care to devise. Yes, arrest and imprisonment may "deter" some, but what good is "deterrence" to the "child" whose mangled and beaten body is placed on public display with a placard exclaiming, "Wouldn't Mind Its Parents!" This sort of example might bring some sort of blind, slavish obedience to the truly timid "children" of the world, but, for the average adults still seeking to find and express themselves, it will only lead to rebellion, revulsion, and secrecy. The "loving parent" will never again know what the child is truly up to. To quote the great child psychologist, Elvis Presley:

> What kid ever changed by being sent to his room? All he did was work harder at not getting caught.

The same rebellion, repulsion, and secrecy will result even if the "child" is not booked, investigated, tried, and jailed—but merely "rehabilitated." Forced "therapy"—in whatever form you care to imagine it—is just as bad and, perhaps, worse.

> *We must abandon
> the prevalent belief
> in the superior wisdom
> of the ignorant.*
>
> DANIEL BOORSTIN

The prerequisite for everything from personal change to spiritual growth is *free will*. If one is not free to *choose* the change he or she wants to make and the method by which that change takes place, even the best of therapies and religious conversions are nothing less than brainwashing.*

After the age of consent, punishment in any form (including enforced education) for any "crime," short of harming the person or property of another, is inhumane, counterproductive—and, besides, Dr. Spock would *not* approve (nor would Mr. Spock, for that matter).

The flip side of paternalism is, of course, *infantilism*.

Infantilism

We live in a culture full of people who *demand* to be "taken care of." Somehow, some people believe that the world not only owes them a living; it also owes them protection, nurturing, and a life free from strife, turmoil, or discomfort. When they *don't* get all the delights they feel they're entitled to, or when they get some of the irritation they feel they shouldn't be subjected to, they become the already-discussed victims: they "grow" into bigger and bigger children.

It's difficult to tell which came first: paternalism or infantilism. Did leaders promise a world free from strife, thus creating in their followers a belief that life should be strife-free; or, did the bellyaching of the masses create potential leaders who, knowing the way to become the leader is to promise the people what they want, promise them the land of milk and honey (with no bees)? Did the serpent promise Adam and Eve God-like status, then Adam and Eve wanted it; or did Adam and Eve want God-like status and the serpent promised them what they wanted?

How infantilism began is in doubt. That it exists today (and how!) is not. The first response to any personal calamity for many people is, "There oughta be a law!" For every thousand people who say this, one person stands and promises, "I'll see that the law is made!" The person is elected, and the law gets made. The next time the calamity happens, the people respond, "This law oughta be enforced!" To get re-elected, the lawmaker promises, "I will see that the law is enforced!" That's how the laws against consensual crimes get made from the bottom up.

---

*I have nothing against brainwashing, by the way. Many people's brains are in desperate *need* of some washing. If one does not, however, voluntarily offer himself or herself to the process of having his or her brain "washed," then the entire process is, at best, a farce, and, at worst, smacks of the totalitarian manipulations made famous in such publications as *1984*, *Animal Farm*, and *National Review*.

From the top down, someone already in a leadership position (often to divert the electorate's attention from his or her lack of success at tackling real problems) will convince the populace—with graphs, expert testimony, and the politicians' all-time favorite, statistics—that there is "danger in this land," and we had better pass and enforce tough laws against *this*, "this" being something the electorate doesn't much like in the first place. It's all reminiscent of Professor Harold Hill in *The Music Man* convincing the townspeople that "the presence of a pool hall" in their community is the beginning of the moral end, that the only way to save the children is to organize a band for them. Professor Hill, of course, just happens to sell band instruments, uniforms, and music lessons. Today's populace believes there's "Trouble in River City" (with a capital "T" and that rhymes with "C" and that stands for *crime*), and follows the leader.

> *Ninety percent of the politicians give the other ten percent a bad name.*
>
> HENRY KISSINGER

In exchange for this illusion of complete protection, we find that one constitutional right (that we previously believed to be inalienable) after another is taken from us. In order to have the *protection* children need, we must be *treated* as children. We are given the rules and restrictions of children. The more that is taken from us in personal freedom, the more we demand in protection. The more protection we are given (or, more accurately, *promised*), the more of our personal freedom we are forced to surrender. It's a vicious circle.

It doesn't work, of course. We give up our freedoms, yes, but where is that security we were promised? Are we safe from every possible negative occurrence in life? Of course not. Has the War on Drugs kept our children safe from drugs? No. It's easier for high school students to buy drugs in high school than to buy alcohol at the liquor store. Has arresting prostitutes ended prostitution? Has persecuting gays ended homosexuality? And if you think hundreds of thousand of arrests over the years have eradicated gambling, I would ask, "Wanna bet?"

The image of the all-powerful, all-loving, stern-when-necessary and nurturing-when-not parent is such a *seductive* one. The evangelists shamelessly exploit this human desire: God the Father gives those who love and obey Him eternal paradise and casts all those who do not obey Him into hell. God rewards his children and smites their enemies. "Just be good little boys and girls," the televangelists tell us, "and we will have the eternal pleasure of watching our enemies suffer forever."

If people want to believe this as part of their religion, that is fine. The trouble arises when this loving/vengeful God becomes the model for government and for law. Then, what is good and what is bad *based upon the interpretation of certain religious experts* becomes the law of the land. That is precisely what has happened in

> *People seem to enjoy things more*
> *when they know*
> *a lot of other people*
> *have been left out of the pleasure.*
>
> RUSSELL BAKER

our country. A certain *interpretation* of the biblical view of right and wrong has been codified into law. The paternal sell this view as right and the infantile accept it.

The more infantile people become, the more rules they demand to know that they are loved, and they demand more punishments of the rule-breakers to know that God is just.

Kill the Messenger!

In olden days, when a messenger brought bad news, the ruler would, naturally, get upset. Rulers, alas, are not famous for their emotional maturity. Alas for the ruler, alas for the country, and alas—especially—for the messenger: he was often killed. A mature ruler, of course, knows that the messenger has nothing to do with the message. Yes, the news means that action must be taken, changes must be made, and perhaps punishments dispensed. The mature ruler gets busy on those. The immature ruler yells, "WHAT? KILL HIM!" Seeing the messenger annihilated on the spot may have given the ruler some visceral satisfaction, but it didn't solve the ruler's—or the country's—problem.

Over time, people would be reluctant to give the ruler bad news: problems would be hidden, discontent glossed over, and difficulties minimized. Without action, the problems, discontent, and difficulties only got worse—sometimes to the point of rebellion, regicide, and revolution. (The three R's of the ancient world for a suppressed people trapped in a nonresponsive government. The modern three R's replaces *regicide* with *riots.*) When the trouble finally reaches the ruler's ears, the ruler is furious. "I don't want any yes-men around me," the ruler yells, quoting Samuel Goldwyn; "I want everybody to tell me the truth, even if it costs them their jobs!" If someone, however, dares to say, "If you'd stop killing the messengers, you'd get more information," more often than not, the ruler would reply, "WHAT? Are you saying it's *my* fault? KILL HIM!" And there goes the country.

Consensual crimes are just messengers.

The irritation, frustration, and turmoil people feel about certain consensual activities only indicate changes need to be made. Some of the changes will be external, some internal; we need to make changes within our country and within ourselves. What these changes will be is not the purpose of this book. It's easy to see, however, we have our work cut out for us: we have some complex problems that can only be solved by more sophisticated responses than, "WHAT? JAIL THEM!"

- Our excessive use of drugs (*all* drugs—the licit and illicit) indicates a deep despair in the country. Drug problems are just bringing us that message. Where despair is greatest, drug use is greatest: the very poor

AIN'T NOBODY'S BUSINESS IF YOU DO

and the very rich. Barrios and boredom produce a need to escape. What
to do about barrios and boredom?
Killing the messenger (jailing drug users) has only made the problem
worse. It's easier to declare war on the
messenger than to do something
about the message.

> *The propagandist's purpose is
> to make one set of people
> forget that certain other sets of
> people are human.*
>
> ALDOUS HUXLEY

- All the variations on the societal norms
  dealing with sex and relationships—
  prostitution, homosexuality, pornography, bigamy, polygamy, adultery—are
  giving us a message: not everyone wants to be in a committed, monogamous, heterosexual relationship; the nuclear family is fine for
  those who want it, but not everyone does. Why should we keep
  pretending otherwise? As a society, we need to become more accepting of the many forms of love, bonding, recreation, and relationship.

- Gambling shows us that human beings love to take risks. Unfortunately, society programs people to play it safe. Safe is fine, but too
  much safety is stifling. Perhaps we should more often view risk-tak-
  ing as exciting rather than dangerous. Then maybe people would
  take their risks starting new businesses, creating new products, and
  expressing themselves. This would help the economy, the culture,
  and the country.

- The prevalence of cults and religious drug use indicate that not
  everyone finds God in the same way. It's not that the established
  religions aren't working; it's that, like marriage, they don't work for
  everyone. If we learn to respond, "Congratulations!" rather than
  "Cult!" when we hear that someone has discovered God in some new
  (to us) and unusual (to us) way, we'd all be more, well, *Christian*.

- Vagrancy is a painful message reminding us of our national poverty.
  The homeless are the tip of an iceberg: there are those who have
  "homes"—but just barely (just barely a home, *and* just barely able to
  pay for it). Whether the solution is the traditional conservative view
  that the individual must be strengthened, or the traditional liberal
  view that a compassionate people will meet the needs of the less
  fortunate, or some combination of the two, or something never tried
  before, each homeless person reminds us that we must do *something*.
  There is another message the homeless give us: we're all awfully
  close to the street. There but for fortune . . .

- The helmet laws and seat belt laws are a reminder of how difficult

> *Consistency requires you to be as ignorant today as you were a year ago.*
>
> BERNARD BERENSON

some people find it to accept the notion that we have the right to go to hell—or to heaven—in our own way, whether in a Hyundai (with or without seat belts) or on a Harley (with or without a helmet). Also, the idea that we can keep others from seriously harming or even killing themselves keeps another message from us: we're all going to die someday. Now *there's* a message we don't want to face. It is, however, one of the few inevitabilities of life. The sooner we accept that we're going to die, the sooner we can start living.

- Unorthodox medical practices and regenerative use of drugs reveal our country's health problem. There are a lot of lessons in this one. First, to paraphrase Shakespeare, "There are more ways of healing in heaven and earth, Dr. Horatio, than are dreamt of in your philosophy." Second, we need to become more responsible for our personal health care; our bodies have a lot more wisdom than we culturally give them credit for. Third, *preventing* disease is the key to health. Fourth, we need to become better consumers. If one man's cure is another man's curse, the man who is cursed needs to learn how to recognize his curses and avoid using them rather than insisting the government make someone's cure illegal.

- Unpopular political beliefs show us that maybe the current government is not doing all it can to create the maximum opportunities for each citizen's life, liberty, and pursuit of happiness. Our fanatic suppression of one such messenger—communism—cost us in the past fifty years, more than 100,000 lives and almost $20 trillion. *That* messenger's gone, but the message remains.

Killing the messenger is a triple threat: it destroys lives (they're only messengers), it disguises real problems (which then get worse), and it wastes precious resources (which could go to solving the problems).

Politics

Politics is the science, practice, and art of *compromise.* You give a little, you get a little. "You want black and I want white? Let's get together and work out which shade of gray we can both live with." "How about black-and-white checks? Checks are *very* fashionable this year."

Consensual crimes are on the short end of any number of political compromises. "We know cigarettes are harmful, but we can't ban them because they're too central to the economy. So, what we'll do is put warning labels on cigarette packages and cigarette ads and, at the same time, step up the enforcement of anti-drug laws so that it will seem as though the government *really does care* about the health and well-being of its citizens."

How certain activities became consensual crimes and others became Big Business is, well, political. For example, it is well

> *I think one of the by-products of the communications explosion is a sort of "corruption fatigue." We've lost our ability to be shocked or enraged by the machinations of politicians. We've been battered with such frequency that we've become indifferent. We're punch drunk with scandal.*
>
> LARRY GELBART

known that the original "pause that refreshes" in Coca-Cola was cocaine, not caffeine. [Trivia question: What are the three familiar flavors that, when combined, make the taste of cola? Answer to come.] The reaction to Prohibition demonstrated that the American public needed *something* in the way of a recreational chemical. It was decided—in classic political compromise—to make alcohol legal again, but to crack down on "real" drugs.

The government could just as easily have decided to make alcohol a "wicked drug," and smile upon the "moderate use" of cocaine in beverages, morphine in "medicines," and hashish in brownies. Why one over another? Alcohol would be easier to control, i.e., *tax*. People, after all, could *grow* marijuana, but few people—once wine and liquor were readily and inexpensively available again—would maintain the fermenting and distilling equipment necessary to produce wine and liquor. Besides, alcoholic beverages took up a lot of space and had to travel in bottles. Cocaine, morphine, hashish, and other drugs were relatively small, and could be smuggled in to avoid taxation. (That Joseph P. Kennedy, while ambassador to England during Prohibition, bought the right to be the exclusive importer of a number of British-made liquors, and that he was politically influential with the people who were making the decision to rescind the Prohibition Act, may have had something to do with alcohol's legality as well.)

At any rate, it was decided to tax alcohol, suppress "drugs," and that—the politicians hoped—would make both the Prohibitionist and the public happy (or, at the very least, not throw the politicians out of office). It worked. Roosevelt stayed in office until his death more than a decade later, marijuana and cocaine became associated with low-lifes, and alcohol became the recreational choice of "ladies and gentlemen of distinction." It could have, however, been precisely the other way around, and would probably have had similar results. (A more complete history of drugs can be found in the chapter, "Recreational Use of Drugs.")

Political compromise is as old as politics itself. In the United States, a particularly tragic compromise was made that directly affected the lives of tens of millions of people and continues to do so to this day. It was found in the first major political document of the United States—the Declaration of Independence.

The Declaration of Independence was a legal document. In it, Thomas Jefferson, a lawyer, had to prove that the acts of King George III were so systematically evil, oppressive, and tyrannical that the thirteen colonies were entitled, not just to *resist* the rule of King George III, but to *revolt* against it. In so doing, Jefferson gave—in good legal form—a list of grievances. As in all legal documents, it is the lawyer's job to make his or her client look good and the opponent look bad. This is done always at the cost of balance and often at the cost of truth. It was Jefferson's job to make King George look truly tyrannical and to make the colonies seem to be poor, innocent, put-upon lambs. (The document would be read by, among others, foreign governments, such as France and Spain, that had to decide which side of the Revolution they would be on.)

The Unanimous Declaration of the Thirteen United States of America begins brilliantly:

> When in the Course of human events, it becomes necessary for one people to dissolve the political bonds which have connected them with another, and to assume among the powers of the earth, the separate and equal station to which the Laws of Nature and of Nature's God entitle them, a decent respect to the opinions of mankind requires that they should declare the causes which impel them to the separation.

> We hold these truths to be self-evident, that all men are created equal, that they are endowed by their Creator with certain unalienable Rights, that among these, are Life, Liberty, and the pursuit of Happiness.

And then politics moved in.

In the first place, "all men" did *not* mean "all humans." It meant, "all white males." Women didn't even get the right to vote for another 144 years. This was not too bitter a political pill to swallow as there was not a woman in any state legislature (by law), and the concept that women should have equal rights was, for the most part (at least to the all-male legislatures), even more radical than violently overthrowing a tyrannical king.

Later, the Native American was savaged. In accusing King George of agitating Indians against the colonists, the Declaration gave the Native American this unfortunate description:

> He has incited domestic insurrections among us and has endeavored to bring on the inhabitants of our frontiers—the merciless Indian savages—whose known will of warfare is an undistinguished destruction of all ages, sexes, and conditions.

This, of course, paved the way for the century of Native American massacres to follow. Only recently, with historical fact and films such as *Dances with Wolves*, has the character of the Native American been even partially redeemed. Of course, it's too late.

Even though it was Native Americans who helped the pilgrim fathers survive the first winters at Plymouth—and although Thanksgiving is celebrated in honor of that event—to portray the Indian as a bloodthirsty savage on the side of King George was politically expedient. As there were no Native Americans and no highly vocal defenders of their dignity in the Continental Congress, the description as written in the first draft survived in the final version of the document.

> *Savages we call them because their manners differ from ours.*
>
> BENJAMIN FRANKLIN

In his original draft of the Declaration of Independence, Thomas Jefferson attacked slavery mercilessly and blamed King George individually for the appalling practice of slavery in the colonies. Jefferson was a smart man, also a lawyer, also one of the largest slave holders in Virginia. He knew he could, in his original draft, condemn slavery as vociferously as he wished. He also knew that there was no chance any wording which even hinted at the abolition of slavery would make it into the final Declaration. The southern states, whose economy depended on slavery, would simply not put up with it, and without the southern states there was no possibility of winning a war against Great Britain. So, Jefferson was able to condemn slavery while still keeping slaves (including one as his mistress, according to some historians) for the remainder of his life.*

By the time the Constitution was written in 1787, the clear direction in thinking—even among many who owned slaves—was that slavery, in and of itself, was an evil and wicked practice. And so, in order to form a union in which the southern states would be a part, politics and compromise ruled again. Article I, Section 9(a) allowed slaves to be imported for at least twenty years, until 1808. (Using the word *migration* to describe the slave trade revealed the sure hand of a lawyer in phrasing the Constitution. This clause also shows that the government doesn't have to *like* something in order to *tax* it.)

> The Migration or Importation of such Persons as any of the States now existing shall think proper to admit, shall not be prohibited by Congress prior to the Year one thousand eight hundred and eight, but a Tax or duty may be imposed on such Importation, not exceeding ten dollars for each Person.

The third paragraph of Article IV, Section 2 of the Constitution—one that many people found to be the most offensive of the entire Constitution—meant

---

*Of the founding fathers who owned slaves, only Washington made a move to free them. In his will, he freed all his slaves upon the death of his wife, Martha.

that slaves who escaped to "free" states would be returned to their "rightful owners."

> No Person held to Service or Labour in one State, under the Laws thereof, escaping into another, shall, in Consequence of any Law or Regulation therein, be discharged from such Service or Labour, but shall be delivered up on Claim of the Party to which such Service or Labour may be due.*

Naturally, the knowledge that the importation of slaves would end in another twenty years, but that keeping and breeding of "domestic slaves" would probably never be illegal, threw the slave trade into high gear. The number of slaves grew from 400,000 to over 8 million by the mid-1800s. The matter would not be settled until 1865 and the Civil War—at a cost of 600,000 lives, the devastation of the South, and the assassination of a president who could have done so much more than merely fight a war.

How did we get off on the Constitution? Didn't I already *have* a chapter about the Constitution—a *long* chapter? What was this chapter about? Oh, yes: politics. Those adults who want to practice consensual activities do so at the peril of laws that are both unjust and outmoded. "No barriers whatever stand today between women and the exercise of their right to vote," said Susan B. Anthony in 1872, "save those of precedent and prejudice." Ms. Anthony, who was born precisely 100 years before women were "given" the vote and who died fourteen years before her dream was achieved, said in the same speech,

> When people enter into a free government, they do not barter away their natural rights; they simply pledge themselves to protect each other in the enjoyment of them through prescribed judicial and legislative tribunals. They agree to abandon the methods of brute force in the adjustment of their differences and adopt those of civilization. The Declaration of Independence, the United States Constitution propose to protect the people in the exercise of their God-given rights.

One hundred years after Susan B. Anthony's 1872 speech, Buffy Sainte-Marie sang of one of the dark nights of the American soul:

> And yet where in your history books
> Is the tale of the genocide basic
> to this country's birth?
> Of the preachers who lied
> How the Bill of Rights failed.

*Meanwhile, the "tyrannical" government of England had ruled in 1772 that "as soon as any slave sets foot in England, he becomes free."

It wasn't until 1943 that the Red Cross stopped typing blood by racial group.

"Blankets for your land!"
So the treaty's a test.
Oh, well, blankets for land
Is a bargain indeed,
And the blankets were those
Uncle Sam had collected
From smallpox diseased
dying soldiers that day.
And the tribes were wiped out.
And the history books censored.

> *I can't understand
> why people are frightened of
> new ideas.
> I'm frightened of the old ones.*
>
> JOHN CAGE

Asked to give a Fourth of July speech in 1852, Frederick Douglass minced few words:

> What, to the American slave, is your Fourth of July? I answer: A day that reveals to him, more than all other days of the year, the gross injustices and cruelty to which he is the constant victim. To him your celebration is a sham.

"Oh, well, that's all behind us now. That's history." No, it's not; with regard to consensual crimes, it is the present. If we don't do something about it, it is also the future. These words from the past may seem overly bitter, but not if you've talked to enough people whose lives were ruined not by consensual activities, but by the laws against consensual activities. These words from the past may seem angry, but not if you've watched one elected official after another tap dance on the Constitution and turn the Bill of Rights into the Bill of Righteousness.

It's all politics.

The loyal opposition is loyal—but to what? Loyal to staying in office, that's for sure. Loyal to maintaining and pandering to the ignorance, intolerance, and arrogance of their constituents.* As Bertrand Russell observed,

> The State is a collection of officials, different for different purposes, drawing comfortable incomes so long as the *status quo* is preserved. The only alteration they are likely to desire in the *status quo* is an increase of bureaucracy and of the power of bureaucrats.

Kenneth Hunter adds,

> The nation's elected representatives . . . maintain the status quo by making the marginal changes required by external forces, rather than grappling directly with worsening problems.

Or, as Laurence J. Peter put it, "Bureaucracy defends the status quo long past

---

*Usually political speeches are neither upsetting nor entertaining nor very much of anything. Usually they resemble those of Warren G. Harding as described by William McAdoo: "His speeches leave the impression of an army of pompous phrases moving over the landscape in search of an idea. Sometimes these meandering words would actually capture a straggling thought and bear it triumphantly a prisoner in their midst, until it died of servitude and overwork."

the time when the quo has lost its status."

The Pecking Order

> *Actions lie
> louder than words.*
>
> CAROLYN WELLS

If you've ever been to a farm where chickens are allowed to run free, the presence of the pecking order is obvious. There is always one miserable, little chicken—emaciated, almost featherless, and covered with little peck sores. This poor chicken is at the bottom of the pecking order.

Chickens—even when food is plentiful—fight with each other over who gets to eat what, when, and where. The fighting is usually subtle—a peck here and a peck there—mostly a reminder between chickens as to which one is higher or lower in the pecking order. The chicken at the top eats anything, anywhere, any time. The chicken at the bottom of the pecking order is lucky to eat at all. Other chickens, especially those toward the bottom, will often keep the lowest chicken from eating at all, even if they don't want the food themselves.

It is well known to a chicken which chickens are above it and which chickens are below it. This pecking order is a source of security for chickens. It lets them know where they stand. It lets them know whom to respect and whom to abuse. It lets them know how they stand in the Divine Plan (or the Divine Peck).

If a chicken feels any displeasure being pecked at, it doesn't take out its frustration on the one doing the pecking. It finds a chicken lower on the pecking order than itself and pecks it. If this newly pecked chicken is unhappy being pecked at, it too does not display its displeasure by pecking back; it finds a chicken even lower on the pecking order and pecks away. This continues down the line until we reach the chicken at the bottom. This chicken simply shrugs its wings (what's left of them) and concludes once again, "Life is not fair."

The pecking order is reminiscent of the cartoon in which there are three fish. The small fish is about to be eaten by the medium-sized fish, which is about to be eaten by the large fish.

The small fish says, "Life is unfair."

The medium-sized fish says, "Life is somewhat fair."

And the big fish says, "Life is fair."

⚖️ ⚖️ ⚖️

If everyone who ever took part in a consensual crime got together, they would clearly make a majority, and consensual crimes would be crimes no more. So why doesn't everyone get together and end this nonsense once and for all? The answer: The Pecking Order.

Society has convinced us that (to para-phrase George Orwell) "all consensual crimes are equally horrible, but some are more equal than others." Gambling, for example, is generally considered less horrible than prostitution. And, within prostitution, *buy-ing* a prostitute is less horrible than *being* one. Even among prostitutes, the call girl who sees three clients per week is of a higher echelon than the hooker who turns three tricks a night. The male prostitutes who work out of classy bars or have an ad

> *There is nothing will kill a man so soon as having nobody to find fault with but himself.*
>
> GEORGE ELIOT

in a newspaper consider themselves several rungs above the street hustler.

Drug use rose from near the bottom of the pecking order in the late 1950s to near the top of the pecking order by the late 1960s, peaking (no pun intended) sometime in the mid-1970s. What with war being declared on drugs in the 1980s, drugs have sunk once again to the lower rungs. There is also a pecking order among drug users. Pot smoking is not as bad as snorting cocaine, which is not as bad as smoking crack, which is not as bad as shooting heroin. The users of psychedelics feel spiritually superior to the pill poppers. Even *how* the same drug is used can cause separation: those who use LSD for "glimpses of enlighten-ment," view with sometimes scorn and sometimes pity those who wash down a tab of acid with a Bud Light and go "party."

Among gays—traditionally *very* low on the pecking order—handsome, muscular, masculine male professionals are toward the upper end of the spec-trum, and drag queens toward the bottom.* Even among drag queens, the ones who can do their own singing rate higher than those who must lip-synch. AIDS has added a sobering new element to the pecking order—to be HIV-positive is negative; to be HIV-negative is positive.

In obscenity, certain words are worse than other words.

"I said the P-WORD."

"So? I said the S-WORD."

"That's awful. But I said the C-WORD."

"That's nothing. I said the F-WORD."

"Well, I said the E-WORD."

"The E-WORD? What's that?"

"I can't say."

I have no intention of detailing the hierarchy of all consensual crimes. Some of it depends on which way the press is blowing. In 1987, Douglas Ginsburg was

---

*JOKE: A mother tells her best friend: "My son just called me. I have some good news and some bad news." Her best friend masks her curiosity with concern: "What's the bad news?" "My son told me he's a homosexual. He's moved in with another man and they're living together as lovers." "That's terrible! What's the good news?" "His lover's a doctor."

denied a place on the Supreme Court solely because he admitted to having experimented with marijuana decades earlier. In 1992, the prevailing wind somehow shifted and, although presidential candidate Clinton admitted youthful experimentation with marijuana, he won the election anyway. Now a former pot smoker *nominates* Supreme Court justices. Sometimes the pecking order is geographical. A polygamist in Ohio would cause a scandal; a polygamist in Utah might have a town named after him. Sometimes it's economic. A drug dealer or pimp in a flashy car is admired in the ghetto, but scorned in the affluent section of town (often more for his *taste* than his *profession*).

> *The big thieves*
> *hang the little ones.*
>
> CZECH PROVERB

As long as one group of consensual crime practitioners can be turned against another group, which can then be turned against another group, and if within each group there is also a pecking order, no one is ever going to notice, "Hey, all us consensual criminals are in the same boat, and *our* boat's bigger than *their* boat!"

Pettiness and Vindictiveness

It's amazing how big pettiness has become. Not only are individuals expanding in their smallness, but the number of petty people has grown. In the past, when people practiced acceptance on a large scale, they were told, "That's big of you." Today, people are praised: "You had your personal prejudice turned into a *law.* Congratulations!"

There have always been petty people, of course, but in the past they were viewed as villains and fools. Shylock was petty. So was Aunt Pittypat. It's when pettiness mixes with religious fervor that people begin dragging out the faggots.* This misuse of religion Nietzsche called,

> The one great curse, the one enormous and innermost perversion, the one great instinct of revenge, for which no means are too venomous, too underhand, too underground and too petty—I call it the one immortal blemish of mankind.

Pettiness is a trait of bickering children—especially spoiled children. Children

---

*I refer here to the bundles of sticks used for burning heretics, witches, and homosexuals. That the word is also a derogatory term for gays (although the two uses have different origins) is a point of playfulness in Charles Ludlam's play, *Camille,* performed by his Ridiculous Theatrical Company to primarily gay audiences in a Greenwich Village theater. One can imagine the fun both audiences and actors had with these lines: MARGUERITE: "I'm cold, Nanine, throw another faggot on the fire!" NANINE: (Waking) "There are no more faggots in the house." MARGUERITE: (Plaintively looking out at the audience) "No faggots in the house? Open the window, Nanine. See if there are any in the street."

use it when attempting to control others; it is also used by parents to control children. Pettiness fits perfectly into the parental/infantile society in which we live. One has a nearly uncontrollable desire to tell these people not only to grow, but to *grow up*.*

⚖️ ⚖️ ⚖️

Pettiness seems to go hand in hand with vindictiveness. The smaller the person, the larger the need for revenge. This may account for the fact that some consensual crimes have stiffer penalties than do most crimes with innocent victims.

But each day brings its petty dust
Our soon-chok'd souls to fill,
And we forget because we must,
And not because we will.

MATTHEW ARNOLD

Putting a man in jail *for life* because of something he was doing in his own bedroom with a consenting adult is clearly the act of petty, vindictive minds. These minds can be found all the way up to and including the majority of the Supreme Court, who, in 1986, upheld such a conviction and sentence. (See the chapter in Part V, "Homosexuality.")

As I watch people inflict their petty morality on the private lives of consenting adults, I wonder, "Don't these people have something better to do?" Does their pettiness grow from excess leisure? Fundamental immaturity? Or are they just plain spoiled? I'm still pondering the source of pettiness. I do know that pettiness is important in the making of new laws against consensual activities, and vindictiveness central to the enthusiastic punishment for breaking the laws we already have.

Righteousness

Righteousness is not just being *right,* but being *so* right that people who believe or act in a way that doesn't honor that rightness can't possibly be right; therefore, they're *wrong.* When this rightness is backed by a religious belief, those who don't "do right" are not just wrong; they are evil, wicked, and under the spell of—if not in league with and actively recruiting for—*Satan.*

When consensual criminals *appear* not to be following the religious beliefs of the righteous, they can choose to follow Jesus' statement, "For whoever is not against you is for you" (Luke 9:50), "For whoever is not against us is for us" (Mark 9:40). Or, they can follow another of Jesus' comments, "He who is not with me is against me" (Matthew 12:30, Luke 11:23). The righteous enthusiastically choose the latter. Choosing the former makes more sense: those who are off committing consensual crimes are not, for the most part, speaking or acting *against* God, Jesus, the Holy Spirit, or even religion; they're just living their lives. So, if they're

---

*Except telling people to grow up begins to suck one into the parental trap, doesn't it? It *is* a complicated game.

> *They hated me without reason.*
>
> JESUS OF NAZARETH
> John 15:25

not against, they're for. No need for the religious to be righteous about this.

If, on the other hand, people take "He who is not with me is against me" to heart, *anyone* who does *anything* not endorsed by their religion is then *against* God, Christ, Jesus, the Holy Spirit, and religion in general. *And that's not right!* So, the righteous—in high dudgeon—get on their high horse, and use their full persuasive power not so much to convict people to Christ, but to convict them as criminals.*

And *righteousness* used to be such a *good* word, too. It meant "to do the right thing," or "to make right use" of something. These are the meanings Jesus had in mind when he said, "Blessed are those who hunger and thirst for righteousness, for they will be filled" (Matthew 5:6), and, "Blessed are those who are persecuted because of righteousness, for theirs is the kingdom of heaven" (Matthew 5:10).** *Doing* right is good. Making *others* do right—by force of law—is wrong. The righteous are, then, the *wrongeous*. (And, they destroyed a perfectly good word, too.)

The Bible says, "Be not righteous over much" (Ecclesiastes 7:16 KJV). Don't the righteous have enough to do keeping their own lives righteous? Isn't worrying about *other people's* righteousness a little "much"? And putting people in jail for their *lack* of righteousness is *too* much.

In the Sermon on the Mount, when Jesus defined righteousness, his definition did *not* include jailing, condemning, accusing, or meddling in the lives of unwilling others in any way. At the beginning of chapter 6 of Matthew, Jesus admonishes, "Be

*The wording of Jesus' three statements is interesting. In the first two, it's directed at "you" and "us." In the third, it's "me." A person seeking guidance for his or her own behavior would look for instructions that include "you" (Jesus' disciples) or "us" (a gathering of the faithful). The teaching, then, is "For whoever is not against you/us is for you/us." The righteous, however, pick the personal statement Jesus made about *himself*—the one in which he used "me." Egomania is one of the attributes of the righteous. (That's why it's often called *self*-righteousness.) That these people would identify with the personal statement of Jesus ("me") and not follow the teachings of Jesus for his disciples ("you"), or for the community of the faithful ("we") (which includes Christ) indicates a lack of humility at best. Even if the latter were the correct choice, the line from The Lord's Prayer, "Forgive us our sins, for we also forgive everyone who sins against us" (Luke 11:4), should handle it. But not for the righteous!

**The original meaning of this beatitude, of course, was for people to do the right things and, if they are persecuted for doing the right things, then "theirs is the kingdom of heaven." With the bigots of this world using the word *righteousness* to cover their bigotry, however, this beatitude takes on a new meaning: those who are persecuted due to the unnecessary righteousness of others get the kingdom of heaven. That means everyone fired, evicted, arrested, jailed, or otherwise persecuted for consensual crimes has the kingdom of heaven. Wouldn't that be a hoot? Won't those righteous religious people be *awfully* upset when Jesus' promise, "So the last will be first, and the first will be last" (Matthew 20:16 [similarly, Mark 10:31, Luke 13:30]), actually comes true?

AIN'T NOBODY'S BUSINESS IF YOU DO

careful not to do your 'acts of righteousness' before men, to be seen by them. If you do, you will have no reward from your Father in heaven." (An admonition obviously not heeded by the vocally righteous.)

Jesus then goes on to define righteousness. It includes giving to the needy, prayer, forgiveness, fasting, storing treasures "in heaven," seeing to it the eyes and the body are "full of light," serving God (not Money), and not worrying about what we eat, drink, and wear, or where what we eat, drink,* and wear comes from. And *that's it*. End of chapter 6.

> *Stop judging by mere appearances, and make a right judgment.*
>
> JESUS OF NAZARETH
> John 7:24

If we continue on to chapter 7, we are told not to judge, not to look for the sawdust in our brothers' eyes when we have a plank in our own, not to give what is sacred to dogs or "cast ye pearls before swine" (KJV). We are also told to ask God for what we want: "Ask and it will be given to you; seek and you will find; knock and the door will be opened to you" (Matthew 7:7—no wonder so many people consider 7 a lucky number).

At the end of Matthew, chapter 7, after defining righteousness, Jesus gives a warning:

> Not everyone who says to me, "Lord, Lord," will enter the kingdom of heaven. . . . Many will say to me on that day, "Lord, Lord, did we not prophesy in your name, and in your name drive out demons and perform many miracles?"
>
> Then I will tell them plainly, "I never knew you. Away from me, you evil-doers!" (Matthew 7:21–23)

And Matthew went on to comment,

> When Jesus had finished saying these things, the crowds were amazed at his teaching, because he taught as one who had authority, and not as their teachers of the law. (Matthew 7:28–29)

So, the next time the righteous give you "Lord, Lord," as justification for supporting the laws against consensual activities, you need only point them to Jesus' own definition of righteousness in Matthew, chapters 6 and 7. (And maybe they'll take the warning at 7:21–23—but I doubt it.)

At this point, I usually add, "More on this in Part IV, 'Consensual Crimes and the Bible,'" but I've said that too often. So, without any further ado, Part IV, "Consensual Crimes and the Bible."

---

*Speaking of drinking, the three familiar flavors that make up cola (and you thought I forgot) are cinnamon, vanilla, and citrus (either lemon or lime). Now you, too, can put together your own regiment for the Cola Wars.

PART IV

CONSENSUAL CRIMES
AND THE BIBLE

Looking for Loopholes

> *If only God would give me*
> *some clear sign!*
> *Like making a large deposit*
> *in my name at a Swiss bank.*
>
> WOODY ALLEN

W.C. FIELDS WAS ON HIS deathbed, reading the Bible. An old friend came in and said, "Bill! You don't believe in God. Why are you reading the Bible?" Fields responded in his familiar cadence, "Looking for loopholes."

I like to think Fields found his loophole. He died on Christmas Day, 1946, in Pasadena, California. To paraphrase Oscar Wilde: "In Pasadena! I fear that hardly points to any very serious state of mind at the last."

Anyone interested in social change—regardless of religious beliefs or lack of them—should read the Bible for no other reason than *it is the book quoted most often to relieve us of our personal freedoms*. It should be read to see what "the other side" is getting so excited about. It should be read from a purely political point of view to, quoting W. C. Fields, "look for loopholes."

Personally, I find it difficult to believe that anyone can read the first four books of the New Testament—Matthew, Mark, Luke, and John, which contain the story of and the direct quotations of Jesus—without concluding, as G. K. Chesterton did in his 1910 book, *What's Wrong with the World*, "The Christian ideal has not been tried and found wanting; it has been found difficult and left untried."

You may, like me, wonder: "Where do these evangelicals get off, taking a nice man like Jesus and using him to justify their ignorance, intolerance, and personal prejudice?"

How can the Prince of Peace be used to justify a *war* on so many things?

How could a man who taught love and forgiveness be used to rationalize hatred and revenge?

Jesus, like all the people who have been jailed for consensual crimes, has been given a bum rap.

ᔕᔕ ᔕᔕ ᔕᔕ

Oh, this section of the book is going to disturb *so* many people. So be it. Those on the so-called religious right will be upset that my interpretation of the Bible is not the same as their own. (My interpretation of the Bible, in fact, is very literal: I read what's there and report on it. It's just that *I* don't read what *they* apparently read—sometimes I wonder whether we're reading the same book.)

The left-leaning secular humanists will be upset that I spend so much time with the Bible—or that I mention it at all. They want to throw out the bath water, the baby, and the bathtub of Bible scholarship. The Bible, they argue, is a religious book and the separation of church and state eliminates any religious book from discussion, be it the Bible, Koran, Mahabharata, Talmud, or *Zen and the Art of Motorcycle Maintenance.*

My point of view—radical as it may be—is that *both* camps could get a lot from reading the Bible.

It may seem strange to suggest that the religious right read the Bible. I have found, in fact, that few of them have. My first question to people who attack personal freedom on biblical grounds is, "Have you read the Bible? Every word? Cover-to-cover?" They hate to admit it, but when pressed (after a few avoidance statements such as, "I know the Bible well," "I've studied the Bible all my life," or "I love the Bible,") their answer is usually, "No."

I have had the most *amazing* discussions with evangelical Christians in which I suggest that they read the book they are quite often holding in their hands. (Somehow, *carrying* the book is more important to them than having *read* it.) They'll quote chapter and verse, and I'll quote it right back at them. They look it up and find that, lo, I know what I'm talking about. After being shaken for a moment, however, most restructure their composure and dismiss me by saying, "The devil can cite Scripture for his purpose."

"Where's that from?" I'll ask.

"Somewhere in the Bible," they fumble.

"No," I say, "It's from Shakespeare, "*The Merchant of Venice,* Act 1, Scene 3, Line 99."

I can just hear these people discussing me with their friends later: "I met one of Satan's legions today! He said the most terrible thing."

"What did he say?"

"He told me to read the Bible!"

"Abominable!" their friends gasp, "What will Satan think of next?"

With those who, for whatever reason, have rejected the Bible outright, I've lost a great many points by saying, "Have you ever read the Bible? Parts of it are quite delightful, especially the first four books of the New Testament. It's full of insight and wisdom."

"Uh, no," they say, although I can see in their eyes, they're thinking, "Another born-again Bible-thumper. God save me!"

"Really? I'll match the philosophy and teachings of Jesus, as a whole, against any philosopher or social scientist you care to name."

They stare at me, "Jesus freak!" writ large across their face.

> *I could not believe that anyone who had read this book would be so foolish as to proclaim that the Bible in every literal word was the divinely inspired, inerrant word of God. Have these people simply not read the text? Are they hopelessly uninformed? Is there a different Bible? Are they blinded by a combination of ego needs and naivete?*
>
> BISHOP JOHN SHELBY SPONG

⚖ ⚖ ⚖

I must admit that I initially turned to the Bible "looking for loopholes." I knew I could pull quotations out of context that would support my point of view. In planning this, I thought of myself in an adversarial relationship: the religious right has presented *its* out-of-context quotations, and has done a good job popularizing them. I could do the same, and make *my* out-of-context quotations support *my* beliefs. Somewhere between the extremes, people would discover something approaching the truth.

Along the way, however, I made an astonishing discovery: There was no need to pull quotations out of context. There was no need for me to ignore certain passages and highlight others. The "scriptural basis" for the evangelicals' claim to righteousness *simply did not exist*. In order to support my opinion I didn't have to—with a certain degree of guilt—leave out "incriminating" passages: the passages were not there.

Certain quotations were *there*, of course, but considering the *context* they were in, no sane human being would take them seriously. (All of the admonitions against "sexual immorality" fall into this category.) Other concepts—promoted loudly by the Bible-quoting moralists of our day—were entirely absent. That Jesus in any way supported the so-called traditional family values, is nonexistent. If anything, Jesus was not *in the least* supportive of the nuclear family. (See the chapter, "Jesus and Traditional Family Values.")

I felt like the defense attorney who discovered the prosecution had no case; not just that they had a *weak* case, but that they had *no case at all*. The witnesses for the prosecution, far from saying, "Yes, I saw him shoot her," said instead, "No, he didn't shoot her; in fact, he was quite nice to her." And these were the witnesses for the *prosecution!* There was no case at all; in fact, there was no crime.*

---

*Although it's not the point of this book, the intolerant interpretation of the Bible by the fundamen-

> *Get your facts first,*
> *and then you can distort them*
> *as much as you please.*
>
> MARK TWAIN

The Bible is a collection of ultimate truths and interim truths. The ultimate truths were true when they were revealed, are true now, and will probably be true for all time (at least as far as this planet goes). The interim truths are those that were given to people in specific situations as they faced specific challenges. When the situations changed and the challenges were met, the truths (rules) no longer applied.*

The Bible, taken as a whole, can be used to praise or condemn practically *any* human activity, thought, belief, or practice. As with the works of Shakespeare, if one looks carefully, one can find a quotation, incident, or story to support or condemn practically anything. The Bible is a massive collection of books covering thousands of years. It's easy to take something out of context and, relying on the ignorance of the listener, show that the Bible—and, therefore, God—is either for or against something.

To say that Shakespeare wrote, "Oh, what a rogue and peasant slave am I," is accurate—but he did not write it as self-description. He put those words in the mouth of Hamlet, that melancholy Dane. Shakespeare didn't necessarily feel that way about himself.

To quote Margaret Mitchell as saying, "I don't know nothin' 'bout birthin' babies," may not be an accurate commentary on Ms. Mitchell's midwifery abilities. Nor is it an accurate commentary on her ability to properly speak the English language. She put the words in the mouth of an uneducated slave. They were not necessarily a reflection of Margaret Mitchell herself.

People who are alive can correct misquotes. Alfred Hitchcock, for example, clarified: "I never said that actors were cattle. What I said was that actors should be *treated* as cattle."

Unfortunately, this ability to illustrate and substantiate nearly anything by misquoting the Bible has been used by a great many people to justify their own prejudices (by proving that "God thinks this way too"), as excuses for grabbing and holding onto power ("It's not what *I* want, it's want *God* wants!"), or as the perfect justification for not taking a fearless look at themselves and making the necessary—although admittedly uncomfortable—personal changes in attitude

---

talists also keeps sincere seekers from a potential source of truth, inspiration, and wisdom. For more on this, please read *Rescuing the Bible from Fundamentalism*, by Bishop John Shelby Spong.

*Those who claim that every word of the Bible is God's divine directive for all people at all times may claim such in *word* but certainly do not follow it in *deed*. As we shall see, none of them would even *consider* following all the commands, rules, and regulations laid out in the Bible.

and behavior.

It's not the Bible *itself* that condemns most consensual crimes, but the *misuse* of the Bible by petty, fearful, manipulative, misguided individuals who deceptively quote from the Bible not as an illumination of truth, but as a justification of their own limited point of view.

⚖ ⚖ ⚖

Allow me to quote Alan Watts at length. He says all I want to say here, and says it much better than I.*

> *The Bible is clear about hate:*
> *Hate is wrong.*
>
> BRUCE HILTON

> [The Bible is] an anthology of ancient literature that contains sublime wisdom along with barbaric histories and the war songs of tribes on the rampage. All this is taken as the literal Word and counsel of God, as it is by fundamentalist sects, which—by and large—know nothing of the history of the Bible, of how it was edited and put together. So we have with us the social menace of a huge population of intellectually and morally irresponsible people.

> [The Bible is a] translation of Hebrew and Greek documents composed between 900 B.C. and A.D. 120. There is no manuscript of the Old Testament; that is, of the Hebrew Scriptures, written in Hebrew, earlier than the Ninth Century B.C. But we know that these documents were first put together and recognized as the Holy Scriptures by a convention of rabbis held at Jamnia (Yavne) in Palestine shortly before A.D. 100. On *their* say-so. Likewise, the composition of the Christian Bible, which documents to include and which to drop, was decided by a council of the Catholic Church held in Carthage in the latter part of the Fourth Century. . . . The point is that the books translated in the . . . Bible were declared canonical and divinely inspired by the authority (A) of the Synod of Jamnia and (B) of the Catholic Church, meeting in Carthage more than 300 years after the time of Jesus. It is thus that fundamentalist Protestants get the authority of their Bible from Jews who had rejected Jesus and from Catholics whom they abominate as the Scarlet Woman mentioned in *Revelation*.

*Some readers may be asking, "Who is Alan Watts?" Alas, Alan Watts does not have the wide audience, readership, or reputation he deserves. In my humble estimation, he was one of the finest philosophers of this century. Although he had a master's in theology and a doctorate in divinity, he seldom had the pretension of calling himself "Dr. Watts" (although, while an Episcopal priest, he probably tolerated the obligatory "Father Watts"). As fine as his writing was, I find his recorded lectures even more delightful. (His tapes and several books are available from his son, Mark Watts, P.O. Box 938, Point Reyes Station, CA 94956.) Although Watts died in 1973, his writings and his lectures are as contemporary, witty, and penetrating as ever. One of his most famous books is called, simply, *The Book*, first published in 1966. The evangelicals had their revenge of sorts when they later published an edition of the Bible (with fundamentalist footnotes) and called it *The Book*.

> *People are much too solemn*
> *about things—*
> *I'm all for sticking pins*
> *into episcopal behinds.*
>
> ALDOUS HUXLEY

As we explored in the chapter, "Consensual Crimes Corrupt the Freedom of the Press," the Bible was a highly manipulated book. In Europe during the Middle Ages, the church and state were essentially one (until that revolutionary concept of the separation of church and state—divided them) and it behooved both the church and the state to underline certain passages and to suppress the rest. The essence of the message that those in power wanted to get across was: Work hard, obey your "parents" (that is, the king, barons, lords, bishops, and other clergy), accept that this life is a "vale of tears" (except for the king, barons, lords, bishops, and other clergy), and if you do a good job of all this working, obeying, and suffering during this "twinkling of an eye" called "life on earth," you will spend all eternity in paradise. If, however, you are idle, disobedient, and devote yourself to a life of pleasure, you will spend all eternity suffering in hell. The "fear of God" kept a small elite rich and fat, while everybody else paid the bills and struggled toward eternal bliss. The oppression didn't stop in Europe, of course: it got missionaried throughout the world. As Bishop Desmond Tutu explained,

> When the missionaries came to Africa they had the Bible and we had the land. They said, "Let us pray." We closed our eyes. When we opened them we had the Bible and they had the land.

The rulers of both church and state knew that if the people found out what the Bible *really* said, there would be rebellion. Sure enough, as soon as enough people *did* find out, there was. It was known as the Reformation, probably the longest nonstop struggle in Western history. It went on for centuries, and continues to smolder today in such hot spots as Northern Ireland. (The unrest is not as much about British control of Ireland, as it is about Protestant control of Catholics.)

And yet, even today—with heaven knows how many translations of the Holy Bible available, in languages as plain as day with footnotes describing obscure references, historical background, and culture—people *still* aren't reading the Bible. I am convinced that if everyone who claims he or she believes in the Bible as the revealed Word of God would simply *read* the thing, consensual crimes would be over overnight.

Alan Watts explained how misinterpretation of the Bible hurts nonbelievers and believers alike:

> As is well known, the enormous political power of fundamentalists is what makes legislators afraid to take laws against victimless "sins" and crimes off the books, and what corrupts the police by forcing them to be

armed preachers enforcing ecclesiastical laws in a country where church and state are supposed to be separate—ignoring the basic Christian doctrine that no actions, or abstentions from actions, are of moral import unless undertaken voluntarily. Freedom is risky and includes the risk that anyone may go to hell in his own way.

> *Why don't you judge*
> *for yourselves*
> *what is right?*
>
> JESUS OF NAZARETH
> *LUKE 12:57*

⚖ ⚖ ⚖

In exploring the Bible, I chose the New International Version (NIV). This is the translation favored by most of the evangelical churches. (I don't want them accusing me of using some "heathen translation.")* Some evangelicals still use the King James Version because the New International Version is—for their tastes—entirely (and dangerously) *too* clear.

The Bible is divided into two sections, the Old Testament and the New Testament. When John Lennon referred to a portion of his writings as "The New Testicle," he was accused of blasphemy. Lennon was, in fact, accurate, and those who accused him were ignorant.

According to the *Dictionary of Word Origins,* the word *testament* has the same root word as *test* and *testify.* They all come from *testicles.*

Throughout history, when people swore an oath, they did so on something important, something sacred. Today people "swear to God," "swear on the lives of my children," and "swear on my mother's grave." In olden days, men would swear on their testicles. At important moments in conversations, men would—like Marky Mark or Michael Jackson—grab their crotches and *swear* they were telling the truth. As castration was a possible punishment for deception, one did not make the gesture lightly—especially in front of the king.

If a man wanted you to do something, and you *really* wanted to show him that you'd do it, to demonstrate your loyalty and intention, where would you grab? Yes, you'd grab him by the Old Testament. Putting your hand under his testicles would be a *test* of your sincerity and the strength of your *testimony.* (And here you thought this section of the book was going to be *boring.* The Bible is a lot more, well, *interesting* than the televangelists have let on. I guess they don't trust us with the truth, the whole truth, and nothing but the truth.) This grabbing became a standard custom in court. A witness, in fact, was once known as the *testis.* (Today we swear on Bibles before testifying or when administering oaths not just because

*The preface of the New International Version shows the fundamentalist influence: "That [the translation scholars] were from many denominations—including Anglican, Assemblies of God, Baptist, Brethren, Christian Reformed, Church of Christ, Evangelical Free, Lutheran, Mennonite, Methodist, Nazarene, Presbyterian, Wesleyan and other churches—helped to safeguard the translation from sectarian bias."

it is considered to be God's holy book, but also because the book contains two testaments, just like most men.)

This information is in the Bible—if they'd only translate it correctly. This, for example, from Genesis 24:1–3 and 9:*

Abraham was now old and well advanced in years, and the Lord had blessed him in every way. He said to the chief servant in his household, the one in charge of all that he had, "Put your hand under my thigh. I want you to swear by the Lord, the God of heaven and the God of earth, that you will not get a wife for my son from the daughters of the Canaanites. . . ." So, the servant put his hand under the thigh of his master Abraham and swore an oath to him concerning this matter.

Now why would he want his servant to place his hand under his *thigh?* If asked, Sunday school teachers invariably say, "It was the custom," never explaining what the custom *really* was. (Chances are, they don't know themselves.) The fact is, *thigh* is a Disneyized translation.

The Hebrew word for what the servant put his hand under is *yarek,* which means "to be soft." According to *Strong's Greek-Hebrew Dictionary,* the word could mean "the generative parts; shank, flank, loins, shaft, side, or thigh." Of these, does *thigh* seem the best choice?

But the most accurate translation might prove, well, *embarrassing.* Here's Abraham—patriarch of Judaism, Christianity, and Islam; whom "the Lord had blessed" "in every way"—asking his servant to put his hand under his (Abraham's) testicles and go find his son a non-Canaanite wife. Imagine what Monty Python could do with *that!* No. Who will question it? (Who but some round-the-bend writer researching a book on consensual crimes?)

Another even more obvious mistranslation of *yarek* is found in Genesis 47:29 and 31:

When the time drew near for Israel to die, he called for his son Joseph and said to him, "If I have found favor in your eyes, put your hand under my thigh and promise that you will show me kindness and faithfulness. . . . Swear to me," he said. Then Joseph swore to him, and Israel worshiped as he leaned on the top of his staff.

*This footnote is for those who are completely unfamiliar with the Bible: The Bible is a collection of "books" (although the word *bible* itself means book). Each book has a series of chapters, and each chapter is divided into verses. These chapter and verse citations are uniform throughout all translations of the Bible and are written as follows: BOOK NAME CHAPTER:VERSE. So, "Genesis 24:1–3 and 9" means the book of Genesis, chapter 24, verses 1 through 3, and also verse 9.

Now how can Joseph put his hand *under* his father's thigh while Israel is *standing up?* Of the available choices ("the generative parts; shank, flank, loins, shaft, side, or thigh"), which is the *only* one you can put your hand *under* when a man is *standing?*

This is the sort of euphemistic nonsense we seem to enjoy in this country. While visiting the United States, Winston Churchill was invited to a dinner party. He asked the woman next to him to please pass the breasts. "Oh, Mr. Churchill," she blushed,

> *Man is an exception,*
> *whatever else he is.*
> *If it is not true that*
> *a divine being fell,*
> *then we can only say*
> *that one of the animals*
> *went entirely off its head.*
>
> G. K. CHESTERTON

"We don't call it *that* in this country. We call it *white meat.*" Churchill thanked her for the English lesson, and the next day sent her a corsage with a note, "Kindly pin this on your white meat."

Keep in mind that the translation we'll be using (NIV) was done by evangelicals and financed by the conservative American (now International) Bible Society. While more accurate than the King James Version (first edition published in 1611), it is, if not bowdlerized, at least *wholesomized.* Even so, I think you'll find what's in the evangelical translation still has little to do with what the televangelists preach.

This is the Bible the evangelicals read and believe. All I ask them to do, from the standpoint of consensual crimes, is practice what it preaches.

⚖️ ⚖️ ⚖️

Where was I? Oh, yes: The Bible is divided into two sections, the Old Testament and the New Testament. The Old Testament contains the story of Judaism; the New Testament, the story of Christianity. If we are to explore Judaism and Christianity in the context of consensual crimes, we must discover what is the core of Judaism and what is the core of Christianity.

Revealing the core of Christianity is easy: It's what Jesus did and said while he was teaching on earth. This, for the most part, is contained in the first four books of the New Testament. (Conveniently, red-letter editions of the Bible have Jesus' words in red.) The remainder of the New Testament is a commentary on Jesus and his teaching.

The core of Judaism, most Judaic scholars agree, is the Ten Commandments, along with the admonition, "Hear, O Israel: The Lord our God, the Lord is one. Love the Lord your God with all your heart and with all your soul and with all your strength" (Deuteronomy 6:4–5).

Is there anything at the core of Judaism and, especially, Christianity that says, "The fundamental beliefs of our religion should be made the law of the land. If people don't follow our beliefs, the government should lock them up"?

Now, even if the Biblical religions *did* say that—loudly and clearly—it wouldn't really matter: the constitutionally guaranteed separation of church and

> *The Bible is for the Government*
> *of the People,*
> *by the People,*
> *and for the People.*
>
> *General prologue to the Wycliffe*
> *translation of the Bible*
> *1384*

state would prevent such a law from being enacted. It would take a constitutional amendment or an overthrow of the United States government before religion could be made law.

Neither Judaism nor Christianity, however, holds as a fundamental belief the concept that nonbelievers should be locked up. The heathens may not be entitled to as many perks as the devout, perhaps, but locked up? No.

We'll also look at Favorite Scriptural References and Bible Stories used as justifications for jailing infidels by those who don't know much about either the Bible or the United States Constitution. Do these passages really say what these people say they say? I say no. But you can read them yourself. As the TV newscasters say, *"You decide!"*

In addition, there are some scriptures and stories that—for some inexplicable reason—the televangelists don't quote. Just because these passages seem to *support* the idea that people should be allowed to do what they choose with their own person and property as long as they don't physically harm the person or property of another, I can't imagine *why* Jerry Falwell hasn't preached a sermon on them or Pat Robertson hasn't written a book about them.

⚖️ ⚖️ ⚖️

For ease of understanding—especially in terms of consensual crimes—allow me to divide the Bible into four parts. The obvious division is between the Old Testament and the New Testament. I'd also like to divide each of those testaments into two parts.

- The first part of the Old Testament consists of its first five books—Genesis, Exodus, Leviticus, Numbers, and Deuteronomy. These were all written by Moses—or inspired by Moses—and are known collectively as the *Pentateuch,* or *Torah.* It chronicles humanity from creation through the acceptance of monotheism (one God) and the establishment of the nation of Israel. It also delineates the laws and precepts of Judaism as practiced at that time. (Judaism has evolved considerably over the past 3,500 years.) The first five books of the Old Testament are explored in the chapters, "The Ten Commandments" and "The Laws of Moses."

- The remaining thirty-four books of the Old Testament are the story of the nation of Israel: its ups, its downs, its successes, its failures, and its eventual dissolution. (These are covered in the chapter, "The Remainder of the Old Testament.") While the *nation* of Israel was destroyed, the *religion* of Judaism burned brightly in individuals, their families, their synagogues, and their communities. What they had lost by the end of the Old Testament was political power. This loss severely interfered with their religious freedoms: every country they tried to live in had other established religions, so from approximately 400 B.C. until after World War II, Jews suffered unbridled prejudice, intolerance, and hatred.

> *I like,*
> *roughly in the order described:*
> *(1) God,*
> *(2) my family and friends,*
> *(3) my country,*
> *(4) J. S. Bach,*
> *(5) peanut butter, and*
> *(6) good English prose.*
>
> WILLIAM F. BUCKLEY, JR.

That Judaism has survived at all (the only ancient religion west of India to do so) is a testament to its central strength ("Love the Lord your God with all your heart and with all your soul and with all your strength" [Deuteronomy 6:5]) and the strength of the Jewish people.

- The first part of the New Testament is its first four books—Matthew, Mark, Luke, and John. They are known as the *Gospels* or "good news." Each of the Gospels tells the complete story of Jesus from a slightly different point of view. Reading the four of them is like watching *Rashomon:* four different people tell the life of one man thirty to sixty years after he died. Of the four authors of the Gospels, Matthew and John knew Jesus personally, Mark probably knew him personally, and Luke did not know him personally but was a good reporter. In these four books are the teachings of Jesus Christ. (Both *Christ* and *Messiah* mean the same thing: the Anointed One.) These are the only four books in the Bible, for the most part, that quote Jesus directly while he lived and taught on earth. (He is also quoted extensively in the last book of the Bible, Revelation, but this was the revealed word of Jesus to John more than sixty years after Jesus' physical death. The Gospels are discussed in the chapters, "Law Versus Grace," "Jesus of Nazareth and Consensual Crimes," "Jesus and Traditional Family Values," "Jesus on Sex and Marriage," and "Jesus and the Separation of Church and State."

- The remaining twenty-three books of the New Testament document the foundation of the Christian religion and the early church. Jesus never discussed religion—religion in the sense of an established organization devoted to the worship of God. He never looked for a building in which people could worship; he went to them. When he sent his disciples out to heal the sick and spread the good news, he divided them and sent them out two by two in all directions. The early church fathers—primarily Peter, James (Jesus' brother), and

> *In his holy flirtation*
> *with the world,*
> *God occasionally drops a*
> *handkerchief.*
> *These handkerchiefs*
> *are called saints.*
>
> FREDERICK BUECHNER

Paul (the converted Roman Pharisee)—struggled with the need to maintain continuity and organization with the spiritual freedom Jesus taught and their belief that Jesus was returning "any day now" to take them all to his father's house. (Please see "The Remainder of the New Testament." It's quite a story.)

In all but one chapter of this section, I will be exploring the Bible from the point of view of "What happened?" rather than "Should we believe that this is God's work?" I will treat the Bible as a history book, asking questions similar to "Who was Napoleon? What did he do? What did he believe? What influence did he have?" Rather than "Did Napoleon do things the right way? Were his beliefs good or bad? Should we have voted for him if he had run for president?"

This attempted "objectivity" (at which I'm sure I will fail many times) does not exist in the chapter, "A Plea for Christian Charity, Tolerance, and (Dare I Say) *Love* for Diversity." This is a chapter for everyone who calls himself or herself "Christian." The assumption is that the reader accepts Jesus as being divine. Those who find such a point of view objectionable can skip that chapter just as they might skip any other sermon given from any other pulpit.

⚖️ ⚖️ ⚖️

Above all, please understand that I do not intend this section of the book to change anyone's *personal* beliefs about God, religion, or methods of worship. This section only deals with the *social* ramifications of the Bible, and those who use the Bible as a reason to support putting people in jail for taking part in certain consensual activities.

Wo(e)man

BEFORE LAUNCHING into the Bible, it is important to understand the role of women in history and, specifically, during the period of time covered by the Bible (the creation of the world until approximately A.D. 100).

The history of women's treatment by men can be summed up in one word: *dreadful*. Women's relationship to men can also be summed up with one word: *property*. Men *owned* women, just as they owned cattle, camels, and children. (Yes, the children belonged to the father. He could do what he wanted with them: sell them, trade them, even kill them. But that's another story.) Women were not considered human beings or even lesser human beings; they were livestock. Their job was to cook, clean, bear children, and take care of them. (Of the children, the father wanted only a male heir and a backup male heir. The rest were a nuisance.)

This system held for quite some time. The first nation to give women the vote—a basic token of humanity and equality in a society—was New Zealand. That was in 1893. Seeing no national upheaval, Australia followed suit—in 1902. Finland was next (1906), followed by Norway (1913). In Soviet Russia, Germany, Austria, Poland, and Czechoslovakia, women had the vote before they did in the United States (1920). Women in France didn't get the vote until 1944; in Italy and Japan, not until 1945 (do we hear the rumbling changes of World War II in there?). In the rest of "civilized" North America, Canadian women didn't get the vote until 1948(!), and Mexican women had to wait until 1953. In Saudi Arabia, women still can't vote.

Being given the vote was called *suffrage*. In reviewing the history of women's suffrage, one begins to think the word was a combination of *suffering* and *rage*. Have a look at some of the popular views expressed during the 131-year struggle

> *Women and people of low birth*
> *are very hard to deal with.*
> *If you are friendly with them,*
> *they get out of hand,*
> *and if you keep your distance,*
> *they resent it.*
>
> CONFUCIUS

in this country (1789–1920 R.I.P.). (Note how similar these arguments are to the arguments of today concerning consensual crimes.)

If there is any conclusion in politics, on which we can securely rely, both from history, and from the laws which govern human action, it is this, THAT UNIVERSAL SUFFRAGE AND FREEDOM NEVER WERE AND NEVER CAN BE CO-EXISTENT.—*John Augustine Smith, president of the College of William and Mary, 1817*

That man says that women need to be helped into carriages, and lifted over ditches, and to have the best place everywhere. Nobody ever helped me into carriages, or over mud puddles, or gives me any best place, and aren't I a woman? I have plowed, and planted, and gathered into barns, and no man could head me—and aren't I a woman? I could work as much and eat as much as a man (when I could get it), and bear the lash as well—and aren't I a woman? I have borne thirteen children and seen them most all sold off into slavery, and when I cried out with a mother's grief, none but Jesus heard—and aren't I a woman?—*Sojourner Truth, 1851*

Nothing could be more anti-Biblical than letting women vote.—Harper's Magazine *editorial, November 1853*

Extend now to women suffrage and eligibility; give them the political right to vote and be voted for, render it feasible for them to enter the arena of political strife . . . and what remains of family union will soon be dissolved.—The Catholic World, *May 1869*

Sensible and responsible women do not want to vote. The relative positions to be assumed by man and woman in the working out of our civilization were assigned long ago by a higher intelligence than ours.—*Grover Cleveland, president of the United States, 1905)*

The suffragettes didn't get much help from their own gender. Women are, after all, human and as easily brainwashed as any other human. And, my, were their brains washed:

> The whole thing [the Women's Suffrage Movement] is an epidemic of vanity and restlessness—a disease as marked as measles or smallpox. . . . Hereafter this outbreak will stand in history as an instance of national sickness, of moral decadence, of social disorder.—*Mrs .Eliza Lynn Linton, March 1892*

The most powerful person in the world during the Victorian Era—Queen Victoria*—was no help at all.

*A woman.

The Queen is most anxious to enlist everyone who can speak or write to join in checking this mad, wicked folly of "Woman's Rights" with all its attendant horrors on which her poor, feeble sex is bent, forgetting every sense of womanly feeling and propriety. . . . It is a subject which makes the Queen so furious that she cannot contain herself.*

🐌 🐌 🐌

A woman carrying a Torah is like a pig at the Wailing Wall.

RABBI MEIR YEHUDA GETZ

In biblical times, if a woman didn't do her job (which included producing a male heir) to the satisfaction of the man, she could be sold into slavery, made the slave of the wife who *could* produce the male heir, or simply abandoned. Divorce was impossible for women; a mere technicality for men.

Other than wife-slave, the other role women filled was that of *courtesan*. Women of exceptional beauty, charm, and intelligence (who were intelligent enough to make the man feel *more* intelligent—sound familiar?)** played a role at *court*.

In short, the woman's role was slave or prostitute—sometimes both.

How women got in this mess is a mystery. Biblically, it is explained thus: Eve was made by God from one of Adam's ribs.*** ("She shall be called 'woman,'" said Adam, "for she was taken out of man.") So, woman was *of man*. When Eve disobeyed God's command and ate of the tree of knowledge of good and evil, God gave women three curses (Genesis 3:16): (1) "With pain you will give birth to children," (2) "Your desire will be for your husband," and (3) "And he will rule over you." With these last two punishments, man has justified (a) allowing men to have many wives, while a woman can only have one husband (it said "for your husband," not "for your husbands") and (b) it is man's *job* to rule over women.

*The Author is tempted to comment on the many powerful closeted homosexuals who are some of the most outspoken critics of gay rights, but the Author realizes that this would be off the point of this chapter—although it has never stopped the Author before—and so he will reluctantly contain himself.

**"I'm furious about the Women's Liberationists," said Anita Loos in 1973. "They keep getting up on soapboxes and proclaiming that women are brighter than men. That's true, but it should be kept very quiet or it ruins the whole racket."

***Because of this biblical passage (Genesis 2:22), it was firmly believed that males had one fewer rib than females. This belief was not challenged (believe it or not) until 1543 when Andreas Vesalius, the first modern anatomist, wrote, "The popular belief that man is lacking a rib on one side and that woman has one more rib than man is clearly ridiculous." Bruce Hilton picked up the story from there: "You can imagine the outraged response of church leaders. Vesalius was accused of being a revisionist, twisting the scriptures to serve his own ends. Called a heretic, he narrowly escaped with his life for stating a fact anybody could have verified. And it still was many years before the holy fathers changed official church policy on the subject."

This, for example, from Paul, written around A.D. 65:

> *In my view women are the bearers of life and the nurturers of life and the idea that we are going to use them in air-to-air combat or in air strikes is ludicrous.*
>
> PAT BUCHANAN
> August 2, 1991

A woman should learn in quietness and full submission. I do not permit a woman to teach or to have authority over a man; she must be silent. For Adam was formed first, then Eve. And Adam was not the one deceived; it was the woman who was deceived and became a sinner. But women will be saved through childbearing—if they continue in faith, love and holiness with propriety. (1 Timothy 2:11–15)

This, after all, is the way God wants it. One must be *literal* about these things: after all, it *is* the Bible.

This is, however, just one of many cases of selected literalism. God's curse to Adam included, "Cursed is the ground because of you; through painful toil you will eat of it all the days of your life. It will produce thorns and thistles for you, and you will eat the plants of the field" (Genesis 3:17–18). Does this mean man should only grow thorns and thistles and eat only "the plants of the fields"? (Previously, God had given him "every seed-bearing plant on the face of the whole earth and every tree that has fruit with seed in it. They will be yours for food" [Genesis 1:29].) Now God's curse was limiting man to "the plants of the field." Man, including Paul, has conveniently forgotten his curse, while scrupulously remembering the woman's. Paul instructed, "Eat anything sold in the meat market without raising questions of conscience" (1 Corinthians 10:25).

Paul, although he didn't necessarily *mean* to, even gave men the slogan they would use to proclaim a night of revelry: "Let us eat and drink, for tomorrow we die" (1 Corinthians 15:32).

Historically, it's difficult to see why women have always been so subservient. (But then, it *is* his-story.) Biologically, women are superior to men in almost every aspect except brute force. Women are more intelligent, live longer, learn faster, and can endure pain longer. In hunter-gatherer tribes, however, (1) they didn't have the brute force to kill the larger beasts (lions, tigers, and men from other tribes), and (2) the latter stages of pregnancy tended to make women less mobile. The importance of hunting, fighting, and mobility may have put the woman in a subservient position.

There was also the maternal instinct. A woman naturally wanted to protect her children—even children conceived in rape, which is, primarily, what sex was in those days. The father could do anything—including murder his children—with impunity. The mother knew this, and began to make concessions. The man knew this, and began to make greater demands. (Battered women today explain their plight in the same terms: "I don't know where I can go," and "I have to stay and protect my children." Sometimes the curse of "your desire will be for your husband" creeps in: "I still love him.")

In time, the game became, "Please the man of the house at any cost." The cost—both to women *and* to men was (and is) enormous. The hunter-gatherer tribes, naturally, rewarded the hunters and gatherers. By the time humans settled down and became farmers, city-dwellers, and stockbrokers—roles in which women can easily do as well as men—the die may have already been cast.

> *Men weren't really the enemy—*
> *they were fellow victims*
> *suffering from an outmoded*
> *masculine mystique*
> *that made them feel*
> *unnecessarily inadequate*
> *when there were no bears to kill.*
>
> BETTY FRIEDAN

Wherever female subservience started, with very few exceptions, it never lets up in the Bible. *Why* women were inferior is not important; *that they were* is. To understand that women were slaves or trinkets is not only central to understanding certain portions of the Old and New Testaments, but, in later chapters, also to understanding the seemingly irrational hatred for male homosexuals and prostitutes.

We certainly don't have to like it, but, to paraphrase Walter Cronkite, "That's the way it was."

The Ten Commandments*

> *My ancestors wandered*
> *lost in the wilderness*
> *for forty years*
> *because even in biblical times,*
> *men would not stop*
> *to ask for directions.*
>
> ELAYNE BOOSLER

PENTATEUCH, OR TORAH, is the law of Moses and forms the central basis of Judaism. These first five books of the Old Testament—Genesis, Exodus, Leviticus, Numbers, and Deuteronomy—were written or directly inspired by Moses, although only Deuteronomy is written in the first person. In the first four books, Moses is referred to as a character, and in Deuteronomy Moses begins using, "I."**

The Book of Genesis covers the creation of the earth; Adam and Eve; Noah and the great flood; and the stories of Abraham, Ishmael, Jacob, Esau, and Joseph.

Exodus tells the story of the Hebrews—the chosen people—their slavery in Egypt, and their deliverance by Moses. Midway through Exodus, they have found themselves—somewhere between 250,000 and 2,000,000 strong—wandering in the desert, being led to the promised land. It is a journey that will take forty years and fill the remainder of Exodus, Leviticus, Numbers, and Deuteronomy.

In these books are the Ten Commandments, as well as the previously noted admonition that is said to be the foundation of the Jewish religion, "Hear, O

---

*No, this chapter does not star Charlton Heston. But what would a chapter entitled "The Ten Commandments" be without at least a *mention* of C.H.? After all, says Heston, "I don't seem to have a twentieth-century face." How shall we feature Mr. Heston? I know; we'll quote Dwight MacDonald's review of Chuck in *Ben Hur*: "Charlton Heston throws all his punches in the first ten minutes (three grimaces and two intonations) so that he has nothing left long before he stumbles to the end, four hours later, and has to react to the Crucifixion. (He does make it clear, I must admit, that he quite disapproves of it.)"

**If all the books were written in the first person, he couldn't get away with inserting comments such as this into the account of a fight with his brother: "Now Moses was a very humble man, more humble than anyone else on the face of the earth" (Numbers 12:3).

> *The pursuit of knowledge*
> *for its own sake,*
> *an almost fanatical love of justice*
> *and the desire for personal*
> *independence—*
> *these are the features of the*
> *Jewish tradition which make me*
> *thank my stars that I belong to it.*
>
> ALBERT EINSTEIN

Israel: The Lord our God, the Lord is one. Love the Lord your God with all your heart and with all your soul and with all your strength" (Deuteronomy 6:4–5).

⚖️ ⚖️ ⚖️

The Ten Commandments are the foundation of Judaism, Christianity, and, to a lesser degree, Islam. Although they have been the basis of laws against consensual activities in the past, only a few give rise to consensual crimes today. (Thank God.) Let's take a look at each.*

I am the Lord thy God . . . Thou shalt have no other gods before me. Some people give more power to gods than to God—and some of these gods are awfully strange. Some people honor fear, guilt, unworthiness, hurt feelings, or anger, more than they honor God. Many people worship the idols of other people's opinions and the gods of greed, pettiness, and vindictiveness more consistently and with more devotion than they have ever worshiped anything divine. And yet, this isn't a crime. If it were, we would have another Inquisition on our hands. The persecution of "cults" in this country, however, can be traced back to these two commandments.

Thou shalt not take the name of the Lord thy God in vain. The religious watchdogs of our morality are more concerned that we don't say anything "dirty" (i.e., about sex) than they are about taking God's name in vain. You hear "goddam" on television from time to time, but you never hear the F-WORD—except on some of those "godless cable stations." (Trivia quiz: Who owns the movie rights to the book, *Joy of Sex?* Answer in a moment.) In many denominations of Judaism, it is forbidden to even *write* the word *God.* When one must refer to God, one writes it, "G-d." Network television—and most popular media—are just as sensitive about the F-WORD. Perhaps the commandment, "Thou shalt not use the F-WORD; and the C-WORD is not recommended," was on the tablet that—according to Mel Brooks—Moses dropped and broke on his way down Mount Sinai. (Answer to trivia quiz: Walt Disney Studios.)

Remember the sabbath day, to keep it holy. In very few places in this country is it still against the law for a retail establishment to be open on the Sabbath. There is, of course, difficulty in establishing what day the Sabbath day *is.* The Muslims celebrate Friday; the Jews celebrate Saturday; and the Christians celebrate Sunday.

---

*These are quoted from Exodus 20:2–17, using the King James Version—all those "thou shalt not's" are, well, *traditional.* That's how we as children learned to distinguish God and Shakespeare from everyone else—if a quotation had a "thou," it was either religious or classical. As I said, I'll be using the New International Version (NIV) for most scriptural references. When I use the King James Version, I'll put "KJV" after the chapter-verse citation.

For the devoutly multireligious, this makes for a long weekend. Those few laws that require certain places to be closed on Sundays (or prohibit certain things being sold on Sunday, such as liquor) are among the last vestiges of Ten Commandment–approved consensual crimes.

Honour thy father and thy mother. Thank heavens breaking *this* one's not a crime; few of us would have passed through our teenage years without at least one jail sentence behind us.

> *The law is not thrust upon man;*
> *it rests deep within him,*
> *to waken when the call comes.*
>
> MARTIN BUBER

Thou shalt not kill. Killing someone, of course, is not a consensual crime—it has an innocent victim. It is illegal, as well it should be. The New International Version translates this commandment as, "You shall not murder." This means, of course, taking the life of another *human being.* It's hard to get through this life without killing *something.* (Someone once defined a vegetarian as a person too insensitive to hear a carrot scream.) There is, however, a sect in India whose members so thoroughly believe in non-harm that they only eat the fruits and nuts that have already fallen from the trees and brush the pathway ahead of themselves with a broom so as not to step on any innocent insects. Needless to say, these people don't accomplish much else.

Thou shalt not commit adultery. Adultery is having sex with someone who is married to someone else or, if you are married, having sex with someone other than your spouse. (There is, of course, the world famous "double adultery," in which two people have sex while married to two other people. I won't discuss triple or quadruple adultery; I have my standards.) Adultery is the last great holdout of the consensually criminal thou-shalt-not's of the Ten Commandments. As of this writing, twenty-seven states have statutes against adultery. Note that the Ten Commandments do *not* prohibit prostitution or homosexual sex— consensual acts which have a lower Harris Poll–approval rating than adultery. The Ten Commandments also do not prohibit sex between unmarried people—*fornication* as they called it back then. On the surface, the rationale for prohibiting one but not the others goes back to the old prejudice that women were considered *property.* Adultery, then, was *theft;* a property violation.

The women-as-property concept is the *emotional* reason that keeps adultery on the law books, although all the other consensual activities in the Ten Commandments are no longer crimes (with the exception of the occasional blue law or cult raid). The idea that women own their own bodies is *slowly* catching on. *(Very* slowly: note the continuing fight over abortion rights.) As the "radical" idea that women—not society, not men—own their own bodies is accepted, the idea that adultery should be illegal may fall away, too.

The underlying reason adultery is forbidden as a *Commandment,* however, is

> *Maybe
> the answer is the
> Ten Commandments.*
>
> JERRY BROWN

that adultery involves *breaking commitments.* People promise to be faithful to each other till death does them part; if one of them steps out, that's a broken agreement. This is not the case with any other sexual dalliance. (Although other sexual unions *may* involve broken agreements, adultery, by definition, *always* does.) The other forms of sexual dalliance are consensual: consenting adults are doing things with their own person and property. The attitudes toward those activities change with time, place, and custom. The Ten Commandments were designed to be universal laws for all time.*

Adultery's being a broken agreement, I believe, is why Jesus was against adultery. (Although this is getting slightly ahead of our story, the only consensual crime Jesus specifically frowned upon was adultery.) The universal law underlying the Commandment is: "Thou shalt not adulterate *yourself* and your relationships by breaking agreements—*any* agreements," or, simply, "Thou shalt keep your agreements." When in the Old Testament God called Israel "adulterous" (as he did many, many times), he wasn't talking about husbands and wives cheating on each other. He was angry that the people of Israel had broken the Covenant—the agreement—he had made with them. If they would keep the Ten Commandments, the Covenant said, God would "bring [them] out from under the yoke of the Egyptians" (Exodus 6:6). Well, he did and they didn't and he didn't like it. Broken agreements seemed to bother the God of the Old Testament quite a bit.

For most people in most times, adultery has probably been the biggest challenge to personal honesty, so the Commandment gives the most difficult example of agreement-keeping. (Today, of course, we have income tax.) The idea is that, if you can stay faithful to your spouse until one of you dies, you can keep *any* agreement. As we shall see, Jesus was not a personal fan of marriage, but, he taught, if you make an agreement, you should keep it. (He also taught that you

---

*Among the Hebrews at that time, "local ordinances" prohibited prostitution, homosexuality, and fornication. This was appropriate for a people wandering in the desert for forty years. They didn't want the nation to shrink into a tribe. Reproduction was important—and awfully difficult while wandering around a desert. Any sexual act that did not potentially lead to children—including masturbation—was forbidden. On the other hand, in Mesopotamia at that time—or even Egypt, whence they had recently exodused—homosexuality, prostitution, fornication, and masturbation were all fine. Mesopotamia and Egypt had no underpopulation problem. (Well, maybe Egypt was hurting a little, after that Red Sea disaster and all. But maybe it wasn't as bad as C. B. De Mille made it out to be. Things always look worse on television.) Yet the Commandment, "Thou shalt not commit adultery," could apply to both the Mesopotamians and the Egyptians. Keeping agreements—about sex or anything else—is a solid, universal policy: the Mesopotamians and Egyptians who chose to follow this Commandment (in whatever form they got it; the Ten Commandments are the basis of most law) lived better lives than those who chose not to.

should pay your taxes. Radical teachings.)

From a legal point of view, however, broken agreements between consenting adults are a matter for *civil*, not *criminal*, law. We can sue people who break contracts, but we can't put them in jail—making them hire a lawyer is punishment enough. Adultery, then, among the sexual variances, is a special case. It should be, however, at worst, a civil case, not a criminal one.

Thou shalt not steal. A crime, an innocent victim, no problem.

> *Men are not made religious by performing certain actions which are externally good, but they must first have righteous principles, and then they will not fail to perform virtuous actions.*
>
> MARTIN LUTHER
> (1483–1546)

Thou shalt not bear false witness against thy neighbour. In our day it's known as *perjury.* It is illegal and there are innocent victims. Amen.

Thou shalt not covet thy neighbour's house, thou shalt not covet thy neighbour's wife, nor his manservant, nor his maidservant, nor his ox, nor his ass, nor anything that is thy neighbour's. And a final "hosanna!" that all these are *not* crimes. We'd *all* be in jail. How often have we coveted our neighbor's house, wife, manservant, maidservant, ox, and so on? If coveting all these things were illegal, then "Lifestyles of the Rich and Famous" would be the most scandalous and banned television show in history (and probably have much higher ratings because of it).

For the most part, then—with the exception of the Big A in twenty-seven states—breaking the Commandments that refer to the *social* morality (the ones with innocent victims) is illegal, and breaking the Commandments that refer to *personal* morality is not.

Nor is it illegal to break the "heart" of the Jewish Law ("Hear, O Israel: The Lord our God, the Lord is one. Love the Lord your God with all your heart and with all your soul and with all your strength.")

In terms of the basis of Judaism, then, synagogue and state are—with one adulteration—separate. These were God's laws—universal and timeless—the Covenant between the chosen people and the God who chose them.

Moses, the Lawgiver, gave a lot of other laws to help the Israelites survive their forty-year desert trek. These are the ones most often quoted by the fundamentalists when condemning this or that consensual crime. (Christians have to go back to Moses for this purpose because Christ didn't say much on the subject.)

Let's look at the Laws of Moses in a radical and almost scandalous way—a way that they are seldom looked at: *in context.*

The Laws of Moses

THE REMAINDER OF EXODUS (the Ten Commandments fall almost precisely midway through the book) and the three books that follow it contain a series of laws—known collectively as the Laws of Moses—which became the basis for Jewish daily living. These were considered necessary laws for a group of people wandering in the desert for forty years and for teaching a polytheistic (pagan) people how to worship one God. The vast majority of these laws, however, are no longer considered necessary for living a pure, good, or holy life—even by the most devout Jew.

The first five books of the Old Testament present a collection of forbidden activities which most of us do on a regular basis (shaving; getting a haircut; wearing clothing woven of two kinds of material; eating rare meat, hot dogs, shrimp, lobster, clams, or oysters). They also present a series of acceptable or even required practices that we wouldn't even dream of doing (animal sacrifices, keeping slaves, stoning people to death for infractions such as cursing their parents).

Let's take a detailed look at just one of these books: Leviticus.* A lot of laws are given over and over. I'll try to avoid too much repetition.

The first seven chapters of Leviticus tell about the various kinds and forms of offerings to God. Chapter 1 tells where and how to slaughter bulls, how to cut them into pieces, and how to arrange them on the burning wood: "and the priest is to burn all of it on the altar. It is a burnt offering, an offering made by fire, an

---

*Please understand that, in this examination, I in no way intend to ridicule, question, or even minimize any of the teachings in the Bible. I simply mean to show that *no one* follows all the teachings of the Bible. Certainly not a single fundamentalist Christian—*not one*. Even the most devout Jew has abandoned burnt offerings, keeping slaves, stoning, and a great many other activities which are permitted or required by the Laws of Moses.

> *When you eat fish,*
> *you don't eat the bones.*
> *You eat the flesh.*
> *Take the Bible like that.*
>
> ROBERT R. MOTON

aroma pleasing to the Lord" (Leviticus 1:9). Sheep and goats to be sacrificed should be males without defect. They are to be slaughtered on the north side of the altar and the blood sprinkled on all four sides of the altar. The entire animal is then cut up and burned on the altar. If a dove or young pigeon is sacrificed, "the priest shall bring it to the altar, wring off the head and burn it on the altar; its blood shall be drained out on the side of the altar. He is to remove the crop with its contents and throw it to the east side of the altar, where the ashes are" (1:15–16). The remainder of the bird is then torn open and burned completely in the fire.

Chapter 2 details the offering of grain. Instructions are given on how the grain, which must always be in the form of "fine flour," can be offered: as is, baked, grilled, or cooked in a pan. When yeast and honey can and cannot be used is carefully explained—but all grain offerings must include salt. Unlike animal sacrifices, which are burned in their entirety, only a portion of the grain offering is burned—"the rest of the grain offering belongs to Aaron and his sons" (2:3). (Aaron was the brother of Moses. Aaron and his sons were the priests in charge of the offerings.)

Chapter 3 concerns itself with the fellowship offering—also known as the peace offering. Here, the animals are slaughtered at the entrance of the Tent of Meeting (the place of worship). Once again, the way to dismember animals and burn them is described. The last verse adds this admonition: "This is a lasting ordinance for the generations to come, wherever you live: You must not eat any fat or any blood" (3:17). This admonition—especially the eating of blood—is repeated throughout the Old Testament. Anytime you've had rare meat or gravy made from pan drippings, you have eaten blood. If you've had a hamburger or hot dog—up to 30% fat—or, ironically, a pastrami sandwich at a kosher deli, you have eaten fat.

Chapters 4, 5, 6, and 7 tell what offerings to bring if you have sinned, how these offerings are to be sacrificed, and which of the offerings are to be burned in their entirety and which of them may be eaten by the priests. (The priests ate *very* well.) The details are extraordinarily precise. When one commits a sin—either intentionally or unintentionally—one becomes "unclean." In order to become clean again, one must make a sacrifice and go through a ritual cleansing. The type and kind of sacrifice for various sins is explained in these chapters.

Chapter 8 describes how Moses ordained his brother Aaron and his sons as priests. They first washed themselves and were anointed with oil. Then a bull was sacrificed and Moses "took all the fat around the inner parts, the covering of the liver, and both kidneys and their fat, and burned it on the altar. But the bull with its hide and its flesh and its offal he burned up outside the camp, as the Lord commanded Moses" (8:16–17). Then they sacrificed one ram in its entirety, then a second ram: "Moses slaughtered the ram and took some of its blood and put it on the lobe of Aaron's right ear, on the thumb of his right hand and on the big toe of his right foot" (8:23). A little later, we learn about the wave offering. "He also took the breast—Moses' share of the ordination ram—and waved it before the Lord as a wave offering, as the

> *I never had any doubt about it*
> *being of divine origin—*
> *point out to me*
> *any similar collection of writings*
> *that has lasted for as many*
> *thousands of years and is still a*
> *best-seller, world wide.*
> *It had to be of divine origin.*
>
> RONALD REAGAN

Lord commanded Moses" (8:29). This form of offering probably grew more popular in time, as all one had to do was *wave* the animal part in the general direction of the Lord and then one could eat it.

> Moses then said to Aaron and his sons, "Cook the meat at the entrance to the Tent of Meeting and eat it there with the bread from the basket of ordination offerings, as I commanded, saying 'Aaron and his sons are to eat it.'" (8:31)

After seven days of spending night and day in the Tent of Meeting—the amount of time it took for the complete ordination—Aaron and his sons were officially priests.

Chapter 9 talks about the many offerings made by Aaron and his sons, and ends with happy news: "Fire came out from the presence of the Lord and consumed the burnt offering and the fat portions on the altar. And when all the people saw it, they shouted for joy and fell face down" (9:24).

Unfortunately, chapter 10 begins with some bad news: Aaron's sons Nadab and Abihu offered the Lord an "unauthorized fire." "So fire came out from the presence of the Lord and consumed them, and they died before the Lord" (10:2). Why they were offering an "unauthorized fire" is not certain, but the signs point to the idea that they were intoxicated: "Then the Lord said to Aaron, 'You and your sons are not to drink wine or other fermented drink whenever you go into the Tent of Meeting, or you will die. This is a lasting ordinance for the generations to come'" (10:8–9). (Any religion that includes drinking wine as part of its service, then, is breaking a Levitical law.) Meanwhile, "when Moses inquired about the goat of the sin offering and found that it had been burned up, he was angry with Eleazar and Ithamar, Aaron's remaining sons, and asked, 'Why didn't you eat the sin offering in the sanctuary area?'" (10:16–17). All in all, it was not a good day for the new priests of Israel.

You will note that we are now more than a third of the way through Leviticus' twenty-seven chapters and, with the possible exception of "lower your intake of animal fats" and "don't get drunk if you are going to officiate in a religious service that utilizes fire," none of the commands applies to the activities of a civilized person today.

Chapter 11 explores the foods that are "clean" and "unclean." This was the beginning of the kosher laws for food. Essentially, you must not eat—or even touch the carcass of—a rabbit, lizard, pig, shrimp, lobster, clam, scallop, eel, octopus, oyster or squid. You may, however, eat "any kind of locust, katydid, cricket or grasshopper. But all other winged creatures that have four legs you are to detest (11:22–23). Well, at least we have locusts, katydids, crickets, and grasshoppers. Anyone who touches the carcass of an unclean animal must wash his clothes and is unclean until evening. If an unclean animal falls on something, the object is unclean and must be put in water until evening; then it will be clean. If the animal falls on or into a clay pot, oven, or cooking pot, the crockery is unclean and must be broken into pieces.

Chapter 12 explores what a woman must do after childbirth in order to become clean again. If she has a boy, she is unclean for seven days, plus an additional 33 days, for a total of 40 days. If she has a girl, however, she will be unclean for two weeks, plus an additional 66 days, for a total of 80 days. When her unclean time following childbirth is over, the woman is to bring a year-old lamb as a burnt offering and a young pigeon or dove as a sin offering. "If she can not afford a lamb, she is to bring two doves or two young pigeons, one for a burnt offering and the other for a sin offering. In this way the priest will make atonement for her, and she will be clean" (12:8).

Chapter 13 (unlucky 13) covers skin diseases and mildew. Verses 1 through 44 explore the many possibilities of skin irritation and delineate which diseases one can have and still be clean and which ones make a person unclean. (Almost all of them fall into the latter category.) With certain diseases (leprosy, for example), one "must wear torn clothes, let his hair be unkempt, cover the lower part of his face and cry out, 'Unclean! Unclean!' As long as he has the infection he remains unclean. He must live alone; he must live outside the camp" (13:45–46). Verses 47 through 59 cover which kinds of mildew can be washed out of clothing (making the clothing or leather article clean again), and which kinds of mildew make an article of clothing or leather permanently unclean, in which case it must be burned.

Chapter 14 tells how one with a skin disease may be made clean again. It is a *very* elaborate procedure, taking at least eight days and involving two birds, two male lambs and one ewe lamb (each a year old and without defect), six quarts of fine flour mixed with oil, and an additional pint of oil. One must shave his entire body twice: "he must shave off all his hair; he must shave his head, his beard, his

eyebrows and the rest of his hair" (14:9).
(What a woman must do in this situation is
not discussed.) The remainder of chapter 14
offers helpful hints on how to clean a house
of mildew. If you're lucky, you'll only have
to scrape out the unclean plaster and apply
new plaster. If you're not so lucky, the
house "must be torn down—its stones, tim-
bers and all the plaster—and taken out of
the town to an unclean place" (14:45).

Chapter 15 discusses a man's nocturnal
emission and a woman's period. Essentially,
these are both unclean acts, and anything the man or woman lies on, sits on, or
touches becomes unclean. Anyone who touches them, or anything they have lain
or sat on, is unclean. The man is unclean until evening and must bring two doves
to be sacrificed, one as a sin offering and the other as a burnt offering. The
woman, however, is unclean for seven days. (So, at least a quarter of a woman's
life is spent "unclean.") After seven days, she brings two pigeons or doves, one as a
burnt offering and one as a sin offering. If a man lies with a woman during her
menstrual period, he is unclean for seven days and must bring two doves or
pigeons, etc. If he lays with a woman, however, he will probably not have a
nocturnal emission that month, so he'll pick up a day. As God points out, "You
must keep the Israelites separate from things that make them unclean, so they
will not die in their uncleanness for defiling my dwelling place, which is among
them" (15:31).

Chapter 16 discusses the elaborate preparations and sacrifices Aaron must
make before he goes into "the Most Holy Place behind the curtain in front of the
atonement cover on the ark, or else he will die" (16:2). In addition to the usual
assortment of burnt offerings, we have a new concept: the *scapegoat*. Two goats
are brought before him. By the casting of lots (dice), it is determined which goat
is to be sacrificed and which goat becomes the scapegoat. On the scapegoat's
head are placed all the sins of the community. The scapegoat is then taken into
the desert where it will die a miserable death—but better the goat than the people
who committed the sins. "[Aaron] is to lay both hands on the head of the live goat
and confess over it all the wickedness and rebellion of the Israelites—all their
sins—and put them on the goat's head. He shall send the goat away into the
desert in the care of a man appointed for the task" (16:21).

Chapter 17 prohibits sacrificing animals in any place other than the Tent of
Meeting. Eating of blood once again is clearly prohibited in any way, shape, or
form. "You must not eat the blood of any creature, because the life of every
creature is its blood; anyone who eats it must be cut off" (17:14).

Chapter 18 contains all the sexual activities that are not acceptable. It's a long
list; here's the *Reader's Digest* version: don't have sex with your stepmother, stepsis-

> Filled with compassion,
> Jesus reached out his hand and touched
> the man.
> "I am willing,"
> he said.
> "Be clean!"
> Immediately the leprosy left him and
> he was cured.
>
> MARK 1:42

ter, "the daughter of your father's wife," your aunt, "a woman and her daughter," a woman and "her son's daughter or her daughter's daughter"; with a woman while she's having her period; with your neighbor's wife. As verse 29 explains, "Everyone who does any of these detestable things—such persons must be cut off from their people" (18:29).

Chapter 19 is a grab bag of laws. It restates many of the laws of the Ten Commandments, but includes such interesting additions as:

Verse 19: "Do not mate different kinds of animals. Do not plant your fields with two kinds of seed. Do not wear clothing woven of two kinds of material."

Verses 20–21: "If a man sleeps with a woman who is a slave girl promised to another man but who has not been ransomed or given her freedom, there must be due punishment. Yet they are not to be put to death, because she had not been freed. The man, however, must bring a ram to the entrance to the Tent of Meeting for a guilt offering to the Lord."

Verse 27: "Do not cut the hair at the sides of your head or clip off the edges of your beard."

Verse 28: "Do not . . . put tattoo marks on yourselves."

Verse 32: "Rise in the presence of the aged, show respect for the elderly. . . ."

Similarly, chapter 20 offers a *potpourri* of sins and punishments. Among the more succulent:

Verse 6: "I will set my face against the person who turns to mediums and spiritists to prostitute himself by following them, and I will cut him off from his people."

Verse 9: "If anyone curses his father or mother, he must be put to death. He has cursed his father or mother, and his blood will be on his own head."

Verse 10: "If a man commits adultery with another man's wife—with the wife of his neighbor—both the adulterer and the adulteress must be put to death."

Verse 11: "If a man sleeps with his father's wife, he has dishonored his father. Both the man and the woman must be put to death; their blood will be on their own heads."

Verse 13 (Falwell's Favorite): "If a man lies with a man as one lies with a woman, both of them have done what is detestable. They must be put to death; their blood will be on their own heads."

Verse 14: "If a man marries both a woman and her mother, it is wicked. Both he and they must be burned in the fire, so that bno wickedness will be among you."

Verse 15: "If a man has sexual relations with an animal, he must be put to death, and you must kill the animal."*

Verse 16: "If a woman approaches an animal to have sexual relations with it, kill both the woman and the animal. They must be put to death; their blood will be on their own heads."

Verse 18: "If a man lies with a woman during her monthly period and has sexual relations with her, he has exposed the source of her flow, and she has also uncovered it. Both of them must be cut off from their people."

> *Homosexuality is Satan's diabolical attack upon the family that will not only have a corrupting influence upon our next generation, but it will also bring down the wrath of God upon America.*
>
> JERRY FALWELL

Verse 27: "A man or woman who is a medium or spiritist among you must be put to death. You are to stone them; their blood will be on their own heads."

Chapter 21 gives more rules for priests and those around them. Highlights include:

Verse 9: "If a priest's daughter defiles herself by becoming a prostitute, she disgraces her father; she must be burned in the fire."

Verse 11: "[The high priest] must not enter a place where there is a dead body."

Verse 13: "The woman he marries must be a virgin."

Verse 14: "He must not marry a widow, a divorced woman, or a woman defiled by prostitution, but only a virgin from his own people. . . ."

Verses 18–20: "No [priest] who has any defect may come near [the altar]; no man who is blind or lame, disfigured or deformed; no man with a crippled foot or hand, or who is hunchbacked or dwarfed, or who has any eye defect, or who has festering or running sores or damaged testicles."

Chapter 22 recounts a great many of the previous admonitions ("If a descendant of Aaron has an infectious skin disease or a bodily discharge, he may not eat the sacred offerings until he is cleansed. He will also be unclean if he touches something defiled by a corpse or by anyone who has an emission of semen, or if

---

*If this seems an unfair punishment—whether your compassion is for the man or the animal—and if you think it could *never* be a law, allow me to quote from William Bradford, governor of Plymouth, Massachusetts (1642): "Ther was a youth whose name was Thomas Granger; he was servant to an honest man of Duxbery, being aboute 16 or 17. years of age. (His father & mother lived at the same time at Sityate.) He was this year detected of buggery (and indicted for the same) with a mare, a cowe, tow goats, five sheep, 2. calves, and a turkey. Horrible it is to mention, but the truth of the historie requires it. He was first discovered by one that accidentally saw his lewd practise towards the mare. (I forbear perticulers.) Being upon it examined and committed, in the end he not only confest the fact with that beast at that time, but sundrie times before, and at severall times with all the rest of the forenamed in his indictmente. And accordingly he was cast by the jury, and condemned, and after executed the 8. of September, 1642. A very sade spectakle it was; for first the mare, and then the cowe, and the rest of the lesser catle, were kild before his face, according to the law, Levit: 20:15, and then he him selfe was executed."

> *Can it be*
> *I am the only Jew*
> *residing in Danville, Kentucky,*
> *looking for matzoh*
> *in the Safeway and the A & P?*
>
> MAXINE KUMIN

he touches any crawling thing that makes him unclean, or any person who makes him unclean, whatever the uncleanness may be" [22:4–5]). It goes on to tell who can and cannot eat the burnt (or, in this case, the cooked) offerings. (The guest of a priest cannot, but the purchased slave of a priest may.) What is and what is not acceptable to the Lord is made more precise.

Verse 22: "Do not offer to the Lord the blind, the injured or the maimed, or anything with warts or festering or running sores. Do not place any of these on the altar as an offering made to the Lord by fire."

Verse 24: "You must not offer to the Lord an animal whose testicles are bruised, crushed, torn or cut."

Verse 28: "Do not slaughter a cow or a sheep and its young on the same day."

Chapter 23 deals with the various festivals. These include the Sabbath (one day a week in which there is absolutely *no*—read my lips: *no*—work), Passover, Feast of the Firstfruits, Feast of Weeks, Feast of Trumpets, Day of Atonement, Feast of Tabernacles, and Feast of Unleavened Bread.

Chapter 24 tells us about the olive oil and the bread that is to be "set before the Lord."

> This bread is to be set out before the Lord regularly, Sabbath after Sabbath, on behalf of the Israelites, as a lasting covenant. It belongs to Aaron and his sons, who are to eat it in a holy place, because it is a most holy part of their regular share of the offerings made to the Lord by fire. (24:8–9)

At this point, chapter 24 takes a rather dark turn. Someone, it seems, has "blasphemed the Name with a curse" (24:11).

> Then the Lord said to Moses: "Take the blasphemer outside the camp. All those who heard him are to lay their hands on his head, and the entire assembly is to stone him. Say to the Israelites: 'If anyone curses his God, he will be held responsible; anyone who blasphemes the name of the Lord must be put to death. The entire assembly must stone him. Whether an alien or native-born, when he blasphemes the Name, he must be put to death. . . .'" Then Moses spoke to the Israelites, and they took the blasphemer outside the camp and stoned him. The Israelites did as the Lord commanded Moses. (24:13–16, 23)

Chapter 25 introduces the Year of Jubilee. Every seven years—Leviticus instructs—the land is to go fallow. Whatever grows there is to be harvested by the poor. This is the Sabbath for the land. Every seventh Sabbath for the land—seven times seven years—becomes the Year of Jubilee. In the Year of Jubilee, all slaves purchased are to be set free, all houses purchased (except houses within walled cities) are to return to their original owner ("Quick! There's only three months until the Year of Jubilee. Let's build a wall."), and all land sold is to return to its original holder. Nothing, it seems, is sold permanently; it is sold only until the Year of Jubilee; all contracts are good for a maximum of forty-nine years. This means that the price of everything must be determined by how many years it is from the time the deal is set until the Year of Jubilee.*

> *If we are not our brother's keeper, at least let us not be his executioner.*
>
> MARLON BRANDO

Chapter 26 tells how wonderful it will be for those who obey *all* the laws and how terrible it will be for those who break even one law. If you obey all the laws, "you will pursue your enemies, and they will fall by the sword before you. Five of you will chase a hundred, and a hundred of you will chase ten thousand, and your enemies will fall by the sword before you" (26:7–8). Paradise! If the laws are not obeyed, however, God "will send wild animals against you, and they will rob you of your children, destroy your cattle and make you so few in number that your roads will be deserted" (26:22). "You will eat the flesh of your sons and the flesh of your daughters" (26:29). God also says, "I will scatter you among the nations and will draw out my sword and pursue you. Your land will be laid waste, and your cities will lie in ruins" (26:33), and "you will perish among the nations; the land of your enemies will devour you" (26:38).

In chapter 27, the last chapter of Leviticus, the price is set for slaves of various ages—males are, of course, worth more than females. A male between the ages of twenty and sixty is worth fifty shekels, and a female between twenty and sixty is worth thirty shekels. "If it is a person between the ages of five and twenty, set the value of a male at twenty shekels and of a female at ten shekels. If it is a person between one month and five years, set the value of a male at five shekels of silver and that of a female at three shekels of silver" (27:5–6).

Leviticus ends on a happy note: tithing. "A tithe of everything from the land, whether grain from the soil or fruit from the trees, belongs to the Lord; it is holy to the Lord. . . . The entire tithe of the herd and flock—every tenth animal that passes under the shepherd's rod—will be holy to the Lord. He must not pick out the good from the bad or make any substitution (27:30, 32–33).

Thus ends Leviticus, just *one* of Moses' four "lawgiving" books of the Pentateuch. Here are selected laws from the other three, Exodus, Numbers, and Deuteronomy:

---

*Did the enforcement of this law create a lot of accountants and lawyers, or were there a lot of accountants and lawyers who, "for the good of the people," created this law? Only Moses knows.

Laws from Exodus

If you buy a Hebrew servant, he is to serve you for six years. But in the seventh year, he shall go free, without paying anything. If he comes alone, he is to go free alone; but if he has a wife when he comes, she is to go with him. If his master gives him a wife and she bears him sons or daughters, the woman and her children shall belong to her master, and only the man shall go free. (21:2–4)

If a man sells his daughter as a servant, she is not to go free as menservants do. If she does not please the master who has selected her for himself, he must let her be redeemed. He has no right to sell her to foreigners, because he has broken faith with her. (21:7–8)

Anyone who curses his father or mother must be put to death. (21:17)

If a man beats his male or female slave with a rod and the slave dies as a direct result, he must be punished, but he is not to be punished if the slave gets up after a day or two, since the slave is his property. (21:20–21)

If a man seduces a virgin who is not pledged to be married and sleeps with her, he must pay the bride-price, and she shall be his wife. If her father absolutely refuses to give her to him, he must still pay the bride-price for virgins. (22:16–17)

Do not allow a sorceress to live. (22:18)

Anyone who has sexual relations with an animal must be put to death. (22:19)

Whoever sacrifices to any god other than the Lord must be destroyed. (22:20)

If you lend money to one of my people among you who is needy, do not be like a moneylender; charge him no interest. (22:25)

Do not blaspheme God or curse God the ruler of your people. (22:28)

You must give me the firstborn of your sons. (22:29)

Do the same with your cattle and your sheep. Let them stay with their mothers for seven days, but give them to me on the eighth day. (22:30)

Do not cook a young goat in its mother's milk. (23:19)

Whoever does any work on the Sabbath day must be put to death. (31:15)

Redeem the firstborn donkey with a lamb, but if you do not redeem it, break its neck. Redeem all your firstborn sons. (34:20)

Do not light a fire in any of your dwellings on the Sabbath day. (35:3)

Laws from Numbers

Whenever the tabernacle is to move, the Levites are to take it down, and whenever the tabernacle is to be set up, the Levites shall do it. Anyone else who goes near it shall be put to death. (1:51)

The Kohathites must not go in to look at the holy things, even for a moment, or they will die. (4:20)

While the Israelites were in the desert, a man was found gathering wood on the Sabbath day. Those who found him gathering wood brought him to Moses and Aaron and the whole assembly, and they kept him in custody, because it was not clear what should be done to him. Then the Lord said to Moses, "The man must die. The whole assembly must stone him outside the camp." So the assembly took him outside the camp and stoned him to death, as the Lord commanded Moses. (15:32–36)

> *As a child my family's menu consisted of two choices: take it or leave it.*
>
> BUDDY HACKETT

[The Levites] must not go near the furnishings of the sanctuary or the altar, or both they and you will die. (18:3)

Only you and your sons may serve as priests in connection with everything at the altar and inside the curtain. I am giving you the service of the priesthood as a gift. Anyone else who comes near the sanctuary must be put to death. (18:7)

From now on the Israelites must not go near the Tent of Meeting, or they will bear the consequences of their sin and will die. (18:22)

So Moses said to Israel's judges, "Each of you must put to death those of your men who have joined in worshiping the Baal of Peor." (25:5)

Laws from Deuteronomy
(which means "repetition of the law")*

The images of their gods you are to burn in the fire. Do not covet the silver and gold on them, and do not take it for yourselves, or you will be ensnared by it, for it is detestable to the Lord your God. (7:25)

If a prophet, or one who foretells by dreams, appears among you and announces to you a miraculous sign or wonder, and if the sign or wonder of which he has spoken takes place, and he says, "Let us follow other gods" (gods you have not known) "and let us worship them," you must not listen to the words of that prophet or dreamer. The Lord your God is testing you to find out whether you love him with all your heart and with all your soul. That prophet or dreamer must be put to death. . . . (13:1–3, 5)

*I will omit most of the repetitions. You are welcome to start skimming here—the test will not include this material. You've probably already gotten the points I plan to make at this chapter's end.

If your very own brother, or your son or daughter, or the wife you love, or your closest friend secretly entices you, saying, "Let us go and worship other gods" . . . do not yield to him or listen to him. Show him no pity. Do not spare him or shield him. You must certainly put him to death. Your hand must be the first in putting him to death, and then the hands of all the people. Stone him to death, because he tried to turn you away from the Lord your God. . . . (13:6, 8–10)

If you hear it said about one of the towns the Lord your God is giving you to live in that wicked men have arisen among you and have led the people of their town astray, saying, "Let us go and worship other gods" (gods you have not known), then you must inquire, probe and investigate it thoroughly. And if it is true and it has been proved that this detestable thing has been done among you, you must certainly put to the sword all who live in that town. Destroy it completely, both its people and its livestock. Gather all the plunder of the town into the middle of the public square and completely burn the town and all its plunder as a whole burnt offering to the Lord your God. It is to remain a ruin forever, never to be rebuilt. (13:12–16)

Do not eat anything you find already dead. You may give it to an alien living in any of your towns, and he may eat it, or you may sell it to a foreigner. But you are a people holy to the Lord your God. (14:21)

At the end of every seven years you must cancel debts. (15:1)

There should be no poor among you. (15:4)

You will lend to many nations but will borrow from none. (15:6)

If there is a poor man among your brothers in any of the towns of the land that the Lord your God is giving you, do not be hardhearted or tightfisted toward your poor brother. (15:7)

There will always be poor people in the land. Therefore I command you to be openhanded toward your brothers and toward the poor and needy in your land. (15:11)

If a man or woman living among you in one of the towns the Lord gives you is found doing evil in the eyes of the Lord your God in violation of his covenant, and contrary to my command has worshiped other gods, bowing down to them or to the sun or the moon or the stars of the sky, and this has been brought to your attention, then you must investigate it thoroughly. If it is true and it has been proved that this detestable thing has been done in Israel, take the man or woman who has done this evil deed to your city gate and stone that person to death. (17:2–5)

The man who shows contempt for the judge or for the priest who stands ministering there to the Lord your God must be put to death. (17:12)

Let no one be found among you . . . who practices divination or sorcery, interprets omens, engages in witchcraft, or casts spells, or who is a medium or spiritist or who consults the dead. Anyone who does these things is detestable to the Lord. . . . (18:10–12)

A prophet who presumes to speak in my name anything I have not commanded him to say, or a prophet who speaks in the name of other gods, must be put to death. (18:20)

> *I would no more quarrel with a man because of his religion than I would because of his art.*
>
> MARY BAKER EDDY

Show no pity: life for life, eye for eye, tooth for tooth, hand for hand, foot for foot. (19:21)

The officers shall say to the army: "Has anyone built a new house and not dedicated it? Let him go home, or he may die in battle and someone else may dedicate it. Has anyone planted a vineyard and not begun to enjoy it? Let him go home, or he may die in battle and someone else enjoy it. Has anyone become pledged to a woman and not married her? Let him go home, or he may die in battle and someone else marry her." Then the officers shall add, "Is any man afraid or fainthearted? Let him go home so that his brothers will not become disheartened too." (20:5–8)

When you march up to attack a city, make its people an offer of peace. If they accept and open their gates, all the people in it shall be subject to forced labor and shall work for you. If they refuse to make peace and they engage you in battle, lay siege to that city. When the Lord your God delivers it into your hand, put to the sword all the men in it. As for the women, the children, the livestock and everything else in the city, you may take these as plunder for yourselves. (20:10–14)

When you go to war against your enemies and the Lord your God delivers them into your hands and you take captives, if you notice among the captives a beautiful woman and are attracted to her, you may take her as your wife. If you are not pleased with her, let her go wherever she wishes. You must not sell her or treat her as a slave, since you have dishonored her. (21:10–11, 14)

If a man has two wives, and he loves one but not the other, and both bear him sons but the firstborn is the son of the wife he does not love, when he wills his property to his sons, he must not give the rights of the firstborn to the son of the wife he loves in preference to his actual firstborn, the son of the wife he does not love. (21:15–16)

A woman must not wear men's clothing, nor a man wear women's clothing, for the Lord your God detests anyone who does this. (22:5)

> Do not plow with an ox and a donkey yoked together. (22:10)

> If a man takes a wife and, after lying with her, dislikes her and slanders her and gives her a bad name, saying, "I married this woman, but when I approached her, I did not find proof of her virginity," then the girl's father and mother shall bring proof that she was a virgin to the town elders at the gate. The girl's father will say to the elders, "I gave my daughter in marriage to this man, but he dislikes her. Now he has slandered her and said, 'I did not find your daughter to be a virgin.' But here is the proof of my daughter's virginity." Then her parents shall display the cloth before the elders of the town, and the elders shall take the man and punish him. They shall fine him a hundred shekels of silver and give them to the girl's father, because this man has given an Israelite virgin a bad name. She shall continue to be his wife; he must not divorce her as long as he lives. If, however, the charge is true and no proof of the girl's virginity can be found, she shall be brought to the door of her father's house and there the men of her town shall stone her to death. She has done a disgraceful thing in Israel by being promiscuous while still in her father's house. (22:13–21)

> If a man is found sleeping with another man's wife, both the man who slept with her and the woman must die. (22:22)

> If a man happens to meet in a town a virgin pledged to be married and he sleeps with her, you shall take both of them to the gate of that town and stone them to death. (22:23–24)

> If a man happens to meet a virgin who is not pledged to be married and rapes her and they are discovered, he shall pay the girl's father fifty shekels of silver. He must marry the girl, for he has violated her. He can never divorce her as long as he lives. (22:28–29)

> No one who has been emasculated by crushing or cutting may enter the assembly of the Lord. (23:1)

> No one born of a forbidden marriage nor any of his descendants may enter the assembly of the Lord, even down to the tenth generation. (23:2)

> No Israelite man or woman is to become a shrine prostitute. (23:17)

> You must not bring the earnings of a female prostitute or of a male prostitute into the house of the Lord your God to pay any vow, because the Lord your God detests them both. (23:18)

> If you enter your neighbor's vineyard, you may eat all the grapes you want, but do not put any in your basket. (23:24)

> If you enter your neighbor's grainfield, you may pick kernels with your

---

Viscount Waldorf Astor owned Britain's two most influential newspapers, The Times and the Observer, but his American wife, Nancy, had a wider circulation than both papers put together.

EMERY KELLEN

hands, but you must not put a sickle to his standing grain. (23:25)

If a man marries a woman who becomes displeasing to him because he finds something indecent about her, and he writes her a certificate of divorce, gives it to her and sends her from his house, and if after she leaves his house she becomes the wife of another man, and her second husband dislikes her and writes her a certificate of divorce, gives it to her and sends her from his house, or if he dies, then her first husband, who divorced her, is not allowed to marry her again after she has been defiled. That would be detestable in the eyes of the Lord. (24:1–4)

> *Anyone who does anything*
> *for pleasure*
> *to indulge his selfish soul*
> *will surely burn in Hell.*
>
> LENNY BRUCE

If brothers are living together and one of them dies without a son, his widow must not marry outside the family. Her husband's brother shall take her and marry her and fulfill the duty of a brother-in-law to her. (25:5)

If two men are fighting and the wife of one of them comes to rescue her husband from his assailant, and she reaches out and seizes him by his private parts, you shall cut off her hand. Show her no pity. (25:11–12)

Whew. Did anyone *ever* get through life without breaking *any* of those laws? And those were just *some* of the laws from *four* of the thirty-nine books of the Old Testament. "If any one of you is without sin" after reading through these four books of the Bible, I'll be glad to continue lawgiving. There are still thirty-four books to go!

I think I've made my points, however, which include

1. Aren't you glad the police aren't out enforcing these laws?

2. The laws of the Bible (the ones we've just reviewed are more than 3,500 years old) make a poor basis for the laws of the United States in the twentieth (or twenty-first) century.

3. We all break God's laws every day—even the ones we try to keep. We're human. But religious people today treat this body of Old Testament law differently: they've decided to *disregard most* of the laws as no longer applicable to life today. Yet these same people cling to a *select few* of the laws as a basis for judging other people's morality and criminality.

4. What justification is there for almost everyone (including most Jewish people) to ignore one biblical law and make another biblical law the basis for imprisonment, persecution, and discrimination? Nothing in the text of the Bible, that's for sure: no forbidden activities are set apart as especially terrible. Then why? People chose what they wanted to ban for whatever reasons they wanted to ban it.

> *I'm not a Jew.*
> *I'm Jew-ish.*
> *I don't go the whole hog.*
>
> JONATHAN MILLER

5. Of the biblical laws against consensual activities, do you want someone else choosing the ones *you* must keep? (That is exactly what is going on in this country.)

6. The next time a televangelist (or senator) quotes Exodus, Leviticus, Numbers, Deuteronomy, or any other book of the Bible as a justification for locking people up, remember the context whence their interpretation of "God's law" comes.

OK, enough laws, now let's go on to *stories.*

Old Testament
Bible Stories

THE REMAINDER OF the Old Testament is the story of the chosen people—the nation of Israel. They raise a lot of armies and fight a lot of battles. When the army can't handle it, God sends in a hero (or, occasionally, a heroine). The heroes and heroines do a lot of assassination. These we hear about in graphic detail. For example,

The Israelites were subject to Eglon king of Moab for eighteen years.

Again the Israelites cried out to the Lord, and he gave them a deliverer—Ehud, a left-handed man, the son of Gera the Benjamite. The Israelites sent him with tribute to Eglon king of Moab. Now Ehud had made a double-edged sword about a foot and a half long, which he strapped to his right thigh* under his clothing. He presented the tribute to Eglon king of Moab, who was a very fat man. After Ehud had presented the tribute, he sent on their way the men who had carried it. At the idols near Gilgal he himself turned back and said, "I have a secret message for you, O king."

The king said, "Quiet!" And all his attendants left him.

Ehud then approached him while he was sitting alone in the upper room of his summer palace and said, "I have a message from God for you." As the king rose from his seat, Ehud reached with his left hand, drew the sword from his right thigh and plunged it into the king's belly. Even the handle sank in after the blade, which came out his back. Ehud did not pull the sword out, and the fat closed in over it. (Judges 3:14–22)

If this sounds like a scene from one of the *Godfather* movies ("I have a message for you from Michael Corleone."), it's probably more than just a coincidence.

---

*Obviously, this use of the word *thigh* does *not* mean "testicles."

Writers of war, crime, and horror movies have used the Old Testament as inspiration for years. The Old Testament is even written in screenplay format with intercutting, long shots, medium shots, and close-ups.

EXTERIOR: LONG SHOT: The king's summer palace.

INTERIOR: MEDIUM SHOT: An upper room of palace.

CLOSE-UP: Ehud: "I have a message from God for you."

MEDIUM SHOT: The king, fascinated, rises from his seat. Ehud pulls out his sword.

CLOSE-UP: The king's face in terror.

CLOSE-UP: The sword pierces the king's belly with a powerful thrust.

CLOSE-UP: Ehud: Determined.

CLOSE-UP: The king's back: The tip of the sword thrusts through the king's clothing.

CLOSE-UP: The king's face in terrified agony.

MEDIUM SHOT: King and Ehud: Ehud completes his thrust.

CLOSE-UP: The king's belly: The handle sinks deep and disappears. Ehud removes his hands from the handle of the sword; fat closes over it.

MEDIUM SHOT: Ehud and the king: The king falls.

CLOSE-UP: Ehud's face: Triumphant.

Let's see how a woman does it:

> Most blessed of women be Jael, the wife of Heber the Kenite, most blessed of tent-dwelling women.
>
> He asked for water, and she gave him milk; in a bowl fit for nobles she brought him curdled milk.
>
> Her hand reached for the tent peg, her right hand for the workman's hammer. She struck Sisera, she crushed his head, she shattered and pierced his temple.
>
> At her feet he sank, he fell; there he lay. At her feet he sank, he fell; where he sank, there he fell—dead. (Judges 5:24–27)

The Old Testament apparently has inspired poets of the Gertrude Stein tradition as well.

When no armies or hit men (Sorry: hit persons) can be found, God handles it Himself. (At Sodom and Gommorah, for example, which we will explore in detail in the chapter, "Homosexuality." Wait until you find out what *really* happened in Sodom.)

The Old Testament is loaded with sex, murder, sex, mayhem, sex, death, sex, dismemberment, and sex. You name it, they do it. If the Bible were a novel published today, it would not be the separation-of-church-and-state people working so hard to keep the Bible from being taught in public schools—it would be the fundamentalists. "This is obscene, pornographic, and contains graphic violence. I don't want my children being taught *this!*" According to the 1993 edition of the *World Almanac and Book of Facts,*

> *God is the Celebrity-Author of the World's Best-Seller.*
>
> DANIEL J. BOORSTIN

> Sex, child abuse, incest, and prostitution were topics unfit for children said Gene Kasmar in his petition to the Brooklyn Center (Minn.) Independent School District to have the Bible taken out of the schools. "The lewd, indecent and violent content of that book are hardly suitable for young students," he wrote in his petition, [and] cited more than 20 pages of examples in the Good Book that frequently refer to concubines, explicit sex, child abuse, scatology, wine, nakedness, and mistreatment of women.

And this all comes from a book translated by fundamentalists who, as we have seen, are stretching their academic integrity by picking the kinder, gentler words. The sex and violence of the Old Testament do not necessarily follow the plot of a Cecil B. deMille movie. In those we get to see an hour and a half of orgies, nudity, debauchery, and other pagan rituals (just so we'll know how *bad* those people *really were*), followed by a battle with one of God's armies (which takes another half an hour with lots of extreme close-ups), to finally show three minutes of the pure, exalted life of the righteous. In the Old Testament, it was not always the bad guys who did the bad things and the good guys who did the good things. David, for example, is by far the most revered, respected, and honored king of Israel. The four major heroes of the Old Testament are Noah, Abraham, Moses, and David. Let's fade into a scene that could be taken from a prime-time soap, "David: King of Israel." (All this is from 2 Samuel, chapter 11.)

> In the spring, at the time when kings go off to war, David sent Joab out with the king's men and the whole Israelite army. They destroyed the Ammonites and besieged Rabbah. But David remained in Jerusalem.
>
> One evening David got up from his bed and walked around on the roof of the palace. From the roof he saw a woman bathing. The woman was very beautiful, and David sent someone to find out about her. The man said, "Isn't this Bathsheba, the daughter of Eliam and the wife of Uriah the Hittite?" Then David sent messengers to get her. She came to him, and he slept with her. (She had purified herself from her uncleanness.) Then she went back home. (2 Samuel 11:1–4)

The "uncleanness" refers to her monthly period. She had performed the ceremonial cleansing rites we discussed earlier. She was, therefore, fit for a king. Note that there is no condemnation of either casual sex, their mutual adultery (Bathsheba was the wife of Uriah, and David, by this time, had many wives) or the king's questionable use of his considerable power to have his way with a beautiful woman. The only concern that we, as readers, might have is that Bathsheba might have been "unclean." This is a rough approximation of the morality that permeates the Old Testament: those "favored by God" do whatever they please (especially to women, foreigners, and anyone who does not believe in and properly worship the God of Israel). Those who want America to return to "the morality of the Bible" are generally those who want the powerful to be able to do whatever they want to the less powerful. But wasn't sleeping with Bathsheba a consensual crime? Isn't that part of their *personal* morality? The *social* morality was not violated, as they did not physically harm the person or property of another (unless David used a threat of force to seduce her). Isn't this, then, a poor example to use? Ah, the story is not over yet. This is just the first commercial break. Let us return now to "David, King of Israel."

> The woman conceived and sent word to David, saying, "I am pregnant."
>
> So David sent this word to Joab: "Send me Uriah the Hittite." And Joab sent him to David. (2 Samuel 11:5–6)

David sends for Bathsheba's husband, Uriah. David realizes that Bathsheba's pregnancy could prove more than a little embarrassing. Uriah's been at war for a while, so he'll know the child is not his. Bathsheba, to save herself from being stoned for adultery, would probably spill the beans about the king. So, David does a little spin control.

> When Uriah came to him, David asked him how Joab was, how the soldiers were and how the war was going. Then David said to Uriah, "Go down to your house and wash your feet." So Uriah left the palace, and a gift from the king was sent after him. (2 Samuel 11: 7–8)

David does a little small talk, a little war talk, and sends the man home. With a woman as beautiful as Bathsheba, David figures Uriah will make love to her. The gift David sent was probably a jug of wine and some kingly food—the sort of things designed to create a romantic evening for Uriah and his wife. Just as J. R. Ewing's best-laid plans were thwarted time and again, however, so David's scheme fails as well.

> But Uriah slept at the entrance to the palace with all his master's servants and did not go down to his house.

God is love, but get it in writing.

GYPSY ROSE LEE

When David was told, "Uriah did not go home," he asked him, "Haven't you just come from a distance? Why didn't you go home?"

Uriah said to David, "The ark and Israel and Judah are staying in tents, and my master Joab and my lord's men are camped in the open fields. How could I go to my house to eat and drink and lie with my wife? As surely as you live, I will not do such a thing!" (2 Samuel 11: 9–11)

> *The husband who decides to surprise his wife is often very much surprised himself.*
>
> VOLTAIRE

What character! What devotion Uriah had for his God, his men, his master, and the ark!* Surely David would see that this was a man of superior moral strength, confess to him his sins, beg his forgiveness, and offer him one of the most powerful positions in the land. But did David do this? To quote John Belushi, "Nooooooo."

> Then David said to him, "Stay here one more day, and tomorrow I will send you back." So Uriah remained in Jerusalem that day and the next. At David's invitation, he ate and drank with him, and David made him drunk. (2 Samuel 11:12–13)

One must begrudgingly admire David's cleverness. Uriah did not feel it was right to "eat and drink and lie with my wife," so, David got him to eat and drink. With two of the three pillars of Uriah's integrity gone, surely the third would fall. (Although it's not stated here, I'd be willing to bet David also had a lot of scantily clad dancing girls at the dinner; if David didn't think of it, Cecil B. deMille certainly would have.) Uriah, however, turned out to be a better man than most.

> But in the evening Uriah went out to sleep on his mat among his master's servants; he did not go home. In the morning David wrote a letter to Joab and sent it with Uriah. (2 Samuel 11:13–14)

It's almost time for another commercial break. We see Joab, in his tent, being given the king's letter by the faithful Uriah. Joab opens the letter, reads it, a look of terrified agony crosses his face (just like King Eglon looked when he was stabbed in the stomach). Joab looks at Uriah, who does not know the contents of the letter.

EXTREME CLOSE-UP OF JOAB'S FACE: He is trying desperately to cover his emotions, but a tear forms in one eye. The music rises to a thundering crescendo.

---

*The ark mentioned is the ark of the covenant in which the stone tablets God gave Moses were kept. It was carried into battle to ensure God's power would be on the side of Israel. The ark was the most sacred object in all of Israel. I would say they worshiped it, but the Israelites firmly believed that idolatry was a sin—and killed countless idolaters to prove it. Let's just say the nation of Israel liked the ark *a whole lot*. This was the same ark, by the way, that Indiana Jones found in *Raiders of the Lost Ark*.

> *Saints are all right in Heaven,*
> *but they're hell on Earth.*
>
> CARDINAL CUSHING

QUICK FADE-OUT. COMMERCIAL. (That scene is not in the Old Testament. I made it up. So, I'm a frustrated screenwriter. So sue me.) We now pause for this public service announcement: According to the International Bulletin of Missionary Research, "Pentecostal and charismatic churches worldwide now count 382 million members, or one for every five Christians. They gain 19 million members per year, and they donate $34 billion to Christian causes." And now, back to our story, in which we discover the contents of King David's letter to Joab, the leader of his army:

> In it he wrote, "Put Uriah in the front line where the fighting is fiercest. Then withdraw from him so he will be struck down and die." So while Joab had the city under siege, he put Uriah at a place where he knew the strongest defenders were. When the men of the city came out and fought against Joab, some of the men in David's army fell; moreover, Uriah the Hittite was dead. (2 Samuel 11:15–17)

WE NOW CUT TO THE PREGNANT BATHSHEBA.

> When Uriah's wife heard that her husband was dead, she mourned for him. After the time of mourning was over, David had her brought to his house, and she became his wife and bore him a son. But the thing David had done displeased the Lord. (2 Samuel 11:26–27)

Well, I should hope so. The Lord decided to punish David. The son born to him and Bathsheba became ill and, after seven days, died. David's period of mourning, to put it mildly, was not a long one:

> Then David got up from the ground. After he had washed, put on lotions and changed his clothes, he went into the house of the Lord and worshiped. Then he went to his own house, and at his request they served him food, and he ate.
>
> His servants asked him, "Why are you acting this way? While the child was alive, you fasted and wept, but now that the child is dead, you get up and eat!"
>
> He answered, "While the child was still alive, I fasted and wept. I thought, 'Who knows? The Lord may be gracious to me and let the child live.' But now that he is dead, why should I fast? Can I bring him back again? I will go to him, but he will not return to me."
>
> Then David comforted his wife Bathsheba, and he went to her and lay with her.* She gave birth to a son, and they named him Solomon. (2 Samuel 12:20–24)

*Just like a man!

The Lord taketh away, and the Lord giveth. The other punishment was a direct attack on his masculinity:

> This is what the Lord says: "Out of your own household I am going to bring calamity upon you. Before your very eyes I will take your wives and give them to one who is close to you, and he will lie with your wives in broad daylight." (2 Samuel 12:11)

Ah, what a scene for some pornographer! *King David's Comeuppance.* For this punishment, we take a deeper look into the royal household. It involves two of David's sons, Amnon and Absalom, and one of David's daughters, Tamar. Amnon is "in love with Tamar" and hatches a plot by which he can have his way with her:

> So Amnon lay down and pretended to be ill. When the king came to see him, Amnon said to him, "I would like my sister Tamar to come and make some special bread in my sight, so I may eat from her hand.
>
> David sent word to Tamar at the palace: "Go to the house of your brother Amnon and prepare some food for him." (2 Samuel 13:6–7)

She does.

> Then Amnon said to Tamar, "Bring the food here into my bedroom so I may eat from your hand." And Tamar took the bread she had prepared and brought it to her brother Amnon in his bedroom. But when she took it to him to eat, he grabbed her and said, "Come to bed with me my sister."
>
> "Don't my brother!" she said to him. "Don't force me. Such a thing should not be done in Israel! Don't do this wicked thing. What about me? Where could I get rid of my disgrace? And what about you? You would be like one of the wicked fools in Israel. Please speak to the king; he will not keep me from being married to you." (2 Samuel 13:10–13)

Although she was only his half sister, marriage between them would still be a violation of the Levitical laws. But, royalty will be royalty:

> But he refused to listen to her, and since he was stronger than she, he raped her.
>
> Then Amnon hated her with intense hatred. In fact, he hated her more than he had loved her. Amnon said to her, "Get up and get out!"*
>
> "No!" She said to him. "Sending me away would be a greater wrong than what you have already done to me."
>
> But he refused to listen to her. He called his personal servant and said, "Get this woman out of here and bolt the door after her." So his servant

---

*Please see previous footnote.

Every man thinks
God is on his side.
The rich and powerful
know he is.

JEAN ANOUILH

put her out and bolted the door after her. She was wearing a richly ornamented robe, for this was the kind of garment the virgin daughters of the king wore. (2 Samuel 13:14–18)

Raping a virgin. Surely that must be one of those Levitical "put them to death" violations. What did the king do?

When King David heard all this, he was furious. (2 Samuel 13:21)

That's all: just furious. The king did nothing about it. Two years later Absalom revenged his sister and had his half-brother Amnon killed. Absalom, exiled, turned against the king and toward politics:

> Whenever anyone approached him to bow down before him, Absalom would reach out his hand, take hold of him and kiss him. Absalom behaved in this way toward all the Israelites who came to the king asking for justice, and so he stole the hearts of the men of Israel. (2 Samuel 15:5–6)

Over the years, Absalom gained enough strength that David fled Jerusalem when he heard Absalom was approaching. Absalom entered Jerusalem and asked a wise man what he should do. The wise man replied,

> "Lie with your father's concubines whom he left to take care of the palace. Then all Israel will hear that you have made yourself a stench in your father's nostrils, and the hands of everyone with you will be strengthened." So they pitched a tent for Absalom on the roof, and he lay with his father's concubines in the sight of all Israel. (2 Samuel 16:21–22)

On the road, David continued to pay his penance when one of his subjects had the audacity to say nasty things to the king. One of the warriors with the king asked, "Why should this dead dog curse my lord the king? Let me go over and cut off his head." (2 Samuel 16:9)

In a fit of noblesse oblige, David said,

> "Leave him alone; let him curse, for the Lord has told him to. It may be that the Lord will see my distress and repay me with good for the cursing I am receiving today." (2 Samuel 16:11–12)

Spoken like a truly repentant king. With this cursing, God apparently figured that poor David had suffered enough. The tide of the war turned, Absalom was killed, David won the battle, and his kingdom was restored. Absalom did not exactly receive a royal burial:

> They took Absalom, threw him into a big pit in the forest and piled up a large heap of rocks over him. (2 Samuel 18:17)

And the concubines? Well, as usual, the women get the short end of every stick:

When David returned to his palace in Jerusalem, he took the ten concubines he had left to take care of the palace and put them in a house under guard. He provided for them, but did not lie with them. They were kept in confinement till the day of their death, living as widows. (2 Samuel 20:3)

⚖ ⚖ ⚖

Oh Lord,
give us the strength to fight
the bastards
and the strength to fight on.

U.S. ARMY CHAPLAIN

There are so many misconceptions about the Bible. As so few people read the Bible as adults, all most people know about the Bible are Sunday School stories and biblical epics. The epics cost so much to make, the producers can't afford to offend anyone; so, all the good parts are left out.

We are told that, after the chosen people left Egypt, God gave them manna in the wilderness. We were told manna was bread. I don't know about you, but I had this image of loaves of Wonder Bread falling from the sky three times a day. In fact,

> The manna was like coriander seed and looked like resin. The people went around gathering it, and then ground it in a handmill or crushed it in a mortar. They cooked it in a pot or made it into cakes. And it tasted like something made with olive oil. (Numbers 11:7–8)

The Bible stories led us to believe that all the Israelites thought Moses was a terrific fellow, and they revered him as their leader and liberator. Well, not always. There were these complaints about the food, you see.

> The rabble with them began to crave other food, and again the Israelites started wailing and said, "If only we had meat to eat!* We remember the fish we ate in Egypt at no cost—also the cucumbers, melons, leeks, onions and garlic. But now we have lost our appetite; we never see anything but this manna!" (Numbers 11:4–6)

Movies and Sunday School certainly lead us to believe that God and Moses had a terrific relationship. Not always, it seems. This manna business put a strain on their relationship. What was wrong with these people? Not only did they have manna, but God had told them, through Moses, "You may eat any kind of locust, katydid, cricket or grasshopper" (Leviticus 11:22). The ingrates—what more could they want?

> Moses heard the people of every family wailing, each at the entrance to his tent. The Lord became exceedingly angry, and Moses was troubled. He asked the Lord, "Why have you brought this trouble on your servant?

*Why doesn't some hamburger chain use that as its slogan?

> *Between projects I go into the park*
> *and bite the grass and wail,*
> *"Why do You make me aware of*
> *the fact that I have to die one day?"*
> *God says, "Please, I have*
> *Chinese people yelling at me.*
> *I haven't time for this."*
> *God is like a Jewish waiter—*
> *he has too many tables.*
>
> MEL BROOKS

What have I done to displease you that you put the burden of all these people on me? Did I conceive all these people? Did I give them birth?* Why do you tell me to carry them in my arms, as a nurse carries an infant, to the land you promised on oath to their forefathers? Where can I get meat for all these people? They keep wailing to me, 'Give us meat to eat!' I cannot carry all these people by myself; the burden is too heavy for me. If this is how you are going to treat me, put me to death right now—if I have found favor in your eyes—and do not let me face my own ruin." (Numbers 11:10–15)

God was not amused. His response to the chosen people:

> Now the Lord will give you meat, and you will eat it. You will not eat it for just one day, or two days, or five, ten or twenty days, but for a whole month—until it comes out of your nostrils and you loathe it. (Numbers 11:18–20)

So God sent a lot of quails but, as with all quails, they came with a curse:

> But while the meat was still between their teeth and before it could be consumed, the anger of the Lord burned against the people, and he struck them with a severe plague. Therefore the place was named Kibroth Hattaavah ["graves of craving"], because there they buried the people who had craved other food. (Numbers 11:33–34)

⚖️ ⚖️ ⚖️

And here we have the one fixed, immutable law of the Old Testament: You had better obey the First Commandment *or else.* "I am the Lord your God, who brought you out of Egypt, out of the land of slavery. You shall have no other gods before me" (Exodus 20:2–3). It's not called the *First* Commandment for nothing. When the other commandments were broken, the people were either punished or they were not. Breaking the First Commandment, however, was *always* punishable:

> You shall have no other gods before me.
>
> You shall not make for yourself an idol in the form of anything in heaven above or on the earth beneath or in the waters below.
>
> You shall not bow down to them or worship them; for I, the Lord your God, am a jealous God, punishing the children for the sin of the fathers to the third and fourth generation of those who hate me. (Exodus 20:3–5)

---

*Somehow, when men are talking, they forget they can't do everything women can do.

Jealous is certainly the right description for God in the Old Testament. In fact, you could almost give God the name Jealousy. Now, don't get mad at *me* for naming God Jealous; that's what he named himself.

> Do not worship any other god, for the Lord, whose name is Jealous, is a jealous God. (Exodus 34:14)

The God of the Old Testament is also not exactly what you would call *mature*. He has trouble taking responsibility for things, even his own jealousy, "They made me jealous by what is no god and angered me with their worthless idols" (Deuteronomy 32:21).

> *Men rarely (if ever) manage to dream up a god superior to themselves. Most gods have the manners and morals of a spoiled child.*
>
> ROBERT A. HEINLEIN

He seems to take everything so *personally*. "I am very jealous for Jerusalem and Zion" (Zechariah 1:14). He reacts like a spurned lover: "I am very jealous for Zion; I am burning with jealousy for her" (Zechariah 8:2).

The entire chapter 23 of Ezekiel is positively astonishing (in its negativity): God gives a heartbroken jealous tirade like nothing the world would see again until, well, Ezekiel, chapter 24. Outside the Old Testament, it wasn't until Othello that the world glimpsed such jealousy, and it wasn't until Frank Sinatra sang, "One for My Baby, and One More for the Road" that the world heard such melancholy. God tells the prophet Ezekiel about two sisters of his close acquaintance (God is not bound by the laws of Leviticus):

> The older was named Oholah, and her sister was Oholibah. They were mine and gave birth to sons and daughters. (Ezekiel 23:4)

The sisters, it turns out, are, in fact, the cities of Samaria and Jerusalem. "Oholah is Samaria and Oholibah is Jerusalem" (Ezekiel 23:4). Alas, all did not go well with God and the two sisters. The sisters seemed to have a roving eye: one was bad; the other was worse:

> Oholah engaged in prostitution* while she was still mine; and she lusted after her lovers, the Assyrians—warriors clothed in blue, governors and commanders, all of them handsome young men, and mounted horsemen. (Ezekiel 23:5–6)

Like all spurned lovers, God goes into explicit detail about his rivals while berating the women who showed the lack of taste in leaving him and the lack of

---

*This is a formal translation of the word. God was not saying they took money for sex, he was calling them sluts, harlots, and whores in the derogatory—not the professional—sense. God considered anyone worshiping other gods a prostitute. As God told Moses just before Moses died, "You are going to rest with your fathers, and these people will soon prostitute themselves to the foreign gods of the land they are entering. They will forsake me and break the covenant I made with them" (Deuteronomy 31:16).

morality to stay faithful:

> She gave herself as a prostitute to all the elite of the Assyrians and defiled herself with all the idols of everyone she lusted after. She did not give up the prostitution she began in Egypt, when during her youth men slept with her, caressed her virgin bosom and poured out their lust upon her. (Ezekiel 23:7–8)

> *Life is God's novel.*
> *Let him write it.*
>
> ISAAC BASHEVIS SINGER

Poor God. But God was to receive even more mistreatment from Oholah's sister, Oholibah:

> In her lust and prostitution she was more depraved than her sister. She too lusted after the Assyrians—governors and commanders, warriors in full dress, mounted horsemen, all handsome young men. I saw that she too defiled herself; both of them went the same way.

> But she carried her prostitution still further. She saw men portrayed on a wall, figures of Chaldeans portrayed in red, with belts around their waists and flowing turbans on their heads; all of them looked like Babylonian chariot officers, natives of Chaldea. (Ezekiel 23:11–15)

So not only is Oholibah into messing around; she also answers the Old Testament equivalent of photo personals. Here was a wall covered with drawings of handsome Chaldeans. One wonders if there was any text. "WARRIORS LOOKING FOR A GOOD TIME. POSSIBLE RELATIONSHIP WITH RIGHT WOMAN. OPEN-MINDED. PRIOR RELATIONSHIPS OKAY. SEND MESSENGERS WITH DRAWINGS OF YOURSELF (NUDE PREFERRED) TO THE GOLDEN RAM INN, CHALDEA, BABYLON."

Now let's return to God's painful account:

> As soon as she saw them, she lusted after them and sent messengers to them in Chaldea. Then the Babylonians came to her, to the bed of love, and in their lust they defiled her. After she had been defiled by them, she turned away from them in disgust. (Ezekiel 23:16–17)

Alas, answering those personal ads seldom works out. Oh, well, Oholibah; chalk one up to experience. God continues:

> When she carried on her prostitution openly and exposed her nakedness, I turned away from her in disgust, just as I had turned away from her sister. Yet she became more and more promiscuous as she recalled the days of her youth, when she was a prostitute in Egypt. (Ezekiel 23:18–19)

Now comes a quote—directly from God's mouth—that, if you put it on a poster and hung it in any church or synagogue in the nation, would be torn down at once and you would be censured, rebuked, and cast out. Frankly, I'm not even sure you could read the next bit on television.

There she lusted after her lovers, whose genitals were like those of donkeys and whose emission was like that of horses. (Ezekiel 23:20)

Can you imagine some pious preacher standing before his congregation and telling them,

> Our sermon today is taken from Ezekiel, chapter 23, verse 20. If you'll all open your Bibles. Those words God spoke more than 3,000 years ago: how they bridge the gap of time and speak so directly to us today. How often have you felt this way? How often have you thought these thoughts—perhaps not as eloquently as God expressed them, but the same idea? I know I have often. Let us pray: Dear God, help us know the deeper meaning of your words. Help us live our lives more fully as set by your word and your example. Amen.
>
> Amen. And now, if you will turn in your hymnals to "The Battle Hymn of the Republic" and sing along with me . . .

> *The only way*
> *of stimulating interest*
> *is to substitute*
> *a performing elephant*
> *in place of a sermon.*
>
> REVEREND LESLIE IRVING

This remembrance of Oholibah's equestrian adventures seems to send God slightly 'round the bend. He no longer addresses Ezekiel; he addresses Oholibah directly:

> So you longed for the lewdness of your youth, when in Egypt your bosom was caressed and your young breasts fondled. (Ezekiel 23:21)

Soon God is so upset that he switches from talking *about* the sisters to directly *addressing* the sisters within the same sentence, and then back again in the next paragraph.

> They even sent messengers for men who came from far away, and when they arrived you bathed yourself for them, painted your eyes and put on your jewelry. You sat on an elegant couch, with a table spread before it on which you had placed the incense and oil that belonged to me.
>
> The noise of a carefree crowd was around her; Sabeans were brought from the desert along with men from the rabble, and they put bracelets on the arms of the woman and her sister and beautiful crowns on their heads. Then I said about the one worn out by adultery, "Now let them use her as a prostitute, for that is all she is." And they slept with her. As men sleep with a prostitute, so they slept with those lewd women, Oholah and Oholibah. (Ezekiel 23:40–44)

Gracious. And the fundamentalists are worried about homosexuals being bad role models for children.

⚖ ⚖ ⚖

> *I read the book of Job last night—
> I don't think God comes
> well out of it.*
>
> VIRGINIA WOOLF

But what does God do about all this jealousy? Does he sit and cry in his beer while pouring his heart out to Ezekiel and the other Old Testament prophets? No.

The Lord is a jealous and avenging God; the Lord takes vengeance and is filled with wrath. The Lord takes vengeance on his foes and maintains his wrath against his enemies. (Nahum 1:2)

He unleashed against them his hot anger, his wrath, indignation and hostility—a band of destroying angels. (Psalm 78:49)

He prepared a path for his anger; he did not spare them from death but gave them over to the plague. (Psalm 78:50)

Pour out your wrath on the nations that do not acknowledge you, on the kingdoms that do not call on your name. (Psalm 79:6)

All our days pass away under your wrath; we finish our years with a moan. (Psalm 90:9)

The mouth of an adulteress is a deep pit; he who is under the Lord's wrath will fall into it. (Proverbs 22:14)*

By the wrath of the Lord Almighty the land will be scorched and the people will be fuel for the fire; no one will spare his brother. (Isaiah 9:19)

See, the Name of the Lord comes from afar, with burning anger and dense clouds of smoke; his lips are full of wrath, and his tongue is a consuming fire. (Isaiah 30:27)

Your sons have fainted; they lie at the head of every street, like antelope caught in a net. They are filled with the wrath of the Lord and the rebuke of your God. (Isaiah 51:20)

Circumcise yourselves to the Lord, circumcise your hearts, you men of Judah and people of Jerusalem, or my wrath will break out and burn like fire because of the evil you have done—burn with no one to quench it. (Jeremiah 4:4)

But I am full of the wrath of the Lord, and I cannot hold it in. "Pour it out on the children in the street and on the young men gathered together; both husband and wife will be caught in it, and the old, those weighed down with years....," declares the Lord. (Jeremiah 6:11)

It goes on and on. Wrath is mentioned 166 times in the Old Testament. Need I mention vengeance, revenge, retribution, chastisement, censure, or reproach? I think not. And what did God do to the two women who scorned him? Did God

---

*I am not saying a *word*.

shrug and quote the Beatles? "'Ob-la-di, Ob-la-da,' Oholah and Oholibah, life goes on. Lordy, how that life goes on." Not hardly:

> This is what the Sovereign Lord says: I will stir up your lovers against you, those you turned away from in disgust, and I will bring them against you from every side—the Babylonians and all the Chaldeans, the men of Pekod and Shoa and Koa, and all the Assyrians with them, handsome young men, all of them governors and commanders, chariot officers and men of high rank, all mounted on horses.

> They will come against you with weapons, chariots and wagons and with a throng of people; they will take up positions against you on every side with large and small shields and with helmets.

> I will turn you over to them for punishment, and they will punish you according to their standards.

> I will direct my jealous anger against you,* and they will deal with you in fury. They will cut off your noses and your ears, and those of you who are left will fall by the sword. They will take away your sons and daughters, and those of you who are left will be consumed by fire. (Ezekiel 23:22–25)

God's anger seems to have spread to *all* those who have *ever* been unfaithful to him. And what is God's justification for all this destruction? Isn't it painfully obvious that he is personally hurt and unable to deal responsibly with his own pain and anger? He directs it at these helpless, albeit libidinous, but otherwise harmless sisters. It may be obvious to any objective observer, but it's not obvious to God. He justifies it in the way those who persecute consensual criminals do (and I bet you thought I forgot what this book was about):

> So I will put a stop to the lewdness and prostitution you began in Egypt. (Ezekiel 23:27)

Oh. So this is all about putting "a stop to the lewdness and prostitution." Uh-huh. If this is the God the fundamentalists follow, no wonder they think he's on their side: he is.

But those who invoke God's will as the reason why laws against consensual activities should be wrathfully enforced seem to forget that, in the more than 2,500 years covered in the Old Testament, God learned an important lesson: suppression doesn't work.

God—the creator of heaven, earth, and the universe—who had, we must presume, more power than currently contained in the combined law enforcement

---

*That's obvious.

agencies of the United States, after demonstrating his powers of destruction time and time again in ways that were more graphic than even televised executions, *could not get even his chosen people to stop worshiping false idols.*

> Ever since Adam
> fools have been
> in the majority.
>
> CASIMIR DELAVIGNE

Does this reflect upon God's poor choice of a chosen people, or does it tell us something about human nature? I vote for the latter. Here were the chosen people, still in bondage in Egypt, watching God bring down plague after plague (blood, frogs, gnats, flies, dead livestock, boils, hail, locusts, darkness, expired firstborn) on the Egyptians while the chosen people remained untouched. They are finally allowed to leave, they do, and they watch as God parts the Red Sea for them and then closes it just in time to swallow up the Egyptian army pursuing them. Pretty remarkable stuff. A more impressive show of force than even the FBI displayed in Waco, Texas.

> And when the Israelites saw the great power the Lord displayed against
> the Egyptians, the people feared the Lord and put their trust in him and in
> Moses his servant. (Exodus 14:31)

But not for long.

The next thing we know, while Moses is on Mt. Sinai chatting with God, his brother, Aaron, is taking everyone's earrings and making them into a golden calf. God expresses his displeasure to Moses, Moses goes down the mountain, organizes a swat team, and tells them, "Go back and forth through the camp from one end to the other, each killing his brother and friend and neighbor" (Exodus 32:27). Three thousand people were killed.* (Moses's brother Aaron was not among them. Hmmmm.)

Did that mass execution work? Nah. Next thing we know, two of Aaron's sons were turned into crispy critters because "they offered unauthorized fire before the Lord, contrary to his command" (Leviticus 10:1). Then some people rebelled, and God sent a fire; then the whole business about eating quail 'til it came out their nostrils and God's subsequent punishment: the Quail Plague (which returned to haunt Murphy Brown for her disobedience to the Lord in 1992); then the Israelites wanted to stone Moses and find a leader who would take them back to Egypt. So God punished "this whole wicked community which has banded together against me," by adding forty years to their desert sojourn and decreeing, "They will meet their end in this desert; here they will die" (Numbers 14:35). Later, another group rebelled: "And the earth opened its mouth and swallowed them with their households and all [their] men and all their possessions," including

*The number of people arrested for consensual crimes every seven hours in the United States.

"their wives, children and little ones"; "250 Israelite men, well-known community leaders who had been appointed members of the council," met their rebellious end when a "fire came out from the Lord and consumed" them; and another 14,700 died in a "wrath [that] has come out from the Lord" in the form of a plague. (All this deterrence can be found in Numbers, chapter 16.) And so even though

> *The wonderful thing about saints is that they were human. They lost their tempers, scolded God, were egotistical or testy or impatient in their turns, made mistakes and regretted them. Still they went on doggedly blundering toward heaven.*
>
> PHYLLIS McGINLEY

> They went down alive into the grave, with everything they owned; the earth closed over them, and they perished and were gone from the community. At their cries, all the Israelites around them fled, shouting, "The earth is going to swallow us too!" (Numbers 16:33–34)

. . . did *that* keep the surviving Israelites from rebelling against God, prevent them from being idle or worshiping idols? No. If I wanted to spend another month researching this book, I might add up the number of people smote (smitten? well, at any rate, *killed*) by God to teach them and everyone else "a lesson."

The lesson was not learned—at least not by the people. Perhaps it was God who had something to learn about this "free will" thing he created in human beings. The Old Testament ends about 433 B.C. Here, in its entirety, is the last chapter of the last book of the Old Testament:

> "Surely the day is coming; it will burn like a furnace. All the arrogant and every evildoer will be stubble, and that day that is coming will set them on fire," says the Lord Almighty. "Not a root or a branch will be left to them.

> But for you who revere my name, the sun of righteousness will rise with healing in its wings. And you will go out and leap like calves released from the stall. Then you will trample down the wicked; they will be ashes under the soles of your feet on the day when I do these things," says the Lord Almighty.

> "Remember the law of my servant Moses, the decrees and laws I gave him at Horeb for all Israel."

> "See, I will send you the prophet Elijah before that great and dreadful day of the Lord comes. He will turn the hearts of the fathers to their children, and the hearts of the children to their fathers; or else I will come and strike the land with a curse." (Malachi 4:1–6)

God sounds a little tired, doesn't he? Just as we have learned to ignore law enforcement officials when they threaten to "step up interdiction" on consensual crimes, or think "yeah, sure," as another elected official proposes a "get tough" campaign, so, too, the chosen people had chosen to filter out most of God's dire warnings. (If you're like me, you probably scanned that last excerpt, asking yourself, "Is he going to say anything new?")

The last verse of the Old Testament, however, is significant:

> He [the Lord] will turn the hearts of the fathers to their children, and the hearts of the children to their fathers; or else I will come and strike the land with a curse. (Malachi 4:6)

People are either going to start loving one another or God's going to end the whole thing. Look at the verse that comes before it: "See, I will send you the prophet Elijah before that great and dreadful day of the Lord comes." The difficulty is with the word *dreadful*. In Hebrew, the word is *yare*. It can mean either to *fear* (which could mean *excitement*) or to *revere*. (Even in English, the word *dread* can mean *terror* and *foreboding*, or it can mean *awe* and *reverence*.) So, if we would say, instead, "That great and reverential day" or "That great and exciting day the Lord comes," it might seem more appealing.

On that day, our hearts will turn, not just to our parents and children; but, in a larger sense, the hearts of the younger generation and the older generation will turn to each other; and, in a larger sense still, all that came before and all that is yet to come will turn their hearts toward one another. "On that great, great come-and-get-it day," we can take the love we need and give the love we've been longing to.

Or . . .

Boom. Crush. Humm. Tittle. Crash. Zap. Oops—or whatever sound you think will accompany the end of the world. "Or else I will come and strike the land with a curse." In Hebrew, the last word of the Old Testament is *cherem*. It doesn't merely mean *curse*; it means "a doomed object," "extermination," "utter destruction," "things which should have been utterly destroyed," or "annihilation." So there was God's choice for our "dreadful" planet: *love or annihilation*. All these threats, random destructions, and wrath were not working. Love or annihilation. If this world was going to work, God would have to move beyond tough love and learn to love tough. But would even *that* work? God would have to stop all this judgment and jealousy and learn to love it all. That would be a lot of work, even for God.

The Official Divine Policy would have to move from *law* to *grace*. God would have to move from *giving* (which he was doing all the time, although human beings—much to God's consternation—seldom realized it), and become *forgiving*.

And if God did all that, would *that* work? No way of knowing. That's the *yare* (fear, excitement, reverence, *and* dread) of populating a planet with creatures who have *choice*. What will they choose? Love or annihilation?

> *Love is a conflict between reflexes and reflections.*
>
> MAGNUS HIRSCHFELD

In 433 B.C., when the last book of the Old Testament was written, the more important question was: What would God decide? He considered the question for about 400 years.

Which did he choose? A few hints: (1) We're still here. (2) According to Christians, there *is* a New Testament.

> *God gives Himself to men*
> *as powerful*
> *or perfect.*
> *It is for them to choose.*
>
> SIMONE WEIL

Law Versus Grace

> *Religion is not obeying rituals, rules, and social action.*
> *It is a means to a transformative interior life.*
>
> PROFESSOR JACOB NEEDLEMAN

THROUGH MOSES, God made a covenant— an agreement, a contract, a promise— with the chosen people. At the time it was made, 3,500 years ago, it was a radical move toward freedom.

Humanity, at that time, lived nomadic, prehistoric existences, or suffered under the absolute rule of ruthless monarchs and warlords. The slavery of many paid for the comforts of a few. Wars were ubiquitous and perpetual.

The covenant offered some distinct advantages, major improvements, and a radical departure from the status quo. A short list:

1. One God rather than many gods. Other religions had a god for everything, and the gods—like humans—did not get along. If you paid too much attention to one god, another god became jealous and *personally* attacked you until you paid more attention to it. Appeasement of the gods was no easy task. There were gods for planting, harvesting, rain, wind, fire, water, air, earth, trees, washing machines, fertility, sun, moon, war, wine, birth, death, and on and on. If it affected your life, a god was in charge of it.

The idea of one omnipotent, omnipresent God was, if nothing else, *simpler.* It saved time, energy, and resources: one only needed to pray to, sacrifice to, and follow the rules of one God. (Each of the many gods had its own set of rules and some of them directly contradicted each other. To follow the rules of one god meant you were insulting another god.)

Polytheism (having many gods) was like working in a corporation with many bosses making noisy and conflicting demands. Monotheism (believing in one God) was like having one Big Boss. Having a Big Boss was easier, but if the Big Boss was ever displeased—look out; there was no entreating another god for help.

> *Religion, which should most*
> *distinguish us from beasts,*
> *and ought most peculiarly*
> *to elevate us,*
> *as rational creatures, above brutes,*
> *is that wherein men often appear*
> *most irrational,*
> *and more senseless*
> *than beasts themselves.*
>
> JOHN LOCKE

That's why many people resisted mono-theism.* (Also, the polytheists threw some *really great* parties.)

2. The end of human sacrifice. The religions that worshiped the polytheistic gods are known as *pagan.* The pagans loved human sacrifice. Firstborn sons, virgins, loved ones—the gods might demand that an individual or a community sacrifice the ones held most dear. (The pagan gods never seemed to demand the sacrifice of the most powerful community leaders or the priests. What a coincidence.) In other words, under paganism, the better you were, the more danger you were in.** Although monotheism under Moses demanded the firstborn male in sacrifice, the first-born son could be "ransomed." Rather than sacrificing your first-born, you could, instead, send a lamb. If you couldn't afford a lamb, you could send two doves. If you couldn't afford two doves, you could send two pigeons. If you couldn't afford two pigeons, what in the name of the Most High were you doing having kids anyway? Allowing the first-born to be ransomed was radical theology back then; and the pagans considered it a sign of weakness, cowardice, and a corrupted moral system.

Under paganism, those who didn't make the ultimate sacrifice, might be required to sacrifice one or more body parts: eyes, ears, nose, fingers, breasts, genitals—or to endure some torture as an appeasement or entreatment. Under monotheism, any of these—including death—might take place as *punishment,* but

*The Catholics fulfilled this need for diversity by inventing patron saints. There's a patron saint for almost everything, but there is never any doubt that the patron saint *serves* God and in no way *competes* with God. There is a patron saint for accountants (Matthew—the tax collector), air travelers (Joseph of Cupertino), authors (Francis De Sales), booksellers (John of God), brides (Nicholas of Myra [If you're concerned that brides have a male patron saint, be consoled that grooms don't have a patron saint at all]), cab drivers (Fiacre), comedians (Vitus ["A funny thing happened on the way to church this morning . . ."]), dentists (Apollonia), firefighters (Florian), funeral directors (Joseph of Arimathea—the man who provided his tomb for Jesus' burial), gravediggers (Antony the Abbot), hairdressers (Martin de Porres), heart patients (John of God—booksellers apparently don't make great demands on him), hotel keepers (Amand), lovers (Valentine), pawnbrokers (Nicholas of Myra [brides and pawnbrokers. Hmmm]), postal workers (Gabriel), social justice (Joseph—let's all say a prayer to Joseph), tax collectors (guess who), television (Clare of Assisi), travelers (Christopher), and women in labor (Anne). In 1988, the remains of Saint Anthony were reported missing from a Franciscan monastery in Kennebunkport, Maine. St. Anthony is the patron saint of missing articles. In 1987, the Citizens Committee for the Right to Keep and Bear Arms petitioned the Vatican to name St. Gabriel Possenti as the "patron of handgunners." St. Gabriel reportedly used a show of marksmanship in 1859 to disarm a group of soldiers in Italy.

**In reviewing the film *The Dragon Slayer*—in which a young man goes to a great deal of trouble to kill a dragon to save his girlfriend, who could at any moment become the next virgin sacrificed to the dragon—Pauline Kael wondered why the man and woman didn't just do what was necessary to have her disqualified on technical grounds.

they were never required by God for adoration.

3. A system of justice. With a few exceptions—such as Mesopotamia—the law was whatever the ruler said it was. It could change daily, hourly. The Ten Commandments replaced this arbitrary system by telling each person within the nation of Israel what could and could not be done. One did not need to second-guess the ruler's mood or worry about his whim. The many other laws of Moses were, at the time, liberating simply because God said, "This is what can and cannot be done. Period." Prior to that, one was always trying to interpret which way the holy and royal winds were blowing. As with believing in one God, rules were simpler. Having a clear set of laws allowed people to worry about other things and get more done.

4. Individual freedom. The Israelites—while they could own slaves—were not slaves themselves. Once their considerable obligations to the community were fulfilled, people were fairly free to go about their business and live their lives. They also followed a certain primitive democracy in which the will of the group prevailed in certain situations. The only rulers, however, were those who could best interpret God's will or give some fairly spectacular demonstrations of God's power.

The covenant, then, was a milestone in civilization. The freedom it introduced was physically represented by the Hebrew people leaving Egypt—where they had been slaves.

God had made several covenants along the way: if Noah built an ark and took two of each kind of animal, his family would be saved and the world would never be destroyed by flood again (the rainbow is the symbol of that covenant); if Abraham would circumcise all male children, he would be the father of many nations; if the people loved God and the Ten Commandments were kept, the descendants of Abraham would possess Canaan, and the Israelites would be God's "treasured possession," with God "showing love to a thousand generations who love me and keep my commandments" (Exodus 20:6).

Which portions of his covenant God had and had not fulfilled, however, became a major political and theological debate—one that continues to this day. There were those who said God had not kept the covenant of a "homeland" for Israel. Others said he did. Among those who said he did, some thought that God had never made Israel his "treasured possession." Some thought he had. Among those who thought he had, some thought that God had not kept his covenant of love. And some thought he had—until humans broke it.

One of those who thought the covenant had been fully kept was King Solomon, who said, "O Lord, God of Israel, there is no God like you in heaven above

> *Belief in a cruel God makes a cruel man.*
>
> THOMAS PAINE

> *It's not listed in the Bible,*
> *but my spiritual gift,*
> *my specific calling from God,*
> *is to be a television talk-show host.*
>
> JAMES BAKKER

or on earth below—you who keep your covenant of love with your servants who continue wholeheartedly in your way" (1 Kings 8:23). But, kings back then had reason to feel more loved than the rest of the world. Even if Solomon was right and God had kept the covenant, Solomon blew it by worshiping another God. "So the Lord said to Solomon, 'Since this is your attitude and you have not kept my covenant and my decrees, which I commanded you, I will most certainly tear the kingdom away from you and give it to one of your subordinates. Nevertheless, for the sake of David your father, I will not do it during your lifetime'" (1 Kings 11:11–12).

By the time of Jeremiah, even God was referring to a new covenant.

> "The time is coming," declares the Lord, "when I will make a new covenant with the house of Israel and with the house of Judah.
>
> "It will not be like the covenant I made with their forefathers when I took them by the hand to lead them out of Egypt, because they broke my covenant, though I was a husband to them," declares the Lord.
>
> "This is the covenant I will make with the house of Israel after that time," declares the Lord. "I will put my law in their minds and write it on their hearts. I will be their God, and they will be my people." (Jeremiah 31:31–33)

By this time, roughly 850 years had passed since Moses made his covenant with God. The number of times the chosen people had broken agreements with God built up a reservoir of unrepented sins that would—spiritually speaking—make our national debt look small. Here was God saying, however, that he was planning to cancel those debts. "I will forgive their wickedness and will remember their sins no more" (Jeremiah 31:34).

But when would this be? God was vague: "The time is coming." In Hosea, chapter 2, verses 16 and 19, he gives these descriptions:

> "In that day," declares the Lord, "you will call me 'my husband'; you will no longer call me 'my master'."
>
> "I will betroth you to me forever; I will betroth you in righteousness and justice, in love and compassion."

Are we are seeing glimpses of a kinder, gentler God? By the time we get to the last book of the Old Testament, Malachi, around 433 B.C., we read,

> "See, I will send my messenger, who will prepare the way before me. Then suddenly the Lord you are seeking will come to his temple; the messenger of the covenant, whom you desire, will come," says the Lord Almighty. (Malachi 3:1)

And so, the chosen people waited for the messenger.

The messenger of the new covenant was called, primarily, by two names: *Christos* or *Christ* and *Messias* or *Messiah*. The former was the Greek and the latter the Hebrew word for "The Anointed One." It referred to one who was anointed by God, one who had the authority and ability to be the "messenger" of the new covenant. Those who accepted Jesus as the messenger referred to him as "Christ"* and seldom as the "Messiah." The Jews who did not accept Jesus as the messenger continued waiting for the Messiah. They continue to wait for the Messiah to this very day.

> *If I have any beliefs about immortality, it is that certain dogs I have known will go to heaven, and very, very few persons.*
>
> JAMES THURBER

The brilliant lyricist, Sheldon Harnick, wrote about this waiting in a song that was, alas, cut from his *Fiddler on the Roof*:

> When Messiah comes he will say to us
> "I apologize that I took so long.
> But I had a little trouble finding you,
> over here a few and over there a few.
> You were hard to reunite
> But everything is going to be all right.
>
> "Up in heaven there how I wrung my hands
> When they exiled you from the Promised Land.
> Into Babylon you went like castaways
> On the first of many, many moving days.
> What a day and what a blow:
> How terrible I felt you'll never know!"
>
> When Messiah comes and his reign begins
> Truth and justice then shall appear on earth.
> But if this reward we would be worthy of
> We must keep our Covenant with God above.
> So be patient and devout
> and gather up your things and get thee out.**

⚖ ⚖ ⚖

I'd like to explore the differences between the old covenant and the new. Whether you accept Jesus as the messenger of the new covenant, you believe the messenger is yet to come, you're not sure whether the messenger has come or

---

*This was a symbolic turning from Judaism. The Hebrews, of course, were Jews, and the Greeks were Gentiles. Using a Gentile term was a way of making a break from the old covenant.

**Mr. Harnick sings this and seventeen of his other songs on *An Evening with Sheldon Harnick* on DRG Records.

> *For if you call me brother now,*
> *forgive me if I inquire*
> *"According to whose plan?"*
>
> LEONARD COHEN

not, or frankly, my dear, you don't give a damn, the study is important from the viewpoint of consensual crimes. Those who use the Bible to justify the laws against consensual activities are following the old covenant—even though most of them *claim* to be Christians. (It's ironic: often the *more* "Christian" they claim to be, the more they follow the old covenant.) So, understanding the attitudes and beliefs of the old and new covenants is useful when asking, "What does either covenant have to do with the laws of the United States of America?" The new covenant would *not* ban, by force of law, *any* consensual activity. It would, of course, have guidelines for *personal* morality, but none for *social* morality between consenting adults.

This discussion is not, repeat, *not* a comparison of Judaism and Christianity. The Jewish people have added 3,500 years of understanding, compassion, and love to the harshness of "an eye for an eye." Many Christian denominations, on the other hand, have added 2,000 years of bigotry, arrogance, and self-righteousness to the simple, graceful teachings of Jesus. In the chapter, "His Master's Voice?" we will, in fact, explore how some modern-day "Christians" are more legalistic and wrathful than even the Pharisees of old.

The primary difference between the old and the new covenant is that the old covenant is based on *law* and the new covenant is based on *grace.* The *law* was, "If you do this, I will reward. If you do that, I will punish you." It was the eye-for-an-eye, tooth-for-a-tooth, I-am-a-wrathful-God theory of management. All favors must be earned, all sins must be punished; all rewards must be earned, all debts must be paid.

Grace means receiving rewards without having to earn them; being forgiven all mistakes without having to atone. Grace was a gift from God; everything received under the law was supposedly made "the old-fashioned way: we *earned* it." The new covenant was remarkably free from restrictions, as God described to to Jeremiah: "For I will forgive their wickedness and will remember their sins no more" (Jeremiah 31:34). This *was* new—no serious restrictions, no harsh punishments. Jesus added only one commandment to the Ten—the only requirement for fulfilling the covenant: "This is my command: Love each other" (John 15:17).

I'll use the terms *law* and *grace* to describe the old and new covenants respectively. (I think I've used the word *covenant* quite enough for one chapter.)

Living under law is based on *judgment.* Every action was judged as either good or bad, based on the law. If one's action was judged good, one would be rewarded. If it was judged bad (far more often), one would be punished. Unrepented judgments were pursued with the relentlessness of a credit card company: every debt was recorded and had to be paid to the last farthing.

Living under grace is based on *forgiveness*. One may transgress (sin), but the transgression is forgiven: "For I will forgive their wickedness and will remember their sins no more" (Jeremiah 31:34). Jesus gave the only requirement for forgiveness under grace: ("Forgive us our debts, as we have also forgiven our debtors" [Matthew 6:12].) If we forgive others, we will be forgiven.

Law is *external:* what you do, how you do it, when you do it, with whom you do it. The control is external; full of crime and punishment, accusers and condemned. Law required external sacrifice of material possessions. Life had to be taken for life to be enhanced. God was a force outside oneself, who had absolute control of the physical universe, including one's life and well-being. The law provided no afterlife. God told Moses he would be "going to rest with your fathers" (Deuteronomy 31:16). Gertrude Stein summed up the prevailing Jewish belief: "When you're dead, you're dead."

Grace is *internal:* the motivation behind an action is more important than the action itself. Jesus criticized the Pharisees, who made sure their external actions looked good while their inner motivations were far from pure. "You are the ones who justify yourselves in the eyes of men," he told them, "but God knows your hearts" (Luke 16:15). On one hand, one can sin by not performing any physical action ("But I tell you that anyone who looks at a woman lustfully," said Jesus, "has already committed adultery with her in his heart" [Matthew 5:28]). On the other hand, you may physically be doing something others consider sinful but, due to your personal motivation, it is a righteous act. Sins that do not involve others, do not require external atonement. Under grace, heaven is within each of us ("The kingdom of God is within you" [Luke 17:21]) and how one responds to what happens is more important than what's happening.

Law counts *sins*. The law preoccupied itself with sin because each sin was counted (judged) and needed to be atoned for. Sin was considered a bad thing—something to be avoided at all costs. Those who sinned were considered evil, wicked, and bad.

Grace teaches *lessons*. Under grace, *sin* simply means "mistake." Each mistake is an opportunity to learn, and grace concerns itself with the *learning* rather than *punishing* the sin. A sin, then, could best be called a mistake, or more appropriately, a *lesson*. If you didn't learn from the lesson, you could always repeat it. Jesus, for example, never berated his disciples for doing something wrong; he only became exasperated with them when they failed to learn quickly enough.*

> *Blessed are the merciful,*
> *for they will be shown mercy.*
>
> JESUS OF NAZARETH
> MATTHEW 5:7

---

*The Hebrew word used most often for *sin* in the Old Testament included not only the concept of an offense, but also to "bear the blame." It included the idea of repentance, cleansing, and purging.

> *God will forgive me the foolish remarks I have made about Him just as I will forgive my opponents the foolish things they have written about me, even though they are spiritually as inferior to me as I to thee, O God!*
>
> HEINRICH HEINE

Law *rejects*. Anyone who doesn't believe the right things or take the right actions is rejected as "unclean."

Grace *accepts*. One doesn't have to *like* what other people do, but one must accept the fact that they are doing it. Jesus only *chose* twelve, but he never *excluded* anyone. (All right: Satan he sent away—but only after he had put up with Satan for a *long* time.) Ironically, some of the most beautiful—and wise—words ever written on acceptance come from the Old Testament (Ecclesiastes 3:1–8 KJV):*

To every thing there is a season,
and a time to every purpose under the heaven:

A time to be born, and a time to die;
a time to plant, and a time to pluck up that which is planted;

A time to kill, and a time to heal;
a time to break down, and a time to build up;

A time to weep, and a time to laugh;
a time to mourn, and a time to dance;

A time to cast away stones, and a time to gather stones together;
a time to embrace, and a time to refrain from embracing;

A time to get, and a time to lose;
a time to keep, and a time to cast away;

A time to rend, and a time to sew;
a time to keep silence, and a time to speak;

A time to love, and a time to hate;

The Greek word used for *sin* in the New Testament meant "to miss the mark (and so not share in the prize)." To sin in the Old Testament, then, means you have acquired something negative. To sin in the New Testament means you've failed to acquire something positive. Hence, the saying, "You are punished *by* your sins (by not getting what you want), not *for* your sins (in retribution for an evil action)." The New Testament word was used in archery to indicate missing the mark. You either "hit" or "sinned." If you sinned, it meant you didn't get the point. That's a good definition of sin: not getting the point.) By comparison, the Old Testament word might have been used for shooting an arrow and hitting something you shouldn't be shooting at. It was *wrong* in the active sense. In the Old Testament case, something was taken away, (a sacrifice or atonement had to be made). In the New Testament sense, nothing is taken away: the "punishment" is that nothing new is added.

*This is the King James version translation. While not always easier to understand, the King James version is often more poetic. It was translated in England at the same time Shakespeare was writing his plays. Sometimes, one must go for the poetry. "To be or not to be, that is the question," while a tad obscure, is far more satisfying than, "Should I kill myself or not?" Besides, the beautiful melody Pete Seeger wrote for these words doesn't fit the New International translation.

a time of war, and a time of peace.

The law decrees *separation*. The Old Testament is full of people being "cut off," "cast aside," and "sent into exile." There were so many offenses for which one could be permanently cut off, it's amazing there was any group left to be cut off from.

Grace devotes itself to *connection*. Grace has no requirements for being connected with oneself, other people, life, spirit, or God. One must simply accept, forgive, and

> *Religion is more like response to a friend than it is like obedience to an expert.*
>
> AUSTIN FARRER

ask. ("Ask and it will be given to you; seek and you will find; knock and the door will be opened to you" [Matthew 7:7].) Asking in the New Testament is often referred to as *repentance*.

Law is preoccupied with *destruction*. This person or that city or this country or that group was always being zapped, or just on the verge of being zapped, or—at the very least—*should* have been zapped.

Grace is obsessed with *creation*. It not only respects, admires, and is grateful for creation (that which has already been created); it is fascinated by the process of creating (or re-creating) anew.

Under law, with all the judgment, retribution, and destruction going on, people naturally *worry*. Their fear of losing what they have or not getting what they want tends to keep people from getting what they want, on the one hand, and keeps them from enjoying what they've got on the other. Not much fun.

Under grace, with gifts from God available in abundant supply, one tends to *trust*. Trusting quiets that need inside for more, more, more, that never seems to rest no matter how many material possessions one obtains. "Is not the thirst when your well is full," asked the Prophet, "the thirst that is unquenchable?"

Law deals in *lack*: "How can I get more?" Grace is *abundant*: "Thank you. I have more than I need."

Law *curses*; grace *heals*.

Law brings *jealousy*; grace brings *freedom*.

Law devotes one to *taking*; grace is for *giving*.

With law, one is *cautious*; with grace, one takes *risks*.

Law makes people *selfish*; grace makes people *want to serve*.

Law promotes *guilt*; grace encourages *corrective action*.

Law springs from and results in *unworthiness*; grace is a wellspring of *worthiness*.

Law promotes *indifference*; grace encourages *involvement*.

Law is *hatred*; grace is *love*.

⚖️ ⚖️ ⚖️

Old Covenant (Law)	New Covenant (Grace)
Judgment	Forgiveness
External	Internal
Rejection	Acceptance
Separation	Connection
Destruction	Creation
Worry	Trust
Lack	Abundance
Cursing	Healing
Jealousy	Freedom
Taking	Giving
Cautious	Risk-taking
Selfishness	Desire to Serve
Guilt	Corrective Action
Unworthiness	Worthiness
Indifference	Involvement

People who reject and separate are preoccupied with destruction and greed; those who curse are jealous, selfish, feel guilty and unworthy; those who are indifferent and hate have no trouble punishing others for taking part in consensual activities. In fact, it's inevitable.

People who accept and connect are devoted to creation and abundance; those who heal, give freely, take risks, and serve encourage corrective action, worthiness, and involvement; those who love tend naturally to give others the freedom to be, learn, grow, and enjoy.

Jesus of Nazareth
and Consensual Crimes

WE WILL EXPLORE NOW the teachings of Jesus as illustrated by his words and incidents from his life, especially as they relate to consensual crimes. This is *not* an "overview of Christianity" or the Christian religion. There are more than one thousand belief systems in this country claiming to be "Christian"—one, sometimes, diametrically opposing another. If you have a belief in a particular religion that calls itself "Christian," please know that I am in no way attempting to criticize or modify that belief. You have a perfect right to believe anything you want and call it whatever you want. That's the essence of religious freedom, and I wouldn't dream of taking it away from anyone.

We will not be taking a religious look, but a *historic, intellectual, analytical* look at the teachings of Jesus as contained in the first four books of the New Testament. Any religious interpretations are entirely for you to make based on whatever criteria you use to formulate your personal beliefs. So, we will not be exploring whether Jesus was or was not the son of God, the *only* son of God, whether Jesus is necessary for personal salvation, or any other aspect of religious belief. (For those who *do* identify themselves as "Christians"—whatever their religion or lack thereof—only the later chapter, "A Call for Christian Charity, Tolerance, and (Dare I Say?) *Love* for Diversity," assumes the divinity of Jesus the Christ.)

I am not even going to question whether what Jesus said was accurately set down, or if the events in his life were accurately chronicled.* We will use *precisely*

*Many modern Bible historians believe that Jesus never said some of the more "hellfire and brimstone" words assigned to him. Their research indicates that these passages were written later to reintroduce fear of eternal damnation notably missing from Jesus' central teachings. If he advised people to worry so little about tomorrow that they shouldn't even concern themselves with the source

> *Both read the Bible day and night,*
> *But thou read'st black*
> *where I read white.*
>
> WILLIAM BLAKE

the same book that those who condemn consensual crimes "in the name of Jesus" use.

If you have a bad opinion of Jesus because of things that people have said or done "in the name of Jesus," it could be that those people used Jesus' name to justify their own prejudices, paranoid delusions, or grabs for power. More evil and wickedness have been done (and continue to be done) "in the name of Jesus" than one could possibly document. Those who have never taken the time to read what Jesus actually said may—mistakenly—blame Jesus for this evil and wickedness. Might I suggest that you read the first four books of the New Testament—as I did—to find out what Jesus himself *said*. This way, the next time someone says he or she is doing something "in the name of Jesus," you can say—as I am—"But he never said that!" or "That's not what he meant at all!" That's why, in this discussion of consensual crimes, we'll be taking the time to explore what Jesus *actually had to say* about them.

The first four books of the New Testament—Matthew, Mark, Luke, and John—tell the story of Jesus' life and teachings. For the most part, they are the only books in the Bible that report what Jesus said while he lived.* They give the story of Jesus' life. The remainder of the New Testament contains Luke's account of the early church (Acts); letters (epistles) written by James and Jude (Jesus' brothers), Peter, John, and Paul to various Christian communities, to set forth doctrine and guidelines for living; culminating with John's apocalyptic vision for the end of the world (Revelation). About half of the New Testament consists of Paul's Epistles.

---

of their food or clothing—that God would provide for all their needs—why would he ask the same people to fear an eternity in hell? In addition, there seem to be passages of great loving which were probably said by Jesus, but not recorded in the four Gospels. (Paul quotes one of the most famous— "It is more blessed to give than to receive" [Acts 20:35]—although it does not appear anywhere in the four Gospels.When Paul quotes this, he refers to it as though it were common knowledge and that his readers would be familiar with the fact that it was Jesus who said it.) These fragments of teachings have been carefully analyzed and many of them have been attributed to Jesus. I have not included these in my consideration. Suffice it to say that—with regard to his own followers—modern Biblical research reveals an even more grace-full Jesus than the Gospels show.

*Jesus appeared to Peter, Paul, and John in visions after his death, resurrection, and ascension. With the exception of Revelation—the last book in the Bible, detailing John's "revelation" from Jesus on what it would be like at the end of the world—Jesus gave more personal direction than universal teaching in his post-ascension visions. He told Paul (then known as Saul), for example, to stop persecuting the Christians. He told Peter to stop worrying about kosher laws and start teaching the Gentiles (pagans) as well as the Jews. Then there is the famous passage already noted, "It is more blessed to give than to receive" (Acts 20:35), as recorded by Paul that somehow slipped by Matthew, Mark, Luke, and John.

The first three Gospels—Matthew, Mark, and Luke—are known as the *synoptic Gospels. Synoptic* means a general view or summary; to give an account from the same point of view. These were written from twenty to fifty years after Jesus' death. The synoptic Gospels seem to rely on each other—the authors of the later two perhaps having read the first—or, at the very least, they relied on similar source material. This material was most likely the written collections of "sayings" circulated, perhaps even while Jesus lived. These "quote books" (scrolls, actually) were quite popular and allowed the essence of a teacher's message to be conveyed in those pre–printing press days. Using these scrolls as a basis, and adding what they knew, remembered, or could discover, Matthew, Mark, and Luke wrote their Gospels (a word which simply means "good news").

> *Christian:*
> *one who believes that*
> *the New Testament is a divinely*
> *inspired book admirably suited*
> *to the spiritual needs*
> *of his neighbors.*
>
> AMBROSE BIERCE

Matthew was one of the chosen twelve apostles, a Jewish tax collector for Rome before he became a disciple. His Gospel was primarily written for Jews, and makes slight variations for his audience. For example, he uses the term "kingdom of heaven" rather than "kingdom of God" because many Jews considered the use of the word *God* too sacred and powerful—they believed it should be reserved only for the most sacred occasions. Matthew also quotes extensively from the body of Jewish scripture that came to be known as the Old Testament, but was known then as the "Law of the Prophets." He did this to prove that Jesus fulfilled all the predictions and qualifications set forth by the prophets and was, in fact, "the Messiah."

Mark was probably John Mark of the Bible and may have known Jesus personally. He could have been part of an inner group—although not one of the chosen twelve—and might have been with Jesus when he was arrested at the Garden of Gethsemene. (An anecdote in Mark 14:51–52 of an unnamed man slipping out of the guards' hands by removing his cloak and running away naked into the night is not recounted anywhere else in the New Testament, and serves no other purpose at that point in the narrative unless Mark was telling us, "This is what happened to me.") Mark also spent a great deal of time with Peter. Mark's Gospel, then, is as close as we come to Peter's story of Jesus. (Peter's epistles are very short and do not discuss the earthly life of Jesus.)

Luke, a physician by training, spent time with both Peter and Paul. He had access to eye witnesses of the major events of Jesus' public life (including several apostles and, perhaps, some of the people Jesus healed) and used his scientific training and excellent command of Greek to write about the life and teachings of Jesus. Although clearly a believer, Luke was a reporter doing a feature story. There is no evidence to indicate that Luke knew Jesus personally.

> *Leaving behind books*
> *is even more beautiful—*
> *there are far too many children.*
>
> MARGUERITE YOURCENAR

John wrote his gospel some time after Matthew, Mark, and Luke. Although it's fair to assume that he read the first three, he did not rely on them, nor the underlying "quote books," as heavily. John accepted the events in the first three Gospels as "given," and added new information. He also wanted to "set the record straight" on a few events—and he does. As the only disciple at the Crucifixion, as well as part of Jesus' "inner circle" (which also included John's brother, James, as well as Peter), he gave accounts and insights Matthew, Mark, and Luke did not.

The four Gospels (also known collectively as *the Gospels)*, then, give us the same life and the same teachings seen from four different viewpoints. If you think that personal agendas and points of view did not affect the Gospels, consider what Mark had to say about a woman: "She had suffered a great deal under the care of many doctors and had spent all she had, yet instead of getting better she grew worse" (Mark 5:26). Compare that with what Luke, the physician, had to say about the same woman: "And a woman was there who had been subject to bleeding for twelve years, but no one could heal her" (Luke 8:43). Whether Luke was protecting his profession or Mark had a bias against physicians—or both—is hard to say. Personal filtering—conscious or unconscious—is inevitable when people write about events—especially events that happened decades earlier.

And yet, with all these differences—sometimes in interpretation and sometimes with the facts themselves—there emerges a pattern of a man who, fundamentally, taught love. That is the essence of Jesus' teaching. He said it himself, quoting the "heart" of the Jewish faith: "'Love the Lord your God with all your heart and with all your soul and with all your mind'" (Matthew 22:37) and he summed up the rest of the Old Testament—the Law of the Prophets—as "Love your neighbor as yourself" (Matthew 22:39). To this, at the very end of his teaching (at the Last Supper), he gave those closest to him a final command—not a request, not a good idea, not even a rule, but a *command:* "A new command I give you: Love one another. As I have loved you, so you must love one another. By this all men will know that you are my disciples, if you love one another" (John 13:34–35).

And how did Jesus love?

1. He healed the sick.

2. He taught love, regardless of rank, station, profession, national origin, financial status, race, creed, color, situation, circumstance, or environment.

3. He attacked hypocrisy, especially among those in power.

4. He taught *grace* rather than *law, acceptance* rather than *judgment,* and *for-*

giveness rather than *punishment*.

And then Jesus made one of the most brilliant moves in the history of human thought. He gave a series of examples that illustrated a being *so* loving, *so* giving, and *so* trusting in God that it was *absolutely impossible* for a *human* being to achieve the ideal. He then *specifically prohibited* any attempts to improve others until you, yourself, were entirely loving, giving, and trusting.

> *The world is equally shocked at hearing Christianity criticised and seeing it practised.*
>
> DR. ELTON TRUEBLOOD

According to Jesus' plan, everyone would be so busy loving, giving, and trusting (or learning to be that way) that there would simply be *no time* to judge others. If one, however, were *tempted* to judge others, giving in to the temptation was *specifically prohibited* by the teachings of Jesus.

When Anita Bryant was at the height (depth?) of her campaign against homosexuals and had the backing of most fundamentalist Christian organizations and celebrities, Dale Evans—a popular Christian lecturer and author—was asked what she thought about homosexuals. Expected to give the knee-jerk reaction ("The Bible says it's an abomination and unnatural, and I'll take God's word for it"), Dale surprised everyone by, instead, stating the essence of Christ's teaching: "I'm too busy loving *everybody* to have any time to hate *anybody*."

It's a marvelous system. Too bad the people who ask for consensual criminals to be punished in the name of Jesus aren't using it.

⚖ ⚖ ⚖

To understand Jesus' point of view on consensual crimes, it's important to understand Jesus' point of view. What was his purpose on earth? What was his message? What were his teachings? By answering these questions, we can more accurately answer the question, "What was Jesus' view on consensual crimes?"

This is only *my* summation of the teachings of Jesus. Again, I encourage you to read Matthew, Mark, Luke, and John yourself and form your own conclusion. I also do not mean to detract from those who believe revelations made after the time Jesus was on earth, nor do I mean to "convert" anyone to my interpretation. (As you will probably see by my interpretation, that is among the *last* things I would want to do.) One need not *believe* or *disbelieve* any of this. The purpose is simply to compare what Jesus *taught* about consensual crimes with what others *say* Jesus taught about consensual crimes.

In a nutshell, my view is that Jesus would no more approve of using his name to lock people up over consensual crimes than he would have approved of using his name to endorse the Spanish Inquisition, the Great Crusades, or the Salem

Witch Hunts.

In a sense, this is a book report: I read the book; now I'm reporting to you what it's about. I find those who want to justify consensual crimes by quoting the teachings of Jesus distort the Gospels as much as someone saying, "Scarlett O'Hara hated Ashley Wilkes," by citing the single passage from *Gone with the Wind* in which she says, "I hate you, Ashley Wilkes! I always hated you and I always will!" Anyone who's even *skimmed* the book in a speed reading course knows that, although she may have said that at one point, it certainly doesn't summarize the general thrust of Ms. O'Hara's feelings toward Mr. Wilkes. "After I took a speed reading course, I read *War and Peace* in twenty minutes," remarked Woody Allen; "it's about Russia." Having spent a bit more than twenty minutes on the first four books of the New Testament, I can say with a great deal of certainty: they're about love.

> *There is no worse lie than a truth*
> *misunderstood*
> *by those who hear it.*
>
> WILLIAM JAMES
> *The Varieties of Religious Experience*
> 1910

⚖ ⚖ ⚖

The basis of Jesus' teaching is this:

1. Jesus is the "messenger of the covenant" (Messiah, Christ) promised by God in the last book of the Old Testament.

> "See, I will send my messenger, who will prepare the way before me. Then suddenly the Lord you are seeking will come to his temple; the messenger of the covenant, whom you desire, will come," says the Lord Almighty. (Malachi 3:1)

2. Jesus came to establish the new covenant, and did so successfully.

3. One always has the choice, in any given moment, whether to live under law or live under grace; that is, moment by moment, one can choose the old covenant or the new covenant. In order to do the things necessary to live under grace (mostly internal), one must believe (trust) that Jesus *was* the messenger. This is always a choice, however, and although one may be *inspired* to make this choice, one must never be *coerced*.

⚖ ⚖ ⚖

As you may recall, the last two verses of the Old Testament are,

> "See, I will send you the prophet Elijah before that great and dreadful day of the Lord comes. He will turn the hearts of the fathers to their children, and the hearts of the children to their fathers; or else I will come and strike the land with a curse." (Malachi 4:5–6)

Jesus identified himself as the messenger of the new covenant, and John the

Baptist as Elijah. (Elijah also dropped by with his good friend Moses to pay Jesus a personal visit on the Mount of Transfiguration. This was witnessed by Peter, John, and James.) As Jesus said,

> "The Father loves the Son and has placed everything in his hands. Whoever believes in the Son has eternal life, but whoever rejects the Son will not see life, for God's wrath remains on him." (John 3:35–36)

> "But do not think I will accuse you before the Father. Your accuser is Moses, on whom your hopes are set." (John 5:45)

> *Had there been a lunatic asylum in the suburbs of Jerusalem, Jesus Christ would infallibly have been shut up in it at the outset of his public career.*
>
> HAVELOCK ELLIS

Jesus was saying: either believe his message of the new covenant, or the covenant of Moses and the wrath of the Old Testament are yours. It is, however, your choice.

> "When a man believes in me, he does not believe in me only, but in the one who sent me. When he looks at me, he sees the one who sent me. I have come into the world as a light, so that no one who believes in me should stay in darkness." (John 12:44–46)

> "Don't you believe that I am in the Father, and that the Father is in me? The words I say to you are not just my own. Rather, it is the Father, living in me, who is doing his work." (John 14:10)

> "I tell you the truth, whoever hears my word and believes him who sent me has eternal life and will not be condemned; he has crossed over from death to life." (John 5:24)

A great misconception about Jesus, I think, is that one has to believe in him *personally,* in order to be "saved." Jesus was saying, I am the messenger: believe in the *message* that we may now live under grace. If you believe in the message, you will do certain things and by doing those things you will receive the grace. For example, if I walked in eating a Haagen-Dazs bar and you asked, "Where did you get that?" and I said, "There's a man outside giving them away for free," you might or might not believe me. If you believed me (or believed *in* me) and wanted a Haagen Dazs bar, you would get up, go outside, and get one. If you did not believe me (believe *in* me) you would not get up, not go outside, and not get a Haagen Dazs bar. Believing in me *personally* is not going to get you the Haagen Dazs bar. Believing in me enough to get up, get out, and get it, is. That's all Jesus was saying: Try these things (which we'll review in a moment), and grace will be yours.

> "For God so loved the world that he gave his one and only Son, that whoever believes in him shall not perish but have eternal life. For God did not

> *The trouble with some of us is that we have been inoculated with small doses of Christianity which keep us from catching the real thing.*
>
> LESLIE DIXON WEATHERHEAD

send his Son into the world to condemn the world, but to save the world through him. Whoever believes in him is not condemned, but whoever does not believe stands condemned already because he has not believed in the name of God's one and only Son." (John 3:16–18)

"If anyone loves me, he will obey my teaching. My Father will love him, and we will come to him and make our home with him. He who does not love me will not obey my teaching. These words you hear are not my own; they belong to the Father who sent me." (John 14:23–24)

Jesus spoke from several levels of consciousness. At times he was the dutiful son of the father; at other times he was the father and the son in one. Expressing himself from the latter state of consciousness got him in no small amount of trouble:

> "I tell you the truth," Jesus answered, "before Abraham was born, I am!" At this, they picked up stones to stone him, but Jesus hid himself, slipping away from the temple grounds. (John 8:58–59)

So, when Jesus says, "I am the light, the truth and the way," he is speaking from that unified consciousness. When he says "The father loves the son and has placed everything in his hands," he is speaking from the consciousness of the dutiful son. When he says, "For God so loved the world that he gave his one and only son, that whoever believes in him shall not perish and have eternal life," he is standing back and observing the process. The statements are not contradictory; it's the same message given from different perspectives.

What is Jesus' teaching? What must we do to achieve "eternal life?" Before exploring this, we must *locate* eternal life, which is referred to by Jesus as the "kingdom of heaven" or the "kingdom of God." These terms are used interchangeably. Jesus probably said the "kingdom of God." As mentioned earlier, Matthew made it the "kingdom of heaven" because the Jews (the primary audience for his Gospel) were offended by the use of the word *God*. He didn't want the book dismissed as blasphemous before anyone had read it. The question, then, is, "Where is the kingdom of God?"

> Once, having been asked by the Pharisees when the kingdom of God would come, Jesus replied, "The kingdom of God does not come with your careful observation, nor will people say, 'Here it is,' or 'There it is,' because the kingdom of God is within you." (Luke 17:20–21)

This, I find, is another primary misconception of Christianity, that the kingdom of God is "out there," "up there," or "beyond the blue horizon." It is, according to Jesus, "within you." When people pray the Lord's Prayer, and begin,

"Our father, who art in heaven, hallowed be thy name," they usually think of God somewhere "out there" in heaven. They may not be thinking of the old man with a white beard on a golden throne, but some contemporary variation of that is usually the case. "Thy kingdom come, thy will be done on earth as it in heaven," most people interpret as "When Jesus returns, then earth will be just like heaven, because only God's will will be done in both places." Unfortunately, that interpretation does not correspond to Jesus' many comments that the kingdom of God was "near," "at hand," and "within you." Consider this passage:

> It is a curious thing that every creed promises a paradise which will be absolutely uninhabitable for anyone of civilized taste.
>
> EVELYN WAUGH

> One day Jesus was praying in a certain place. When he finished, one of his disciples said to him, "Lord, teach us to pray, just as John [the Baptist] taught his disciples." He said to them, "When you pray, say: 'Father, hallowed be your name, your kingdom come. Give us each day our daily bread. Forgive us our sins, for we also forgive everyone who sins against us. And lead us not into temptation.'" (Luke 11:1–4)

Note the first line: "Father, hallowed be your name, your kingdom come." That is a complete sentence. "Father, hallowed be your name," is an invocation: it calls forth the kingdom of God. "Your kingdom come," is a statement that the invocation was successful; God delivered what was requested: the kingdom of God. This might be called more accurately an *attunement*, or tuning in to the kingdom of God already present within each of us. It works just as well with the more traditional interpretation of the Lord's Prayer, with only minor changes in punctuation:

> "Our Father in heaven, hallowed be your name. Your kingdom come. Your will be done on earth as it is in heaven." (Matthew 6:9–10)

The idea that the kingdom of God will not be established until Jesus *physically* returns is also contradicted in this statement:

> And [Jesus] said to them, "I tell you the truth, some who are standing here will not taste death before they see the kingdom of God come with power." (Mark 9:1)

We know that everyone who was standing there has tasted death. Did Jesus return in the Second Coming during their lifetimes? No. Did some of them experience "the kingdom of God come with power" within themselves and within many others? Absolutely. Either Jesus was not an accurate interpreter, nor an accurate predictor of the future, or the kingdom of heaven is, as Reverend Ike puts it, "not that pie in the sky by and by."

While on the subject of misconceptions (not to mention controversy), many claim that only Jesus could work miracles or, at best, others can only work the miracles Jesus worked, and no more. Any attempt to do more receives the accusatory questions, "Who do you think you are? Greater than Jesus?" I'll let Jesus answer that one:

> "I tell you the truth, anyone who has faith in me will do what I have been doing. He will do even greater things than these, because I am going to the Father." (John 14:12)

> "And I will ask the Father, and he will give you another Counselor to be with you forever—the Spirit of truth. The world cannot accept him, because it neither sees him nor knows him. But you know him, for he lives with you and will be in you." (John 14:16–17)

> "All this I have spoken while still with you. But the Counselor, the Holy Spirit, whom the Father will send in my name, will teach you all things and will remind you of everything I have said to you." (John 14:25–26)

One can, therefore, do the things Jesus did, do greater things, and be divinely connected to a Jesus-requested, God-given counselor who will teach "all things and will remind you of everything" that Jesus taught. Say *that* to many fundamentalists, however, and you'll be accused of practicing a New Age religious cult.

⚖️ ⚖️ ⚖️

First, let's establish the *basic laws* of Jesus' teachings. What was the *foundation* upon which everything else rested?

> One of the teachers of the law came and heard them debating. Noticing that Jesus had given them a good answer, he asked him, "Of all the commandments, which is the most important?" "The most important one," answered Jesus, "is this: 'Hear, O Israel, the Lord our God, the Lord is one. Love the Lord your God with all your heart and with all your soul and with all your mind and with all your strength.' The second is this: 'Love your neighbor as yourself.' There is no commandment greater than these."

> "Well said, teacher," the man replied. "You are right in saying that God is one and there is no other but him. To love him with all your heart, with all your understanding and with all your strength, and to love your neighbor as yourself is more important than all burnt offerings and sacrifices."

> When Jesus saw that he had answered wisely, he said to him, "You are not far from the kingdom of God." And from then on no one dared ask him any more questions. (Mark 12:28–34)

If we were busy loving God, Jesus maintains, life would be *heavenly*. Not that *everyone* needs to be doing this to make *our* life heavenly: just us. By loving God, we get the benefit of the loving. "The love I give you is secondhand," as a poet once wrote, "I feel it first." If we are loving God with all our heart, soul, and mind, we will feel only love in our heart, soul, and mind.

But that law had been around since the time of Moses. It was repeated time and again in the Law of the Prophets (the Old Testament). What did Jesus bring to it? The "message" on *how* to do it:

> *They brought to the Pharisees the man who had been blind. Now the day on which Jesus had made the mud and opened the man's eyes was a Sabbath. Some of the Pharisees said, "This man is not from God, for he does not keep the Sabbath."*
>
> JOHN 9:13–14, 16

> "Do not think that I have come to abolish the Law or the Prophets; I have not come to abolish them but to fulfill them. I tell you the truth, until heaven and earth disappear, not the smallest letter, not the least stroke of a pen, will by any means disappear from the Law until everything is accomplished." (Matthew 5:17–18)

Some use this passage as the justification for selectively choosing various Old Testament restrictions as being endorsed by Jesus. They want to fulfill "the smallest letter" of the law—the smallest letter of the law *they* chose that *everyone else* should fulfill. This is not, however, what Jesus was saying. One must include his definition of the Law of the Prophets:

> "So in everything, do to others what you would have them do to you, for this sums up the Law and the Prophets." (Matthew 7:12)

This is known as the Golden Rule. It is an ancient teaching. Five hundred years before Jesus, Confucius said, "What you do not want done to yourself, do not do to others." To continue with Jesus,

> "Anyone who breaks one of the least of these commandments and teaches others to do the same will be called least in the kingdom of heaven, but whoever practices and teaches these commands will be called great in the kingdom of heaven. For I tell you that unless your righteousness surpasses that of the Pharisees and the teachers of the law, you will certainly not enter the kingdom of heaven." (Matthew 5:19–20)

Jesus was not talking about every minuscule prohibition of the Old Testament; he was talking about loving God, the Ten Commandments, and the Golden Rule. To this, at the Last Supper,

> "A new command I give you: Love one another. As I have loved you, so you must love one another. By this all men will know that you are my disciples, if you love one another." (John 13:34–35)

Later, he stated it more succinctly,

"My command is this: Love each other as I have loved you." (John 15:12)

The Golden Rule, as golden as it was, is subject to tarnishing: manipulative people manipulate it to their own manipulative ends. One might say,

"If I took drugs, I'd want someone to come in and stop me. That's how I'd want to be treated. When we tell the government to do that, that's asking the government to fulfill the Golden Rule."

"Would you want to be stopped by force?"

"If necessary, yes. If education failed and I was still taking drugs, yes, I would want someone to come in, by force, and stop me."

"You'd want them to throw you in jail?"

"Well, maybe not jail, but certainly a treatment center."

"Where they would lock you up until you were cured?"

"Yes."

"Who would determine when you were 'cured'?"

"Well, somebody qualified; a doctor, I suppose."

"And who would pick the doctor?"

"I suppose there would be some sort of committee who could decide, and they could turn their findings over to a judge, and the judge could determine which doctor to evaluate me, and then the judge would either accept or reject the doctor's recommendation, and . . . I'm getting confused."

That's the problem with using *force* to enforce the Golden Rule: things get very confused. Also oppressive, arbitrary, and unjust. All those for-their-own-good-and-the-good-of-society rules are variations of the Golden Rule being turned into the Golden Ruler.

So, Jesus added a command which brought "love God" down to earth, and which gave a concrete example of *how* to implement the Golden Rule. Jesus' command instructed us to love each other *as Jesus loved*. And how did Jesus love?

> He called his twelve disciples to him and gave them authority to drive out evil spirits and to heal every disease and sickness. (Matthew 10:1)

> "As you go, preach this message: 'The kingdom of heaven is near.' Heal the sick, raise the dead, cleanse those who have leprosy, drive out demons. Freely you have received, freely give." (Matthew 10: 7–8)

That, essentially, is what he did: he taught and he healed. This, for Jesus, was life; this, for Jesus, was love. He taught that "The kingdom of heaven is near." A lot nearer than anyone suspected: inside themselves. He also healed the sick—not just physically, but emotionally, mentally, and spiritually. He also inspired people

---

---

to heal themselves. ("Your faith has healed you" [Matthew 9:22; Mark 5:34, 10:52; Luke 8:48, 18:42].) He encouraged, cajoled, prodded, and (mostly) inspired (by example) people toward the kingdom of God. Only *once* did he use physical force—when he drove the money changers from the temple. Even then, he only used the physical force of a *man*, and not the significant spiritual force that he obviously possessed. (If you can raise the dead, you can raze a marketplace.)

> *Police arrested Emmet Wheat, of Hayward, California, for hitting eighteen vehicles with his flatbed truck, injuring twelve people. He crashed into the highway center divider after littering three miles of the Nimitz Freeway with dented vehicles. "He said the Lord had spoken to him," Karen Wheat recounted, "and that the Lord told him he could drive through cars."*
>
> NEWS ITEM

This lack of Old Testament wrath irritated his disciples: they wanted to see some of that vengeful-God pyrotechnics. In that, alas, Jesus was a disappointment.

> When the disciples James and John saw this, they asked, "Lord, do you want us to call fire down from heaven to destroy them?" But Jesus turned and rebuked them, and they went to another village. (Luke 9:54–56)

John and James were brothers. Jesus called them the Sons of Thunder, probably because they made such old covenant comments. Jesus saved his wrath for the Pharisees, and while he was brilliant at destroying their arguments and the traps they set for him, he never attempted to destroy them physically. (Although I sometimes wish he had—excuse, please, my un-Christian thought; just call me "Son of Thunder III.")

That does, however, bring us to Jesus' three primary tools for obtaining and maintaining the kingdom of God. They are (1) prayer, (2) acceptance (nonjudgment), and (3) forgiveness.

1. Prayer. Jesus frequently went off alone to pray. Based on the prayers that were recorded, he seems to have used various techniques of meditation and contemplation as well. After feeding "about five thousand men, besides women and children" with five loaves of bread and two fishes,

> He went up on a mountainside by himself to pray. When evening came, he was there alone. (Matthew 14:23)

Jesus prayed a great deal, and for many reasons. Among them *rejuvenation* . . .

> Yet the news about him spread all the more, so that crowds of people came to hear him and to be healed of their sicknesses. But Jesus often withdrew to lonely places and prayed. (Luke 5:15–16)

strength . . .

> "Watch and pray so that you will not fall into temptation. The spirit is willing, but the body is weak." (Matthew 26:41 and Mark 14:38)

healing . . .

> *When we talk to God,*
> *we're praying.*
> *When God talks to us,*
> *we're schizophrenic.*
>
> LILY TOMLIN

After Jesus had gone indoors, his disciples asked him privately, "Why couldn't we drive [the evil spirit] out?" He replied, "This kind can come out only by prayer." (Mark 9:28–29)

inspiration, guidance . . .

One of those days Jesus went out to a mountainside to pray, and spent the night praying to God. When morning came, he called his disciples to him and chose twelve of them, whom he also designated apostles. (Luke 6:12–13).

and the ever-popular *requests** . . .

"But I have prayed for you, Simon, that your faith may not fail." (Luke 22:32)

Jesus also had some pretty nifty experiences while praying:

About eight days after Jesus said this, he took Peter, John, and James with him and went up onto a mountain to pray. As he was praying, the appearance of his face changed, and his clothes became as bright as a flash of lightning. (Luke 9:28–29)

When all the people were being baptized, Jesus was baptized too. And as he was praying, heaven was opened and the Holy Spirit descended on him in bodily form like a dove. And a voice came from heaven: "You are my Son, whom I love; with you I am well pleased." (Luke 3:21–22)

2. Acceptance (nonjudgment). The Greek words Jesus used to describe judgment *(krino* and *krima)* meant to *evaluate* something, and then *apply the law* to it. Once one chooses the law, one is bound by the law. One is no longer living in grace. Therefore, if you *judge* by the law, you *get judged* by the law.

"Do not judge, or you too will be judged. For in the same way you judge others, you will be judged, and with the measure you use, it will be measured to you." (Matthew 7:1–2)

But isn't it *human* to judge others? Absolutely—all too human.

"You judge by human standards; I pass judgment on no one." (John 8:15)

With enough prayer (attunement), the concept of judging doesn't even arise. When we judge anyway (and we will, we will), Jesus teaches us to move immediately (or as quickly as possible) on to . . .

3. Forgiveness. The Greek word for forgiveness is *aphiemi,* which means "to forsake, lay aside, leave, let alone, let be, let go, let have, omit, put away, send away, yield up." In other words, *let go of it* and move on with your life.

"And when you stand praying, if you hold anything against anyone, for-

---

*Requesting forgiveness, for example, is known as repentance.

give him, so that your Father in heaven may forgive you your sins." (Mark 11:25)

The technique for being forgiven, then, is forgiveness and repentance (asking for forgiveness),

> "For if you forgive men when they sin against you, your heavenly Father will also forgive you. But if you do not forgive men their sins, your Father will not forgive your sins." (Matthew 6:14–15)

"So watch yourselves"(Luke 17:3), said Jesus.

> *I've tried by tender and conscientious nursing to keep my grudge against you alive, but I find it has died on me.*
>
> ALEXANDER WOOLLCOTT

> "If your brother sins, rebuke him, and if he repents, forgive him. If he sins against you seven times in a day, and seven times comes back to you and says, 'I repent,' forgive him." (Luke 17:3–4)*

ᛘ ᛘ ᛘ

That's the technique, as Jesus taught it, for moving from law to grace: prayer, acceptance (nonjudgment), forgiveness. Any one of those three will move a person from judgment to grace *if only* he or she applies it. That's the trick, of course: remembering to apply it, and doing so with enough faith, commitment, and abandon (trust) to make it work. The goal is to live in a state of grace at all times. This is perfection. ("Be perfect, therefore, as your heavenly Father is perfect" [Matthew 5:48].) As human beings, however, we'll never achieve perfection. That's life. Even the human part of Jesus had to admit this: "'Why do you call me good?' Jesus answered. 'No one is good—except God alone'" (Luke 18:19).

And here, in my estimation, is one of Jesus' most brilliant concepts: As soon as you're perfect, you can then judge others; until that time, keep working on yourself. Since there will always be *some* work to do on ourselves, there will never be any time to judge others. Not judging others keeps us in a state of grace. When we *do* judge, we should forgive the people we've judged at once: since we weren't perfect, we had no business judging them in the first place. This forgiveness moves us back into grace, and the upward spiral continues. Brilliant. As quoted earlier, here's how Jesus summed it up:

> "Why do you look at the speck of sawdust in your brother's eye and pay no attention to the plank in your own eye? How can you say to your brother, 'Let me take the speck out of your eye,' when all the time there is

---

*Peter, looking for a loophole (brothers can be *awfully* exasperating), was hoping that the eighth time he could judge instead of forgive. Jesus filled *that* loophole: "Then Peter came to Jesus and asked, 'Lord, how many times shall I forgive my brother when he sins against me? Up to seven times?' Jesus answered, 'I tell you, not seven times, but seventy-seven times'" (Matthew 18:21–22). And that's per *day.*

> *We have grasped the
> mystery of the atom
> and rejected
> the Sermon on the Mount.*
>
> GENERAL OMAR BRADLEY

a plank in your own eye? You hypocrite, first take the plank out of your own eye, and then you will see clearly to remove the speck from your brother's eye." (Matthew 7:3–5)

This is taken from the Sermon on the Mount, thus intended by Jesus for the widest possible audience. The use of the word *hypocrite*, then, is a strong one. He almost exclusively reserved the term for the Pharisees, who were *professional* hypocrites. In the days of Jesus, it was one of the harshest words you could use. That he would apply it in a public lecture to people who had traveled days, perhaps weeks, to hear his message is shocking. It's a way of saying, *Wake up! Listen to this!* "You hypocrite, first take the plank out of your own eye, and then you will see clearly to remove the speck from your brother's eye."

The remainder of the Sermon on the Mount—and most of Jesus' teachings—gives further suggestions on perfection. Jesus played with people: "You have this point down? Good. Before you judge anyone, though, how about this point? Oh, you have that one down, too? Very good. But *just before* you judge, how about *this one?*" He loved doing this—especially with the self-righteous.

> A certain ruler asked him, "Good teacher, what must I do to inherit eternal life?" . . . Jesus answered, . . . "You know the commandments: 'Do not commit adultery, do not murder, do not steal, do not give false testimony, honor your father and mother.'" (Luke 18:18, 20)

After listing each of these, one can almost hear Jesus pausing and waiting for a reaction: Adultery? Murder? Stealing? Giving false testimony? By this time, Jesus is either in the presence of a saint or someone with a conveniently poor memory. Invariably, it was the latter. Who *hasn't* stolen something at some time? Who hasn't borne false witness (lied) at some time? In exasperation, Jesus pulls out the one *everybody's* broken, "Honor your father and mother." And how does this ruler respond?

> "All these I have kept since I was a boy," he said. (Luke 18:21)

Uh-huh. Right. Time for Jesus to pull out the nuclear warheads:

> When Jesus heard this, he said to him, "You still lack one thing. Sell everything you have and give it to the poor, and you will have treasure in heaven. Then come, follow me."

> When he heard this, he became very sad, because he was a man of great wealth. (Luke 18:22–23)

Gotcha! That's the thing about life: there's always a *gotcha*. We are never so perfect that, by Jesus' teachings, we have the right to judge another. In fact, we don't even have the right to judge *ourselves.* That, quite simply, is God's job.

Here are some levels of perfection Jesus suggests obtaining before judging another's lack of perfection.

> "Do not worry about your life, what you will eat or drink; or about your body, what you will wear. Is not life more important than food, and the body more important than clothes? Look at the birds of the air; they do not sow or reap or store away in barns, and yet your heavenly Father feeds them. Are you not much more valuable than they?

> *I believe in God, only I spell it Nature.*
>
> FRANK LLOYD WRIGHT

> "Who of you by worrying can add a single hour to his life?

> "And why do you worry about clothes? See how the lilies of the field grow. They do not labor or spin. Yet I tell you that not even Solomon in all his splendor was dressed like one of these. If that is how God clothes the grass of the field, which is here today and tomorrow is thrown into the fire, will he not much more clothe you, O you of little faith?

> "So do not worry, saying, 'What shall we eat?' or 'What shall we drink?' or 'What shall we wear?' For the pagans run after all these things, and your heavenly Father knows that you need them. But seek first his kingdom and his righteousness, and all these things will be given to you as well.

> "Therefore do not worry about tomorrow, for tomorrow will worry about itself. Each day has enough trouble of its own." (Matthew 6:25–34)

Do I hear an "Amen!" on that last one?

Some have accused Jesus of not having a sense of humor. I find that Jesus has quite a good sense of humor. As we continue with the Sermon on the Mount, see if you can spot the "in" joke:

> "You have heard that it was said, 'Love your neighbor and hate your enemy.' But I tell you: Love your enemies and pray for those who persecute you, that you may be sons of your Father in heaven. He causes his sun to rise on the evil and the good, and sends rain on the righteous and the unrighteous. If you love those who love you, what reward will you get? Are not even the tax collectors doing that? And if you greet only your brothers, what are you doing more than others? Do not even pagans do that?" (Matthew 5:43–47)

The person recording this was Matthew who, before he was called by Jesus, was a tax collector. Tax collectors were despised—the very personification of Roman exploitation and Roman rule—but one imagines Jesus liked to kid Matthew about it, even with thousands of people listening in. Jesus continues:

> "Do not give dogs what is sacred; do not throw your pearls to pigs. If you

do, they may trample them under their feet, and then turn and tear you to pieces." (Matthew 7:6)

Here Jesus cautions against judgments hidden under the guise of "good advice." Keep your pearls of wisdom to yourself, he cautions, because the world has never treated its great teachers well—as the world would prove with him a short while later. Just in case Jesus hasn't gotcha yet, he continues:

> "But I tell you, Do not resist an evil person. If someone strikes you on the right cheek, turn to him the other also.* And if someone wants to sue you and take your tunic, let him have your cloak as well. If someone forces you to go one mile, go with him two miles. Give to the one who asks you, and do not turn away from the one who wants to borrow from you." (Matthew 5:39–42)

"Come on, Jesus! Isn't that God's job?" some protest. "Doesn't God take care of the lilies of the fields and the birds of the air?" Well, if that is true, then judging is God's job too. Assuming God-like attributes (such as the right to judge) gives one God-sized responsibilities. For any last vestiges of righteousness standing, Jesus pulls out the heavy artillery:

> "It has been said, 'Anyone who divorces his wife must give her a certificate of divorce.' But I tell you that anyone who divorces his wife, except for marital unfaithfulness, causes her to become an adulteress, and anyone who marries the divorced woman commits adultery." (Matthew 5:31–32)

There goes Ronald Reagan's right to judge. (And Ronald Reagan is the man who, if evangelicals had a pope, would have ascended to the office immediately upon leaving the presidency—although he probably wouldn't have had to wait that long.)

> "You have heard that it was said, 'Do not commit adultery.' But I tell you that anyone who looks at a woman lustfully has already committed adultery with her in his heart." (Matthew 5:27–28)

They even got Jimmy Carter on that one. Okay, so you have absolutely no libido and have not sinned in, with, or around sex. Next?

> "You have heard that it was said to the people long ago, 'Do not murder, and anyone who murders will be subject to judgment.' But I tell you that anyone who is angry with his brother will be subject to judgment." (Matthew 5:21–22)

> *No man ever believes that the Bible means what it says:*
> *he is always convinced that it says what he means.*
>
> GEORGE BERNARD SHAW

---

*A Quaker was slapped by an enemy. The Quaker dutifully turned the other cheek, which was slapped also. "Now that the Scriptures have been fulfilled," the Quaker said, removing his coat, "I shall proceed to beat the hell out of thee."

You can't get angry without judging someone, and if you judge someone, you're out of grace. If Jesus had hired an advertising agency, the commercial might say, "Are you feeling out of grace? Have you been angry with your brother and feel subject to judgment? Well, then, try FORGIVENESS! for fast, fast, fast relief. That's FORGIVENESS! F-O-R (ting, ting, ting,) G-I-V-E (ting, ting, ting, ting) N-E-S-S (ting, ting, ting, *ting*). Now available in Family Size for family-strength forgiveness."

> *We must be on guard against giving interpretations of scripture that are far-fetched or opposed to science, and so exposing the word of God to the ridicule of unbelievers.*
>
> **SAINT AUGUSTINE**
> (354–430)

Jesus demonstrates he can be as Old-Testament as the rest of them:

> "If your right eye causes you to sin, gouge it out and throw it away. It is better for you to lose one part of your body than for your whole body to be thrown into hell. And if your right hand causes you to sin, cut it off and throw it away." (Matthew 5:29–30)

With this passage (terribly uncharacteristic of Jesus) he demonstrates either (a) everything in the Bible is *not* to be taken literally, or (b) those who *claim* to follow the Bible's literal teaching who have any eyes or hands left are hypocrites. And what was his advice to hypocrites?

> "First take the plank out of your own eye, and then you will see clearly to remove the speck from your brother's eye." (Matthew 7:5)

Even the footnote in a fundamentalist Bible I have cautions, "Jesus is not teaching self-mutilation." *But that's what it says.* By being unreasonable beyond even the point of a fundamentalist's reason, Jesus bluffs them into submission. If they don't follow his teaching literally, what grounds do they have to insist that any other teaching be followed literally? And if they don't follow this teaching, they are not obeying the Lord, and are, ergo, not perfect. Therefore, they don't get to judge. As I say, Jesus was brilliant.

⚖ ⚖ ⚖

All laws against consensual crimes are based on some group of people—perhaps even the majority of people—judging that what another group of people does is wrong. According to Jesus' teachings, however, until the group doing the judging can demonstrate perfection, they have no business doing so. They should, as the saying goes, "mind their own ten acres," and apply themselves wholeheartedly toward perfection—*their own.*

It could even be argued that—short of changing money in temples—the teaching of Jesus has *nothing* to do with this physical world. It is a spiritual path with little or no comment to make on government. Although Jesus had plenty of criticism for the Pharisees, the leaders of a spiritual path who attacked him, he

> *What one Christian does
> is his own responsibility,
> what one Jew does
> is thrown back at all Jews.*
>
> ANNE FRANK
> *Diary entry,
> May 22, 1944*

was remarkably silent about the governors of Judea, or Rome (who would mercilessly persecute Christians in later years), or King Herod (whose father murdered all babies over the age of two in an attempt to destroy Jesus).* He was a firm believer in separation of church and state simply because *he did not care about the state: his eyes were set on higher (inner) sights.*

---

*This shows Jesus' remarkable self-restraint or disinterest—or both: as he was being led away from Herod's court to his Crucifixion, he did not yell out, "All those children your father killed: it didn't work. I was the one he was after!"

Jesus and the
Separation of Church and State

JESUS OF NAZARETH WAS clearly in favor of separation of church and state. Few things in the Bible are more certain. His teaching was spiritual: he had no interest in this world. Short of appointing twelve disciples, he didn't even bother setting up a church or any other formal organization to carry on his teachings. His disinterest in the governments of this world—and the world itself—is profound.

"My kingdom is not of this world." (John 18:36)

"You are from below; I am from above. You are of this world; I am not of this world." (John 8:23)

The *only* organization he left behind was that he designated twelve men as his disciples with Peter as their leader. That was it. When turning over his authority to his disciples, he even warned against political involvement:

"The kings of the Gentiles lord it over them; and those who exercise authority over them call themselves Benefactors. But you are not to be like that. And I confer on you a kingdom, just as my Father conferred one on me." (Luke 22:25–26, 29)

So, even the kingdom Jesus passed on to his disciples was not a kingdom of this earth. Time and again, his statements indicated he had no interest in the corporeal governments of this world:

"Heaven and earth will pass away, but my words will never pass away." (Matthew 24:35)

"What good will it be for a man if he gains the whole world, yet forfeits his soul?" (Matthew 16:26)

Then a teacher of the law came to him and said, "Teacher, I will follow you wherever you go." Jesus replied, "Foxes have holes and birds of the air have nests, but the Son of Man has no place to lay his head." (Matthew 8:19–20)

Even when he was *offered* absolute political power on earth, he turned it down.

The devil led him up to a high place and showed him in an instant all the kingdoms of the world. And he said to him, "I will give you all their authority and splendor, for it has been given to me, and I can give it to anyone I want to. So if you worship me, it will all be yours." Jesus answered, "It is written: 'Worship the Lord your God and serve him only.'" (Luke 4:5–8)

Anyone with political ambitions would have been tempted. "What I'll do," one might connive, "is beat the devil at his own game. I'll take over the kingdoms of the world, but turn them into kingdoms of heaven. That way God's law will rule on earth, and no one will worship the devil anymore. He'll lose his power, and we will have won." Beating the devil at his own game: Oh, *if only* those well-intended but deeply misguided religious activists would simply follow the words of their own Savior, "Worship the Lord your God and serve him only," this world—and perhaps even the next—would be a lot better off.

Even when Jesus was offered a kingdom on earth by the will of the people, he rejected it:

After the people saw the miraculous sign that Jesus did, they began to say, "Surely this is the Prophet who is to come into the world." Jesus, knowing that they intended to come and make him king by force, withdrew again to a mountain by himself. (John 6:14–15)

That was Jesus' version of William Tecumseh Sherman's 1884 message to the Republican National Convention: "I will not accept if nominated and will not serve if elected." As a clear indication that the evangelicals are 180° from Jesus' teachings, one need only observe the 1988 presidential candidacy of Pat Robertson. He gave up his television ministry in order to run. The voters were, to put it mildly, underwhelmed. Jesus turns down kingdoms that are offered to him in favor of his ministry. Robertson turns down his ministry in favor of kingdoms that few wanted to give him.

Not that everyone was happy with Jesus' not-of-this-earth attitude. The Jews wanted a restoration of their homeland, the promised land, the land of milk and honey. They wanted it *on earth* and they wanted it *in Palestine*. This was the land God promised them, and on this land they wanted their kingdom. The Jews didn't want to be told that the kingdom of heaven was within themselves. They wanted a warrior with the full arsenal of God's destruction to send the Romans packing, get rid of the pagans, and wipe out those damned Samaritans. Even Peter—who would receive the keys to the spiritual kingdom—didn't get it:

> But when Jesus turned and looked at his disciples, he rebuked Peter. "Get behind me, Satan!" he said. "You do not have in mind the things of God, but the things of men." (Mark 8:33)

> *And what of the curious resemblances between Protestant churches and courts of law? The minister and the judge wear the same black robe and "throw the book" at those assembled in pews and various kinds of boxes, and both ministers and judges have chairs of estate that are still, in effect, thrones.*
>
> ALAN WATTS

In fact, *none* of them understood Jesus' ministry while Jesus lived. After his resurrection, Jesus returned and found his disciples moping down a road. Because he did not *look* like Jesus, they did not recognize him. They were not on the lookout for his *spirit*. Jesus, incognito, asked what was troubling them. They responded,

> "He was a prophet, powerful in word and deed before God and all the people. The chief priests and our rulers handed him over to be sentenced to death, and they crucified him; but we had hoped that he was the one who was going to redeem Israel." (Luke 24:19–21)

They were disappointed because they had lost their redeemer. They wanted the kingdom of Israel restored, not the kingdom of heaven (as Jesus had defined the kingdom of heaven). It was not until the Holy Spirit visited them—an entirely spiritual action—that they *finally* got it.

⚖ ⚖ ⚖

The concept of separation of church and state was unknown at the time of Jesus. It was, in fact, unknown until the time of the Enlightenment more than 1600 years later. That Jesus was so vehemently opposed to political activities was remarkable. All other spiritual leaders wheedled for power. They had to. Without the support of the corporeal government, the religious leaders might find themselves eliminated because some *other* religion gained favor with the ruler and wanted all the "infidels" wiped out. Religious leaders made sure that God's miracles were paid for in corporeal favors. But Jesus had none of it. Take this story for example:

> While he was saying this, a ruler came and knelt before him and said, "My daughter has just died. But come and put your hand on her, and she will live." Jesus got up and went with him, and so did his disciples.

> When Jesus entered the ruler's house and saw the flute players and the noisy crowd, he said, "Go away. The girl is not dead but asleep." But they laughed at him. After the crowd had been put outside, he went in and took the girl by the hand, and she got up. News of this spread through all

that region. (Matthew 9:18–19, 23–26)

Note that Jesus did not make—or even request—any conditions of the ruler. Certainly raising a daughter from the dead is worth more than just a few political favors. Jesus asked for none, and there's no record of his receiving any.

Not only was Jesus disinterested in political matters; he was disinterested in civil matters as well.

Someone in the crowd said to him, "Teacher, tell my brother to divide the inheritance with me." Jesus replied, "Man, who appointed me a judge or an arbiter between you?" (Luke 12:13–14)

He then, of course, proceeded to teach them about the Spirit.

⚖ ⚖ ⚖

> *I never saw a contradiction between the ideas that sustain me and the ideas of that symbol, of that extraordinary figure [Jesus Christ].*
>
> FIDEL CASTRO

Two of the most famous incidents of the New Testament show Jesus' attitude toward church and state. He was as opposed to state intervention by the church as he was to church intervention by the state.

> When it was almost time for the Jewish Passover, Jesus went up to Jerusalem. In the temple courts he found men selling cattle, sheep and doves, and others sitting at tables exchanging money. So he made a whip out of cords, and drove all from the temple area, both sheep and cattle; he scattered the coins of the money changers and overturned their tables. To those who sold doves he said, "Get these out of here! How dare you turn my Father's house into a market!" (John 2:13–16)

He was not against money-changing or sheep-selling; he was, however, opposed to either taking place *in the temple.* Although he clearly did not have a high opinion of money-changers and sheep-sellers ("It is written, 'My house will be called a house of prayer,' but you are making it a 'den of robbers'" [Matthew 21:13]), it is doubtful that he would have upset their tables had the "den of robbers" been across the street from the temple. Jesus felt so strongly that the temple should be used as "a house of prayer" and not be involved in material matters at all (even though the livestock was being sold for religious sacrifice in the temple and the money changers were there so foreigners could pay the temple tax) that he resorted to physical violence. As I mentioned before, this is the only recorded incident of Jesus using physical violence.

There is nothing more intimate to the function of government than taxes. No taxes, no government. How Jesus dealt with taxes is central to his view on separation of church and state. Among the Jews in Palestine at the time of Jesus, many (including some of his disciples) believed that if the Jews stopped paying taxes, the

Romans would find it no longer profitable to stay in Judea, and they would leave. Israel would then be restored. Paying taxes, then, was far more controversial than it is even today. There were few economic or political reasons for Rome to be in Israel other than tax collecting. Even so, Jesus' stand was firm. When asked whether Caesar's tax should be paid, Jesus answered,

> "Show me the coin used for paying the tax." They brought him a denarius, and he asked them, "Whose portrait is this? And whose inscription?" "Caesar's," they replied. Then he said to them, "Give to Caesar what is Caesar's, and to God what is God's." When they heard this, they were amazed. So they left him and went away. (Matthew 22:19–22)

The wages of sin are death, but by the time taxes are taken out, it's just sort of a tired feeling.

PAULA POUNDSTONE

That is the *essence* of the separation of church and state. It is one powerful group saying to the other: You do what you do best, we'll do what we do best; and we'll leave each other alone so that we can both do our best.

Jesus did, however, get his revenge on the tax collectors: he took one.

> As Jesus went on from there, he saw a man named Matthew sitting at the tax collector's booth. "Follow me," he told him, and Matthew got up and followed him. (Matthew 9:9)

So, Matthew, rather than writing the history of Roman taxation, wrote one of the four histories of the life of Jesus.

⚖ ⚖ ⚖

For more than thirty years, the most heated issue surrounding the separation of church and state has been prayer in schools. The evangelicals would have us believe (as they do) that *not* to allow prayer in publicly funded schools is "anti-Christian." In fact, praying in public *at all* goes against the teachings of Jesus:

> "And when you pray, do not be like the hypocrites, for they love to pray standing in the synagogues and on the street corners to be seen by men. I tell you the truth, they have received their reward in full. But when you pray, go into your room, close the door and pray to your Father, who is unseen. Then your Father, who sees what is done in secret, will reward you." (Matthew 6:5–6)

Jesus was, therefore, opposed to public prayer *of any kind*. He prayed in public on very few occasions: his baptism, the Last Supper, and on the cross. Even when he prayed just prior to his arrest and Crucifixion, he did so in private:

> Then Jesus went with his disciples to a place called Gethsemane, and he said to them, "Sit here while I go over there and pray." (Matthew 26:36)

When he prayed the Lord's Prayer, he did it as *instruction* on how to pray, not as a prayer itself. Of the more than sixty times the words *pray, prayer,* or *prayed* are said by or descriptive of Jesus, only three relate to praying in public.

Jesus did, however, teach working with others as part of his technique for receiving things.

> "Again, I tell you that if two of you on earth agree about anything you ask for, it will be done for you by my Father in heaven. For where two or three come together in my name, there am I with them." (Matthew 18:19–20)

> The aim of the law
> is not to punish sins.
>
> JUSTICE OLIVER WENDELL
> HOLMES

This even suggests that like-minded believers gather for fellowship. (Jesus never had anything remotely resembling "church services.") It does *not* contradict his earlier comment that prayer should be done in private. Certainly public schools are among the *least* private places on earth, and Jesus is firmly on the side of the "infidels" when it comes to prayers not belonging in school.

It's also interesting to note that "so help me God" sneaked into the presidential oath of office, even though the Constitution specifically does not include it. Surely Jesus would be happy that most civil courts, swearing-in ceremonies, and even the presidential oath of office includes an acknowledgment of God and a request of his help. Not so.

> "But I tell you, Do not swear at all. Simply let your 'Yes' be 'Yes,' and your 'No' 'No'; anything beyond this comes from the evil one." (Matthew 5:34, 37)

If someone, however, recommended that the next presidential inauguration eliminate the phrase, "so help me God," guess who the fundamentalists would say was in league with "the evil one"?

⚖ ⚖ ⚖

Those who rattle on and on saying that the United States was founded as a "Christian nation" (which I trust we have historically disproved in the chapters, "Laws against Consensual Activities Are Unconstitutional," and "Laws against Consensual Activities Violate the Separation of Church and State, Threatening the Freedom of and from Religion") obviously don't maintain that this country has followed the teachings of *Jesus* since its inception. If it had, those thirteen states would probably still be thirteen states.

Imagine, for example, if the cavalry had followed Jesus' admonition, "If someone strikes you on the right cheek, turn to him the other also" (Matthew 5:39), during the elimination of the Native Americans:

"Sir, the Indians are here. They want Fort Jefferson."

"Fine, fine; let's give them Fort Monroe, too."

Or imagine the plight of the legal profession if they were, by law, forced to follow the advice, "And if someone wants to sue you and take your tunic, let them have your cloak as well" (Matthew 5:40).

"Hello? This is Roy Coen. I hear your client is suing my client for $10 million. *That's ridiculous!* He's got to take *$20 million!*"

> *Christianity neither is, nor ever was a part of the common law.*
>
> THOMAS JEFFERSON
> February 10, 1814

No, we're not a Christian nation, thank God: We are a nation of free men and women who have the right to worship what we believe in the way we believe best. Our founding fathers had the good sense to follow the teachings of Jesus when it came to the issue of separation of church and state. Would that we continue in the faith of our fathers.

Jesus and Traditional Family Values

ONE OF THE MOST ABSURD claims made by the evangelicals is that their interpretation of "traditional family values" is supported by Jesus. It is not. In fact, nothing could be further from the truth.

The traditional family according to the evangelicals is a husband and wife, faithful to each other until death do them part, and their children. The husband's purpose is to (a) worship God, (b) earn a living, (c) protect his children, and (d) cleave to his wife. The wife's duty is to (a) worship God, (b) worship her husband, (c) love her children, and (d) take care of the house.

Of these, Jesus would certainly support (a), putting God above all things, and (c), Jesus did love children. (Make that *other people's* children: he didn't have any himself.)

> People were bringing little children to Jesus to have him touch them, but the disciples rebuked them. When Jesus saw this, he was indignant.* He said to them, "Let the little children come to me, and do not hinder them, for the kingdom of God belongs to such as these. I tell you the truth, anyone who will not receive the kingdom of God like a little child will never enter it." And he took the children in his arms, put his hands on them and blessed them. (Mark 10:13–16)

The rest of the evangelicals' interpretation simply does not fit. The idea that if you're not in such a family you are somehow failing God is *completely* foreign to the teachings of Jesus.

*Here is an example, by the way, of seeing Jesus from different points of view. Mark says Jesus was indignant with his disciples for not letting the children come to him. When Matthew tells this story, Jesus' indignation is omitted. Luke also leaves out the indignant Jesus. John does not mention the incident at all.

Jesus never married. Within the Jewish tradition, not marrying was almost a sacrilege. Everyone married. The Jews, traditionally not believing in an afterlife, believed that this life—one's only life—centered around four activities: (1) loving God; (2) keeping his commandments; (3) having children; and (4) passing on the tradition to the next generation. People received the tradition from their parents, and they owed it to their children. It was considered a *personal failing* for a Jew not to succeed in *any* of these four areas. A child, turning against Judaism, was seen as turning against his or her parents. The child's lack of faith was also considered to be a *personal failing* on the part of the parents. Not until their son had produced a son and the baby was circumcised (God's covenant with Abraham) did the Jews believe they could, as God told Moses, "rest with their fathers."

And they didn't have long to do it, either. The average life span was around thirty-five. Jewish males were considered men at thirteen. It was then a boy had his bar mitzvah; he declared to the community, "Today I am a man," and the responsibilities of manhood were upon him. By this time, he knew a trade (which he entered into), and he married. (Marriages, like the son's profession, were almost always arranged by the parents.) The first child was expected within the year. This gave the grandparents a few "golden years" with their grandchildren.

By not marrying and fulfilling his obligation to God, his family, and his ancestors, Jesus became an outcast. The pressure upon him could hardly have been more intense, and yet he resisted.

But then, Jesus came from an unusual family. To begin with, his lineage is uncertain. At the beginning of Matthew's Gospel, a lineage from God through David and down to Jesus is given. In Luke, from David on, we have an entirely different lineage. Some explain this by saying one was the lineage of Joseph and the other was the lineage of Mary; others explain it by saying one was the lineage of Joseph and the other the keepers of the Christ consciousness. Or, maybe either Matthew or Luke got it wrong (which is unlikely, because one was a tax collector and the other a physician—two professions known for their accuracy—bad handwriting, perhaps, but accuracy). Whatever the explanation, there is some confusion about Jesus' genealogy.

Mary, as is well known, was a virgin. This is no doubt true, physically, but the word *virgin* in Greek is *parthenos*. This meant simply "a maiden." Some scholars say it also meant a woman of independent means, a woman free to choose her own husband. This degree of independence was rare among women at the time. As an example of this independence, when Mary was told by an angel that she was going to have a child, she was also told that a relative of hers, Elizabeth, was six months pregnant. As soon as the angel left, "Mary got ready and hurried to a town in the hill country of Judea, where she entered Zechariah's home and greeted Elizabeth" (Luke 1:39–40). She remained with them for three months. This shows a person of independent means, or at least an independent spirit.

Elizabeth was no wallflower herself.

> *I'm one of those*
> *cliff-hanging Catholics.*
> *I don't believe in God,*
> *but I do believe*
> *that Mary was his mother.*
>
> MARTIN SHEEN

> On the eighth day they came to circumcise the child, and they were going to name him after his father Zechariah, but his mother spoke up and said, "No! He is to be called John." They said to her, "There is no one among your relatives who has that name." (Luke 1:59–61)

This was utterly shocking behavior. Zechariah was a priest in the temple, and his wife knew her place during religious ceremonies, such as circumcision, and her place was to keep quiet. That she spoke up was bad enough. That she demanded a name that had never been used in the family was appalling. But she had to do it: this child was to speak for Elijah and point the way to the Lord of the New Covenant. "John the Baptist" sounded a lot better than "Zechariah the Baptist." And, after all, men named Zechariah are often called Zack, and "Zack the Baptist" just didn't have the right ring.

If Mary and Elizabeth hadn't been the mothers of John the Baptist and Jesus the Christ, they might have been great organizers for women's suffrage in ancient Judea.

When Joseph found out about Mary's pregnancy "before they came together," he "did not want to expose her to public disgrace; he had in mind to divorce her quietly" (Matthew 1:18–19). For him to quietly divorce her (that is, break off the betrothal) showed great compassion on Joseph's part. It also shows him to be something of a renegade. He could have invoked the law of Moses:

> If a man takes a wife and, after lying with her . . . no proof of the girl's virginity can be found, . . . the men of her town shall stone her to death. (Deuteronomy 22: 13, 20, 21)

Although they weren't stoning people as much in Jesus' day (Moses lived 1,500 years earlier), for Mary to be pregnant outside of marriage was a scandal. Joseph protected her—at the cost of his own reputation. By breaking off the engagement, Joseph would be seen by the community as a man who did not keep his word. By not revealing Mary's condition—which he was charged by law to do—he demonstrated a similar independent spirit. Then Joseph had an angelic visitation, and was told to marry Mary. The family Jesus grew up in, then, was not the traditional family of its day.

☙ ☙ ☙

Generally, Mary is portrayed as knowing about her son's divinity from the beginning, and Jesus is portrayed as the most loving and devoted son in the world. The New Testament, however, paints quite a different picture.

Little is known about the childhood of Jesus. Both Mark and John pick up the story when the adult Jesus is baptized by John the Baptist. Matthew skips from the family moving to Nazareth, when Jesus was still a small child, to the baptism. Luke gives the most complete account, which is sketchy at best.

When Mary and Joseph took Jesus to Jerusalem as an infant to sacrifice "a pair of doves or two pigeons" and consecrate him as their firstborn, a man "moved by the spirit" said that Jesus was "a light for revelation to the Gentiles and for glory to your people Israel" (Luke 2:32). What follows, however, is interesting.

> The child's father and mother marveled at what was said about him.
> (Luke 2:33)

It indicates Mary and Joseph did not know quite what they were holding in their hands.

At this we have a fade-out, and are told only

> The child grew and became strong; he was filled with wisdom, and the
> grace of God was upon him. (Luke 2:40)

When Jesus was twelve, his parents took him to Jerusalem for their annual celebration of the Passover. Jerusalem during Passover was like Disneyland on Walt Disney's birthday or New York City on New Year's Eve: crowded, jubilant, and exciting. That Jesus was exposed to this cosmopolitan influence each year indicated that not only he, but his family, were far more sophisticated than the small-town-son-of-carpenter images we've been given. In his twelfth year,

> After the Feast was over, while his parents were returning home, the boy
> Jesus stayed behind in Jerusalem, but they were unaware of it. (Luke 2:43)

This indicates Jesus, too, had an independent spirit. Here they are, leaving Jerusalem for Nazareth—quite a trek—and Mary and Joseph must have assumed he was with them. Besides, Mary and Joseph had at least six other children—four of them boys.* Jesus, the eldest, was expected to be responsible. As neither Mary

---

*We know there were four boys and at least two girls—there may have been more. Some of them may have come after Jesus was twelve, so it is impossible to know how many children were traveling with them. It was not, however, just Jesus, Mary, and Joseph living alone together, loving one another and praising God all day.

nor Joseph knew where Jesus was, they must have assumed he knew when the caravan was leaving, and would be there. (Caravans were the jumbo jets of their day.)

> Thinking he was in their company, they traveled on for a day. Then they began looking for him among their relatives and friends. When they did not find him, they went back to Jerusalem to look for him. After three days they found him in the temple courts, sitting among the teachers, listening to them and asking them questions. Everyone who heard him was amazed at his understanding and his answers. When his parents saw him, they were astonished. His mother said to him, "Son, why have you treated us like this? Your father and I have been anxiously searching for you." (Luke 2:44–48)

Just like a mother! Here is Jesus at twelve—almost a man—trying out his developing manhood in his Father's profession and, apparently, doing well at it. And what does she do? She scolds him, right in front of all those elders and teachers, giving the standard parental double whammy of guilt: "Why did you treat us this way?" and "We've been worried sick!"* Jesus, for his part, is hardly the apologetic child:

> "Why were you searching for me?" he asked. "Didn't you know I had to be in my Father's house?" But they did not understand what he was saying to them. Then he went down to Nazareth with them and was obedient to them. But his mother treasured all these things in her heart. (Luke 2:49–51)

This final vignette from Jesus' childhood tells us a bit more about their relationship. Jesus was "dutiful," but obviously not devoted. Given his druthers, it's obvious he would rather stay in the house of his Father where he "had to be." It also indicates, once again, that Mary and Joseph did not realize the significance of Jesus' mission on earth.

> But they did not understand what he was saying to them. (Luke 2:50)

That it took them three days to figure out that Jesus would be in the temple indicates that they hardly saw Jesus as the Messiah. But, no matter how much trouble he caused them, "his mother treasured all these things in her heart." ("My son, Jesus; talking to the teachers in the temple; how sweet.") On this tableau of

---

*Psychologists tell us that we recreate our parental relationships with our adult companions. Consider this, for example, from Jesus' early days of gathering his disciples: "Very early in the morning, while it was still dark, Jesus got up, left the house and went off to a solitary place, where he prayed. Simon [Peter] and his companions went to look for him, and when they found him, they exclaimed: 'Everyone is looking for you!'" (Mark 1:35–37)

satisfied (but far less knowledgeable than we've been led to believe) motherhood, we fade out.

⚖ ⚖ ⚖

We fade back in again, eighteen years later when Jesus is around thirty. He is about to be baptized by John the Baptist.

> *I was a loner as a child. I had an imaginary friend—I didn't bother with him.*
>
> GEORGE CARLIN

The next day John saw Jesus coming toward him and said, "Look, the Lamb of God, who takes away the sin of the world! This is the one I meant when I said, 'A man who comes after me has surpassed me because he was before me.' I myself did not know him, but the reason I came baptizing with water was that he might be revealed to Israel."

Then John gave this testimony: "I saw the Spirit come down from heaven as a dove and remain on him. I would not have known him, except that the one who sent me to baptize with water told me, 'The man on whom you see the Spirit come down and remain is he who will baptize with the Holy Spirit.' I have seen and I testify that this is the Son of God." (John 1:29–34)

Whatever this may indicate spiritually, from a family point of view, it shows that Jesus did not come from a close-knit family. With Elizabeth a relative and Jesus and John being born six months apart, had there been regular family gatherings of *any* kind in the thirty years from their births to the baptism, John certainly would have known Jesus.

⚖ ⚖ ⚖

And now, Jesus performs his first public miracle—thanks to mother. It was at a wedding feast in Cana. *Usually* this story is told in the following way:

> Jesus, who was a loving and devoted son, went to a wedding feast with his mother, at her request. As the bride and groom were friends of Jesus' mother, when they ran out of wine Jesus' mother was disturbed.
>
> "Mother, I see you are disturbed. What may I do?"
>
> "I am concerned because my dear friends have run out of wine and it will be an embarrassment to them."
>
> "Would you like me to turn some water into wine, dear Mother?"
>
> "Oh, Jesus, you are such a true and devoted son."
>
> "My love for my mother is so great, I can deny her nothing." (Mothers 11:26)

Well, it didn't *quite* happen that way. This is one of the events in the New Testament we know happened fairly close to the way it is told. It was written by

John, who knew both Jesus and Mary better than anyone else. John never refers to himself by name in his Gospel, but by the phrase, "the disciple whom he loved." After Jesus' death, Mary went to live with John. So, John is the best possible witness for this scene, and here is how he describes it:

> On the third day a wedding took place at Cana in Galilee. Jesus' mother was there, and Jesus and his disciples had also been invited to the wedding. When the wine was gone, Jesus' mother said to him, "They have no more wine."

> *When I was a boy, my family took great care with our snapshots. We really planned them. We posed in front of expensive cars, homes that weren't ours. We borrowed dogs. Almost every family picture taken of us when I was young had a different borrowed dog in it.*
>
> RICHARD AVEDON

"Dear woman, why do you involve me?" Jesus replied. "My time has not yet come." (John 2:1–4)

Not exactly the anything-you-say attitude we have been led to believe. The phrase "dear woman" is hardly a term of endearment. The word *dear*, in fact, is not part of the original. The word Jesus uses is *gune*, which means, "wife" or "woman." Peter uses it, for example, when he denies Christ.

> A servant girl saw him seated there in the firelight. She looked closely at him and said, "This man was with him." But he denied it. "Woman, I don't know him," he said. (Luke 22:56–57)

It's also the word Jesus used when he referred to the adulteress, and the word the crowd used when they referred to the adulteress. As we have seen, neither wives nor women were held in the highest esteem. There were a great many more affectionate terms Jesus could have used, even the more neutral word *meter*, which means "mother."

Jesus is saying, in essence, that he is not yet ready to perform a public miracle, that his mother knows this, and why is she bothering him with this problem of the wine? What does his mother do? *She completely ignores him.* John continues,

> His mother said to the servants, "Do whatever he tells you." (John 2:5)

Mary starts involving other people. One can almost hear her saying, "My son will take care of the wine problem. Servants! Come over here! Help my son make some more wine. Do whatever he tells you." Jesus performed the miracle, and, according to John, "thus revealed his glory." Imagine: being spiritually outed by your mother!

Apparently, Jesus was not too upset with his mother because, "After this he went down to Capernaum with his mother and brothers and his disciples. There they stayed for a few days" (John 2:12).

Then he went on to Jerusalem where he upset the tables of the money-changers in the temple, upset the Pharisees, and no doubt upset his mother if she came along.*

⚖️ ⚖️ ⚖️

> And the thing is,
> if I try to be cool and tell him
> he can get an earring,
> he'll get a <u>nose</u> ring.
> Or by the time my son
> is in high school
> it will be nose bones,
> or something like that.
>
> DAVE BARRY

One of the most important passages indicating Jesus' relationship with his family is found in the third chapter of Mark and also in Matthew (12:46–50) and Luke (8:19–21). By the time Jesus began his ministry, we know that he had four brothers and at least two sisters. There is never a mention again of Joseph, who probably had died. Jesus is remarkably successful as a healer and teacher. Concerning "traditional family values," here is one of the most significant—and least quoted lines—in the entire Bible:

> When his family heard about this, they went to take charge of him, for they said, "He is out of his mind." (Mark 3:21)

If you were successfully teaching and your mother and brothers thought you were out of your mind and planned "to take charge of" you, what would you do? That's just what Jesus did: he didn't go near them. He stayed in the house where he was protected by his followers and sent to his mother and brothers his true message concerning "family values":

> Then Jesus' mother and brothers arrived. Standing outside, they sent someone in to call him. A crowd was sitting around him, and they told him, "Your mother and brothers are outside looking for you."
>
> "Who are my mother and my brothers?" he asked.
>
> Then he looked at those seated in a circle around him and said, "Here are my mother and my brothers! Whoever does God's will is my brother and sister and mother." (Mark 3:31–35)

Jesus' point of view about who is and is not family is hardly obscure. It has simply and conveniently been ignored by those who have alternate agendas.

⚖️ ⚖️ ⚖️

Considering Jesus' relationship with his brothers, this incident from the book of John is telling:

> But when the Jewish Feast of Tabernacles was near, Jesus' brothers said to him, "You ought to leave here and go to Judea, so that your disciples may see the miracles you do. No one who wants to become a public figure acts in secret. Since you are doing these things, show yourself to the world."

---

*There's no record that she did. John's account of the life of Jesus shows him upsetting the tables of the money-changers at least one year before his Crucifixion. The other Gospels—and most movies—put the events closer together in time. We know his mother was present at the Crucifixion, but we don't know where she was when he drove the money-changers from the temple.

For even his own brothers did not believe in him. (John 7:2–5)

If it wasn't for John's comment, "For even his own brothers did not believe in him," it might sound as though his brothers were encouraging him to make his teachings more widely known. In fact, with the information John provides us, we know that they are, at best, encouraging him to "go public" so he'll get this whole savior thing out of his system, or, at worst, they are taunting him with some sibling, "We dare you! We double dare you!" Jesus handles them as any typical misunderstood sibling might: he deceives them.

> *Helvidius was condemned for suggesting that Mary went on to have other children, even though his critics had to do some fancy selecting— leaving out any mention of Jesus' brothers, for example.*
>
> BRUCE HILTON

> "You go to the Feast. I am not yet going up to this Feast, because for me the right time has not yet come." Having said this, he stayed in Galilee. However, after his brothers had left for the Feast, he went also, not publicly, but in secret. (John 7:8–10)*

⚖ ⚖ ⚖

In his hometown of Nazareth, Jesus was not exactly remembered as "Little Jesus, Boy Messiah":

> Jesus left there and went to his hometown, accompanied by his disciples. When the Sabbath came, he began to teach in the synagogue, and many who heard him were amazed. "Where did this man get these things?" they asked. "What's this wisdom that has been given him, that he even does miracles! Isn't this the carpenter? Isn't this Mary's son and the brother of James, Joses, Judas and Simon? Aren't his sisters here with us?" And they took offense at him.

> Jesus said to them, "Only in his home town, among his relatives and in his own house is a prophet without honor." He could not do any miracles there, except lay his hands on a few sick people and heal them. And he was amazed at their lack of faith. (Mark 6:1–6)

Like so many others, Jesus found it difficult to "be himself" "among his relatives and in his own house."

> They got up, drove him out of the town, and took him to the brow of the hill on which the town was built, in order to throw him down the cliff. But he walked right through the crowd and went on his way. (Luke 4:29–30)

You can't go home again. On another occasion, Jesus was preaching and a woman (no doubt an early Catholic) interrupted his teaching.

---

*He did not, by the way, stay "secret" for long: he was healing, teaching, and arguing with the Pharisees almost immediately. Water is wet; rocks are hard; saviors save.

> *The Jewish boy with parents alive*
> *is a fifteen-year-old boy*
> *and will remain*
> *a fifteen-year-old boy*
> *until they die.*
>
> PHILIP ROTH
> *Portnoy's Complaint*

As Jesus was saying these things, a woman in the crowd called out, "Blessed is the mother who gave you birth and nursed you."

He replied, "Blessed rather are those who hear the word of God and obey it." (Luke 11:27–28)

Jesus did not say, "Yes, and . . ." Nor did he quote George M. Cohan and say, "My mother thanks you, my Father thanks you, and I thank you." He said, "Blessed rather . . ." *Rather* means, "No, what you said is not correct, here is the truth." Jesus somehow felt the need to correct the impression that his mother was especially "blessed."

⚖ ⚖ ⚖

And what tender farewell did Jesus have for his mother? Here are his final words to her, spoken while he was on the cross:

> When Jesus saw his mother there, and the disciple whom he loved standing nearby, he said to his mother, "Dear woman, here is your son," and to the disciple, "Here is your mother." From that time on, this disciple took her into his home. (John 19:26–27)

That's it. No, "I love you," no "Sorry," no "See you later." We know these words are fairly accurate because "the disciple whom he loved" was John, who also relays this story. Again, there is the word *woman*, which the translators attempt to soften by preceding it with the word *dear* not in the original Greek text.

After Jesus' childhood, Mary is conspicuous in her absence. Except for sometimes being mentioned as one of the women who followed Jesus, *every* incident involving Jesus' mother in the books of Matthew, Mark, Luke, and John has already been detailed in this chapter. There is no record of Jesus returning to her after his resurrection, and in the remainder of the New Testament, she is mentioned only *once*.

None of this is intended to denigrate Mary in any way. It is merely intended to show that Jesus' relationship with his blood relatives—including his mother—was far closer to *normal* than we have been led to believe.

⚖ ⚖ ⚖

When it came time to gather his chosen family (his disciples), Jesus concerned himself not at all with what their "traditional" families (that is, their blood relatives) might think, say, or feel.

> As Jesus was walking beside the Sea of Galilee, he saw two brothers, Simon called Peter and his brother Andrew. They were casting a net into

the lake, for they were fishermen. "Come, follow me," Jesus said, "and I will make you fishers of men." At once they left their nets and followed him. Going on from there, he saw two other brothers, James son of Zebedee and his brother John. They were in a boat with their father Zebedee, preparing their nets. Jesus called them, and immediately they left the boat and their father and followed him. (Matthew 4:18–22)

> *"For this cause shall a man leave his mother and father and cleave to his flesh"— I mean, "cleave to his wife."*
>
> PAT ROBERTSON
> *"Larry King Live"*
> August 17, 1992

Peter was married and had children; John and James, as we are told in this passage, have a father. (They also have a *mother*, whom we will get to in a moment.)

> Peter said to him, "We have left all we had to follow you!"
>
> "I tell you the truth," Jesus said to them, "no one who has left home or wife or brothers or parents or children for the sake of the kingdom of God will fail to receive many times as much in this age and, in the age to come, eternal life." (Luke 18:28–30)
>
> Still another said, "I will follow you, Lord; but first let me go back and say good-by to my family." Jesus replied, "No one who puts his hand to the plow and looks back is fit for service in the kingdom of God." (Luke 9:61–62)
>
> Another disciple said to him, "Lord, first let me go and bury my father." But Jesus told him, "Follow me, and let the dead bury their own dead." (Matthew 8:21–22)

In this, it must be understood that Jesus did have compassion for the relationship others had with their families:

> As he approached the town gate, a dead person was being carried out— the only son of his mother, and she was a widow. And a large crowd from the town was with her. When the Lord saw her, his heart went out to her and he said, "Don't cry." Then he went up and touched the coffin, and those carrying it stood still. He said, "Young man, I say to you, get up!" The dead man sat up and began to talk, and Jesus gave him back to his mother. (Luke 7:12–15)

It was simply that Jesus was making it very clear to his followers that those who chose a spiritual path had no room for attachment to *anything* of this earth, including relatives:

> "If anyone comes to me and does not hate his father and mother, his wife and children, his brothers and sisters—yes, even his own life—he cannot be my disciple." (Luke 14:26)

Being the messenger of the new covenant in a world that firmly believed in the old covenant would—as Jesus well knew—cause turmoil, and turmoil is always reflected in the family.

> *"Family" this and "family" that.
> If I had a family I'd be furious that
> moral busybodies are taking the
> perfectly good word <u>family</u> and
> using it as a code for censorship
> the same way "states' rights" was
> used to disguise racism
> in the mid-sixties.*
>
> JOHN WATERS

"Do not suppose that I have come to bring peace to the earth. I did not come to bring peace, but a sword. For I have come to turn 'a man against his father, a daughter against her mother, a daughter-in-law against her mother-in-law—a man's enemies will be the members of his own household.' Anyone who loves his father or mother more than me is not worthy of me; anyone who loves his son or daughter more than me is not worthy of me; and any one who does not take his cross and follow me is not worthy of me." (Matthew 10:34–38)

No, traveling from law to grace was not a "family plan" journey:

"From now on there will be five in one family divided against each other, three against two and two against three. They will be divided, father against son and son against father, mother against daughter and daughter against mother, mother-in-law against daughter-in-law and daughter-in-law against mother-in-law." (Luke 12:52–53)

It gets worse:

"Brother will betray brother to death, and a father his child. Children will rebel against their parents and have them put to death. All men will hate you because of me, but he who stands firm to the end will be saved." (Mark 13:12–13)

⚖ ⚖ ⚖

Who was Jesus' family, then? As he explained, "Whoever does God's will is my brother and sister and mother." Luke gave this description of his traveling household:

Jesus traveled about from one town and village to another, proclaiming the good news of the kingdom of God. The Twelve were with him, and also some women who had been cured of evil spirits and diseases: Mary (called Magdalene) from whom seven demons had come out; Joanna the wife of Cuza, the manager of Herod's household; Susanna; and many others. These women were helping to support them out of their own means. (Luke 8:1–3)

This passage is fascinating on several accounts. First, there is no mention of Jesus' mother or brothers among this group. Second, Mary Magdalene, contrary to popular belief, was *not* the adulteress saved from being stoned, nor was she ever characterized in the Gospels as a prostitute—unless one of those "seven demons" had a promiscuous nature. Third, Joanna, the wife of the manager of Herod's household, Cuza, followed Jesus at great peril to herself and her husband: King

Herod disliked Jesus because he thought of him as John the Baptist returned, and he still felt guilty about beheading John. One can imagine that this caused marital discord between Joanna and her husband. Nonetheless, Joanna followed Jesus. Fourth, the women were "helping to support [Jesus and his disciples] out of their own means." As has been shown time and time again, in one church after another, it is the men who get the credit but the women who do the work. In this case, it appears that women financed Jesus' ministry. Where do we ever hear about this in Sunday sermons? The image of Jesus and a band of twelve men, walking along and discussing the meaning of life, is not accurate. They were a traveling entourage, with women supplying essential support.

> *What is a family?*
> *They're just people*
> *who make you feel less alone*
> *and really loved.*
>
> MARY TYLER MOORE

One of the women who followed Jesus was the mother of Zebedee's sons, James and John. Zebedee himself, meanwhile, is never heard from again. The last we see or hear of him is when his sons run off to join Jesus. "Without delay he called them, and they left their father Zebedee in the boat with the hired men and followed him" (Mark 1:20). So, not only did Zebedee's sons, but also Zebedee's wife followed Jesus. Zebedee, one must assume, stayed behind with the hired men, and one can only imagine his thoughts about this charismatic Jesus.

The mother of John and James, meanwhile, was doing mother stuff:

> Then the mother of Zebedee's sons came to Jesus with her sons and, kneeling down, asked a favor of him.
>
> "What is it you want?" he asked.
>
> She said, "Grant that one of these two sons of mine may sit at your right and the other at your left in your kingdom." When the ten heard about this, they were indignant with the two brothers. (Matthew 20:20–21, 24)

Mothers, sibling rivalry . . . just a normal family!

⚖ ⚖ ⚖

This chapter covers just about everything Jesus did or said about blood relatives. Not exactly "Leave It to Beaver," is it? But what did Jesus have to say about other relationships, like marriage and sex? If he didn't teach traditional family values, surely he taught morality with regard to sex.

Oh, yes—far stricter than most Christians care to know.

Jesus on Sex and Marriage

> *Men and women
> will retain
> their sex
> in heaven.*
>
> **POPE JOHN PAUL II**

HOW DID JESUS REALLY FEEL about sex? It's a hard question to answer because (a) he seldom talked about it and (b) the one time he did, his answer did not prove very popular. "It is better," religious leaders throughout the centuries have decided, "to assume that *Jesus* was a good man, that *we* are good men, so the way *we* feel about sex must be the way *he* felt about sex."

Here, however, is what Jesus had to say:

When they were in the house again, the disciples asked Jesus about this. He answered, "Anyone who divorces his wife and marries another woman commits adultery against her. And if she divorces her husband and marries another man, she commits adultery." (Mark 10:10–12)

A hard teaching this, but it leads directly to Jesus' true feelings about sex:

The disciples said to him, "If this is the situation between a husband and wife, it is better not to marry."

Jesus replied, "Not everyone can accept this word, but only those to whom it has been given. For some are eunuchs because they were born that way; others were made that way by men; and others have renounced marriage because of the kingdom of heaven. The one who can accept this should accept it." (Matthew 19:10–12)

For Jesus himself, then, marriage was out of the question, and the ideal was celibacy. That quote, "Not everyone can accept this word," is one of Jesus' most noteworthy understatements. Nonetheless, he counsels, "The one who can accept this should accept it."

The word *eunuch* in Greek is *eunouchos,* which means "a castrated person," or "an impotent or unmarried man." It's doubtful that Jesus is recommending all

> Mr. Mercaptan went on
> to preach a brilliant sermon
> on that melancholy
> sexual perversion
> known as continence.
>
> ALDOUS HUXLEY

males become castrated. His suggestion is to abstain from marriage and sexual activity. That he means "a renunciation of marriage" and not "castration" when he refers to *eunuchs* is obvious by the use of the word in the sentence:

"For some are eunuchs because they were born that way; others were made that way by men; and others have renounced marriage because of the kingdom of heaven." (Matthew 19:12)

"Some are eunuchs," "others were made that way" "and others have renounced marriage" show that *eunuchs, that way,* and *renounced marriage* all refer to the same thing; within the sentence they are interchangeable. In the East and the Middle East, the idea that one would give up marriage and sex to achieve higher spiritual states was, by the time of Jesus, well established. The belief that sexual, creative, and spiritual energy were the same energy expressed in different ways was neither new nor unfamiliar. (It's more unfamiliar in America today than it was in Judea then.)

In the phrase, "others have renounced marriage because of the kingdom of heaven," *because* is a poor translation, suggesting one might *offend* the kingdom of heaven by having sex, in the way that one might offend the host of a dinner party by having sex on the table between courses. The Greek word here is *dunamai,* which means "to be able or possible; can, could, may, might, be possible, be of power." It might be better to say *in order to obtain* the kingdom of heaven, or *to reach* it rather than *because of.* The phrase *the kingdom of heaven* is a translation of the Greek word *ouranos,* which means "the sky, the abode of God, happiness, power, eternity, and the Gospels (the good news)." One would not give up sex *because of* these things, but *in order to reach* these things. The reward of celibacy is great, but so is the cost. "Not everyone can accept this word, but only those to whom it has been given. . . . The one who can accept this should accept it."

Note that Jesus is not laying out absolute rules: if you *can* you *should;* if you can't, well, *c'est la vie.* (Translation: move to France.)

Does Jesus expect perfection? Hardly. That's why marriage poses a problem: within it is the potential for broken agreements. If one is single and "slips," no one is harmed other than the person slipping. If married, however, slipping means breaking one's word with another, and that's not good. Again, the larger sense of *adultery* is invoked: not keeping one's word; not being faithful to one's promise; adulterating one's integrity. Jesus' message, then, was, "fornication is a lesser sin than adultery, so before you get married be *absolutely sure* that this is the *only person* you plan to have sex with *for the rest of your life,*" or "if you're going to work without a net, be really good on the tightrope."

⚖️ ⚖️ ⚖️

Let's take a slight flashback to the scene preceding the one in which the disciples conclude, "if this is the situation between husband and wife, it is better not to marry."

> Some Pharisees came to him to test him. They asked, "Is it lawful for a man to divorce his wife for any and every reason?"
>
> "Haven't you read," he replied, "that at the beginning the Creator 'made them male and female,' and said 'For this reason a man will leave his father and mother and be united to his wife, and the two will become one flesh'? So they are no longer two, but one. Therefore what God has joined together, let man not separate."
>
> "Why then," they asked, "did Moses command that a man give his wife a certificate of divorce and send her away?"
>
> Jesus replied, "Moses permitted you to divorce your wives because your hearts were hard. But it was not this way from the beginning. I tell you that anyone who divorces his wife, except for marital unfaithfulness, and marries another woman commits adultery." (Matthew 19:3–9)

> JUDGE:
>
> *You want a divorce on the grounds that your husband is careless about his appearance?*
>
> WIFE:
>
> *Yes, your honour—he hasn't made one for three years.*

Jesus seemed to enjoy out-Phariseeing the Pharisees. Just when they thought he would want to liberalize the law again, he would give Scripture a more conservative interpretation than even the Pharisees had given. (And *that* was not easy.) The sole reason Jesus gives for making divorce valid is "marital unfaithfulness." In other words, if the commitment is broken, it's broken. Once broken by the other party, the deal's off. Again, this goes back to the underlying importance of commitments not just in sexual fidelity, but in all human relations.

Jesus is also standing up for women's rights. In this, he was unique, in all the Bible. As women were considered property, marriage and divorce were a man's prerogative; the woman had no say in the matter. The Law of Moses, as the Pharisees pointed out, said that all a man had to do to get a divorce was "give his wife a certificate of divorce and send her away." Who needs all those expensive divorce courts? Jesus was saying, however, that women *do* count; that an agreement with a woman (wife) is as binding on the man as it is on the woman; and that only if the *woman* breaks the agreement does the man have a right to break his. This was the equivalent of saying, "Before you sell your property, your property must first give permission." Shocking. It was so conservative, it was radical.

In order to find scriptural proof for his conservative-radical point, Jesus goes all the way back to Genesis and the story of Adam and Eve. It's hard to tell whether Jesus actually meant this, or whether he was making a far-out point in order to goad the Pharisees. As we shall see in the chapter, "His Master's Voice?"

> For a while we pondered whether to
> take a vacation or get a divorce.
> We decided that a trip to Bermuda
> is over in two weeks,
> but a divorce is something
> you always have.
>
> WOODY ALLEN

Jesus loved saying things in public that would (a) impress the people and (b) irritate the hell out of the Pharisees. Certainly quoting Genesis would please the people, but using it as an argument against divorce would irritate the Pharisees. Genesis was written by Moses. The Pharisees could not accuse Jesus of defying the Law of Moses without seeming to attack another of Moses' sacred writings. Once again, they were trapped.

But Jesus was making a larger point. It's found in the phrase, "at the beginning, the Creator made them male and female . . . and the two will become one flesh" (Matthew 19:4–5). There he was going into the ancient past—about as ancient as history on the planet earth gets. As a look into the future, he claimed,

> "At the resurrection people will neither marry nor be given in marriage;
> they will be like the angels in heaven." (Matthew 22:30)

Jesus, then, is juxtaposing the past with the future, pointing out that we are caught somewhere between our "at the beginning" desires to "become one flesh" and our post-resurrection nature to "be like the angels." It's the old beast versus beatific question, "Are we animals or are we angels?" The answer, as always, is, "Yes." Later he recommends that his disciples—those who can handle it—stay unmarried and celibate; to the general public (and, perhaps, to irritate the Pharisees) he gives the equally idealistic advice, "What God has joined together, let man not separate." Quite a range of behavior there. According to the teachings of Jesus, one is not right and one is not wrong: both—although obviously opposites—were recommended by Jesus. Which path should one person take and which path should another take? The answer does not lie in the *path*, but in the *person*. Celibacy or marriage is for "only those to whom it has been given."

⚖ ⚖ ⚖

But this is not a book about choosing one's sexual expression: it is a book that explores the question, "What should *the law* do about sexual expression (or any other activity) between consenting adults?" Well, how did Jesus treat those who had a sexual expression different from his own or an expression different from one he recommended? Without exception, his attitude went beyond tolerance, well into acceptance and often veering on celebration.

Take, for example, his exchange with the "woman at the well":

> Jacob's well was there, and Jesus, tired as he was from the journey, sat
> down by the well. It was about the sixth hour. When a Samaritan woman
> came to draw water, Jesus said to her, "Will you give me a drink?" (His dis-

ciples had gone into the town to buy food.) (John 4:6–8)

The Jews and the Samaritans hated each other. The Samaritans were a mixed race of Jews and Gentiles, so the Jews found the Samaritans unnecessarily fallen and the Samaritans found the Jews unnecessarily righteous. The feud was so bitter that Samaritans would provide no food, water, or shelter to Jews passing through Samaria. So, there sits Jesus alone by a well, around noon, and who should appear but a Samaritan woman.

> *To justify Christian morality because it provides a foundation of morality, instead of showing the necessity of Christian morality from the truth of Christianity, is a very dangerous inversion.*
>
> T. S. ELIOT

We've already explored the attitude toward women during biblical times, and this was a *Samaritan woman*. Even worse, however, was that she was drawing water at noon. No woman in her right mind drew water from a well at noon. It was done in the cool of morning or the cool of evening. In a "Saturday Night Live" skit many years ago, Gilda Radner, dressed in a formal evening gown, stumbles out of an apartment building in Manhattan around noon and hails a cab. It is painfully obvious to everyone that she had not spent the night in her own apartment. The Samaritan woman stumbling out to get water at the crack of noon indicates she was probably truant for a similar reason. Nevertheless, Jesus strikes up a conversation. They talk for a while about Samaritans, Jews, water, and "living water," and Jesus asks her to call her husband.

> "I have no husband," she replied.
>
> Jesus said to her, "You are right when you say you have no husband. The fact is, you have had five husbands, and the man you now have is not your husband." (John 4:17–18)

Jesus has "read her beads." He accurately told her of her past and her present: he knew all about her, and he talked to her anyway. He even asked her for water. (As a Jew, for him to take water from a Samaritan would make him "unclean.") They talked for a while about where one worships—on mountain tops or in Jerusalem—and Jesus concludes, "True worshipers will worship the Father in spirit and truth." (John 4:23)

> The woman said, "I know that Messiah" (called Christ) "is coming. When he comes, he will explain everything to us."
>
> Then Jesus declared, "I who speak to you am he." (John 4:25–26)

Zap! Jesus had never revealed his messiahship to anyone—not even his disciples. It would not be until the end of his life at his trial that he again directly admits to being the Messiah (or the Christ). (His favorite reference for himself was "the Son of Man.") That Jesus would reveal he was *the* messenger to a

Samaritan five-time divorcee living with yet another man, indicated that Jesus was not only accepting of physical, cultural, and lifestyle differences; he was *oblivious* to them. He saw not the body, not the history, not the behavior, not the gender, not the religion, but the *person*.

> Just then his disciples returned and were surprised to find him talking with a woman. But no one asked, "What do you want?" or "Why are you talking with her?" (John 4:27)

> *If Jesus had wanted to make a woman an Apostle He could have done so.*
>
> PAMPHLET AGAINST THE ORDINATION OF WOMEN TO THE PRIESTHOOD 1985

If lawmakers, like the disciples, can't understand *why* certain people have certain sexual variances, the least they could do is behave *like* the disciples, and simply *not ask*.

> Many of the Samaritans from that town believed in him because of the woman's testimony, "He told me everything I ever did." So when the Samaritans came to him, they urged him to stay with them, and he stayed two days. And because of his words many more became believers. (John 4:39–41)

⚭ ⚭ ⚭

As to Jesus' relationship with those who vary from today's sexual norms, the incident of Jesus and the centurion is telling:

> When Jesus had entered Capernaum, a centurion came to him, asking for help. "Lord," he said, "my servant lies at home paralyzed and in terrible suffering."
>
> Jesus said to him, "I will go and heal him." (Matthew 8:5–7)

Matthew uses the Greek word *pais*, which means "boy," and Luke (7:1–10) uses *doulos*, or "slave." That a Roman officer would seek out a Jewish healer for a servant shows a deeper relationship than simply master-servant. We also know the depth of the relationship was not based on the amount of time the servant had spent with him: being a "boy," he would not be, say, the slave who raised the centurion from birth. The boy-slave was what was often referred to as a *body slave*, a young man who would wash, groom, and take care of the personal needs of his master—including sexual ones. Body slaves were very common among Roman officers—especially while on a campaign or stationed outside Rome: only the highest officers were allowed to bring their wife (or wives), and, even then, many found a male body slave a more practical traveling companion. Bisexuality was commonplace in Rome, as it had been in Greece. Even Julius Caesar was said to be "every man's wife and every woman's husband" by Curio the Elder. It was not a pejorative comment, but merely one of his many accomplishments.

When the centurion arrived (or, in Luke's account, sent emissaries) and expressed concern over the slave-boy, the centurion's relationship with the boy was obvious. It made no difference to Jesus. He agreed to heal the boy. This was remarkable in that Jesus was addressing his teachings to the Jews, not the Gentiles, and the centurion and the boy would clearly be of the Gentile/pagan category. According to Luke, the centurion had helped build a synagogue and was a friend of the Jewish people, but it's doubtful that would have influenced Jesus very much. Jesus was a pushover for *faith*.

> *Plato argued that pairs of homosexual lovers would make the best soldiers and the Thebans actually formed an army of such pairs in what turned out to an extraordinarily successful experiment.*
>
> JOHN BOSWELL

> The centurion replied, "Lord, I do not deserve to have you come under my roof. But just say the word, and my servant will be healed. For I myself am a man under authority, with soldiers under me. I tell this one, 'Go' and he goes; and that one, 'Come,' and he comes. I say to my servant, 'Do this,' and he does it."

> When Jesus heard this, he was astonished and said to those following him, "I tell you the truth, I have not found anyone in Israel with such great faith." Then Jesus said to the centurion, "Go! It will be done just as you believed it would." And his servant was healed at that very hour. (Matthew 8:8–10, 13)

Similarly, Jesus had no condemnation for effeminate men or eunuchs. After all, he described himself metaphorically as a eunuch when referring to his own sexuality. Within the Jewish culture, however, eunuchs and effeminate men were outcasts.

> So he sent two of his disciples, telling them, "Go into the city, and a man carrying a jar of water will meet you. Follow him." (Mark 14:13)

Carrying water in Israel was definitely "woman's work." Telling his disciples to look for "a man carrying a jar of water" would be the same as saying today, "Look for a man in a dress, high heels, and a bouffant hairdo." That Jesus would have either a eunuch or an effeminate male lead his disciples to the upper room where the Last Supper would be held is one of Jesus' many statements of acceptance, inclusion, and compassion.

⚖ ⚖ ⚖

No incident from the Gospels, however, more clearly shows how Jesus wants his followers to behave toward those who have "sinned" sexually than the one in which he saved the adulteress from being stoned. The Pharisees were constantly trying to trap Jesus, and offered him one double bind after another. The damned-if-you-do-damned-if-you-don't challenge of the adulteress was probably their best.

> The teachers of the law and the Pharisees brought in a woman caught in adultery. They made her stand before the group and said to Jesus, "Teacher, this woman was caught in the act of adultery. In the Law Moses commanded us to stone such women. Now what do you say?" They were using this question as a trap, in order to have a basis for accusing him. (John 8:3–6)

> *Robert Benchley and I had an office so tiny that an inch smaller and it would have been adultery.*
>
> DOROTHY PARKER

If Jesus said, "Don't stone her," he would—according to the law—be as guilty as she. The Pharisees would have grounds to stone him, too. On the other hand, if he said, "Go ahead and stone her," he would be affirming the law and denying grace. If he did not answer, he would be seen as a man without convictions. It's important to note that adultery was a sexual transgression which Jesus frowned on. It was prohibited by the Seventh Commandment, and he had affirmed the Ten Commandments on several occasions.

> But Jesus bent down and started to write on the ground with his finger. When they kept on questioning him, he straightened up and said to them, "If any one of you is without sin, let him be the first to throw a stone at her." Again he stooped down and wrote on the ground. (John 8:6–8)

Brilliant. Jesus took the responsibility from a faceless crowd self-righteously fulfilling God's law and placed it in the hands of each person, saying, "If you've *never* made a mistake, go ahead: throw the first stone." He was restating his fundamental teaching: "First, take the plank out of your own eye, and then you will see clearly to remove the speck from your brother's eye" (Matthew 7:5). He was saying, yet again, "Until you're perfect, don't judge." Here, in fact, he was taking it a step further: "If you *ever* have sinned, don't judge." So much for judgment. So much for throwing stones.*

Note that he made no physical move to become involved. Unlike in the movies, he does not try to protect her or shield her. He does not pick up a rock and offer it to individual after individual and, with withering eye contact, one by one turn their indignation into shame. No, he simply stops his writing, says his truth, and continues his writing. (Would that *all* writers could be so detached to the outcome of their words. This one certainly isn't.)**

---

*As the joke goes, at this point a woman steps from the crowd and throws a stone that hits Jesus directly on the forehead. Jesus looks at the woman while rubbing the bump on his head, and says to her in exasperation, "Mother, would you stop it!"

**By far the best—and scripturally most accurate—film about the life of Jesus is Franco Zefferelli's *Jesus of Nazareth.*

At this, those who heard began to go away one at a time, the older ones first, until only Jesus was left, with the woman still standing there. Jesus straightened up and asked her, "Woman, where are they? Has no one condemned you?"

"No one, sir," she said.

"Then neither do I condemn you," Jesus declared. "Go now and leave your life of sin." (John 8:9–11)

> *I have looked on*
> *a lot of women with lust.*
> *I've committed adultery*
> *in my heart many times.*
> *God recognizes I will do this*
> *and forgives me.*
>
> PRESIDENT JIMMY CARTER

He does not demand prayer, fasting, or atonement through any sacrifice. He simply tells her to leave her life of sin. Corrected behavior is the best apology.

If each elected official, before voting on the next law to take away yet another consensual freedom, would reflect on his or her own personal transgressions, unpopular preferences, and unsuccessful experiments, maybe we'd have that Christian nation after all.

⚖ ⚖ ⚖

Besides adultery, didn't Jesus condemn other casual sexual practices? Jesus *does* use the term *sexual immorality* once in the Gospels; the same mention is recorded by Matthew (15:19) and Mark (7:21). This is often pulled out of context to prove that whatever *might* be considered "sexually immoral" today was condemned by Jesus. It's a perfect example of quoting the *letter* while entirely missing the *spirit* of the message. The phrase is not only taken out of context within its sentence, but the sentence is taken out of context within its message. The message is a very good one: a major statement of moving from law to grace. Jesus is, once again, explaining to the Pharisees how hypocritical they are. He then makes a general announcement to the crowd:

> Again Jesus called the crowd to him and said, "Listen to me, everyone, and understand this. Nothing outside a man can make him 'unclean' by going into him. Rather, it is what comes out of a man that makes him 'unclean.'" (Mark 7:14–15)

With this statement, Jesus ends the elaborate ritual of "clean" and "unclean" that made up so much of the law. That, combined with his elimination of animal sacrifice ("I desire mercy, not sacrifice" [Matthew 9:13, 12:7]), had effectively wiped away what most people—particularly the Pharisees—considered to be the law. He affirmed the heart of the law: one God, love God, the Ten Commandments, the Golden Rule (the essence of the Law of the Prophets), and added "love one another." *All other* general laws and restrictions were swept away. This infuriated the Pharisees and puzzled the rest. It's as though someone said, oh,

"People shouldn't be put in jail anymore for consensual crimes." It was a great moment of good news (gospel). Nobody got it. Mark tells us in 7:17: "After he had left the crowd and entered the house, his disciples asked him about this parable." Matthew picks up the story:

Peter said, "Explain the parable to us."

"Are you still so dull?" Jesus asked them. "Don't you see that whatever enters the mouth goes into the stomach and then out of the body?" (Matthew 15:15–17)

This is another one of those, shall we say, *modified* translations. "Out of the body" really means (now how do *I* say it discreetly?), "out your butt." Jesus is upset with his disciples ("Are you still so dull?") so he gives it to them in straightforward earthy terms: "What goes into your mouth goes through your stomach and out your butt," although the term was probably even more graphic than "butt." But you can't have Jesus saying, "out your butt," *but*, let's continue.

"But the things that come out of the mouth come from the heart, and these make a man 'unclean.'" (Matthew 15:18)

He then gives examples:

"For out of the heart come evil thoughts, murder, adultery, sexual immorality, theft, false testimony, slander." (Matthew 15:19)

Looking at this list, "evil thoughts" and "sexual immorality" stand out. Amongst all these activities that potentially have innocent victims, what are evil thoughts and sexual immorality doing in there? The answer is that (a) the list is incomplete and (b) "sexual immorality" is a poor translation. It's so poor, in fact, that one begins to wonder whether the evangelical translators of this Bible weren't looking for loopholes themselves. The Greek word they're translating is *porneia*. It means: "harlotry (including adultery and incest); idolatry:—fornication." That is the complete definition—in order—from *Strong's Hebrew-Greek Dictionary*. Doesn't "sexual immorality" as a translation seem unnecessarily vague? It does to this minor wordsmith. The word refers primarily to taking part in pagan ritualistic sex. We'll discuss paganism in greater detail in the next chapter, "The Remainder of the New Testament," but for now, just know that the pagans were, well, *pagan*. They performed live human sacrifices (usually with unwilling sacrificees), ritual deflowering (usually with unwilling flowers), mutilation (usually with unwilling mutilants) and similarly inconsiderate behavior. In this context, "immoral" means sexual practices with *unwilling* victims or other *pagan* acts that have nothing to do with the sexual activities practiced between consenting adults today and so soundly condemned by the evangelicals "in the name of Jesus."

In addition, the list from Matthew is incomplete. Mark, in telling of precisely the same incident, quotes Jesus as giving a fuller list:

> For from within, out of men's hearts, come evil thoughts, sexual immorality, theft, murder, adultery, greed, malice, deceit, lewdness, envy, slander, arrogance and folly. (Mark 7:21–22)

Here, again, Jesus lays out a *spiritual* teaching that is far more strict than the laws of *any* government can ever be—and far

> *Adultery is in your heart not only when you look with excessive sexual zeal at a woman who is not your wife, but also if you look in the same manner at your wife.*
>
> POPE JOHN PAUL II

more strict than *any* human could follow without making many, many "sins" (mistakes). If we jail people for greed, malice, deceit, envy, slander, arrogance and folly, who wouldn't be in jail? The combination of a bad translation and taking the poorly translated term "sexual immorality" out of context, then, provide the evangelicals with the foundation for condemning every sexual act *they* find "immoral." It's a foundation that is beyond shaky; it's downright deceptive.

⚖️ ⚖️ ⚖️

That's it. That's all Jesus has to say about sex. In order to make it look as though Jesus condemned sex, however, religious leaders have tortured his teaching in a manner that is nothing short of *pagan*. Whatever followers of Jesus do with their *own* sexuality, however, is between them, their conscience, and God. How Jesus treated those who fell short of either his personal standards or his teachings is a matter of record: *at no time* did he suggest temporal punishment for *any* sexual activity. Even when he went so far as to condemn lust to the point of saying,

> "But I tell you that anyone who looks at a woman lustfully has already committed adultery with her in his heart. If your right eye causes you to sin, gouge it out and throw it away. It is better for you to lose one part of your body than for your whole body to be thrown into hell. And if your right hand causes you to sin, cut it off and throw it away. It is better for you to lose one part of your body than for your whole body to go into hell." (Matthew 5:28–30)

Even if one wanted to interpret this comment literally (and I've never heard of a single Christian, no matter how fundamental, who does), it does not say—as the Law of Moses did—that the *community* or the *elders* or any other external force should do the gouging and the cutting. The adulterers themselves are their own judge, jury, and executioners. As far as the rest of the world goes, it ain't nobody's business (except God's and theirs) if they do.

The Remainder of the
New Testament

> *Christianity is one beggar
> telling another beggar
> where he found bread.*
>
> D. T. NILES

A T THIS POINT, some people may be saying, "Perhaps the teachings of Jesus don't justify laws against consensual activities, and, yes, the Old Testament is full of rules and regulations that we no longer follow, but the *revealed word* in the remainder of the New Testament does have certain restrictions, and I believe that—as part of the New Testament—these restrictions apply to all Christians." Allow me to answer this in some detail.

First, even if that statement were absolutely true, the doctrine of the separation of church and state (which we explored in the chapter, "Laws against Consensual Activities Violate the Separation of Church and State, Threatening the Freedom of and from Religion") would (or at least, *should)* make it impossible for our government to pass a law because most Christians believe it's right—even if (a) those Christians form a majority of the population, or (b) it is the most marvelous personal life enhancement belief on earth.

But let's look at the remainder of the New Testament—a history and set of guidelines for the very early Christian church—and see if, indeed, all the admonitions and restrictions given for that time would apply to even the most devout Christians today.

The first book after Matthew, Mark, Luke, and John is Acts. It tells of the acts of the apostles, and was written by Luke. As mentioned earlier, Luke probably never knew Jesus personally. He did, however, spend time with Peter and the other apostles, and, it appears, a good deal of time with Paul. Acts opens with Jesus being taken into heaven forty days after the Resurrection. The Twelve (now, The Eleven) choose a replacement for Judas, who had hung himself. Matthias was chosen—by the casting of lots—to round out the twelve. (How, then, anyone can say that gambling is forbidden by the New Testament is beyond me.)

A little more than a month later—the day of Pentecost—the Holy Spirit descended upon the apostles in the form of tongues of fire. They were filled with such joy and enthusiasm (the word *enthusiasm* comes from two words, *en* meaning "with" and *theos* meaning "God") that some people "made fun of them and said, 'They have had too much wine'" (Acts 2:13). Peter had to explain to the crowd: "These men are not drunk, as you suppose. It's only nine in the morning!" (Acts 2:15).

Here the apostles worked their first miracle. As they spoke to the crowd, each member of the crowd heard the words in his or her own language. About three thousand people caught the spirit and were baptized that day.

The apostles were so successful in working miracles and healing the sick that the Sanhedrin—the ruling body of Jerusalem run by the Pharisees—warned Peter and John to knock it off. Peter and John, now buoyed by the spirit, paid them little mind. The pure love and spontaneous affection of these first Christians was touching.

> All the believers were together and had everything in common. Selling their possessions and goods, they gave to anyone as he had need. (Acts 2:44–45)

> All the believers were one in heart and mind. No one claimed that any of his possessions was his own, but they shared everything they had. (Acts 4:32)

> There were no needy persons among them. For from time to time those who owned lands or houses sold them, brought the money from the sales and put it at the apostles' feet, and it was distributed to anyone as he had need. (Acts 4:34–35)

(How anyone could say that communism—not the totalitarianism and atheism practiced in Russia, but pure communism—is inherently anti-Christian is a puzzlement.)

Part of what appears to be complete fiscal irresponsibility on the part of the early Christians came from the belief that Jesus was going to return *any day now* and physically take his followers to "the Father's house" with him. This probably grew from a misunderstanding of a promise Jesus made at the Last Supper:

> "My children, I will be with you only a little longer . . . Where I am going, you cannot come."

> Simon Peter asked him, "Lord, where are you going?"

> Jesus replied, "Where I am going, you cannot follow now, but you will fol-

low later."

Peter asked, "Lord, why can't I follow you now? I will lay down my life for you."

Then Jesus answered, "Will you really lay down your life for me? I tell you the truth, before the rooster crows, you will disown me three times!" (John 13:33, 36–38)

> *Tolerance comes with age.*
> *I see no fault committed*
> *that I myself*
> *could not have committed*
> *at some time or other.*
>
> GOETHE

And he did. Peter was not yet ready to die for Jesus. Peter had complained previously, "We have left everything to follow you!" (Matthew 19:27). Then Peter was thinking about wives and children and fishing nets. He had forgotten he still had his body—the final attachment.

It's not that Jesus hadn't warned them before the Last Supper:

> Then Jesus said to his disciples, "If anyone would come after me, he must deny himself and take up his cross and follow me. For whoever wants to save his life will lose it, but whoever loses his life for me will find it." (Matthew 16:24–25)

Perhaps Jesus was telling them that *when they individually die*, that is, when they give up the body, *then* they will enter the spiritual kingdom of which he spoke. Back to the Last Supper:

> "In my Father's house are many rooms; if it were not so, I would have told you. I am going there to prepare a place for you. And if I go and prepare a place for you, I will come back and take you to be with me that you also may be where I am. You know the way to the place where I am going." (John 14:2–4)

Yes, we "know the way to the place where I am going"; that is: we all know how to die. It is one of the few things that all human beings, eventually, master.* Jesus prays to his Father:

> "I will remain in the world no longer, but they are still in the world, and I am coming to you. Holy Father, protect them by the power of your name—the name you gave me—so that they may be one as we are one." (John 17:11)

So, when one *leaves the world*, he or she goes to the Holy Father. The apostles thought Jesus would return physically, very soon, and take them all at once. They

---

*I should point out that this Jesus-returns-to-get-you-when-you-die theory is simply what *I* get when I read John, chapters 13 through 17, and compare the predictions made at the Last Supper to what happened in the remainder of the New Testament. After his ascension, Jesus *did* send the Counselor—the Holy Spirit—but he did *not* physically return to take his followers with him *en masse*. He must have meant something else by "I will come back and take you to be with me that you also may be where I am." Physical death is the only time for this that makes sense to me.

> *Now the Lord is the Spirit,*
> *and where the Spirit of the Lord is,*
> *there is freedom.*
>
> 2 CORINTHIANS 3:17

all left eventually, but by ones and by twos. In the meantime, the Holy Spirit had come and proved *most* effective. Could the return of Jesus be far behind? So, they lived day-by-day, intoxicated with the love and the joy of the Holy Spirit.

"I have told you this so that my joy may be in you and that your joy may be complete. My command is this: Love each other as I have loved you." (John 15:11–12)

It should be noted, however, that the early Christian economic system did not prove too successful. From almost the beginning of his ministry, Paul gathered money from the outlying churches for the needy Christians of Jerusalem.

This leads us to what is commonly known as the First Sin in the new church. It seems there were a husband and wife, Ananias and Sapphira, who sold a piece of property and gave the money to the church, but kept a portion for themselves. Peter so soundly rebuked Ananias that "he fell down and died" (Acts 5:5). Ananias was carried out and his wife was brought in. She knew about retaining a portion of the money from the sale of the land, but did not know that her husband had recently moved on to a piece of afterlife real estate. She, too, lied to Peter about the money, and, after being rebuked by Peter, "fell down at his feet and died" (Acts 5:10). "Great fear seized the whole church and all who heard about these events" (Acts 5:11). Well, I would imagine so.

⚖ ⚖ ⚖

As must happen to all groups, The Twelve became Organization Men. Soon they delegated their more administrative duties to seven men chosen by all the disciples, so that the Twelve could give their "attention to prayer and the ministry of the word" (Acts 6:4). One could almost imagine them saying to each other, "All we do anymore is paperwork and handle petty disputes. We don't have any time to heal the sick or spread the good news!" So, they chose seven administrative assistants, apparently headed by Stephen, "a man full of faith and of the Holy Spirit" (Acts 6:5). Stephen was eventually seized and, after a stirring speech in front of the Sanhedrin, stoned to death—the first Christian martyr.

At this point the story takes an abrupt shift. We are introduced to "a young man named Saul" (Acts 7:58). In fact, we have here a major turning point in the entire New Testament: Saul, who later became Paul, wrote most of it. This is also a major turn in the history of Christianity itself. Saul was the son of a Pharisee, and a Pharisee himself. Unlike the Jews of Palestine, however, who were a people conquered by and subservient to Rome, Saul was a Roman citizen. How much

Saul had to do with the condemning of Stephen in the Sanhedrin is not known. He probably supervised the stoning (he watched the cloaks of people who were doing the stoning, and, by tradition, the one in charge of the stoning did not take part in it), and, at the very least, "Saul was there, giving approval to his death" (Acts 8:1).

Saul—a true Pharisee—then began a widespread persecution of the Christians. "Saul began to destroy the church. Going from house to house, he dragged off men and women and put them in prison" (Acts 8:3).

> *A saint is a dead sinner*
> *revised and edited.*
>
> AMBROSE BIERCE

This persecution went on for an unspecified period of time. While Saul was traveling to Damascus, about 150 miles from Jerusalem, to arrest Christians, Jesus appeared to him and, basically, told him to knock it off. And blinded him. Saul was led to Damascus and, for three days, was blind and did not eat or drink anything.

Then Jesus appeared before one of the Christians of Damascus named Ananias (not the stingy Ananias who, by all accounts, was still dead, but another Ananias). Jesus told Ananias where to find Saul, and that Saul would be the one to take Jesus' message to the Gentiles. (More on this important message soon.) Ananias told Saul what Jesus had said, and the "scales fell from Saul's eyes, and he could see again" (Acts 9:18).

Saul was baptized and immediately began preaching in the synagogues of Damascus that Jesus was the Christ—much to the puzzlement of those who wondered, "Isn't he the man who raised havoc in Jerusalem?" (Acts 9:21). The Jews in Damascus, who had been taught to hate Christians by people like Saul, conspired to kill him. Saul had to escape by night, being lowered down the city walls in a basket.

He was, understandably, not immediately welcomed by the Christians in Jerusalem. Eventually, however, they decided his conversion was genuine. Saul took the Christian name Paul.

⚖ ⚖ ⚖

Now comes the first major internal crisis in the new church. Initially, the news that Jesus was the Christ (or the Messiah) was meant for the Jews. The Jews, after all, believed in one god, and spent their entire lives waiting and preparing for the Messiah.

Those who were not Jews were known as Gentiles. Today we think of Gentiles as primarily Christians; that's because most of the non-Jews in this country are Christians. The word *gentile*, in fact, simply means non-Jewish. It could refer to atheists, Hindus, Muslims, or any other non-Jew. In the time of Jesus and the early church, most Gentiles (that is, most non-Jews) were pagans.

A pagan is anyone who believes in more than one god. At the time of Jesus, only the Jews believed in one god. (In fact, monotheism is probably the most significant and radical contribution the Jewish people made to the history of theology and religion.)

As we've already explored, the Gentiles, or pagans, believed in many gods. There was a god of fertility, a god of weather, a god of war, and on and on. There was also a head god—Isis, Zeus, Jupiter (or Jove). The head god, however, was usually just the president of a loosely knit club of gods, each having almost absolute power over the respective areas of life or afterlife that it controlled.

To understand Paul's ministry, one must know just how, well, *pagan* the pagans could be. They were not, as depicted in most biblical films, a few semi-naked bodies dancing in front of some golden idol to some strange-sounding music. The Jews in that day sacrificed grain, birds, lambs, goats, and cattle; the pagans added humans to the list of sacrifices. These humans were not necessarily willing sacrifices, either. It was a time of slavery and conquered nations. When a nation was conquered, its inhabitants were either killed (often in sacrifice to one or more of the gods) or enslaved. Some of these slaves were raised for the express purpose of sacrifice, just as livestock was raised for that purpose.

As God demanded the "firstborn" and "unblemished" animals for sacrifice, most physically perfect specimens were considered more appealing to the pagan gods. Virginity, innocence, and youth were particularly prized.

As fertility was of primary concern—for the continuation of a family lineage, the reproduction of one's livestock, and the growth of crops—sex and sexuality permeated pagan religious practices. Virgins were often deflowered (usually unwillingly) prior to the sacrifice, either by the priest himself or by a "sacred" phallic instrument. (Archaeology has discovered evidence of phallic worship on every continent of the world.) Sometimes the deflowering and sacrificing happened in one motion as the virgin was impaled on a particularly well-endowed pagan idol.

(Please excuse the graphicness of all this; it does serve a purpose. I'm trying to show that, when the early church leaders complained about "sexual immorality," the sexual immorality of the day was *really* immoral.) Emperor Nero would chain nude men and women to stakes, dress himself in animal skins, come out of his "den," and devour their sexual organs. Pretty pagan, eh? It wasn't until A.D. 390 that the Roman government made a law against human sacrifices in pagan rituals.

In addition to sacrifices, there were feasts. Here, the excesses of wine, food, and sex were raised to an art form. (The Romans routinely excused themselves from banquets, went outside, vomited, and returned to start anew.) This frenzied singing, dancing, eating, drinking, and sexual activity (which today might be called a rock concert) was named after the Latin word for "secret rites," *orgia,* or *orgy.* The most remarkable of these was the Roman Bacchanalia, a sort of pagan Mardi Gras, in honor of the god Bacchus.

Pagan temples often employed temple prostitutes, both male and female, for a variety of purposes. Physical ecstasy was considered a sure sign of the presence of certain gods. Temple prostitutes were carefully trained to use sexual energy to bring about religious experiences. The Emperor Tiberius had children trained to gratify him as he was swimming. He called them his "minnows."

> *Everyone would like to behave*
> *like a pagan,*
> *with everyone else*
> *behaving like a Christian.*
>
> ALBERT CAMUS

And let's not forget what—besides "ordinary" food and drink—pagans *consumed.* Cannibalism was not uncommon. It was widely believed that the spirit or essence of others could be received by eating their flesh or drinking their blood.* Partaking of the body or blood of sacrificial victims—sometimes while they still lived—was not uncommon in pagan rituals.

In addition to all this, the Gentiles were also the ones who had been persecuting the Jews for generations.

The term *gentile* was often used by the Jews in the most vile and loathsome manner. The Jews believed the Gentiles were—spiritually speaking—brutal heathens, who were neither prepared for, nor entitled to, the kingdom of God. To even *eat* with Gentiles made a Jew "unclean." Peter ate with Gentiles and then, bowing to community standards, he stopped. For this, he was soundly criticized by Paul.

The dilemma was resolved for Peter by a vision. He saw all the animals forbidden to him as a Jew by Leviticus. A voice told him, "'Kill and eat.' 'Surely not, Lord!' Peter replied. 'I have never eaten anything impure or unclean.' The voice spoke to him a second time, 'Do not call anything impure that God has made clean'" (Acts 10:13–15). Peter later interpreted this vision to mean that the ritualistic laws of Moses had been lifted and that the Holy Spirit was available to Jews and Gentiles alike.

Nevertheless, it continued to be church policy that, before a Gentile could

---

*This was the basis of the Last Supper, in which Jesus turned the bread and wine into his body and blood and encouraged his disciples to eat and drink. "Whoever eats my flesh and drinks my blood remains in me, and I in him" (John 6:56). This was a way in which Jesus separated himself and his followers from the Law of Moses, as the eating of human flesh and the drinking of *any* kind of blood was specifically forbidden to Jews. He also used this to separate his true followers from those who were not. Prior to the Last Supper, when Jesus only *talked* about the drinking of his blood and the eating of his body, John tells us, "Then the Jews began to argue sharply among themselves, 'How can this man give us his flesh to eat?'" (John 6:52) and "From this time many of his disciples turned back and no longer followed him" (John 6:66).

become a Christian, he or she first had to become a Jew. This meant that men had to be circumcised—no small sacrifice in the days before anesthetics and antibiotics.

> *A man is accepted into a church*
> *for what he believes*
> *and he is turned out*
> *for what he knows.*
>
> MARK TWAIN

Around A.D. 50—roughly twenty years after the ascension of Jesus—the Council at Jerusalem was convened to decide who could and could not be saved. The Christians who still thought of themselves as Pharisees said, "The Gentiles must be circumcised and required to obey the law of Moses" (Acts 15:5). Peter and Paul both recommended that the kingdom of God be opened to all who believed. James, a brother of Jesus, as he seemingly presided over the conference, made a politically expedient compromise:

> "It is my judgment, therefore, that we should not make it difficult for the Gentiles who are turning to God. Instead we should write to them, telling them to abstain from food polluted by idols, from sexual immorality, from the meat of strangled animals and from blood." (Acts 15:19–20)*

From A.D. 50 onward, Christians were made up of converted Jews who were very strict and converted Gentiles (pagans) who were very loose. Much of the New Testament, then, tells the Jews to "loosen up!" and warns the Gentiles to "straighten up!"

Few (if any) Christians today worry about the edicts laid down at the Council at Jerusalem. I'm sure that even the most devout Christian has not gone into a restaurant and asked, "Is this chicken killed by strangulation or by apostle-approved, God-fearing Christian decapitation?" Whether some strange restaurateur sacrificed the animal to an idol, or whether blood was or was not used, similarly goes unresearched. And, as mentioned earlier, the sexual immorality which concerned the council was the kind practiced by Charles Manson and Jeffrey Dahmer, not the sort of interlude immortalized in the song, "Strangers in the Night."

Before listing some other New Testament prohibitions that are seldom considered sinful today, and certainly are not illegal, let's consider some of the pressures the early church leaders faced and how it shaped the writings.

1. When the Holy Spirit hit, the new Christians had a genuine mystical experience. Mystical experiences are handled differently by different people. Just as some people, when they drink, become deep and reflective, while others become foolish and reckless; so too, mystical experiences can lead to either profundity or foolishness. Paul's letters—the earliest surviving Christian writings—are, for the

---

*Even so, Paul—who knew the value of compromise and the importance of appearances—circumcised Timothy before taking him on one of his missionary journeys "because of the Jews who lived in that area" (Acts 16:3).

most part, stern warnings to members of the early churches to "knock it off!" (as Jesus had told him). We get a distorted picture of Paul because what survives is a series of letters in which he is "putting out fires"—admonishing the Jewish Christians to stop being so rigid and non-loving, and admonishing the Gentile Christians to stop being so loose and fun-loving. We also get a distorted view of Peter through his surviving writings. He goes on at such great length about "false teachers" that he begins to sound almost paranoid.

> *Humor is*
> *a prelude to faith and*
> *Laughter is*
> *the beginning of prayer.*
>
> REINHOLD NIEBUHR

2. A belief circulated within the early church that went something like this: "Since all of our sins are forgiven, and since Jesus already died for our sins, and since I am already saved because of my belief, then I can do anything I want without fear of reprisal. I can sin as much as I like because, after all, my sin is already forgiven—even before I commit it. I live under grace and not the law, so there is no reason for me to behave." As you can imagine, this disturbed the church leaders to no end. "Yes, you *are* saved, but being saved doesn't mean you don't have to behave," was the message of many of the Epistles. The relationship between sin and grace remains to this day, in fact, a thorny theological question.

3. To this "anything-goes" belief, some followers added a second—even more distressing—element: "If God gives me grace in proportion to my sins, then the more I sin, the more grace I'll get. Therefore, it's *good* to sin because it means that God will pour more grace upon me." In other words, the wheel that squeaks gets the grease and the Christian who sins gets the grace. Again, the church leaders had to inform their misguided believers that the basic supposition (that God sends more grace to sinners because, after all, sinners need more grace) may be correct, but that the conclusion (that people should sin more to get more grace) was faulty. (See Romans 6 for Paul's discussion of these issues.)

4. The early church leaders had a *church* to build. They were putting together a collection of people who often distrusted and sometimes downright hated each other—not just Jews versus Gentiles, but antagonistic nationalities, races, economic groups, professions; all the prejudices that separate us today—only worse. Jews who suffered under the tyranny of Roman occupation were now, as Christians, asked to sit down and break bread with their Roman "brothers." Slaves were told not to revolt, but to love their slavery and their owners—even if the slaves were being mistreated (1 Peter 2:18, 1 Timothy 6:1, and Colossians 3:22). The rich were asked to accept the poor as equals, and the poor were asked to forget about the oppression of the rich. Nations that had been fighting each other for generations were asked to love each other. Keeping these disparate individuals from turning back to the ingrained habits of Judaism and paganism, and keeping them

together as one church, was no easy task. The difference between Jesus and James was that James felt responsible to the church, whereas Jesus felt responsible only to the truth. James made a compromise so as not to upset the Pharisees. Jesus would probably have let the Pharisees be upset. Jesus' message was clear to both Paul and to Peter—"teach the Gentiles." He did not say, "Convert them to Judaism, or some compromised version thereof, and then teach them." He said, simply, "Teach them." Although the Council at Jerusalem decreed it was no longer necessary, Paul circumcised Timothy anyway, so that Timothy would be more acceptable to the Jews. Compromise, politics, church-building.

๑ ๑ ๑

As the old saying goes, "When brains run out, rules begin." That's what the early church leaders found themselves increasingly doing—setting rules because some of their followers' brains (that is, common sense and maturity) ran out. Like the Laws of Moses, some of these rules are universal and apply to followers of Christ today; others applied to specific situations that are not part of the modern world. Here, then, is only a partial listing of rules and regulations given in the New Testament that today are followed by few Christians and are enforced by absolutely no police departments.

The following are laws given by Paul to the Romans who were, for the most part, pagans. Much of the book of Romans, then, forbids various pagan practices.

> To mark the end of taking a vow, cut off your hair. (Acts 18:18)
>
> Do not make images of God "to look like mortal man." (Romans 1:23)
>
> Do not be arrogant. (Romans 1:30 and 11:20)
>
> Do not envy, have strife or malice, or deceive. Do not gossip, slander, be insolent, arrogant, or boastful. (Romans 1:29–30)
>
> Do not disobey your parents. (Romans 1:30)
>
> Do not be senseless, heartless, or ruthless. (Romans 1:31)

As to the last three points, "those who do such things deserve death" (Romans 1:32). (In this precise context [Romans 1:26–27], by the way, Paul condemns homosexuality and puts it on the same level with envy, having strife or malice, deception, gossip, slander, insolence, arrogance, boastfulness, senselessness, heartlessness, ruthlessness, and disobeying one's parents.*)

---

*What Paul was actually condemning in this example was *unnaturalness*; heterosexuals were losing their "natural" desires and lusting after members of their own sex. Precisely the same example could

"You who pass judgment on someone else, . . . at whatever point you judge the other, you are condemning yourself." (Romans 2:1)

Do not be self-seeking. (Romans 2:8)

Do not "brag about your relationship to God." (Romans 2:17)

"What advantage, then, is there in being a Jew, or what value is there in circumcision? Much in every way!" (Romans 3:1–2)

Do not boast. ("It is excluded" [Romans 3:27].)

> *[Paul's] letters contain some things that are hard to understand, which ignorant and unstable people distort, as they do the other Scriptures, to their own destruction.*
>
> **2 PETER 3:16**

"For there is no difference between Jew and Gentile." (Romans 10:12)*

Envy is a good way to save people's souls. "Inasmuch as I am the apostle to the Gentiles, I make much of my ministry in the hope that I may somehow arouse my own people [the Jews] to envy and save some of them." (Romans 11:13–14)

"Love must be sincere." (Romans 12:9)

"Be devoted to one another in brotherly love. Honor one another above yourselves." (Romans 12:10)

"Be . . . patient in affliction." (Romans 12:12)

"Share with God's people who are in need. Practice hospitality." (Romans 12:13)

"Bless those who persecute you; bless and do not curse." (Romans 12:14)

"Do not be proud, but be willing to associate with people of low position. Do not be conceited." (Romans 12:16)

"Do not repay anyone evil for evil." (Romans 12:17)

"If it is possible, as far as it depends on you, live at peace with everyone." (Romans 12:18)

"Do not take revenge." (Romans 12:19)

"If your enemy is hungry, feed him; if he is thirsty, give him something to

be given that homosexuals, when lusting after members of the opposite sex, are being equally "unnatural." Here, Paul is condemning unnaturalness in all forms—that is, not being in accord with one's own nature (as in "to thine own self be true")—not condemning specific homosexual activity. This example from Paul—taken out of context and misinterpreted—is what evangelicals point to in condemning homosexuality.

*Reading this, how could *any* Christian church tolerate the church-sanctioned antisemitism which began in the Christian world by the fourth century and did not let up—even in the United States—until after World War II? This question is not intended to open the Jews versus Christians debate, but merely to demonstrate that precepts clearly written in the New Testament are not necessarily followed by either Christians or the governments they create.

drink." (Romans 12:20)

"Everyone must submit himself to the governing authorities, for there is no authority except that which God has established. The authorities that exist have been established by God. Consequently, he who rebels against the authority is rebelling against what God has instituted, and those who do so will bring judgment on themselves. Therefore, it is necessary to submit to the authorities, not only because of possible punishment but also because of conscience." (Romans 13:1–2, 5)*

> *No sooner had Jesus knocked over the dragon of superstition than Paul boldly set it on its legs again in the name of Jesus.*
>
> GEORGE BERNARD SHAW

"Give everyone what you owe him . . . let no debt remain outstanding." (Romans 13:7–8)

Do not be drunk, do not dissent, do not be jealous (Romans 13:13). (Also prohibited equally amongst those are "orgies" and "sexual immorality and debauchery.")

"One man's faith allows him to eat everything, but another man, whose faith is weak, eats only vegetables." (Romans 14:2)

"The man who eats everything must not look down on him who does not, and the man who does not eat everything must not condemn the man who does." (Romans 14:3)

"Who are you to judge someone else's servant?" (Romans 14:4)

"You, then, why do you judge your brother? Or why do you look down on your brother?" (Romans 14:10)

"Therefore let us stop passing judgment on one another. Instead, make up your mind not to put any stumbling block or obstacle in your brother's way." (Romans 14:13)

"If your brother is distressed because of what you eat, you are no longer acting in love. Do not by your eating destroy your brother for whom Christ died." (Romans 14:15)

"Do not destroy the work of God for the sake of food." (Romans 14:20)

"Each of us should please his neighbor for his good, to build him up." (Romans 15:2)

"Accept one another." (Romans 15:7)

Paul's letters to the Corinthians are often quoted. They comprise two books of the New Testament, first and second Corinthians. When the letters were written, Corinth, Greece, was a city of 250,000 free persons and approximately

---

*Had the founding fathers been as "Christian" as the fundamentalists claim and had followed this advice, we would never have fought the revolutionary war.

400,000 slaves. It had at least twelve pagan temples—including one to Aphrodite, which employed more than 1,000 temple prostitutes.*

No jealousy or quarreling. (1 Corinthians 3:3)

"The wisdom of this world is foolishness in God's sight." (1 Corinthians 3:19)

Do not be proud. (1 Corinthians 4:6)

"To this very hour we go hungry and thirsty, we are in rags, we are brutally treated, we are homeless. We work hard with our own hands. When we are cursed, we bless; when we are persecuted, we endure it; when we are slandered, we answer kindly. Up to this moment we have become the scum of the earth, the refuse of the world. Therefore I urge you to imitate me." (1 Corinthians 4:11–13, 16)

> *God's service spells freedom.*
>
> JUDAH HALEVI

Do not be arrogant. (1 Corinthians 4:18)

"It is actually reported that there is sexual immorality among you, and of a kind that does not occur even among pagans: A man has his father's wife." (1 Corinthians 5:1)**

"Your boasting is not good." (1 Corinthians 5:6)

"You must not associate with anyone who calls himself a brother but is sexually immoral or greedy, an idolater or a slanderer, a drunkard or a swindler. With such a man do not even eat." (1 Corinthians 5:11)

Do not bring civil lawsuits against each other. (1 Corinthians 6:1–8)

Neither greedy nor drunkards nor slanderers will inherit the kingdom of God (nor will swindlers, the sexually immoral, idolaters, adulterers, male prostitutes, nor homosexual offenders***). (1 Corinthians 6:9–10)

"'Everything is permissible for me'—but not everything is beneficial. 'Everything is permissible for me'—but I will not be mastered by anything." (1 Corinthians 6:12)

"It is good for a man not to marry," or, in an alternate NIV translation, "It is good for a man not to have sexual relations with a woman." The King James version: "It is good for a man not to touch a woman." (1 Corinthians 7:1)

"The husband should fulfill his marital duty to his wife, and likewise the

---

*One Bible study teacher said that first and second Corinthians could now be called first and second Californians.

**Cicero noted that incest was practically unheard of in Roman society. In this case "his father's wife" refers to a stepmother, not a natural mother.

***Do you think "homosexual offenders" means "people who offend homosexuals"?

wife to her husband. Do not deprive each other except by mutual consent and for a time, so that you may devote yourselves to prayer. Then come together again so that Satan will not tempt you because of your lack of self-control. I say this as a concession, not as a command. I wish that all men were as I am. But each man has his own gift from God; one has this gift, another has that." (1 Corinthians 7:2–3, 5–7)

"Now to the unmarried and the widows I say: It is good for them to stay unmarried, as I am. But if they cannot control themselves, they should marry, for it is better to marry than to burn with passion." (1 Corinthians 7:8–9)

"To the married I give this command (not I, but the Lord): A wife must not separate from her husband. But if she does, she must remain unmarried or else be reconciled to her husband. And a husband must not divorce his wife." (1 Corinthians 7:10–11)

"Now about virgins . . . I think that it is good for you to remain as you are." (1 Corinthians 7:25–26)

"Are you married? Do not seek a divorce." (1 Corinthians 7:27)

"Are you unmarried? Do not look for a wife." (1 Corinthians 7:27)

"But if you do marry, you have not sinned; and if a virgin marries, she has not sinned. But those who marry will face many troubles in this life, and I want to spare you this." (1 Corinthians 7:28)

"From now on those who have wives should live as if they had none." (1 Corinthians 7:29)*

"He who marries the virgin does right, but he who does not marry her does even better." (1 Corinthians 7:38)

"Do not grumble." (1 Corinthians 10:10)

"Nobody should seek his own good, but the good of others." (1 Corinthians 10:24)

"The head of the woman is man. Every man who prays or prophesies with his head covered dishonors his head. And every woman who prays or prophesies with her head uncovered dishonors her head. If a woman does not cover her head, she should have her hair cut off." (1 Corinthians 11:3–6)

"A man ought not to cover his head, since he is the image and glory of God; but the woman is the glory of man. For man did not come from

---

*Can't those in jail for failing to pay child support in this "Christian nation" just quote Paul and get out?

woman, but woman from man; neither was man created for woman, but woman for man." (1 Corinthians 11:7–9)

"For this reason, and because of the angels, the woman ought to have a sign of authority on her head." (1 Corinthians 11:10)

"Does not the very nature of things teach you that if a man has long hair, it is a disgrace to him, but that if a woman has long hair, it is her glory? For long hair is given to her as a covering." (1 Corinthians 11:14–15)

> *An avidity to punish is always dangerous to liberty. It leads men to stretch, to misinterpret, and to misapply even the best of laws. He that would make his own liberty secure must guard even his enemy from oppression; for if he violates this duty he establishes a precedent that will reach to himself.*
>
> THOMAS PAINE

"When you come together to eat, wait for each other." (1 Corinthians 11:33)

"Women should remain silent in the churches. They are not allowed to speak, but must be in submission, as the Law says. If they want to inquire about something, they should ask their own husbands at home; for it is disgraceful for a woman to speak in the church." (1 Corinthians 14:34–35)

"Do not peddle the word of God for profit." (2 Corinthians 2:17)

"Each man should give what he has decided in his heart to give, not reluctantly or under compulsion, for God loves a cheerful giver." (2 Corinthians 9:7)

"Delight in weaknesses, in insults, in hardships, in persecutions, in difficulties." (2 Corinthians 12:10)

Paul's letter to the Galatians was written to Christian Jews, who called themselves Judaizers.

"All who rely on observing the law are under a curse." (Galatians 3:10).

"Now that faith has come, we are no longer under the supervision of the law." (Galatians 3:25)

"If you let yourselves be circumcised, Christ will be of no value to you at all." (Galatians 5:2)

"You who are trying to be justified by law have been alienated from Christ; you have fallen away from grace." (Galatians 5:4)

The remainder of Paul's letters are addressed to Christian pagans and Christian Jews alike.

Those who are the sons of God were chosen as such "before the creation of the world" and such salvation was "predestined." (Ephesians 1:4, 5)

"The law with its commandments and regulations" is abolished. (Ephesians 2:15)

"Be completely humble and gentle; be patient." (Ephesians 4:2)

"Do not let the sun go down while you are still angry." (Ephesians 4:26)

"Get rid of all bitterness, rage and anger, brawling and slander, along with every form of malice." (Ephesians 4:31)

"Nor should there be . . . foolish talk or coarse joking." (Ephesians 5:4)

"Have nothing to do with the fruitless deeds of darkness, but rather expose them. For it is shameful even to mention what the disobedient do in secret." (Ephesians 5:11–12)

> *The man who is always worrying*
> *whether or not his soul*
> *would be damned*
> *generally has a soul*
> *that isn't worth a damn.*
>
> OLIVER WENDELL HOLMES

"Be very careful, then, how you live—not as unwise but as wise, making the most of every opportunity, because the days are evil." (Ephesians 5:15–16)

"Therefore do not be foolish." (Ephesians 5:17)

"Do not get drunk on wine." (Ephesians 5:18)

"Wives, submit to your husbands as to the Lord. For the husband is the head of the wife as Christ is the head of the church, his body, of which he is the Savior. Now as the church submits to Christ, so also wives should submit to their husbands in everything." (Ephesians 5:22–24)

"The wife must respect her husband." (Ephesians 5:33)

"Children, obey your parents." (Ephesians 6:1)

"Fathers, do not exasperate your children." (Ephesians 6:4)*

"Slaves, obey your earthly masters with respect and fear, and with sincerity of heart, just as you would obey Christ. Obey them not only to win their favor when their eye is on you, but like slaves of Christ, doing the will of God from your heart. Serve wholeheartedly, as if you were serving the Lord, not men, because you know that the Lord will reward everyone for whatever good he does, whether he is slave or free." (Ephesians 6:5–8)

"Do nothing out of selfish ambition or vain conceit, but in humility consider others better than yourselves." (Philippians 2:3)

"Each of you should look not only to your own interests, but also to the interests of others." (Philippians 2:4)

"Do everything without complaining or arguing." (Philippians 2:14)

Don't become circumcised. "Watch out for those dogs, those men who do evil, those mutilators of the flesh." (Philippians 3:2)

"Many live as enemies of the cross of Christ. Their destiny is destruction, their god is their stomach, and their glory is in their shame. Their mind is on earthly things." (Philippians 3:18–19)

*Children of Bible-believing Christians: take note.

"Do not be anxious about anything." (Philippians 4:6)

"Whatever is true, whatever is noble, whatever is right, whatever is pure, whatever is lovely, whatever is admirable—if anything is excellent or praiseworthy—think about such things." (Philippians 4:8)

"See to it that no one takes you captive through hollow and deceptive philosophy, which depends on human tradition and the basic principles of this world rather than on Christ." (Colossians 2:8)

> *[Freedom is] keeping open the channels of revelation, preserving the Word of Truth and communicating the Spirit of Life.*
>
> CHRISTOPHER DAWSON

"He forgave us all our sins, having canceled the written code, with its regulations, that was against us and that stood opposed to us; he took it away, nailing it to the cross." (Colossians 2:13–14)

"Therefore do not let anyone judge you by what you eat or drink, or with regard to a religious festival, a New Moon celebration or a Sabbath Day." (Colossians 2:16)

"Since you died with Christ to the basic principles of this world, why, as though you still belonged to it, do you submit to its rules: 'Do not handle! Do not taste! Do not touch!'? These are all destined to perish with use, because they are based on human commands and teachings. Such regulations indeed have an appearance of wisdom, with their self-imposed worship, their false humility and their harsh treatment of the body, but they lack any value in restraining sensual indulgence." (Colossians 2:20–23)

"Clothe yourselves with compassion, kindness, humility, gentleness and patience." (Colossians 3:12)

"Bear with each other and forgive whatever grievances you may have against one another." (Colossians 3:13)

"Slaves, obey your earthly masters in everything; and do it, not only when their eye is on you and to win their favor, but with sincerity of heart and reverence for the Lord." (Colossians 3:22)

"Make it your ambition to lead a quiet life, to mind your own business and to work with your hands, just as we told you, so that your daily life may win the respect of outsiders and so that you will not be dependent on anybody." (1 Thessalonians 4:11–12)

"Test everything. Hold on to the good." (1 Thessalonians 5:21)

"Keep away from every brother who is idle . . . We hear that some among you are idle. They are not busy; they are busybodies. Such people we command and urge in the Lord Jesus Christ to settle down and earn the bread they eat." (2 Thessalonians 3:6, 11–12)

"If a man will not work, he shall not eat." (2 Thessalonians 3:10)

> *The good news is that*
> *Jesus is coming back.*
> *The bad news is that*
> *he's really pissed off.*
>
> BOB HOPE

"If anyone does not obey our instruction in this letter, take special note of him. Do not associate with him, in order that he may feel ashamed." (2 Thessalonians 3:14)

Do not devote yourself to "myths," "endless genealogies," and "meaningless talk." (Timothy 1:4, 6)

"Lift up holy hands in prayer, without anger or disputing." (1 Timothy 2:8)

"Dress modestly, with decency and propriety, not with braided hair or gold or pearls or expensive clothes, but with good deeds, appropriate for women who profess to worship God." (1 Timothy 2:9–10)

"A woman should learn in quietness and full submission." (1 Timothy 2:11)

"Do not permit a woman to teach or to have authority over a man; she must be silent." (1 Timothy 2:12)

"Adam was formed first, then Eve. And Adam was not the one deceived; it was the woman who was deceived and became a sinner." (1 Timothy 2:13–14)

"Women will be kept safe through childbirth—if they continue in faith, love and holiness with propriety." (1 Timothy 2:15)

Some early Christians apparently had more than one wife.*

"For everything God created is good, and nothing is to be rejected if it is received with thanksgiving." (1 Timothy 4:4)

"Do not rebuke an older man harshly, but exhort him as if he were your father. Treat younger men as brothers, older women as mothers, and younger women as sisters, with absolute purity." (1 Timothy 5:1–2)

"Stop drinking only water, and use a little wine." (1 Timothy 5:23)

"All who are under the yoke of slavery should consider their masters worthy of full respect, so that God's name and our teaching may not be slandered." (1 Timothy 6:1)

Do not have "an unhealthy interest in controversies and quarrels about words." (1 Timothy 6:4)

"People who want to get rich fall into temptation and a trap and into

---

*This makes sense—what were the polygamists who converted to do? When Paul gives the requirements to become a church elder, his first requirement, in more than one reference, is to have only *one* wife. This clearly implies that some early Christians—even those who might potentially be considered for the position of elder in the church—had more than one wife. (1 Timothy 3:2, 1 Timothy 3:12, and Titus 1:6.)

many foolish and harmful desires that plunge men into ruin and destruction." (1 Timothy 6:9)

"Command those who are rich in this present world not to be arrogant nor to put their hope in wealth, which is so uncertain, but to put their hope in God, who richly provides us with everything for our enjoyment. Command them to do good, to be rich in good deeds, and to be generous and willing to share." (1 Timothy 6:17–18)

> *It's going to be fun to watch and see how long the meek can keep the earth after they inherit it.*
>
> KIN HUBBARD

"Warn them before God against quarreling about words; it is of no value, and only ruins those who listen. Avoid godless chatter, because those who indulge in it will become more and more ungodly." (2 Timothy 2:14, 16)

"Don't have anything to do with foolish and stupid arguments, because you know they produce quarrels." (2 Timothy 2:23)

"The Lord's servant must not quarrel; instead, he must be kind to everyone, able to teach, not resentful. Those who oppose him he must gently instruct, in the hope that God will grant them repentance leading them to a knowledge of the truth, and that they will come to their senses and escape from the trap of the devil, who has taken them captive to do his will." (2 Timothy 2:24–26)

"But mark this: There will be terrible times in the last days. People will be lovers of themselves, lovers of money, boastful, proud, abusive, disobedient to their parents, ungrateful, unholy, without love, unforgiving, slanderous, without self-control, brutal, not lovers of the good, treacherous, rash, conceited, lovers of pleasure rather than lovers of God—having a form of godliness but denying its power. Have nothing to do with them." (2 Timothy 3:1–5)

"Avoid foolish controversies and genealogies and arguments and quarrels about the law, because these are unprofitable and useless. Warn a divisive person once, and then warn him a second time. After that, have nothing to do with him." (Titus 3:9–10)

The letter to the Hebrews was, obviously, intended for Jews who had converted to Christianity, but its authorship is unknown. Some scholars say Paul wrote it, but others dispute this. The teachings, however, are consistent with Paul's other epistles.

Joyfully accept the confiscation of your property. (Hebrews 10:34)

If you have the faith of Rahab the prostitute, you will not be killed with those who are disobedient. (Hebrews 11:31)

"Strengthen your feeble arms and weak knees." (Hebrews 12:12)*

"Do not forget to entertain strangers, for by so doing some people have entertained angels without knowing it." (Hebrews 13:2)

"Remember those in prison as if you were their fellow prisoners, and those who are mistreated as if you yourselves were suffering." (Hebrews 13:3)**

"Keep your lives free from the love of money and be content with what you have." (Hebrews 13:5)

> *A person from the provinces may move to the city and be horrified by what he sees there, as appears to have been the case with many early Christian writers.*
>
> JOHN BOSWELL

"Do not be carried away by all kinds of strange teachings." (Hebrews 13:9)

"Obey your leaders and submit to their authority." (Hebrews 13:17)

From James, Brother of Jesus

"If any of you lacks wisdom, he should ask God, who gives generously to all without finding fault, and it will be given to him." (James 1:5)

"The one who is rich . . . will pass away like a wild flower. For the sun rises with scorching heat and withers the plant; its blossom falls and its beauty is destroyed. In the same way, the rich man will fade away even while he goes about his business." (James 1:10–11)

"Everyone should be quick to listen, slow to speak and slow to become angry, for man's anger does not bring about the righteous life that God desires. Therefore, get rid of all moral filth and the evil that is so prevalent and humbly accept the word planted in you, which can save you." (James 1:19–21) (Here, immorality is connected to anger and lack of patience, not sexuality.)

"If anyone considers himself religious and yet does not keep a tight rein on his tongue, he deceives himself and his religion is worthless." (James 1:26)

"Religion that God our Father accepts as pure and faultless is this: to look after orphans and widows in their distress and to keep oneself from being polluted by the world." (James 1:27)

"Has not God chosen those who are poor in the eyes of the world to be rich in faith and to inherit the kingdom he promised those who love him? But you have insulted the poor. Is it not the rich who are exploiting you? Are they not the ones who are dragging you into court? Are they not the

---

*It's amazing that some enterprising entrepreneur has not opened a Christian gym (the 12:12 Gym?) using Hebrews 12:12 to drum up business.

**Amen, amen.

ones who are slandering the noble name of him to whom you belong?" (James 2:5–7)

"I will show you my faith by what I do. A person is justified by what he does and not by faith alone. In the same way, was not even Rahab the prostitute considered righteous for what she did when she gave lodging to the spies and sent them off in a different direction.* As the body without spirit is dead, so faith without deeds is dead." (James 2:18, 24–26)

> *Tolerance implies a respect for another person, not because he is wrong or even because he is right, but because he is human.*
>
> JOHN COGLEY

"Not many of you should presume to be teachers." (James 3:1)

"You adulterous people, don't you know that friendship with the world is hatred toward God? Anyone who chooses to be a friend of the world becomes an enemy of God."** (James 4:4) (Note that, here, adultery is connected with materialism, not sex.)

"Grieve, mourn and wail. Change your laughter to mourning and your joy to gloom. Humble yourselves before the Lord, and he will lift you up." (James 4:9–10)

"But you—who are you to judge your neighbor?" (James 4:12).

"As it is, you boast and brag. All such boasting is evil." (James 4:16)

"Anyone, then, who knows the good he ought to do and doesn't do it, sins." (James 4:17)

"Now listen, you rich people, weep and wail because of the misery that is coming upon you. Your wealth has rotted, and moths have eaten your clothes. Your gold and silver are corroded. Their corrosion will testify against you and eat your flesh like fire. You have hoarded wealth in the last days. You have lived on earth in luxury and self-indulgence. You have fattened yourselves in the day of slaughter." (James 5:1–3, 5)***

"Above all, my brothers, do not swear—not by heaven or by earth or by anything else." (James 5:12)

From Peter, the Apostle

"Have sincere love for your brothers, love one another deeply, from the heart." (1 Peter 1:22)

"Therefore, rid yourselves of all malice and all deceit, hypocrisy, envy, and

---

*When, in the Old Testament, the walls of Jericho fell and the city was destroyed, only Rahab, a prostitute, and her family were saved because she had hidden the spies of God prior to the battle.

**Some people have misinterpreted this passage to label environmentalists "enemies of God."

***Do you get the feeling that James is not exactly enamored of rich people?

slander of every kind." (1 Peter 2:1)

"Submit yourselves for the Lord's sake to every authority instituted among men: whether to the king, as the supreme authority, or to governors, who are sent by him to punish those who do wrong and to commend those who do right." (1 Peter 2:13–14)

"Slaves, submit yourselves to your masters with all respect, not only to those who are good and considerate, but also to those who are harsh." (1 Peter 2:18)

> *Archbishop: a Christian ecclesiastic of a rank superior to that attained by Christ.*
>
> H. L. MENCKEN

"Your beauty should not come from outward adornment, such as braided hair and the wearing of gold jewelry and fine clothes." (1 Peter 3:3)*

"Husbands, in the same way be considerate as you live with your wives, and treat them with respect as the weaker partner and as heirs with you of the gracious gift of life, so that nothing will hinder your prayers." (1 Peter 3:7)

"Finally, all of you, live in harmony with one another; be sympathetic, love as brothers, be compassionate and humble." (1 Peter 3:8)

"Do not repay evil with evil or insult with insult, but with blessing, because to this you were called so that you may inherit a blessing." (1 Peter 3:9)

"For you have spent enough time in the past doing what pagans choose to do—living in debauchery, lust, drunkenness, orgies, carousing, and detestable idolatry." (1 Peter 4:3) (Note that from this list Peter singles out idolatry as the worst, calling it "detestable.")

"The end of all things is near." (1 Peter 4:7)

"Offer hospitality to one another without grumbling." (1 Peter 4:9)

"Each one should use whatever gift he has received to serve others, faithfully administering God's grace in its various forms." (1 Peter 4:10)

From John, the Apostle

"Anyone who claims to be in the light but hates his brother is still in the darkness." (1 John 2:9)

"Do not love the world or anything in the world." (1 John 2:15)

"If anyone loves the world, the love of the Father is not in him. For everything in the world—the cravings of sinful man, the lust of his eyes and the boasting of what he has and does—comes not from the Father but from

---

*Heeding this advice would make the Home Shopping Network the most immoral show on television.

the world." (1 John 2:15–16) (Here, lust is equated with cravings and boasting and is not necessarily sexual lust.)

"No one who is born of God will continue to sin because God's seed remains in him; he cannot go on sinning, because he has been born of God. This is how we know who the children of the devil are: Anyone who does not do what is right is not a child of God; neither is anyone who does not love his brother." (1 John 3:9–10)

> *Tolerance is the positive and cordial effort to understand another's beliefs, practices, and habits without necessarily sharing or accepting them.*
>
> JOSHUA LIEBMAN

"Anyone who hates his brother is a murderer." (1 John 3:15)

"If anyone has material possessions and sees his brother in need but has no pity on him, how can the love of God be in him?" (1 John 3:17)

"Dear children, let us not love with words or tongue but with actions and in truth." (1 John 3:18)

"If anyone says, 'I love God,' yet hates his brother, he is a liar." (1 John 4:20)

"And he has given us this command: Whoever loves God must also love his brother." (1 John 4:21)

"If anyone sees his brother commit a sin that does not lead to death, he should pray and God will give him life. I refer to those whose sin does not lead to death. There is a sin that leads to death. I am not saying that he should pray about that. All wrongdoing is sin, and there is sin that does not lead to death." (1 John 5:16–17)

"Many deceivers, who do not acknowledge Jesus Christ as coming in the flesh, have gone out into the world. Any such person is the deceiver and the antichrist. If anyone comes to you and does not bring this teaching, do not take him into your house or welcome him. Anyone who welcomes him shares in his wicked work." (2 John 1:7, 10–11)

From Judas (Jude), Brother of Jesus

Do not "pollute [your] own bodies, reject authority and slander celestial beings." (Jude 1:8)

Do not grumble, find fault, boast, or flatter others for your own advantage. (Jude 1:16)

And, finally,

Do not go to bed with any woman named Jezebel. (Revelation 2:22)

⚖️ ⚖️ ⚖️

Well, as I said at the end of the list of Old Testament regulations, Whew! Mixed in with some beautiful ideals (few of which, however, are easily put into practice) and universal truths, the remainder of the New Testament contains more of the same: rules that applied only to Judean and Mediterranean Christians in the first century—rules that changed even during the time of the New Testament ("to circumcise or not to circumcise"), rules that are routinely ignored by even the most devout Christian today.

Do the writers of the Epistles distinguish some restrictions and admonitions as being more important than others? Do they classify some behaviors as more sinful than others? For the most part, no. Each writer had his personal preferences, of course, (James hated the rich; Paul loved obedience) and often wrote his letters with a specific purpose in mind ("Shape up, you Corinthians!"). But nowhere in the remainder of the New Testament is, say, homosexuality singled out as more sinful than, say, anger, nor is prostitution more condemned than drunkenness.

Once one knows the historical context—the challenges the early church leaders faced—and once one has actually read Acts and the Epistles to understand their teachings in the textual context, then Jesus' fundamental message, "Love one another" shines through—"through a glass, darkly" (1 Corinthians 13:12) in some places, but it does shine through.

There are those who have quoted, do, and will continue to quote portions of the New Testament out of context to serve their own personal agendas. This is too bad. The early church leaders tried to bring Jesus' message of love to a world full of hate. Now their words are used by those who want to bring more hate to a world already hurting.

The early church leaders deserve better than that.

So does the world.

His Master's Voice?

Let's leave religion
to the televangelists.
After all,
they're the professionals.

CHEVIOT
"Max Headroom"

NEW TESTAMENT TRIVIA QUIZ: In establishing the new covenant of grace, who was Jesus' primary opponent? (a) The devil, (b) Sickness, (c) Death, (d) Evil spirits, (e) The Pharisees.

The answer is (e) The Pharisees.

Jesus had very little trouble with (a) The devil. Early on, Jesus spent forty days in the desert being tempted by the devil and seemed, at most, disinterested. The devil could only offer him worldly things and Jesus was noticeably not of this world. Nor did (b) Sickness trouble him. There's no record of his being sick, and he seemed to be able to cure any illness in just about anyone (except when he returned to his hometown of Nazareth and the townspeople's lack of faith prevented him from doing great miracles). Of course, (c) Death was no obstacle. He raised up one person after another,* and eventually raised up himself. And (d) Evil spirits were

*After raising up several people who had recently died—about whom skeptics probably said, "Oh, they weren't dead; they were just stunned," as the pet-shop owner said of the parrot in the famous Monty Python sketch—Jesus raised up Lazarus, who had not only been dead four days, but was *decomposing.* ("But, Lord . . . by this time there is a bad odor " [John 11:39].) *This* was a raising of the dead that could not be denied. It, however, did not sit well with the Pharisees: "So the chief priests made plans to kill Lazarus as well [they were already planning to kill Jesus], for on account of him many of the Jews were going over to Jesus and putting their faith in him" (John 12:10–11). We hear no more about this, but it raises the question: if the Pharisees had killed Lazarus, would Jesus have raised him from the dead again? And if Jesus did, would the Pharisees kill Lazarus *again?* This has great possibilities for another Monty Python sketch, or a Terminator-type movie set in biblical times. The Pharisees could kill Lazarus in more and more elaborate ways, and Jesus could raise him up and make him whole again. Great special effects opportunities, lots of violence, lots of miracles—something for everyone. Perhaps we should call it *Lazaruated,* followed by *Lazaruated II: The Pharisees Strike Back,* followed by *Lazaruated III: The Return of Jesus.* I know, I know, you're asking yourself, "Why is this man writing political books when he should be making movies?" Because if I

easy: he seemed to have complete dominion over those. (Although he once got in trouble when he took some evil spirits from a man and sent them into a herd of pigs. The pigs ran in the water and drowned. This made for some unhappy pig farmers.) It was (e) The Pharisees who created Jesus' greatest problems, including, not insignificantly, his Crucifixion.

The Pharisees, while a minority, were political. They knew how to posture, thus appearing more righteous and, therefore, more deserving of leadership than others. They took advantage of every photo opportunity. They were in the right place at the right time doing the piously right thing. Being political, the Pharisees cared more how they *appeared* than what they *did*. They fasted twice a week, *and the world knew it.* "Oh, those Pharisees: they fast twice a week; what holy men!"

The Pharisees controlled Jerusalem's ruling body, the Sanhedrin. Only Rome's occupation of Jerusalem kept them from having complete power. Rome allowed the Pharisees to inflict traditional physical punishments on those who violated Jewish law. Rome would not allow the Pharisees to put people to death. Those damn Romans, interfering with God's plan! Although formal executions were not allowed, stonings for offenses such as adultery did take place, but they were written off by Rome as "mob action." If the Pharisees didn't approve of a teacher—such as John the Baptist or Jesus, they had to ask the secular power of Rome, or King Herod (Rome's puppet government in Judea), to execute the dissident. The Pharisees could order their Temple Guard, however, to arrest anyone who bothered them.

The Pharisee's self-appointed mission was to maintain "traditional Jewish values" in a time of social upheaval. One of their self-appointed tasks was to separate true prophets from false prophets. They "investigated" all reports of prophets, but it was merely show; the Pharisees *knew* that a prophet could only rise from within the ranks of the righteous: the Pharisees. Anyone not raised as a Pharisee didn't have the proper credentials for prophesy. The punishment for being a false prophet was death. One holy person after another fell before the judgment of the Pharisees. Said Jesus:

> "Woe to you, teachers of the law and Pharisees, you hypocrites! You are like whitewashed tombs, which look beautiful on the outside but on the inside are full of dead men's bones and everything unclean. In the same

made movies, I'd probably make political movies, and we already have an Oliver Stone. Which reminds me: Why did Oliver Stone have so much difficulty finding a casting director for his first film? Because in Hollywood, it's hard to find someone without sin, and only someone without sin could cast the first . . . oh, never mind, let's get back to the text.

way, on the outside you appear to people as righteous but on the inside you are full of hypocrisy and wickedness." (Matthew 23:27–28)

The Pharisees were well versed in Scripture. They could quote chapter and verse to justify any behavior they found expedient. It's the same when a civilian talks law with a lawyer: the lawyer isn't always right—just better trained.

The most dangerous part about the Pharisees, however, was that they *believed*

> *Moralizing and morals are two entirely different things and are always found in entirely different people.*
>
> DON HERALD

that what they were doing was right. They didn't see themselves as hypocrites; they saw themselves as exemplary spiritual leaders. They didn't see themselves as murdering people for expressing new religious points of view; they saw themselves as keeping the people safe from false prophets. While they certainly felt themselves spiritually superior to "ordinary" men, they were willing to share the benefit of their superior learning and discipline by sacrificing their personal time to take leadership roles in the synagogues. They did what they did because they honestly believed they were the chosen among God's chosen people.

These were the "teachers of the law" and, almost by definition, would be the greatest obstacle in Jesus' mission to replace law with grace. While ordinary people were moved by the miracles of Jesus, the Pharisees denounced them as sorcery—punishable by death. While the people found the teachings of grace liberating and appealing, the Pharisees found them blasphemous—punishable by death. While the people found the Pharisees to be ideal role models for achieving righteousness and godliness, Jesus found them hypocritical "vipers." From the Pharisee point of view, Jesus' attitude was punishable by death *at once!* (No, there was no law stating that disrespect for the Pharisees was punishable by death, but the Pharisees did, after all, represent the Law and, as such, anyone who spoke against the Pharisees also spoke against the Law, and *that* was punishable by death.)

The Pharisees, then, (a) represented strict adherence to the letter of the law, while violating the spirit of the law; (b) inflicted harsh punishments for violation of the law (such violations as determined by the Pharisees); (c) went directly against the spirit of the law by strict enforcement of the letter of the law; (d) knew everything and *knew* they knew everything, so could not be taught anything; and (e) were hypocritical in their holier-than-thou attitudes. It wasn't the Pharisees themselves whom Jesus opposed; it was this set of values and behavior.*

---

*Jesus liked certain individual Pharisees, and vice versa. He told Nicodemus, a Pharisee, that he was very close to the kingdom of heaven. Joseph of Arimathea, also a Pharisee, asked Pilate for the body of Jesus and laid him in his own tomb. Jesus ate with Pharisees, just as he ate with tax collectors, pagans, and prostitutes. As always, Jesus chose his companions for themselves, not their station, occu-

> *Fine words and
> an insinuating appearance
> are seldom associated
> with true virtue.*
>
> CONFUCIUS

Even though the Pharisees wanted Jesus out of the way, to say that he was "murdered by the Jews," and hold modern Jews responsible, is as absurd as saying Jesus was "murdered by Rome" (he was executed by Roman officials), and blame the citizens of Rome today. On the contrary, our country's Jewish leaders are some of the clearest voices for tolerance, reason, and justice, while some Christians are today's greatest Pharisees. In fact, the two greatest "Christians" of our time—Jerry Falwell and Pat Robertson—are our two greatest Pharisees.

⚖ ⚖ ⚖

Let's take a look at the religious right in this country, and compare what they do and teach with what Jesus said about the Pharisees. This is not an exhaustive look—that's a book in itself; this discussion limits itself to those hypocrisies that directly affect the laws against consensual activities and the enforcement of those laws.

> "Thus you nullify the word of God for the sake of your tradition. You hypocrites! Isaiah was right when he prophesied about you: 'These people honor me with their lips, but their hearts are far from me.'" (Matthew 15:6–8)

While the religious right quotes the Bible right and right (I was going to say "left and right" but that might be misconstrued), they seldom quote Jesus. (When they *do* quote Jesus, they quote him out of context.) What they quote is the Old Testament and portions of the New Testament covering events which took place after Jesus' time. The religious right would like us to believe that Paul's scolding the pagans—who sacrificed unwilling humans to their gods—applies to us today. Of course, it does not. They ignore the fact that Jesus summed up the entire Old Testament (the Laws and the Prophets) with the simple phrase, "So in everything, do to others what you would have them do to you" (Matthew 7:12). From the Law of Moses, he pulled only "love God," and the Ten Commandments (which is plenty). To this he added, "Love one another. As I have loved you, so you must love one another" (John 13:34). Jesus' commands are not sufficient justification for locking people up or behaving as if "a war has been declared" on fundamentalist Christian beliefs. But does this stop the Pharisees of today? No.

> "They worship me in vain; their teachings are but rules taught by men." (Matthew 15:9)

pation, or outward actions.

Without Jesus to back them up, the religious right relies on concepts such as "traditional American values," "family values," and "the American way." With great piety, they discuss the "faith of our fathers," "the pride of the pilgrims," and the "Christian nation." They misquote and misrepresent the American founding fathers mercilessly. And all to justify their hatred of anyone who is "different." They use the Bible to justify prejudice, exclusion, and persecution. They contradict Jesus' fundamental message, which is love *everyone*, not just those who believe what you believe or do what you do.

> *Distrust all men in whom*
> *the impulse to punish is powerful.*
>
> FRIEDRICH NIETZSCHE

> "Woe to you, teachers of the law and Pharisees, you hypocrites! You have neglected the more important matters of the law—justice, mercy and faithfulness." (Matthew 23:23)

Since the Civil War, the churches that make up the religious right have not taken a leadership stand on any positive social change. Quite the contrary, they have opposed social change. Whether it be the treatment of blacks, Jews, immigrants, homosexuals, or any minority (including the majority minority: women), the evangelicals have quoted chapter and verse to prove that one group or another doesn't even deserve the "privileges" it already has. The way the evangelicals treat gays, for example—frequently calling them "perverts" from the pulpit—is only the most recent example of their injustice, lack of mercy, and unfaithfulness to Jesus' word and example of love.

> "If you had known what these words mean, 'I desire mercy, not sacrifice,' you would not have condemned the innocent." (Matthew 12:7)

Just as the blacks after the Civil War, at the height of religious racial intolerance, went off and formed their own churches and had far more directly spiritual experiences (which were, of course, condemned and ridiculed by the oh-so-proper whites), so, too, some of today's outcasts have gone off and—on their own or in small groups—had visitations by the Holy Spirit, healings, and mystical experiences that rivaled experiences people had during and immediately following Jesus' time. It's a fitting irony—but one foretold by Jesus.

> "I tell you the truth, the tax collectors and the prostitutes are entering the kingdom of God ahead of you." (Matthew 21:31)

The leaders of the religious right have the love of power, righteousness (read: intolerance), fame, and money in their hearts. They pray—loudly and often—but only for effect.

> "You Pharisees clean the outside of the cup and dish, but inside you are

full of greed and wickedness." (Luke 11:39)

When Jesus had finished saying these things, the crowds were amazed at his teaching, because he taught as one who had authority, and not as their teachers of the law. (Matthew 7:28–29)

> Moral indignation
> permits envy or
> hate to be acted out
> under the guise of virtue.
>
> ERICH FROMM

The lack of spiritual connectedness, compassion, and love of religious right leaders is evident to all but their most devout followers.

"But I know you. I know that you do not have the love of God in your hearts." (John 5:42)

If one were to tell the Pharisees of old—or the leaders of the religious right today—that they have no love in their hearts, they would cite twenty-seven specific examples in which they were loving *that week*. Tell them that they lack true humility, and they will cite forty-six specific instances in which they *were* humble—several of which happened on national television (and they'll play you the video). Tell them they neither love nor teach Jesus, and they will say you are inspired by Satan. Black is white and white is black, love is hate and hate is love, and the Prince of Peace will lead us all off to holy war.

"Be on your guard against the yeast of the Pharisees, which is hypocrisy." (Luke 12:1)

"Beware of the teachers of the law. They like to walk around in flowing robes and love to be greeted in the marketplaces and have the most important seats in the synagogues and the places of honor at banquets. They devour widows' houses and for a show make lengthy prayers." (Luke 20:45–47)

The leaders of the religious right love to be photographed with presidents, governors, and dignitaries of all kind. They dress well (by their standards, anyway), travel first class, and seem to want for nothing. Meanwhile, all this luxury is financed primarily by widows, unemployed people, and the working poor, who send $5 and $10 donations, genuinely believing they are doing something for Jesus.

"No servant can serve two masters. Either he will hate the one and love the other, or he will be devoted to the one and despise the other. You cannot serve both God and Money." The Pharisees, who loved money, heard all this and were sneering at Jesus. (Luke 16:13–14)

The other effective money-raiser is fear. The religious right's ministries fight one "conspiracy" after another. They see every minority with "an agenda" and the agenda invariably is "recruiting your children" and "destroying the principles on which this great nation was founded." So, to save our way of life, our children, and the country itself, *send money.* ("There's an 800 number on your screen right now . . .")

> "Woe to you experts in the law, because you have taken away the key to knowledge. You yourselves have not entered, and you have hindered those who were entering." When Jesus left there, the Pharisees and the teachers of the law began to oppose him fiercely. (Luke 11:52–53)

I am patient with stupidity, but not with those who are proud of it.

EDITH SITWELL

The key to knowledge, as taught by Jesus, was prayer, nonjudgment (acceptance), and forgiveness. All three—although they do get occasional lip service—are not part of what the religious right teaches. Followers are not told to "go within" (where Jesus said the kingdom of heaven are) and listen for the voice of "the counselor" (the Holy Spirit) for guidance. The leaders will take care of any communications with God, thank you very much. The leaders of the religious right want their followers to listen to *them,* not to any "voices" the followers may have inside themselves.

The idea of nonjudgment and acceptance is a joke. Sermons, speeches, and teachings of the religious right are full of one hellfire-and-damnation judgment after another. Only those who accept Jesus, and practice that acceptance of Jesus *the right way,* are acceptable. Everything else is "abominable."

These spiritual leaders seldom discuss forgiveness, but rely on "repentance." To them this means, "Change your ways *to our ways* and *then* you will be forgiven." What they mean by "your ways," of course, is any ways that they do not personally approve of as *the* way (that is, *their* way—the One Way).

> "And you experts in the law, woe to you, because you load people down with burdens they can hardly carry, and you yourselves will not lift one finger to help them." (Luke 11:46)

Because the religious right teaches guilt, but not forgiveness, it heaps on its followers responsibilities (blame) for situations they cannot effectively deal with themselves. For example, the religious right teaches that God will hold *each person in this country* responsible for the 30 million abortions (which they categorize as "the murder of innocent little babies") performed since 1972. "If there's anything you could have done you didn't do, then God will hold *you* responsible." *Never mind* the 30 million illegal abortions that took place from 1952 to 1972 (and the women who died from them)—as long as it's legal now, *you* are responsible. That's why anti-abortion protesters are so frantic, why one can shoot and kill a doctor outside an abortion clinic and sincerely believe he is doing "God's work," and why Jerry Falwell can excuse the shooting by saying, "Let's not forget the doctor was a mass murderer."*

"Woe to you, teachers of the law and Pharisees, you hypocrites! You travel over land and sea to win a single convert, and when he becomes one, you make him twice as much a son of hell as you are." (Matthew 23:15)

The religious right points with great pride to its "overseas rescue missions," in which the "rescuing" that's going on is not so much feeding hungry mouths (although a little of that goes on because it makes good video) as it is "rescuing" human souls. In America we are supposed to keep *our* "traditional values," but around the world people are supposed to "cast off" *their* traditional values in favor of the Americanized version of "Christianity." These converts are then supposed to preach "Christianity," which is, of course, nothing but the religious right's own political conservatism. People in foreign countries are encouraged to become politically active, not for social change and justice within that country, but for policies that will favor the right-wing conservative causes the religious right so firmly believes are one and the same with Christianity. The communists in their heyday never had a group of infiltrators as numerous, organized, and well-financed (by people who think they're feeding the poor of the world) as the standard-bearers of the American political-religious right.

"For John came neither eating nor drinking, and they say, 'He has a demon.' The Son of Man came eating and drinking, and they say, 'Here is a glutton and a drunkard, a friend of tax collectors and "sinners."' But wisdom is proved right by her actions." (Matthew 11:18–19)

One thing's for sure: with the religious right, there are no *discussions* any more. If you don't agree with them on everything, you hate Jesus. Pure and simple. No matter what position you take, if it's not the position *they* take, your reasoning will be knocked down by one "scriptural" argument after another. That these arguments often contradict each other doesn't seem to matter.

Then they hurled insults at [a blind man healed by Jesus] and said, "You are this fellow's disciple! We are disciples of Moses!" (John 9:28)

If you do anything that's not "in the name of Jesus," it doesn't count. You can heal the sick, feed the poor, and teach the truth, but if you don't do it in the name of Jesus, you're just another part of the devil's work. The "secular humanists" (as the evangelicals call them) are some of Satan's greatest warriors. Those humanists go out and do good *for the sake of humanity* and not for the sake of Jesus. Can you imagine! What a sacrilege! The religious right teaches that suffering is good

___

*"The Old Time Gospel Hour," May 2, 1993.

because it leads one to Jesus, and anything that alleviates suffering except in the name of Jesus is bad because it postpones the sufferer's ultimate conversion. So, people who do good are bad. The more effective one is at making positive change, the more one will be seen as the agent of the devil.

> *My religion is to do good.*
>
> THOMAS PAINE

> All the people were astonished and said, "Could this be the Son of David?" But when the Pharisees heard this, they said, "It is only by Beelzebub, the prince of demons, that this fellow drives out demons." (Matthew 12:23–24)

For these people, it is better to fail in the name of Jesus than to succeed in the name of humanity.

> Another time he went into the synagogue, and a man with a shriveled hand was there. Some of them were looking for a reason to accuse Jesus, so they watched him closely to see if he would heal him on the Sabbath. Jesus said to the man with the shriveled hand, "Stand up in front of everyone." Then Jesus asked them, "Which is lawful on the Sabbath: to do good or to do evil, to save life or to kill?"

> But they remained silent. He looked around at them in anger and, deeply distressed at their stubborn hearts, said to the man, "Stretch out your hand." He stretched it out, and his hand was completely restored. Then the Pharisees went out and began to plot with the Herodians how they might kill Jesus. (Mark 3:1–6)

The Pharisees of today ignore one miracle after another if it's not performed in Jesus' name. When they can't ignore it, they call it the devil's work.

> "I have shown you many great miracles from the Father. For which of these do you stone me?" (John 10:32)

And, of course, the religious right demand more laws against consensual acts—and the strict enforcement of the laws already on the books—in the name of Jesus.

> "A time is coming when anyone who kills you will think he is offering a service to God." (John 16:2)

⚖️ ⚖️ ⚖️

Probably the religious right's single most dangerous tactic is using the "born again" spiritual experience to convert people to a conservative political point of view. Whether one believes this born-again experience is a gift from God, or simply a psychological reaction to certain pressure and release of pressure is beyond the scope of this book. That there *is* an experience characterized by

> *The modern conservative is*
> *engaged in one of man's oldest*
> *exercises in moral philosophy,*
> *that is the search for*
> *a superior moral justification*
> *for selfishness.*
>
> JOHN K. GALBRAITH

euphoria, exultation, and joy is a documented fact, both historically and scientifically. In the throes of this experience, the Quakers and Shakers got their names. The "Holy Rollers" did not refer to gamblers, but to those in spiritual ecstasy rolling around on the floor.

To program political views into the freshly plowed "Fields of the Lord," to take a moment of spiritual or psychological liberation and use it for political indoctrination, must rate among the most reprehensible actions in civilized society.

⚖ ⚖ ⚖

For Christians, Easter is a day of great celebration, second only to Christmas. For many Christians, in fact, Easter is a greater day of celebration than Christmas: on Christmas the Christ Child was born; on Easter, Jesus, the man, was resurrected, proving he was not just a prophet or a martyr, but the Christ. It is also a day that ends—with joy and triumph—the agony and mourning of the Crucifixion. For Christians, it is a day of great rejoicing.

What, however, was the theme for the 1993 Easter Sunday sermon on Jerry Falwell's "The Old Time Gospel Hour"? The resurrection was never mentioned: there was not *one word* about Jesus conquering death so that we may all have eternal life. Nor was there a *mention* of the Crucifixion. Nor was there an Easter bonnet, Easter egg, or Easter bunny in sight. I don't know *why* I was expecting *some* mention of Jesus on Easter. Perhaps I'm just too old fashioned for "The Old Time Gospel Hour."

The sermon was exclusively about what has been Falwell's pet subject for the past thirty-seven years: What is *politically* wrong with America? If Falwell dislikes something politically, it is, automatically and without further argument, both immoral and unChristian. (No, more than *un*Christian: *anti*-Christian.) *We are under attack.* ("We" being "all good Christians," "all good Americans" [those two being synonymous] and the innocent, bright-eyed, oh-so-easily-influenced-by-any-outside-stimulus-of-the-devil children of the aforementioned good Christian Americans.)

The show opens with Falwell not preaching, but peddling: he looks directly and sincerely into the camera from what is supposed to be his office (but is obviously a television set) and pitches four of his sermons ("a $100 value!") for "only $35." The set of four sermons is collected under the general title, "Who Killed America?" One of the sermons in the packet of four was today's sermon. If Falwell mentioned Easter in his sermon, you see, it would date the entire video package, and make it less saleable in the future. All good marketers know not to mention a holiday on a show that you want to sell year 'round, and Falwell *is* a good marketer.

"The Old Time Gospel Hour" is not a religious show, but an infomercial for the religious right.

Jerry Falwell, of course, inspired the Moral Majority, which inspired the bumper sticker, "The Moral Majority is Neither." The Moral Majority did well by Falwell: it made him famous, rich, and fat. In the late 1980s, he declared "victory," and disbanded the organization. What really happened was that the Moral Majority had stopped making money because Falwell had run out of things to hate. Oh, there was still plenty to hate (from Falwell's perspective); hating just wasn't raising enough money any more. Even the War on Drugs didn't raise much money: *everyone* had declared war on *that*. So Jerry shut down the Moral Majority.

> *God bless you*
> *and keep you safe from anything*
> *as dangerous as knowledge.*
>
> ALEXANDER WOOLLCOTT

What brought Falwell back out of the closet? Homosexuality, of course.

In the fall of 1992, an obscure fundamentalist church in the California desert began selling a videotape taken at a Gay Pride parade. It was carefully edited by the church to show only the most salacious homosexual activity: men kissing, men wearing dresses, lesbians walking about with their hooters out—and all of them not going to church on Sunday. You could get nearly the same footage of heterosexuals by going to Fort Lauderdale during spring break or videotaping any fraternity beer bash. Nonetheless, it was presented as an example of what every town in America would look like twenty-four hours a day if the "Gay Agenda" came to pass. The tape was outrageously successful. It put a struggling church located in the California desert on the map, making it rich, famous, and powerful. Tens of thousands of copies of the tape were sold. Political commentators said it tipped the scales in the Colorado referendum in which voters narrowly decided that gays were not entitled to civil rights, and it was shown to the Joint Chiefs of Staff before they came out against gays in the military.

Falwell must have watched this phenomenon from his church in Lynchburg, Virginia, and chewed his nails (and everything else that wasn't nailed down). He had been against the *homa-sex-ya'alls* for *years*. He thought that vein of hatred had been fully mined. He was wrong. There was still gold in that thar homophobia, and *damn* if some other fundamentalist preacher hadn't struck the Mother Lode! Like the phoenix of old, Jerry girded his loins, put on his girdle, and set out for the gold rush again.

Falwell sent his camera crews to cover the Clinton inauguration. Of the many inaugural balls, it seemed that the gays and lesbians had one of their own (Gasp!). Jerry's crew videotaped hours and hours of men in tuxedos dancing with men in tuxedos, women in formals dancing with women in formals, men in tuxedos

> *Among life's perpetually*
> *charming questions is whether*
> *the truly evil*
> *do more harm than*
> *the self-righteous and wrong.*
>
> JON MARGOLIS

dancing with men in formals, women in tuxedos dancing with women in formals, men in formals dancing with men in formals, women in tuxedos dancing with women in tuxedos, women in tuxedos dancing with men in formals, and even (can't these perverts get anything straight?) men in tuxedos dancing with women in formals. It's what "Arthur Murray's Dance Party" would have looked like if Liberace had been the guest host.

Yes, Jerry put together a video of this, and, over images of men kissing men and women kissing women (which you can buy for "only $35, and charge it to your Visa or MasterCard, so call toll-free now, and it's all tax deductible"), Falwell tells us that President Clinton "is considering" legislation to make homosexuals "a minority." Does this imply gays are currently a majority? No, Falwell explains, once gays are recognized as a minority, they are entitled to *equal rights!* They would be protected from job discrimination (Horrors!), entitled to equal housing (Terrors!), and might even be permitted to get married (No!) to each other (No! No!). Then Falwell crosses even his own line between reality and illusion. If we didn't know Falwell better, it might seem like simple paranoia, but, knowing Falwell as we do, we know it's nothing but a good fund-raising technique, one of Falwell's favorites: If he can scare the be-Jesus out of people with dishonest and outrageous statements, he can scare the money out of them too. Falwell explains that the federal government could require a certain number of homosexuals to be hired by private churches. Over videos carefully selected to show gays to be as salacious as possible, Falwell asks, "Do you want gays working in *your* church, preaching Sunday sermons, educating *your* children?" The idea that the federal government is going to shove homosexuality down our throats and down the throats of our children *in church* is enough to open pocketbooks, purses, and checkbooks all across the country.

But buying a video is not enough—one must also *vote.* Falwell, you see, has discovered the 900 number. Legitimate network current affairs programs have used 900 numbers to have their audiences vote on controversial subjects for some time. The charge is nominal, usually 50 cents, and any profits are usually donated to charity. Falwell, too, has 900 numbers; one to call if you support protecting our children from federally imposed homosexuality, the other to call if you're in favor of perverts, perverts everywhere. Either call costs you $1.95 per minute. The money—after the phone company takes its cut—goes to Jerry Falwell. If you oppose homosexual rights, Falwell will send your name to the White House stating your position (which Falwell has kindly worded for you, including biblical citations). Falwell will also be kind enough to add your name to his mailing list, as you are obviously a right-thinking, all-American Christian. (Besides, you might

want to buy some of his tapes, books, sermons, or even send your children to his university.) If you support gay rights, Falwell
does nothing. No petition to the White
House, no mailing list, no solicitations for
videos, books, sermons, and your *children*
are not welcome at his university. He keeps
your $1.95 per minute anyway.

> *He's all buttoned up*
> *in an impenetrable*
> *little coat of complacency.*
>
> ILKA CHASE

Speaking of education, Falwell also
regularly gives an extended pitch for Liberty
University—there, over images of Falwell
roughhousing with the guys, talking re-
spectfully to the girls, roughhousing with the guys, talking respectfully to the
girls, and roughhousing with the guys—we are told that this institute of higher
learning has no co-educational dorms; no drugs; no alcohol; no secular, humanis-
tic, atheistic teachings (such as evolution); no Marxist, Leninist, communist
propaganda (the kind you might find at, say, the Democratic National Headquarters); no Godless liberalism; and—most important of all—"no sex outside of
marriage." With all these restrictions, it's no wonder that the pitch is directed
toward "parents and grandparents" and not at the potential students themselves.

One thing there's obviously plenty of at Liberty University, however, is white
people. Of the dozens, perhaps hundreds of students shown in the promotional
video, I spotted precisely two students who were darker than Debby Boone. One
must suspect from this footage that—at Liberty University—either (a) the term
racial minority is given new and vibrantly literal meaning, or (b) Falwell wants the
parents and grandparents to *think* the term *racial minority* is given new and vibrantly literal meaning.

The whole idea is that your children or grandchildren will be *safe* at Liberty
University—safe from drugs, safe from alcohol, safe from radical politics, safe
from homosexuals and other minorities. Your child or grandchild will even be safe
from his or her own lust. One assumes the school motto is *"Non libertas Liber-
taum"* ("No liberties are taken at Liberty"). It appears, however, that one is even
kept safe from *thought*. That this sort of highly edited curriculum makes one
unprepared for most jobs in the real world, much less for most institutes of higher
education ("No, I've never read Marx, but I've memorized the entire Book of
Leviticus"), is not discussed. That this comfortable Christian cocoon might produce someone capable of getting a job only at a Baptist church is likewise never
mentioned.

As the weeks passed, I continued watching "The Old Time Gospel Hour" (it's
like a traffic accident—can't look at it; can't look away). The videos taken at the
gay inaugural ball (under the title "Exposé of the Clinton Inaugural Gala") must
have been a hit. Falwell sent a camera crew to the 1993 gay march on Washington,
and brought back even more "shocking and disgusting" video of men kissing

> His studie was but litel
> on the Bible.
>
> GEOFFREY CHAUCER
> *The Canterbury Tales*
> 1387

men, women kissing women, and (prepare yourself) men marrying men and women marrying women.*

If Falwell was the Pharisee I believed him to be, I wondered how long it would take me to discover hypocrisy. The rules of my little game were: it had to be *his* hypocrisy and he had to be hypocritical on *his own* terms. It didn't take long. In fact, I had my choice. On his show of May 2, 1993, Falwell said *17 times* that this was the absolute last and final week to get a copy of the "Exposé of the Clinton Inaugural Gala." Two weeks later, he offered it again. I faxed a letter to Jerry, pointing out his, shall we say, discrepancy, just in case his misrepresentation was inadvertent. No: he meant it. The next week he offered the "Exposé of the Clinton Inaugural Gala" again. Again, he said it was the last week. The following week, guess what? Yes, more Clinton Inaugural Galas. But this time, he actually *admitted* that he had previously said, "this is the last week," on *two other* videos, and sure enough, he was offering *them again*. He freely admitted that he was going to, in his own words, "renege," "change my mind," and "go back on my word." Isn't this commonly known as *lying*? Well, what had Falwell said about lying and its consequences on recent shows? He had quoted Revelation:

> But the fearful, and unbelieving, and the abominable, and murderers, and whore mongers, and sorcerers, and idolaters, and all liars, shall have their part in the lake which burneth with fire and brimstone: which is the second death. (Revelation 21:8 KJV)**

According to God (according to Falwell), "all liars" fall into the same category as "the fearful, and unbelieving, the abominable, and murderers, and whore mongers, and sorcerers, and idolaters." All, then, are *abominable*.

The reason we should all join God in hating homosexuals, Falwell claims, is because God condemns it. He cites (over and over) this passage:

---

*I wonder if Falwell is aware of the service he is doing to the gay and lesbian community. First, he's exposing children to images of men kissing men and women kissing women, children who would *never* be exposed to this until they were old enough to see an R-rated Hollywood feature. Even then, they would have to look carefully, as same-sex kissing takes place about twice per year in Hollywood movies. By showing the same images week after week, however, Falwell uses the well-known psychological technique, "repetition brings acceptance," and conditions his audience—however subconsciously—to be accepting of homosexuality. No matter how repulsed one may initially be at seeing two men kissing, lesbians shirtless, or a man dressed up like Snow White, after seeing the same images over and over again, one becomes acclimated, and eventually decides, "So what?" Maybe I shouldn't include this footnote. I think I will. No, maybe not. Well, if you read this footnote, you know I've included it. But don't tell Jerry.

**Falwell uses the King James Version: he doesn't want his followers to actually *understand* this stuff, only to understand his interpretation of it.

Thou shalt not lie with mankind, as with womankind: it is abomination. (Leviticus 18:22 KJV)

So, lying is as much an abomination as to "lie with mankind, as with womankind." And what does Reverend Falwell say about ministers who are not morally up to snuff? This from his Easter Sunday sermon, April 11, 1993:

> But I do not believe that when a preacher's ever guilty of moral default, he should ever be allowed in the pulpit again. Period.

> *A lie will easily get you out of a scrape, and yet, strangely and beautifully, rapture possesses you when you have taken the scrape and left out the lie.*
>
> C. E. MONTAGUE

By his own standards, by his own Bible verse, and by his own admission, Falwell was no longer fit to preach. I wrote and asked him for his resignation. Do you think he resigned? Do you think he even wrote back? Do you think Falwell would say no to a Hostess Twinkie?* The answer to all three of these questions is the same.

(I purchased the "Exposé of the Clinton Inaugural Gala" and "The March on Washington" videos, and guess what I got in the mail? A letter from Jerry, *begging* for more money to help save America from the homosexuals. If I sent $49, he'd send me even *more* "uncensored" videos! How many hours of gay video can one Christian take?)

Jerry knows he's got to mine this prejudice as quickly as he can. Science has fairly well proven that most homosexuality is not a choice, but something people are born with. This being the case, homosexuality must then be God's will, and if it's God's will, good Christians must accept it—no matter how much it may hurt.

On March 21, 1993, Falwell said,

> We must evangelize America beyond any past efforts. . . . With more than 200 television stations now carrying "The Old Time Gospel Hour" worldwide, I am recommitted to giving the pure Gospel of Jesus Christ to a lost world.

In the eight or so shows broadcast since then, I have not seen Falwell spend more than one minute per hour "giving the pure Gospel of Jesus Christ" to anyone. It's politics, politics, politics, hate, hate, hate, fear, fear, fear. It's the same anti-gay, anti-women (one of the tapes he sells is "Why True Christian Women Do Not Participate in the Feminist Movement"**), anti-Clinton (to the sins of

---

*Falwell is amazingly cooperative: I was watching "The Old Time Gospel Hour" one day, and wondered, "How overweight *is* he, anyway?" Within five minutes he told me. (He said he was 59 years old, 6'1" and 282 pounds. That makes him 89 pounds overweight.) Gee: interactive television!

**A typical quote: "Calling a woman a 'Christian feminist' is a contradiction in terms. It is much like saying, 'Christian prostitute.' If a woman takes the Bible seriously, she cannot be a committed

communism and onanism, Falwell apparently wants to add Clintonism), anti-choice, and anti-ACLU (which he calls the "American Communist Lawyers Union").

At first, I thought that by this lack of focus on Jesus, Falwell was just breaking yet another promise. Then it dawned on me: This *is* what he considers "giving the pure Gospel of Jesus Christ to a lost world." He has so thoroughly left behind the separation of church and state that he actually *believes* his $99\frac{44}{100}\%$ political "Old Time Intolerance Hour" *is* "The Old Time Gospel Hour." "We must again learn to view governmental action from God's viewpoint," he explains. He then goes on to say,

> A great American, Pat Robertson, recently said: "Man's law is important, but it must reflect God's law to be truly valid. . . . What a gift our forefathers have given us. By their example we learn that it is our right and duty as citizens to judge the laws and the lawmakers of this nation by the laws of God in the created order and in God's Word, and then to act."

Although Jerry Falwell and Pat Robertson think of themselves as the prima donnas of rival opera companies (they kiss in public but bitch about each other in private), they will quote even each other when desperate to prove a point.

⚖ ⚖ ⚖

Pat Robertson hosts the daily "700 Club" (named after his first 700 devoted donors), is the founder of the Christian Broadcasting Network (CBN), writes best-selling books on what God would do if He only had control of Washington, is the ringleader of the Christian Coalition, and runs for president whenever he is "forced" to. Between Falwell and Robertson, from the standpoint of consensual crimes, Robertson is far more dangerous.

In 1989, Robertson formed the Christian Coalition, a tax-exempt "social welfare organization" which gathers money from Christians and puts it into political campaigns. Not directly, mind you, but in the form of "voter information pamphlets" which supposedly tell where candidates stand on particular issues in a supposedly fair and balanced way. Of course, they are neither fair nor balanced. The conservative candidate (almost always a Republican) is the knight in shining armor for God's righteous forces and his or her opponent is, at best, anti-Christian and, most likely, in league with the devil. The Christian Coalition sent out 40

> *A religion that requires persecution to sustain it is of the devil's propagation.*
>
> HOSEA BALLOU
> (1771–1852)

Christian and a feminist at the same time." Or, "In the event, young lady, you are being persuaded by some feminist to join the movement, you have to make a major choice in your life. You must reject the Bible if you do it." Or, "I have difficulty understanding why Norman Lear [founder of People for the American Way] so aggressively promotes feminism since his last divorce settlement cost him $125 million. One would think he would be angry with women."

million such "voter information pamphlets" in support of George Bush during the 1992 presidential campaign. That didn't help, but sometimes it does. In 1990, the Christian Coalition sent out 350,000 pieces of literature at the last minute to help Jesse Helms win what many thought was a lost senatorial campaign.

The Christian Coalition campaigned heavily in the 1993 Los Angeles mayoral race, sending out 450,000 pamphlets, and its candidate won. The next morning on the

> KING: God told you to be for George Bush. Is that true? Did you say that?
> ROBERTSON: I'm not sure if I did . . .
> KING: Pat—Did you, Pat?
> ROBERTSON: I may have, to some of my close friends . . .
> KING: Pat!
> ROBERTSON: Yes! I think he's going to win.
>
> "Larry King Live"
> August 17, 1992

"700 Club," Pat Robertson gloated that "Christian-bashing politics and anti-Christian campaign tactics" were no longer going to work. He showed the "Christian-bashing," "anti-Christian" commercial prepared by his candidate's opponent. The commercial was *only* anti–Pat Robertson. Christ and Christianity were never mentioned. If one criticizes Pat Robertson's role in the political process, then, one is *of course* bashing Christianity and is anti-Christian. Or so Pat Robertson wants his followers to believe. Scarier still, Pat Robertson probably believes it himself.

That same morning on the "700 Club," Robertson interviewed, via satellite, the gushingly grateful new senator from Texas, also backed by the Christian Coalition. One by one, election by election, Robertson is pocketing elected officials at all levels of government, right up to and including the United States Senate. They owe Robertson political favors, and the political favor Robertson wants is for God's law to become man's law. More accurately, it is for Pat Robertson's *interpretation* of God's law to become man's law.

The goose laying all these political golden eggs is the "700 Club." It's an hour-long Monday-through-Friday right-wing Christian infomercial modeled after "Good Morning, America" ("Good Morning, Conservatives"). Other "700 Club"– golden eggs include Regent University, of which Robertson is chancellor; the Christian Broadcasting Network, run by Robertson's son; and "a lavish faux– eighteenth century motel called the Founders Inn, whose walls are adorned with gigantic oil portraits of George Washington, Thomas Jefferson and . . . Pat Robertson,"* as Joe Conason described it in the April 27, 1992, issue of *The Nation*.

The "700 Club" has a set format. Robertson chats amiably with Ben, Robertson's sidekick, who is as obedient to Robertson as he supposedly is to Jesus. Then we go to "CBN News" which, in network-reporting style (on-air reporter, stock footage, interviews, sound bites, and lots of graphics), a news story is told from an unabashedly politically conservative point of view. We then go back to Pat and Ben, who chat about it. In case anyone missed the point (liberals are Godless

*Can you spot the one "Christian" in this trio?

heathens and conservatives are America's only hope), Robertson calmly lets us know God's point of view on every political and social issue, while Ben leads him on with question after question, as though Robertson were somehow shy—even reluctant—to share his personal point of view. "Ah, shucks, Ben, I don't know. But if I had to take a guess . . ." and then he moves in with an obviously well-prepared kill. After a report on Hurricane Andrew, for example, Robertson revealed its true cause: the fact that God had removed "his blessing" from America. "If we're not a Christian nation," Robertson said, "why should God give us his blessing?" Why indeed? Next news item.

Then it's time for guests. These are either celebrities paying homage, authors of Christian books, experts pontificating on current events, politicians looking for votes, or entertainers looking for a little PR—typical morning talk-show fare, but everyone must acknowledge Christ as Lord at least once during the interview. And then there are the Geraldo-like guests designed to keep viewers glued to their sets with personal stories involving tantalizing, even scandalous, twists of fate. An example: "This Christian mother and father of three children have AIDS. Their story later in our show. But now . . ." It makes for good sound bites. The husband and wife, as it turns out, don't have AIDS, but are infected with "the AIDS virus." They got it through "heterosexual promiscuity" prior to their conversion to Christ. Two and a half years after being "rooted in the Lord" they discovered their condition, but, "praise the Lord," none of their children is HIV-positive. (Thank God, indeed.) That the "700 Club" is telling its viewers AIDS is also transmitted by heterosexuals is good news. The bad news? On the "700 Club" Christians are *not* encouraged to use condoms; children should *not* be instructed in condom use; and condoms should *not* be passed out in public schools. The *only answer* to stop the spread of AIDS is complete and total *abstinence* until marriage. Period. Sometimes they come *so close* to making sense on this show.

This facade of journalistic integrity is reminiscent (and why shouldn't it be?) of Robertson's 1990 book, *The New Millennium.* In his book, Robertson goes along just fine outlining, with proper statistical background, some real problems in America (the national debt, violent crime, and so on) and then, suddenly, he makes a sharp turn to the right, another sharp turn to the right, another sharp turn to the right, another sharp turn to the right, and then retraces his ground. Like most commentators who *only* turn right or *only* turn left, he winds up going around in circles. Violent crime is caused by feminists (by destroying the American family, which erodes society, which raises immoral children, who go out and commit violence). The national debt was caused by homosexuals. (I won't torture you with the logic of *that* one.) The rhetoric harkens back to Hitler who blamed *everything* on (a) the International Jewish Conspiracy, (b) communism, (c) the impurity of the Aryan race, (d) homosexuality, and, most often, (e) all of the above.

The "700 Club" spends at least two minutes of each hour praying. Good. One can only take so much politics. And then there's fund-raising. That gets a lot more than two minutes each hour, but not as much as politics—except during fund-raising periods.

> *Watch out*
> *that you are not deceived.*
> *For many will come in my name,*
> *claiming, "I am he,"*
> *and, "The time is near."*
> *Do not follow them.*
>
> JESUS OF NAZARETH
> LUKE 21:8

Yes, Robertson loves saving souls. He also loves getting conservative Christian voters on his mailing lists. In 1992, Robertson declared his Christian Coalition's goal:

> We want to see a working majority of the Republican Party in the hands of pro-family Christians by 1996 or sooner.

If that comes to pass—and there's not much reason why it should not—by the new millennium, I'll be able to publish a book the size of this one just *listing* the consensual crimes.

⚖ ⚖ ⚖

I'm not against Falwell and Robertson because they are politically conservative; I'm against them because they are against fundamental freedoms. They don't believe we, as adults, have the right to do with our person and property as we see fit, as long as we do not physically harm the person or property of another. Why? "Because it's *against God's law*." Who says? "*God does!*" Where? "*Just read the Bible!*" I did, and as this rather lengthy section of this book shows, "It's not there." Alan Watts offers his perspective:

> Fundamentalists veer to the extreme right wing in politics, being of the personality type that demands strong external and paternalistic authority. Their "rugged individualism" and their racism are founded on the conviction that they are the elect of God the Father, and their forebears took possession of America as the armies of Joshua took possession of Canaan, treating the Indians as Joshua and Gideon treated the Bedouin of Palestine. In the same spirit the Protestant British, Dutch and Germans took possession of Africa, India and Indonesia, and the rigid Catholics of Spain and Portugal colonized Latin America. Such territorial expansion may or may not be practical politics, but to do it in the name of Jesus of Nazareth is an outrage.

Amen.

A Plea for Christian Charity, Tolerance, and (Dare I Say) *Love* for Diversity

> *If you love Jesus,*
> *work for justice.*
> *Anybody can honk.*
>
> BUMPER STICKER

THE WORDS OF MY SERMON* today are three: read the Gospels. The Gospels of course, are the first four books of the New Testament. I did. My conclusions—from the standpoint of consensual crimes at any rate—are contained in this section of the book. But please don't take *my* word for it: read the Gospels for yourself and form your own conclusions. This is my plea to Christians: *read what the Christ had to say.*

It's not a major undertaking: an hour a night for a week should take care of it—and that includes reading all the historical footnotes. If you want the "Cliff's Notes" version, get a red-letter edition and just read the words in red (Jesus' words). This should take no more than two hours. If you're like me, you'll find yourself saying time and again, "I didn't know Jesus said that," or "Oh, *that's* what he meant."

I do not see how anyone can read the words of Christ, believe them, commit to follow them, and *still* be in favor of laws against consensual activities. Practicing Christians may not *take part* in any of the consensual crimes; they may teach their children not to take part in them; and they may encourage others not to take part in them; but they will *not* force people, by law, not to take part in them. The true Christian, as I see it, will pray for people who have vices, not jail them.

In previous chapters, I have given example after example of Jesus' attitude toward consensual crimes. No example is clearer than Jesus saving the adulteress from being stoned. At risk to his own life, he got involved (he could have walked away) and saved someone from being punished for a consensual crime that he

---

*If you don't consider yourself a Christian, you are welcome to nod off during my sermon—just as most Christians do. Come to think of it, *everybody* nods off during my sermons. Perhaps I'll publish a book: *The Sominex Sermons* by Reverend Peter McWilliamzzz.

> *The responsiblity of tolerance
> lies in those who have
> the wider vision.*
>
> GEORGE ELIOT

personally taught was a sin. Christians should always, before judging, ask themselves, "Am I without sin?" If the answer is no, Christians then are called to work on perfecting themselves, not on punishing others. Even Jesus, who met the criterion of "no sin," and *could* have thrown the first stone, did not.

"Woman, where are they? Has no one condemned you? Then neither do I condemn you. Go now and leave your life of sin." (John 8:10, 11)

As Christians, follow the example of Christ: of consensual crimes, even those you firmly believe to be sins, learn to say, "Neither do I condemn you."

⚖ ⚖ ⚖

As Christians, it's important to understand that the separation of church and state is there for the benefit of the *church,* not the benefit of the state. The freedom both of and from religion guaranteed in the First Amendment allows each person to believe what he or she believes *without* the state taking sides. In any way. Period. *All* religions must demand complete and absolute neutrality from the state in *all* religious matters—including those that favor the religious belief you happen to hold. This does not mean the state is *against* religion or "hostile to Christianity" (as the Falwells and the Robertsons would have you believe), but that the state favors religion *so much* and trusts its citizens *so much* that it provides a completely level and neutral field in which they can plant any crop, play any game, or build any structure they see fit.

Everyone in this country is part of a religious minority. The Catholic church has more members than any other Christian denomination. That would seem to make Catholics the majority. If all the Protestant churches combined, however, *they* would be the majority, and the Catholics would be a minority. Even the broad, sweeping term, "This is a Christian nation," is true only if each person gets to define what Christianity is and is not. Any number of self-proclaimed Christians will point to another self-proclaimed Christian's belief and declare, *"That's not Christianity!"* Without separtation of church and state, factions would be fighting one another, each one trying to gain control of the government so that its view of God becomes *the* view of God—*or else.* The majority of Christians—splintered into minority groups—would find themselves on the receiving end of that "or else."

Hence, the separation of church and state. It's there for the believers, not the state. The state, frankly, could care less. Historically, the state has been able to use *any* religious point of view for its own ends. What begins as purely religious intolerance—if popular enough—soon becomes incorporated into the state. It becomes institutionalized. The government runs it. The Spanish Inquisition was begun by the church, but was eventually controlled by Spain. The examples of government misusing religion are endless. Using the Bible, you can prove *anything you want*. That is entirely too tempting for political despots— or even government clerical workers. As soon as we allow something—*anything*—to supersede the Constitution as the "supreme

> *Tolerance implies*
> *no lack of commitment*
> *to one's own beliefs.*
> *Rather it condemns*
> *the oppression*
> *or persecution*
> *of others.*
>
> JOHN F. KENNEDY

law of the land," we have not invited God, but the devil, to be the leader of the nation. Consider the dialog between Sir Thomas More and Roper, his future son-in-law.* More is encouraged to arrest someone. "On what charge?" asks More. "That man's bad!" More is told.

MORE: There's no law against that.

ROPER: There is: God's law.

MORE: Then God can arrest him.

ALICE: While you talk, he's gone.

MORE: And go he should if he were the devil himself until he broke the law.

ROPER: So, now you give the devil benefit of law.

MORE: Yes. What would you do? Cut a great road through the law to get after the devil?

ROPER: Yes! I'd cut down every law in England to do that.

MORE: Oh. And when the last law was down and the devil turned round on you, where would you hide, Roper, the laws all being flat? This country is planted thick with laws from coast to coast—man's laws, not God's laws—and if you cut them down, and you're just the man to do it, do you really think you could stand upright in the winds that would blow then? Yes, I give the devil benefit of law *for my own safety's sake*.

The law that keeps prayer out of school is the same law that keeps prayer free at home. As soon as children are taught to pray in school, they will then be taught *what* to pray in school. Whose decision shall that be? As soon as the Bible is read daily in classrooms, the question will arise, "Who decides *what* is read?" I could select twenty minutes of Bible readings that Jerry Falwell would not let me read in his church, nor would Pat Robertson allow me to read on the "700 Club." I could select such violence and explicit sexual activity that I doubt I could even read it on primetime network television.

*From Robert Bolt's screenplay, *A Man for All Seasons*.

> *Example is not the main thing
> in influencing others.
> It is the only thing.*
>
> ALBERT SCHWEITZER

The irony is that the people who want the Bible read in the schools the most are the very people who would lose the most if the Bible were accurately *understood* by the majority of Americans. If people knew the story of the Bible as well as they know the plot of *Gone with the Wind*—or even *The Wizard of Oz*—the fundamentalists would lose their control.

It is the duty, then, of all Christians to staunchly defend the separation of church and state *for their own safety's sake.*

ᘓ ᘓ ᘓ

Although we are not a Christian nation, Christianity is the most popular religious belief. Almost 60% of the population belongs to one of the more than one thousand Christian denominations. It's essential to point out, however, that Christians are Christian by *choice*, not by *force*.

Free will is an essential part of Christian belief. *Freely choosing* to love God and to follow the teachings of Christ is what makes a Christian a Christian. If God (whom we must assume to be all powerful) wanted to make *everyone* believe in Jesus and follow his teachings, the laws of Christ would be as immutable as the law of gravity. Just as *every* human requires oxygen to live, God could have easily designed it so that, with each breath, we would *automatically* think, "Praise Jesus." This is not the case. Although people may profess undying love while there's a gun to their head or after sufficient torture, true love is freely given.

Because they legislate religious behavior, laws against consensual activities want to take our freedom of choice away. When one must, by law, love God in a certain way, the sweetness of love and choice are gone *for the individual doing the choosing*. I've discussed in many other areas of this book the unfairness to those who *don't want to believe;* here I'd like to point out the dangers for those who *do* believe.

From an individual Christian point of view, without the option *not* to love Jesus, how can one know one truly does love Jesus? It is only by having the choice *not* to love someone that we know we truly love him or her. Those who want to make this a Christian nation *by law* want to, in essence, return to arranged marriages. If marriage were mandatory and spouses were selected by others, we would have a lot more marriages, but there would be a lot less love within them. Even in arranged marriages where people get along just fine and actually do love one another, there's always that nagging doubt, "But is this the one *I* would have chosen?"

So it is with Christianity. If we had one state-run religion, mandated by law, with one view of Jesus who must be loved and obeyed *or else*, there would always be the nagging doubts, "Would I have come to love Jesus on my own?" and "Is this the way I would have chosen to love him?" Christians use their love of Christ in every decision every day. State-mandated religion—in any form—undermines one's basic love of Jesus, one's basic belief system, and adds an underlying doubt to every choice in life.

God gave us free will for a purpose—to make our choices meaningful. Without choice, free will cannot be. State-mandated religion, which removes choice and renders free will meaningless, is clearly not part of God's plan.

> *I hate people*
> *who are intolerant.*
>
> LAURENCE J. PETER

⚖ ⚖ ⚖

From my point of view, it is the duty of all Christians to work at *removing* the laws against consensual activities—even those they personally do not practice and may personally find sinful. It's important that Christians do this both to preserve the freedom to choose *in all aspects of life*, as well as an expression of good, old-fashioned Christian charity.

One can be in favor of freedom without endorsing everything a free person might do.

I often wonder what Jesus might say if he saw his suggestions for living a more loving, accepting, and grace-filled life being used to lock up those who did *not* follow his suggestions. I wonder if he might pick up yet another whip and drive not the money changers this time, but the *Pharisees* from the temple, yelling as he did the last time he cleansed the temple,

> "'My house will be a house of prayer; but you have made it a den of robbers.'" (Luke 19:46)

Referring directly to the Pharisees of his day, Jesus told a parable which may apply to our time. It begins,

> "A man planted a vineyard. He put a wall around it, dug a pit for the winepress and built a watchtower. Then he rented the vineyard to some farmers and went away on a journey. At harvest time he sent a servant to the tenants to collect from them some of the fruit of the vineyard. But they seized him, beat him and sent him away empty-handed. Then he sent another servant to them; they struck this man on the head and treated him shamefully. He sent still another, and that one they killed. He sent many others; some of them they beat, others they killed." (Mark 12:1–5)

Perhaps when Jesus said, "'I tell you the truth, whatever you did for one of the least of these brothers of mine, you did for me'" (Matthew 25:40), perhaps "the least of these brothers of mine" might be those who want to take part in a consensual crime. What are the fruits of the vineyard they were entitled to? Well, what *are* the fruits of God's teaching? Charity? Compassion? Understanding? Acceptance? And what did these brothers get from this "Christian nation"? They've been arrested, jailed, beaten, destroyed, and, in some cases, killed. Jesus continues with the parable:

> "He had one left to send, a son, whom he loved. He sent him last of all, saying, 'They will respect my son.' But the tenants said to one another, 'This is the heir. Come, let's kill him, and the inheritance will be ours.' So they took him and killed him, and threw him out of the vineyard." (Mark 12:6–8)

If the vineyard was the church of God, or at least God's teachings, and Jesus is the Son of God, and Jesus' teaching was "Love one another as I have loved you," then haven't the Pharisees of today taken that son (in the form of those teachings), killed him, and thrown him out of the vineyard?

Try suggesting to one of the Pharisees that laws against consensual activities should be eliminated for no other reason than simple Christian mercy.

> "'I desire mercy, not sacrifice.' For I have not come to call the righteous, but sinners." (Matthew 9:13)

> "If you had known what these words mean, 'I desire mercy, not sacrifice,' you would not have condemned the innocent." (Matthew 12:7)

> "Shouldn't you have had mercy on your fellow servant just as I had on you?" (Matthew 18:33)

Shouldn't we open the jail cells in the name of Jesus and proclaim, as he did,

> "Go home to your family and tell them how much the Lord has done for you, and how he has had mercy on you." (Mark 5:19)

And shouldn't we do it, not just for the least of our brothers, but for ourselves as well?

> "Blessed are the merciful, for they will be shown mercy." (Matthew 5:7)

Yes, the people who are in jail for consensual crimes are sinners, but aren't we all? If we want mercy, isn't the technique to show mercy?

Go ahead: say that to one of the Pharisees currently claiming to be the true representative of God's vineyard (his church). Do you know what you'll hear? You will be accused of being mislead, uneducated in Scripture, and in need of some good pastoral counseling. If you persist, the Pharisee will declare that you are in league with the devil, and you will be dismissed. To continue the parable,

> "What then will the owner of the vineyard do? He will come and kill

---

> *The churches must learn humility as well as teach it.*
>
> GEORGE BERNARD SHAW

those tenants and give the vineyard to others." (Mark 12:9)

Did the Pharisees hearing this in the time of Jesus suddenly wake up and see the error of their ways? No.

> Then they looked for a way to arrest him because they knew he had spoken the parable against them. But they were afraid of the crowd; so they left him and went away. (Mark 12:12)

If the Pharisees of today cannot be turned out of the vineyard, they should at

> *So mainline Christians allow the television preachers to manipulate their audiences, most times to their own financial gain, by making the most absurd biblical claims without their being called to accountability in the name of truth.*
>
> BISHOP JOHN SHELBY SPRONG

least be afraid of the people. The people of the vineyard are other Christians. I believe that the vast majority of Christians do not condone the hatred taught in Jesus' name by Pharisees like Falwell and Robertson. And yet, when the public thinks of American "Christian leaders," who comes to mind? If Christians do not speak against them, Falwell and Robertson and their friends will, by default, become the spokespersons for the entire Christian community. I'm not saying that anyone do anything to *stop* their preaching: freedom of religion extends to them as well. It is up to *God* to throw them out of the vineyard. It is, after all, God's vineyard. But the good, tolerant, merciful Christians can speak of goodness, tolerance, and mercy to the point that the Pharisees of today, like the Pharisees of old, would be "afraid of the crowd; so the Pharisees went away." If every time a Pharisee's voice cried out in hatred, another Christian voice spoke up firmly in the name of love, the Pharisees would not cry out in hatred quite so often nor quite so loudly.

It's important that this voice of love be heard by those who are not Christian. All that millions of people in this nation know about Christianity is the false Jesus of hatred they are told is the authority for putting them in jail if they get caught enjoying their simple pleasures. Heaven knows how many gay people, for example, think Jesus was actually *against* homosexuality. It's absurd. How many homosexuals, then, have never taken the time to explore the teachings of Jesus? The same is true for any group of consensual "criminals" you care to name. The caring Christian majority needs to speak out in defense of *all* minorities—*especially* those they do not personally belong to. Jesus suggested loving your enemies because, after all, who doesn't love their friends? So too, should Christians love sinners. And a concrete way of loving them is to stop putting them in jail for sinning, as long as they haven't physically harmed the person or property of a nonconsenting other.

When will we return to a time when the most well-known preacher of the day is fighting for civil rights and not punishing religious wrongs? We don't have to go back very far for an example: only about thirty years to the time of the

Reverend Dr. Martin Luther King, Jr. Now, of course, every church says it was on Dr. King's side "from the early days." If every church member who now claims to have "marched with Dr. King" had marched with Dr. King, there wouldn't have been room enough for all of them to stand, much less march. Listen to Dr. King himself writing from his jail cell in Birmingham, Alabama, in 1963:

> *Though we cannot think alike, may we not love alike? May we not be of one heart though we are not of one opinion?*
>
> JOHN WESLEY

So often the contemporary Church is a weak, ineffectual voice with an uncertain sound. So often it is an archdefender of the status quo. . . .

When I was suddenly catapulted into the leadership of the bus protest in Montgomery, Alabama, a few years ago, I felt we would be supported by the white Church. . . . Instead, some have been outright opponents, refusing to understand the freedom movement and misrepresenting its leaders; all too many others have been more cautious than courageous and have remained silent.

Yes, if you begin to speak out, as a Christian, in favor of abolishing the laws against consensual activities, you may not get much support from your church. So be it. The question is: "Do you want to be on the side of what's *popular* now, or on the side of what is *right?*" Dr. King again:

Called to be the moral guardian of the community, the Church at times has preserved that which is immoral and unethical. Called to combat social evils, it has remained silent behind stained-glass windows.

If good Christians don't become involved in the fight for freedom, then freedom will be seen as the result of humanism, and Christianity will be identified with suppression. Once again, Dr. King:

I would be the last to condemn the thousands of sincere and dedicated people outside the churches who have labored unselfishly through various humanitarian movements to cure the world of social evils, for I would rather a man be a committed humanist than an uncommitted Christian.

The silent Christian, by default, is seen as supporting Jerry Falwell, Pat Robertson, and their ilk. To ask a question from the civil rights movement, "Which Side Are You On?"

⚖ ⚖ ⚖

Whom did Jesus spend time with? Who were his friends, his followers, his chosen twelve? Fishermen, women, "sinners," prostitutes, zealots, and even the lowest of the low, a tax collector. Jesus celebrated diversity. Why shouldn't the Christians of today do the same? People with diverse lifestyles can—when fully accepted—contribute enormously to Christianity and our understanding of Christ.

Consider, for example, what just three homosexuals added to Christian culture. If Leonardo da Vinci had been jailed, we would not have his *Last Supper*, the most famous image of not only that event, but of how Jesus himself appeared. If the Pope had burned Michelangelo, rather than employed him to paint the ceiling, we would never have the Sistine Chapel and—from the panel, "The Creation of Adam"—our most popular image of God. If the church had executed King James I of England for his homosexual activities, we would not have the King James translation of the Bible.

> *In the evening of life*
> *we shall be judged on love,*
> *and not one of us is going*
> *to come off very well,*
> *and were it not for my absolute*
> *faith in the loving*
> *forgiveness of my Lord*
> *I could not call on him to come.*
>
> MADELEINE L'ENGLE

The list goes on and on for almost any consensual crime you'd care to name. Isn't the heart of Christ big enough to find room for all comers? And can't Christians be secure enough in their own faith that they can tend their vines in the garden while others tend tomato plants, rutabagas, and squash in their own? In freely sharing the fruits of the harvest, perhaps our neighbors—appreciating the richness of our wine—will plant a few vines. And, perhaps, we will raise a few tomato plants of our own.

> "Blessed are those who hunger and thirst for righteousness, for they will be filled.
>
> "Blessed are the merciful, for they will be shown mercy.
>
> "Blessed are the pure in heart, for they will see God.
>
> "Blessed are the peacemakers, for they will be called sons of God.
>
> "Blessed are those who are persecuted because of righteousness, for theirs is the kingdom of heaven." (Matthew 5:6–10)

PART V

THE CONSENSUAL CRIMES
A CLOSER LOOK

The Consensual Crimes:
A Closer Look

> We must learn to
> distinguish morality
> from moralizing.
>
> HENRY KISSINGER

ENTIRE BOOKS CAN BE (and have been) written on each of the consensual activities currently prohibited by law. While the books already written have pretended to present "balanced views," almost all have reflected the bias of the writer, the publisher, or, in some cases, the sponsoring organization.

In this section of the book, I make no such pretense. This is *not* a "balanced look." The child who said, "The Emperor wears no clothes," did not make a balanced statement. A balanced statement might have been, "The Emperor is a fine and noble person who in almost all instances exercises great wisdom in his choices and is known for his fine taste in clothing which has manifested itself over the years in a display of tasteful, elegant, and sometimes spectacular attire. It is, in fact, fair to say that our Emperor is among the best dressed emperors in history. I wonder, then, why on this particular day the Emperor, in all his wisdom, has chosen not to wear any clothing." That statement, of course, went beyond balance, passed swiftly through diplomacy, and came perilously close to elephant droppings before arriving at the truth of the matter. In this section of the book, I will spare you the preamble.

In order to put people in prison for something, it is essential for the ordinary citizen to believe that the activity the person is being put in jail for is particularly odious. If it does not harm the person or property of another, the general population must believe that the action is *so* vile and *so* inherently evil that merely *allowing* it to take place within a society corrupts that society irreparably. Those who want to keep something illegal, then, must (a) keep their hands in the political pie, so that laws can be passed, enforced, and not repealed, and (b) use everything that is known about psychology, advertising, and public relations to make

> *If I go to*
> *church on Sunday*
> *and cabaret*
> *all day Monday,*
> *well, it ain't nobody's*
> *business if I do.*
>
> FROM THE SONG BY
> PORTER P. GRAINGER
> & EVERETT ROBBINS

the population think that "a menace" is being kept at bay and that the moralists—far from being seen in their true light as destroyers of freedom and individual choice—are super-heroes in the never-ending battle for truth, justice, and the American way.

This section of the book, then, is designed to counter those negative impressions in the small way that limited space allows. As with all human activities, the activities currently set aside as illegal have built-in pros and cons, ups and downs, rewards and risks. The negative PR against each of these consensual crimes, however, has stressed only the cons, downs, and risks. The average person, then, has a distorted view. My purpose here is to mention a few of the pros, ups, and rewards so that, when combined with the conditioned programming we already have, the reader may be left with a more balanced view.

Because of this approach, it may seem as though I am *endorsing* one, another, or all of the consensual crimes. I am not. I am endorsing the *freedom* for each person to take part in any or all of them—as a participant or merely a curiosity seeker, in reality or only in the imagination—without fear of being jailed. Exploring any new activity is fearful enough without the fear of jail being added to it. Exploring is a matter of free choice.

A free society of free individuals must, of necessity, have free choice. The moralists in their paternalistic splendor want us to believe that, yes, we can handle certain choices (such as whom we can marry), but we cannot handle others (such as the gender of the person we marry, the number of people we can be married to at once, and who gets to wear the wedding dress). "These laws are not for *you*," they tell us, "these laws are for all those *weaker vessels* who, if given the freedom, will abuse it, and then where will we be?" The moralists attempt at every turn to suck us into their own superiority. They want us to join the ranks of their paternalism. "You and I, of course, can take part in our simple pleasures without overdoing it," they tell us, "but whereas we use it to *amuse* ourselves, *they* use it to *abuse* themselves." When we get to the top of the power structure, *then* we will have total freedom.

Such nonsense. It's the power game and the pecking order—squared.

In fact, people who want to take part in the currently illegal consensual activities already do. Following the repeal of Prohibition, for example, after a minor burst of curiosity, alcohol consumption actually went down. Some people discovered they had problems with alcohol, and stopped drinking altogether. Others found that, when drinking stopped being clandestine, it wasn't as much fun. Still others found that one or two drinks a couple times a week were all they wanted. With alcohol readily available, they stopped overindulging because they no longer had to compensate for the scarcity. As we shall see in the discussion between William F. Buckley, Jr., and Professor Gazzaniga in the chapter, "Recreational Use of Drugs," the percentage of people who *abuse* rather than *use* a substance or activity will be roughly the same whether that substance or activity is illegal or not.

Which brings me to a few overall points I would like to make or reiterate:

1. Use is not abuse.

2. You need not personally support or take part in any activity in order to support another person's freedom to take part in it.

3. One person's meat is another person's poison; one person's poison is another person's meat. (I'm such a *phrasemaker*.)

4. While we can control our *actions*, we cannot control our needs, desires, or preferences.

5. Although, in order to exist, a society must have certain mores, rules, and codes of behavior, putting these mores, rules, and codes of behavior into the hands of the criminal justice system is the least effective method to bring about compliance.

6. *Your* freedom of choice is paid for by giving *others* their freedom of choice.

⚖ ⚖ ⚖

If you've ever taken part in a consensual activity that is—or at that time was—against the law, you probably came to the conclusion, "All the bad things they said about this don't seem to be true; at least they're certainly not true about *my* doing *this.*" If you came to that conclusion about *one* of the consensual crimes, it's true about all of them. It may not be true about *you* with all of them, but just as you found one of them was not anywhere near as harmful, degrading, or demoralizing as you were led to believe, other people find that, for them, one or another of the consensual crimes is far from criminal.

I was reading an article about myself in a magazine once in which I was misquoted, the facts were distorted, and I was shown to be a generally sleazy person simply because that particular publication happens to make money by "exposing" the darker side of individuals. I certainly *have* my darker side, but they didn't take the time to find it; they merely made one up. I finished the article and concluded (a) I didn't know I was worthy of such public abuse; I'm flattered, (b) there is nothing true here at all, (c) this publication has no integrity, and (d) I certainly hope that right-minded people will *know* that this publication has no integrity and won't believe all these things about me. I turned the page, and there was a headline revealing an unsavory fact about someone else. I immediately

> I can't stand to sing the same song the same way two nights in succession. If you can, then it ain't music, it's close order drill, or exercise or yodeling or something, not music.
>
> BILLIE HOLIDAY

> *So little time,*
> *so little to do.*
>
> OSCAR LEVANT

thought, "I didn't know that!" and believed the scandalous tidbit with all my heart. In the time it took me to turn the page, my mind had immediately snapped back to the conditioning, "If it's in print, it must be true." The unjust trashing I had received was an anomaly, I concluded, and I was fully prepared to believe the trash revealed about all the other "victims."

That's how we all are, I think, about the consensual crimes. Even if we explore one and decide, "There's no reason why this should be illegal," we fail to apply that reasoning to all the other consensual crimes. Somehow the one we explored, enjoyed, and either incorporated into our lives or moved on from is the exception, and all the other rules are just and honorable. It's not so. The emperor wears no clothes.

The emperor never has.

IN CONGRESS. JULY 4, 1776.

The unanimous Declaration of the thirteen united States of America,

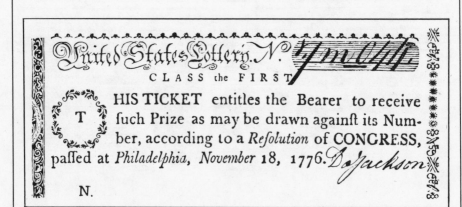

Gambling

> The urge to gamble is so universal
> and its practice so pleasurable
> that I assume it must be evil.
>
> HEYWOOD BROUN

THERE SEEMS TO BE something in human beings that likes to (a) predict the future, and (b) be rewarded when right. The destinies of individuals, peoples, and entire nations have rested on someone saying, "I think it will go *this way*." If this tendency is not inborn, it is ingrained early on. One of the most frequent interchanges between even young children is, "Wanna bet?" "Yeah! How much?"

The leaders of big business—who already have more than enough money to live ostentatiously for the rest of their lives—often say, "I'm in business because I *enjoy* it. It's a game!" Part of the excitement of the game of business is that it's a *gamble;* people evaluate data, make conclusions, and place their bets. (In business, it's known as *taking risks.*)

Gambling is as American as 1776. Guess how the fledgling colonies raised money to pay the Continental Army and fight the revolutionary war? The lottery ticket on the facing page should give you more than a clue. Gambling was perfectly legal in this country until the 1820s when, guess what? Yes, our old friends the evangelicals had their revivals and declared gambling—along with drinking, promiscuity, and all the rest—a sin against God. By 1830, most forms of gambling were outlawed.* (It's a good thing for Liberty that the evangelicals held less influence in France—the Statue of Liberty was paid for by a series of lotteries.)

The Civil War and the expansion of the Wild West re-established legalized gambling, but by the early 1900s the evangelicals held sway again and, as they

---

*How the evangelicals concluded gambling was anti-scriptural considering that the eleven remaining apostles chose a replacement for Judas by throwing dice is beyond me. But then, a lot of the evangelicals' conclusions are beyond me. ("Then they cast lots, and the lot fell to Matthias; so he was added to the eleven apostles" [Acts 1:26].)

were doing with alcohol, re-established the prohibitions on gambling. (By 1910, even Nevada had outlawed it.)

Today, we see increasing acceptance of gambling. The fund-raising through raffles, Bingo, and even "Las Vegas Nights" keeps many churches from openly opposing gambling, and the government can hardly call gambling a social menace: thirty-two states run lotteries, and the number is increasing.

> *Gambling in a big city*
> *is like cancer.*
> *Clap a lid on this thing*
> *before it spreads.*
>
> "DRAGNET"

Neither church nor state can, without transparent hypocrisy (neither minds hypocrisy, mind you, but that *transparent* hypocrisy might cause trouble), strongly oppose gambling—church and state both rely on gambling as a source of income. At the same time (and for the same reason), neither is going to say, "Gambling hasn't done any harm, so let's remove the laws against it." With the exception of Nevada, Atlantic City, and a handful of cities that allow poker clubs, church and state have a monopoly on gambling, and they're not about to give it up. (Having the full force of criminal law enforcement to eliminate competition makes gambling not just a monopoly, but a monopoly at gunpoint.)

The major objection people seem to have to gambling these days is not so much that it's *wrong*, but that their towns would start looking like Las Vegas: gaudy casinos, ostrich plumes, and red velour everywhere. People don't fear *gambling;* they fear bad taste.*

That legalized gambling would cause no threat to community standards is clearly evident from observing the situation in New York City. The police once spent heaven knows how much money and time raiding bookie joints. But then the city opened Off Track Betting (OTB) outlets in storefronts all over the city. These storefronts are near schools, churches, day care centers, you name it. They have hardly become magnets for crime and corruption. In fact, there's hardly a better example than OTB to illustrate that addiction to gambling is no fun. The men and women who populate the storefronts appear to be mostly *numb*. When the results of a race are announced, most silently drop their tickets to the floor (ripping up losing tickets is a movie cliché), and a handful unenthusiastically shuffle over to the payoff window. It appears to be *no fun at all*.

⚖ ⚖ ⚖

In terms of people throwing away their money by gambling, nothing could be worse than the state-run lotteries. Here we have, essentially, robbery by bureauc-

---

*Frankly, this is a fear that I share. The only comfort I can offer is that, if the zoning laws of Cambridge, Massachusetts, can get McDonald's to build a modest brick structure with no golden arches, local zoning ordinances can also see to it that casinos are built with something less than 247,000,000 flashing lights out front.

AIN'T NOBODY'S BUSINESS IF YOU DO

racy. The odds in state-run gambling are *so bad* that wherever organized crime has decided to compete with state-run gambling, organized crime is not just winning, but *flourishing*. This is because state governments spend hundreds of millions of dollars in advertising designed to entice *new* gamblers into the arena. Most people find that, after buying a few lottery tickets, they're no longer interested in that form of gambling. The government, then, needs to encourage more people who have never gambled before to begin gambling. As law professor and expert on gambling I. Nelson Rose wrote in the *Los Angeles Times*,

> *The gambling known as business looks with austere disfavor upon the business known as gambling.*
>
> AMBROSE BIERCE

> Lottery tickets are the only consumer products actively promoted and sold by the state. The state does not sell toothpaste, or even promote brushing your teeth. But it tells people they should gamble. The main marketing concern is how to attract new players, who otherwise wouldn't gamble.

Those who decide gambling is for them soon begin shopping around for better odds. They're not hard to find. Most people, however, spend their money on other pastimes. Lottery commercials are clearly targeted toward the poor. (Stockbrokers pitch their ads toward the rich.*) Even if one wins a million-dollar lottery, is one really a millionaire? Hardly. Although the payoff rules vary from state to state, large jackpots are usually paid off over, say, twenty years. That's $50,000 a year. Not bad, of course, but then taxes are taken off the top. That's up to 40% of $50,000, or about $20,000. Which means, an income of $30,000 per year. Still very good, but not exactly enough to buy all those things you planned to buy when you became "a millionaire," and certainly not enough to live up to the expectations of all your friends who now want to be lavishly entertained by "a millionaire." After twenty years, your money's gone. (Those who live off lotteries get neither retirement nor health benefits.) More than one "instant millionaire" regretted ever winning.

One would think the government, just out of *shame*, would allow other forms of betting. Shame, however, is not something governments are famous for. With gambling available in many churches, every supermarket in thirty-two states, and a phone call away to any stockbroker or OTB, should it really matter whether one wants to gamble on the turn of a wheel, the turn of a card, or the turn of events on Wall Street?

---

*I was once told by a senior editor of the *Wall Street Journal* that the paper was "the most elaborate scratch sheet in the world."

Recreational Use of Drugs

CONSUMERS UNION—the highly respected, scrupulously impartial organization responsible for *Consumer Reports*—studied the drug problem in this nation long and hard. Its conclusions—not yet published—are:

This nation's drug laws and policies have not been working well; on that simple statement almost all Americans seem agreed. . . . They are the result of mistaken laws and policies, of mistaken attitudes toward drugs, and of futile, however well-intentioned, efforts to "stamp out the drug menace." [What we have in this country is] aptly called the "*drug problem* problem"—the damage that results from the ways in which society has approached the drug problem.

The Consumers Union report made six recommendations. I quote:

1. Stop emphasizing measures designed to keep drugs away from people.

2. Stop publicizing the horrors of the "drug menace."

3. Stop increasing the damage done by drugs. (Current drug laws and policies make drugs more rather than less damaging in many ways.)

4. Stop misclassifying drugs. (Most official and unofficial classifications of drugs are illogical and capricious; they, therefore, make a mockery of drug law enforcement and bring drug education into disrepute. A major error of the current drug classification system is that it treats alcohol and nicotine—two of the most harmful drugs—essentially as non-drugs.)

5. Stop viewing the drug problem as primarily a national problem, to be solved on a national scale. (In fact, as workers in the drug scene confirm, the "drug problem" is a collection of local problems.)

> *There's no greater threat to our independence, to our cherished freedoms and personal liberties than the continual, relentless injection of these insidious poisons into our system. We must decide whether we cherish independence from drugs, without which there is no freedom.*
>
> WILLIAM VON RAAB
> *Commissioner*
> *U.S. Customs Service*

6. Stop pursuing the goal of stamping out illicit drug use.

The report, which is nearly six hundred pages long, concludes,

These, then, are the major mistakes in drug policy as we see them. This Consumers Union Report contains no panaceas for resolving them. But getting to work at correcting these six errors, promptly and ungrudgingly, would surely be a major step in the right direction.

I lied. I'm sorry. The previous excerpts were *not* from a "yet unpublished" report. The report *was* published in 1972; it is more than twenty years old. It was published by Consumers Union in book form, *Licit and Illicit Drugs.** It asked for its proposed changes to be made "promptly and ungrudgingly." Far from doing that in 1972, our most recent "Drug War" *began* in 1982. As the line from the song, "Where Have All the Flowers Gone?" laments, "When will they ever learn, when will they ever learn?"

⚖️ ⚖️ ⚖️

It's amazing how little Americans know about drugs. Considering that we spend $40 billion per year to make 1,100,000 arrests and have sacrificed a good number of our personal freedoms and physical safety to the War on Drugs, it might be valuable to take a look at the "enemy."

Opiates

The opiates are opium, morphine, and heroin. All three come from the opium poppy. They are generally known as *narcotics*.

At first, opium was smoked. It wasn't smoked, actually; it was heated until it gave off vapors—but did not yet "smoke"—and the vapors were inhaled. The active ingredient of opium, morphine, went directly to the bloodstream and to the brain. This was the method favored in China and by the Chinese immigrants imported to the U.S. to build the transcontinental railroads.

For medical and white-middle-class use, however, the morphine was extracted from the opium and either injected or "eaten." Morphine was first separated from

---

*This book is, alas, out of print. It is one of the finest I've seen on the subject. The copy I borrowed from the library had an added humorous/sobering note. Someone had gone through the book carefully looking for negative reports on drug use. He or she did not find many. On every twentieth page or so, a sentence or two would be highlighted—often out of context—along with comments written in the margin such as, "Society thinks there's no social harm." The phrase, this library-book scribbler must have determined, was categorically disproven by the underlined sentences. The sentences, however, were a facetious misstatement of the case, and the remainder of each chapter went on to prove that there was no appreciable social harm.

opium in 1806. Any oral ingestion was referred to as "eating." Opium eating was usually drinking some concoction or another made with morphine. These included *laudanum*, an alcohol-morphine mixture, and any number of patent medicines. In addition to pain killing, morphine was known for its tranquilizing and relaxing effects. Many of the patent medicines were marketed to women to cure their anxiety, nervousness, and menstrual cramps. By the 1890s, men went to the saloons to drink and women stayed home and "ate opium." Eugene O'Neill wrote eloquently and touchingly about his mother's morphine addiction in his play, *Long Day's Journey into Night.*

> *I always wanted to blunt and blur what was painful.*
> *My idea [in taking drugs] was pain reduction and mind expansion, but I ended up with mind reduction and pain expansion.*
>
> CARRIE FISHER

Physicians referred to morphine as G.O.M. or "God's Own Medicine." The introduction of the hypodermic syringe in the mid-1800s thrilled medical doctors. Morphine was proven to be an excellent injectable substance, and the Civil War an ideal laboratory to experiment with morphine's injectable painkilling qualities. The doctors went a little overboard, it seems, as many soldiers returned from the war addicted to morphine. For quite some time, in fact, morphine addiction was known as the "soldier's disease."

Nevertheless, by 1880, physicians recommended G.O.M. for fifty-four "diseases" including anemia, insanity, and nymphomania. The addictive quality of morphine, however, did not concern doctors. Although many people needed the drug daily, as long as they were able to get the drug, morphine addicts functioned normally in society. The idea here is that most addictions are only troublesome when the addictive substance is taken away. As a culture today, we are addicted to—among many other things—electricity, packaged foods, and automobiles. As long as these things are readily available, we don't notice our addiction to them. If one—or all three—were taken away, we would immediately exhibit the symptoms of classic addictive withdrawal.

I mentioned earlier Dr. William Stewart Halsted, widely recognized as "the father of modern surgery" and one of the four founders of Johns Hopkins Medical Center. Dr. Halsted died at the age of 70, having revolutionized surgery (the sterile operating room was one of his many contributions). He enjoyed a thirty-two year marriage characterized by "complete mutual devotion," good health, and the admiration of his peers. In 1969, Sir William Osler's "Secret History" of the medical center revealed that Dr. Halsted had been addicted to morphine until the end of his life. Dr. Osler, one of the other founders of Johns Hopkins, wrote,

> He had never been able to reduce the amount to less than three grains [180 milligrams] daily; on this he could do his work comfortably, and maintain his excellent physical vigor.

A daily injection of morphine is certainly not recommended operating room procedure, but the history of Dr. Halsted is hardly the stereotype of narcotic addiction that we have come to believe.

In 1898, heroin was synthesized from morphine by the Bayer company, the folks who gave us aspirin. They were looking for a better painkiller than aspirin—and they found it. *Unfortunately,* it had this minor drawback: it was almost as addictive as tobacco. Heroin is four to eight times more potent than morphine. Knowing this, why would anyone risk addiction? The answer may be found in this description:

> Heroin's most valued effect is the ecstatic reaction that it gives after being intravenously injected; within seconds, a warm, glowing sensation spreads over the body. This brief but intense rush is then followed by a deep, drowsy state of relaxation [that] lasts two to four hours and then gradually wears off.

That was not an enticement from a drug catalog or some pusher, but the description from the *Encyclopedia Britannica.* No matter how addictive heroin may be, however, most ill effects and almost all heroin fatalities are due to the laws against the drug and not the drug itself.

It is impossible to accurately determine the strength and purity of heroin purchased on the street. Practically all overdoses occur because users cannot accurately determine a dosage level. In addition, most of the negative effects people associate with heroin addiction (premature aging, ill health, and what Roseanne Roseannadanna might describe as "looking *awful*") come not from the heroin, but from the impure substances used to cut the heroin. From the time heroin is imported, it is cut—that is, diluted—at least six times by six different individuals (or organizations). When drug dealers cut heroin, they're not too fussy about what they use: anything that's white and dissolves in water will do—laxatives, powdered milk, baking soda, quinine, or any other substance at hand. By the time the heroin reaches the end user, more than 90% of the "white powder" is something other than heroin. All these "additives" may be perfectly fine for the stomach, but can play havoc on the body when directly injected into the bloodstream. When a heroin addict refers to being made ill by "bad dope," he or she is referring not to the quality of the heroin, but the content of the contaminants.

Although heroin is the opiate most effective in killing pain, it is not available by prescription. What is readily available on street corners is not available for use in hospital wards. People are suffering needlessly at this very moment because the moralists of our time are concerned that heroin manufactured for medical use will be used "recreationally." To control the personal habits of would-be heroin users, then, innocent hospital patients in advanced stages of degenerative disease must suffer.

All of the opiates have the same active ingredient, morphine, in different degrees of concentration. While the most addictive of all *illegal* substances, they're seldom deadly, and the primary harm they cause is due to their illegality.

> *A prohibition law strikes a blow at the very principles upon which our government was founded.*
>
> ABRAHAM LINCOLN

Cocaine, Crack, Amphetamines

Cocaine is simply a stimulant, an energizer. In the early 1500s, when the Spanish conquistadors conquered the Incas, they discovered the coca leaf was a gift more prized than silver or gold. "Priests and supplicants were allowed to approach the Altar of the Inca only if they had coca leaf in their mouths," writes Edward M. Brecher in *Licit and Illicit Drugs*. For religious and superstitious reasons, the conquistadors themselves did not chew the coca leaves, but used the practice as a method to encourage the Incas to work harder and produce more. Although coca leaf chewing never caught on in Europe or North America, wine drinks prepared with the coca leaf were very popular when first marketed in 1886 as a "remarkable therapeutic agent." Gounod, who wrote "Ave Maria," and Pope Leo XIII were regular imbibers of "Mariani's wine," a popular cocaine-wine concoction. Coca-Cola, also originated in 1886, contained cocaine from the coca plant and caffeine from the kola nut.

Cocaine, first synthesized from the coca leaf in 1844, was used as a local anesthetic, to fight fatigue, and as an antidepressant. Here's how one doctor described it in 1884:

> I take very small doses of it regularly against depression and against indigestion, and with the most brilliant success. . . . In short it is only now that I feel I am a doctor, since I have helped one patient and hope to help more.

This same doctor wrote to his fiancée:

> If you are forward you shall see who is the stronger, a gentle little girl who doesn't eat enough or a big wild man *who has cocaine in his body.* [Italics in original.] In my last severe depression I took coca again and a small dose lifted me to the heights in a wonderful fashion. I am just now busy collecting the literature for a song of praise to this magical substance.

The "Song of Praise" to cocaine and its therapeutic benefits was published in a medical journal in July 1884. The young doctor's name was Sigmund Freud.

Amphetamines were first synthesized in 1887, but their effect as a cocaine-like stimulant was not noted until 1927. In 1932, an amphetamine marketed under the trade name Benzedrine replaced cocaine as the "power drug" of choice. Several film historians report that *Gone With The Wind* never would have been made without producer David O. Selznick's twenty-two-hour Benzedrine-inspired days. World War II could be called the Benzedrine War—the American, British, German, and Japanese armed forces were all given amphetamines to counteract fatigue, elevate mood, and heighten endurance. After World War II, "pep pills" replaced caffeine for many students, cross-country truck drivers, and athletes.

> *Creation is a drug*
> *I can't do without.*
>
> CECIL B. deMILLE

A small minority of users were not content with the increased well-being and productivity cocaine and amphetamines supplied, so they began injecting themselves with amphetamines (the "speed freaks") and, later, smoking cocaine in preparations known as "freebase," "ice," or "crack." As long as people regulate their use of these more concentrated and directly ingested forms to avoid "burnout," there is nothing intrinsically more addictive or harmful about mainlining amphetamines or smoking crack than there is in cocaine or amphetamines themselves. This is not to say that they are not addictive—cocaine and amphetamines are, although less addictive than tobacco or opiates—but to single out "crack" as though it were some newly discovered instant addicter and destroyer of humanity is a gross misrepresentation.

The most popular legal drug in the Cocaine, Crack, and Amphetamines category is caffeine. It is the most popular drug in the world. I must caution you, however, that the National Institute on Drug Abuse has the following to say about caffeine:

> **Dependence:** A form of physical dependence may result with regular consumption. In such cases, withdrawal symptoms may occur if caffeine use is stopped or interrupted. These symptoms include headache, irritability, and fatigue. Tolerance may develop with the use of six to eight cups [of coffee] or more a day. A regular user of caffeine who has developed a tolerance may also develop a craving for the drug's effects.

> **Dangers:** Poisonous doses of caffeine have occurred occasionally and have resulted in convulsions, breathing failure, and even death.

These are roughly the same dependence and dangers of the other stimulants: cocaine, crack, and amphetamines.

Among other atrocities, those who make war on certain drugs will have to answer the charge of attempted destruction of the English language. *Narcotic* means "inducing sleep or stupor,"—or at least that's what it *once* meant. While this does describe the opiates, precisely the *reverse* is true of the stimulants: cocaine and amphetamines. To lump these two types of drugs—opiates and stimulants—into a category (narcotics) which, in fact, only applies to the opiates, is an unnecessary attack upon the perfectly good word *narcotic*. The reason for this languagecide is that once the American public believed narcotics were bad, then the easiest thing to do was lump every other drug the government wanted to control into that category. The same tactic is used today with all the "hot" words: *cults, perverts, child abusers,* and, ever faithful, *narcotics*.*

Psychedelics

The psychedelics include peyote, mescaline, psilocybin, and that relative newcomer, LSD. We will explore peyote and LSD in the next chapter, "Religious Use of Drugs."

Marijuana (Hemp, Cannabis)

Marijuana was among the first plants cultivated by human beings. Approximately 10,000 years ago, at the same time humans began making pottery and working metal, they began weaving hemp fiber.**

As Jack Herer points out in his book, *The Emperor Wears No Clothes,*

> From at least the 27th to 7th century B.C. up until this century, cannabis was incorporated into virtually all the cultures of the Middle East, Asia Minor, India, China, Japan, Europe, and Africa for its superior fiber, medicines, oils, food, and for its meditative, euphoric, and relaxational uses. Hemp was one of our ancestors' most important overall industries, along with toolmaking, animal husbandry and farming.

Homer refers to a drug brought by Helen to Troy that sounds remarkably like marijuana, and Dr. Robert P. Walton, an American physician, found passages from Pliny, *The Arabian Nights,* Herodotus, Marco Polo, and others clearly indicating that marijuana was raised in the ancient world for purposes *other* than making rope.

In 1903, Dr. C. Creighton, a British physician, pointed out several references to marijuana in the Bible. I am not convinced.*** Others claim the use of the word *calamus* means cannabis. In passages such as this from the Song of Songs:

---

*Narcotics has been shortened to simply *drugs* to fit limited headline space and television newscast time. At least *drugs* is more accurate.

**As we shall see in the chapter, "Hemp for Victory," in addition to its medicinal and recreational uses—which we will primarily explore in this chapter—the hemp plant is and has been an excellent source of cloth, rope, canvas (which was named after *cannabis*), paper (early drafts of the Declaration of Independence were written on hemp paper), fuel, and even food.

***Those who want to know God's opinion of marijuana need look no further than Genesis 1:29: "Then God said, 'I give you every seed-bearing plant on the face of the whole earth and every tree that has fruit with seed in it. They will be yours for food.'"

> *There's been no top authority*
> *saying what marijuana*
> *does to you. I tried it once*
> *but it didn't*
> *do anything to me.*
>
> JOHN WAYNE

Your plants are an orchard of pomegranates with choice fruits, with henna and nard, nard and saffron, calamus and cinnamon, with every kind of incense tree, with myrrh and aloes and all the finest spices. (Song 4:13–14)

Or this from Ezekiel:

Danites and Greeks from Uzal bought your merchandise; they exchanged wrought iron, cassia and calamus for your wares. (Ezekiel 27:19)

The Hebrew word for calamus is *qaneh*. It could mean "reed, rod, shaft, tube, stem (the radius of the arm), beam, balance, bone, branch, calamus, cane, stalk." Qaneh is used sixty-two times in the Old Testament in many different contexts. None of them seems to directly relate to marijuana use. In Job 31:22, however, the New International Version translates *qaneh* to mean *joint*. Well, I thought, this is *very* contemporary. As it turns out, it refers to the shoulder joint: "then let my arm fall from the shoulder, let it be broken off at the joint."

Whether used in the Bible or not, hemp use is historically proven in many other documents. Hemp in its many forms—industrial, spiritual, or recreational—was a valuable commodity.

Although the Greek and Roman civilizations certainly had access to the ingestible forms of hemp, wine was the intoxicant of choice. The early Christians inherited this preference. The pagans, however, supplemented wine with various "herbs," one of which was hemp. The use of any intoxicant other than alcohol, then, became associated with paganism, and the Christian world turned its back (and eventually its wrath) on such practices. The use of any plant product for consciousness-altering was considered a form of witchcraft, banned by the Church, and later enforced by the Inquisition. In 1430, for example, Joan of Arc was accused of using "witch" herbs so that she could hear her "voices." The most popular "witch herb" was cannabis. In 1484, Pope Innocent VIII proclaimed that cannabis, among other herbs, was central to satanic worship. From that point until the end of the Inquisition, lighting up could have led to burning at the stake.

Hemp continued to be grown, of course, as a raw material for manufacture. The sails and ropes on Columbus's ships were made of hemp, as were the sails and ropes on the Mayflower. When the Mayflower arrived in 1620, marijuana had been grown on the American continent for almost a decade: the Jamestown settlers brought it to Virginia in 1611 and cultivated it for its fiber.* As Edward M.

---

*Only the flowering tops of the marijuana plant contain enough THC, the psychoactive element of marijuana, to create a high. Smoking a length of hemp rope, for example, will only make you sick. Again, more on the industrial use of hemp in the chapter, "Hemp for Victory."

Brecher wrote,

> Marijuana was introduced into New England in 1629. From then until after the Civil War, the marijuana plant was a major crop in North America, and played an important role in both colonial and national economic policy. In 1762, Virginia awarded bounties for hemp culture and manufacture, and imposed penalties upon those who did not produce it.

> *The greatest service which can be rendered any country is to add a useful plant to its culture.*
>
> THOMAS JEFFERSON

As hemp grew practically everywhere, it was common knowledge that smoking the flowering tops of the plant created intoxication. As tobacco at that time was smoked primarily for its high and usually in a pipe, the paraphernalia and the practice for pot smoking—as well as the plant itself—were readily at hand.

Marijuana was also one of the few painkillers in colonial America. George Washington, who had dental problems his entire life, was obviously concerned about the medicinal uses of marijuana. His journal for August 7, 1765, states "—began to seperate [*sic*] the Male from the Female Hemp at Do—rather too late." It was the belief then that the *unfertilized* female plants produced the best resin for making hashish. Washington's comment that he was "rather too late" indicates that he wanted unpollinated female plants. Other than medicinal or recreational use, there is no reason to concern oneself with whether or not the male plants had fertilized the female plants.* This journal entry also implies Washington was not *obsessed* with getting the most powerful hashish from his plants—if he had been, he would have kept a closer eye on them.

Throughout the 1800s, cannabis was prescribed for a number of conditions. It was listed in the *United States Pharmacopoeia* as *extractum cannabis* or *Extract of hemp,* and was so listed until 1942. In 1851, the United States *Dispensatory* reported of extract of hemp:

> The complaints in which it has been specially recommended are neuralgia, gout, rheumatism, tetanus, hydrophobia, epidemic cholera, convulsions, chorea, hysteria, mental depression, delirium tremens, insanity, and uterine hemorrhage.

By the second half of the 1800s, fluid extracts of hemp were marketed by Parke Davis, Squibb, Lilly, and Burroughs Wellcome. Grimault and Sons manufactured cannabis cigarettes as an asthma relief. All these products were sold at modest prices without a prescription at neighborhood pharmacies. (Those were the days when drug stores were *drug stores.*)

---

*The hemp plant is botanically quite advanced: some plants are male, some are female, and some are androgynous. Most species in the plant kingdom are merely androgynous.

Recreationally, hemp was generally eaten or smoked in the form of hashish, a concentration of the THC-containing portions of the hemp plant. Hashish was freely imported, and the World's Fairs and International Expositions from the 1860s onward often featured the Turkish Hashish Smoking Exposition. At the 1876 Centennial Exposition in Philadelphia, the Turkish Hashish Exposition was most popular, and fairgoers were encouraged to return again and again to "enhance" their enjoyment of the fair.

For the most part, however, Americans in the mid- to late 1800s either drank extracts of cannabis or ate hash. From the Civil War onward, the Ganjah Wallah Hasheesh Candy Company sold a popular intoxicating hash candy. A typical ad read:

> **Hasheesh Candy.**—The Arabian "Gunje" of Enchantment confectionized.—A most pleasurable and harmless stimulant.—Cures Nervousness, Weakness, Melancholy, &c. Inspires all classes with new life and energy. A complete mental and physical invigorator. Send for circular. Beware of imitations. 25 cents and $1 per box. Imported only by the Gunjah Wallah Co., 476 Broadway, N.Y.

And then there were Alice B. Toklas's favorite, "hash brownies," but actually called Haschich Fudge. Here, from her 1954 *Alice B. Toklas Cook Book,* is the recipe (which I certainly do *not* recommend your making, and *certainly* not eating. It is presented here solely for its historical, gastronomical, and literary value.)

HASCHICH FUDGE
(which anyone could whip up on a rainy day)

This is the food of Paradise—of Baudelaire's Artificial Paradises: it might provide an entertaining refreshment for a Ladies' Bridge Club or a chapter meeting of the DAR. In Morocco it is thought to be good for warding off the common cold in damp winter weather and is, indeed, more effective if taken with large quantities of hot mint tea. Euphoria and brilliant storms of laughter; ecstatic reveries and extensions of one's personality on several simultaneous planes are to be complacently expected. Almost anything Saint Theresa did, you can do better if you can bear to be ravished by *"un évanouissement reveillé."*

Take 1 teaspoon black peppercorns, 1 whole nutmeg, 4 average sticks of cinnamon, 1 teaspoon coriander. These should all be pulverised in a mortar. About a handful each of stoned dates, dried figs, shelled almonds and peanuts: chop these and mix them together. A bunch of *canibus sativa* can be pulverised. This along with the spices should be dusted over the mixed fruit and nuts, kneaded together. About a cup of sugar dissolved in a big pat of butter. Rolled into a cake and cut into pieces or made into balls about the size of·a walnut, it should be eaten with care. Two pieces are quite sufficient.

Obtaining the *canibus* may present certain difficulties, but the variety known as *canibus sativa* grows as a common weed, often unrecognized, everywhere in Europe, Asia and parts of Africa; besides being cultivated as a crop for the manufacture of rope. In the Americas, while

> *Woodbury, GA.—Few families in this rural Georgia town were left untouched by a federal investigation that culminated in the arrest of 62 people on charges of selling crack.*
> *The accused sellers include a sherriff's deputy, a retired policeman and a 68-year-old woman.*
>
> ASSOCIATED PRESS
> April 25, 1993

often discouraged, its cousin, called *canibus indica,* has been observed even in city window boxes. It should be picked and dried as soon as it has gone to seed while the plant is still green.

Only the poor and lower classes smoked (or ate) the hemp plant itself. Liquid extract of cannabis, hashish candy, and hashish itself were readily and inexpensively available. Why bother with the plant? Ah, but we're getting ahead of our story, including how marijuana was named *marijuana,* and no longer called hemp or cannabis. We'll get to that shortly.

Marijuana is not a narcotic. Like alcohol, it is not sleep-inducing unless taken in large quantities. Unlike tobacco or opiates, it is nonaddictive. To quote from the Consumers Union Report, "the lethal dose is not known; no human fatalities have been documented."

How and Why Drugs Became Illegal

One might wonder after reading the United States Constitution how Congress can justify making laws against drug sale, use, and possession. As we have seen, the enumerated powers given Congress by the Constitution have to do with keeping the national borders strong, keeping the business environment healthy, and collecting taxes. It would take the legal word-bending of a *lawyer* to stretch the enumerated powers enough to include making laws against drugs. Alas, one thing Congress has plenty of is lawyers.

Here, then, is the abbreviated story of how and why drugs became illegal. It is filled with more abuses, horrors, deceptions, and possible harm than any drug has *ever* done.

Prior to 1883, there were no federal laws against the manufacture, sale, use, or possession of drugs. As drugs had been available since before the Pilgrims arrived, the United States seemed to survive—even thrive—with no drug restrictions whatsoever. The primary "drug problem" was alcohol—not marijuana, morphine, or cocaine.

State governments were free to regulate drugs because, as you will recall, it was not until the early twentieth century that the Supreme Court decided the constitutional guarantees on the federal level applied to state laws as well. This is why states could pass laws prohibiting alcohol without amending their state constitutions. The states were free to regulate and make illegal whatever they saw fit. For the most part, however, even state laws against drugs did not begin to appear until the late 1800s.

In California, in 1875, a blatantly racist law against opium was directed against the Chinese. Prejudice against Chinese immigrants was high. The city of San Francisco prohibited establishments where opium was smoked. The law—like all drug laws that followed—failed: The large, well-run opium houses closed, but were immediately replaced by smaller, less reputable opium dens. A similar law was passed in Virginia City, Nevada, and similarly failed to work. Rather than realizing that such laws don't work, the Nevada *state* legislature made even more stringent laws. The state laws didn't work any better than the city laws, but that didn't stop other cities and states from passing laws. When *all* these laws failed, the United States Congress got involved. (Sound familiar?)

In 1883, Congress used its constitutional power to "lay and collect taxes, duties, imposts, and excises" to heavily tax imported smoking opium.* That was the foot in the door. What followed was a wedge of misuses and abuses of power that not only tore the door off the hinge; it ripped away the entire front of the house. Once taxation was used to *act on a moral belief* (in this case that the Chinese were debauching the youth of America by enticing the innocent young into their opium dens) rather than using taxation to *raise revenue*, the die had been cast. The power to tax, then, was no longer what the founding fathers had intended—a way to raise money—but had become a way to legislate morality as well.

If there is any doubt about the intent of the founding fathers, here is the complete text of that enumerated power:

> To lay and collect taxes, duties, imposts, and excises to pay the debts and
> provide for the common defense and general welfare of the United States;
> but all duties, imposts and excises shall be uniform throughout the United
> States.

People looking for a loophole will argue that the "general welfare of the United States" is much advanced by laws requiring behavior consistent with *their* moral standards and beliefs. A literal reading of the Constitution, however, shows that not to be the case.

---

*Real Americans were opium eaters or injectors, not smokers, so the racism in regulating drug use reached all the way to Washington.

Making matters even worse, as this was a prohibition act *pretending* to be a tax bill, its enforcement fell under the Department of the Treasury. From 1883 until 1968, the Secretary of the Treasury had the dual duty of not only Collector of the Tax, but Keeper of the Public Good. Even if the United States *needed* a Keeper of the Public Good, putting it in the same department as the tax collectors and money counters of the nation was probably the worst choice.*

> *The country's first drug ban explicitly targeted the opium of "the heathen Chinee." Cocaine was first banned in the south to prevent an uprising of hopped-up "cocainized Negroes."*
>
> DAUN BAUM
> *The Nation*

Once the precedent that the federal government could legislate morality was established, no one gave a second thought to the law passed five years later prohibiting altogether the importation of certain kinds of opium and preventing the Chinese in America from importing opium at all. The United States Treasury was now *giving up* revenue (the tariff on the opium imported by the Chinese into America) in exchange for regulating moral behavior. The anti-Chinese prejudice was such that the United States Treasury was permitted to abandon its primary mission—collecting and spending money—in exchange for this new mission. Over the next thirty years, taxes on smoking opium went up, went down; smoking opium was banned altogether; the ban was lifted and reinstated again. During this time, the tax ranged from $6 per pound to $300 per pound. All that these regulatory and restrictive efforts accomplished, however, was building the Chinese underworld (the "tongs"), corrupting the Treasury Department, and increasing the nation's opium smoking at least nine fold. The Secretary of the Treasury wrote the Speaker of the House of Representatives on January 12, 1888, "Although all possible efforts have been made by this Department to suppress the traffic, it has found it practically impossible to do so." The United States government, of course, responded with more laws and more law enforcement officers.

As this onslaught only affected "the heathen Chinee" and not "Americans," no one much cared. All other forms of opium were perfectly legal and modestly taxed. Why should anyone worry about defending the rights of the Chinese? If they wanted to smoke opium, it was said, they could go back to China. A legal precedent, however, was set by the racist, anti-immigrant, smoking opium restrictions.

---

*The Secretary of the Treasury is still the Keeper of the Public Good in—among other areas—cult control. The Bureau of Alcohol, Tobacco, and Firearms (ATF) masterminded the raid on the Branch Davidians in Waco, Texas. (It was only after the ATF had thoroughly botched it up that the FBI was called in to *blow* it up.) The ATF is under the Department of the Treasury, using the power to tax as the reason to control. The Secretary of the Treasury gave the go-ahead to make the raid. Why wasn't he watching the national debt instead?

> *I say that you cannot administer a
> wicked law impartially.
> You can only destroy.
> You can only punish.
> I warn you that a wicked law,
> like cholera, destroys everyone
> it touches—its upholders
> as well as its defiers.*
>
> JEROME LAWRENCE
> & ROBERT E. LEE
> *Inherit the Wind*

⚖️ ⚖️ ⚖️

The next major step in federal drug enforcement was the 1906 Pure Food and Drug Act. This act said that all patent medicines containing drugs had to say so on the label and, with later amendments, had to state the amount of the drug. This requirement was a positive step, in that it allowed people to regulate the kind and amount of drugs they took. It was only later that this act became yet another weapon in the arsenal used for the federal attack on individual choice. (More on the Pure Food and Drug Act in the chapter, "Regenerative Use of Drugs and Other Unorthodox Medical Practices.")

⚖️ ⚖️ ⚖️

The next major move by the federal government—and the great-granddaddy of all federal drug restrictions—was the Harrison Narcotic Act of 1914. The bill's chief proponent was then–Secretary of State William Jennings Bryan, staunch fundamentalist, Prohibitionist, and famed orator. His oratory on behalf of Woodrow Wilson won Wilson the presidential nomination, and Wilson appointed him Secretary of State in appreciation. Eleven years later, Bryan would lead the prosecution in the Scopes Monkey Trial, winning a conviction against the schoolteacher who had the audacity to teach Darwin's "unbiblical" theory of evolution in the public schools.

The Harrison Act, in fact, did not prohibit drugs. The act only regulated and taxed the importation and distribution of "opium or coca leaves, their salts, derivatives, or preparations, and for other purposes." It seemed reasonable to regulate, not prohibit, opium, cocaine, and their derivatives. "It is unlikely that a single legislator realized in 1914," wrote Edward M. Brecher, "that the law Congress was passing would later be deemed a Prohibition law."

Even in the *National Report on Drugs, Crime, and the Justice System*, published in December, 1992, the United States government admits,

> The Act was ostensibly a revenue measure that required persons who prescribe or distribute specific drugs to register and buy tax stamps.

The Oxford English Dictionary defines *ostensibly* as "under mere profession or pretense." The government admits, then, that the law was deceptive. It deceived the legislators who passed it and the public who accepted it. The only people who complained at first were physicians. This from the *National Report*:

> From the first, the Treasury Department held that medical maintenance
> of opiate addicts (treatment through declining usage) was not permissible,

but physicians opposed this view. . . . Initial enforcement included arrests of physicians, pharmacists, and unregistered users.

Six months after the passage of the Harrison Act, an editorial in *American Medicine* stated,

> Narcotic drug addiction is one of the gravest and most important questions confronting the medical profession today. Instead of improving conditions, the laws recently passed have made the problem more complex. . . . Abuses in

the sale of narcotic drugs are increasing . . . a particular sinister sequence . . . is the character of the places to which [addicts] are forced to go to get their drugs and the type of people with whom they are obliged to mix.

> *Prohibition goes beyond the bounds of reason in that it attempts to control a man's appetite by legislation, and makes a crime out of things that are not crimes.*
>
> ABRAHAM LINCOLN

In 1918, the Secretary of the Treasury appointed a committee to look into the drug problem. The committee found that, since the passage of the Harrison Act, underground traffic was flourishing, "dope peddlers" had established a national organization, smuggling was rampant, and the use of the forbidden substances had increased. What did the government do? Well, of course, it made new and stricter laws.

In 1922, it created the Federal Narcotics Control Board. In 1924, it banned the importation or manufacture of heroin in any form, even for medical purposes. Since that time, one of the most effective painkillers known to humanity has been missing from the pharmacopoeia of physicians. Although in 1925 Dr. Lawrence Kolb concluded, after an elaborate study, "If there is any difference in the deteriorating effects of morphine and heroin on addicts, it is too slight to be determined clinically." In 1967, the President's Committee on Law Enforcement and Administration of Justice came to the same conclusion: "While it is . . . somewhat more rapid in its action, heroin does not differ in any significant pharmacological effect from morphine." Has either of these reports changed the government's mind? Come now. That "cocaine is a narcotic" and that "heroin addiction is significantly worse than morphine addiction" are but two of the government-instigated myths that the government refuses to let die.

It was, in fact, the heavy restrictions placed on morphine that turned addicts to heroin. Like hard alcohol in place of beer and wine during Prohibition, heroin—being more concentrated—was easier to transport and smuggle. People who were content to drink morphine began injecting heroin simply because heroin was more available and the cost-per-high was lower. (As we shall see shortly, the same is true today in the relationship between crack and cocaine.)

Did the new and stricter laws work? Here is an excerpt from an editorial in the

June 1926 issue of the *Illinois Medical Journal*:

> The Harrison Narcotic law should never have been placed upon the statute books of the United States. It is to be granted that the well-meaning blunderers who put it there had in mind only the idea of making it impossible for addicts to secure their supply of "dope" and to prevent unprincipled people from making fortunes and fattening upon the infirmities of their fellow men.
>
> As is the case with most prohibitive laws, however, this one fell far short of the mark. So far, in fact, that instead of stopping the traffic, those who deal in dope now make double their money from the poor unfortunates upon whom they prey. . . .
>
> The doctor who needs narcotics used in reason to cure and allay human misery finds himself in a pit of trouble. The lawbreaker is in clover.

> *Cocaine habit forming?*
> *Of course not.*
> *I ought to know,*
> *I've been using it for years.*
>
> TALLULAH BANKHEAD

The government's reaction? Why, of course, more laws and stricter enforcement of the laws already on the books. As the *National Report on Drugs, Crime and the Justice System* tells us:

> In 1930, the Federal Bureau of Narcotics (FBN) was created within the Treasury Department under the direction of Commissioner Harry Anslinger.

Enter one of the true villains of the piece—particularly with regard to marijuana prohibition—Commissioner Anslinger. From 1930 until he was forced out of office by President Kennedy in 1962, Anslinger ran the FBN with the same tight reins—and questionable ethical procedures—that his contemporary J. Edgar Hoover held at the FBI.

⚖️ ⚖️ ⚖️

By 1932, the evangelicals were in desperate need of a Cause and a Leader. Their previous Cause, Prohibition, was obviously running out of steam, as had their previous Leader, William Jennings Bryan. (Shortly after winning the glorious victory for the literal interpretation of the Bible in the Scopes Monkey Trial, he literally ran out of steam and died.) After prohibition the evangelicals turned to keeping creationism taught in the public schools, censoring those disgraceful Hollywood movies, and ending the drug menace. In the latter Cause, they gladly cleaved to the bosom of their new leader, Commissioner Harry Anslinger.

Poor Harry. Try as he might, he never obtained the recognition and personal glory Hoover did at the FBI—or even that of Postmaster-turned-Hollywood-censor Hayes (with his *Hayes* Office and *Hayes* Production Code).*

---

*Anslinger came *really close* once to becoming a household name. From 1943 to 1948, he had the

For some reason, Anslinger had a real seed under his dentures when it came to the subject of marijuana. Yes, he was ruthless in pursuing all those other narcotics violators—the coke-heads and the junkies—but there was something about marijuana that infuriated him. Perhaps it was because marijuana was not officially labeled a narcotic, thus not under his jurisdiction. Perhaps it was his racism. Perhaps he wanted a drug to call "his own" and hold proudly before the evangelicals as David had held the head of

> *Our laws are telling people,*
> *"If you're concerned*
> *about getting caught,*
> *don't use marijuana,*
> *use cocaine."*
> *Well, that is not necessarily*
> *what people want to do.*
>
> JUDGE JAMES GRAY

Goliath. Perhaps he wanted to be a hero in the Hearst papers, as Hearst was suddenly printing provocative anti-hemp stories. Perhaps he was on the take from DuPont. Perhaps it was some combination of these.

In the mid-1930s, machinery was perfected that would allow the hemp fiber to be more easily and economically separated from the plant. This meant paper, clothing, and other manufactured articles could be produced at prices far more competitive than ever before. This did not sit well with two American giants: William Randolph Hearst and the DuPont Corporation. Hearst not only printed newspapers; he made the paper on which to print them. If hemp became the primary source of paper, not only would much of Hearst's paper-making machinery become obsolete, but all those forests he purchased could only be used as backdrops for Marion Davies movies. Hearst began attacking the recreational uses of hemp at every possible opportunity.

Earlier, Hearst had successfully turned public opinion against Hispanics. Many believe he and fellow yellow-journalism baron Joseph Pulitzer had started the unnecessary Spanish-American War. Hearst used the Mexican term for hemp, *marijuana,* in his many salacious anti-hemp stories. Most Americans never associated marijuana with the hemp their grandfathers grew, or the extract of cannabis their grandmothers took. Hearst's headlines included such joys as

NEW DOPE LURE, MARIJUANA, HAS MANY VICTIMS

MARIJUANA MAKES FIENDS OF BOYS IN 30 DAYS

HOTEL CLERK IDENTIFIES MARIJUANA SMOKER
AS "WILD GUNMAN" ARRESTED FOR SHOOTINGS

FBN collect evidence on the drug use of every major musician in the country, including Thelonius Monk, Louis Armstrong, Les Brown, Count Basie, Jimmy Dorsey, Duke Ellington, Dizzy Gillespie, Lionel Hampton, Cab Calloway, and the studio musicians of many popular radio programs. Few arrests were made because Anslinger had a dream: he wanted his agents to move in and arrest them all *on the same night*. That would be front page news all over the country. He would be truly famous. Alas, his immediate supervisor, Assistant Treasury Secretary Foley, pulled the plug on Anslinger's jukebox. "Mr. Foley disapproves!" the secretary wrote on Anslinger's elaborate plans. Poor Harry.

And guess who was quoted in Hearst's papers as saying, "If the hideous monster Frankenstein came face to face with the monster marijuana he would drop dead of fright"? Yes, none other than "H. J. Anslinger, head of the Federal Narcotics Bureau." Hearst's paper went on to "report,"

> This is not overstatement. Users of the marijuana weed are committing a large percentage of the atrocious crimes blotting the daily picture of American life.
>
> It is reducing thousands of boys to CRIMINAL INSANITY.
>
> And ONLY TWO STATES have effective laws to protect their people against it.
>
> The marijuana weed, according to Mr. Anslinger, is grown, sold, and USED in every State in the Union. He charges, and rightly, that this is not a responsibility of one State, but OF ALL—and of the federal government.

DuPont, meanwhile, had just patented a process for making paper from wood pulp (which Hearst would use extensively in the years to come). The process, which relied heavily upon DuPont chemicals, was *not* necessary in manufacturing paper from hemp. Additionally, DuPont had recently taken German patents and perfected the miracle fiber *nylon*, to be manufactured from coal tar and petroleum products. Inexpensive, readily grown hemp fibers would put a damper on two of DuPont's future money makers, paper production and textiles.

Make of these facts what you will. One thing is certain: Hearst and DuPont made a fortune thanks to the prohibition on hemp.*

⚖ ⚖ ⚖

Anslinger used his position of authority to encourage states and cities to ban marijuana. In 1935, Anslinger announced,

> In the absence of Federal legislation on the subject, the States and cities should rightfully assume the responsibility for providing vigorous measures for the extinction of this lethal weed, and it is therefore hoped that all public-spirited citizens will earnestly enlist in the movement urged by the Treasury Department to adjure intensified enforcement of marijuana laws.

By 1937, forty-six of the forty-eight states, as well as the District of Columbia had laws against marijuana. At Anslinger's urging, marijuana was labeled a nar-

---

*Anslinger was appointed head of the Federal Bureau of Narcotics by his uncle-in-law, Andrew Mellon, Secretary of the Treasury under Herbert Hoover. Mellon was the largest stockholder in Mellon Bank, one of two banks with which DuPont exclusively did business. This is, of course, entirely coincidental and has absolutely nothing to do with the discussion at hand.

cotic and had the same strict penalties as morphine, heroin, and cocaine.

Meanwhile, the wild press continued in Hearst newspapers and magazines. Commissioner Anslinger took quill in hand himself on occasion—his prose as bad as his politics. This, for example, from *American Magazine* of July 1937:

> *Of course drugs were fun. And that's what's so stupid about anti-drug campaigns: they don't admit that. I can't say I feel particularly scarred or lessened by my experimentation with drugs. They've gotten a very bad name.*
>
> ANJELICA HUSTON

> An entire family was murdered by a youthful [marijuana] addict in Florida. When officers arrived at the home they found the youth staggering about in a human slaughterhouse. With an ax he had killed his father, mother, two brothers, and a sister.

> He seemed to be in a daze. . . . He had no recollection of having committed the multiple crime. The officers knew him ordinarily as a sane, rather quiet young man; now he was pitifully crazed. They sought the reason. The boy said he had been in the habit of smoking something which youthful friends called "muggles," a childish name for marihuana [*sic*].

I don't know about you, but I've never met a pot smoker that *ambitious.*

In Hollywood, in his famous Production Code, Mr. Hayes prohibited any positive mention of drugs. (Cigarettes, of course, were just fine.) Hollywood joined in the propaganda madness (at Hearst's encouragement?) and made the now-classic *Reefer Madness.*

In 1937, Anslinger rushed through Congress the Marijuana Tax Act. Anslinger had waited because the question of whether or not it was acceptable to use the tax provisions of the Constitution to justify prohibitions was before the Supreme Court. On March 29, 1937, the Supreme Court decided that machine guns could be prohibited by first passing an act taxing them, then using the tax-law to ban them altogether.

On April 14, 1937, the Marijuana Tax Act was introduced to Congress.

The testimony before the congressional committee was, for the most part, provided by Anslinger, Anslinger employees, and Anslinger reading Hearst newspaper articles, some of which he had written. The hearings were reminiscent of the scene from John Huston's film, *The Bible,* in which John Huston, playing Noah, has a conversation with God, also played by John Huston. The film was produced and directed by John Huston. The narrator: John Huston.

Curiously, neither Hearst, DuPont, nor Anslinger had by 1937 created the myth that marijuana use leads to heroin addiction. During the House hearings, a representative remarked, "I am wondering whether the marijuana addict graduates into heroin, and opium, or a cocaine user." Commissioner Anslinger replied,

> No, sir; I have not heard of a case of that kind. The marijuana addict does

not go in that direction.*

> *The great masses of the people . . . will more easily fall victims to a big lie than to a small one.*
>
> ADOLF HITLER
>
> *Mein Kampf*
> 1933

And how many doctors were heard in the congressional hearings in 1937? Precisely one. He represented the American Medical Association. The AMA opposed the bill. At least twenty-eight medicinal products containing marijuana were on the market in 1937, the doctor pointed out; drugs containing marijuana were manufactured and distributed by the leading pharmaceutical firms; and marijuana was recognized as a medicine in good standing by the AMA.

An editorial in the *Journal of the American Medical Association* (May 1, 1937) vigorously opposed the legislation:

> After more than 20 years of federal effort and the expenditure of millions of dollars, the opium and cocaine habits are still widespread. The best efforts of an efficient Bureau of Narcotics, supplemented by the efforts of an equally efficient Bureau of Customs, have failed to stop the unlawful flow of opium and coca leaves and their components and derivatives, on which the continuance and spread of narcotic addiction depends.

Like the Harrison Narcotics Law before it, the Marijuana Tax Act claimed—even in the title of the bill—only to *tax* marijuana. It was yet another deception perpetrated on Congress and the American people: the intent of the bill was never to tax, but to prohibit. Beyond mere deception, however, the Big Lie to Congress was yet to come.

In testifying before the congressional committee, the doctor sent by the AMA said the AMA had only realized "two days before" the hearings that the "killer weed from Mexico" was indeed cannabis, the benign drug used and prescribed by the medical profession for more than a hundred years. Said Dr. Woodward,

> We cannot understand, yet, Mr. Chairman, why this bill should have been prepared in secret for two years without any intimation, even to the profession, that it was being prepared.

Anslinger and the committee chairman, Robert L. Doughton,** denounced and curtly excused Dr. Woodward. When the marijuana tax bill came before Congress, one pertinent question was asked from the floor: "Did anyone consult with the AMA and get their opinion?"

Representative Vinson answered for the committee, "Yes, we have . . . and they

---

*With another 18 years to prepare, however, Anslinger got it "right." Still commissioner, Anslinger testified before a senate committee in 1955 that "Eventually if used over a long period of time [marijuana] does lead to heroin addiction."

**According to Jerry Colby, author of the book, *DuPont Dynasties*, Robert Doughton was a key DuPont supporter in Congress.

AIN'T NOBODY'S BUSINESS IF YOU DO

are in complete agreement."

The Big Lie. The bill passed, and became law in September 1937.

⚖️ ⚖️ ⚖️

Anslinger was furious with the AMA for opposing him before the congressional committee. As the commissioner of the Federal Bureau of Narcotics, he could prosecute any doctors who prescribed narcotics for "illegal purposes." Which purposes were "illegal" was pretty much Anslinger's call. Through 1939, more than 3,000 doctors were prosecuted. In 1939, the AMA made peace with Anslinger and came out in opposition to marijuana. From 1939 to 1949, only three doctors were prosecuted by the FBN for illegal drugs of any kind.

In 1944, Mayor Fiorello La Guardia and the New York Academy of Medicine released the La Guardia Marijuana Report, which, after seven years of research, claimed that marijuana caused no violence and had certain positive medical benefits. In a rage, Anslinger banned all marijuana research in the United States. He attacked La Guardia vehemently.

In 1948, however, Anslinger voluntarily dropped the "marijuana causes violence" argument. He made, in fact, a complete about-face when he testified before Congress in 1948 that marijuana made one *so* tranquil and *so* pacifistic that the communists were making abundant supplies available to the military, government employees, and key citizens. Marijuana was part of a Communist Plot aimed at weakening America's will to fight.

That this statement was a complete reversal of his congressional testimony only eleven years before went completely unnoticed. Anti-communism put Anslinger back in the public eye, along with his good friend Senator Joseph McCarthy. It was later revealed by Anslinger in his book, *The Murderers,* and also by Dean Latimer in his book, *Flowers in the Blood,* that Anslinger supplied morphine to McCarthy on a regular basis for years. Anslinger's justification? So that the communists could not blackmail such a fine American just because he had a minor drug problem.

In 1970, in passing the Controlled Substances Act, the federal government shifted its constitutional "excuse" for jailing people from taxation to the federal government's constitutional right to regulate interstate traffic. This is as dramatic a violation of the Constitution as the taxation excuse, but it fit the government's plan better. Under this law a bureaucrat—usually not elected—decides whether or not a substance is dangerous and how dangerous that substance is, in order to determine which drugs are illegal. There's no more messing around with legislatures, presidents, or other bothersome formalities. When MDMA (ecstasy) was

> As a first-time drug law offender,
> I was sentenced to 27
> non-parolable years in prison.
> The amount of time was based on
> liquid waste found in the garage
> and unprocessed chemicals.
> There were no drugs.
>
> DAVID A. NICHOLS
> May 29, 1993

made illegal, no elected official voted on that. It was done "in house." People are now in jail because they did something that an administrator declared was wrong. The Controlled Substances Act was circulated to the states, where it was enthusiastically received; most states have modeled their programs on the federal plan. There is no longer a need, then, to lie to legislators: the agency heads and their minions simply decide what is, and that's the way it is.

Today, the Federal Bureau of Narcotics is, like its former director Anslinger, no more. How's this for a bureaucratic shuffle: In 1968, the Federal Bureau of Narcotics (FBN) was transferred from the Treasury Department to the Justice Department, where it was merged with the Bureau of Drug Abuse Control (BDAC) to form the Bureau of Narcotics and Dangerous Drugs (BNDD). In 1973, the Bureau of Narcotics and Dangerous Drugs (BNDD), the Office for Drug Abuse Law Enforcement (ODALE), and the Office of National Narcotics Intelligence (ONNI) all combined to form the Drug Enforcement Administration (DEA). (I hope you're paying attention: there will be a quiz.) When war was declared in 1982, one agency was not enough, so more were created in 1988: the National Drug Enforcement Policy Board (NDEPB) and the Office of National Drug Control Policy (ONDCP). The director of ONDCP was given the title that Mr. Anslinger (anti-communist sentiments notwithstanding) would have killed for: The Drug Czar.

Who would have thought we would have a czar in the same Washington that gave us Joseph McCarthy, the Bay of Pigs, and the Cold War? Oh, well. Long live the revolution.

⚖️ ⚖️ ⚖️

As we're in the midst of a Drug War, this chapter could go on forever. As is typical in wartime, each day we are inundated with news—some heartening, some discouraging. For example, in *Newsweek,* June 14, 1993, we read,

> Fed up with mandatory sentences, about 50 senior federal judges have refused to hear any more drug cases. Others have disobeyed sentencing rules and a few have resigned in protest. "You get a kid who makes a mistake. If he's involved with enough drugs then it's a 10-year minimum mandatory sentence and he has to do 8-½ years. To me, that's ludicrous," says J. Lawrence Irving, who quit the federal bench in San Diego in 1990.

Fifty federal judges refusing to hear drug cases is unprecedented. Heartening, but then, on the same page,

> An 18-year-old Alabama high-school senior [was] sentenced to 10 years for

federal drug conspiracy because she told an undercover agent where to meet her boyfriend to buy LSD.

Discouraging. Again.

So, allow me to end this section on recreational drug use in an unusual way: by quoting at length from the *National Review.*

One might think, if I wanted a supporting point of view, I would quote at length from, oh, the *Nation,* the *New Republic,* or maybe *High Times* (the latter if I were desperate). But, no, the sanest words I've read

> *Nothing will ever be attempted if all possible objections must be first overcome.*
>
> DR. SAMUEL JOHNSON

in a while on drugs come from a discussion between William F. Buckley, Jr., and Michael S. Gazzaniga, Professor of Neuroscience at Dartmouth Medical School. I would like to thank Mr. Buckley for his permission to quote from this discussion at length.* So, this from the February 5, 1990, issue of the *National Review.* First, the magazine gives Professor Gazzaniga's credentials:

> Professor Gazzaniga is the Andrew W. Thompson Jr. Professor of Psychiatry (Neuroscience) at Dartmouth Medical School. He is editor-in-chief of the *Journal of Cognitive Neuroscience* (MIT Press) and his most recent book is *Mind Matters* (Houghton Mifflin, 1988).

> BUCKLEY: It is said that the drug crack is substantively different from its parent drug, cocaine, in that it is, to use the term of Professor van den Haag, "crimogenic." In other words a certain (unspecified) percentage of those who take crack are prompted to—well, to go out and commit mayhem of some kind. Is that correct?

> GAZZANIGA: No, not in the way you put it. What you are asking is: Is there something about how crack acts on the brain that makes people who take it likelier to commit crime?

> Let's begin by making it clear what crack is. It is simply cocaine that has been mixed with baking soda, water, and then boiled. What this procedure does is to permit cocaine to be smoked. Now any drug ingested in that way—i.e., absorbed by the lungs—goes more efficiently to the brain, and the result is a quicker, more intense experience. That is what crack gives the consumer. But its impact on the brain is the same as with plain cocaine and, as a matter of fact, amphetamines. No one has ever maintained that these drugs are "crimogenic."

> The only study I know about that inquires into the question of crack breeding crime reports that most homicides involving crack were the re-

---

*In fairness, I should point out that Mr. Buckley is *not* a fan of my assertion that all laws against consensual activities should be repealed. He was kind enough to read the Introduction and Part I of this book prior to publication and give me his feedback. After reading his opinion, I began my reply with the punch line of an old joke, "Other than that, Mrs. Lincoln, how did you like the play?"

sult not of the use of crack, but of dealer disputes. Crack did not induce users to commit crimes. Do some crack users commit crimes? Of course. After all, involvement in proscribed drug traffic is dangerous. Moreover, people who commit crimes tend to use drugs at a high rate, though which drug they prefer varies from one year to the next.

BUCKLEY: You are telling us that an increase in the use of crack would not mean an increase in crime?

GAZZANIGA: I am saying that what increase there would be in crime would not be simply the result of the pharmacology of that drug. Look, let's say there are 200,000 users/abusers of crack in New York City—a number that reflects one of the current estimates. If so, and if the drug produced violent tendencies in all crack users, the health-care system would have to come to a screeching halt. It hasn't. In fact, in 1988 the hospitals in New York City (the crack capital of the world) averaged only seven crack-related admissions, city-wide, a day. The perception of crack-based misbehavior is exaggerated because it is the cases that show up in the emergency rooms that receive public notice, and the whole picture begins to look very bleak. All of this is to say: when considering any aspect of the drug problem, keep in mind the matter of selection of the evidence.

It is prudent to recall that, in the past, dangerous and criminal behavior has been said to have been generated by other drugs, for instance marijuana (you remember *Reefer Madness?*). And bear it in mind that since cocaine is available everywhere, so is crack available everywhere, since the means of converting the one into the other are easy, and easily learned. It is important to note that only a small percentage of cocaine users actually convert their stuff to crack. Roughly one in six.

BUCKLEY: Then would it follow that even if there were an increase in the use of crack, the legalization of it would actually result in a decrease in crime?

GAZZANIGA: That is correct.

BUCKLEY: Isn't crack a drug whose addictive power exceeds that of many other drugs? If that is the case, one assumes that people who opt to take crack do so because it yields the faster and more exhilarating satisfactions to which you make reference.

GAZZANIGA: That is certainly the current understanding, but there are no solid data on the question. Current observations are confounded by certain economic variables. Crack is cheap—

BUCKLEY: Why? If cocaine is expensive, how can crack be cheap?

GAZZANIGA: Cocaine costs $1,000 per ounce if bought in quantity. One ounce can produce one thousand vials of crack, each of which sells for $5. The drug abuser is able to experience more drug episodes. Crack being cheap, the next high can come a lot more quickly and since there is a down to every up, or high, the cycle can become intense.

So yes, crack is addictive. So is cocaine. So are amphetamines. The special punch of crack, as the result of going quickly via the lungs to the brain, may prompt some abusers to want more. By the way, it is the public knowledge that crack acts in this way that, as several studies document, causes most regular cocaine users to be cautious about crack. The casual-to-moderate user very clearly wants to stay in that category. So, all you can say is that there is a *perception*, widely shared, that crack is more addictive. Whether it is, isn't really known. One thing we do know is that crack does not begin to approach tobacco as a nationwide health hazard. For every crack-related death, there are three hundred tobacco-related deaths.

> *Every form of addiction is bad,*
> *no matter whether*
> *the narcotic be alcohol*
> *or morphine or*
> *idealism.*
>
> CARL JUNG

Another example of hyperbole is the recent claim that there were 375,000 "crack babies" born last year; how could that possibly be, when the government (the National Institutes on Drug Abuse) informs us that there were only 500,000 crack *users* last year? Exaggeration and misinformation run rampant on this subject.

BUCKLEY: Well, if crack were legally available alongside cocaine and, say, marijuana, what would be the reason for a consumer to take crack?

GAZZANIGA: You need to keep your drug classifications straight. If your goal were, pure and simple, to get high, you might try crack or cocaine, or some amphetamine. You wouldn't go for marijuana, which is a mild hallucinogen and tranquilizer. So, if you wanted to be up and you didn't have much time, you might go to crack. But then if it were absolutely established that there was a higher addiction rate with crack, legalization could, paradoxically, diminish its use. This is so because if cocaine were reduced to the same price as crack, the abuser, acknowledging the higher rate of addiction, might forgo the more intensive high of crack, opting for the slower high of cocaine. Crack was introduced years ago as offering an alluring new psychoactive experience. But its special hold on the ghetto is the result of its price. Remember that—on another front—we know that 120-proof alcohol doesn't sell as readily as 86 proof, not by a long shot, even though the higher the proof, the faster the psychological effect that alcohol users are seeking.

BUCKLEY: Is there evidence that the current consumption of drugs is restrained by their illegality? We have read that ninety million Americans

> *No major American decision*
> *was ever made without*
> *the influence of*
> *alcohol, nicotine, caffeine—*
> *often all three.*

have experimented, at one time or another, with illegal drugs. Would more than ninety million have experimented with them if drugs had been legal?

GAZZANIGA: I think illegality has little if anything to do with drug consumption—and, incidentally, I am certain that far more than ninety million Americans have at some point or other experimented with an illegal drug.

This gets to the issue of actual availability. Drugs are everywhere, simply everywhere. In terms of availability, drugs might just as well be legal as illegal. Now it has been argued that legalization will create a different social climate, a more permissive, more indulgent climate. It is certainly conceivable, primarily for that reason, that there would be greater initial use—the result of curiosity. But the central point is that human beings in all cultures tend to seek out means of altering their mental state, and that although some will shop around and lose the powers of self-discipline, most will settle down to a base rate of use, and a much smaller rate of abuse, and those rates are pretty much what we have in the United States right now.

BUCKLEY: Then the factor of illegality, in your opinion, does not weigh heavily? But, we come to the critical question, if ninety million (or more) Americans have experimented with the use of drugs, why is drug abuse at such a (relatively) low level?

GAZZANIGA: If you exclude tobacco, in the whole nation less than 10 per cent of the adult population abuses drugs. That is, 9 to 12 million adult Americans abuse drugs. That figure includes alcohol, by the way, and the figure remains fairly constant.

Consider alcohol. In our culture alone, 70 to 80 per cent of us use alcohol, and the abuse rate is now estimated at 5 to 6 per cent. We see at work here a major feature of the human response to drug availability, namely, the inclination to moderation. Most people are adjusted and are intent on living productive lives. While most of us, pursuing that goal, enjoy the sensations of euphoria, or anxiety reduction, or (at times) social dis-inhibition or even anesthesia, we don't let the desire for these sensations dominate our behavior. Alcohol fills these needs for many people and its use is managed intelligently.

It is worth noting that the largest proportion of this drug is sold to the social drinker, not the drunk, just as most cocaine is sold to the casual user, not the addict. Now, early exposure to alcohol is common and inevitable, and youthful drinking can be extreme. Yet studies have shown that it is difficult to determine which drunk at the college party will evolve into a serious alcoholic. What is known is that the vast majority of early drinkers stop excessive drinking all by themselves. In fact, drug use of all types drops off radically with age.

BUCKLEY: Wait a minute. Are you telling us that there is only a 10 per cent chance that any user will become addicted to a drug, having experimented with it?

GAZZANIGA: The 10 per cent figure includes all drugs except tobacco. The actual risk for abuse of some drugs is much lower. Consider last year's National Household Survey (NHS) which was carried out by the National Insti-

> *It's gotten to where defense attorneys in federal drug cases can do their clients about as much good as Dr. Kevorkian can do his— quietly shepherd them through to the least painful end.*
>
> DAN BAUM

tutes on Drug Abuse. It is estimated that some 21 million people tried cocaine in 1988. But according to the NHS only three million defined themselves as having used the drug at least once during the month preceding their interview. Most of the three million were casual users. Now think about it. *All* the cocaine users make up 2 per cent of the adult population, and the addicts make up less than one-quarter of 1 per cent of the total population. These are the government's own figures. Does that sound like an epidemic to you?

BUCKLEY: But surely an epidemic has to do with the rate at which an undesirable occurrence is increasing. How many more cocaine users were there than the year before? Or the year before that?

GAZZANIGA: The real question is whether or not more and more Americans are becoming addicted to something. Is the rate of addiction to psychoactive substances going up? The answer to that is a flat no. Are there fads during which one drug becomes more popular than another as the drug of abuse? Sure. But, when one drug goes up in consumption, others go down. Heroin use is down, and so is marijuana use. That is why the opiate and marijuana pushers are trying to prove their purity—so they can grab back some of their market share, which apparently they have done for heroin in New York City.

But having said that, you should know that the actual use of cocaine and all other illicit drugs is on the decline, according to the NHS. The just-published National High School Survey carried out by the University of Michigan reports that the same is true among high-school students. Crack is used at such a low rate throughout the country that its use can hardly be measured in most areas.

BUCKLEY: Well, if a low addiction rate is the rule, how do we come to terms with the assertion, which has been made in reputable circles, that over 40 per cent of Americans fighting in Vietnam were using heroin and 80 per cent marijuana?

GAZZANIGA: Stressful situations provoke a greater use of drugs. Vietnam was one of them. But what happens when the soldiers come home?

> *Marijuana is not much more*
> *difficult to obtain than beer.*
> *The reason for this is that a liquor*
> *store selling beer to a minor stands*
> *to lose its liquor license.*
> *Marijuana salesmen don't have*
> *expensive overheads,*
> *and so are not easily punished.*
>
> WILLIAM F. BUCKLEY, JR.

That point was examined in a large study by Dr. Lee Robbins at Washington University. During the Vietnam War, President Nixon ordered a study on the returning vets who seemed to have a drug problem. (Nixon didn't know what he was looking for, but he was getting a lot of flak on the point that the war was producing a generation of drug addicts.) Dr. Robbins chose to study those soldiers returning to the United States in 1971. Of the 13,760 Army enlisted men who returned and were included in her sample, 1,400 had a positive urine test for drugs (narcotics, amphetamines, or barbiturates). She was able to re-test 495 men from this sample a few months later. The results were crystal clear: Only 8 per cent of the men who had been drug positive in their first urine test remained so. In short, over 90 per cent of them, now that they were back home, walked away from drug use. And all of them knew how to get hold of drugs, if they had wanted them. Incidentally, Dr. Robbins did a follow-up study a couple of years later on the same soldiers. She reported there had not been an increase in drug use.

BUCKLEY: Aha! You are saying that under special circumstances, the use of drugs increases. Well, granted there was stress in Vietnam. Isn't there stress also in American ghettos?

GAZZANIGA: If you live in poverty and frustration, and see few rewards available to you, you are likelier than your better-satisfied counterpart to seek the escape of drugs, although the higher rate of consumption does not result in a higher rate of addiction. Virtually every study finds this to be the case with one possibly interesting twist. A recent Department of Defense study showed that drug use in the military was lower for blacks than for whites, the reverse of civilian life. (It is generally agreed that the military is the only institution in our country that is successfully integrated.) In short, environmental factors play an important role in the incidence of drug use.

BUCKLEY: So you are saying that there are social circumstances that will raise the rate of consumption, but that raising the rate of consumption doesn't in fact raise the rate of addiction. In other words, if 50 per cent of the troops in Vietnam had been using crack, this would not have affected the rate at which, on returning to the United States, they became addicted. They would have kicked the habit on reaching home?

GAZZANIGA: That's the idea. Drug consumption can go up in a particular population, fueled by stress, but the rate of addiction doesn't go up no matter what the degree of stress. Most people can walk away from high drug use if their lives become more normal. Of course, the stress of the ghetto isn't the only situation that fuels high drug consumption. Plenty of affluent people who for some reason or another do not find their lives rewarding also escape into drugs.

BUCKLEY: If it is true, then, that only a small percentage of those who take crack will end up addicted, and that that is no different from the small percentage who, taking one beer every Saturday night, will become alcoholics, what is the correct way in which to describe the relative intensity of the addictive element in a particular drug?

Nothing is less productive than to make more efficient what should not be done at all.

PETER DRUCKER

GAZZANIGA: That is an interesting question and one that can't satisfactorily be answered until much more research is done. There are conundrums. Again, it is estimated that 21 million people tried cocaine in 1988. Yet, of those, only 3 million currently use it, and only a small percentage are addicted. As for crack, it is estimated that 2.5 million have used it, while only a half million say they still do, and *that* figure includes the addicted and the casual user. Some reports claim that as many as one half of crack users are addicted. As I have said, crack is cheap, and for that reason may be especially attractive to the poor. That is a non-pharmacological, non-biological factor, the weight of which we have not come to any conclusions about. We don't even have reliable data to tell us that crack creates a greater rate of addiction than, say, cocaine. My own guess is it doesn't. Remember that the drug acts on the same brain systems that cocaine and amphetamines do.

BUCKLEY: To what extent is the addictive factor affected by education? Here is what I mean by this: Taking a drug, say heroin or cocaine or crack—or, for that matter, alcohol—is a form of Russian roulette, using a ten-cartridge revolver. Now, presumably, an educated person, concerned for his livelihood, wouldn't take a revolver with nine empty cartridges and one full cartridge, aim it at his head, and pull the trigger. But granted, decisions of that kind are based on ratiocinative skills. And we have to assume these skills don't exist even among college students. If they did, there would be no drinking in college, let alone drug taking. Comments?

GAZZANIGA: Most people perceive themselves as in control of their destiny. They do not think the initial exposure will ruin their lives, because of their perceived self-control, and they are right. Take the most difficult case, tobacco—the most highly addictive substance around. In a now classic study, Stanley Schachter of Columbia University formally surveyed his highly educated colleagues at Columbia. At the same time, he polled the working residents of Amagansett, a community on Long Island where he summered. He first determined who were ongoing smokers, and who had been smokers. He took into account how long they had smoked, what they had smoked, and all other variables he could think of.

> *Adulation is all right*
> *if you don't inhale.*
>
> ADLAI STEVENSON

It wasn't long before the picture began to crystallize. Inform a normally intelligent group of people about the tangible hazards of using a particular substance and the vast majority of them simply stop. It wasn't easy for some, but in general they stopped, and they didn't need treatment programs, support programs, and all the rest. Dr. Schachter concluded, after this study, that it is only the thorny cases that show up at the treatment centers, people who have developed a true addiction. For those people, psychological prophylactics, including education, are of little or no value. Yet it is these people that are held up as examples of what happens when one uses drugs. This is misleading. It creates an unworkable framework for thinking about the problem. Most people can voluntarily stop using a psychoactive substance, and those people who do continue to use it can moderate their intake to reduce the possibility of health hazards. This is true, as I say, for most substances, but I repeat, less true for tobacco because of its distinctively addictive nature. The people who unwisely continue to use tobacco tend to smoke themselves into major illness even though they are amply warned that this is likely to happen.

BUCKLEY: So no matter how widely you spread the message, it is in fact going to be ignored, both by Ph.D.s and by illiterates?

GAZZANIGA: If they are real abusers, yes. That is the reason for the high recidivism rate among graduates of drug treatment centers. Here we are talking about the true addicts. Education appears not to help the recalcitrant abusers, who are the ones that keep showing up at health centers.

Yet, manifestly, education contributes to keeping the abuse rate as low as it is. I think the message gets to the ghetto, but where there are other problems—the need for an artificial reward—drugs are going to be taken by many people because the excruciating pain of a current condition overrides long-term reason. In short, the ghetto citizen or the psychologically isolated person might well decide that the probability of living a better life is low, so grab some rewards while you can.

BUCKLEY: In that case, education, even in the popular media, is likely to influence primarily the educated classes. That has to mean that the uneducated class will suffer more addiction than the educated class.

GAZZANIGA: Well, again, people in the lowest socio-economic status will continue to consume more drugs, but that doesn't change the addiction rate. Still, legalization shouldn't change the current figures, since drugs are literally available everywhere in the ghetto. They are also available on every college campus. They are available in prisons! I suppose if one wants to conjure up fresh problems brought on by legalization, they will center on the folks living on Park Avenue, where drugs are less easily secured, not the ghetto. Legalization of drugs would reduce crime in the ghetto, and much that is positive would follow. The vast majority of the crime network ought to crumble. The importance of that cannot be underestimated.

BUCKLEY: What would be your prediction, as a scientist, of what the advent of [drugs sold legally and without prescription to adults in a kind of] Federal Drugstore, combined with a program of intensified education, would accomplish in the next ten years?

> *It seems as if the Department [of Justice] sees the value of the Bill of Rights as no more than obstacles to be overcome.*
>
> PROFESSOR SANFORD H. KADISH

GAZZANIGA: Drug-consumption rates will bounce around, related as they are to environmental factors, fads, and a host of other factors. Drug-abuse rates will not change much, if at all. Yet many of the negative social consequences of keeping drugs illegal will be neutralized. The health costs of drug abuse will always be with us. We should try to focus on those problems with more serious neurobiologic and neurobehavioral research and help where we can to reduce the percentage that fall victim. I am an experimental scientist, and like most people can see that the present system doesn't work. We need to try another approach. If, for whatever reason, legalization doesn't improve the situation, it would take five minutes to reverse it.

Thank you, Mr. B. and Professor G. I was so fascinated by the discussion, I have no comments to make. Ah, good conversation: what a drug.

I close this chapter with this quote from the National Institute of Justice, from a program sponsored by the Police Foundation:

> The goal of legalizing drugs is to bring them under effective legal control. If it were legal to produce and distribute drugs, legitimate businessmen would enter the business. There would be less need for violence and corruption since the industry would have access to the courts. And, instead of absorbing tax dollars as targets of expensive enforcement efforts, the drug sellers might begin to pay taxes. So, legalization might well solve the organized crime aspects of the drug trafficking problem.

On average, drug use under legalization might not be as destructive to users and to society as under the current prohibition, because drugs would be less expensive, purer, and more conveniently available.

Peyote—Mystic Fruit of Mexico

By Count A. N. MIRZAOFF

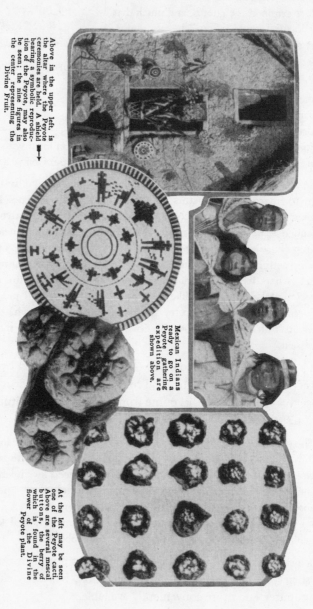

Above in the upper left, is the altar where the Peyote ceremonies are held. A shield bearing a symbolic reproduction of the Peyote, may also be seen; the nine figures in the center representing the Divine Fruit. →

Mexican Indians ready to go on a Peyote gathering expedition are shown above.

At the left may be seen one of the Peyote cacti. Above are several mescal buttons, the berry of which is found in the flower of the Divine Peyote plant

Religious Use of Drugs

> I have sworn upon the altar of God
> eternal hostility
> against every form of tyranny
> over the mind of man.
>
> THOMAS JEFFERSON

L ONG BEFORE THE WHITE MAN traveled with hempen sails to find religious freedom in a New World, the natives on a land mass now called North America used sacramental plants to achieve union and communion with nature, the universal brotherhood, and the Great Spirit.

The Incas chewed coca leaves, but *only* for spiritual purposes and *only* with the permission of their leader, the Inca. The conquistadors from Spain turned what was once a sacrament into a reward for work and, later, for the energy to do more work. Changing the purpose and use of coca leaves was but one part of the destruction of a great civilization.

Indigenous tribes throughout North America ate parts of the peyote cactus as an expression of thanksgiving, a request for guidance, or in support of a brother who wanted to give thanks or seek direction. Peyote was always used in a formal, ceremonial way, and "recreational" use was considered a sacrilege. It took the white man—who knew or cared so little about the Native American way—until 1899 to find out what was going on and make it illegal. Oklahoma passed a law against peyote in 1899, and New Mexico outlawed it in 1929. Not until the 1960s, when a sufficient number of white people began seeking that mystical experience, was peyote considered "a menace" that had to be controlled nationally. Today in Oregon, for example, possession of peyote is punishable by ten years in prison. Many Native Americans think so much of peyote that they carry a symbolic peyote button in a richly ornamented bag hung around their neck. Just *wearing* this religious symbol can get you a decade in the white man's prison. In 1988, the United States Supreme Court ruled that Native Americans were not entitled to constitutional protection under the freedom of religion clause of the First Amendment with regard to the use of peyote.

> *We are not clear as to*
> *the role in life of these chemicals;*
> *nor are we clear as to*
> *the role of the physician.*
> *You know, of course,*
> *that in ancient times there was*
> *no clear distinction between*
> *priest and physician.*
>
> ALAN WATTS

Humans have always sought ways to alter everyday consciousness. This is usually achieved either through drastic changes in normal behavior, or by ingesting a consciousness-altering substance.

In the middle of the garden were the tree of life and the tree of the knowledge of good and evil. And the Lord God commanded the man, "You are free to eat from any tree in the garden; but you must not eat from the tree of the knowledge of good and evil, for when you eat of it you will surely die." (Genesis 2:9, 16–17)

The serpent told Eve that by eating of the tree of the knowledge of good and evil, "you will be like God." This was an unbearable temptation.

> When the woman saw the fruit of the tree was good for food and pleasing to the eye, and also desirable for gaining wisdom, she took some and ate it. She also gave some to her husband, who was with her, and he ate it. (Genesis 3:6)

But there were two trees in the middle of the garden: the tree of life and the tree of the knowledge of good and evil. They *could* have eaten of the tree of life, but did not. Instead, they listened to the serpent, who convinced them that knowing good from evil was a God-like quality. They were given bad advice. They ate from the wrong tree. *They made a poor religious choice.*

Which is a more fundamental aspect of God: *life* or *knowing good from evil?* Obviously, life. *Everybody* knows how to judge good from evil. That hardly makes anyone God-like. But who can give life? As no one once wrote, "Good and evil are judged by fools like me, but only God can give life to a tree."

Ironically, we continue to believe the serpent's misinformation *to this day.* Nowhere do we apply this misinformation *more* than in our quest for religion. Religions are layered thick with rules, rights and wrongs, goods and evils. The very conflict over which is the *good* religion and which is the *evil* religion has caused more discord, disagreement, war, oppression, and death than any other single factor in history. A difference of opinion is what makes horse races; a difference of religious opinion is what makes Inquisitions, holy wars, and just about every law against consensual activities. In the words of Justice Walter P. Stacy,

> It would be almost unbelievable, if history did not record the tragic fact, that men have gone to war and cut each other's throats because they could not agree as to what was to become of them after their throats were cut. Many sins have been committed in the name of religion.

Don't people realize that when they try to force others to do "good," they are following the advice of the serpent?

Instead, why don't we look at the *life* in alternate religions? *"How* do you worship? *What* do you believe? What is the *essence* of your teaching? What in your religion sustains you, nurtures you, gives you life?" These are questions that help us understand the *life* in other religions. Far too many "religious" people merely ask, "Do you believe that our Lord Jesus Christ was the only Son of God, and only through Him can one achieve eternal life?" or "Have you accepted

> *It is well for people who think*
> *to change their minds occasionally*
> *in order to keep them clean.*
> *For those who do not think,*
> *it is best at least to rearrange*
> *their prejudices once in a while.*
>
> LUTHER BURBANK

Jesus Christ as your personal Lord and Savior?" Only an enthusiastic and convincingly sincere, "Yes! Praise Jesus!" proves to them you're not an unsaved—therefore, evil—heathen.

Isn't it obvious that all this judging is the same thing as eating from the tree of the knowledge of good and evil and not eating from the tree of life?

ふふ ふふ ふふ

In the West, we have a strong bias that religious experiences should be obtained through *altered action* rather than *sacramental ingestion.* Prayer, fasting, penance, and personal sacrifice are all acceptable means to achieving greater connection with God and Spirit. Ingesting chemicals, sacramental plants, or other consciousness-altering substances is not. Even in the churches that practice Holy Communion—in which one does ingest something—the act is often viewed by the communicants as *symbolic,* a *remembrance* of the Lord's Supper. Few believe that the communion wafer or the piece of bread and sip of wine *actually contain* the transformative energy of the Christ and the Holy Spirit. Even if they *believe* it's there, they don't *experience it* often. If asked why they don't experience it every time, they usually answer, "I have not done enough to prove myself worthy." Back to physical actions, and to that contradiction in terms: *earning grace.*

The irony is that most intense religious experience is based on a *chemical change.* Sometimes the chemical comes from outside oneself, and sometimes it is produced by the human body in response to a mental, emotional, or physical change. Either way, chemicals change—or shift—people's consciousness.

Human consciousness is an electrochemical process. *What* we are aware of and *that* we are aware is due to an elaborate biochemical-electrical arrangement that is a miracle of nature—the human nervous system. A slight alteration in its delicate balance creates a shift in consciousness. Any number of stimuli can trigger the chemical-electrical shift that leads to the change in consciousness. A single thought can do it. We can be on an airplane with someone we dearly love, and the single thought, "Did I leave the water running in the bathtub?", can change our feelings from delight to uptight. Conversely, we could be "worried sick" about a loved one's well-being and, on hearing of his or her safety, become ecstatic. In both cases, *a thought* produced an electrochemical change which produced a change in consciousness.

All the "acceptable" techniques for achieving religious experiences involve chemical change. Prayer is changing one's focus—altering what one is thinking. Fasting causes a significant biochemical change. Even the "born again" experience as practiced by many churches is based on psychological pressure ("You are a sinner and you will spend all eternity in hell") and relief ("Accept Jesus and you will spend all eternity in paradise"), which can produce profound biochemical change.

This is not to say that *other factors*—such as God's intervention, Spirit touching to earth, or Jesus the Christ appearing in one's heart—don't play a part in religious experiences. It is simply to point out that immediately prior to—or simultaneous with—them, the body's electrochemical functioning changes.

When we have a shift in consciousness, our *belief* usually determines whether or not the shift is perceived as a religious experience. If we connect a certain positive feeling with God, for example, each time we have that feeling, we think of God. If we attach that same pleasant feeling to our spouse, each time we feel that feeling, we will think of our spouse. If we attach the very same feeling to our favorite television program, each time we feel that feeling, we will think of our favorite television program.

If you have a certain shift of consciousness and are convinced that it is a mystical experience, and a sign that you are progressing toward God, that would be a positive religious experience. If, however, you believed that precisely the same shift in consciousness was a psychotic episode and an indication that you were getting progressively more insane, you would probably perceive it as a negative psychological experience.

A change of consciousness is an *event*, an *experience.* If we choose to give that experience religious meaning, it becomes a religious experience. If we choose to associate it with someone we are in love with, it becomes a romantic experience. If we choose to associate it with our favorite television show, it becomes a video experience. We could even choose to associate it with something wicked and evil ("This is the devil tempting me."), and the same experience would be a negative one.

⚖ ⚖ ⚖

It takes very little chemical change to bring about a profound shift in consciousness. LSD, for example, is not measured in *milligrams,* or thousandths of a gram, but in *micrograms*—millionths of a gram. As few as 25 micrograms—that is, twenty-five millionths of a gram—can bring about a profound change in consciousness that lasts many hours. After Dr. Albert Hofmann accidentally ingested LSD on April 16, 1943, he described his experiences :

> *Not a shred of evidence exists in favor of the idea that life is serious.*
>
> BRENDAN GILL

> I was seized with a feeling of great rest-lessness and mild dizziness. At home, I lay down and sank into a not unpleasant delirium, which was characterized by ex-tremely excited fantasies. In a semiconscious state, with my eyes closed (I felt the daylight to be unpleasantly dazzling), fantastic visions of extra-ordinary realness and with an intense kaleidoscopic play of colors as-saulted me. After about two hours this condition disappeared.

Note that there's not much talk about *God* in there, or even mystical experi-ence. In fact, at first people thought the LSD experience closely resembled the delirium of extreme schizophrenia and explained, perhaps, the paintings of Vin-cent van Gogh. (He was not *interpreting* those swirling sunflowers—he was paint-ing what he *saw*.) LSD, it was thought, should be taken by therapists so that they might understand the working of the schizophrenic mind. An architect took LSD so that he might better design a mental institution—a place that would be seen as healing and comforting from an "insane" person's point of view.

Others thought LSD would be useful in therapy because it produced such a pronounced shift from ordinary consciousness. It could be the chemical equiva-lent of electroshock therapy. If insane people could be sufficiently jarred from their insanity—even for a brief period of time—perhaps their reality could be restructured, through therapy, into a healthier pattern.

Still others—such as author Aldous Huxley and Harvard professors Timothy Leary and Richard Alpert—thought that LSD opened the "doors of perception" (as Huxley called it) through which human consciousness could glimpse mystical visions. They maintain that LSD opened the consciousness through which all the great spiritual teachers—Buddha, Zoroaster, Krishna, Jesus, Mohammed, and so many others—had their insights and revelations. In his 1969 book, *High Priest*, Timothy Leary compares the first four verses of Genesis to the same experience that Dr. Albert Hofmann described as "not unpleasant delirium."

> In the beginning God created the heavens and the earth. Now the earth was formless and empty; darkness was over the surface of the deep, and the spirit of God was hovering over the waters. And God said, "Let there be light," and there was light. God saw that the light was good, and He separated the light from the darkness. (Genesis 1:1–4)

> In the beginning was the TURN ON. The flash, the illumination. The elec-

tric trip. The sudden bolt of energy that starts the new system.

The TURN ON was God.

All things were made from the TURN ON and without Him was not any thing made.

In this TURN ON was life; and the life was the light of men.

It has always been the same.

It was the flash that exploded the galaxies, from which all energy flows. It was the spark that ignites in the mysterious welding of amino-acid strands that creates the humming vine of organic life. It is the brilliant neurological glare that illuminates the shadows of man's mind. The God-intoxicated revelation. The Divine union. The vision of harmony, samadhi, satori, ecstasy which we now call psychedelic.

> *Instant gratification takes too long.*
>
> CARRIE FISHER

Some thought LSD produced psychoses; others thought it produced enlightenment. Some thought Jesus was crazy; some thought he was the son of God. In both cases, how people *approached* the experience significantly influenced the *results* of that experience.

Those who took LSD thinking it was going to simulate schizophrenia left the LSD experience thinking, "Oh, that's what it's like to be crazy." Many of those who took LSD fully expecting mystical revelation got mystical revelation. Many of those who went to Jesus thinking he was crazy came away convinced that he was crazy. Those who went believing he was the son of God came away convinced he was the son of God. *("Your faith has made you whole.")*

In the 1960s and early 1970s, hundreds of thousands—perhaps millions—accepted the Huxley-Leary-Alpert interpretation and, for the most part, had experiences they would describe as religious. The "set and setting" was vitally important. The *set* was the mind-set: One had to ask oneself, "Am I taking part in this experience for kicks or for illumination?" The latter was strongly recommended. The *setting* was where you took the LSD, whom you took it with, and what physical activities were planned: music, silence, readings aloud from the New Testament or the Tibetan Book of the Dead. One had a *guide* who had had the experience before, and could provide safety, support, and encouragement to "go to God." (Hell, in that set and setting, *vodka* would give mystical experiences.)

Less than ten years later, the "next generation" was "dropping acid" before a relatively uneventful evening of disco dancing. "The Bee Gees! Jesus!" the psychedelic old-timers would lament. "What happened to the *Beatles*? And why are they going to a *disco*? If they want to go out, why don't they go to a *real* religious experience—like seeing *2001: A Space Odyssey* in Cinerama?"

Soon "acid" became synonymous with *any* orally taken consciousness-changing substance: tranquilizers, strychnine, it didn't matter. People were looking for a "trip," not a journey; a "high," not a higher state of consciousness.

Some of the original "mystical" LSD takers went on to explore God in more traditional ways: LSD was advertised as only *one door* to the house of perception; how you moved in was up to you. Richard Alpert took an ancient route, went to India, and became Ram Dass. Timothy Leary took the techno route and became fascinated with space travel, computers, and cyberspace. As Joni Mitchell described it, "Some turned to Jesus, some turned to heroin," and some turned into their parents. Whatever the outcome, LSD was a bright flash between the black and white '50s and the technicolor '70s. What people did with that flash was entirely up to them.

> *Every happening,*
> *great and small,*
> *is a parable*
> *whereby God speaks to us,*
> *and the art of life*
> *is to get the message.*
>
> MALCOLM MUGGERIDGE

⚖ ⚖ ⚖

Throughout history, humans have sought the tree of life. Realizing that eating from the tree of the knowledge of good and evil was not the right choice, people have sought to "return to the garden" by ingesting substances from the plant, mineral, and animal kingdoms. Some worked; most didn't.*

We have in our country today a situation in which sincere seekers cannot seek. They are entitled to use the traditional methods as much as they please, but only those tried and accepted by "our Judeo-Christian forefathers." People can pray, fast, retreat into a monastery or convent, and that's okay. (As long as they don't overdo it, of course: then they'd be *crazy* and not *Christed.*) Changing consciousness through external actions that produce internal chemical reactions is acceptable. *Ingesting* chemicals is not. *"It's just not done."* If you do it, you are not taking part in a sacrament, but committing a sacrilege. You will be *punished* for it; not only in the hereafter, but *here.*

We'll explore further the absurdity of jailing people for religious beliefs in the chapter, "Unconventional Religious Practices." The point of this chapter is: although ingesting chemicals may not be part of the Judeo-Christian tradition, it certainly has a long and dignified history in the *human* tradition. To deny Americans—native or immigrant—the right to explore chemical sacraments is not only an interference with people's religious freedom, but yet another example of imposing Judeo-Christian religious beliefs on others by force of law.

---

*Many of these worldwide explorations—past and present—are described in Terence McKenna's book, *Food of the Gods.* (Not to be confused with a Greek cookbook by the same name.)

Regenerative Use of Drugs
and Other Unorthodox Medical Practices

> *Unless we put medical freedom
> into the Constitution,
> the time will come
> when medicine will organize itself
> into an undercover dictatorship.*
>
> DR. BENJAMIN RUSH
> *a signer of the*
> *Declaration of Independence*

HOW CAN SOMETHING START OUT SO good and wind up so bad? That's the question I ask myself each time I think about the Food and Drug Administration (FDA). It began as such a good idea: constitutionally sound, designed to educate and protect the citizens of the United States. Now it regularly raids alternative healers, keeps healing and rejuvenative drugs away from those who might benefit, dictates what is and is not proper healing, and wants to even more severely limit our ability to buy vitamins, minerals, and other nutritional supplements. The FDA has, like Dr. Frankenstein's experiment, gone awry.

In the early 1900s, prepared foods and packaged medicines were a mess. As Upton Sinclair described in *The Jungle*, his 1906 exposé of the meatpacking industry, meatpackers would pack anything into skins and call it meat. Sawdust, rat droppings, the digestive tracts of animals and all that they contained were ground together and sold as "pure beef sausage." One could never be sure if a quart of beef stew contained an entire *quart* of beef stew—or even if it contained beef. Over-the-counter (patent) medicines might contain alcohol, morphine, cocaine, and not list the ingredients or strength of concentration on the label.

Normally, it would be left to the states to regulate food and drugs through local health codes, honest-weight restrictions, and other local regulatory laws. With improvements in packaging, transportation, and marketing, however, by the turn of the century a great many products were traveling across state lines. This brought them under the jurisdiction of the federal government: regulation of interstate commerce was one of the powers enumerated to Congress. Section 8 of the Constitution—the powers granted to Congress—states, "(c) To regulate Commerce with foreign Nations, and among the several States, and with the

Indian Tribes."

In 1906, Congress passed the Pure Food and Drug Act, which established that foods and drugs should be "unadulterated," and that their contents be clearly labeled. This was a much-needed regulation. The patent medicine people didn't like it, of course, because many of their concoctions were nothing but sugar water. It wasn't that the medicine makers were afraid people would find out their medicines contained drugs, but that people would discover the medicines didn't contain drugs. (Morphine, cocaine, and alcohol were—then as now—more expensive than water, sugar, and food coloring.) The packaged-food industry certainly didn't want to change its practices. "Beef" meant "some kind of meat, for the most part" and everybody knew it, so where was the problem? Why should "beef" have to come from cattle? Picky. Picky. Picky. Although the Pure Food and Drug Act may have seemed bad for business on the surface, it was good for business overall: it was enacted less to protect the consumer than to provide a level playing field on which all businesses could fairly compete. "The business of government is business." That, of course, is not what politicians admitted in *speeches;* it was merely what they actually practiced. On the rostrum, they all sounded like Teddy Roosevelt, who said in 1910:

> The object of government is the welfare of the people. The material progress and prosperity of a nation are desirable chiefly so far as they lead to the moral and material welfare of all good citizens.

Right. By 1910, however, the administrators of the Pure Food and Drug Act were getting a little *too* concerned with the "welfare of all good citizens." The act had this little loophole: What is "adulterated" and who decides what is "adulterated"?

According to the book, *The Big Drink: The Story of Coca-Cola* by E. J. Kahn, proponents of the Pure Food and Drug Act often cited Coca-Cola as a reason why the government needed to regulate packaged products. Here, they claimed, was a beverage, supposedly as safe as sarsaparilla, that contained cocaine. Eventually, Coca-Cola removed the cocaine, but when the act was passed in 1906, Coca-Cola was taken to court not for containing cocaine without labeling it, but for marketing a "mislabled" product: the drink contained no coca (cocaine) and little kola. To make sure Coca-Cola still provided "the pause that refreshes" the company replaced the real thing (cocaine) with a wallop of caffeine. Adding caffeine to products was not permitted by the Pure Food and Drug Act—that was "adulteration." The case continued in court for nine years, and Coca-Cola eventually agreed to make changes in its manufacturing process and to list its ingredients—

Half of the modern drugs could well be thrown out of the window, except that the birds might eat them.

DR. MARTIN HENRY FISCHER

which included neither coca nor kola—but did include caffeine. The requirement to list its ingredients removed the mystery of what Coca-Cola contained, opening the doors for other cola competitors, and setting the stage for the infamous Cola Wars.*

In 1927, the enforcement of the law moved from the Bureau of Chemistry (a division of the Department of Agriculture) into its own bureaucratic structure: the Food, Drug, and Insecticide Administration—a formidable, respectable name if there ever was one. Not surprisingly, in 1931 it dropped the Insecticide from its title and became the Food and Drug Administration.

> *Sailing round the world
> in a dirty gondola
> Oh, to be back in the land of
> Coca-Cola!*
>
> BOB DYLAN

The FDA was then given the power to ban "harmful" additives. By what criteria do we define "harmful" additives? If there is a known lethal dose, should something be prohibited? If that were the case, salt could never be used as an additive. For the most part, whatever the FDA *decided* was harmful *was* harmful. The decisions were (and are) capricious at best.

⚖ ⚖ ⚖

The original Pure Food and Drug Act (also known as the "Wiley Act") only required that food not be "adulterated" or "misbranded" when shipped across state lines. In 1912, the act was amended to prohibit false therapeutic claims. The problem with that is the same as determining what is "harmful": Who is to say what is and is not therapeutic?

For example, the placebo effect is a scientifically proven fact: if you take an absolutely worthless substance and *believe* it's going to make you better, it tends to make you better. Good old mind-over-matter—the placebo is a way of tricking matter (the body) into minding the mind. Bona fide, licensed, reputable physicians use placebos every day—with the approval of both the Food and Drug Administration and the American Medical Association. The doctor will charge the full amount for an office visit, write a prescription, send the patient to a pharmacy to pay a large amount of money for sugar pills. Whether it's belief in the doctor, in the pills, in getting out of the house and paying some money, or a combination of all those factors, one thing is certain: people who take the sugar pills get better faster than people who are told by the doctor, "There's nothing I can do about this; it will have to run its course."

And so it was with the patent medicines. If advertising copy (and patent medi-

---

*As previously noted, the cola taste is made by combining the flavors of citrus (lemon or lime), cinnamon, and vanilla. Cocaine and kola have nothing to do with it.

cines were the largest advertisers in the country at the turn of the century) could convince you that Mother's Soothing Syrup *would* cure your cold, the cold got cured sooner than it would absent Mother's Soothing Syrup. If the medicine didn't work, the most the government could do was require that the manufacturer issue a refund. This is simple, responsible Consumerism 101: Try it; if it works, great; if it doesn't work, you get your money back.

Can you imagine what our health care system would be like if it worked on this simple principle? If you went to the doctor and didn't get cured, you wouldn't have to pay. But no: it doesn't work that way—the FDA and AMA have convinced us that a medical professional is entitled to full pay for "a good try." Meanwhile, they prohibit others from even trying.

The 1912 law put the burden of proof on the government: a manufacturer had to be clearly defrauding the public. This was not stringent enough, however, and in 1938 the Federal Food, Drug, and Cosmetic Act was passed. Since then it has been up to the *manufacturer* to prove—scientifically—that its drugs are effective. Good-bye placebo effect. (For patent medicines, at least. For the AMA—*fine!*)

Then, in 1962, in the wake of the tragedy of thousands of deformed infants whose mothers had taken thalidomide during pregnancy, Congress unanimously passed legislation increasing the FDA's powers to limit drug sales and, in 1976, expanded those powers to include all "medical devices."

⚖ ⚖ ⚖

While the spirit behind strengthening the FDA was certainly a good one; the results have been anything but. Yes, we can buy foods relatively free of rat droppings (FDA guidelines restrict the *amount* of animal droppings and insect parts permitted in foods, but do not prohibit them altogether), and while it's good to know that hemorrhoid cream has actually shrunk a "hemorrhoidal tissue" here or there, much of what the FDA currently does amounts to nothing more than dictating what does and does not heal people.

Just as people should have the freedom to find and worship God as they choose, so too should they have the freedom to find, maintain, and enhance their own health as they choose.

The FDA neither believes nor supports this contention. Only medicine as the FDA and the AMA (it's hard to tell them apart most of the time) define medicine *is* medicine. Everything else is *quackery*. Quackery, according to the FDA, is not just misguided medical practices that American consumers need to be educated about; quackery is fundamentally *evil*, and those who traffic in it—both suppliers and consumers—must be *punished*.

♎ ♎ ♎

The quackery of yesteryear is the sound medical practice of today; the sound medical practice of yesteryear is utter foolishness today.

George Washington, for example, was literally bled to death. It was the medical belief in Washington's day that, when ill, "pressure" had to be relieved and the "evil humors" had to be bled off. The sicker one was, the more he or she was bled, and the more often. Now, of course, we know that people need their blood the most when they are ill. There's hardly a practice or procedure that was considered sound medical science 200 years ago that someone wouldn't be arrested for attempting today—and with good reason. As Thurman Arnold observed,

> The principles of Washington's farewell address are still sources of wisdom when cures for social ills are sought. The methods of Washington's physicians, however, are no longer studied.

Conversely, to suggest fifty years ago that diet, exercise, or vitamins would help prevent or cure heart disease would be considered blatant quackery. *Bed rest* was what was needed if you had a weak heart, medical doctors told us, and lots of *red meat*. People were *arrested* for suggesting that exercise, reduced meat diets, and vitamin supplements would help the heart. Now the same techniques are part of standard medical practice.

All this restriction came about because the FDA took a leap that defies logic. This from the official FDA history:

> It was recognized that no drug is truly safe unless it is also effective, and effectiveness was required to be established before marketing—one of the major advances of medical history. [Emphasis added.]

How can one equate *safety* with *effectiveness*? A safe drug is one I can put in my body and know that, as long as I take it in recommended doses, will not cause me to shrivel up and die. An effective drug is something else again. Yes, if one takes an ineffective drug when one could, instead, be taking an effective drug, the illness may become worse, and this is not good. To say, however, that the ineffective drug is *not safe* is confusing the issue and torturing the language. Saying a drug cures something that it does not makes the manufacturer guilty of *false advertising*, not of marketing *unsafe substances*.

It is this fundamental misconception at the FDA that makes equating *effective* with *safe*—far from "one of the major advances in medical history"—one of the major *retreats* in medical history. The *most* that the government can do is warn the consumer of the potential risks—which include the risk that the drug or medical

---

Despite the belief that handwashing is the most important measure to prevent the spread of infection in hospitals, less than one third of physicians wash their hands between patients.

THE AMERICAN HOSPITAL
ASSOCIATION
1992

> *Upjohn Co., which makes Halcion, the most widely prescribed sleeping pill in America, has confirmed that it submitted incomplete data on the side effects of the controversial drug to the Food and Drug Administration when it sought approval to sell the drug here.*
>
> THE WASHINGTON POST

procedure may not be effective at all. Instead of, for example, giving certain products the "FDA seal of approval," the FDA wants to remove all products that do *not* have the FDA seal of approval. The FDA also wants to arrest those products' manufacturers. I shouldn't say the FDA *wants* to do this—*it's doing it right now.*

According to *Science* magazine, it costs, on average, $231,000,000 and takes twelve years to do the necessary testing on a drug in order for it to receive FDA approval. If complications arise, the cost can be considerably more. This sheer financial burden keeps any number of useful drugs off the market. Pharmaceutical companies often don't bother with the necessary testing because it feels it will not make back its investment. Even if a pharmaceutical company moves full speed ahead, cures are still, for the most part, twelve years from the market. The FDA guidelines are known to be so strict and so all-pervasive that Lees can say of its Relaxed Riders jeans: "If they were any more relaxing, we'd need FDA approval."

Even worse than suppressing newly discovered drugs is the fact that drugs discovered years ago will *never* receive FDA approval and therefore can *never* be marketed. The drug MDMA, for example, was synthesized years ago, and is thus part of the public domain. Sometime in the mid-1970s the drug was found to have potentially beneficial results in psychological therapy. In the 1980s, after the drug—marketed as *ecstasy**—became very popular recreationally, it was made illegal and will probably never be made legal again, certainly not by current FDA guidelines. Who is going to spend twelve years and $231,000,000 proving the safety and effectiveness of a drug that anyone can then manufacture? No pharmaceutical company in the known world, that's for sure.

These many hurdles are keeping essential drugs and treatments from the American public. Jane S. Smith observes in her 1990 book, *Patenting the Sun: Polio and the Salk Vaccine,*

> As Jonas Salk has often remarked, it would be impossible to repeat his polio work today, when such ventures need to be passed by human-subject review boards and peer review boards and various other qualifying agencies. In 1952 you got the permission of the people involved and went out and did it, and then wrote up your results in a scientific journal. If something terrible happened, the blame would be on your head and the blood on your hands, and of course your career would be over—but in the planning stages, at least, life was a great deal easier for the medical experimenter than it has since become.

*The man who discovered the modern use of MDMA said he wanted to call it *empathy,* but thought *ecstasy* would sell better. Ah, marketing.

By today's standards, the Salk vaccine (which was used widely starting in 1953) would not have been available until the mid-1960s—providing that Dr. Salk could have found a pharmaceutical company willing to gamble $231,000,000 on his vaccine. With current FDA guidelines, polio might be a common disease even today.

⚖️ ⚖️ ⚖️

Imagine what the FDA would have to say about these unorthodox medical practices:

> *In the scheme of things I'm not as important as Dr. Jonas Salk.*
>
> TOM SELLECK

> They came to Bethsaida, and some people brought a blind man and begged Jesus to touch him. He took the blind man by the hand and led him outside the village. When he had spit on the man's eyes and put his hand on him, Jesus asked, "Do you see anything?"
>
> He looked up and said, "I see people; they look like trees walking around."
>
> Once more Jesus put his hands on the man's eyes. Then his eyes were opened, his sight was restored, and he saw everything clearly. (Mark 8:22–25)
>
> There some people brought to him a man who was deaf and could hardly talk, and they begged him to place his hand on the man.
>
> After he took him aside, away from the crowd, Jesus put his fingers into the man's ears. Then he spit and touched the man's tongue. He looked up to heaven and with a deep sigh said to him, "Ephphatha!" (which means, "Be opened!"). At this, the man's ears were opened, his tongue was loosened and he began to speak plainly. (Mark 7:32–35)

Spitting! Can you imagine!

⚖️ ⚖️ ⚖️

As Julian Whitaker, M.D., points out:

> In medical school I was taught that the *only* tools that work to help people are drugs and surgery. In the twenty years since then, I have seen that much of what I was taught is just plain *wrong.*
>
> The medical establishment has been *wrong* about the big killers and cripplers like heart disease, stroke, cancer, diabetes, high blood pressure, obesity, and arthritis. *Wrong* about the origins of these diseases. And *wrong* about how to remedy them. Their record is shameful.
>
> As young doctors we all take a solemn oath to uphold human life and well-being above all else. Sadly, it seems today's physicians care more about their *profession* than their *patients.*

> *We must free science and medicine from the grasp of politics.*
>
> PRESIDENT BILL CLINTON

Traditional Western medicine is known as *symptomatic* medicine. It diagnoses and treats *symptoms*. This is fine—and for the elimination of certain symptoms there is nothing like symptomatic medicine. To pretend, however, that symptomatic medicine represents the full range of healing and health enhancements available is a severely limited view. In fact, the human life span has doubled in the past 400 years primarily for two reasons—neither of them medical: *plumbing,* which took septic waste away from homes, streets, and cities; and *transportation,* which made fresh fruits and vegetables available year-round. The majority of lives saved by modern medical science can be summed up by the Three A's: Anesthesia (which permits surgery), Antiseptics, and Antibiotics.

While symptomatic medicine is marvelous (and I wouldn't live—in fact, probably wouldn't be alive—without it), it does not justify our current attitude, which was summed up by George Bernard Shaw: "We have not lost faith, but we have transferred it from God to the medical profession." Many of the more *holistic* (that is, treating the *whole* person) and alternative methods of obtaining, maintaining, and enhancing health should be, if not encouraged, at least not *forbidden* by the FDA.

The Food and Drug Administration is intimately connected with the American Medical Association and the handful of pharmaceutical companies that create and manufacture the vast majority of prescription drugs. Working at the FDA, being on the board of the AMA, and working for one or another of the large pharmaceutical companies, is like playing musical chairs. The high-paying jobs—the gold ring on the merry-go-round—are at pharmaceutical companies. The best way to get a raise is to become a "public servant" for a couple of years and spend some time at the FDA or AMA.

Politicians frequently own pharmaceutical stocks. For example, when George Bush took office as vice president, the *New York Times* reported, "The Vice President still owned the Eli Lilly stock upon taking office. It was his most valuable stock holding." Dan Quayle's family owns an enormous amount of stock in Eli Lilly. When Bush left the CIA in 1977, he was made the director of Eli Lilly (supposedly by Dan Quayle's father), a post he held until 1979. While vice-president, Bush made what the *New York Times* called "an unusual move" when he "intervened with the Treasury in March in connection with proposed rules that would have forced pharmaceutical companies to pay significantly more taxes" (*New York Times,* May 19, 1982). When politicians are willing to do something as bold and public as intervene to preserve a tax loophole, imagine how vigorously they will support laws that "ostensibly" (to quote the government) promote the public good (and incidentally benefit the pharmaceutical companies). Alternative healing methods directly threaten the profitable prescription drug business. Here—as with the banning of marijuana—we see not just old-time religion, but good old corporate greed as a motivating factor. To quote Dr. Whitaker again:

> The U.S. government's recommended daily allowances (RDA) for vitamins and minerals are insufficient. Powerful food lobbies work overtime to keep these figures low. A nutrition label may proudly state it contains 100% of the RDA for Vitamin C. And since the RDA for Vitamin C is only 60 mg per day, the product looks good. But consider that some medical research puts the optimal intake of Vitamin C at 3,000 mg per day. Now, the manufacturer's claim seems ridiculous, as it contains only 2% of the optimal intake.

> *Taking vitamin E supplements daily for at least two years appears to dramatically reduce the risk of heart disease.*
> *Separate studies of men and women who took daily vitamin E supplements had about a 40 percent lower risk of heart disease.*
>
> NEW ENGLAND JOURNAL OF MEDICINE
> May, 1993

And now the FDA wants to limit vitamin supplements to the recommended daily allowance. Larger doses would require a doctor's prescription. This means that (a) doctors will be paid to write the prescriptions and (b) only certain authorized pharmaceutical companies will be able to manufacture the pills. Is the FDA *really* concerned that we're all taking too much vitamin C?

The FDA does not, by the way, sit quietly in Washington rubber-stamping its approval or disapproval on various proposals. It has its own army of armed agents who—augmented by state and local law enforcement authorities—make raids. For example, here is how Saul Kant, Director of the Life Extension Institute, described a typical FDA raid:

> On February 26, 1987, an armed force of about 25 FDA agents, U.S. marshals, and members of the Hollywood, Florida police department smashed down the glass doors of our store at 2835 Hollywood Boulevard, and stormed into our nearby warehouse with guns drawn. As Bill Feloon, the vice president of the Foundation, was trying to leave the warehouse to find out what was going on at the building, he suddenly found himself staring down the barrel of a .45 caliber pistol, which belonged to a member of a second group of FDA agents, U.S. marshals, and police officers, who were simultaneously attacking the warehouse.

The FDA can, overnight, put a small nutritional supplement manufacturer like the Life Extension Institute out of business.

⚖️ ⚖️ ⚖️

To say that the FDA sometimes overreacts is an understatement. When some truly despicable person laced Tylenol with cyanide in 1982, resulting in seven deaths, guess what the FDA did? Every time you open a bottle or a package of practically *anything,* you have your answer: tamper-resistant packaging. Notice it's called tamper-*resistant* packaging and not tamper*proof* packaging. That's because *no* packaging is truly tamper*proof.* Any deranged person with a hypodermic needle can poison any product wrapped in plastic, paper, or cellophane. To make the food and drug supply truly tamper*proof* would require metal and glass packaging for *everything* from candy bars to loaves of bread to boxes of cereal.

Nonetheless, the FDA requires certain tamper-resistant packaging on certain consumable products. How much time do you spend each day removing tamper-resistant packaging? If it's only a minute a day, over 70 years of package opening, you will have wasted 425 hours thanks to FDA overreaction. More than 17 *days* (and these are 24-hour days) of your life will be spent complying with an FDA regulation which fails to "solve" a problem we don't even have.

"Well," one might protest, "since that time we haven't had any cyanide in our Tylenol." Yes, and how much cyanide did we have in our Tylenol *before* the restrictions? Fortunately, whoever was insane enough to do it in the first place stopped doing it. Voluntarily. And, thank God, there have been few "copycat" occurrences. But this had nothing to do with tamper-resistant packaging. As previously noted, the vast majority of our packaging is outrageously tamperable. If some nut wanted to randomly poison innocent people, he or she still could.

⚖ ⚖ ⚖

It is our right to seek the health care we choose. Whether it's taking drugs not yet approved by the FDA, visiting "unorthodox" healers (from chiropractors to acupuncturists to witch doctors to faith healers to prayer therapists), purchasing health machinery (did you know you can't buy *oxygen*—or even plastic tubing used to *transport* oxygen—without a prescription?), or anything else that does not physically harm the person or property of another, it ain't the FDA's business if we do. (But, FDA, *please* keep the rat droppings and insect parts in my frozen pizzas down to an absolute minimum!)

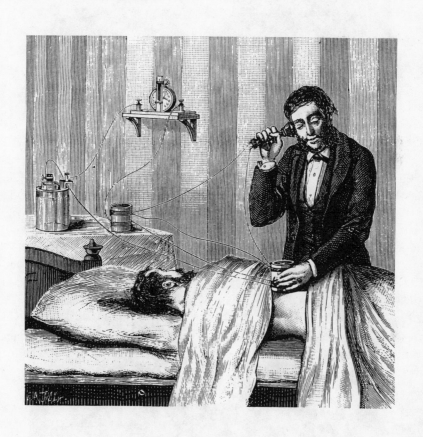

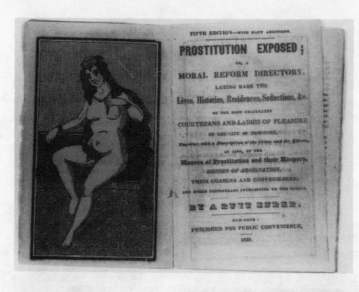

Prostitution

LET'S FACE IT: we're all whores. We've all done things we wouldn't have done if it weren't for the money. We've all worshiped at the shrine clearly labeled "In God We Trust." We've all done something with our bodies we wouldn't have done if we hadn't been getting paid for it.

We do things every day that we wouldn't do if we had a million dollars, or ten million dollars, or a hundred million dollars, or a billion dollars.* When we reach the point of having so much money we no longer have to put out, we start buying. We become the procurer, the customer, the john. But please don't be upset—we're all in good company:

I'm a whore. All actors are whores. We sell our bodies to the highest bidder. —*William Holden*

I do everything for a reason. Most of the time the reason is money.—*Suzy Parker*

People think I sit here and push buttons and get things accomplished. Well, I spent today kissing behinds.—*Harry S. Truman*

I did it for the loot, honey, always the loot.—*Ava Gardner*

I went into the business for the money, and the art grew out of it. If people are disillusioned by that remark, I can't help it. It's the truth.—*Charlie Chaplin*

I've been in trouble most of my life; I've done the most unutterable rubbish, all because of money. I didn't need it . . . the lure of the zeros was simply too great.—*Richard Burton*

---

*The difference between a million dollars and a billion dollars is that a million dollars is a stack of $100 bills . . . wait—I've said that already. Twice.

> *I'm a marvelous housekeeper.*
> *Every time I leave a man,*
> *I keep his house.*
>
> ZSA ZSA GABOR

Sometimes I feel like an old hooker.
—*Cher*

That place [Disneyland] is my baby, and I would prostitute myself for it.—*Walt Disney*

Sometimes at the end of the day when I'm smiling and shaking hands, I want to kick them.—*Richard Nixon*

I am never quite sure if I am one of the cinema's elder statesmen or just the oldest whore on the boat.—*Joseph L. Mankiewicz*

The only reason I'm in Hollywood is that I don't have the moral courage to refuse the money.—*Marlon Brando*

I made appearances at cocktail parties in Florida for $500 a pop, pretending to be an old friend of the host.—*Mickey Rooney*

I'd love to sell out completely. It's just that nobody has been willing to buy.—*John Waters*

"Well," some might protest, "they're not talking about *sex* there."

Okay: let's talk about sex.

First, let's accept that, in prostitution, there's no difference between buyer and seller. Culturally we are conditioned that the seller (the prostitute) is degraded and the buyer (the customer) is a mere adventurer. Logically, however, if one of them *must* be seen as self-degraded, it would have to be the customer. One who has to *buy* sex is in a sadder situation than one who is simply filling an economic necessity.

I, however, would prefer to view prostitution as a purely economic exchange, inherently no more or less degrading than any other professional relationship for either buyer or seller. The same arguments against prostitution—either buying or selling—could be made against any professional service: psychologist, psychiatrist, doctor, lawyer, priest, minister—you name it.

"You mean you *sell* your knowledge of God?"

"Well, not exactly, I, well . . ."

"Do you get paid for it?"

"Well, I do get a salary, yes. A small stipend."

"Do you have to do any manual labor; I mean, do you have to landscape the grounds or sweep out the church or anything?"

"No, but I do have other duties."

"Such as?"

"I counsel people, I have administrative duties in the church, I perform marriage ceremonies . . ."

"You get *paid* to officiate in the spiritual union of two human beings? Do you do *anything* in your job in which you are not the representative of God?"

"Well, there is the administrative work."

"Do you have training in administration?"

"No. Part of my pastoral duties is running the church."

"But you don't have a degree in administration."

"No, my degree is in Divinity."

"So, you sell Divinity."

"Well, if you put it that way—you know, you're really distorting this whole thing."

> *Losing my virginity*
> *was a career move.*
>
> MADONNA

Yes, it *is* a distorted way of looking at it. It is, however, the same distortion people apply to prostitution. Some people become prostitutes because they like it; others become prostitutes because they feel they are providing a service; many people become prostitutes because—all things considered—it's the best job they could get. Other than the unjustified cultural taboos against it, prostitution is no more degrading than any other job, and, in talking with prostitutes, one discovers that many find prostitution less degrading than other jobs.

"I make good money. That's why I do it," commented one prostitute; "if I worked at McDonald's for minimum wage, then I'd have low self-esteem."

One of the myths about prostitution is that it is full of drugged-out, washed-out, otherwise worthless men and women. This is not the case. "I find that the women, generally, are ambitious, clever, intelligent, gregarious, and usually like people," says Margo St. James, founder of C.O.Y.O.T.E., the organization for prostitutes' rights. C.O.Y.O.T.E. stands for Call Off Your Old Tired Ethics. "The profession itself is not abusive; it's the illegality; it's the humiliation and degradation that is dealt to them at the hands of the police."

Norma Jean Almodovar agrees, and she knows whereof she speaks: Ms. Almodovar was a Los Angeles police officer for ten years and, tired of the corruption and *genuinely* immoral acts she was asked to condone daily, she quit and became a prostitute. For this affront, she was targeted by the police, entrapped, arrested, and jailed. If a prostitute went on to become a police officer, her friends would probably throw her a party. When a police officer became a prostitute, however, the police considered it a personal insult and felt they had to do something about it. Ms. Almodovar's story is told in her 1993 book, *Cop to Call Girl: Why I Left the LAPD to Make an Honest Living as a Beverly Hills Prostitute.* In her book, she gives her views on whether or not prostitution is degrading:

> That really depends on the individual involved or how one views sex. It was not degrading to me because I think that sex is a positive, nurturing act, and whether it is given out of love or rendered as a service, as long as it is consensual it is still positive.

> *It is a silly question to ask a prostitute why she does it. These are the highest-paid "professional" women in America.*
>
> GAIL SHEEHY

On a scale of the pain or pleasure human beings can inflict on each other, if murder, rape, and torture are the worst, certainly giving another person an orgasm must be among the best. I cannot fathom how one could think that making another human being feel good for a fee could be degrading or demeaning unless it is degrading to make other people feel good.

If the reason society continues to arrest men and women who engage in prostitution is that it is degrading, then perhaps someone could explain how going to jail, being strip-searched, checked for lice, and asked to undress in front of dozens of insensitive guards and inmates somehow resolves this problem. Jail and prison were degrading to me, not prostitution.

When asked if prostitution is immoral, Ms. Almodovar replied,

> Morality is the belief of the person. I don't consider it immoral. Everyone who works "sells" one or more parts of his or her body. Athletes, actors, actresses, and construction workers "sell" their body. The body is what is needed to engage in physical work. It would be difficult to engage in any profession without the use and therefore "sale" of one's body.
>
> Perhaps because the genitalia is involved, people object to prostitution. In a free society people should be able to engage in behavior that others find immoral or objectionable as long as no force or fraud is involved. As an adult I feel confident that I can make my own moral judgments. For me it is not immoral to make other people feel good in a sexual way and receive payment for providing the service.

People are often surprised to learn that many prostitutes actually *enjoy* their work. Like all professionals who feel they are filling a need, prostitutes can feel a profound psychological satisfaction. Here is what Barbara, a Los Angeles prostitute, had to say:

> I derive a great deal of satisfaction knowing that I'm turning some guy on, more than he's ever been turned on in his life. And I know I'm turning him on more than his wife. That's not that difficult to do, because the average American housewife, from what I've been able to tell through the husband, most definitely is not very adept. Most of them have this typical Anglo-Saxon–American guilt complex, and use sex as a tool against their husbands. They definitely don't know how to give pleasure to their husband.*

---

*The same can certainly be said about men by women, which, perhaps, is the reason the number of male prostitutes is growing.

Which brings us to the question, "Why do people visit prostitutes?" First, we must accept that sex and the desire to be lovingly touched are human needs. (If not a need, after enough time they're certainly high on the list of "wants.") As such, it's like eating—although sexual needs usually do not need to be fulfilled as often as the need to eat. Those who are not having their sexual needs fulfilled in other areas of their lives tend to go to prostitutes; just as those who don't cook—or have someone to cook for them—sometimes buy prepared food or go to restaurants.

From a simple beginnin',
just see how her sinnin' has paid.
She's the picture of happiness
now that she's mastered a trade.

SHELDON HARNICK

Sex always involves some sort of *trade*. Those who are attractive enough trade (exchange) their attractiveness with other people; their attractiveness is the coin with which they pay for sex. Some people have a good personality; they trade charm for sex. Others spend time with and do things for the people (or person) they have sex with. Some people trade the exclusivity of their emotional affection, tenderness and care. The list of what people "spend" in order to have sexual and sensual needs fulfilled is a long one.

Those who are too busy, not very attractive, too shy, or who simply don't want to be bothered with "the dating game" sometimes visit prostitutes. People also visit prostitutes because they want a "walk on the wild side"; some have a specific sexual fantasy they would like fulfilled. (Here, I am not necessarily talking about outrageously kinky things: many men, for example, visit prostitutes simply to receive oral sex.) There is no more need to pity or censure someone who visits prostitutes than there is to pity someone who doesn't always get home-cooked meals. Perhaps the person doesn't want all that comes with those home-cooked meals; it just isn't worth it. Perhaps the person hasn't found someone who wants to stay home and cook his or her meals. Or perhaps the person is simply tired of home-cooked meals and wants a little variety.

Some people are hypocritical about their purchase of sex: they know their interest in another is primarily sexual, and will "buy" that person with candy, flowers, dinners, shows, concerts, and, perhaps, a few words of affection. They might even pay for sex by using that famous word, *love*.

People on the receiving end of this deception are sometimes deceived—but often, they're playing the game too. They want the attention, flattery, companionship, and experiences ("I haven't been to that new restaurant, have you?"), and are willing to trade sex for those (provided, of course, they feel loved—or at least *liked*).

⚖️ ⚖️ ⚖️

There are two reasons prostitution is so despised in our culture: hatred of women and the taboos against paganism. As we explored earlier, in ancient times

> *Lawyers and tarts are the two*
> *oldest professions in the world.*
> *And we always aim to please.*
>
> HORACE RUMPOLE

women were valued for either domestic abilities (having children, raising children, keeping house, making clothes, cooking food) or entertainment (sex, pleasant talk, sex, dancing, sex, and sex). As women were not viewed as *human beings* but as necessary (and often troublesome) means to an end, a split developed in which women were seen by the roles that they fulfilled. This evolved into what we call today the "madonna/whore complex." A woman is either put on a pedestal, protected, taken care of, seen as "the mother of my children and the light of my life"; or she is to be used for sex, emotionally and perhaps physically abused, and seen as really nothing more than "a slut." In the minds of many men, women must fall into one of these two categories. One seldom goes from the whore category to the madonna category, but the slide from madonna to whore (at least in the eyes of the man) is fairly common.

This degrading view of women, combined with man's belief in his innate superiority, produces an inbuilt hostility to women who *charge* for sex. To the sexist male this is like a cat charging to be petted: it seems to be a defilement of the natural order. In ancient times, however, one of the very few bargaining tools women had was sex, and, of course, they used it. Men resented women for this, persecuted them further, and the separation became broader and deeper.

In the ancient Judaic culture, the only woman of independence was the prostitute. No other trades were open to women. All professions were filled by men. Everything was owned by men. The only valuable commodity a woman had was her body and her charm. Women became whores because they didn't want to prostitute themselves to one man in marriage. Prostitution was considered not only against the "natural" order of things; it was also a *sacrilege*. While it was against religious law (certainly in ancient Judaism), what men really resented about prostitution was the *independence*. Prostitutes, then, were the lowest of the low, although in many cases they were the only women who had any degree of freedom whatsoever.

In pagan cultures, however, women could aspire to a very different profession: temple (or sacred) prostitute. Pagans believed that physical pleasure signified the presence of the gods. Sexual pleasure—among the greatest of physical pleasures—was one of the gods' greatest gifts. Not only was sex pleasurable; it was also essential to fertility and, in agrarian cultures, fertility was life. The fertile ground gave of its crops; the fertile livestock gave of their young; the fertile trees gave of their fruit. Human fertility was necessary for the propagation of the species. Everything was viewed in sexual terms: the rain falling on the receptive earth, the seed planted in the receptive ground, the net thrown into the receptive sea.

In this system, the feminine (receptive) quality was not just appreciated; it was worshiped. The temple prostitute—whether female or male*—developed this quality to an art. (Or, at least, to a level of professional excellence.) Yes, the male had the seed, but what good was that alone? A thousand seeds might make a single meal. Planted in fertile ground, however, a thousand seeds become a harvest; a field of abundance.

*After I die,
I shall return to earth as
a gatekeeper of a bordello
and I won't let any of you enter.*

ARTURO TOSCANINI
to the NBC Orchestra

The temple prostitute performed many functions. She was the High Priestess (or he was the High Priest) of the temple. She or he would make offerings to the goddess or god of the temple, explore erotic visual delights through dance, play music, write and recite poetry, prepare sumptuous food, and concoct potions of love. The temple prostitute was, of course, also well trained in the arts of massage, touch, and erotic stimulation.

Sex was a sacrament; orgasm, a religious experience. The community respected and revered the sacred prostitute as much as any priest or priestess. Prostitution was a high calling, an honorable and exalted position.

In our Judeo-Christian heritage, however, paganism simply did not fit. In the Old Testament, there was *one God;* that God was a *man,* and demanded obedience, not orgasm. The temple prostitute was a sign of civilization, of refinement. Upon leaving Egypt (where there were lots of temples and lots of prostitutes), however, the Israelite became a nomadic tribe of warriors. Nomads and warriors are not famous for temples and civilization. Even the sacred place that housed the ark of the covenant was the *tent* of meeting—not a building. No, for the Jews to wander in the desert for forty years and be successful warriors, all this pagan frivolity had to go. Among the most popular of the pagan frivolities—not surprisingly—was the temple prostitute.**

In the New Testament, as we have explored, Paul (in particular) denounced pagan practices at every opportunity.*** Paul speaks specifically against the tem-

---

*As we shall see in the "Homosexuality" chapter, the ancient world was not divided into homosexuals and heterosexuals, but active and passive. Men could be temple prostitutes as easily as women, and often were.

**When the nation of Israel finally settled down, civilization and its frivolities returned—up to a point. Some of the songs of David (Psalms) and the song of Solomon (Song of Songs) could have been written to, by, or about sacred prostitutes. These songs were certainly more pagan than puritan in content.

***Some pagan practices did survive, however: the actual date of Christmas has nothing to do with the birthdate of Jesus, but was the pagan celebration of the winter solstice. The pagans-turned-Christians simply refused to give up that celebration, so the Christian fathers, wisely, declared it Jesus' birthday celebration, and the festivities continue annually to this day.

> *Women were in such short supply in Louisiana in 1721 that the government of France shipped twenty-five prostitutes to the colony. By this action the government hoped to lure Canadian settlers away from Indian mistresses.*
>
> ONE NIGHT STANDS
> WITH AMERICAN HISTORY

ple prostitutes, not prostitution in general. It was not simple sex, however, that Paul opposed, but the violent human sacrifices and mutilations that he called "immoral." The kinkiest consensual sex of today is awfully vanilla when compared to some pagan rituals.

⚖ ⚖ ⚖

Prostitution, of course, continued through the centuries, and only became a serious civil problem with the outbreak of syphilis in the 1500s. Everyone knew that syphilis was spread by sex, but no one knew how to prevent the disease. The solution, then, was to ban prostitution (and casual sex in general), as a health measure.

Many claim that there is a parallel today with AIDS. The difference between AIDS and syphilis, of course, is that we now know how to reduce the risk of spreading AIDS. ("If you have sex, use a condom.") Sex being their profession, prostitutes are better versed in the prevention of sexually transmitted diseases than the average "amateur." Just as doctors, dentists, and other healthcare workers routinely put on rubber gloves for standard medical procedures, so, too, do prostitutes routinely insist the customers wear condoms. Most prostitutes, in fact, have techniques for applying condoms that are nonobtrusive and erotic.

In study after study, prostitutes who are not intravenous drug users have a lower rate of HIV infection than the general population. Prostitutes do not spread AIDS, any more than drug use spreads AIDS. What spreads AIDS is unsafe sex and the use of contaminated needles. When the purchase of sex is legalized and the use of drugs is legalized, both of these transmission routes will be almost completely eliminated. Where prostitution is legal, prostitutes are professionals. They know how to protect themselves and their clients. For example, a study of 535 prostitutes working in legal Nevada brothels showed that *none* of them was infected with HIV. Prostitutes also show a lower incidence than the general public of all other sexually transmitted diseases as well. Prostitutes also know how to (discreetly) examine a client for signs of other sexually transmitted diseases. They know what herpes sores look like, for example, and are not going to fall for the I-just-caught-it-in-my-zipper deception that some men try to use in a moment of passion. Prostitutes also know how to satisfy their clients in safe ways even if the client *does* have a sexually transmitted disease. (Masturbation, for example, can be very erotic and very safe.)

It is unsafe sex that spreads AIDS and other sexually transmitted diseases, and unsafe sex can only be eliminated through education, not by prohibiting prostitution.

⚖️ ⚖️ ⚖️

Prostitution is not disgusting, but what's happening today *in connection with* prostitution is. In several cities, the names of men arrested for soliciting prostitutes are published in the newspaper. These men have not been *convicted*, mind you—just arrested. Some cities send letters to wives and employers. Spurred by the laws, vigilante groups of moralists have formed. One group writes down license numbers of cars driving in areas known for prostitution, gets the owner's address from the department of motor vehicles (which cooperates in this "effort"), and calls the wives and employers telling them drivers were seen "looking for prostitutes." Some cities use the assets forfeiture laws and confiscate cars—permanently—even for a first offense.

> *Remove prostitutes from human affairs, and you will destroy everything with lust.*
>
> ST. AUGUSTINE

It's obscene.

The police are thoroughly corrupted by the techniques they must use in order to enforce the laws against prostitution. According to the *Washington Post*,

> The police engage in substantial perjury to avoid the charge of entrapment and to obtain sufficient evidence for conviction "beyond a reasonable doubt." And perhaps even more upsetting, the police often must suppress their best evidence because they cannot admit having sex with the prostitute before the arrest.

The illegality of prostitution also creates an unsafe environment for the women. Those who object to prostitution because they find that it "degrades women" should realize that the women who take part in prostitution may or may not be degraded by the job, but are *certainly* degraded by the rape and other violence that can take place because prostitutes must ply their trade in clandestine ways and in clandestine places. Further, these rapes and other acts of violence against prostitutes are seldom if ever reported to the police. If they are, the police dismiss them with a comment, "That's part of the game. If you don't want it, don't be a hooker," or simply respond, "You can't rape a whore."

As with all consensual crimes, arresting women for prostitution sets them on a life of crime. As Margo St. James describes,

> 70% of all women who are in jail today were first arrested for prostitution. When a woman is charged for a sex crime, it's a stigma that lasts her lifetime, and it makes her unemployable.

⚖️ ⚖️ ⚖️

Like entering any other profession, becoming a prostitute is a choice. Exercising free choice of professions is certainly guaranteed to us by the Constitution

> *Prisons are built*
> *with stones of Law,*
> *Brothels with bricks of Religion.*
>
> WILLIAM BLAKE

and the Bill of Rights, as long as the profession we choose doesn't harm the person or property of a nonconsenting other. We may not treat "sex workers" (as some prostitutes prefer to be called) with the reverence that once was given the sacred prostitute, but sexual professionals are entitled to the respect, protection against violence, and freedom to make a living that anyone else has.

Pornography, Obscenity, Etc.

<table>
<tr><td>

JACK PAAR:

*What do you think about
pornography?*

OSCAR LEVANT:

It helps.

</td></tr>
</table>

CENSORSHIP APPLIES TO basically three subjects: (1) Sex, (2) Violence, and (3) Ideas. Of the three, censorship of ideas is by far the most serious. It is also, by far, the most subtle.

A major motivation behind censorship is *paternalism.* "You are not able to deal with this information," the censor says; "therefore—for your own protection—we will keep it from you." The variation on that, of course, is *"You and I* will not be corrupted by this, but *they*—those poor uneducated, unsophisticated, unwashed masses—will not be able to handle it, so, for their own good and the good of society, we'll ban it."

The other major motivation—far more pernicious—is to *protect power.* Here, someone or some group with power decides, "If this information got out, it might prove damaging to my (our) power, so I'd (we'd) better suppress it." What usually follows that statement is a long list of justifications—if the justifications didn't precede it—which generally run along the lines of, "It's not true anyway," "This is distorted and will confuse people," "The people saying this have ulterior motives," "This is inflammatory," "This is un-American," and so on.

All censorship is a violation of the First Amendment:

> Congress shall make no law respecting an establishment of religion, or
> prohibiting the free exercise thereof; or abridging the freedom of speech,
> or of the press; or the right of the people peaceably to assemble, and to
> petition the Government for a redress of grievances.

It was a brilliant move for the founding fathers to put all of these guarantees together in one amendment. Almost all censorship is based on the religious and/ or political beliefs of those in power. The bottom-line justification for censorship

> *If the First Amendment means anything, it means that a state has no business telling a man, sitting alone in his own house, what books he may read or what films he may watch.*
>
> JUSTICE THURGOOD MARSHALL
> *From a unanimous Supreme Court decision, 1969*

is invariably (a) "It's immoral!" (meaning, of course, against their religious beliefs), and/or (b) "It's un-American!" (which means it doesn't agree with their view about the kind of government America should have and the way that government should be run). Most censorship violates our First Amendment rights to (a) freedom of and from religion and (b) "petition the government for a redress of grievances." Even if the "freedom of speech, or of the press" clause were not in there, applying the remainder of the First Amendment would eliminate almost all censorship as we know it.

But just in case the primary justification for all censorship—that is, religious and political suppression—was missed, the founding fathers added the freedom of speech and press clause: "Congress shall make no law . . . abridging the freedom of speech, or of the press." As I've asked before, what could be clearer than that? The only limitation on this freedom is, as always, directly threatening the person or property of innocent people with physical harm. Supreme Court Justice Oliver Wendell Holmes expressed this in his famous example from 1919:

> The most stringent protection of free speech would not protect a man in falsely shouting fire in a theatre and causing a panic. [The] question in every case is whether the words used are used in such circumstances and are of such a nature as to create a clear and present danger that they will bring about the substantive evils that Congress has a right to prevent.

One could not, then, in supervising the demolition of a building, give the order, "Blow it up," knowing that there still were people inside. The willful murder of those people cannot be protected by saying, "Well, I was just exercising my right of free speech." Unfortunately, over the years, the "clear and present danger" of "substantive evils" that Justice Holmes gave as exceptions to the First Amendment rights have been interpreted beyond his obvious physical example of knowingly starting a panic in a public theater by yelling "Fire!" The "clear and present danger" has been interpreted as a potential danger to our national *morality*—and we've already established the source of most "morality."

In 1991, for example, the Supreme Court decided that nude dancing by performers in a Las Vegas bar was *not* protected by the First Amendment. This dancing, the Court held, was on the level of shouting "Fire!" in a crowded theater. How far *backward* we have gone from '19 to '91. This is considered a landmark decision. As Stanford University law professor Gerald Gunther explained,

> The court is saying that public morality trumps legitimate rights of expression. That's never happened before.

In the past, one had to define the "clear and present danger" by comparing whether or not the censored material would potentially cause the same physical harm as shouting, "Fire!" in a crowded theater. Now, the "clear and present danger" need only be as potentially harmful as consenting adults dancing nude in front of other consenting adults, in a bar—*in Las Vegas*. What a wonderful gift the Supreme Court gave us in 1991 to celebrate the 200th birthday of the passage of the Bill of Rights.

> *Fear of serious injury cannot alone justify suppression of free speech and assembly. . . . It is the function of speech to free men from the bondage of irrational fears.*
>
> LOUIS BRANDEIS

⚖ ⚖ ⚖

I'll explore the censorship of political ideas more fully in the chapter, "Unpopular Political Views." For now, let me turn to the two other favorites of censorship: sex and violence.

With censorship, we find another conservative-liberal division over which activity justifies "bending" the First Amendment. When either side wants to censor, conservatives usually want to censor the sexual; liberals generally want to censor violence. Neither camp uses the word *censor*—they use words such as *curb, protect, control, modify, limit,* and so on.

Might I remind both camps that *any* "abridging" is a violation of the First Amendment?

⚖ ⚖ ⚖

The Problem with Pornography

The problem with pornography is that it is done so *poorly*. "There is no such thing as a moral or an immoral book," said Oscar Wilde more than one hundred years ago. "Books are well written, or badly written. That is all." Nothing much has changed since then. In 1993, Calvin Tomkins wrote in the *New Yorker:*

> Of all the minor art forms, pornography has remained the least developed. Certified pornographic masterworks, from Sappho to Nabokov, can be counted on the fingers of one hand. The best-known critical theorists of the form, from Anthony Comstock to Jesse Helms, have had the disadvantage of being morons. The National Endowment for the Arts supports pornographic experiment unwillingly, at best, and our popular culture contents itself with unimaginative increases in the gross annual depiction of bare skin and earnest copulation.

Violence has its artists—Sam Peckinpah, Francis Ford Coppola, Ridley Scott. Where are pornography's artists? Twenty years ago, *Deep Throat* got publicity just because it had *a plot*. What have we got today? Mapplethorpe and Madonna?

Once upon a time, some of our best artists gave us our erotica. Today the Bible is used as a reason to censor. Not long ago, it was used as a method to *avoid* the censor.

Michelangelo was able to do a magnificent male nude statue by calling it "David" (the model's real name was probably something closer to Tadzio). Michelangelo was also able to place a reclining male nude in the very center of the ceiling of the Sistine Chapel (the pope's personal chapel, for heaven's sake) by calling it "Adam."

Gustave Doré (1832–1883), who had a taste for subjects not acceptable in his own time (although his obvious love for sex and violence would be right at home in our time), was able to create some of the most bizarre art of the nineteenth century simply by illustrating Bible stories. Because he had the good sense to call his etchings, "The Deluge" and "Jehu's Companions Finding the Remains of Jezebel," his work was welcomed in the same Victorian parlors and praised by the same Victorian social leaders who probably would have put him in jail if he had accurately entitled his etchings, "Naked Man, Naked Woman, and Four Naked Children Writhing in the Water and on a Wet Rock" and "Selected Body Parts of an Attractive Young Woman Being Examined by Four Men Prior to Being Eaten by Dogs." Because he was clever, however, *Doré's Bible* became so popular many people assumed that he wrote the text, too.

"I don't think pornography is very harmful," Sir Noel Coward summed it up in 1972, "but it is terribly, terribly boring."

In 1967, Congress established and funded a National Commission on Pornography. Its report, published in 1970, found that it was not *pornography*, but the puritanical attitudes *toward* pornography that cause problems in America. The report said the problems stemmed "from the inability or reluctance of people in our society to be open and direct in dealing with sexual matters." In surveys, the commission found that only 2% of Americans thought sexually explicit material was a significant social problem. The report recommended that all legislation interfering with the right of adults to read, obtain, or view explicit sexual material be repealed.

The findings of this exhaustive study did not happen to fit the personal morals of Washington's power structure—from President Nixon on down. Nothing was done about repealing the laws.

When President Reagan put together another commission to study pornography, he did it *right—extreme* right. Attorney General Edwin Meese carefully selected eleven God-fearing (and, apparently, *sex-fearing*) Americans. One of the Meese Commission members was James C. Dobson, who wrote:

That is what the pornographers are doing to my country. They are hammering down the supporting columns and blasting away the foundations. We must stop the devastation before the entire superstructure crashes to the earth! With the diligent prayers and personal involvement of God-fearing people, we can save the great edifice called America. But there is not a minute to lose. "But each one is tempted when he is carried away and enticed by his own lust. Then when lust has conceived, it gives birth to sin; and when sin is accomplished, it brings forth death." (James 1:14–16, NASB) [italics in original]

> *Whenever*
> *they burn books,*
> *they will also,*
> *in the end,*
> *burn people.*
>
> HEINRICH HEINE

Is there any doubt where his personal sense of morality comes from? And does the rhetoric sound familiar? It is part of what Donna A. Demac, in her book, *Liberty Denied: The Current Rise of Censorship in America,* calls (quoting Hugh Hefner) "sexual McCarthyism":

> The antipornography movement of the 1980s represents yet another attempt by certain groups to impose their morals on the rest of society. What makes these efforts more threatening than those of the past is the extent to which they have been abetted by federal, state, and local authorities. The climate engendered by initiatives such as the Meese Commission has been described with only a bit of hyperbole by Hugh Hefner as "sexual McCarthyism."

The Problem with Violence

The problem with violence is that it is not violent enough. According to the National Coalition on Television Violence, by the age of eighteen, the average American will have seen 250,000 acts of violence and 40,000 attempted murders on television. And yet, how realistic will they be? Not very. When people are shot on TV, they grab the part of their body that is shot, fall over (if they are *severely* hurt), and continue with the written dialog. The dialog usually includes an obligatory "Ow" or "Ouch" or "Ahh" and then adds such stellar commentary (which *must* be a holdover from radio) as, "Why did you shoot me?" "My arm! [leg! chest! head!]" and the classic "I've been shot!" No matter how much dialog the victims have or how long it takes for the paramedics to arrive, we see very little blood. We seldom even see holes in clothing, and almost never see holes in flesh.

In real life, when someone is shot, he or she goes into shock. Blood is—to put it mildly—abundant. Shock is not pretty: pasty face, severe trembling, eyes rolling toward the back of the head. Coherent dialog seldom passes the lips, but dinner frequently does—on the way out. Vomiting often accompanies shock. [CAUTION: The next two paragraphs are going to get a little graphic. Skip them if you want

> *People want to know why I do this,*
> *why I write such gross stuff.*
> *I like to tell them*
> *I have the heart of a small boy—*
> *and I keep it in a jar on my desk.*
>
> STEPHEN KING

to avoid explicit descriptions of violence. Now that I have your complete attention, I'll continue.]

Even movies famous for violence are not allowed to go as far as real life. In *The Godfather, Part III*, for example, one of the villains is killed by being stabbed in the throat with his own eyeglasses. As originally filmed, the character coughed and sprayed large quantities of blood from his mouth. In order to avoid an X rating, however, the scene had to be re-shot, sans spraying.

In *The Godfather, Part II*, when the Godfather (played by Robert DeNiro) becomes the Godfather by committing his first murder, he sticks the revolver in the mouth of his victim and, bang. In the movie, we see a little bit of brain and blood splatter on the door behind him. The scene was shot for television sans splattering. In fact, even the movie version was incredibly tame. The *AMOK Assault Video* contains a news clip that was too graphic even for the evening news (if you can imagine that). It showed a politician who had been caught with his hand in the cookie jar. He called a press conference. There he proclaimed his innocence, protested the unfairness of his persecution, pulled out a .357 Magnum, put it in his mouth, and pulled the trigger. What the camera captured then is certainly enough to convince anyone *not* to play with firearms—or enter politics. After his head exploded (a look at the Zapruder film in the movie *JFK* will give you an idea), blood *poured* from his nose and mouth. Although he was clearly dead, the blood kept gushing. We didn't see this in *The Godfather, Part II.**

The other myth perpetrated in television and movies is how little people bruise and how quickly they heal. The day after a severe beating, the hero has a few red marks, a little white tape, and that's about it. In real life, he'd look *terrible.* Two days after a beating, in the movie, he's fine. In real life, two days after a beating you look *worse* than you did the day after the beating.

All of this sanitized violence only makes real violence a more acceptable solution to problems. It's not that violence is shown, and that causes violence; it's that violence is shown as the *solution* to problems; *that* causes violence. "A single death is a tragedy, a million deaths is a statistic," said Joseph Stalin (who should know). If, however, the way in which each of those million died and the suffering they went through had to be viewed one at a time in great detail, perhaps it would no longer be a statistic, and perhaps such tragedies would happen less often.

Portraying violence in all its gory would probably have these positive effects:

---

*A friend told me that, when he was a boy, his father committed suicide with a shotgun. "What did you do?" I asked. "What could we do?" my friend replied. "We painted the room and we moved."

1. Far fewer people would watch violent programs. In television, people vote with their remotes. In magazines, movies, and newspapers, they vote with their purchase. If enough people vote no, fewer violent acts would be depicted.

2. People would be less likely to take part in violence. In your own home, you'd be less likely to shoot someone because you wouldn't want all that blood, vomit, and other internal fluids on your floor (wall, ceiling, couch, fish tank, etc.). You would also assiduously avoid situations where violent harm to your own person was remotely possible. One California judge sentences teenage drunk driving offenders to witness an autopsy of a traffic fatality caused by a drunk driver. It's been remarkably effective. Such a cold, forensic reality of violence would remove any sense of glamour from either hurting or being hurt. It's the human equivalent of the idea, "If each person had to kill his or her own dinner, there would be a lot more vegetarians."

> *After seeing <u>Rambo</u> last night I know what to do next time this happens.*
>
> PRESIDENT RONALD REAGAN
> *following the hijack of an airplane carrying American passengers*
> *1985*

⚖️ ⚖️ ⚖️

The Problem with Censorship

The problem with censorship can be summed up in two words: *who decides?*

If someone other than the end consumers—voting with their purchases, attendance, or remote controls—decides what should or should not, can or cannot, must or must not be said, depicted, or offered for sale, who should that person be? And who decides who that person should be? And who decides if those people are doing a good job deciding? Ultimately, censorship comes down to *taste*. What offends me may enlighten you. Do you want *me* deciding—based on my taste and construct of morality—what *you* should or should not be exposed to?

Most censors don't stop at what offends them, of course: their overheated imaginations begin conjuring up what might offend this person or that group, and pretty soon *everything* is "pornographic." Many start sounding like Mervyn Griffiths-Jones, the prosecuting attorney in the 1960 trial to keep *Lady Chatterly's Lover* banned:

> You may think one of the ways in which you can test this book is to ask yourself the question: would you approve of your own son and daughter, because girls can read as well as boys, reading this book? Is it a book you could have lying in your own house? Is it a book you would wish your wife or your servant to read?

So much of what we'd want to censor depends on where we stand, what we're standing on, and whom we're standing with—rather than simply what we can't stand. Shelley Winters, tongue well in cheek, pointed out,

> I think nudity on the stage is disgusting, shameful and unpatriotic. But if I were twenty-two with a great body, it would be artistic, tasteful, patriotic and a progressive, religious experience.

In addition, besides deciding what's good and what's bad, who decides what the punishment should be for violating these standards? For example, consider this comment from a young artist:

> Anybody who sees and paints a sky green and pastures blue ought to be sterilized.

This may seem to be a trivial, even silly, comment for a young artist to make, but what if this young artist sets aside his art and turns to the art of politics? What if he gains enough power to fulfill not only his censorship dreams, but to inflict the punishments he finds appropriate? Well, that's precisely what happened. The artist-turned-politician who detested green skies and blue pastures had tens of thousands sterilized, and presided over the most sterile artistic period in the history of Europe—and these were the least of his crimes. As I'm sure you've guessed, the censor was Adolph Hitler. Which brings us to the F-WORD.

The F-WORD

In our use of language, we go beyond the hypocritical directly into the silly. When I say, "F-WORD," you know precisely which word I mean. Isn't it silly, though, that if I actually *use* that word, I would be unnecesarily giving ammunition to those who want to attack this book not for its *ideas*, but for the use of a single word.

As a writer, I don't mind that the F-WORD is taboo. Being taboo gives it extra power. It's good that certain words have the power that only complete prohibition can provide.

In the film *Mommy Dearest*, Joan Crawford meets with the Board of Pepsi Cola, who think they have the better of her. She drops the demure and dignified act long enough to deliver the line, "Don't [F-WORD] with me, fellas: this ain't my first time at the rodeo." The line is most effective.

When Walt Disney Productions decided to make non-children's films (I can't say "adult films," because that has other connotations), they started Touchstone Pictures. Touchstone had a rule: only two F-WORDS per picture. That was fine. The creators carefully selected the two points in the film where the F-WORD would have the most impact.

Having a few words forbidden allows for creative people to be even more

> *I am mortified to be told that, in the United States of America, the sale of a book can become a subject of inquiry, and of criminal inquiry too.*
>
> THOMAS JEFFERSON

delightfully creative. Woody Allen, for example:

> Some guy hit my fender the other day, and I said unto him, "Be fruitful, and multiply." But not in those words.

Or, Dorothy Parker:

> Ducking for apples—change one letter and it's the story of my life.

When all words are accepted—even expected—language deteriorates. As the British journalist Sir William Connor described,

> All were swearing steadily and quietly and all were using the same time-dishonoured Army oaths with such lavishness that made it necessary to split words open in the middle in order to cram all the obscenities in.

Alexander Woollcott replied to a critic about the unnecessary use of "God damn," which was the F-WORD of his day:

> When you speak of "three unnecessary 'God damns'" you imply that there is such a thing as a *necessary* God damn. This, of course, is nonsense. A God damn is never a necessity. It is always a luxury.

"I was arrested for using a ten-letter word that began with 'c,'" said Lenny Bruce, "and I would marry no woman who was not one."

⚖ ⚖ ⚖

God forbid that any book should be banned. The practice is as indefensible as infanticide.

REBECCA WEST

From the standpoint of consensual crimes and freedom of speech, (if I may paraphrase Lenny Bruce) we must use that marvelous ten-letter word that begins with "t" (and certainly no one would marry me who didn't have a great deal of it): *toleration.* If I don't want Jerry Falwell editing my books, I must forgo the luxury of editing his sermons. (But I can dream, can't I?) To have a freedom ourselves, we must pick up the banner of that great light of the Enlightenment, Voltaire, and declare: "I disapprove of what you say, but I will defend to the death your right to say it."*

As long as we keep censoring things, we are lost in the *symptoms* of our society's problems, thus ignoring the problems themselves. Pornography, for example, doesn't degrade women; women are degraded by our culture, and certain forms of pornography reflect that. Yes, we have a serious problem with the way women are treated in our culture, and pornography is a symptom, but let's not kill the messenger. Let's get the message and *do something about it.*

Similarly, violence is a messenger. The idea that problems can be solved

---

*In fact, he never said that. What he said was the less quotable, "I never approved either the errors of his book, or the trivial truths he so vigorously laid down. I have, however, stoutly taken his side when absurd men have condemned him for these same truths."

> *Without censorship,*
> *things can get terribly confused*
> *in the public mind.*
>
> GENERAL WILLIAM
> WESTMORELAND

through violence causes violence. We have a problem with drugs? Let's declare a war on drugs! We have a problem with crime? Let's declare war on crime! We have a problem with violence? Let's declare war on violence! It's this deeply ingrained American attitude that we can solve any problem with enough force (violence) that creates, feeds, and rewards the epidemic of violence we are currently experiencing.

"Military solution" is an oxymoron.

The actual depiction of violence in TV, movies, and song, in fact, has little effect. As Jon Stewart observed:

> The song "Cop Killer" doesn't make me want to murder a policeman any more than Julie Andrews singing "Climb Ev'ry Mountain" makes me want to go hiking.

Again, let's get the message. Let's do something about the false notion that violence solves problems. Let's not kill the messenger.

Violations of Marriage:
Adultery, Fornication, Cohabitation, Bigamy, and Polygamy

Is MARRIAGE SUCH a *fragile* institution that it must be defended by putting all dissenters in jail?

The obvious answer: "No—there will always be a fairly large percentage of people who *want* a lifelong, monogamous, formal, committed relationship with a partner of the opposite sex to keep the $32 billion bridal industry humming." Then why, I wonder (just as I wonder why it's called the *bridal* industry and not the *bridal and groomal* industry or simply the *wedding* industry), why must there be so many *laws* to encourage, support, and protect marriage?

When it comes to *professional* relationships, the law recognizes just about every kind. In business, there are sole proprietorships, limited partnerships, corporations, and any number of other government (and, more importantly, IRS) recognized relationships. Individuals have *Entrepreneur*; small corporations have *INC.*; and large corporations have *Fortune, Forbes,* and the *Wall Street Journal.* There's a governmental institution to cater to the needs, whims, and desires of every size business: small businesses have the Small Business Administration, large corporations have the Congress, and multinational mega-giants have the president of the United States. Businesses of all sizes are honored and respected in the community; real estate brokers are anxious to rent or sell them property; the government is anxious to provide growth incentives and tax breaks; and banks are anxious to loan them money in the time-honored tradition of the-less-you-need-it-the-more-they-want-to-loan-it-to-you. The laws and customs are neatly in place for mergers, takeovers, and creating and dissolving professional relationships of all shapes, sizes, and forms.

> *It doesn't matter what you do
> in the bedroom as long as
> you don't do it in the street
> and frighten the horses.*
>
> MRS. PATRICK CAMPBELL

Why is it, then, when it comes to *personal* relationships, there is only one legally recognized, community approved, IRS sanctioned relationship: one man and one woman promising sexual fidelity until one of them dies? Only in this relationship—known as marriage—do people get the tax breaks, bank loans, realtor acceptance, and Welcome Wagon visits.

Further, consenting adults entering into personal, romantic, or erotic relationships *other* than marriage might find themselves in jail. If you're 63 and a 22-year-old fashion model finds your charm, sex appeal, and $500 million net worth absolutely irresistible, and this model, as Stephen Sondheim put it, "marries you a little," there may be a few raised eyebrows. Although eventually you'll probably be raising alimony payments, one thing you *won't* have to raise is bail. If, however, the same financial relationship were offered in more straightforward terms, in all fifty states (with the exception of a few counties in Nevada) you'd be arrested for solicitation, prostitution, or pandering.

Even if you firmly believe in, staunchly support, and passionately desire a one-on-one, monogamous, committed, lifelong partnership, if you happen to want that with a member of your own sex, that's illegal in all fifty states. Let's say you're heterosexual, then—*so* heterosexual, in fact, that you want to marry *two* members of the opposite sex. Sorry, that's a little *too* heterosexual: just one to a customer, please. To paraphrase Oscar Wilde, bigamy is having one spouse too many; monogamy is the same. The standard reply to a man who says, "I am married to a beautiful woman and a wonderful cook," or the woman who says, "I'm married to a successful businessman and a wonderful lover," is, "Oh? You're a bigamist?"

The principle that if you steal a hundred dollars you're a crook, but if you steal a billion dollars you're a multinational business genius, also seems to hold true between bigamy and polygamy. *Webster's New World Dictionary,* the *American Heritage Dictionary,* and the venerable *Oxford English Dictionary,* define *bigamy* as a crime, whereas *polygamy* is not.* Perhaps the dictionaries were following the example of the "old party of Lyme" in William Monkhouse's limerick:

> There was an old party of Lyme,
> Who married three wives at one time.
> When asked, "Why the third?"
> He replied, "One's absurd,
> And bigamy, sir, is a crime!"

---

*Don't take this oversight seriously: if you were a polygamist in this country, you would probably be arrested on several counts of bigamy.

Generally, polygamy is thought of as one man with several wives. As the King in *The King and I* explains it:

> A woman is like a blossom
> with honey for just one man.
> The man must be like the honey bee,
> and gather all he can.
> To fly from blossom to blossom,
> the honey bee must be free.
> But blossom must not ever fly
> From bee to bee to bee.

Anna, the Welsh schoolteacher tutoring the children of the King of Siam's "favorite" wives, has an alternate view:

> In your pursuit of pleasure, you
> have mistresses who treasure you.
> They have no ken of other men,
> beside whom they can measure you.
> A flock of sheep, and you the only ram.
> No wonder you're the wonder of Siam!

There is no reason, of course, why the woman cannot have many husbands. The word *polygamy*, in fact, is not attached to gender. A man with several wives technically practices *polygyny;* a woman with several husbands practices *polyandry.*

We know Cleopatra, for example, was not exactly the queen of denial, and only World War II went through more Russians than Catherine the Great. Mae West, in her play *Catherine Was Great,* played the Russian empress on Broadway. In her curtain speech, West told the audience,

> I'm glad you like my Catherine. I like her too. She ruled thirty million people and had three thousand lovers. I do the best I can in two hours.

In a few parts of the country—particularly among Mormons—polygamy (or, more accurately, polygyny) is quietly accepted. Some Mormons, in fact, consider polygamy their religious right. It is certainly true that polygamy, as a religious tenet of Mormonism, was driven out by this country's traditional religious intolerance and the government's willingness to give such intolerance full force of law. Professor Robert Allen Rutland tells the story:

> From 1831 onward the Mormons, whose religion embraced the practice of polygamy, had been hounded from settlement to settlement, and in 1844 their leader, Joseph Smith, and his brother were lynched by an Illinois mob; the surviving believers then trekked from the Mississippi to their New Zion in present-day Utah. After Congress outlawed bigamy in 1862 Mormons challenged the law, claiming that it violated their guarantee to worship freely. The high court decision upheld the law and kept Utah out of the Union until 1896.

> *The plural of spouse*
> *is spice.*
>
> CHRISTOPHER MORLEY

> *You can point to any item*
> *in the Sears catalog and*
> *somebody wants to sleep with it.*
>
> DETECTIVE STANLEY
> WOJOHOWICZ
> *Barney Miller*

Brigham Young, who led the Mormons from Illinois to Utah, had at least twenty wives and fathered forty-seven children. "He is dreadfully married," wrote Artemus Ward. "He's the most married man I ever saw in my life."

⚖ ⚖ ⚖

As of August 1993, adultery (sex with someone who is married, or sex with anyone other than your spouse if you are married) is illegal in twenty-seven states. Oral sex (called *sodomy* in some states)—either giving or receiving—is illegal for consenting heterosexual adults in fourteen states. Even missionary style, conventional, heterosexual sex between unmarried consenting adults is illegal in nine states. Cohabitation (living as married with someone you're not married to) is illegal in ten states.*

And let's not forget local ordinances. There are any number of laws—such as this one from Long Beach, California—which sound more like a passage from a Sidney Sheldon novel than a legal statute:

> No person shall indulge in caresses, hugging, fondling, embracing, spooning, kissing, or wrestling with any person or persons of the opposite sex . . . and no person shall sit or lie with his or her head, or any other portion of his or her person, upon any portion of a person or persons, upon or near any of the said public places in the city of Long Beach.

⚖ ⚖ ⚖

Any guess where all these restrictions come from? Almost invariably they are religious in origin. In their attempt to protect "the American family," fundamentalists are, in fact, destroying the institution of marriage. Lifelong, monogamous marriage is a relationship that a great many people are naturally drawn to. But when society programs those *not* drawn—for whatever reason—to that particular relationship to believe that they *should* or even *must* be married, people who have no business being in that relationship muck it up for those who want to be.

It's like visiting Disneyland. Some people naturally *love* the place. As long as only those who are naturally drawn to Disneyland visit Disneyland, it is "the happiest place on earth." If, however, everyone were forced by *law* to visit Disneyland, then those who were not congenitally suited for Disneyland would—with their noticeable displeasure, rebellious acts, and disparaging comments—ruin it for those who naturally wanted to be there.

---

*In three states—Arizona, Florida, and New Mexico—you can have sex if you're not married, but you can't live together. What sort of morality is *that* set of laws teaching?

AIN'T NOBODY'S BUSINESS IF YOU DO

That's the state of marriage in America today. When people who really *want* to be married marry people who think they *should* get married, both end up suffering. If people who *want* to get married marry people who also *want* to get married, the likelihood of success is far greater. Meanwhile, if the people who don't want to get married, but think they *should* get married, no longer are told they *should* get married, they are free to explore and enter into whatever sort of relationship they *do* want. (Psychiatrists say that 20% of the American public has no appreciable sex drive whatsoever.)

> *I was thrown out of NYU for cheating—with the Dean's wife.*
>
> WOODY ALLEN

If business law had an equivalent to the laws concerning personal relationships, it would say, "If you're in business, you must have one partner, and only one partner, and keep that partner, until one of you dies." Can you imagine the state of business in America? The same is true of the state of personal relationships.

If we allow people to follow their hearts (and what else should they primarily follow in romantic relationships?) and allow relationships the freedom to grow, dissolve, merge, and interact with the same legal freedoms and protections we give business, then everyone—including (and perhaps especially) those who want a traditional marriage—would be a lot better off.

This topic, of course, is the subject of its own book. From a legal point of view, to sanction (reward, in fact) only one kind of relationship and punish other relationships—as long as the alternative relationships do not physically harm the person or property of nonconsenting others—is simply not the law's business.

Homosexuality

CALL ME DIMWITTED, thickheaded, or just plain insensitive, but the consensual crimes that seem the *silliest* to me are the ones directed against homosexuality. Why should anyone care about whom other people love, feel affection for, date, live with, marry, or have sex with? I just don't get it.

I also don't understand the *astonishing* prejudice against gay people.* The *New York Times* reported findings of the Governor's Task Force on Bias-Related Violence:

> In one of the most alarming findings, the report found that while teenagers surveyed were reluctant to advocate open bias against racial and ethnic groups, they were emphatic about disliking homosexual men and women. They are perceived "as legitimate targets that can be openly attacked," the report said. . . . The feelings were as strong among twelve-year-olds as among seventeen-year-olds. Many students added gratuitous vicious comments about homosexuals; that was not the case with other groups.

Gays seem to be at the bottom of the pecking order: no matter how far down the pecking order another group is, its members still feel superior to and have no problem picking on gays. It also seems that groups that hate each other and disagree on absolutely everything find one common point of agreement: homosexuality is bad, wrong, evil, wicked, and all the rest. Take, for example, Jerry Falwell and L. Ron Hubbard. One would think these two individuals were about

*As you may have noticed, I use the terms *homosexual* and *gay* almost interchangeably. Some gays prefer *gay*, some prefer *homosexual*. One group (a minority, as of this writing) likes the word *queer*. When I use *gay* or *homosexual*, I automatically mean both men and women; so, if I say "gays" or "homosexuals," I mean "lesbians and homosexual men." If I offend anyone with my selection of words, I apologize. No disrespect is intended.

as far apart as possible on any spectrum you'd care to name. The fact that one is dead and the other is not is just the *beginning* of their differences. Falwell dismisses Hubbard's creation, the Church of Scientology, as just another "satanic cult." On the subject of homosexuality, however, Falwell and Hubbard seem to find some common ground. We've already established how Falwell feels about "perverts." Here are some excerpts from L. Ron Hubbard's *Dianetics,* the "15 million copy bestseller":

> The sexual pervert (and by this term Dianetics, to be brief, includes any and all forms of deviation . . . such as homosexuality, lesbianism . . .) is actually quite ill physically. . . . He is also so far from normal and so extremely dangerous to society that the tolerance of perversion is as thoroughly bad for society as punishment for it.

> To make a pervert is, rather, something on the order of kicking a baby's head in, running over him with a steamroller, cutting him in half with a rusty knife, boiling him in Lysol, and all the while with crazy people screaming the most horrifying and unprintable things at him.

As Dr. Edward W. Bauman, United Methodist pastor who for more than twenty years conducted a Bible class on television in the Washington, D.C., area, observed,

> The thing that impressed me most, however, and moved me deeply was the discovery of the incredible amount of suffering experienced by homosexuals. For centuries the church refused to serve them Holy Communion. They were often stripped, castrated, marched through the streets, and executed. In Hitler's Germany they were exterminated by the thousands in the furnaces and gas chambers.

> In our own country, gay persons are disowned by their families, ridiculed and rejected by society, made the object of cruel jokes, and forced to laugh at the jokes lest their "secret" be revealed.

> They are barred from jobs and housing, often living in loneliness, seeking companionship in sordid places and in devious (and dangerous) ways. They have become the "lepers" of our society. How many young people are there who lie awake at night, terrified by these "feelings," with no one to talk to?

 ᛟ ᛟ ᛟ

What causes such deep and unreasonable hatred? I've explored the question in some detail, and the answers I discovered were surprising. Before giving the reasons, allow me to give a little background.

Prior to the late 1800s, the concept of homosexuality did not exist. The idea that one would exclusively feel romantically and sexually drawn to a member of the same sex was not considered. Yes, there was certainly homosexual *activity*, but this had always existed. The Hebrews, for example, did not have a word for homosexuality. When they wanted to describe the forbidden activity, they had to say, "Do not lie with a man as one lies with a woman; that is detestable" (Leviticus 18:22). Similarly, the

> *Athenians attributed the establishment of their democracy to a pair of gay lovers.*
>
> JOHN BOSWELL
> *Christianity, Social Tolerance, and Homosexuality*

Greeks had no word for homosexual. Paul had to explain: "Even their women exchanged natural relations for unnatural ones. In the same way the men also abandoned natural relations with women and were inflamed with lust for one another" (Romans 1:26–27). There was no word, then, for a man who only went to bed only with men or a woman who went to bed only with women.

To even *ask* the question never arose. It would be as unusual as asking today, "Are you a hot dog eater or a hamburger eater?" The idea that one preference would exclude the other made no sense. Even if one has not had a hot dog in twenty years, one would never think of defining oneself as a *hamburgerist* or, if a person had never had a hamburger in his or her life but adored hot dogs, we would not label such behavior as that of "a hotdogger."

In societies of ancient Greece and Rome, sexual activity with either sex was perfectly acceptable. To *exclusively* go to bed with one sex or the other, in fact, was considered a bit odd—something like eating nothing but raw vegetables might be considered today. In the ancient world, the distinction was: "Were you the *dominant* or the *passive* partner in the sex act?" In relationships between men, the dominant partner was praised, and the passive partner was condemned. Why? Because to play the passive partner meant a man *voluntarily played the part of a woman.*

We're back again to the anti-woman prejudice. Why would a *man* want to play the part of a *woman?* To do so was considered unnatural, self-deprecating, and perverse. If slaves or captives did it, well, that was acceptable: they *had* to. But for a *man* who had a *choice* to take the passive role in sex was considered personally degrading.

And therein lies the seed of the prejudice. It wasn't that homosexual activity was wrong; it was *playing the woman's role* in homosexual activity that was considered perverted.

Alexander the Great—whose masculinity was never in doubt—had as a primary sexual partner a castrated Persian boy. Alexander also had a wife. No one questioned the arrangement. Alexander played the dominant role in both relationships. He was a man. Both Alexander's wife and the Persian boy were treated with the respect due the ruler's favorites, but with little admiration.

In the pagan temples, the male and female sacred prostitutes were nearly interchangeable. One would be more likely to request a certain *type* than gender. One would have a preference for, say, blonds, not for either men or women. For a male to serve as a temple prostitute was acceptable because, after all, he was in service to a god.

As we have seen, any number of prohibitions in both the Old and New Testaments were abandoned a long time ago. And yet, the one against homosexuality remained because the bias against women remained. That's the first reason homosexuality has continued to be viewed in a negative light long after the practical reason (it doesn't propagate the species) no longer applied.

The second reason homosexuality is so feared and despised is that *homosexuality is too close to home.* It's fairly easy for, say, white people to become tolerant of black people because white people are not black. White people seldom think, "I think I'll have black skin for the next two hours." White people and black people are so fundamentally different—in terms of skin color—that white people almost never say, "I wonder if I'm really black?"

This security is not felt with homosexuality. On a purely sexual level, the human animal responds to lubricated friction. It doesn't much matter whether this lubricated friction is being applied by a man, a woman, a machine, or a well-trained dog; human sexual response on the biological level is automatic. (Yes, we are sexually turned on more when our *psychological* preferences in partners are met, but here, I'm referring only to the biological responses.)

It is also true that human beings can feel affection—even love—for members of their own sex. Affection is not a tidy emotion. It tends to dip—all by itself—into mental, emotional, physical, sensual, and even sexual levels of awareness and expression.

When one first realizes that he or she is actually *capable* of some kind of sexual and/or emotional response with a member of the same sex, panic ensues. Before children are even *aware* of their sexuality, they know that homosexuality is bad. Very bad. Among boys eight years or older, one of the most pejorative names they can call each other is, "faggot!" Later, when they become aware of their sexuality and find—even for a moment—that it flashes in the direction of the same sex, there's trouble in River City.

At this point, one has the choice to (a) confront one of the greatest and most pervasive taboos in our culture or (b) deny the inner reaction vehemently by supporting the taboo enthusiastically. Almost invariably, (b) is the choice. It's an old psychological truism: the more you want to taste of the forbidden fruit, the more you condemn it. Shakespeare realized this, and assumed his audience understood the concept so well that he made it a joke: "The lady doth protest too much, methinks."* That line has been met by the laughter of recognition for almost four hundred years.

By soundly condemning homosexuality outwardly, one avoids facing even the *possibility* that one *might*—just maybe—feel love for or be capable of responding sexually to a member of one's own sex.

> *It is a great injustice to persecute homosexuality as a crime, and cruelty too.*
>
> SIGMUND FREUD

Those are the two fundamental reasons I've found for the longevity, depth, and breadth of the anti-gay prejudice in this country. To keep that prejudice in place, however, requires more than just a handful of false assumptions, taboos, gross exaggerations, and outright lies. Let's call them *myths*.

⚖ ⚖ ⚖

Hating gays seems to be the only fashionable prejudice left. Maybe that's why it's dying so hard—some people just can't *stand* to be without at least *one* unjustifiable hatred. Some stores sell t-shirts with sayings such as "Homophobic and Proud of It" and "Club Faggots, Not Seals." What other minority is subjected to such unchallenged, violent hatred? As with most prejudices, the hatred of gays is based on a series of misconceptions. Our culture seems to have more myths about gays than most. Let's see if we can shine a little light on a few of them.

Myth #1: *Homosexuality is unnatural.* In order to see what *is* natural, we must look to nature. In nature, every mammal has been observed in the wild taking part in same-sex activities, affection, and bonding. In some animals, homosexuality increases during times of overpopulation—sort of nature's birth control.

In nature, by the way, what is decidedly *not* natural is monogamy—especially for life. The only mammals who even *sometimes* mate for life are foxes, wolves, gibbons, beavers, dik-diks, coyotes, the elephant shrew and, perhaps, geese. (Pairs of female geese and gulls, however, have been observed in bonded partnerships. They sit on the eggs, raise the young, and go about life's activities as a couple. Ganders are required only once per mating season, and any gander seems to do.) Some animals mate for a season; most animals mate and move on.**

---

*Hamlet, Act III, Scene 2, Line 242.

**I stuck to mammals for this example because the lower forms of life—while natural—are positively *inhuman*. You could say, for example, that the praying mantis "mates for life," only because, while the male shudders in orgasm, the female bites his head off. Then she eats him. The male praying mantis is an animal that comes and goes at the same time. Maybe that's why he's always praying. Sexually faithful until death? Undeniably. We all know how the black widow spider becomes a widow and why there is no such thing as a black widower (some animals just get so *hungry* after

> *Homosexual activity occurs under some circumstances in probably all known human cultures and all mammalian species for which it has been studied.*
>
> WARREN J. GADPAILLE, M.D.
> Comprehensive Textbook of Psychiatry

From a purely human point of view, homosexual behavior has been recorded in every culture that kept detailed enough records. Sociologists and anthropologists have documented homosexual behavior in every country on earth—including in tribes that have had no contact with any outside human beings until the arrival of the anthropologists. Any behavior observed among all races, all peoples, all cultures, and in all countries must certainly be considered natural for humans.

Myth #2: *People are either homosexual or heterosexual.* Not true. People do tend to specialize—partially because people are conditioned to think they *should* specialize. Sexual behavior is a *continuum* with exclusive heterosexuality on one end and exclusive homosexuality on the other. People, however, can be found at any point along that spectrum. A corollary to Myth #2 is:

Myth #3: *Homosexuality is contagious.* The myth goes something like this: If you try a homosexual experience and find it even marginally enjoyable, a seed (more like a virus) has been planted, and, eventually, you will wind up a full-fledged, card-carrying, flag-waving homosexual. This is simply not the case. You can't "catch" homosexuality any more than you can "catch" heterosexuality (although the latter myth is supported by the concept that "the love of a good woman" will "cure" a gay man). In either case, even a successful liaison with the gender one is not naturally drawn to will have little, if any, lasting effect.

I'm amazed at the power those who propound the you-can-catch-homosexuality theory give to homosexuality. How could it be so *powerful* that, with only a small dose, it would suddenly take over an otherwise robust heterosexual? This myth probably springs from observing some individuals who had severely suppressed their homosexuality, but once they got one foot out the closet door, there was no stopping them. ("I am not just out of the closet," the greeting card reads, "I am sitting in the living room with my feet propped up watching television.") We pretty much are what we are, and neither homosexuality nor heterosexuality can be "caught." The next myth seems to contradict this myth but, like different aspects of a used-car salesman's pitch, they don't have to support each other for

sex). Here's how Phyllis Lindstrom explained the birds and the bees—well, at least the bees—on "The Mary Tyler Moore Show": "Did you know the male bee is nothing but the slave of the queen? And once the male bee has, how should I say, *serviced* the queen, the male dies. All in all, not a bad system." Earthworms have male sexual organs on one end and female sexual organs on the other. They cannot, however, fertilize themselves. To mate, earthworms lie next to each other—how can I say this without becoming numerical?—head-to-toe and simultaneously and mutually play both male and female. Amoebas seem to have the best idea—the simplest, anyway: when they've had enough of themselves, they just *divide*. When one discusses what's *natural*, then, one has quite a range of behaviors to choose from.

people to believe them. "The American public," said Pat Robertson, "has a very short memory." And this is a man who *knows*.

Myth #4: *Homosexuality is a choice*. It has been established for some time that one's sexual orientation is part of the basic personality and formed before the age of two. The most recent studies, however, both behavioral and biological, indicate one's sexual orientation is genetic, something one is born with. Whether it happens

> *My lesbianism is an act*
> *of Christian charity.*
> *All those women out there*
> *are praying for a man,*
> *and I'm giving them my share.*
>
> RITA MAE BROWN

before birth or it happens by age two, the determination of sexual preference can hardly be considered a *choice*. One can, of course, *choose* not to follow one's preference, but this is not the sort of choice the proponents of this myth mean. They mean that gay people choose to be gay in the same way that they might sit down and choose which program to watch on television, which team to bet on in the Super Bowl, or whether or not they want pepperoni on their pizza.

The idea behind this myth is: a perfectly normal, well-adjusted heterosexual is sitting around one day and just *decides* to go gay, as one might decide to move to Antarctica or try to flush hockey pucks down the toilet. It is truly aberrant behavior, but *it is his or her choice*. Implied in this choice, of course, is a certain hostility to God, parents, society, and the American way. It's as though being gay is an act of *rebellion:* by a rebel with lots of flaws.

Gays don't *choose* to be gay; they *discover* they're gay. Like heterosexuals, they find themselves increasingly attracted (romantically as well as sexually) to one gender or the other. The bisexuals find themselves attracted to both. (Even though, as Woody Allen says, "Bisexuality immediately doubles your chances for a date on Saturday night," discovering one's bisexuality must be more confusing than discovering one is primarily gay or straight.)

Like being left- or right-handed, there is little "choice" to one's sexual preference. Allow me to give you an example. Clasp your hands together by interlocking your fingers. Is your right thumb on top or your left? Now switch your clasp, so that the *other* thumb is on top. Feel unnatural? Well, for *half* the population, this way is natural—it's the way they formed their clasp when first asked. Although one feels normal to you and one does not, when did you *choose* which was which? At what age? Who offered you the choice? The answer to these questions is also the answer to the question, "When did gays choose to be gay?"

To discover one is (or might be) gay can—considering the many cultural prejudices—be traumatic, and one can be in denial for quite some time. With society screaming, "Stay in the closet!" and nature pleading, "Get out! Get out!" one *does* have the choice of which voice one listens to. In this way—and in this way only—is homosexuality a choice.

Myth #5: *Homosexuals recruit others.* This is a myth that grew out of the evangelical camp where proselytizing, testifying, missionizing, and converting are basic tenets of the faith. Evangelicals somehow feel that gays have the same *zeal* to spread a gay-spell that they have to spread a God-spell. It's a simple matter of the evangelicals projecting their tactics on the gays. As with most projections, the image is distorted—and very wrong.

> *As a mother,*
> *I know that homosexuals*
> *cannot biologically reproduce*
> *children; therefore, they must*
> *recruit our children.*
>
> ANITA BRYANT

Gays have no desire to "recruit" heterosexuals into becoming homosexual. A gay person may, individually, want to have sex with a heterosexual of the same sex whom he or she finds attractive; the gay person may even make a pass. This gay person is making a personal statement of desire and not fulfilling a recruitment quota. ("If you recruit ten heterosexuals this month, you get this beautiful 26-piece set of Tupperware!") Additionally, gays who are out of the closet may offer support and encouragement to gays who are miserably in the closet, but that's about as far as it goes. Besides, the whole idea of recruitment rests on the concept that homosexuality is a *choice*, and every homosexual knows that just ain't so.

Myth #6: *You can spot a gay a mile away.* In 1985, when Rock Hudson publicly admitted his homosexuality, I was visiting two gay friends in Maine. Both men were in their eighties and had been lovers in 1925. In this rather remote region of Maine (is there any other kind of region in Maine?) the people did not have what you would exactly call a *cosmopolitan* view of life. They had somehow heard about Rock Hudson (an issue of *People* must have washed ashore in a bottle). They were shocked, stunned, numb. Not since the news of Kennedy's assassination (which they found out about in 1971) had the people of this town been so in shock. "Rock Hudson?" "No." "He couldn't be." "He doesn't look . . ." "Rock Hudson was such a *man*." My two friends and I were visiting the general store (yes, it was called the general store) and that's all anyone could talk about. I wondered what this group of shoppers would say if I told them that the dear, sweet, elderly men they were expressing their astonishment to had been lovers in Paris sixty years before, *and* that they regularly had dinner with Gertrude Stein and Alice B. Toklas—two lesbians. But I figured, no, one Rock crumbling that week was enough. Besides, they'd probably think a lesbian was someone from Lesbania.

Some gay men are effeminate; most are not. Some straight men are effeminate; most are not. Some lesbians are masculine; most are not. Some heterosexual women are masculine; most are not. According to the organization that considers itself an *expert* on homosexuality, the Pentagon, "feminized males make up only a small proportion of homosexuals, perhaps 10 percent. Thus 90 percent . . . display no overt behavioral stigmata." (Oooo. "Behavioral stigmata." The Pentagon uses such *macho* terms.) Regarding effeminacy in men, remember the most notorious ladies' man in history, Casanova, could probably not walk into a pool hall today and order a *creme de menthe* without being beaten silly with pool cues. Casanova was—like many men of his era—foppish. It was something men strived for. It indicated refinement, discernment, taste. All those King Louises of France wore wigs that even Dolly Parton

> *Can it matter where or in whom you put it?*
>
> ANTONY

would find too elaborate. And let's not forget our own founding fathers: satin pants, powdered wigs, make-up and all.

Linking effeminacy with homosexuality is primarily an American assumption. In the 1880s, Oscar Wilde toured America and lectured widely on *aesthetics*. He carried a lily on stage and was as much an aesthete as an Irishman could possibly be. The press ridiculed him, he ridiculed America, his lectures sold out, and everybody loved it. "A man in Leadville, Colorado," Wilde would say, "sued the railroad company because the reproduction of the Venus deMilo he ordered arrived without arms." Wilde would pause for dramatic effect while breathing in the fragrance of his lily. "The man collected on his claim." At the time he was touring the United States, Wilde was a married man with two children. No one linked his studied effeminacy with sexual preference any more than they linked it to Ireland, lecturers, or playwrights. In 1895, however, when Wilde was found guilty of being a "sodomite" and, in 1897, when Havelock Ellis used the word *homosexuality* in his *Studies in the Psychology of Sex*, Americans linked the two: "So, there are homosexuals, Oscar Wilde is a homosexual, so *that's* what they're like." Ironically, had America used as a stereotype one of its homegrown homosexuals of that era— such as the rough and rugged Walt Whitman—we might all have a very different view of how to "spot" homosexuals. It would be just as inaccurate, but different.

Myth #7: *There aren't enough gays to really worry about.* The percentage of primarily homosexual people in this country is estimated at from one to ten percent. One percent seems low—if it were one percent, that would mean more than *half* the nation's gay population traveled to the capital for the 1993 March on Washington. This is unlikely.* But the *number* of gays is unimportant. As the *Los Angeles Times* editorialized on April 25, 1993,

> What does all this mean in regard to current debates about the place of homosexuals in American society? It means exactly nothing.
>
> Whether homosexuals are 1% of the population or 10% or some figure in

---

*There is a rumor that 1,000,000 gays did not show up—that only 247 gays came, and the rest were Jerry Falwell's camera crews.

between, they are beyond any argument or cavil 100% entitled to the same protection under the law and the enjoyment of the same rights that everyone else is guaranteed. That specifically includes the right to be free from discrimination and intimidation in employment, housing and schooling. It means the right to be protected from hate-inspired physical assaults. It means the right to privacy as that right applies to everyone else.

Gays have been—and continue to be—hidden from view in the media, except in the form of (a) psychotic killers, or (b) effeminate jokes. The first time the word _homosexual_ was uttered in a film was 1961. When plays and novels featuring gay characters were made into movies, those characters turned into heterosexuals who were simply "too sensitive." Film biographies completely expunged any mention of a gay hero's true sexual preference. For example, when the story of Lorenz Hart's life was filmed as _Words and Music,_ the movie had him overcoming people's prejudice against him for "being too short." The oddest example was probably _Night and Day,_ in which Cary Grant, a bisexual, played Cole Porter, a homosexual, as a heterosexual. Even today, "sophisticated" films avoid homosexuality. Peter Biskind reported in _Premiere_ that in the novel, _Fried Green Tomatoes at the Whistle Stop Café,_ "the two main characters engage in a robust lesbian relationship. Where was the lesbianism when the novel was adapted for the screen?"

Myth #8: _God is opposed to homosexuality._ Oh dear, haven't we done enough Bible study for one book? We have covered most of the condemnations of homosexual acts in the Bible and, as I trust was clear, the context in which those condemnations were given include activities that most people now do every day. To select homosexual behavior out of those and pretend that God still hates that, but has come to accept and, in some cases, even encourage the rest of them is indefensible. As John Boswell points out in his book, _Christianity, Social Tolerance, and Homosexuality,_

> The very same Christian Scriptures which are thought to condemn homosexual acts condemn hypocrisy in the most strident terms, and on greater authority: And yet Western society did not create any social taboos against hypocrisy, did not claim that hypocrites were "unnatural," did not segregate them into an oppressed minority, did not enact laws punishing their sin with castration or death. No Christian state, in fact, has passed laws against hypocrisy _per se_, despite its continual and explicit condemnation by Jesus and the church.

There is one Bible story, however, we have not told: Sodom and Gomorrah. The "sin of Sodom" was apparently so bad that they named a consensual crime after it.

Sodomy has become synonymous with homosexual anal sex, perversion, and degeneracy too despicable to mention. Sodomy, in fact, is a grab-bag legal term that encompasses anything the legislative moral fathers of a given state find personally disgusting. It can include anal sex between men or between men and women (including married couples); oral sex between men, between women, men and women (including married couples); and sex between humans and animals.

> *We need laws that protect everyone.*
> *Men and women,*
> *straights and gays,*
> *regardless of sexual perversion*
> *. . . ah, persuasion.*
>
> BELLA ABZUG

In August 1982, a Mr. Hardwick was in his bedroom engaging in an act of sodomy with another consenting adult male. Sodomy is defined in Georgia (the state where this took place) as when one "performs or submits to any sexual act involving the sex organs of one person and the mouth or anus of another." In this case, it was Mr. Hardwick's mouth and the other man's sex organ. A police officer came in and, without a warrant, arrested them both. Mr. Hardwick took the case as far as the Supreme Court. What did the Supreme Court have to say? "The Constitution does not confer a fundamental right upon homosexuals to engage in sodomy." Mr. Hardwick is currently in prison—for life.

One wants to play the Supremes to the Supremes: "Stop! In the Name of Love."

But what *is* the sin of sodomy? (And what ever happened to Gomorrahy?)

> Now the men of Sodom were wicked and were sinning greatly against the Lord. (Genesis 13:13)

We gather they must have been doing something not very nice. But what was it? Five chapters later we find:

> Then the Lord said, "The outcry against Sodom and Gomorrah is so great and their sin so grievous that I will go down and see if what they have done is as bad as the outcry that has reached me. If not, I will know." (Genesis 18:20–21)

But what is the sin? We still have not been told. In the next chapter, we finally get to the meat of the story:

> The two angels arrived at Sodom in the evening, and Lot was sitting in the gateway of the city. When he saw them, he got up to meet them and bowed down with his face to the ground. "My lords," he said, "please turn aside to your servant's house. You can wash your feet and spend the night and then go on your way early in the morning."
>
> "No," they answered, "we will spend the night in the square." But he insisted so strongly that they did go with him and entered his house. He pre-

> *The New Testament takes no demonstrable position on homosexuality. To suggest that Paul's references to excesses of sexual indulgence involving homosexual behavior are indicative of a general position in opposition to same-sex eroticism is as unfounded as arguing that his condemnation of drunkenness implies opposition to the drinking of wine.*
>
> JOHN BOSWELL

pared a meal for them, baking bread without yeast, and they ate.

Before they had gone to bed, all the men from every part of the city of Sodom—both young and old—surrounded the house. They called to Lot, "Where are the men who came to you tonight? Bring them out to us so that we can have sex with them." (Genesis 19:1–5)

Now, is the sin sodomy—as in consensual anal or oral intercourse—or is it something else? Obviously the sin is *rape*, not consensual sodomy. Further, the sin is *inhospitality*. In desert regions, not being hospitable—that is, denying a traveler essential food and water; or, worse, taking advantage of a traveler in some way—was a sin second only to murder. Certainly, if travelers come out of the desert looking for water and get raped instead, that's pretty sinful—whether the travelers are men, women, or, in this case, angels. We'll get to other comments made about what the sin of Sodom was in a moment, but let's continue with our story. These are the parts the televangelists never get around to reading on television:

> Lot went outside to meet them and shut the door behind him and said, "No, my friends. Don't do this wicked thing. Look, I have two daughters who have never slept with a man. Let me bring them out to you, and you can do what you like with them. But don't do anything to these men, for they have come under the protection of my roof." (Genesis 19:6–8)

I don't want to sound like a *prude*, but isn't Lot supposed to be the hero of this piece? And here he is offering this rowdy crowd his two virgin daughters so that the crowd might "do what you like with them." If Lot had offered *himself*, that might be noble. "Take me, but leave my guests and daughters alone." Frankly, in comparing the sins of raping two strangers and offering your two virgin daughters to an unruly mob, I think the latter is worse. Maybe I'm just too old-fashioned for the Old Testament.

The angels blind the nasty mob, pull Lot into the house to safety, send Lot and his family on their way, and destroy Sodom and Gomorrah; Lot's wife turns to look back and becomes a pillar of salt; and then the story gets exciting again: Lot's daughters show that kinkiness runs in the family:

> He and his two daughters lived in a cave. One day the older daughter said to the younger, "Our father is old, and there is no man around here to lie with us, as is the custom all over the earth. Let's get our father to drink wine and then lie with him and preserve our family line through our father."
>
> That night they got their father to drink wine, and the older daughter went in and lay with him. He was not aware of it when she lay down or

AIN'T NOBODY'S BUSINESS IF YOU DO

when she got up. (Genesis 19:30–33)

That must have been some wine.

The next day the older daughter said to the younger, "Last night I lay with my father. Let's get him to drink wine again tonight, and you go in and lie with him so we can preserve our family line through our father." So they got their father to drink wine that night also, and the younger daughter went and lay with him. Again he was not aware of it when she lay down or when she got up. So both of Lot's daughters became pregnant by their father. (Genesis 19:34–36)

VICTIM'S GRIEVING WIDOW:

Do you know what it's like to be married to a wonderful man for fourteen years?

DETECTIVE DREBIN:

No, I can't say that I do. I did . . . uh . . . live with a guy once, though, but that was just for a couple of years. The usual slurs, rumors, innuendoes— people didn't understand.

"POLICE SQUAD!"

Okay, enough peeking into the caves of the morally upright. Let's return to defining the sin of Sodom. Nowhere in the remainder of the Bible—Old or New Testament—is the sin of Sodom defined as sex between consenting male adults. Here are the sins of Sodom (this is God speaking, by the way):

Hear the word of the Lord, you rulers of Sodom; listen to the law of our God, you people of Gomorrah!

Learn to do right! Seek justice, encourage the oppressed. Defend the cause of the fatherless, plead the case of the widow.

See how the faithful city has become a harlot! She was once full of justice; righteousness used to dwell in her—but now murderers! Your silver has become dross, your choice wine is diluted with water. Your rulers are rebels, companions of thieves; they all love bribes and chase after gifts. They do not defend the cause of the fatherless; the widow's case does not come before them. (Isaiah 1:10, 17, 21–23)

This sounds more like Washington, D.C., than West Hollywood to me.

Now this was the sin of your sister Sodom: She and her daughters were arrogant, overfed and unconcerned; they did not help the poor and needy. They were haughty and did detestable things before me. Therefore I did away with them as you have seen. (Ezekiel 16:49–50)

"Arrogant, overfed and unconcerned; they did not help the poor and needy. They were haughty . . ." Sounds more like a couple of televangelists I could name. Note, there is still no specific mention of same-sex activities.

Each time Jesus mentions Sodom and Gomorrah, he does so in connection with inhospitality:

If anyone will not welcome you or listen to your words, shake the dust off your feet when you leave that home or town. I tell you the truth, it will be more bearable for Sodom and Gomorrah on the day of judgment than for that town. (Matthew 10:14–15)

Or, perhaps, ingratitude (or just plain stupidity):

> And you, Capernaum, will you be lifted up to the skies? No, you will go down to the depths. If the miracles that were performed in you had been performed in Sodom, it would have remained to this day. But I tell you that it will be more bearable for Sodom on the day of judgment than for you. (Matthew 11:23–24)

The only Biblical passage that even mentions sexual behavior that *might* apply to homosexuality is this from Jude:

> In a similar way, Sodom and Gomorrah and the surrounding towns gave themselves up to sexual immorality and perversion. They serve as an example of those who suffer the punishment of eternal fire. In the very same way, these dreamers pollute their own bodies, reject authority and slander celestial beings. (Jude 7–8)

As we previously explored, "sexual immorality" and "perversion" refer to violent practices of idolatry—including human sacrifice—and not what goes on between consenting adults in their own bedrooms.

According to Methodist pastor Dr. Edward Bauman,

> The real irony is that homosexuals have been the victim of inhospitality for thousands of years in the Christian nations of the world. Condemned by the church and the state, they have been ridiculed, rejected, persecuted, and even executed. In the name of an erroneous interpretation of the crime of Sodom, the true crime of Sodom has been continuously perpetrated to our own day.

In his book, *Can Homophobia Be Cured?*, Bruce Hilton presents an amusing reversal on the role of gays in the church:

WHY HETEROSEXUAL MEN SHOULD NOT BE ORDAINED

1. According to divorce statistics, fewer than half of them are able to maintain a long-term relationship.

2. The literature is full of tales of clergymen becoming sexually involved with women of the congregation.

3. Three out of four straight males in the United States admit to being unfaithful to their long-term partners.

4. Thousands of straight men are in jail for molesting little girls. A shocking percentage of these victims were their own daughters.

5. Straight males are the driving force behind the declaration of wars—the only other activity described in the Social Principles as "incompatible with

---

> *People should not be surprised when a morally offensive lifestyle is physically attacked.*
>
> THE VATICAN

Christian teaching."

6. Jesus saved his harshest words for the self-righteousness of groups like the Pharisees and Sadducees—which, if they lived according to the code they promoted, were made up of straight males.

⚖️ ⚖️ ⚖️

As an intermission from debunking negative images, let's have some positive Biblical images of male affection:

After David had finished talking with Saul, Jonathan became one in spirit with David, and he loved him as himself. From that day Saul kept David with him and did not let him return to his father's house. And Jonathan made a covenant with David because he loved him as himself. Jonathan took off the robe he was wearing and gave it to David, along with his tunic, and even his sword, his bow and his belt. (1 Samuel 18:1–4)

After the boy had gone, David got up from the south side of the stone and bowed down before Jonathan three times, with his face to the ground. Then they kissed each other and wept together—but David wept the most. Jonathan said to David, "Go in peace, for we have sworn friendship with each other in the name of the Lord, saying, 'The Lord is witness between you and me, and between your descendants and my descendants forever.'" (1 Samuel 20:41–42)

"Saul and Jonathan—in life they were loved and gracious, and in death they were not parted. They were swifter than eagles, they were stronger than lions." (2 Samuel 1:23)

"I grieve for you, Jonathan my brother; you were very dear to me. Your love for me was wonderful, more wonderful than that of women." (2 Samuel 1:26)

⚖️ ⚖️ ⚖️

Myth #9: *God made Adam and Eve, not Adam and Steve.* Yes, God *did* make Adam and Steve, as well as Adam and Eve, and Eve and Genevieve—some people just don't like it that way.

Myth #10: *Homosexuals are promiscuous.* Some are; most are not. The same can be said of heterosexuals. In fact, almost *anything*—good or bad—that can be said about homosexuals can also be said of heterosexuals. Homosexuals are indistinguishable from heterosexuals except in whom they love and whom they go to bed with.

Myth #11: *Homosexuals can't control their sex drives.* When you consider how well most homosexuals have controlled not just their sex drives, but their conver-

> *The grounds for this membership revocation are the standards for leadership established by the Boy Scouts of America, which specifically forbid membership to homosexuals.*
>
> LETTER TO EAGLE SCOUT
> JAMES DALE
> August 10, 1991

sations, their innuendoes and even their inferences for so many years, it seems as though homosexuals have *remarkable* control. If closeted gays have been able to keep their homosexuality secret from friends and co-workers, *obviously* they can keep their sexual urges under control should they happen to stumble out of the closet.

The idea that gays have no sexual control is brought up repeatedly during discussions on whether or not gays are fit to serve in the military. All the reasons why gays shouldn't serve boil down to one: the excessive prejudice of the *heterosexuals* against homosexuality would make the heterosexuals somehow unfit for combat. The pro-prejudice group argues, "Wouldn't *you* be uncomfortable if some gay guy kept trying to hit on *you?*"

What the heterosexuals in the military are obviously afraid of is that the gays in the military—should they be allowed to come out—would start hitting on the heterosexuals with the same levels of determination and deception that the heterosexual men use to hit upon women. *The heterosexual men, then, are afraid to be treated the way they treat women.* Well, who can blame them? That gay men will behave as disreputably as straight men is an unfair projection on the part of straight men. Give the gays a chance. If the gays do treat the straights the way the straights treat women, one can only quote the phrase from the street: "What goes around, comes around."

As to women in the military, here's this herstorical tidbit from the June 21, 1993, issue of *Newsweek:*

> General Dwight D. Eisenhower received some unsettling news while he was in occupied Germany after World War II. There were, he was told, a significant number of lesbians in his Women's Army Corps (WAC) command. He called in Sgt. Johnnie Phelps and ordered her to get a list of all the lesbians in the battalion. "We've got to get rid of them," he barked. Phelps said she'd check into it. But, she told the general, "when you get the list back, my name's going to be first." Eisenhower's secretary then interrupted. "Sir, if the general pleases, Sergeant Phelps will have to be second on the list, because mine will be first." Dumbfounded, Ike realized he'd lose many of his key personnel if he persisted. "Forget that order," he told Phelps.

Myth #12: *Homosexuals spread AIDS.* AIDS is a disease spread by unsafe sexual contact (primarily intercourse) and dirty hypodermic needles. Gays have taken great care to educate their community, practice safe sex, and take care of those unfortunate enough to have caught the disease. The way caring individuals—gays, straights, it doesn't matter—rose and continue to rise in service to their

AIN'T NOBODY'S BUSINESS IF YOU DO

fellow humans brings tears to my eyes. Because most gays have changed their sexual activities and are now practicing safe sex, new infections in the gay community have leveled off. Meanwhile, infections are on the rise in the heterosexual community. The myth "If you don't go to bed with someone gay you won't get AIDS" is hurting the heterosexual community far more severely than it's hurting the homosexual community.

> *One-third of all*
> *teenage suicides*
> *are gays and lesbians.*
>
> U.S. DEPARTMENT OF HEALTH

Worldwide, AIDS is primarily a heterosexual, not homosexual, disease. It is a sexually transmitted disease that—for whatever reason—entered the gay community in the United States and stayed fairly contained there for a number of years. It is now spreading through the heterosexual community, and will continue to do so until the heterosexual community realizes that AIDS is not a "gay disease" and that any sexually active person—male, female, gay, straight—can get it. *If you have sex, use a condom.* There's hardly a gay person in this country who does not know the rule of safe sex. Can the same be said of heterosexuals?

Myth #13: *AIDS is God's curse upon homosexuals.* Crises bring out the best in people—and the worst. They also bring out the best people—and the worst. I do not believe that God curses anyone. I do believe, however, that God challenges. One of the biggest challenges in my life right now is how to deal with ignorant, arrogant, politically active people who say things like, "AIDS is God's curse upon homosexuals." I can remember the words of Jesus, "Forgive them, Father, for they know not what they do," but then I remember Jesus said that moments after he was nailed to the cross.

Unconventional Religious Practices

> *A cult is a religion with no political power.*
>
> TOM WOLFE

WE ARE SHOCKED and saddened by the events in Waco, Texas. We grieve with the families on both sides who lost loved ones.

The federal government is conducting investigations to find out what happened at the Branch Davidian compound in Waco to prevent similar occurrences in the future. While we think such an investigation is appropriate, we oppose any attempt to define what is a valid religion or set the parameters of a proper church.

Under the religious liberty provisions of the First Amendment, government has no business declaring what is orthodox or heretical, or what is a true or false religion. It should steer clear of inflammatory and misleading labels. History teaches that today's "cults" may become tomorrow's mainstream religions.

The United States is a religiously diverse country. We treasure its religious pluralism. Such diversity is a natural and expected result of our constitutionally protected religious liberty and is a source of strength, not weakness. These religious contours add to the American landscape, they do not detract from it. In the midst of our national mourning, we must fend off any inclination to shrink from our commitment to religious pluralism or to seek security at the expense of liberty.

This heady freedom is not absolute. It should be exercised responsibly. Religion is no excuse for violent or criminal conduct that harms other people or threatens public safety or welfare. Absent some compelling justification, however, government should not restrict religious exercise. And force—if ever appropriate—must be employed as a last resort.

Public discourse should be conducted with integrity. The nation's leaders ought to measure their words carefully and temper their passion with reason.

Government must resist any temptation to retreat from our "first freedom." To deny religious liberty to any is to diminish religious liberty for all.

෪ ෪ ෪

I didn't write the first part of this chapter. It was taken, verbatim, from a document entitled, "Religious Liberty at Risk," and signed by American Baptist Churches in the U.S.A.; American Civil Liberties Union, Washington Office; American Conference on Religious Movements; Americans United for Separation of Church & State; Association of Christian Schools International; Baptist Joint Committee on Public Affairs; Church of Scientology International; Center for Theology/Public Policy; Episcopal Church; First Liberty Institute; General Conference of Seventh-Day Adventists; Greater Grace World Outreach; National Association of Evangelicals; National Council of Churches of Christ; Presbyterian Church (U.S.A.), Washington Office; Union of American Hebrew Congregations.

Quite a diverse list. The federal government's attack on the Branch Davidians in Waco, Texas, demonstrated: (a) how little the government cares about religious freedom; (b) how quickly the people of this country can be talked out of protecting others' religious freedoms; (c) how willing the press is to ingest and regurgitate exaggerations, half-truths, and outright lies; and (d) how much danger *all* of our freedoms are in.

෪ ෪ ෪

When I visited the Holy Land, everyone said, "You must visit Masada!" Masada is located in a desert so rolling and barren that traveling there literally makes you seasick. Every five minutes the bus would stop so we could all get out and readjust our equilibriums, so we would not have to readjust our lunch (outwards). When we got there, we found that Masada is at the top of a mesa that goes waaaaaay up. It is in the middle of nowhere. Getting off the bus, I wondered, "I have to walk all the way to the elevator in this heat?" No, of course not: there *is* no elevator. You have to walk *all the way up to the top.* Did I mention this was in the middle of a desert? Did I mention it was *very* hot? Did I mention this was near the Dead Sea? (The heat killed it.) We had to climb 1,424 feet straight up. (Well, *almost* straight up.)

At the top of the mesa (the least they could have done was given us credit for climbing a *mountain)* is the ruins of a stone fortress built as a castle by Herod the Great. (Yes, the one who had all male children under the age of two killed in an effort to wipe out the Christ child.) As a fortress, it was occupied by Rome from 4

B.C. until A.D. 66, when Jewish Zealots took it by surprise ("Surprise!"). In A.D. 70, when Jerusalem was destroyed by Rome, the Masada garrison was the last remnant of Jewish rule in Palestine. Although outrageously outnumbered (15,000 to less than 1,000), the Jews refused to surrender. It took the Romans two years to build an enormous ramp (Did I mention the mesa was 1,424 feet high? That it was in the middle of the desert? That it was very hot?) so that they might attack the fortress at the top.

> I believe there is
> something out there
> watching over us.
> Unfortunately,
> it's the government.
>
> WOODY ALLEN

The Jews decided they would prefer death to Roman slavery. (And they had two years to think about it, too.) They scratched their names on potsherds and drew lots to determine the order of death. Of the almost 1,000, only seven women and children—who had hidden in a water conduit—survived. According to the *Encyclopedia Britannica:*

> In the twentieth century, Masada has become a symbol of Jewish national heroism, and the difficult ascent* is regularly performed by Israeli youth groups.

Those who committed suicide at Masada—which included women and children—are known as the Patriots of Israel. Looking at the endless expanse of nothingness surrounding Masada—literally nothing except the Dead Sea as far as the eye can see (at 1,424 feet) in any direction—one wonders why the Romans bothered. It was a matter of national pride, it seems. That a band of Jewish Zealots could hold out against Rome was more than the pride of Rome could bear. Roman soldiers were told to capture the fortress at all costs, and they did. Why did the Jews commit suicide? It was a statement of religious and political freedom. The world would know they would not be captured by Rome. Jews would not be prisoners; Jews would not be slaves. Suicide was the only way this statement could be made.

⚖ ⚖ ⚖

On November 18, 1978, approximately the same number of people—912, in this case—took part in a mass suicide because they felt, religiously and politically, at the end of the line. This was the "Jonestown Massacre." And yet, why do most people in this country compare the mass suicide of Jim Jones's People's Temple with the Holocaust rather than Masada? The fact that I'm even *asking* this question is going to infuriate some people. The question is, however, central to exploring the religious intolerance we feel in this country today. Our view of "cults" can be traced directly to the national fear and loathing we feel about Jonestown.

*See, I told you it was difficult.

> *Who says I am not*
> *under the special protection*
> *of God?*
>
> ADOLF HITLER

Can we look at the event in Jonestown and what led up to it without in any way endorsing Jim Jones's philosophy, tactics, motives, or teachings? Jim Jones and what he taught, in fact, is not important. What *is* important is that people *chose* to follow his teachings. For this discussion, *what* they believed is not as important as *that* they believed.

To compare what happened at Jonestown to the Holocaust *or* Masada is equally absurd. If parallels have to be drawn, however, there are more to be drawn between Jonestown and Masada than between Jonestown and the Holocaust.

In the Holocaust, Jews were forced from their homes, at gunpoint, and taken to concentration camps where they were executed. It was done entirely by force, and entirely against their will. That it was taking place at all was kept a secret from the German people, and from the world. The full ramification of the Holocaust was only discovered after the war. Hitler told the world that the Jews were merely being "relocated." The only "choice" the Jews had—if it can be called a choice at all—was to leave their countries by stealth. But where in this world could they have found safety? Antisemitism was everywhere, including America, and was accepted in every country of the world as "the way things ought to be."

The people who died in Jonestown had a choice. They chose to follow Jim Jones. They chose to sell everything they had. They chose to move from California to Guyana. They chose to stay in Guyana. When Jones announced the time for the mass suicide had come, only one voice spoke out in protest, not against the mass suicide, but only against including the children. Most people who died sincerely believed the murder of their children and their own suicide was a *religious and political act*. That they were brainwashed into believing this is a given. That—for whatever reason—they *chose* to take part in this brainwashing is the important fact.

The difference between Jonestown and Auschwitz is obvious: Hitler had not brainwashed the Jewish people; he had only brainwashed those who murdered them into believing that such murder was righteous. The comparison between Jonestown and Masada doesn't hold up because the Jews at Masada had nowhere to go. They would wind up prisoners and slaves of Rome. The members of Jonestown, however, were still American citizens and could have returned to the United States and continued with their lives.

Comparisons to either Masada or the Holocaust, then, are useless. The point is that today, the vast majority of people in our country would instantly subscribe to the Holocaust comparison rather than the Masada comparison. Why is this? Why is it when we hear the word *cult*, we immediately think, "evil, bad,

Jonestown"? What is there to learn from the Jonestown incident that applies to our discussion of consensual crimes, unorthodox religious beliefs, and government intervention? What triggered the Jonestown suicide? What prompted Jim Jones to say, "Today is the day"?

The answers to this—and particularly the answer to the last question—have a great deal to teach us. There was a sign in Jonestown, above the place where Jim Jones lectured his followers. The sign, a slight misquoting of George Santayana, read,

> *We have just enough religion*
> *to make us hate,*
> *but not enough*
> *to make us love one another.*
>
> JONATHAN SWIFT
> (1667–1745)

THOSE WHO DO NOT REMEMBER THE PAST ARE CONDEMNED TO REPEAT IT.

Our government did not remember the past, and repeated it in Waco, Texas, less than fifteen years later. As a nation, however, it was hard for us to remember a past so carefully hidden from us. Jonestown was a powder keg, ready to explode at any minute. One person brought the match to Jonestown. The ghost of that person brought the match to the equally explosive Branch Davidian compound in Waco, Texas.

It is not a *person* I want to blame here, but the *ideas* this person represents. The ideas are the all-American concepts, "Problems are best solved by force," and "You're different; I don't like it; you'd better change." The combination of these two beliefs—deeply ingrained in the American character—was responsible for Jonestown, Waco, and all the laws against consensual activities today.

⚖ ⚖ ⚖

The quotes in this next section come from the 1982 book, *Raven: The Untold Story of Rev. Jim Jones and His People.* It was written by Tim Reiterman. Reiterman is a reporter who investigated and wrote about the People's Temple prior to the Jonestown incident; accompanied United States Congressman Leo J. Ryan on his visit to Jonestown; left Jonestown within an hour of the mass suicide; and was wounded during the airstrip murders of Congressman Ryan, three other reporters, and a defecting People's Temple member.

To say that Reiterman despised Jim Jones, everything he did, everything he taught, and everything he stood for, is an understatement along the lines of saying, "Simon Wiesenthal was not fond of Adolf Hitler." Reiterman, in fact, considers Jones an American Hitler, Jones's personal staff as "Gestapo," and titled the chapter on the mass suicide itself, "Holocaust." When he describes the actions of Congressman Ryan, then, we know that Reiterman is in no way trying to cast a favorable light upon Jim Jones. In fact, one of the people to whom Reiterman dedicated his book was "Representative Leo Ryan."

> When I hear a man preach,
> I like to see him act
> as if he were fighting bees.
>
> ABRAHAM LINCOLN

From Congressman Ryan's point of view in 1978, Jim Jones had three *significant* strikes against him: (1) he had weird religious beliefs, (2) he was a communist, and (3) he had led 1,200 American citizens to a foreign country to establish a religious/political "paradise."

For reasons we shall explore later, Jones is remembered today as primarily a "cult leader"—that is, people followed him because of his strange religious beliefs. In fact, they followed him for his political beliefs as well. He was an avowed socialist—which all good Americans, at that time, knew meant *communist*. He would preach in his San Francisco temple:

> "I see some," he said raising his voice, "are not aware what God is. The only thing that brings perfect freedom, justice and equality, perfect love in all its beauty and holiness is socialism. *Socialism!*"

Jones' beliefs were so political that in choosing the title for his book, *Raven*, Reiterman used this quote from Jones: "I come with the black hair of a raven. I come as God Socialist!" What the religious right is doing today with conservatism, Jim Jones did in the 1970s with socialism: use religious fervor to whip up political action.*

It was not just our country's anti-communist fervor (at its peak in 1978); it was also religious intolerance (which is only peaking now) that prompted Congressman Ryan to become personally involved.

Some of the relatives of the more than 900 who had followed Jones to Guyana formed a group called Concerned Relatives. They were concerned that their loved ones had moved to a primitive South American country, that they followed blindly the dictates of a charismatic leader, that they had sold everything they owned and donated the money to this leader's church (temple), and that some of them— tired of the Concerned Relatives' concern—had broken off all communications. On March 14, 1978, they had yet another reason to be concerned:

In a letter addressed to members of both houses of Congress, Temple mem-

---

*This is one of the great unlearned lessons of Jonestown, but not the one we are focusing on in this chapter. The parallels between the rise of Jim Jones and that of Pat Robertson and Jerry Falwell are astonishing. All three began by preaching the word of God and Jesus, winning converts, and then becoming increasingly political. Once politics was equated with God in the minds of their followers, politics took over almost completely. Watch "The Old Time Gospel Hour" or "The 700 Club" and you'll find clearly political programs that mention God, as opposed to religious programs that mention politics. It was not that way at the beginning: "The Old Time Gospel Hour" preached the gospel, and "The 700 Club" saved souls. The only difference is that Jones's *personal* political beliefs were far left and Falwell's and Robertson's political beliefs are far right. The technique all three used— convert them with God; then turn them to politics—was the same.

ber Pamela Moton complained of alleged harassment and threatened: "I can say without hesitation that we are devoted to a decision that it is better even to die than to be constantly harassed from one continent to the next."

On April 11, 1978, about fifty Concerned Relatives protested in front of the San Francisco temple:

> At the head of the list of grievances, the relatives excerpted the "decision to die" statement sent to Congress by the Temple.

> *A way of life that is odd or even erratic but interferes with no rights or interests of others is not to be condemned because it is different.*
>
> WARREN E. BURGER
> *Chief Justice*

To the question that people often ask, "What did Jim Jones and his followers want?" at least one answer was abundantly clear: they wanted to be left alone. The Concerned Relatives, however, thought they knew what was best. "You're different; I don't like it; you'd better change." "Problems are best solved by force," and that was how they wanted the government to react. They found in Washington a sympathetic ear in the person of Congressman Leo J. Ryan.

Reiterman describes Ryan as

> a rebellious Irish Catholic and political maverick, [who] had little reverence for either churches or the Temple's friends in high places. Most important, he was a compassionate man, and he had been moved by the appeals [Concerned Relatives] made to him. Independent, brash, tenacious, Ryan would be no easy mark for Jim Jones.

The combination of (perhaps misguided) compassion, rebelliousness, independence, brashness, and tenacity—driven by the two above-mentioned all-American concepts—was the spark that ignited Jonestown.

Ryan found no support in Congress for his trip.

> Travel guidelines of the Foreign Affairs Committee [of which Ryan was a member] compelled Ryan to try to find a colleague to join him for the Jonestown expedition. His letters to his colleagues interested only one committee member, Representative Ed Derwinski of Illinois—and he would bow out at the last moment.

Ryan decided to go anyway. Both the United States State Department—well trained in diplomacy—and the government of Guyana gave Ryan advice, all of which he ignored.

> At the September [1978] meeting, the State Department advised Ryan against including four or five Concerned Relatives whom Ryan had mentioned as possible companions. The same position was taken in November when the group had expanded to eighteen relatives and nine news media representatives, all unofficially traveling with Ryan's congressional delegation. In the interim the Temple, through an Embassy official, told Ryan that it wanted no press coverage; it already went without saying they

> *Religion may
> in most of its forms
> be defined as
> the belief that the gods
> are on the side
> of the Government.*
>
> BERTRAND RUSSELL

did not want their avowed enemies, the Concerned Relatives. And at the same time, Guyanese Ambassador Mann, who had his own very personal tie to the Temple, informed the Embassy that Guyana would not and could not force Jonestown to open its gates to Ryan's group.

Although Ryan was compassionate, he was also a politician. The maverick congressman invading the communist cult stronghold made a great story. Nine newsmen accompanied him including a camera crew from NBC News, reporters from the Washington Post, *San Francisco Examiner,* and *San Francisco Chronicle.* For journalistic balance, a reporter from the *National Enquirer* went along, too.

> So the congressman wound up with a national television network, the two major newspapers in his congressional district and the most prominent newspaper in the nation's capital.

At the airport, just before they were to take off, Reiterman reported, "a Guyanese official advised us not to take the Guyana flight because we would be turned back upon landing."

> [Ryan] ignored warnings and plunged ahead, despite State Department advice that Jonestown was private property, despite the Temple's discouraging letters. On the plane [Ryan was] holding court to an audience of press and [Concerned] relatives. . . . If Jones stopped him from entering Jonestown, Ryan reasoned, he wanted it on film.

Arriving in Guyana, Ryan was told by a member of the People's Temple that Jones was "very ill." (The State Department claims it attempted to tell Ryan about Jones's illness before Ryan left Washington, but Ryan didn't want to hear about it.) Ryan was also told what he had been told many times before: that he was not welcome in Jonestown. The United States embassy in Guyana, although sympathetic with the plight of the Concerned Relatives, could do nothing to help.

> He was miffed about the State Department's hands-off attitude. In private, he swore, "I'm going to have something to say about this when I get back."

The two attorneys who represented the People's Temple in the United States made an emergency trip from the United States in an attempt to reason with Ryan. When Ryan heard they were coming, it had the reverse effect.

> Late Thursday, sensing the Temple's hardening resistance and some disenchantment within his own entourage, Ryan's language took a tougher turn. Thinking the Temple might plan to use the attorneys to stall him, he

held out a threat, implying that he might stir up investigations of the Temple's tax-exempt status, as well as its handling of social security checks.

We reporters felt restless, too, and skeptical of Ryan's ability to break through the Temple's stone wall. His assurances had begun to ring hollow. . . . In a frank confrontation, Don Harris [of NBC News] told Ryan: "Leo, we don't know if we can trust you."

> *The greatest dangers to liberty lurk in insidious encroachment by men of zeal, well-meaning but without understanding.*
>
> JUSTICE LOUIS D. BRANDEIS

The congressman's credibility with the press—hence with his own constituency and the American public—was on the line. When the two attorneys arrived, "Ryan stood firm." The two lawyers, knowing the power of Congress, urged Jones to let Ryan and his party in. "You can tell Congress to go f— themselves, and if you do that I can't live with it," one of his attorneys told Jones by radio. "I am imploring you to open it to the world and let them come in."

Finally Jones agreed, "All right. Come on down."

The plane Ryan had chartered, however, would only hold twenty passengers. There were nine newsmen, and eighteen Concerned Relatives. It was Ryan's decision as to who would go and who would stay. In the choice between compassion and politician, Ryan was a congressman.

With all nine newsmen and the two attorneys aboard the plane, there would be space for only four of the relatives who had come so far for reunions with loved ones. Clearly, Ryan's first priority was focusing the world's attention on Jonestown.

When they arrived at Jonestown, only the reporter for the *National Enquirer* was turned away. (Communists!) The remainder were transported to Jonestown and found Jones, as they had been told, very ill. His speech was slurred, and he had little ability to concentrate. As to Jonestown itself, it was a settlement in the middle of a jungle. Huts, houses, dormitories, and wooden structures were constructed, and the land was being used for agriculture. Even the highly skeptical Reiterman conceded that—had the shootings and mass suicide not taken place—he would "describe the place as physically impressive and the people as generally appearing happy and healthy." When Ryan addressed the group at Jones's invitation, temple members showed how happy and satisfied they were with their choice to be there:

Sounding as friendly as a political stumper, [Ryan] said, "This is a congressional inquiry and . . . from what I've seen, there are a lot of people here who think this is the best thing that happened in their whole life." An explosion of hand-clapping cut off his declaration as the entire nine hundred settlers, Jones included, took to their feet and sustained the applause for what seemed an eternity. The metal roof nearly shook, and those of us at the head table looked around in amazement. . . .

Ryan quipped, "I'm sorry you can't all vote in San Mateo County." Jones jumped up: "We can, by proxy." Then he added more quietly, "You have my vote." Again a roar of approval reverberated through the pavilion.

While a band played and the Jonestown residents danced, Jones conducted an informal interview with the reporters and Ryan. "There's no barbed wire here," Jones told them. "We don't have three, let alone three hundred, who want to leave."

> Interviews by Ryan and [Ryan's aide] Jackie Speier since their late afternoon arrival tended to support that conclusion. Not a single relative of the Concerned Relatives in Jonestown had accepted an invitation to leave with the Ryan party.

Ryan once again faced public humiliation. He had claimed the media would find a hellhole where American citizens were being held captive practically at gunpoint. What they found, while no "paradise," was a physically ill leader and happy, dancing people.

"If they don't want us in America," Jones asked the reporters, "why not let us live in peace?"

> In recent years, some had questioned whether the Temple was, in reality, a church. It is a church, Jones said, explaining that Jesus also had commanded his followers to sell their possessions.

By the next day, Ryan had found twelve people—mostly in two families—who wanted to return with him to the United States. This seemed to shatter Jones, who was unable to convince them to stay.

> In a low, resigned voice, Jones told the Bogue family, privately, "There's always a place, just know there's always a place for you. Always a place."

Meanwhile, Ryan quietly celebrated his victory.

> At one point, Leo Ryan stood back as the Temple leadership and their attorneys pulled close together to parley in low tones. "How are things going, Leo?" I asked. "Are many leaving with us?"
>
> He cocked back his head, then dropped his chin to his chest and out of the corner of his mouth said with a touch of bravado: "Looks like about a dozen. There are more every minute. They're coming out of the woodwork." Ryan was vindicated and he knew it; no one could say any longer

that he was on a political witch hunt, or chasing headlines. . . . The gloom in the other camp was oppressive. From the rank and file to the higher-ups, not a soul could summon a smile.

Twelve out of more than 900 may not seem like much, but Jones referred to each of his members as his "children" and they called him "Dad." Ryan had brought with him the one temptation some of his followers could not resist: blood relatives. "We're gonna go back," one of those leaving told Jones. "I've got my whole family back there. . . . It's not that I don't think what you're doing here is wonderful, cuz I do."

The second blow to Jones happened shortly thereafter.

> *The highest proof of virtue is to possess boundless power without abusing it.*
>
> LORD MACAULAY
> 1843

> [As] departure time raced nearer, NBC set up for their finale. In the news media, it is known as a confrontation interview, usually done at the conclusion of an investigation, with the prime target.

The NBC crew nailed Jones, and they got it all on video. Ill, disoriented, mourning the loss of his "children," and knowing he was defeated at every turn in his confrontation with Ryan (or, more accurately, Ryan's confrontation with him), Jones must have felt humiliated by what NBC captured on video.

While Ryan was saying good-bye—in an episode not witnessed by any of the media—one of the members of the People's Temple attacked Ryan with a knife. Jones's attorneys and members of the People's Temple wrestled the knife from the man. Ryan was unharmed.

> When Ryan picked himself up, he was angry. Then he composed himself. Jones stood to one side, silently, as if in a trance; he had not lifted a hand or protested in any way, and did not apologize now. He only listened as Ryan promised that his recommendation and report to Congress would remain unchanged, providing the attacker was arrested. Jones agreed to call the police only after the lawyers instructed him to do it.

So now Ryan was giving Jones yet another ultimatum: call the police on one of his "children" or face unspecified threats when Ryan got back to Washington. Ryan got on the transport with the reporters and the departing members of the People's Temple, and they left Jonestown.

One can only imagine Jones's feelings at that moment. Ryan—uninvited and unwelcome—had used threats to enter Jonestown and brought with him members of the Concerned Relatives, who were central in taking away several of Jones's "children." He had also brought another group whom Jones specifically requested Ryan *not* bring: the press. Jones's humiliation would be reported to the world. It was even on videotape. Telling them he was ill was not enough—Ryan

> *Politics is the art*
> *of looking for trouble,*
> *finding it whether it exists or not,*
> *diagnosing it incorrectly,*
> *and applying the wrong remedy.*
>
> ERNEST BENN

came anyway. Based on the success of the four Concerned Relatives to "rescue" their loved ones, more would come. Ryan would almost certainly escort them back personally. The media would come too, of course. More, next time. While Ryan supervised the dismantling of the People's Temple, person by person, the media would record it all. Jones was certain there was a conspiracy within the government to destroy him and his temple.

"Obviously, there is a conspiracy. Someone shot at me and missed me by a couple of inches. We went through a week of hell."

But who would do such a thing? "Who conspired to kill Dr. Martin Luther King, Malcolm X and John Kennedy? Every agency of the whole government is giving us a hard time. Somebody doesn't like socialism."*

There is only one statement Jones could make that showed how little he and his followers cared about this life and this world, and how much contempt they had for the government that hounded them from one country and now followed them to another: that was to imitate the Jewish patriots at Masada and commit mass suicide. The order went out (presumably from Jones): Kill Ryan and prepare for the mass suicide.

Does this rationale in any way *excuse* what Jim Jones did? Of course not. Although he had the right to commit suicide and his adult followers had the right to follow along, killing others—Ryan, the newsmen, defectors, and children—is and was wrong. This profile of Jones's psychological state might explain, however, how close to an explosion the powder keg was, and how the solution of suicide was "logical"—almost inevitable—for Jones.

Jones and his followers firmly believed that there was a better life beyond this one. Death was the doorway to that life, and was welcome. The group practiced for mass suicides over and over. The only regret most members had after these experiences was that they were not "the real thing." Here is an excerpt from a letter to Jones, entitled "The Real Thing," written in a childish scrawl by one of his followers:

> If the potion we drank had been the real thing, then it would have been the end. . . . The rest of the people would be in peace with our loving leader if it was the real thing there would be no more pain and no more suffering. We would be in peace today. That would have been the best way

---

*Even Jones felt persecuted for his *political* and not his *religious* beliefs. Again, we will explore shortly why he is primarily remembered as a demented *religious* leader and not as a demented *political* leader.

AIN'T NOBODY'S BUSINESS IF YOU DO

to die. . . . If it was real, of course we would have been free. We would have died the best way. . . . Thank-you Dad

A large vat of Grape Flavor Aid was prepared and heavily mixed with cyanide. Liquid Valium was also available. As previously mentioned, only one person verbally objected, and that was only to request that the children be allowed to live. It seemed everyone knew before it happened what was going to happen. Nine members left, even before Ryan had left camp, telling friends they were going on a "jungle picnic." Others left after the mass suicide had begun. One woman unknowingly slept through it all in her cabin. Before it began, Jones sent his two lawyers away on a pretext. There's an audio tape of the final hour of the People's Temple. Far from the belief that people were drinking the Flavor Aid at gunpoint, what we hear for the most part are the voices of people who (with more emotion than Jim Jones liked) willingly said good-bye to this world in preparation for the next. Among the last recorded words are these from Jones:

> "We've set an example for others. One thousand people who say: we don't like the way the world is.

> "Take our life from us. . . . We didn't commit suicide. We committed an act of revolutionary suicide protesting the conditions of an inhumane world."*

At the airstrip, Ryan, three newsmen, and one of the defectors were killed. Jones was found near his wife, a single bullet through his brain.

ॐ ॐ ॐ

Understandably, the Jonestown suicide made a deep impression on the American people. A survey taken in the early 1980s indicated that, as a news item, only Pearl Harbor and the assassination of John F. Kennedy made a greater impact. What could possibly cause 912 Americans to sell all they owned and commit mass suicide in a South American jungle? Yes, they were communists, and yes, they were mostly from California, but *even so,* what could have possessed them? The members of the People's Temple who did not move to Guyana provided few answers. There were very few temple members left in the United States, and the media inundation was overwhelming. They scattered. One held a news conference, made a statement defending Jim Jones, excused himself, walked into an adjacent room, and shot himself. Great for headlines; bad for explanations.

The "Jonestown Massacre" was ripe for exploitation. It was exploited. The anticommunists, however, didn't need any more ammunition: since the beginning

---

*Again, Jones viewed this as a *political* and not *religious* act.

> *A serious problem exists in our society as a result of the emergence of groups, popularly called "cults," using mind control (undue influence) and unethical means to recruit and retain followers. Association with these groups can be harmful to followers and disruptive to families, friends and society.*
>
> CULT AWARENESS NETWORK

of the Cold War, they had stockpiled—literally—a nuclear arsenal. Everyone in the country *knew* communism was terrible; people didn't need to be convinced further. Besides, the Jonestown mass suicide didn't quite fit the profile of the "communist menace" the anti-communists wanted to portray. Whereas a military power attacking our borders with tanks and pelting us with nuclear warheads was considered a threat by most citizens, few Americans felt that they were likely to follow a charismatic leader to Guyana. Being controlled by someone to the extent of committing suicide was a concept to which few Americans could relate. Hence Jonestown—while puzzling, even fascinating—was not seen as a communist menace.

Enter, stage right, the Cult Awareness Network. The Cult Awareness Network (CAN) went national in 1980. It claimed to be an expert on this "new" American phenomenon, cults, and both press and legislators ate it up. If a journalist had a clandestine organization to investigate or a member of Congress received a letter from a constituent expressing concern that a loved one had joined a mysterious organization, who ya' gonna call? Cultbusters!

Over the years, the FBI and CIA had done an excellent job tracking organizations that even *might* be communistic, socialistic, fascistic, or in some way politically "un-American." There was a gap in the FBI's knowledge, however, when it came to unconventional religious groups—a gap CAN was more than happy to fill. CAN pontificated on what was and was not a cult. Its spokespersons were quoted in the media and the Congressional Record as "experts on cults."

But what were CAN's credentials? How is the relative cultness or noncultness of an organization determined? Who or what was funding CAN? *Don't ask so many questions.* The Cult Awareness Network was performing a valuable service for the press and for Congress: it provided quick answers to complex questions at no cost. It provided "experts" who were willingly quoted so, if an organization was mistakenly accused, it wasn't the fault of the press or of Congress, but of the Cult Awareness Network.

To concerned relatives of those who had loved ones in one of CAN's "cults," CAN provided graphic details of the horrors the members might be subjected to. CAN also recommended *deprogrammers.*

A deprogrammer is someone who kidnaps a cult member, holds the member in a secluded spot against his or her will, and uses every brainwashing technique known to man (and man knows many) to bring the "poor, misguided" cult member "back to reality." Reality, of course, is what the relatives of the cult member (the relatives who are paying dearly for the deprogrammer's "skill") want their loved one's reality to be.

These intensive brainwashing sessions are most effective. Over time, the victim generally begins identifying with his or her captors. Just as the American soldiers captured during the Korean War began "voluntarily" making pro-communist statements, and just as Patty Hearst "became" a member of her captor's Symbionese Liberation Army, so, too, do the majority of the kidnaped cult members become enthusiastic supporters of CAN. In the cases where the "deprogramming" is not successful or wears off, police

> *The arts of power and its minions*
> *are the same in all countries*
> *and in all ages.*
> *It marks its victim; denounces it;*
> *and excites the public odium*
> *and the public hatred,*
> *to conceal its own abuses*
> *and encroachments.*
>
> HENRY CLAY
> 1834

are hesitant to arrest and district attorneys hesitant to prosecute deprogrammers for a charge as serious as kidnapping (which, of course, is precisely what it is) because so many *concerned* and *well-meaning* family members (who paid for it and are, therefore, accomplices in a highly criminal act) tearfully tell their stories of concern. When a case does go to court, juries are not likely to convict. The deprogrammer and concerned relatives were, after all, doing it for the cult member's *own good* and making a stand against those *evil cults.*

Creating the anti-cult atmosphere in this country is one of the Cult Awareness Network's greatest achievements. CAN has succeeded in making the word *cult* evoke immediate hostility, revulsion, and fear, as *communist* once did, and as *homosexual, child molester,* and *drug addict* still do. Most people believe, if a group or individual is evil enough to even be *accused* of such a despicable act, they deserve everything they get. Cult members are not innocent until proven guilty; *they're guilty.* When it comes to wiping out such evil, ordinary rules of law do not apply. There isn't time. The need to eradicate it is too great. The means justifies the end, and the end is an America free of such contagion.*

⚖ ⚖ ⚖

The Cult Awareness Network is conveniently vague about what constitutes a cult. This allows *CAN* to be the final arbiter in such matters. The guidelines are general enough to include practically any religion, private club, fraternity, sorority, or magazine subscription. Most of the criteria even describe the Cult Awareness Network itself.

---

*Based on the success of the Cult Awareness Network, several copy-cat (copy-CAN?) organizations have arisen—some of them to stay afloat, some of them to sink again. Most are right-wing religiously based, and proclaim that *any* organization smaller than, say, the Roman Catholic Church that does not follow the cultbusters' fundamentalist beliefs is a cult. (They also refer to cults as "spiritual counterfeits.") You can safely assume *any* group that calls any other group a "cult" (a term acknowledged as derogatory in religious circles; the terms *New Religious Movements,* or *NRMs,* describe small spiritual groups without bias) does so either to get publicity or protect itself, and because it does not believe in religious freedom.

The Cult Awareness Network seems to object to the idea that "religious, therapy/self-awareness, political, commercial or New Age" groups should use sales techniques to gain new members, or that they should use persuasion to keep the members they already have. The Cult Awareness Network draws absolutely no line between *violent* and *nonviolent* sales and persuasive techniques. The underlying supposition is that "nontraditional" religious groups are automatically wrong and not entitled to employ the same marketing techniques so successfully used by Coca-Cola, *Encyclopedia Britannica*—or the Cult Awareness Network.

From my point of view, a "destructive cult" is one that uses *physical force* or *threats* of physical force either to recruit or to keep its members from leaving. In other words, unless an organization commits a *crime* according to the definition we have discussed repeatedly (physically harming the person or property of a nonconsenting other), it is not a "destructive cult." If physical force or the threat of physical force is not used, should the government become involved? No. Just because the Cult Awareness Network brands a religious organization it doesn't happen to like—for whatever reason—a "cult" is no reason for government action.

By this definition, then, those who kidnap people and "convert" them by force—such as deprogrammers do—are members of a "destructive cult," and those the Cult Awareness Network brands as destructive cults (including such benign organizations as Transcendental Meditation, LifeSpring, and the Hunger Project) are not destructive cults at all. They may be cults, in the sense that (by Robert Altman's definition) they don't have enough members to make a minority, but destructive? Hardly. *Kidnapping* is destructive. Brainwashing while being held by physical force is destructive. *Choosing* to take part in an unconventional religious practice can potentially only physically harm the person or property of those who choose to take part in it. That's not the law's business.

⚖️ ⚖️ ⚖️

Which brings us to Waco, Texas. Before the raid, during the standoff, and after the fiery end, guess who was feeding government agencies, the press, and members of Congress "information" and providing "consultations"? CAN you guess? Yes, the Cult Awareness Network. According to an article in the *Los Angeles Times* shortly after the conflagration,

> The network's president . . . was quoted by the *Houston Post* on April 9 as saying that the FBI should use any means necessary to arrest Koresh, including lethal force. Soon after the initial February 28 federal raid, another "deprogrammer" named Rick Ross, long associated with the net-

work, said on television that he had "consulted" with the ATF before the raid. The network's former executive director, Priscilla Coates, raised allegations of child abuse.

It was astonishing to watch how the press, Congress, and other elected officials swallowed whole and reported as fact the information provided by the Cult Awareness Network. After the raid, when the facts about David Koresh and the Branch Davidians were known, most people agreed that the federal government *never should have been there in the first place.* If there were violations of the law, they were a matter for *local* and not *federal* intervention. A year before the armed raid by the Bureau of Alcohol, Tobacco, and Firearms (ATF), the district attorney for Waco, Texas, Victor Feazell, thoroughly investigated charges similar to the ones which supposedly justified a military attack on the compound by one hundred armed federal officers. The Branch Davidians were exonerated on all counts. "We treated them like human beings, rather than storm trooping the place," Feazell said, "and they were extremely polite and cooperative."

According to an article in the *Washington Post* by E. J. Dionne, entitled "Have We All Gone Bloody Mad?"

> Words like "fanatics" and "cults" are getting thrown around as if they explain all we need to know about Waco—as if there's something suspicious about all forms of religious commitment.

Franklin Littell, a Methodist minister and the chairman of the American Conference on Religious Movements, wrote:

> Fortunately for the bureaucrats of the [Bureau of Alcohol, Tobacco, and Firearms], the public had been brainwashed to suspect anything called a "cult." A few lonely historians of religion had tried to point out that "cults," always unpopular in their origin, often settled down and enjoyed bemused acceptance by the majority—or at least toleration.

> The Christian movement itself had begun as a "cult." The Church of Jesus Christ of Latter Day Saints ("Mormons") had begun as a despised and persecuted "cult," its Prophet and his brother murdered by an anti-cult mob. Yet the LDS is now considered one of the most economically, politically and religiously edifying forces in America's pluralistic society.

Even if it *had been* a matter for federal intervention, the we're-going-to-make-a-bold-frontal-attack-with-the-news-media-in-tow approach of Congressman Ryan was met with precisely the same predictable results as Ryan received: death and destruction. As the *National Catholic Reporter* stated,

---

> *The Joy of Sects*
>
> *Title of cover story by*
> PAUL BOYER
> *in the New Republic*
> May 17, 1993

SWAT teams were not trained for nonviolent tactics. The FBI agents are apocalyptists, too. They want to exercise decisive force against "evil." Thus, catastrophe was predictable. In the lingo of the Vietnam War, "We had to destroy the village in order to save it."

Dean Kelley, a religious counselor at the National Council of Churches, commented:

> Few commentators seem to have asked what was the heinous offense or imminent peril that prompted the Sunday morning attack on the sect's headquarters. . . . Were the Branchites planning to take over Baylor University and subject the faculty to forced conversion? . . . There's been talk of "illegal" weapons in the premises—though most of them were admittedly acquired legally and openly. One wonders what an "illegal firearm" would be in Texas anyway, short of a bazooka firing nuclear warheads.*

When the Bureau of Alcohol, Tobacco, and Firearms was noticeably in over its head, whom (in addition to the Cult Awareness Network, who probably said, "See? We told you they were dangerous!") did the ATF call? The National Council of Churches? Other religious experts? Negotiators skilled in religious extremism? No. According to Alexander Cockburn, writing in the *Los Angeles Times,* the government repeatedly rejected "mediation offered by prominent religious groups." To solve its problem it called in *more force:* the FBI. The FBI decided the solution was even *more force:* it borrowed a tank from the army and began poking holes in the walls of the compound and, according to Cockburn in the *Los Angeles Times:*

> For six hours the FBI pumped CS2 into a compound containing children too small to wear the gas masks allegedly stockpiled by the Davidians. It now seems likely that the M-60 tank knocked over kerosene for the compound's lamps (which the Feds knew were about) and almost everyone burned alive.

Force, force, and more force. Cockburn's *Los Angeles Times* analysis concludes:

> And as a final horrible irony in this saga of Nazi-like affront to religious tolerance, the deprogrammers are demanding that they be allowed to exercise their dark arts on the burned Davidian survivors so that they testify correctly and desist from maintaining—as they have—that no mass suicide was under way. The FBI says "this is worth considering."

---

*The Branch Davidians do have scriptural reference for arming themselves: "Then Jesus asked them, 'When I sent you without purse, bag or sandals, did you lack anything?' 'Nothing,' they answered. He said to them, 'But now if you have a purse, take it, and also a bag; and if you don't have a sword, sell your cloak and buy one'" (Luke 22:35–36). Some might think, however, the Branch Davidians took this a little too far—and didn't read this scripture far enough. "The disciples said, 'See, Lord, here are two swords.' 'That is enough,' he replied" (Luke 22:38).

⚖️ ⚖️ ⚖️

Those two American beliefs: "You're different; I don't like it; you'd better change" and "Problems are best solved by force"—so perfectly embodied by the actions of Representative Leo J. Ryan—surfaced once again in the federal attack on the Branch Davidians in Waco, Texas. We didn't learn the lesson when Ryan used the formidable power of the United States government to force his way into Jonestown, and we don't seem to have learned a lesson now that the ATF and the FBI have forced their way into the Branch Davidian compound. The "enemy" is always the "charismatic cult leader" and not our national inability to tolerate charismatic cult leaders. If it's different, we believe, it must be stopped—by force.

> *Indeed I tremble for my country when I reflect that God is just.*
>
> THOMAS JEFFERSON

That's what all laws against consensual activities are: the force of law against people who do things that are "different." Because of this, our religious freedoms are in serious danger. Ironically, they are being torn down by people in the name of God. In the name of God, when will this end?

By the way, did I tell you who's the president of the Cult Awareness Network? Patricia Ryan, Representative Leo J. Ryan's daughter.

PROSECUTOR ON KNEES IN PRAYER

PASSIONATE APPEAL TO JURY TO END MENACE OF FOREIGN REDS.

From OUR OWN CORRESPONDENT

NEW YORK, Monday.

The amazing trial ended to-day at Charlotte, North Carolina, when seven labour leaders, members of the Textile Workers' Union, were found Guilty in the second degree of the murder on June 9 of Mr. Aderholt, the chief of police of Gastonia, North Carolina, where a strike of textile workers has been a long time in progress.

Throughout the trial Communism rather than individuals appeared to be on trial, and the prosecutor in his summing up devoted more attention to the political and religious views of the defendants than to the crime with which they were charged.

"FIENDS INCARNATE"

During his final speech he knelt in prayer before the jurors, rolled on the floor to illustrate Aderholt's death, and held the hand of Aderholt's widow as he pleaded with the jurors to end the menace of foreign Communists.

These he described as "fiends incarnate who came sweeping like a cyclone to sink their fangs in the heart and life blood of my community."

The jurors, before whom witnesses had been impeached because they would not affirm their belief in a God who after death would punish wrong-doing, heard the prosecutor demand: "Do you believe in the flag of the United States? Do you believe in the State of North Carolina?"

The jury took only a few minutes to decide that the defendants were guilty, and sentence was deferred. All except one of the defendants hail from outside the State of North Carolina, having been sent by their union to organise the textile workers.

Unpopular Political Views

> *If our democracy is to flourish*
> *it must have criticism,*
> *if our government is to function*
> *it must have dissent.*
> *Only totalitarian governments*
> *insist upon conformity and they—*
> *as we know—do so at their peril.*
>
> HENRY STEELE COMMAGER
> 1947

THE UNITED STATES CONSTITUTION is a fascinating document. It has within itself the rules by which it can be changed, modified, or eliminated altogether. This flexibility allows the United States to have one of the oldest continuing governments in the world.

Some people, however, believe that the Constitution needs to be "protected" from even the *idea* of another system of government. Ironically, those who, in order to defend the Constitution, suspend people's constitutional right to advocate another form of government are the ones who destroy the Constitution—not those who proclaim the Constitution should be replaced with another document. That the people may someday vote out our current form of government and replace it with another is a risk inherent in our form of government. Those who try to eliminate the risk are, simultaneously, destroying the present system.

It has always amazed me that the people who claim the greatest allegiance to the Constitution and our form of government should trust either so little. Why do people seem to think our system of government is so fragile that it can't stand on its own among other ideas of government? Why do they assume a system of government that's been able to flourish for more than 200 years is some fragile butterfly? It is, in fact, an iron butterfly, a system that becomes stronger by being challenged, just as we become stronger through exercise. When not challenged, our government—like us—becomes flabby, self-indulgent, and complacent.

⚖ ⚖ ⚖

Now that the "communist menace" has been safely laid to rest, I trust I can make a few frank observations about communism, the United States' reaction to the "communist threat," and how great a menace or threat it really was. Prior to

1989, as someone accurately observed, the only state-sponsored religion in the United States was anti-communism. One of the tenets of this religion was that if you did *anything* but denounce communism in *anything* but the most virulent terms, you were a communist. Now that it's all over, however, and we can use the word *communist* without prefacing it with *damn* or *God damn,* let's take a look at the growth of anti-communism in the United States.

We never really hated *communism* a s much as we hated the way communism was practiced in the Soviet Union, which was *totalitarianism*. In fact, it wasn't so much totalitarianism we didn't like, it was *Stalinism*. In fact, it wasn't so much Stalinism we didn't like, but *Stalin*.

It was not hard to hate Joseph Stalin. Of few people in history can one say, "He was responsible for the death of millions." *Countries* have been responsible for the death of millions, but *individuals* who can claim this distinction are few. Stalin is one of the few. His politics in a nutshell: Kill those who oppose you; terrorize those who support you. Using this method, Stalin succeeded, by 1924, in gaining total and absolute control of Russia. He rounded up millions of dissidents, put them in prison camps (the *Gulags*) and, essentially, starved them to death.

That Stalin was a monster may not have been good for any number of Russian people, but historically, it was good for the United States. If Stalin had been a weaker leader (like Mussolini), he probably would have joined ranks with Hitler in the 1930s (like Mussolini) and Hitler would have won World War II.

⚔ ⚔ ⚔

Although *communal* societies have existed throughout history, what we now call *communism* was first proposed by Karl Marx and Friedrich Engels in the mid-1800s. Suggesting that everything be owned *in common* was, naturally, a threat to *anyone* in power, and *everyone* in power was opposed to it. Marx and Engels's book, *The Communist Manifesto,* published in 1848, began:

> A specter is haunting Europe—the specter of Communism. All the powers of old Europe have entered into a holy alliance to exorcise this specter: Pope and Czar, Meternich and Guizot, French Radicals and German police spies.

For the next seventy years, communism made for stimulating political discussion. In 1918, however, the communists won the Russian Revolution—under the leadership of Vladimir Lenin—and the first communist state was established.

In the United States, by 1918, communism, socialism, anarchism, or any *ism* other than Americanism was soundly denounced. In early 1920, for example, a national "Red Scare" resulted in the arrests of 2,700 communists, anarchists, and other "radicals." The most famous case during this time was that of Sacco and Vanzetti. They were arrested in Massachusetts in 1920, found guilty in 1921, and executed in 1927 primarily due to their unpopular political beliefs. (They were vindicated on July 19, 1977, in a proclamation by Massachusetts Governor Dukakis.)

> *A reactionary is someone with a clear and comprehensive vision of an ideal world we have lost.*
>
> KENNETH MINOGUE

Prior to his execution, Nicola Sacco wrote in a letter to his son Dante:

> Help the weak ones that cry for help, help the prosecuted and the victim . . . they are the comrades that fight and fall . . . for the conquest of the joy of freedom for all the poor workers. In this struggle for life you will find more love and you will be loved.

Meanwhile, in Germany, Hitler won the support of the bankers and the industrialists with his virulent anti-communist stance.

In Russia, along came Stalin. After three years in a seminary, Stalin saw the light and became a professional revolutionary. By 1922, Stalin was the general secretary of the Communist Party. Although shortly before his death in 1924, Lenin wrote a "testament" urging that Stalin be removed from his post for inappropriate and arbitrary conduct, Stalin succeeded Lenin as leader of the Soviet Union in 1924. Throughout the remainder of the 1920s and the 1930s, Stalin repeatedly sought European and American support in forming an alliance against Adolf Hitler. England, France, and America, however, were not interested in dealing with a "communist," forcing Stalin to enter into a nonaggression pact with Hitler in 1939. While this did not make Hitler and Stalin allies, each agreed not to interfere with the military aggression of the other. This gave Hitler the green light to attack Poland, which he promptly did. World War II was underway.

⚖ ⚖ ⚖

In 1911, at the age of twenty-nine, Franklin Delano Roosevelt said, "There is nothing I love as much as a good fight." This being the case, Roosevelt certainly got what he loved: he was assistant secretary of the Navy during World War I; ran a losing vice-presidential race in 1920; was stricken with polio in 1921, leaving him permanently disabled; successfully ran for president in 1932; battled the Depression during the 1930s; and led the Allies to victory in World War II.

In the 1930s, while enacting and administering some of the most sweeping socialistic programs in American history (the New Deal), Roosevelt remained, in

> *No democracy can long survive*
> *which does not accept*
> *as fundamental*
> *to its very existence*
> *the recognition of*
> *the rights of minorities.*
>
> FRANKLIN D. ROOSEVELT

speeches, violently anti-communist. While running for presidential re-election in 1936, for example, he made this speech:

> I have not sought, I do not seek, I repudiate the support of any advocate of Communism or of any other alien "ism" which would by fair means or foul change our American democracy.

Note "by fair means or foul." What Mr. Roosevelt was saying—and it has certainly been practiced by American politicians before and since—is that communism should not be tolerated even if it were introduced by "fair means." In other words, even if the communists were legally voted into office, it would be unacceptable to President Roosevelt. That the successful 1936 presidential candidate (and the liberal candidate at that) could make hostile statements ("I repudiate the support of any advocate of Communism"), indicated the tenor of the times—a tenor which became increasingly shrill over the years.

But it wasn't really the American communists Roosevelt disliked:

> I do not believe in communism any more than you do but there is nothing wrong with the Communists in this country; several of the best friends I have got are Communists.

When the discussion turns to Stalin, however, Roosevelt applied the nastiest word one could use in 1940, *dictatorship:*

> The Soviet Union, as everybody who has the courage to face the fact knows, is run by a dictatorship as absolute as any other dictatorship in the world.

In other words, Roosevelt thought Stalin was another Hitler. Roosevelt even had trouble with the Russian people:

> I don't know a good Russian from a bad Russian. I can tell a good Frenchman from a bad Frenchman. I can tell a good Italian from a bad Italian. I know a good Greek when I see one. But I don't understand the Russians.

In a radio broadcast on October 1, 1939, Churchill shared Roosevelt's uncertainty of Russia:

> I cannot forecast to you the action of Russia. It is a riddle wrapped in a mystery inside an enigma.

In addition to being the leader of the Soviet communists, financing communist movements in America, murdering millions, and other assorted distastefulness, the former seminary student had also become an outspoken enemy of *all* religion. When it was suggested he might want to make a political alliance with the pope, Stalin replied, "The pope? How many divisions has *he* got?" Stalin was responsible for the adjective *godless* being grafted onto *communism,* a phrase which did not help Stalin's, or communism's, standing in American popularity polls.

Anti-communism may have been a national religion in the United States before World War II, but it became a national hysteria after the war. During the Cold War, the general public labeled Russia, who had been our vital ally only a few years earlier, our vilest enemy. If the American people had remembered some details about World War II and its peace settlement, they might have seen the "communist menace" in a more realistic perspective, and the U.S. might not have spent so much money and destroyed so many lives fighting communism.

> *If Karl,*
> *instead of writing a lot*
> *about capital,*
> *had made a lot of it*
> *it would have been much better.*
>
> KARL MARX'S MOTHER

⚖ ⚖ ⚖

In the 1930s, the mood of America was isolationist. We had fought World War I "to keep the world safe for democracy," and here it was, less than twenty years later, and the Europeans were about to go at it again. The conflict was referred to as the coming "European war" and Americans wanted none of it. With the Depression, Americans had enough troubles of their own. In 1937, we were about as likely to return to fight in Europe as we would return to Vietnam today. Various politicians attempted to tell the American people that this war was *different*—there was this man named *Hitler,* but the American people, for the most part, were not buying. In October of 1937, Roosevelt compared Hitler with a disease:

> War is a contagion. The epidemic of world lawlessness is spreading. When an epidemic of physical disease starts to spread, the community approves and joins in a quarantine of the patients in order to protect the health of the community against the spread of the disease. . . . There must be positive endeavors to preserve peace.

In a campaign speech on October 30, 1940, President Roosevelt, campaigning for an unprecedented third term, said:

> And while I am talking to you mothers and fathers, I give you one more assurance. I have said this before, but I shall say it again and again and again: Your boys are not going to be sent into any foreign wars.

No less an American hero than Charles Lindbergh visited Germany and returned to inform the American people that there was no comparison between the air power of England and the air power of Germany: Germany would win the European war. Unless we wanted to go over and fight for ourselves, Lindbergh suggested the path of strict neutrality. His voice was persuasive. He was a realist, but did not take into consideration two factors: first, the tenacity of the British

> *I have been forced
> to the conclusion
> that we cannot win
> this war for England,
> regardless of how much
> assistance we extend.*
>
> CHARLES A. LINDBERGH
> 1941

people; and, second, their good sense in making Winston Churchill their prime minister in 1940.

Far from being neutral in the European conflict, Roosevelt leaned heavily toward England. Churchill said, "Give us the tools," and Roosevelt did. Through a program known as lend-lease, the United States supplied Great Britain with ships, airplanes and armaments. The resulting surge in industrial output, more than any other single factor, helped bring America out of its Depression. Although America was not sending fighting men into the European conflict, the United States was no longer officially neutral.

⚖️ ⚖️ ⚖️

Throughout the 1930s, Winston Churchill, though not holding a public office, had made repeated warnings to England about Nazi Germany. The warnings were ignored. In Churchill's 1936 book, *While England Slept,* he wrote:

> I have watched this famous island descending incontinently, fecklessly, the stairway which leads to a dark gulf.

Once Hitler's tanks rolled into Poland, then captured Paris, England saw Churchill had been right all along. They made him prime minister, and he sailed to America where he charmed the armaments out of the United States.

Things went from bleak to worse; the darkness just before the dawn got considerably darker still, and there was no dawn in sight. The only alliance that could *possibly* beat Hitler would be one between Roosevelt, Churchill, and Stalin. As much as these three differed, they enthusiastically agreed on one crucial subject: their hatred for Herr Hitler.

Roosevelt's reference to Hitler as "a contagion" only grew stronger as the '40s rolled in. Churchill was, to say the least, considerably more outspoken. From a radio broadcast on September 11, 1940, Churchill purred:

> This wicked man Hitler, the repository and embodiment of many forms of soul-destroying hatred, this monstrous product of former wrongs and shame.

When Hitler, suddenly and without warning, broke the nonaggression pact and attacked Russia in June of 1941, Churchill found himself defending Russia.

> Hitler is a monster of wickedness, insatiable in his lust for blood and plunder. Not content with having all Europe under his heel, or else terrorized into various forms of abject submission, he must now carry his work of butchery and desolation among the vast multitudes of Russia and of Asia. The terrible military machine, which we and the rest of the civilized

world so foolishly, so supinely, so insensately allowed the Nazi gangsters to build up year by year from almost nothing, cannot stand idle lest it rust or fall to pieces. . . . So now this bloodthirsty guttersnipe must launch his mechanized armies upon new fields of slaughter, pillage and devastation.

Secretly, of course, Churchill was thrilled. He knew Hitler's invasion of Russia would take the pressure off England and provide additional evidence to the United States that Hitler respected no treaty, territory, or bounds of decency. Hitler would not take over Europe and leave America alone: Hitler's goal was world domination. The attack on Russia made it no longer a European war, but a world war. On July 14, 1941, Churchill said,

> We will have no truce or parley with you [Hitler], or the grisly gang who work your wicked will. You do your worst—and we will do our best.

By the end of 1941, Pearl Harbor was attacked and the United States was in the war. This achieved, Churchill paused for a moment of self-congratulation with a touch of British wit:

> When I warned [the French] that Britain would fight on alone whatever they did, their generals told their prime minister and his divided cabinet, "In three weeks England will have her neck wrung like a chicken." Some chicken; some neck.

Like Churchill, Stalin was vindicated in his warnings of Hitler's danger. On November 6, 1942, with Hitler's army only fifty miles from Moscow, Stalin did not flinch:

> The Hitlerite blackguards . . . have turned Europe into a prison of nations, and this they call the new order in Europe.

In late 1943, Roosevelt, Churchill, and Stalin met face to face in Teheran. Although still holding the weakest hand, Stalin was in a better negotiating position than anyone had previously thought possible: he had received a gift from Mother Russia. As she had done with Napoleon in 1812, the worst Russian winter in recent memory attacked Hitler's finest army with a fierceness Hitler had yet to encounter during the war. Although the newsreels sent back to Berlin showed naked German soldiers rollicking in the snow and having a jolly good time, the reality was far more somber. The snows of winter and the mud of spring made either advance or retreat nearly impossible. Tens of thousands died, the army was demoralized, and Hitler was faced with his first retreat in the entire war. Roosevelt, Churchill, and Stalin became, if not comrades, certainly allies.

In his 1943 Christmas Eve Fireside Chat, President Roosevelt assured the people of the United States:

I believe that we are going to get along very well with [Stalin] and the Russian people—very well indeed.

⚖ ⚖ ⚖

> *If Stalin had learned to play cricket the world might now be a better place to live in.*
>
> ARCHBISHOP R. DOWNEY

By early 1945, all was not so rosy. In February, the "Big Three" gathered in Yalta in the U.S.S.R. Roosevelt had been elected to a fourth term in office. He was, however, very ill. Stalin found Roosevelt's weakened condition pathetic: born rich, well-educated, a lawyer, disabled in adulthood by a disease that struck mostly children, and now in perpetual ill health. That Americans would elect this man as their leader only four months before indicated the weakness of capitalism and the West. Stalin, three years older than Roosevelt, was still robust. A leader, Stalin felt, must be strong, and strength begins with physical power. The very name *Stalin*—which he chose for himself when he became a revolutionary—meant "man of steel."

Stalin was feeling strong. What he brought to the conference table was not insignificant: Stalin had lost 20 million people in the war, compared to Roosevelt's 407,000, and Churchill's 378,000. There was no doubt that had Stalin given in to Hitler in 1941, the war would be over and Hitler would be the winner. Stalin considered himself, then, a full partner in the war and, as an equal victor, was entitled to a full share of the spoils. Roosevelt and Churchill had other ideas.

It wasn't that Churchill and Roosevelt wanted to take *more* of the spoils than Stalin; Churchill and Roosevelt wanted to *give it back to the Germans.* Stalin was incensed. When you lose a war, you lose your land: that's what wars were about. If you win a war, you win the land—*especially* when you are the one *attacked.* Stalin had not lost 20 million Russians for nothing: he had every intention of expanding the Soviet empire, and that was going to include his fair share of Germany.

Roosevelt and Churchill had no designs on Europe—particularly Germany. Germany, they felt, still belonged to the German *people:* had they not been taken over by Hitler and his SS, they would never have gone to war. Besides, argued Roosevelt and Churchill, Stalin was playing by the *old* rules of war; Roosevelt and Churchill claimed they were fighting for *ideology,* not land.

Stalin had never heard such nonsense. He maintained that all Germans seriously opposed to Hitler had left Germany, been eliminated, or were in concentration camps. The vast majority of the people Roosevelt and Churchill wanted to give Germany back to were firmly behind Adolf Hitler, and had been since at least the first military victories. Besides, this is what happened at the end of World War I, only twenty-seven years before: Germany was given back to the German people, who, within two decades, had rearmed and started another world war.

Stalin thought Roosevelt and Churchill's claim that the United States and England fought wars for ideological reasons was particularly ironic: America had declared war on millions of Native Americans, taken their land, and built a country using the forced labor of African Americans who were savagely taken from their homeland. Less than a hundred years before the Yalta Conference, the United States was still actively involved in the "relocation" of millions of Native Americans and the "migration" of millions more African Americans. How, wondered Stalin, could Roosevelt—less than fifty years after the last Indian surrender, which happened not just within Roosevelt's lifetime, but within Roosevelt's *memory* (he would have been sixteen at the time)—have the nerve to tell Stalin that the rules of war had now been "civilized"? Only three months before the Yalta Conference, on November 4, 1944, while campaigning in Boston, Roosevelt acknowledged:

> *The Marxist analysis has got nothing to do with what happened in Stalin's Russia: it's like blaming Jesus Christ for the Inquisition in Spain.*
>
> TONY BENN

> All of our people all over the country—except the pure-blooded Indians— are immigrants or descendants of immigrants, including even those who came over here on the Mayflower.

And how dare Roosevelt criticize Stalin's prison camps (the *Gulags*)? Didn't Roosevelt have more than 100,000 Japanese-American citizens rounded up and, without trial, sent to prison camps in the United States? And, speaking of Japan, why was Japan in this war?

Until the mid-1800s, Japan was a fiercely isolationist "floating kingdom." It was content to be completely uninvolved with the rest of the world and remain "floating in the middle of the sea." In 1853, Commander Perry arrived with his gunboat diplomacy. He was intent not on conquering, but on opening trade routes. (Much more civilized than war.) If, however, the United States had left Japan in its 1853 feudal, shogun-dominated state, it would have been about as formidable in the 1940s as, say, Guam. Only eighty-eight years after the American gunboats forced Japan to become a trading partner, who was surprised that Japan would take its revenge by dropping bombs on the modern-day American gunboats at Pearl Harbor?

In a speech to the United States Congress nineteen days after Pearl Harbor, Winston Churchill asked indignantly, "What kind of people do [the Japanese] think we are?" They think, Sir Winston, that we are a pushy people who would use gunboats to open up trade with a country that wanted nothing more from the world than to be left alone. "They want to be left alone, do they? Well, bring on the artillery!"

> *I can retain neither
> respect nor affection
> for a Government which
> has been moving from wrong
> to wrong in order to defend
> its immorality.*
>
> MOHANDAS K. GANDHI

And as for England, although Churchill gave speeches which included lines such as, "We do not covet anything from any nation except their respect," Britain was still, in fact, an imperialist nation: England dominated several countries and had absolutely no intention of giving up control after World War II. Although by 1945 the sun *occasionally* set upon the British empire, it was not sundown for long. India was the perfect example. England had occupied and exploited the country for hundreds of years, and it was not about to stop now. Let us not forget Winston Churchill's words about the man who would eventually force England to leave: Mahatma Gandhi.*

> It is . . . nauseating to see Mr. Gandhi, a seditious Middle Temple lawyer now posing as a fakir of a type well known in the East, striding half-naked up the steps of the Vice-regal Palace, while he is still organizing and conducting a defiant campaign of civil disobedience, to parley on equal terms with the representative of the King Emperor.

So, perhaps Germany would be Russia's India, or, perhaps it would be Russia's Africa, supplying slave labor for Russian agriculture, or, perhaps Russia would populate Germany and "relocate" the Germans as the United States had the Native Americans.

Stalin maintained, whatever he planned to do with his portion of Germany after the war was *his* business, and it was not that of either England or the United States.

To add insult to injury, Roosevelt and Churchill wanted to bring France in as a full partner in the postwar division of Germany. France! Its "impregnable" Maginot line was a joke: Germany simply took Belgium and went around it. France fell within six weeks. France refused an alliance with the Soviet Union when Stalin offered it in the 1930s. Why should Stalin give away any of Germany to them? By rights, France should be part of the spoils to be divided: it had lost to Germany, and now Germany was about to lose to the Allies. In Stalin's view, France had surrendered its sovereignty in 1940.

Roosevelt, Churchill, and Stalin reached a compromise: Russia would agree to remain in the war until the victory in Japan was won; Germany would be occupied by four countries, including France; Russia would have full control of the countries east of Germany, but Poland would be guaranteed a representative form of government; and a United Nations would be formed as soon as the war was over.

---

*On a visit to England, Gandhi was asked, "What do you think of Western Civilization?" He thought for a moment and replied, "That would be a good idea."

And so, back to war.

⚖️ ⚖️ ⚖️

President Roosevelt died on April 12, 1945, the victory of the largest battle in his career—World War II—clearly in sight: Germany surrendered less than a month later. Vice-president Truman took over as president and the nation simultaneously mourned the loss of Roosevelt and celebrated the victory in Europe. Harry S Truman was, if nothing else, a realist.

> *You can no more win a war than you can win an earthquake.*
>
> JEANNETTE RANKIN

> My choice early in life was either to be a piano-player in a whorehouse or a politician. And to tell the truth there's hardly any difference.

In his first message to Congress on April 16, 1945, he gave his view of the post-war world:

> The responsibility of the great states is to serve and not to dominate the world.

This concept was directly counter to Stalin's, who believed that three powers had won the war and three powers should divide the world. When Truman, Churchill, and Stalin gathered at Potsdam on July 17, 1945, the chill of the coming Cold War was in the air. As at Yalta, Stalin brought the same trump card: war casualties. In terms of the dead, Stalin paid a higher price than all the Allied countries combined. (Roughly half of *all* World War II casualties were Russian.) To the Potsdam Conference, however, Truman (whose favorite game was poker) came to the table holding a wild card that would guarantee him a winning hand after hand: the day before the conference began, on July 16, the first atomic bomb was exploded at Alamogordo, New Mexico.

Although Roosevelt may not have been strong physically, he was smart. When Roosevelt took office in 1932, he organized what was called the Brain Trust. He sought the power of intellect, ideas, and creativity to help solve the formidable problems facing the country. World War II was won because, at the beginning of the war, the West, inferior in armaments, had a slight *technological* advantage. Although Britain did not have the air power (brute force) of Hitler's Luftwaffe, England had radar, giving it *information*. Before a British plane left the ground, Air Command knew where the German planes had entered English airspace, how many there were, and at what speed they were flying. Without radar, England would have lost the war.

Another example of brain over brawn was the British mathematical genius who, early in the war, broke the Nazi code. By intercepting radio communications, Britain knew the German ship and submarine movements, as well as other vital military information. Germany was quite certain it was protected by its "unbreakable" code. One brain unlocked the information without which England would have fallen.*

Hitler appreciated brains and technology, too. His "flying bombs" brought untold destruction to British cities. When his rocket bomb, the V-1, was developed, the devastation was so great and the potential devastation so awesome that the news was kept from the British people. What cost Hitler some of his best technology—and the war—was his uncontrolled antisemitism. The finest Jewish scientists, mathematicians, and inventors either died in Hitler's concentration camps or fled the country. One was Albert Einstein. On August 2, 1939, he wrote a letter to President Roosevelt discussing the wartime possibilities of $E = mc^2$:

> This new phenomena [atomic energy] would also lead to the construction of bombs. . . . A single bomb of this type, carried by boat and exploded in a port, might very well destroy the whole port, together with some of the surrounding territory. However, such bombs might very well prove to be too heavy for transportation by air.

Einstein was right to flee from Hitler, wrong about how large the bombs would be, but right about their potential destruction.** This, too, was information Truman brought to the Potsdam poker table: an atomic bomb *could* be carried by airplane. Its use, then, was not limited to seaports. No target was safe: not Hiroshima, not Nagasaki, not Moscow.

Stalin, in direct contrast to the technological West, fought the war in the time-honored tradition of "throw more troops at the enemy." In creating the love of country and fear of retribution necessary for whole towns and regimens to fight to the bitter end, Stalin was a genius. When it came to ideas, well, let's just say that Stalin would never have been part of Roosevelt's Brain Trust.

And so the Hot War, for all practical purposes, ended with the hottest-ever

---

*The man who broke the code, Alan Turing, also happened to be a homosexual. After the war, rather than being treated as a war hero, he was persecuted for his sexual preference. He was arrested in 1952 for "gross indecency" and placed on probation with the condition that he submit to "treatment" for his homosexuality. Two years of "treatments" failed to "cure" him of his homosexuality. On June 7, 1954, he dipped an apple in cyanide, ate it, and died.

**In the brain versus brawn department, Stalin wanted Russian troops to be the first to enter Berlin: they were. The taking of Berlin was a great show of force and a display of power. The Americans, meanwhile, were busy scurrying off the German scientists—led by Wernher von Braun—who had developed the V-1 rocket. Stalin wanted the brawn; America wanted von Braun. Herr von Braun became the head of the U.S. space program. When the first rocket to the moon was about to be launched, a reporter asked von Braun, "How do we know this won't land on London?"

manmade flash in the New Mexico desert on July 16, and the Cold War began on July 17 as Truman and Stalin sat down at the poker table in Potsdam.

"Deal," said Truman coolly.

With the atomic bomb, the United States no longer needed Russia's support in the invasion of Japan. The atomic bomb also neutralized Stalin's implied threats concerning Europe that "There are 20 million more Russians where those came from." Stalin knew that England and the United States were not willing to risk high casualties in order to have their way on post-war Germany. Stalin, on the other hand, was willing. England and the United States had this funny quirk: they actually *cared* about how many troops they lost. Stalin found this a weakness in war: as a general, he only cared if there were more troops left. Stalin mercilessly exploited what he saw as the West's weakness. At Yalta it had worked. At Potsdam it did not. The West now had the power to, with one bomb, succeed where both Napoleon and Hitler had failed: to destroy Moscow.

> *The belief in the possibility of a short decisive war appears to be one of the most ancient and dangerous of human illusions.*
>
> ROBERT LYND

With the bomb, the West did not just have the winning hand: it owned the casino. Stalin backed off, licked his wounds, and began making other plans. Some say we should have continued the war until Stalin was eliminated; others say Stalin should have been given the Germany he wanted. One side said destroy him; another side said make him a friend. The United States did neither. Stalin left Potsdam humiliated but not weakened. The Cold War had begun.

⚖ ⚖ ⚖

Publicly, the Potsdam Conference was labeled a success. U.S. Undersecretary of State Dean Acheson issued the following statement:

> Never in the past has there been any place on the globe where the vital interests of American and Russian people have clashed or even been antagonistic . . . and there is no reason to suppose there should be now or in the future ever such a place.

Truman immediately began a plan to rebuild Europe and give it back to the Europeans—including the Germans. Congress approved the spending of—in today's dollars—the equivalent of $100 billion. This rebuilding of Europe has usually been couched in humanitarian terms and, from one point of view, it was a humanitarian venture. Stalin, however, saw it as a military action against Russia and an insult to him personally. The rebuilding of Europe was even administered by a general and named after him: the Marshall Plan.

Here was the West, returning German control to Germany. Russia shared a

> *All through history it's
> the nations that have given most
> to the generals and the least
> to the people that have been
> the first to fall.*
>
> HARRY S TRUMAN

border with Germany. England was across the English Channel, and America was across the Atlantic Ocean. Just as Hitler had not invaded England or the United States, Stalin reasoned, so, too, Germany's next leader would invade Russia first.

On a more immediate level, Stalin perceived the United States as "buying" the favor of the European people. These were the *enemies*. Where was the money for the *allies?* The United States would have a strong presence in Europe—perhaps strong enough in a few years to take over Russia. Stalin began rebuilding Russia, but always with a cautious eye on the West.

Soon, practically all contact between the East and the West was cut off. This rapid deterioration was, officially, kept from the American people, but rumors abounded. After meeting with President Truman at the White House on February 12, 1946, Churchill joked with the reporters,

> I think "No Comment" is a splendid expression. I am using it again and again.

By the time Churchill addressed Westminster College in Fulton, Missouri, on March 5, 1946, however, the lines of the Cold War were drawn—and given a name:

> From Stettin in the Baltic to Trieste in the Adriatic an iron curtain has descended across the Continent.

At Nuremberg, only a handful of Nazis were punished; in Japan, the emperor not only got to live, but got to continue as emperor. Germany and Japan were now our friends. Russia, on the other hand, was the new enemy. Anti-communism grew into a frenzy.

In 1949, Stalin exploded a bomb: the same atom bomb Truman had exploded at Potsdam. Russia now had The Bomb. The balance of power tipped, this time in Stalin's favor. Something had to be done! Scapegoats had to be found! They were.

In 1951, Julius and Ethel Rosenberg were tried and convicted for "wartime espionage." Their crime: passing along atomic secrets to the Russians. Their sentence: death. Whether the Rosenbergs were guilty of actually passing information to Russia, whether the information they passed was of any value in developing the bomb, or even if there were any "atomic secrets" to pass, did not really matter. What mattered was that Julius and Ethel Rosenberg were long-time members of the American Communist Party. That was enough. Scapegoats only have to be goats, not guilty. Although either Truman or Eisenhower could have granted clemency, neither did. The Rosenbergs were executed on June 19, 1953.

But they were only the most obvious scapegoats. Russia's atomic bomb had

AIN'T NOBODY'S BUSINESS IF YOU DO

also lit a fire under the already overheated Senator Joseph McCarthy. The McCarthy witch hunts began.

Had this era not produced so much tragedy, it would be a good theme for a comedy. Looking back, Joseph McCarthy was absolutely *ridiculous*. Take, for example, these three statements of his made on February 9, 10, and 20, 1950. From these statements, can you answer the question, "How many communists are there in the State Department?":

> *They'll nail anyone*
> *who ever scratched his ass*
> *during the national anthem.*
>
> HUMPHREY BOGART

- I have here in my hand a list of 205 that were known to the Secretary of State as being members of the Communist Party and who, nevertheless, are still working and shaping policy in the State Department.

- Last night I discussed Communists in the State Department. I stated that I had the names of 57 card-carrying members of the Communist Party. Now, I want to tell the Secretary this: If he wants to call me tonight at the Utah Hotel, I will be glad to give him the names of those 57 card-carrying members.

- There is a serious question whether I should disclose names to the Senate. I frankly feel, in view of the number of cases—there are 81 cases—that it would be a mistake to disclose the names on the floor. I should be willing, happy and eager to go before any committee and give the names and all the information available.

He made statements that were so illogical any child should have been able to see through them. In 1951, for example:

> The Communists within our borders have been more responsible for the success of Communism abroad than Soviet Russia.

McCarthy was, in fact, a raving paranoid. Consider this quote from Richard Hofstadter's book, *The Paranoid Style in American Politics*, taken from a speech given by McCarthy on the Senate floor, June 14, 1951:

> How can we account for our present situation unless we believe that men high in this government are concerting to deliver us to disaster? This must be the product of a great conspiracy, a conspiracy on a scale so immense as to dwarf any previous venture in the history of man. A conspiracy of infamy so black that, when it is finally exposed, its principals shall be forever deserving of the maledictions of all honest men.

Although Truman later claimed, "I've said many a time that I think the Un-American Activities Committee in the House of Representatives was the most un-American thing in America!" he was remarkably silent about it while he was president and while it was happening. Dwight D. Eisenhower, who took over the presidency on January 20, 1953, gave speeches (such as this at Columbia University on May 31, 1954):

> The tendency to claim God as an ally for our partisan values and ends is the source of all religious fanaticism.
>
> REINHOLD NIEBUHR

Here in America we are descended in blood and in spirit from revolutionaries and rebels—men and women who dared to dissent from accepted doctrine. As their heirs, may we never confuse honest dissent with disloyal subversion.

Nevertheless, Eisenhower did little to interfere with the House Un-American Activities Committee. It took individual citizens, refusing to cooperate with the committee, to slow the committee from the Stalinesque purge it so desperately wanted. On May 16, 1953, Albert Einstein wrote:

> Every intellectual who is called before one the committees ought to refuse to testify, i.e., he must be prepared . . . for the sacrifice of his personal welfare in the interest of the cultural welfare of his country. . . . This kind of inquisition violates the spirit of the Constitution.
>
> If enough people are ready to take this grave step they will be successful. If not, then the intellectuals of this country deserve nothing better than the slavery which is intended for them.

Those who failed to cooperate by "naming names of known communists" were fired, blacklisted, and jailed. To give you an idea of the sort of power the committee thought it had, consider this from Representative J. Parnell Thomas during a House Un-American Activities Committee hearing to a witness who claimed a constitutional right:

> The rights you have are the rights given to you by Committee. We will determine what rights you have and what rights you have not got.

The United States was so caught up with its own internal anti-communist witch hunt that it failed to notice the most important event of 1953: the death of its enemy. With Stalin's passing in 1953, the Cold War *could* have been over. All this witch hunting was, apparently, too much fun (and there were darker motives, which we shall get to shortly), so it continued. In 1956, when the Soviet Communist Party denounced Stalin's "policies and personality" (and there's not much more about a political leader you can denounce than that), once again the door was wide open for a warmer relationship with Russia: we could all blame the Cold War on Stalin, declare the hostilities over, and get on with our lives. Although Stalin's replacement, Nikita Khrushchev, pursued a policy of "peaceful coexistence" and even toured the United States in 1959 (visiting Disneyland and the set of the film *Can-Can*), he canceled a 1960 Paris Summit Conference when a United States reconnaissance plane was shot down over Russia. The flying of illegal spy planes over Russia was hardly a gesture that would help end the Cold

War.

To prove that Khrushchev was another Stalin with world domination on his mind, one phrase was repeated over and over: "We will bury you." Khrushchev said this at the end of a longer speech given at the Polish Embassy in Moscow on November 18, 1956. The speech ended:

> *If we maintain our faith in God, our love of freedom, and superior global air power, I think we can look to the future with confidence.*
>
> GENERAL CURTIS LeMAY
> February 1956

> About the capitalist states, it doesn't depend on you whether or not we exist. If you don't like us, don't accept our invitations, and don't invite us to come and see you. Whether you like it or not, history is on our side. We will bury you.

The last two sentences, however, do not appear in either *Pravda* or the *New York Times*, both of which printed the complete text of the speech. How did these lines get added? And why? Even the translation, "We will bury you," is inaccurate: a better translation would be, "We will walk on your graves," which only implies disrespect; "We will bury you" implies aggression.

Joseph McCarthy's paranoia proved highly contagious. The whole country got a bad case of anti-communism. (I use, here, the "contagion" analogy Roosevelt used to describe Hitler.) Consequently, FBI Director J. Edgar Hoover became a bestselling self-help author. In his 1958 book, *Masters of Deceit: The Story of Communism and How to Fight It*, Hoover tells us how to spot a communist—and why communists are so difficult to spot:

> The communist official will probably live in a modest neighborhood. His wife will attend the corner grocery store, his children attend the local school. If a shoe store or butcher shop is operated by a Party member, the official will probably get a discount on his purchases.

> Most Party officials drive cars, usually older models. They are generally out late at night, attending meetings. Except for special affairs, communist activity is slight early in the morning. The organizer, coming in around midnight or one o'clock, will sleep late. But that doesn't mean all day. One Southern official was severely censured for sleeping too late; to solve the problem the Party bought him an electric alarm clock.

But it wasn't just the paranoia of McCarthy, Hoover, and others. For anti-communism to continue as the country's bedrock fundamental, accepted-without-question belief required a much deeper motive. The questions, "Who perpetuated the religion of anti-communism?" and "Why?" were answered by President Dwight David Eisenhower on January 17, 1961. During his farewell address to the American people, three days before turning over the presidential reins to John F. Kennedy, he said:

> *We must especially beware of*
> *that small group of selfish men*
> *who would clip the wings*
> *of the American Eagle*
> *in order to feather their own nests.*
>
> FRANKLIN D. ROOSEVELT

This conjunction of an immense military establishment and a large arms industry is new in the American experience. The total influence—economic, political, even spiritual—is felt in every city, every statehouse, every office of the federal government. . . .We must not fail to comprehend its grave implications.

In the councils of government, we must guard against the acquisition of unwarranted influence, whether sought or unsought, by the military-industrial complex. The potential for the disastrous rise of misplaced power exists and will persist.

Eisenhower spilled the beans and went off to play golf. Ike slipped it into his speech and slipped out of town. His warning went right over the heads of the American public, where, for the most part, it dangles even today.

Without the threat of communist aggression, the build-up of the military—and its blank-check policy with industry—would have been entirely unnecessary. If Russia was our friend, who would be our enemy? There was none. A wartime economy, however, is *terrific* for industry. In a wartime economy, industry makes guaranteed profits with no fear of competition or need for efficiency. The typical defense contract reads: Spend what you need, deliver it when you can, and add a 15% profit. What industry wouldn't want *that* kind of contract rather than competing for profits in a free marketplace? Capitalism is *work*. Defense Department contracts are *play*.

Just as a wartime economy does not require industry to follow the precepts of capitalism, so, too, in time of war, the military is not required to follow democratic principles. The military structure, of course, is precisely the opposite of a democracy; the will of the people is not communicated from below: orders are passed down from above. For those who love power, democracy is inconvenient. The military is the power seeker's paradise.

So, the profit-hungry industrialists and the power-hungry militarists were busy destroying capitalism and democracy *in the name of defending capitalism and democracy*.

John F. Kennedy knew of the military-industrial complex's power—his father made quite a lot of money with a more primitive form of this economic system. Kennedy did what he could to work within it. He attempted, for example, to switch from war production to space production. The "space race" was not sold to the American public as a way of advancing humanity's scientific knowledge, but as a way to "beat the Russians to the moon." Kennedy hoped to redirect the anti-communist sentiment into a peacetime activity that would keep the military-industrial complex happy. Alas, a race to the moon was not enough. The military-industrial complex needed a war. The military-industrial complex thought Vietnam held all the delicious possibilities of Korea. Kennedy resisted. Many assassination buffs maintain that this resistance is what got Kennedy killed.*

According to Stanley Karnow's book, *Vietnam: A History,* Lyndon Baines Johnson, at a 1963 Christmas party with military-industrial complex types, told them, "Just get me elected and you can have your damn war."

> *If the United States gives up [in Vietnam] the Pacific Ocean will become a Red Sea.*
>
> RICHARD M. NIXON
> October 15, 1965

Whatever the origins of the Vietnam War, it didn't turn out the way *anyone* wanted. Poor Johnson. Here was a president who passed more civil rights legislation than any in history, and the people he thought would praise him for his agenda of social change were the very ones who attacked him for attacking the Vietnamese. By 1968, Johnson was fed up, and chose not to run again for president. By this time, however, as one commentator noted, "Our fear that communism might someday take over most of the world blinds us to the fact that anti-communism already has."

The perfect military-industrial presidential candidate? Richard Milhous Nixon. Here's the man who had, as vice-president, successfully defended American industry against none other than Nikita Khrushchev in Moscow in the Kitchen Debates. He was also prone to making such statements as, "What are schools for if not indoctrination against communism?" What, indeed?

(Not that his opponent, Hubert Horatio Humphrey, could for a moment be considered soft on communism. Humphrey said, "The greatest risk is communist aggression, communist conquest, and communist advance." The *greatest* risk? Oh, Hubert, say it ain't so.) As a staunch pro-capitalist with strong anti-communist credentials, Nixon could do some things that no liberal democrat would *dare* to do. For example, as Gore Vidal described it, "Nixon sort of *wandered over* to Communist China one day in 1972 and made friends with them all." Well, *that* was a billion fewer communists to worry about. But those Russians. We still had to worry about them.

---

*This is presented as conspiracy-buff theory *only*, not as fact. For an entertaining—and disturbing—view of this theory, see Oliver Stone's film, *JFK.* (The director's cut is available on video and recommended over the theatrical cut.) For an overview of the conspiracy debvate, read the book of the film, which includes 97 reactions and commentaries from historians, journalists, and others, as will as 340 research notes used by Stone and Zachary Sklar in writing the screenplay. If the Kennedy assassination was a military-industrial plot, making it appear to be the work of a self-confessed "socialist" with a Russian wife, photographed handing out "Fair Play for Cuba" leaflets, was quite clever. The sheer *economy* of such a move, however, directly counters military procedure. With one assassination, it wipes out the most powerful opponent to the Vietnam War and strengthens America's anti-communist and anti-Russian sentiments. That seems just *too* efficient for the military.

After the Vietnam War was lost in 1973, the domino theory fell. One country after another in Southeast Asia did *not* fall to communist aggression. U.S.–Soviet relations entered into a period of *detente*, which is Russian for, "We're both really tired; why don't we rest for a while?" Presidents Ford and Carter were happy with this policy. So, apparently, were most of the American people. Ronald Reagan was not.* There was a term once used in the press, *Afghanistanism*, which meant, "reporting obscure stories of foreign news because there's nothing else to write about." Prior to the Soviet invasion of Afghanistan, the doings in Afghanistan were an example of the most obscure and meaningless foreign news story possible. But because Russia had invaded it, Reagan was for defending it. He also found pockets of subversive communism in South America, Central American, and, of course, America. The Cold War heated up, but Russia was not ready for another round. It was bankrupt. As the Iron Curtain came crashing down in the late 1980s and early 1990s, what we found was not a political superpower, but a near–third-world country without roads, industry, communications, or viable economy. If Russia hadn't been Russia, we would have been giving it foreign aid for decades. As it turns out, Russia was just "putting on a show." (Even the film of Russia's first space walk was later proven to be shot in a film studio.)

Commentators differ as to when the Cold War could have ended. Some say Stalin could have been made a friend in 1945. Others say it could have ended after Stalin's death in 1953. Others say after Stalin's denouncement by even Russia in 1956. John Chancellor's theory, as reported in his book, *Peril and Promise: A Commentary on America,* and in the 1993 *World Almanac and Book of Facts* is:

> The Cold War was a necessity when it began, when the Soviet regime posed a genuine threat to democratic governments. It was a necessity at least until Khrushchev put missiles in Cuba in 1962. After that, its own momentum kept the Cold War going until it was stopped by the internal contradictions of the communist system. But while it lasted, life in the U.S. was shaped by it.

If Chancellor's analysis is correct, the Vietnam War was completely unnecessary. Some commentators say after the fall of Vietnam and the failure of communism to spread throughout the Mideast, there was no need for the massive nuclear and military build-up that continued taking place. Looking back, few except the

---

*When I say "Ronald Reagan" I mean, of course, the people who were behind him. We know he was—literally—only an actor. To say he was the star player in the Military-Industrial-Complex Playhouse is probably not unfair.

extreme right accept the necessity for the multi-trillion dollar military build-up during the Reagan-Bush years.

Who (or what) kept the fact that Russia was bankrupt from the American people for so long? It wasn't Russia—U.S. intelligence knew it well. Why weren't we told? Do you suppose the initials M-I-C had something to do with it?

⚖ ⚖ ⚖

> HELEN THOMAS:
>
> *Mr. President, would your view of Communism have been different if you had gone to Russia twenty years ago and saw how they laughed, cried, and were human?*
>
> PRESIDENT REAGAN:
>
> *No. They've changed.*

What did the Cold War cost us? We can start with the 118,000 American military deaths and 256,000 injuries suffered since 1945—most of which resulted from various anti-communist military conflicts. We can add to that a good portion of the accumulated Defense Department budget from 1945 to 1993: a mere $20 trillion. If we hadn't wasted much of this amount in unnecessary defense, the national debt—currently dragging us down—would be a national surplus. In this country alone, the Defense Department has left behind 11,000 sites which are contaminated either by radioactive materials or toxic chemicals. And then there are all those Vietnam veterans, a disproportionate number of whom fill the ranks of the homeless.

One more thing: these people are still in charge. Maybe not the same *people*, but the same organizations. The Military-Industrial-Complex Playhouse plays on. They're just having a little trouble finding a new leading player: Bush failed, and Quayle never got out of the bush. Casting, however, continues in earnest. The religious right keeps the campfires burning, and liberals who worry more about stomping out drug use than preventing others from stomping on the Constitution throw napalm on those campfires. Meanwhile, the War on Drugs is being sold to the American public with the same techniques as the War on Communism. "What's next?" one wonders.

What may be next is any political thought that doesn't fit into the conservative Democrat/Republican range. Libertarians, for example—even though their basic philosophy seems completely in tune with the Constitution—are routinely characterized as kooks who want to let vicious criminals run in the streets—machine guns in hand. Liberals are deluded do-gooders. One of the reasons Michael Dukakis lost so badly in his presidential bid was that his opponents succeeded in labeling him "a liberal"; Clinton took great pains to avoid it.

⚖ ⚖ ⚖

The solution to the Cold War—or any other war against unpopular political views, including the war against consensual crime—was given in 1961 by George F. Kennan in his book, *Russia and the West under Lenin and Stalin:*

> *When the tyrant has disposed of foreign enemies by conquest or treaty, and there is nothing to fear from them, then he is always stirring up some war or other, in order that the people may require a leader.*
>
> PLATO

If we are to regard ourselves as a grown-up nation—and anything else will henceforth be mortally dangerous—then we must, as the Biblical phrase goes, put away childish things; and among these childish things the first to go, in my opinion, should be self-idealization and the search for absolutes in world affairs: for absolute security, absolute amity, absolute harmony.

John Chancellor talks about the end of the Cold War:

The Cold War was won by the west, but there were no victory celebrations, no ticker-tape parades. For Americans, the Cold War didn't have a real ending. It just stopped, like a movie projector that had run out of film.

There's lots more film available for that projector, however, and we must be careful to know a movie when we see one. A consensual crime—drug use—currently monopolizes that projector. Other reels are being edited and, if sufficiently menacing political enemies cannot be found, consensual criminals will have to do. Note the horror films the Pentagon (not to mention Jerry Falwell) had ready when it was suggested the military acknowledge the gays already in its ranks. Films are available for all the other consensual crimes, as well—for them to surface, all it takes is someone in power—or a sufficient number of the American people—to seriously suggest legalization.

For a preview, call your favorite bigoted person and suggest that your favorite consensual activity be legalized. Before you can say "the United States Constitution and its Bill of Rights," the projector will be threaded, the house lights dimmed, and the next show begun at the Military-Industrial-Complex-Cineplex. Let the good times roll.

Suicide and Assisted Suicide

> *Beware!*
> *To touch these wires*
> *is instant death.*
> *Anyone found doing so*
> *will be prosecuted.*
>
> sign at a railroad station

THERE CAN BE NO more fundamental statement concerning individual freedom and responsibility than this: *Our bodies and our lives belong to ourselves.* Our bodies do not belong to the state, to our relatives, or to our friends.

The laws against suicide and assisted suicide run directly counter to this concept. These laws spring from our cultural unwillingness to face the reality of death, and the religious belief that "only God can take a life."*

The laws against suicide are obviously the silliest laws in the world: if one is successful, who gets punished? Just as there was once Christian and unchristian burial, with suicides receiving unchristian burial, perhaps we should have different sections of the morgue: one for those who simply *died* and one for those who died *criminally.* If one does not succeed at suicide, then are we to assume that arresting and locking that person up is somehow going to help? "Where am I?" "You're in a jail cell. You attempted suicide. You're going to spend the next ten years of your life here." Terrific.

When Derek Humphrey's book on suicide, *Final Exit,* was published, it caused an *absolute scandal.* You would think he had divulged some great mystical secret; as though we all didn't know that the means to end our own life is in our own hands, and always at hand. *That* we can commit suicide at any time is a given. The only thing that laws against suicide force one to do when committing suicide is use techniques that are either messy, painful, dangerous to others—or all three.

*It is ironic that those who are the most ardent supporters of laws against suicide and assisted suicide based on religious grounds are precisely the ones who usually support capital punishment. Could we have a little consistency here, please?

> *Razors pain you;*
> *Rivers are damp;*
> *Acids stain you*
> *And drugs cause cramp;*
> *Guns aren't lawful;*
> *Nooses give;*
> *Gas smells awful;*
> *You might as well live.*
>
> DOROTHY PARKER

In attempting suicide, there's always the chance that one will wind up not dead, but a vegetable. It is this fear that causes people to use fail-safe (that is, absolutely guaranteed) methods of suicide that either hurt (hanging, slitting wrists in a warm bathtub), are messy (bullets in the head), or could potentially harm others (jumping off buildings, high-speed car crashes). The standard technique of "taking a bottle of sleeping pills," is uncertain at best. If one takes too few, one may wind up a vegetable. If one takes too many, one may vomit before sufficient medication is absorbed through the stomach and may wind up a vegetable.

All of this is so unnecessary because, with the proper number of pills, a simple injection, or inhaling carbon monoxide or nitrous oxide, one can peacefully and painlessly die.

When one chooses to die, shouldn't one have the right to do it in the presence of friends and loved ones? In more than half the states (and the number is growing), the law says no. If you do invite friends or loved ones to be there, you put them at risk for being charged with "assisted suicide," "accessory to suicide," or even murder. (First degree murder in at least two states.) So many suicide notes contain messages such as, "I'm so sorry we couldn't be together at the end, but I did not want to endanger you. I thought this way was best."

Note that I haven't said a *word* about motivation. One's motivation to commit suicide is not the issue here. What is at issue is the fundamental right to make decisions about one's own life. *Without government intervention.* Suicidal thoughts are a *symptom* of emotional depression. Our culture's taboo against suicide often keeps people who are thinking about suicide from talking about it. By talking about it, people can often get the emotional and psychological support they need to see them through a tough time. When people are afraid to talk about it, the pressures can increase to the point that they actually *do* something about it. If suicide itself were not forced to be—by law—such a lonely activity, we might have fewer suicides. Even if we do not, however, there is no reason for laws that make one's last moments painful and lonely.

Nowhere is the concept of assisted suicide and the cruelty of making it illegal more pronounced than when individuals are unable to take their own lives. People in advanced stages of life-threatening illness, for example, either don't have the use of their limbs or are unable to gather the proper drugs or paraphernalia by which they might deliver themselves. Here, suicide is *only* available through assistance. By filling out the proper legal documents ahead of time, people can clearly indicate the point of deterioration after which they choose to no longer live. When this point is reached, death then becomes a medical procedure.

We accept the fact that if one makes a living will, his or her life will not be artificially extended through the use of life support systems. Once the life support systems are removed, however (an accepted medical procedure), have you considered what death might be like for that person? To find out, exhale completely and do not take your next breath while you continue reading. (Please try this.) If one is taken off artificial respiration, he or she no longer has the ability to inhale. Death may come "within a matter of minutes," but what are those minutes like? "Well, they'll be given painkilling medications, won't they?" To the degree prescribed by law, yes. These are, however, sometimes woefully inadequate. To take a breath (as you probably are noticing if you are attempting the experiment) is a powerful biologic imperative. The lack of oxygen can sometimes rouse one from the limited legal dosages of painkilling medication. Of course, this torture may go on for days. One might be able to rouse oneself to, say, two breaths per minute. Or, one's lungs may be filling up with fluids in what the doctors acknowledge will be the inevitable form of death. Here, one is permitted to slowly drown. If intravenous feeding tubes (medically considered a form of life support) are removed, one dies of dehydration; this while one is starving to death.

> *To save a man's life*
> *against his will*
> *is the same as killing him.*
>
> HORACE
> B.C. 65–8

People who take part in the "death watch," in hospitals where the end is near, often ask the doctors, "Isn't there something you can give [him or her]?" The answer: no. Certainly not by law. That some hospital personnel quietly give larger doses of drugs than necessary is a well-known and generally accepted medical fact. The administration of these drugs, of course, must be kept absolutely confidential. The family, then, cannot know the moment of death. (In fact, such medical mercies are usually performed when no one is present.)

The desire to be with loved ones when they die is a strong one. Once a person who is clearly dying has indicated his or her desire to die after a certain point of deterioration—why should being with that person for the final moments be a matter of chance? The days—sometimes weeks—of waiting around hospitals twenty-four hours a day, being afraid to leave even for a moment because that might be when the loved one dies, are an unnecessary torture on those being left behind.

As Charlotte Perkins Gilman wrote in her suicide note:

> Human life consists in mutual service. No grief, pain, misfortune or "broken heart" is excuse for cutting off one's life while any power of service remains. But when all usefulness is over, when one is assured of an unavoidable and imminent death, it is the simplest of human rights to choose a quick and easy death in place of a slow and horrible one.

ॐ ॐ ॐ

In contemplating suicide when death is imminent and there is nothing ahead but pain and suffering, I find it fascinating to consider these passages from the New Testament. Mark (15:23) tells us that just before the Crucifixion "they offered [Jesus] wine mixed with myrrh, but he did not take it." Matthew (27:34) says, "There they offered Jesus wine to drink, mixed with gall; but after tasting it, he refused to drink it." Gall and myrrh—especially when combined—were strong narcotics, and perhaps poison. One of the definitions in the *Oxford English Dictionary* for *gall* is "poison, venom." It was the custom, prior to crucifixion, to give prisoners a narcotic to ease the pain. Jesus, however, turned this down before the Crucifixion. After three hours, however, John (19:28–30) tells us:

> Later, knowing that all was now completed, and so that the Scripture would be fulfilled, Jesus said, "I am thirsty." A jar of wine vinegar was there, so they soaked a sponge in it, put the sponge on a stalk of the hyssop plant, and lifted it to Jesus' lips. When he had received the drink, Jesus said, "It is finished." With that, he bowed his head and gave up his spirit.

Could it be Jesus knew that, in his weakened condition, the drugged wine would be sufficient to carry him off? Was it the same gall-myrrh-laced wine he had been offered earlier, or was it wine belonging to the centurions that had no intoxicants other than alcohol in it? Having accomplished all he needed to do on earth ("knowing that all was now completed"), and knowing there was nothing but pain ahead (crucifixions could go on for days), did Jesus knowingly use the wine to end his earthly life? The only additional clue we have comes from Mark (15:44–45), in which Joseph of Arimathea asks Pilate for the body of Jesus:

> Pilate was surprised to hear that he was already dead. Summoning the centurion, he asked him if Jesus had already died. When he learned from the centurion that it was so, he gave the body to Joseph.

Could it be that the religious restrictions to suicide and assisted suicide—under certain conditions—are based on something other than the life and teachings of Jesus?

ॐ ॐ ॐ

Again, I am not discussing the ethics of when *others* decide your life is over, but the rights you yourself have to determine when you no longer want to live. If individuals—for spiritual, religious, or any other reasons—choose to hang on until God or nature determines their last breath, they certainly have that right.

What I am speaking of here is abolishing laws that prohibit people from taking their own lives, either with or without the assistance of others.

Life is a precious possession. As with all of our possessions, how we use, manage, and eventually say good-bye to life is our own business, not the law's.

> *Who knows?*
> *Maybe my life belongs to God.*
> *Maybe it belongs to me.*
> *But I do know one thing:*
> *I'm damned if it belongs*
> *to the government.*
>
> ARTHUR HOPPE

THE TITANIC MARITIME MEMORIAL ACT OF 1985

TUESDAY, OCTOBER 29, 1985

House of Representatives,
Committee on Merchant Marine and Fisheries,
Washington, DC.

The committee met, pursuant to call, at 1:40 p.m., in room 1334, Longworth House Office Building, Hon. Walter B. Jones (chairman of the committee) presiding.

Present: Representatives Jones, Anderson, Studds, Hughes, Carper, Bosco, Tallon, Thomas, Ortiz, Manton, Shumway, Fields, Schneider, McKernan, Franklin, Chappie, Saxton, and Bentley.

OPENING STATEMENT OF HON. WALTER B. JONES, A U.S. REPRESENTATIVE FROM NORTH CAROLINA, AND CHAIRMAN, MERCHANT MARINE AND FISHERIES COMMITTEE

The CHAIRMAN. The meeting will come to order, please.

Without objection from any part of the members of the committee, the TV cameras will be on during the session.

Is there any objection?

If not, so ordered.

This morning the Oceanography Subcommittee held a hearing on the issue of shipwrecks. This afternoon we will listen to testimony concerning a particular shipwreck of such unique significance as to merit its own hearing.

Many consider it to have been the greatest of all maritime disasters. Like most people, I was intrigued by the recent discovery of the *Titanic*. Shortly thereafter, I introduced H.R. 3272. This bill memorializes the shipwreck of the *Titanic* as a gravesite to the more than 1,500 passengers who perished with her.

Immediately after this tragedy occurred in April 1912, the Senate held hearings to learn of its cause. Seventy-three years later, this committee will reopen discussion of the *Titanic* disaster.

However, the purpose of our meeting today is to establish a record by which Congress can determine how the United States should now proceed, given the fact that the *Titanic* has finally been located.

Some folks would like to see the shipwreck salvaged immediately. Others feel strongly that she should remain undisturbed where she rests on the ocean floor.

H.R. 3272 will ensure that we give thoughtful consideration to all of these views before any activities proceed.

The Titanic Laws:
Public Drunkenness, Loitering, Vagrancy,
Seat Belts, Motorcycle Helmets,
Public Nudity, Transvestism

> *If you have ten thousand regulations you destroy all respect for the law.*
>
> SIR WINSTON CHURCHILL

THIS IS A CHAPTER in which we explore a variety of other consensual crimes. Each one demonstrates yet again (a) the government does not trust its citizens to take care of themselves; (b) the moralists of our time don't believe in the ancient wisdom, "live and let live"; (c) if we put a bunch of lawyers together, call them "lawmakers," give them a hefty salary, and provide them with nearly unlimited power . . . they will make laws; (d) if we ask the police, "Would you rather enforce *these* laws, or laws against *real* crimes?" they become far more interested in protecting people from *themselves* than from criminals.

I named this chapter "The Titanic Laws" not because these laws are so huge, enormous, or gargantuan (they are, in fact, only gargantuan in their pettiness). I named it after the ship, *H.M.S. Titanic.* I am not about to give a lecture on how the United States is a "ship of state" we believe is "unsinkable" and the "iceberg of consensual crimes" created by the "frigidity" of the moralists threatens to sink us, and most of us will drown in the icy waters of our own indifference. No, this chapter was named after an actual law, passed by the Congress of the United States after extended and expensive debate, and signed into law by President Ronald Reagan on October 21, 1986—just in time for Halloween.

The Titanic Maritime Memorial Act of 1985 makes it illegal for any U.S. citizen to buy, sell, or own anything that went down with the Titanic. This flies in the face of maritime salvage laws that have worked successfully since long before the formation of the United States. The Titanic Maritime Memorial Act is also yet another unnecessary hindrance to free enterprise and our rights as citizens to buy, sell, or own whatever we choose. The lawmakers wanted to allow the *Titanic* to rest "undisturbed" on the ocean floor and discourage salvage operations by elimi-

> *Reader, suppose you were an idiot.*
> *And suppose you were*
> *a member of Congress.*
> *But I repeat myself.*
>
> MARK TWAIN

nating the American market. I don't know about you, but ever since hearing about this law I have *desperately* wanted to own a piece of the *Titanic*. Call me a rebel without a pause, but *anything* will do: a rusty bolt, a broken tea cup, an ice cube.

In order for such a nonsensical law to pass, the bill had to discuss such concepts as not disturbing the graves of those brave passengers who sank in mid-Atlantic in 1912. Well, a great many of the bodies were recovered and properly buried. The rest were eaten by fishes long ago. (Perhaps we should pass a law saying that no fishing can take place within 300 miles of the *Titanic* to make sure we don't eat any of those fish who might be descendants of fish who nibbled on one of those "brave" passengers. Or perhaps we should just nuke the whole area to punish all those fish who don't respect graves.)

⚖ ⚖ ⚖

Speaking of federal laws, death, and the ocean, did you know that "burial of cremated remains shall take place no closer than three nautical miles from land"? This is to make sure that the remains "will have minimal adverse environmental impact." And, did you know that you have to report all such burials "within 30 days to the (EPA) Regional Administrator of the Region from which the vessel carrying the remains departed"?

When a body is cremated, it is exposed to 1800- to 2000-degree heat for $1\frac{1}{2}$ to 3 hours. Nothing is left but some brittle bones, which are ground up—one's ashes are not really ashes; they are ground calcium—and placed in a container. What remains is about two quarts of, well, *remains*.

The Environmental Protection Agency (EPA) permits raw sewage, toxic waste, and poisons of various kinds (within certain limits) to be dumped into lakes, streams, and directly offshore. Outrageously sanitized ground calcium, however, must go outside the three-mile limit. One also wonders, "What does the Regional Administrator *do* with all those reports? What does he or she need them for? Is it possible that there could be *so much* ash dumping in a certain section of ocean outside the three-mile limit that the Regional Administrator would be forced to cordon off a segment of the ocean? Give people the job of administrating, and they'll create things to administrate.

⚖ ⚖ ⚖

Granted, disturbing the "International Maritime Memorial to the men, women, and children who perished aboard" the *Titanic* (I was quoting from the law there) and dumping Uncle Nathan's ashes only 2½ miles and not 3 miles from shore do not exactly fill the police blotters or jail cells, but let's consider a crime that does: *public drunkenness.* More than 6% of all arrests in 1991—881,100—were for public drunkenness. This is, simply, being drunk in public—not operating a motor vehicle, trespassing, or disturbing the peace (they each have their own arrest categories). No, public drunkenness is someone staggering down the street or leaning against the pro-

> *All casual drug users should be taken out and shot.*
>
> DARYL GATES
> *Los Angeles Chief of Police*

verbial lamp post. Like loitering (another 93,400 arrests) or vagrancy (38,500 arrests), public drunkenness is generally considered one of those "discretionary laws": the police make the arrest or not based on their own discretion. Police are not supposed to arrest *everyone* who appears drunk in public (imagine the jail load on New Year's Eve if that were the case), but those who are, well . . . what?

Here's the problem with discretionary laws: what is the criterion of discretion? Not having specific criteria allows law enforcement officers to write the law, try the case, and enforce it on the spot. Ultimately (and inevitably), this leads to a police state. Those who make the laws, those who arrest people for breaking the laws, and those who decide whether the suspects are guilty or not are kept in three distinct groups for a very good reason: to protect our freedom. Any breach of that system invites trouble.

As it is, the public drunkenness, loitering, and vagrancy laws can be used as excuses by unethical law enforcement officers to arrest people they happen not to like. "I smell alcohol on your breath. I'm taking you in for public drunkenness." You won't be convicted, generally, but a night in a jail cell is punishment enough. Sue the officer for false arrest? Right. That means hiring a lawyer. Out of the jail cell and into the fire.

Please keep in mind that if public drunkenness, loitering, or vagrancy become trespassing, disturbing the peace, vandalism, or obstructing traffic, then arrests are in order. Yes, it may be uncomfortable seeing drunks, loiterers, and vagrants staggering, loitering, and being vague on public streets, but that's the price we pay for keeping them *public* streets and not "Official Police Property."

⚖ ⚖ ⚖

Seat belt laws and helmet laws are perfect examples of the government not trusting us to make our own decisions about our own lives. But—with seat belt laws in particular—there's a lot more than mere paternalism in the works. Here politics, power, and simple greed enter—trap door, center. This from *Consumer Reports,* April 1993:

The single most significant safety improvement is the air bag, an improvement that auto manufacturers fought every step of the way.

The first air-bag regulations were promulgated by the National Highway Traffic Safety Administration in 1970. But when auto makers complained that air bags were too expensive, the Nixon administration quashed the rule.

An air bag standard was reissued in 1977, under Jimmy Carter, but was revoked again, in 1981, when the Reagan Administration caved in to auto makers' complaints.

After the Supreme Court ruled that the Administration unlawfully rescinded the rule, a new air-bag standard was issued in 1984. But the auto makers again succeeded in watering it down, so that it required only "passive restraints." Those could be air bags or "automatic" safety belts, or a combination—at the carmaker's discretion.

This is where the seat belt laws came from. The federal government *forced* states to enact mandatory seat belt laws. (If the states wanted to continue receiving federal highway funding, they had to pass seat-belt laws.) Yes, this was a major intrusion upon the rights of drivers—especially drivers who believed they were safer without seat belts. (A minority, but certainly entitled to risk their own lives on their opinion.) The reason for these seat belt laws is that Detroit did not want to include the air bags—which automatically protect the driver and passenger better than seat belts do—and the Nixon and Reagan administrations went along with the auto makers.

Instead of telling the American public the truth, however, Detroit and the federal regulators regaled us with one story after another about how many lives would be saved, how many injuries prevented, and how kind the federal government was to force the states to enact these laws. However, to continue from the *Consumer Reports* article:

> A driver's-side air bag increases the driver's chance of surviving a crash by 29 percent. That's on top of the margin afforded by wearing lap-and-shoulder belts. Had all cars on the road in 1991 been equipped with a driver's-side air bag, some 4,000 people killed that year would have survived.

That's 80,000 people over the past twenty years—*without* the mandatory seat belt law. So, really: does the federal government *care* about us? Not unless we're a major lobby. What's especially galling is the sanctimonious attitude with which the government takes away our personal freedoms and convinces us it's for our own good, while, in reality, it's allowing people to die unnecessarily every day because it caved in to political and economic pressure from a powerful lobby. To quote again from *Consumer Reports:*

> Now that safety has become a major selling point, no carmaker wants to mention that air-bag technology was developed in Detroit more than 20 years ago and left unexploited for nearly as long. Neither do the ads touting safety mention the years of delay and lives lost through auto maker opposition.

And, I might add (as if I haven't already), through inappropriate government action.

I do not participate in any sport with ambulances at the bottom of a hill.

ERMA BOMBECK

⚖ ⚖ ⚖

Laws that require motorcycle riders to wear helmets were passed not due to the lobbying of the motorcycle industry (no motorcycle air bag has yet been perfected), but due to a general public dislike (shared by many law enforcement officers) of motorcyclists. It's not the argument, "Helmet laws will save motorcyclists' lives," that convinces people to favor such laws, but the argument, "People are more severely injured in motorcycle accidents if they aren't wearing a helmet, so insurance rates and the potential financial burdens to society go up." No one seems to worry much about the "cost to society" of cigarettes, alcohol, prescription drugs, or any of the other legal-lethal activities. Motorcyclists opposed to helmets claim their vision, hearing, and the mobility of their head are impaired by the helmet; they feel they are more likely to get into an accident. Further, they claim, if you're going to be killed in a motorcycle accident, you're going to be killed: helmets probably won't help that much. According to the General Accounting Office, of the more than 3,000 motorcycle deaths in the United States in 1990, 45% of the riders were wearing helmets.

But safety is not the issue: personal choice is. The motorcycle rider who is more seriously injured or even killed because he or she is not wearing a helmet hurts himself or herself only. If insurance companies and states want to require special insurance coverage for those who choose to ride without helmets, that's fine: those who take risks should see to it that they are not a financial burden on society. Health insurance companies that offer better rates to nonsmokers are, in effect, charging smokers higher rates. That's fair. Charging motorcyclists a premium to not wear a helmet is also fair.* Insisting that a cyclist wear a helmet *or*

---

*Ironically, that premium would probably not be very high, as death costs insurance companies less than serious injury. If it's true that people not wearing helmets die more often, then it must mean that those wearing helmets, rather than dying, sustain serious injuries. A serious injury could cost an insurance company hundreds of thousands, perhaps millions of dollars. Death is a one-time pay-

> *Gradually,*
> *without noticing it,*
> *you turn into a Republican*
> *and judge everything*
> *on the basis of whether or not*
> *it will increase your taxes.*
>
> DAVE BARRY

else is not fair.

People obviously don't want helmet laws. In 1967, the federal government issued another of its financial ultimatums: if a state didn't enact a helmet law, it ran the risk of losing highway funding. By 1975, all but three states (as diverse as California, Illinois, and Utah) had complied (succumbed?). In 1976, when Congress rescinded the ruling, twenty-nine states repealed their laws. Now the federal government is back with a let's-do-helmet-laws-again attitude.

Allow me for a moment to view with the cold eye of an insurance actuary a motorcyclist's potential for hurting others. A motorcyclist involved in a serious accident becomes a projectile: the rider's motorcycle stops, the rider does not, and we have a human rocket flying through space. If this human rocket hits something or someone, the human rocket is *more* dangerous wearing a heavy, hard helmet than not. To reduce potential injury to nonconsenting others, then, the law should *prohibit* motorcycle helmets. Okay. Enough actuarial thinking. Let's return to the question: "Why helmet laws?"

When the California helmet law was passed in 1991,* the California Highway Patrol "lobbied heavily," according to the *Los Angeles Times,* for the law's passage. Why? What possible business is it of the California Highway Patrol to force its concept of personal safety on motorcycle riders? Wouldn't the California Highway Patrol's precious lobbying time be better spent getting more highway patrol officers, better equipment, or making sure Ted Turner doesn't colorize old episodes of "Highway Patrol"? Yes, it may be that the Highway Patrol thought it was saving lives, or could it be—as some pro-choice motorcycle helmetists claim—that the Highway Patrol wanted to separate the "bad" cyclists from the "good" cyclists? (The "bad" cyclists don't want to wear motorcycle helmets; the "good" cyclists may or may not want to, but will because "it's the law.") Now the Highway Patrol knows a "bad" cyclist on sight: no helmet.

There's also the matter of *fines:* a first offense is $100, second offense $200, third offense $250. With enough offenses, "bad" motorcycle riders will lose their licenses. If they ride anyway, they'll go to jail. Just where "bad" motorcycle riders belong. In the first year of California's helmet law, close to $1 million worth of tickets were written. If enough laws like this are enacted on relatively powerless,

---

ment to the survivors. From the cold-hearted view of insurance companies, in fact, those *not* wearing helmets might be entitled to a rate *reduction.*

*Yes, as soon as most of the other states repealed their laws, California had to get one. The Marine Corps motto is *Semper fidelis,* always faithful. The California motto is *Semper differens,* always different. By the way, do you know what George Washington's family motto was? *Exitus acta probat:* the end justifies the means. Really.

AIN'T NOBODY'S BUSINESS IF YOU DO

marginally unpopular groups, the rich, powerful people won't have to pay any income tax at all. (Do they anyway?) Well, before I get *too* cynical about this one, let's move on to a much more exciting topic: public nudity.

⚖ ⚖ ⚖

By public nudity, I'm not referring to flashers or other aggressive, pseudo-sexual behavior. I'm referring to people who want certain beaches set aside on which clothing

is optional. Frankly, I don't think nudity in public should be a major concern for the same reason I don't think we need to concern ourselves about people wearing fried eggs on their foreheads or those who want to heavily rouge their nostrils and skip down the street singing "Rudolph the Red-Nosed Reindeer."* I mean, how many people actually *want* to do it?

Even if something is illegal, if people really want to do it, a certain number of them do it. How many people have you actually *seen* shopping nude in the supermarket? How many people have confessed to you how satisfying it was to walk in the nude amongst the nude paintings at the Metropolitan Museum of Art? In the many lists of "secret fantasies" I have read, "walking around Sears Roebuck nude"—or doing anything else nude that didn't involve Tom Cruise or Sharon Stone—did not make the list.

The laws against nudity make no sense. The idea that Jerry Falwell can go topless while Cindy Crawford cannot, for example, is an absolute affront to logic, common sense, and the 5,000-year human struggle for aesthetic taste. The reason that women should wear more clothing than men goes back to the old possession concept: "This is my *property*,"sayeth the man, "and you can't even *look* at it." In the 1890s, for a woman to show an ankle in public was scandalous. By 1910, it was the calf. By the 1920s, it was the knees. By the 1950s, two-piece bathing suits were all the rage (and scandal). Today, in England, women appear topless regularly in magazines, newspapers, and even on television. It's been going on for years. England has not exactly fallen into complete moral decay because of it. When are we going to learn that if it's okay for the gander, it's okay for the goose?

Other than a spate of streaking in the early 1970s (which was more about shock than nudity), the only real social nudity we've been confronted with in our country is at beaches. Some people like more of their fun exposed to the sun than others. The police in Pinellas County, Florida, began locking up nudists who

---

*JOKE QUIZ: Test your ability to write a joke. The punch line is, "Rudolph the Red knows rain, dear." Make up a joke to precede this punch line. Submit your entry to Famous Joke-Writers' School, Westport, CT, for a *free* evaluation. Neatness and originality count.

frequented an isolated beach. "Come on, deputies," Don Addis chided them in the *St. Petersburg Times*, "If that's all you've got to do with your time, go join a Big Brother program or something." Mr. Addis continued,

A member of the sheriff's marine unit, it says here, came jogging along the beach posing as an average, everyday gawker then pulled a badge. That undercover technique will have to do for now, until the rubber naked-person suits arrive.

At first the deputies approached the beach from the open sea in their official boats in hopes of catching skinny-baskers unaware. I wonder how long it took them to figure out why that wasn't working. (You'd think they would have learned something from the Normandy invasion. By the time the Allied forces came ashore, the Germans all had their clothes on.)

Meanwhile, down at the Addis-Holtz Behavioral Research Institute and Sub Shop, laboratory rats are being used extensively in the study of nudity, with the aim of helping humans afflicted with the dread condition. One group of rats was dressed in tiny little polyester suits, complete with shirts, ties, hats, two-tone wingtip shoes, socks and colorfully patterned boxer undershorts. Another group of rats was left unclothed.

It was found that the rats without clothes mated more readily than those trussed up to the incisors in off-the-rack ratwear. Conclusion: Nudity causes lust in rats.

The findings have been challenged in some scientific circles on the grounds that researchers failed to take into account the possible effects of (1) embarrassment on the part of rats whose undershorts had trombones printed on them, (2) fear of criticism from Mr. Blackwell and (3) chafing.

With 2,000 beaches closed in 1992 due to unacceptable levels of water pollution, don't we have more important things to concern ourselves with than whether or not some mammals are exposing their mammary glands on beaches?

"And what about the children?" some ask. In 1920, it was considered scandalous for a man to appear in any public arena other than prize-fighting (which had an all-male audience) with his shirt off. Children *raised* not seeing men with their shirts off were naturally a bit giggly and curious as the first daring shirtless men began appearing on beaches, in magazines, and in movies. Today, because it's what children are raised with, no one thinks of a topless male as a threat to the morality of children. After a similar period with topless women (or even fully nude adults), the children will adjust (a lot faster than their parents, probably), life will go on, and police can go catch real criminals. Remember: children are born naked. They seem to like nothing better than getting naked. It's *adults* who teach them what parts of their bodies are and are not shameful to expose. A child has absolutely no natural guilt about this at all.

But, again, I don't think we'll see much nudity in public. Being nude just isn't very *convenient*. Without clothing, things tend to *flop around*; and then there is the time-honored question: where do you *carry* things? Where to carry a fountain pen is easy,* but what about notebook, wallet, and key chain?

> *So long as a man rides his hobbyhorse peaceably and quietly along the King's highway, and neither compels you or me to get up behind him, —pray, Sir, what have either you or I to do with it?*
>
> LAURENCE STERNE
> 1759

The most publicized nudity case of the past several years is the man who padded around the University of California, Berkeley, campus wearing sandals, a bookbag, and nothing else. This went on for months; his fanny appeared in every publication but *Christian World* (where it might have appeared: I must admit I'm not a regular reader), and the campus did not seem to either disintegrate or lose its academic credentials—although it did lose a bit of its radical chic when it finally banned nude students. But, while we may shed a tear for American freedom, we need not shed a tear for the formerly nude stude: he's writing a book about his adventures. As J. P. Morgan once said, "The first man gets the oyster, the second man gets the shell." To paraphrase this slightly: "The first nudist gets the book, the second nudist gets booked."

⚖️ ⚖️ ⚖️

Okay, so you think women's clothing is important. You think it should be worn. Well, some men would agree with you: they *love* wearing women's clothing. While some men want to come *out* of the closet, other men want to go *into* the closet: Dolly Parton's.

Now why on *earth* should transvestism be illegal? As a Frenchman accurately observed in the 1930s, "Mae West is the greatest female impersonator in the world!" Somehow in this country, as long as a female impersonator has been a female, it's been okay: Jayne Mansfield, Marilyn Monroe, Zsa Zsa Gabor.** Just as Charlie Chaplin used to refer to his Tramp character as "the little fellow," so Bette Midler referred to her outrageous stage persona when honoring a male female impersonator who impersonated her: "He did a better Bette than I."

The closest we've come to accepting a male female impersonator is Liberace.

---

*Behind your ear, of course.

**Paul Krassner wrote in *The Realist* that gays were planning to boycott Zsa Zsa Gabor because she'd made some derogatory comments about lesbians, but the gays couldn't figure out what to boycott.

> *The will of the people is the only legitimate foundation of any government, and to protect its free expression should be our first object.*
>
> THOMAS JEFFERSON
> *First Inaugural Address*
> 1801

Of course, it's hard to tell exactly *what* Liberace was, or what he was impersonating. Was he impersonating a Rockette? A Las Vegas showgirl? Wayne Newton? A piano player? Whatever it was, it made Lee (as all his close friends called him) famous, rich ("I cried all the way to the bank"), and well loved.

Liberace followed Quentin Crisp's advice, detailed in Quentin's book, *How to Become a Virgin:* if what you're doing causes people to cross the street to avoid you, confess every detail of what you're doing on television. This is the act of national cleansing. All your sins are forgiven. You become a virgin again. More importantly, you become a *celebrity* virgin. People will now cross the street—at great peril to their lives—in order to shake your hand and say, "I saw you last night on the *telly!*"

While Quentin never hovered over audiences at Caesar's Palace suspended by piano wire (the best use of a piano Liberace made in his entire career), Quentin made his daring—and personally more dangerous—statement that if boys will be girls, well, *c'est la vie.* In the 1930s in England, he wore make-up, scarves, and reddened his hair with henna. He was beaten up fairly regularly for his independence, but he persisted.

His flamboyance also made him highly unemployable, so he took a job as a nude model for state-run art schools. His manner of dress did not concern them, for obvious reasons. As all models worked for the government, the title of Quentin's autobiography is *The Naked Civil Servant.* When the rationing at the beginning of World War II was announced, he went out and bought two pounds of henna.

Sting immortalized Quentin Crisp's courage to be himself against the most impossible odds in his song, "Englishman In New York."

> Takes more than combat gear to make a man,
> Takes more than a license for a gun.
> Confront your enemies, avoid them when you can—
> A gentleman will walk but never run
>
> If "manners maketh man" as someone said,
> Then he's the hero of the day.
> It takes a man to suffer ignorance and smile:
> Be yourself no matter what they say

In his liner notes for his album, . . . *Nothing Like the Sun,* Sting explains,

> I wrote "Englishman In New York" for a friend of mine who moved from
> London to New York in his early seventies to a small rented apartment in

the Bowery at a time in his life when most people have settled down forever. He once told me over dinner that he looked forward to receiving his naturalization papers so that he could commit a crime and not be deported. "What kind of crime?" I asked anxiously. "Oh, something glamorous, non-violent, with a dash of style" he replied. "Crime is so rarely glamorous these days."

> *Of course, the last thing my parents wanted was a son who wears a cocktail dress that glitters, but they've come around to it.*
>
> **DIVINE**

"To me," Quentin said, "a movie star has to be something you couldn't have invented for yourself if you sat up all night." He speaks of Evita Perón with only half-veiled envy:

> In England, spelling primers begin with the words "The cat sat on the mat." No wonder literacy is at a low ebb, when the first glimpse of it is this banal and even distasteful piece of information. But in Argentina, spelling books begin with "I love Evita."
>
> The crowning moment of her entire career was when she stood up in her box in the opera house in Buenos Aires and made a speech. She lifted her hands to the crowd, and as she did so, with a sound like railway trucks in a siding, the diamond bracelets slid down from her wrists. When the expensive clatter had died away, her speech began, "We, the shirtless . . ."
>
> You may not believe in Mrs. Perón, but the Argentinians did. So much so that when she died they petitioned the Pope to make her a saint. His Holiness declined; but if he'd consented, what a triumph for style that would have been! A double fox stole, ankle-strap shoes, and eternal life. Nobody's ever had that.

Of course, most transvestites are not as flamboyant as Evita. Chuck Shepherd, John J. Kohut, and Roland Sweet, in their *More News of the Weird*, report,

> In 1989 jazz musician Billy Tipton died of a bleeding ulcer, leaving an ex-wife and three adopted sons. While the funeral director was preparing the body for burial, he discovered the 74-year-old saxophonist-pianist was really a woman. "He'll always be Dad," said one of Tipton's boys.

Contrary to popular misbelief, a good number of transvestites—both male and female—are also heterosexual. Just because they want to get dressed up like the opposite sex does not necessarily mean they want to go to bed with the same sex. Some have successful heterosexual marriages, and enjoy the most delightful shopping expeditions with their spouses. It must be reminiscent of the scene on an episode of "Soap" in which the Billy Crystal character is discovered by his mother in one of her dresses. "What are you doing wearing my dress?" she yells, taking a hard look at him. She takes a closer look. "Oh! You wear it with a belt." All horror vanishes, and the mother gets some sound wardrobe tips from her son.

Laws against transvestism, obviously, spring from the hatred of women: "Why would a *man* want to get dressed up like a *woman?*" The fear of homosexuality that grew out of that same irrational disgust has kept the laws against cross-dressing on the books: "normal" heterosexual men don't want to be "tricked" into falling for a "woman" who's really a man. What a waste of testosterone! And what an *embarrassment.* Who wants to feel like the Charles Durning character in *Tootsie?* Falling for Dustin Hoffman in drag. How demeaning. And then he winds up your son-in-law no less! No, there's gotta be a law against this.

᎐᎐ ᎐᎐ ᎐᎐

If we'd all treat our lives more as comedies than potential tragedies, a great many of the laws against consensual activities—which are enacted and perpetuated due to our fears of possible tragic outcomes—would disappear.

Now, if you'll excuse me, I have an appointment to meet my *Titanic* artifacts dealer. He says he has a genuine knife from the first-class dining room. He described it to me on the phone. I don't know, though. There have been so many phony *Titanic* artifacts floating around (no pun intended) since that Titanic law was passed. I don't know whom to believe anymore. It took me three weeks to discover the VCR my dealer *claimed* was from the captain's cabin, couldn't *possibly* have been from the captain's cabin. A good friend of mine (whom I trust) says he already *owns* the VCR from the captain's cabin, and why would the captain have *two* VCRs? This dealer had me going there for a while: he said one VCR was for Beta and one was for VHS. But I caught him in his lie: *they didn't have VHS in 1912.*

Yes, without the government protecting us it is more dangerous out there, but tonight I may wind up with a knife from the first-class dining room of the most famous ship in history, a knife manufactured by one of the most renowned knife makers in the world: *Ginsu.*

PART VI

QUESTIONS ANSWERED, ANSWERS QUESTIONED

Separation of Society and State

IN DEFENDING THE LAWS against consensual activities, some ask: "Shouldn't the laws of the state describe—or at least reflect—what is acceptable and not acceptable to a broad segment of society?"

My answer: Absolutely not.

The government—which makes and administers the laws—is there to keep physical violence from being inflicted on its citizens, whether that violence comes from foreign governments, groups of citizens, or individuals. A government that provides a level playing field for commerce and keeps everyone's person and property relatively safe from the physical harm of others is doing a good job. As Thomas Paine wrote in his 1776 pamphlet, *Common Sense,*

> Society in every state is a blessing, but Government, even in its best state, is but a necessary evil; in its worst state, an intolerable one.

Society, on the other hand, determines acceptable and unacceptable social behavior. Many of society's rules are so thoroughly accepted we don't even think about them. That we speak primarily English in the United States is purely a matter of custom. That we eat certain animals and don't eat others (horse is very popular in France), sleep in a bed (the Japanese do not understand why we need a bed*room*), bury our dead (cremation is the only thing people from India understand), and so much more, are all purely matters of custom. Although one, in this country, *can* speak Croatian, eat horse, sleep on a futon, and be cremated, the vast majority of people choose not to.

The reason? Our conditioning. "Society attacks early," B. F. Skinner pointed out, "when the individual is helpless." This is society's first line of defense: We do certain things, don't do other things, and behave in certain ways because that's how we were trained. Much of the time we do what we do because (a) it's the only thing we know (Are you fluent in any other language besides English?), (b) it's what we're comfortable with (Would you feel comfortable eating a horseburger?), or (c) we have to *get along in society.*

That last one—getting along in society—is what keeps us in place when cultural conditioning fails. Even as rebellious a rascal as George Bernard Shaw acknowledged the need for society—and its power:

> It is hard to fight an enemy
> who has outposts
> in your head.
>
> SALLY KEMPTON

> Nobody can live in society without conventions. The reason why sensible people are as conventional as they can bear to be is that conventionality saves so much time and thought and trouble and social friction of one sort or another that it leaves them much more leisure time for freedom than unconventionality does.

The more we pull away from society's norms, the more society pulls away from us. We can, quite legally, be total renegades—and totally ostracized. If we wore aluminum foil clothing, never washed, communicated only with grunts and squeaks, walked backwards, and lived off live grasshoppers, we might occasionally find ourselves as a guest on "Geraldo," but we would never be a guest at a dinner party, be rented an apartment, or offered much work (except, perhaps, for organic pest control during grasshopper infestations). If our behavior is sufficiently eccentric, society punishes without the law's help at all.

Prior to complete isolation, however, any number of societal punishments keep us in line—sometimes literally. It is not, for example, illegal to take cuts in front of someone at an automated teller machine (on second thought, it probably *is* illegal *somewhere*). And yet, very few people take cuts. Some wait their turn because they believe in fair play; others because they're afraid of disapproval. (In Los Angeles we wait because we're afraid someone in line might be carrying a gun.) The *reason* there are no laws against taking cuts is that most people understand the fairness of lines and agree to cooperate. Most of those who don't believe in fairness do believe in avoiding barrages of negative comments. The very small minority who *do* take cuts do not cause enough of a problem to warrant legal regulation.

Most of us *want* to fit into society. A cartoon appearing in *The Realist* many years ago showed a line of sack-clothed bearded men—one looking just like another—holding identical signs that read, "We protest the rising tide of conformity." Even the rebels follow certain *counter* social mores in order to be accepted in the counterculture society. To get (or keep) a job, a living arrangement, or a love, we will conform to any number of standards—without a police officer in sight.

Society has the means to change itself without anyone changing a single civil

law. Thirty years ago, for example, an earring on a man would mean that he (a) was
gay, (b) was a pirate, or (c) had drunk a bottle of Mr. Clean. Today, earrings are *de rig-
ueur* as a proof of heterosexuality among
certain groups of men. No one had to write
a law, enforce a law, or repeal a law regarding earrings on men. As Lewis Thomas explained,

> *Never speak disrespectfully
> of Society, Algernon.
> Only people who can't get into it
> do that.*
>
> OSCAR WILDE
> *The Importance of Being Earnest*

> We pass the word around; we ponder
> how the case is put by different people;
> we read the poetry; we meditate over
> the literature; we play the music; we change our minds; we reach an un-
> derstanding. Society evolves this way, not by shouting each other down,
> but by the unique capacity of unique, individual human beings to compre-
> hend each other.

Imagine if *every* "rule" we have in society required a law, law enforcement,
court time, and jail space. Several laws, for example, have been proposed to make
English the national language of the United States. These laws have been dismissed, for the most part, because they were entirely unnecessary. Not only were
they unnecessary; they were unenforceable. Although the proposals sparked interesting debates (one congressman said, "Jesus spoke English, and that's good
enough for me"), people realized such laws were futile. I wish people would
realize the same thing concerning consensual crimes.

Not only is the law's help thoroughly inappropriate; society doesn't *need* the
law's help: society does just fine on its own. In fact, society has far more power
over the individual than law enforcement does. "Order is not pressure which is
imposed on society from without," José Ortega y Gasset wrote in 1927, "but an
equilibrium which is set up from within."

Society, in fact, does not *mind* that some people flout its regulations: some
people *must* be outside society in order for those inside society to know they're
inside. If *everybody* were "in," then *nobody* would be "in." The very fact that some
people are "out" makes being "in" worthwhile. Only *religions* live under the misguided notion that everyone must or should be "good."

Religion deals in absolutes; society deals in relativity. "In the land of the blind,
the one-eyed man is king," is a *social* statement. From a religious point of view,
neither the blind nor the one-eyed man stands a better chance. Indeed, in the land
where looking at a woman with lust is a sin, the blind man stands a better chance;
all are, however, expected to go to God.

From the government's point of view, which drug one uses recreationally should
make no more difference than, say, whether or not one wears an earring. Those
behaviors are primarily a matter of fad and fashion that the government has no
business becoming involved in. Society makes its recommendations about such

> *He who is unable to live in society,*
> *or who has no need because*
> *he is sufficient for himself,*
> *must be either*
> *a beast or a god.*
>
> ARISTOTLE

relatively trivial topics. The government has far more important issues to consider than the current currents on earrings, drug choices, or sexual preferences between consenting adults.

What I'm calling for is not just a separation of church and state, but a separation of society and state. (Whether there should be a separation between church and society is for church and society to work out between themselves.) This is a book about government intervention in private lives. The government has no more business being the enforcer of social policy than it has being the enforcer of religious belief.

Many who would classify themselves as anti-communists are often the same people who argue that a legitimate role of government is to help regulate society. Don't they know that that is a basic tenet of communism? As Mikhail Bakunin, the Russian political theorist, wrote more than one hundred years ago,

> I detest communism, because it is the negation of liberty. . . . I am not a communist because communism concentrates and absorbs all the powers of society into the state.

In 1978, Alexander Solzhenitsyn revealed that a century hadn't changed things:

> I have spent all my life under a Communist regime, and I will tell you that a society without any objective legal scale is a terrible one indeed. But a society with no other scale but the legal one is not quite worthy of man either.

Both the church and society have lasted longer than any government. The *people* need the government to keep forced intrusions of both religion and society out of their lives. Our country is doing just the opposite. Instead of saying no to religion and to society, the government of the United States is saying no to individuals seeking personal freedom. Allowing religion and society to supersede individual rights is the reverse of the way things should be—if one considers the Constitution the supreme law of the land. Some people do not, of course: they consider religious and/or cultural beliefs to be more important. I, for one, do not agree. Those who want the government run by religion or by society are free to propose a constitutional amendment. Until such an amendment is ratified, however, this is still a free country. As usual, Thomas Jefferson said it best. At the age of seventy-seven, he wrote,

> I know no safe depository of the ultimate powers of the society but the people themselves; and if we think them not enlightened enough to exercise their control with a wholesome discretion, the remedy is not to take it from them, but to inform their discretion.

Education, Not Legislation

> *The only fence against the world*
> *is a thorough knowledge of it.*
>
> JOHN LOCKE
> 1693

IN ORDER TO MAKE intelligent choices, we must have accurate information about the potential consequences of those choices. Learning about those potential consequences—how to maximize the positive ones and how to minimize the negative ones—is the essence of education. True education is not deciding what is right or wrong and then convincing the student of the wisdom of the decision. That's propaganda. True education says, "Here are the possible rewards; here are the potential risks; here's how to maximize the rewards and minimize the risks; you make the choice."

Nowhere do we need true education more than in the area of consensual crimes: it seems that all we've had for the longest time is *propaganda*—both negative and positive. Society teaches us that committing consensual crimes is always bad, always wrong, always dangerous, and always deadly. The indulgers, on the other hand, teach that society is *entirely* wrong, that there are no risks, that there are no dangers—they're all a figment of the military-industrial complex's imagination. Neither of these approaches is valid; neither is true education.

Much of what passes for drug education, for example, is not education at all, but simply scare tactics; terrors for children. The idea (as one popular billboard depicts) that snorting cocaine is the same as sticking a pistol in your nose and pulling the trigger is absurd. One famous television commercial shows an egg being dropped into a frying pan (which must be heated to at least 3,000 degrees); as the egg fries and burns, a voice-over says, "This is your brain. This is your brain on drugs." This is not only untrue; it's also a waste of good food.

All this propaganda is as transparently silly as the supposed documentary films from the '30s: *Sex Madness, Cocaine Madness,* and the ever-popular *Reefer Madness.*

In these films, ordinary, healthy (but, one must admit, terribly boring), young men and women are driven insane by, respectively, sex, cocaine, and marijuana.

One television commercial sponsored by the Partnership for a Drug Free America shows a wholesome young ghetto child having to jump over fences, run down alleys, and hide behind trees in order to make the journey from school to home without drug dealers forcing him to take drugs. This modern-day misinformation causes a person to conclude, "I know what they're saying here is wrong; therefore *everything* they say is wrong; therefore *everything* I want to do must be right."

> The highest result of education is tolerance.
>
> HELEN KELLER

A society that lies to its people divides itself: some people believe everything they're told and others believe nothing they're told. Both attitudes are dangerous to the health and well-being of a society. The misinfomercials from the Partnership for a Drug Free America only show those already ignorant of drug use how right their righteous position is, while further alienating those who know that eggs in frying pans and children hiding behind trees have nothing to do with drugs.

Who pays for all this propaganda? Who finances the Partnership for a Drug Free America? Some of its contributors *could* be said to have vested interests in *not* making additional drugs legal.

According to *The Nation*,

> the Partnership for a Drug Free America received $150,000 each from Philip Morris (Miller beer and Marlboro cigarettes), Anheuser-Busch (Budweiser) and R. J. Reynolds (Camel) over 1988–91. Other contributors: American Brands (Jim Beam and Lucky Strike), Pepsico, and Coca-Cola. Contributing pharmaceutical companies included Bristol-Meyers Squibb, CIBA-Geigy, Dow, DuPont, Glaxo, Hoffman-La Roche, Johnson & Johnson, Merck, Pfizer, Schering-Plough, Smith-Kline and Warner-Lambert.

It's not just the Partnership for a Drug Free America propagandizing; media over the years have thought they were somehow helping by spreading scare stories as fact, or by dramatizing extreme cases of abuse as though they were everyday occurrences.

Two 1967 "Dragnet" episodes are a perfect example. (These weren't the gritty *film noir* episodes of the 1950s, but the technicolor episodes of the '60s. *Film noir* was better.) Jack Webb, the producer, director, star, etc., must have considered himself a one-person war on drugs. In one episode, Detective Sergeant Joe Friday takes a night-school class in "sensitivity training." No one in the class knows he's a cop. One of the participants admits to having taken drugs. Friday thinks he sees marijuana in the man's notebook. He arrests his classmate. The man is sent up the river. Meanwhile, the teacher of the class is outraged. People were encouraged to open up, to share, to be vulnerable and honest, and along comes an unannounced policeman who arrests a class member for doing just that. The professor wants to throw Friday out of the class. Friday asks for the class to decide: he'll give his point of view, and then they can vote. What follows is an impassioned speech (well, as impassioned as Jack Webb can get, which is not very impassioned) about the dreadful things that he, as a Los Angeles cop, has seen drugs do to people. The speech goes on and on, one horror story after another. The class, initially hostile, sees the light, and votes to let Friday stay. If this were high school, they probably would have elected him class president.

> *I've over-educated myself*
> *in all the things*
> *I shouldn't have known.*
>
> NOEL COWARD

An even more amazing "Dragnet" episode tackled another drug. A young man is picked up. He has his head stuck in the sand, one side of his face painted blue, the other side painted yellow, and is carrying a pocketful of sugar cubes. He is babbling about seeing the "pilot light" at the center of the earth and then believes he is becoming a tree. Guess what drug he was on? Based on the cubes in his pocket, it was either a sugar rush or LSD.

Yes, the scientist in the lab confirms it is LSD. The scientist in the lab seems to know a great deal about LSD, although his specialty is forensics. (According to "Dragnet," there is precisely one scientist in the entire Los Angeles Police Department. He was played by the same actor, week after week: don't want to confuse the home audience with more than one scientist on a show.* This scientist could answer every question from, "What kind of gun could make a hole that size in a man?" to "We found this goldfish on the floor of the victim's apartment. Can you check it for fingerprints?")

The scientist, as it turns out, doesn't know that much about LSD after all. Although he looks very authoritative in his white science-coat, and is surrounded by the paraphernalia of scientific investigation, not one of the "facts" he reveals in his five-minute lecture on the horrors of LSD is known to medical science. Although we now know LSD is a Truly Bad Thing, the boy cannot be arrested: alas, there is no law against LSD. "I sure hope they give you boys something to fight with out there real soon," the scientist says. Friday nods grimly.

The boy is now back to his normal self. He wipes the blue and yellow grease-paint off with his mother's handkerchief. His parents want to take him home. Not so fast: Friday wants to book 'em. "I happen to know there is no law against LSD,"

---

*That this same actor occasionally played a judge *might* have caused some audience confusion *except* when he played a scientist he always wore *white* and when he played a judge he always wore *black*.

> *If you're not growin',*
> *sit down.*
>
> SERGEANT JOE FRIDAY
> *to a hood getting up from a table*
> *"Dragnet"*

says the father. Friday looks frantically at his captain. He pleads to his captain with a look that says, "I want to book him. I already *said*, 'I want to book him.' Please, help me find some way to book him!" The captain, an old hand at all this, says, "Book him on a 601." While the boy is taken to juvenile hall, Friday's voice-over explains a 601. It has something to do with suspicion of intent to commit conspiracy to corrupt your own morals in a way that is particularly disagreeable to Los Angeles police sergeants.

When the boy is released from juvenile hall, he commits the worst sin in Joe Friday's book: disrespect for Joe Friday. The boy has the nerve to call Friday "Sherlock." From his look, it's obvious that Friday doesn't know what the boy is talking about, but Friday knows it's not good.

Meanwhile, two teenaged girls are at police headquarters. They apparently spent the day "tripping." One of them describes how she watched Los Angeles melt; either that, or she stumbled into a movie theater showing *The House of Wax*. The girls show us what it's like to "come down" from an LSD trip. It looks like a combination of extreme nausea and severe menstrual cramps. Not at all appealing. Oh, by the way, they purchased their LSD from the boy.

Six months pass. The captain comes in and hands Joe Friday a booklet. It is the new law declaring LSD a "dangerous substance." Joe Friday is like a kid at Christmas. The captain is Santa Claus. "When does this law go into effect?" Friday asks, his eyes ablaze. "Forty-eight hours," the captain tells him. These men are high, truly high. They've just gotten a fix of the drug they love most: a new law. Forty-eight hours. Just enough time to roll out the (dum-da-dum-dum) dragnet.

In search of the boy, they visit an LSD party. It looks something like "Laugh In's" cocktail party, but much slower and without jokes. Friday calls some uniformed police. They arrive within thirty seconds. (Ah, the good old days.) Everyone at the party is arrested. Talk about a bad trip. The boy, unfortunately, is not there. Fortunately, however, a pharmacy calls in: they have just sold 1,000 empty gelatin capsules to a young man fitting the description of the boy. Friday goes to the pharmacy. Yes, after being shown mug shots, the pharmacist (who has precisely *one* shelf with about twelve bottles of pills on it) gives Friday the address of where the capsules were delivered. (Which means the boy came in, ordered 1,000 empty gelatin capsules, which must weigh about five ounces, and then said, "Here, deliver these." Yes, this boy was *clearly* on drugs—or the scriptwriter was.)*

The landlady happily provides Detective Friday with a passkey. Friday enters (apparently having no use for that seven-letter four-letter word: *warrant*) and finds

---

*Maybe the guy who plays the scientist and the judge also writes the scripts.

a friend of the boy, who says of the boy, "He kept taking more and more pills. He kept wanting to go far out, far out, far out . . ." "He made it," intones Friday, "he's dead." Dum-da-dum-dum.

After the commercial, we are told that a coroner's inquest found the boy died of an LSD overdose. (Barbiturates are mentioned somewhere in there, parenthetically.) Yes, ladies and gentlemen, for the first and only time in history, LSD kills.

> *Education's purpose is to replace an empty mind with an open one.*
>
> MALCOLM S. FORBES

"Dragnet" was famous, of course, for Joe Friday's sardonic and ironic comment just before the final dum-da-dum-dum. In keeping with that tradition, here is my sardonic and ironic comment: Detective Sergeant Joe Friday stoically acknowledged defeat and celebrated victory in the same way. He lit up a cigarette. According to the American Heart Association, cigarette smoking is the #1 cause of heart disease. Jack Webb, a life-long smoker, died of a heart attack on December 23, 1982.

Dum-da-dum-dum.

⚖ ⚖ ⚖

Yes, that was 1967. A hipper, trendier show for the hipper, trendier '80s was "Miami Vice." It was *so cool* to catch drug dealers. The only burning question, however, was: how did Crockett afford thousands of dollars in new designer clothes and other hip paraphernalia each week on a Miami detective's salary? Yes, it was cool to put the bad guys away, but never forget the most essential American lesson: There is nothing cooler than money.

Even films such as *The Gene Krupa Story* perpetuated the myth that, if you even *tried* marijuana, within six months you would be hopelessly addicted to heroin, which, as everyone knew, meant an agonizing death in the gutter three months later—but only after pulling everything you ever had and everyone you ever knew into the gutter with you.

Well, as millions of Americans (including our current president) learned, that's simply not the case. In fact, pot doesn't lead to *anything*. That's the problem with pot; it tends to make one nonproductive (except, perhaps to eat and watch television). Pot seems to give some people abundantly creative ideas, but it also seems to prevent them from putting very many of them into action. The typical pothead is someone who has lots of dreams, very few of which come true.

What I just did was education. I told people the genuine dangers of pot-smoking, and now they can choose for themselves. If people are willing to be nonproductive, they are welcome to smoke pot. If people who currently smoke pot find themselves not as productive as they'd like to be, they might abstain from pot for a while. If their productivity increases, they know what the choice is: getting

> *There should be some schools*
> *called deformatories*
> *to which people are sent*
> *if they are too good*
> *to be practical.*
>
> SAMUEL BUTLER

stoned or getting more things done. Who says people should value getting things done over getting high? Not me. It's a *personal choice.*

The purpose of education is to make the choices clear to people, not to make the choices for people.

⚖ ⚖ ⚖

Education comes from the Latin word *educare,* which means to draw forth what is within. I believe that people already know where they want to go in life, and have an intuitive sense of what they want to do. The job of the people who have been down the many paths it takes to achieve one's heart's desire is not to tell others what to do or where to go, but simply to provide a road map accurately describing where each experience is. Rather than saying, "Go to the lakes and stay away from the mountains," the true educator would say, "The lakes are over here and the mountains are over there," and then give *factual* descriptions of the possible pleasures and potential dangers of each.

It's not very helpful to say, "The mountains are too high." Too high for whom? Too high for what? If the educator overlays a personal fear of heights onto the information about the mountain, he or she is not truly educating, but merely passing along a prejudice. Perhaps the student finds heights exhilarating and is looking for the next mountain to climb.

Tom Boyer explained that the difference between deciding and educating can be seen in the difference between American and Italian warning signs. In America, signs by high voltage power lines say, "Do not touch." In Italy the signs say, "You touch, you die." In America the choice is made for you: do not touch. In Italy the consequences are clearly laid out (you touch, you die), and the choice is left to you.

Cigarettes are readily available, seductively advertised, and you may even be offered one from time to time, and yet, the vast majority of the American public simply chooses to say no. Only the most unbalanced person would respond to the friendly offer of a cigarette with, "What? Are you trying to get me hooked? Are you a recruiting agent for one of the tobacco companies? You should be put in jail!" The answer is simply: "No, thank you," and people go about their business.

Cigarette consumption has dropped dramatically in this country during the past two decades, and that's not due to government restrictions or prohibitions. The kingpins of the tobacco industry were not rounded up. A tobacco czar was not appointed to arrest and prosecute all the tobacco lords. A person caught selling a cigarette to another did not have his or her home confiscated, was not sent to jail for tobacco trafficking. Habitual cigarette users ("nickies") were sentenced neither to jail nor to mandatory rehabilitation programs.

No. Cigarette consumption in this country has dropped thanks to one thing: education.

It is through education that people think of cigarettes as hazardous, not glamorous. The federal government played only a small part in this educational process (a *very* small part, in the person of former Surgeon General C. Everett Koop. Koop was to cigarettes what Ralph Nader was to Corvairs). The educators were, for the most part, non-profit organizations funded by voluntary donations—the American Cancer Society, the American Lung Association, the Heart Association, and several others. Their factual and undeniable information was picked up by the media, and the attitude of an entire nation changed in a short time.

> *There is no slavery but ignorance.*
> *Liberty is the child of intelligence.*
>
> ROBERT G. INGERSOLL

(The tobacco industry, of course, continues to claim that cigarette smoking is *good for you*. The Tobacco Institute claims that "all this smoking-is-harmful nonsense" is merely a conspiracy engineered and paid for by the people who make those "Thank You for Not Smoking" signs. My favorite no-smoking sign is, "If you're smoking in here, you'd better be on fire.")

⚖️ ⚖️ ⚖️

Calling unreasonable scare tactics *education* only produces some people who are unreasonably scared and others who are unreasonable. Trying to wipe out drug abuse with the commercials from the Partnership for a Drug Free America is, as Alan Watts put it, "Like trying to kill mosquitoes with a machine gun." As Maria Montessori wrote in *The Montessori Method,*

> Discipline must come through liberty. . . . We do not consider an individual disciplined when he has been rendered as artificially silent as a mute and as immovable as a paralytic. He is an individual *annihilated*, not *disciplined*.

As Franklin Delano Roosevelt pointed out,

> Knowledge—that is, education in its true sense—is our best protection against unreasoning prejudice and panic-making fear, whether engendered by special interest, illiberal minorities, or panic-stricken leaders.

Or all three.

Fail-Safe Safety Devices

> The ordinary
> "horseless carriage"
> is at present a luxury for the
> wealthy; and although its price
> will probably fall in the future,
> it will never, of course, come into
> as common use as the bicycle.
>
> THE LITERARY DIGEST
> October 14, 1899

TECHNOLOGY HAS MOVED AHEAD at a rapid pace. At the turn of the century, the consensus in the medical community was that the human body could not withstand traveling at the inconceivable rate of a mile a minute. Today, many drivers complain that the 55 MPH speed limit won't let them routinely travel faster than a mile a minute. And even though many of us travel daily at speeds once considered humanly impossible, the technology for devices to prevent these mile-a-minute missiles (automobiles) from being operated by incapable drivers is no further along than it was when the first carriage moved without a horse in 1885.

In that same year, 1885, mass communication consisted of newspapers, phonograph cylinders, and illustrated monthlies. Our view of the world came from paintings, etchings, and stereopticon slides. Communication took place by letter or the quaint old custom of visiting people and talking with them.* In an emergency, one could send a telegram (by going to a Western Union office), and a handful of people had telephones. The business world gravitated around the ticker tape, and the carrier pigeon was still in use. That was about it.

Today we have radio, telephones, VCRs, computers, mobile telephones, fax machines, movies, televisions (with a hundred cable channels), Walkmen, boomboxes, home stereo, car stereo, as well as all the other communication devices of the earlier days.** And yet, with all the technological advancements in spreading

---

*Archaeological remnants of the day refer to a form of communication known as *conversation*. It is believed that through this "conversation" information was somehow conveyed between people. This is, however, merely speculative. Nothing more is known about this mysterious "conversation."

**Except for that mysterious "conversation." Also, the carrier pigeon, as a species, is extinct.

information, no technology exists that enables people to select the kind of information they want to receive. Right now, those who don't want to be exposed, or their children to be exposed, to certain material must rely on minor variations of the censorship practiced in Victorian times.

It's time technology better served the nonconsenting.

> *Traffic signals
> in New York
> are just rough guidelines.*
>
> DAVID LETTERMAN

⚖️ ⚖️ ⚖️

It's hard to imagine the kind of damage a 3,000-pound metal and glass object traveling a mile a minute can do. Hard, that is, until you see a traffic accident. Then we look and look away all at the same time. We like to think that degree of devastation is a fluke of nature. (It's not.) We like to think it won't happen to us. (You have a 2% chance of dying in a traffic accident.) Most of these accidents are caused by a driver *not being capable of operating a motor vehicle at that time.*

At the risk of stating the obvious, people who are not capable of operating a motor vehicle—for whatever reason—have no business operating it; not because they may harm themselves, but because there is a very good chance they may harm nonconsenting others. Of this country's 44,000 annual traffic deaths, 22,000 are alcohol related. Of the 22,000 that are *not* alcohol related, a good many happen because the drivers are too stoned (on drugs other than alcohol), emotionally upset, physically impaired, senile, exhausted, or in some way physically, mentally, or emotionally incapable of driving.

A simple device, installed in each car, could prevent the majority of deaths caused by these impairments.

Let's call this device, for lack of a better name, the "Tester." Imagine a panel on the dashboard with a numeric keypad, like those on touch-tone telephones. Above the keypad is a screen to display numbers and brief messages. There is also a slot, about the size of a credit card. The Tester works like this:

When you want to use the car, first insert your driver's license, which would act and look like a credit card. The Tester reads your driver's license, as an automated teller machine reads your credit card, and then asks for your four-digit personal identification number (PIN), much as a teller machine would. Your PIN is known only to you, but is encoded in your license. After your four-digit personal identification number is successfully given, the screen displays seven random numbers—the number of digits in a phone number. You must then, within a certain period of time and with a certain degree of accuracy, enter those numbers on the keypad. Once you complete this procedure, which should take less than a minute, the car is ready to operate normally.

That extra minute will keep a good many unlicensed and incapable drivers off the road.

Driving is *not* an inalienable right. We must meet certain standards of knowledge, ability, and competence before we receive a *license* to drive. A great many car accidents are caused by people whose licenses have been revoked or suspended, or people who don't have licenses at all. Without a license, people have no business—and certainly no right—to drive a car. If, potentially, they could only hurt themselves, they *would* have the right. The potential for hurting innocent

> *The last-ditch stand against "accidents" will be the car. After seat belts, after air bags, after drunken driving and speed, there will be changes in the car.*
>
> JOHN BARBOUR
> *Chicago Tribune*

others, however, moves driving into the realm of licensing. Hang gliding, for example, should require no license. The chances of harming anyone but yourself are extremely slim. The chances of an incompetent person hurting someone with a car, on the other hand, are very high.

The Tester assures that only licensed drivers are using automobiles. Your PIN means that your license can't be used if it's stolen. Because it's encoded in your driver's license, however, the PIN works in any car. Yes, sophisticated license thieves will have machinery to read PINs, but the average would-be license-and-car thief would find the lack of a PIN a sufficient deterrent.

The Tester can be programmed so that each car will accept only certain licenses. This deters theft and keeps unauthorized family members from "accidentally" using the wrong car. Or, a car can accept any license *except* those specifically excluded (very handy in recent divorces).

After one has been authorized by the state (through licensing) and by the owner of the car (who has selected which licenses can and cannot operate the car), the randomly generated seven-digit number appears. If one cannot see, read, comprehend, or lacks the hand-eye coordination necessary to enter seven randomly generated digits into a keypad, that person has no right (based on his or her demonstrated lack of ability) to operate a motor vehicle.

If one fails to accurately enter the number, a new number is generated. If the second attempt is not successful, the person gets one more try, and a third randomly generated number appears. As with baseball, three strikes and you're out—at least for the inning. The Tester then displays the message, "TRY AGAIN IN 15 MINUTES," and then keeps track of the time ("TRY AGAIN IN 14 MINUTES," "TRY AGAIN IN 13 MINUTES," and so on). During this mandatory waiting period, one can chill out, warm up, breathe deeply, or do whatever one must do to meet the minimum mental and physical standards for operating an automobile. After a driver fails three consecutive tests (nine times in a row failing to enter a seven-digit number correctly), the Tester shuts the car down for two hours and suggests, "CALL A CAB." (The Tester would, however, allow a different license to be entered and the car to be driven by a competent driver.)

The Tester controls the link between the engine and the transmission. The car cannot be put in gear unless the Tester signals its okay. This allows you to start the car and use the heater, air conditioner, radio, tape player, telephone, or any car function other than moving it.

There is, of course, an emergency button, which overrides the Tester entirely and allows one to start the car and drive it immediately. Pushing the emergency button, however, automatically activates the emergency flashers and beeps the horn once every two seconds. This alerts law enforcement officers that you need aid, and they will be happy to supply it. It also alerts other motorists on the road that you have an emergency and, perhaps, they might want to get out of your way (or stay out of your way, whichever applies).

As with all fail-safe devices, this one has built-in drawbacks, the primary one being that someone else can enter the code for an inebriated, stoned, or otherwise incompetent friend. Yes, this could be made illegal. But, again, the solution lies in education and creating the cultural belief that overriding the fail-safe system for another is neither an act of kindness, friendship, or love. In fact, it could be seen as an act of indifference and dismissal. A true friend would offer a ride, call a cab, or walk the person around the block a few times.

No, this system will not get *every* incompetent driver off the road.* It's designed to keep some of the most blatant offenders off the road. We must handle the problem of incompetent drivers *at its source:* not banning the alcohol or drugs that contribute to the incompetency, but stopping the problem at the point it becomes a problem: when an incapable driver gets behind a steering wheel.

⚖ ⚖ ⚖

People are offended by a broad variety of expressions. Others may not be offended themselves, but want to shield their children from certain images, words, or ideas. The battle between the freedom to express and the freedom from being inflicted upon has been an ongoing struggle. The First Amendment ("Congress shall make no law . . . abridging the freedom of speech . . . ") insists that we err on the side of expression; that is, being more concerned about protecting one's freedom to express than others' freedom from being offended.

We could, however, use technology to simultaneously allow for freer expression *and* keep material people consider offensive away from them and their chil-

---

*Accountants would probably have no trouble entering randomly generated numbers in their sleep, much less when drunk. But then, how often do accountants get drunk? "You don't want to see me drunk," said one accountant. "When I get drunk, all I do is talk about stock options."

dren. Let's call this fail-safe device the "Sensor." This device would attach to any television set and senses when certain types of programming are being played through the set.* Any time something was played, a signal indicating the *content* of what was being played would go along with it. The Sensor—always on guard—would sense when a type of programming you didn't want was being broadcast. The Sensor would then black out the screen, or the sound, or both, depending on whether the objectionable

> *The means by which we live have outdistanced the ends for which we live. Our scientific power has outrun our spiritual power. We have guided missles and misguided men.*
>
> MARTIN LUTHER KING, JR.

material was trying to enter your home audibly, visually, or both. The *range* of what could be edited out is quite extensive: 999 different variables of "Sensorship" would not be difficult to program into the device. Those ever-popular censorship categories of sex and violence can each have 100 variables, breaking them down precisely into what can and cannot be told or shown: which body parts shouldn't be mutilated (or fondled), which types of people cannot be tortured (or tickled), and, in general, how far one can go (ditto).

Then there's language. One hundred words could have forbidden status. (We'll ask George Carlin to select them.) Every potentially objectionable word from *annihilate* to *zipper* will—if you select it—never darken your TV speaker again. Then there are political points of view. Do you want the far right taken out? The far left? The moderate right? The moderate left? Maybe you just don't want any talk of politics at all. There are many religious points of view. Whose don't you want to hear? Those could be eliminated. Which countries have you heard too much about? Off the map! Which celebrities are you tired of? Bye, bye, Zsa Zsa. The list can go on and on.

Another possibility (but, boy, is this one going to have a hard time passing Congress) is that the Sensor could be set to eliminate certain types of commercials, commercials for certain products or, commercial messages altogether. This would give us an advanced form of zapping.

⚖ ⚖ ⚖

The ideas behind these fail-safe devices (which are only in the idea stage, obviously) are just an indication of what technology can do to make everyone physically safer—and free people from being exposed to some of the objectionable aspects of other people's freedom. The possibility for using technology—rather than unenforceable, unworkable, unjust laws—to regulate potentially harmful behavior is vast but largely untapped.

---

*The Sensor would monitor anything that went through the television, including VCRs, laser disks, cable, satellite dish, or any other future video developments.

What About the Children?

ONE OF THE ONGOING psychological debates for the past century has been *heredity versus environment.* In determining personality, what's more important: the gene pool or whether the children have a swimming pool? Ancestors or a Stairmaster? Our genes or our jeans?

Since World War II, the popular conclusion has leaned toward environment. The baby boom generation was raised by parents who, for the most part, *exhausted* themselves creating the ideal environment for their offspring. (Well, *my* mother's awfully tired.) Doctor Spock was there every step of the way; since 1946, only the Bible has sold more copies than *Baby and Child Care.* The media generally supported the idea that how you treated your children determined how your children would turn out. In time, the focus of these articles, talk shows, and books shifted slightly: the way you are now is the way your parents raised you—it's their fault.

Believing that environment is the cause of what we become has created a generation of defeated, guilty parents and spoiled, blaming children. Everything that goes wrong in a child's adult life (and who hasn't had *something* go wrong?) is blamed on his or her parents (or lack of parents). All stereotypical therapy sessions begin, "Tell me about your childhood." There the *cause* of all adult miseries is found: too much love, not enough love; too much discipline, not enough discipline; too much privacy, not enough privacy; too much emphasis on achievement, not enough emphasis on achievement; the list is endless.

There's only one problem with this belief: it no longer has any scientific basis.

An exhaustive study designed to answer the question, "Which affects us more: heredity or environment?" resulted in a conclusion that was more, well, *conclusive* than any of the scientists working on the study thought it would be. That conclusion? (The envelope, please.) Who we are is shaped, almost entirely, by *heredity.*

The study examined identical twins, separated at birth. One twin might have been raised in poverty, the other in a mansion; one in an agnostic household, the other in a religious household; one in a "stable home environment," the other in a succession of institutions and foster homes; one by members of his or her own race, the other by members of another race; one in the country of his or her birth, the other in a foreign country. The variety of environmental conditions could hardly have been more diverse (within the limitations of what we call "Western civilization").

> *Her origins are so low,*
> *you'd have to limbo under*
> *her family tree.*
>
> MINISTER
> *"SCTV"*

Each twin was independently subjected to extensive psychological tests, which determined more than one hundred factors of personality. (Tendency toward optimism or tendency toward pessimism, cautious or daring, outgoing or withdrawn—all those characteristics we use to describe who we and other people are.) The result? Identical twins turned out to be *identical.* Beyond all statistical probability, it was heredity, not environment, that shaped the personality of the twins. Regardless of their environmental backgrounds, within each set, the twins were, essentially, the same person.

The results of this study did not make the lead story on the network evening news, although their impact on our individual lives is probably more important than whatever was—or the topics of all lead stories for the entire month. That our heredity has more to do with shaping us than our environment affects nearly every aspect of our lives, including our discussion of consensual crime.

⚖ ⚖ ⚖

I've always been something of an environmentalist myself (in the heredity versus environment sense of that term), and I took the results of this study with a grain of salt about the size of the iceberg that sank the Titanic. How could all the magnificence and mellifluence of a human being be contained in a fertilized egg the size of a pinprick? But then I had one of those miraculous learning experiences in which I am gently told, "Yes, Peter, you've been *wrong* all these years."*

I bought a butterfly farm. *Why* I bought a butterfly farm, heaven knows. (Doesn't *everyone* doing research on a book about consensual crimes buy a butterfly farm?) The caterpillars arrived by UPS in a transparent plastic cup. They were

---

*These gentle learning experiences happen about three times a day. On a slow day. I, however, usually don't learn from the gentle reminders. The less-gentle reminders ("Wrong, wrong, *wrong."*) are usually ignored by me as well. The School of Hard Knocks ("WRONG! WRONG! WRONG!") and the University of Adversity *("WRONG! WRONG! WRONG!")* eventually drum it in my head. I furrow my brow and arrive at the brilliant conclusion, "Maybe I should reconsider this."

black and brown fuzzy things about half an inch long. They looked like cut-up pipe cleaners. (Remember pipe cleaners? Do they still make pipe cleaners? Do children still make things from pipe cleaners?) The caterpillars were about as active as pipe cleaners. They just *lay* there. I thought they were dead. I had paid $29.95 for five dead pipe-cleaner fragments. At the bottom of the plastic cup was some green stuff that resembled pesto sauce after two days in the refrigerator (or Alfredo sauce after two months in the refrigerator). The instructions informed me that the sauce was a sort of leaf and water puree—the only thing the caterpillars would need to turn into butterflies.

> *The tragedy and magnificence of Homo Sapiens together rise from the same smokey truth that we alone among the animal species refuse to acknowledge natural law.*
>
> ROBERT ARDREY

After a day the pipe-cleaner fragments started moving around, eating, and getting bigger. After about a week, as though somebody had fired a signal gun, they all crawled up the side of the cup, attached themselves to the lid of the cup and just hung there. The next thing I knew, there were five chrysalids hanging from the lid of the cup. And, each of these chrysalids had *iridescent gold highlights.* (Pardon me while I rhapsodize about nature for a bit. I've lived a sheltered life.) These highlights were not just yellow, they were *gold;* reflective, shining *gold.* The pipe-cleaner fragments had been black and brown and all they did was eat green stuff. *Where did the gold come from?*

The instructions that came with the butterfly farm told me that now it was time to put together the butterfly house. I assembled the cardboard-and-cellophane house (which any eight-year-old could do in fifteen minutes. It took me about two hours.). I put the chrysalids inside. Sure enough, ten days later: butterflies. They had about a two-inch wingspan and contained just about every color imaginable. All these colors (plus iridescent gold on the chrysalids) from black and brown things eating green stuff. As they drank sugar-water from an eyedropper, I felt like a proud papa.

I read that these butterflies (Painted Lady, they are called) migrate two thousand miles in the fall, and migrate two thousand miles back again in the spring. How do black and brown things, eating green stuff and drinking only sugar-water do *that?* Sometimes millions of butterflies fly together. They have set migratory routes, like birds. How do they do *this?* I have trouble getting four friends together for dinner. (I should point out that the Painted Lady butterfly does all this without the slightest degree of parental supervision—the female lays her eggs and is gone forever.)

After about a week, I set the butterflies free. It was just as well—I didn't put the butterfly house together quite right and it was falling apart. I'm afraid my butterflies began life in substandard housing. As I let them go and saw them fly

> *Science teaches those who immerse themselves in it to know the workings of God in Nature. As the depth of their understanding grows, its students cannot fail to learn the interdependence of all creation. This is even more than the brotherhood of man, this is the harmony of all nature.*
>
> MAGNUS PYKE

away, it seemed like a scene from one of those Coronet films we saw in elementary school. The music would swell, I'd be waving good-bye to the butterflies who would fly around me in one last good-bye (they didn't, but this is how it would happen in the film) and my voice-over would say: "Yes, I gave the butterflies the gift of life, but they taught me *about* life. I now know the power and the wonder of heredity, and the potential unseen deep within each gene." The title of this film would probably be something like *DNA at Work and Play*.

All this showed me how much there was in a caterpillar's genes; how much more, then, must there be in human genes? If the DNA can tell a million butterflies where to gather and how to get to Mexico, it can certainly carry a hundred or so personality traits.

Considering this, a child is more like a tree to be watered and weeded than a hunk of clay to be molded and sculpted. In growing a tree (or a child) one can provide good soil (a good home), fertilizer (food), staking (education), pruning (discipline), shade (shelter), disease prevention (good health care), protection from predatory insects (protection), and most important of all, water (love). Given all this, however, the truth is that the tree (the child) grows itself and becomes the kind of tree (adult) that it becomes.

Yes, watering, mulching, fertilizing, and protecting from disease and predatory insects are important, but when the tree reaches maturity, an apple tree will produce apples and not lemons. What sort of fruit—in the form of a personality—a human being will produce is a mystery. The intermingling of two gene pools is a gamble, a risk. There are certain statistical, predictable outcomes,* but no guarantees. There are too many wild cards in the deck. Eight aces are possible. So are eight jokers.

ふ ふ ふ

Although a great many human characteristics are determined by heredity, religious preference is *not*. This biological reality irritates religious parents no end. When their progeny does not follow the faith of their fathers—or follows it in form only, with no degree of inner passion or conviction—the parents wonder, "What did we do wrong?" It's an inappropriate question. It's like a gifted musician asking, "Why doesn't my child like music?" A painter asking, "Why can't my child draw?" Or a singer asking, "Why can't my child carry a tune?" The answer is:

---

*One predictable outcome: two black-haired, brown-eyed parents living in Southern California will *always* produce blond-haired, blue-eyed children.

some children do, and some children don't; some children will, and some children won't. It is something the child decides. Agnostic families have produced devoutly religious children, and devoutly religious families have produced agnostic children.

> *The course of a river is almost always disproved of by the source.*
>
> JEAN COCTEAU

Yes, the child can go through the religious motions—just as a musician's child can take lessons, a painter's child can take classes, and a singer's child can study voice—but, in time, when the direct influence of the parents or the need to please them is no longer dominant, the commitment falls away. It happens so often among Catholics, there is a term for it: *lapsed Catholic.* A letter I received from an evangelical church said that seven out of ten children from evangelical households will not themselves follow an evangelical religion. That children don't inherit religious beliefs is no failing on the part of either the Catholics or the evangelicals—it is simply what's been happening throughout the recorded history of religions. The Old Testament is a history of children who did not want to follow their parents' faith, or of children who wanted to follow another faith, or of children who didn't want to follow any faith at all. The children who refused to pay lip service were cast off, disowned, and sometimes put to death.

The modern-day disappointed religious parents who blame themselves for their children's lack of devoutness and devotion suffer needlessly thinking they are somehow responsible. Even from a purely religious point of view, isn't it God's job to call those whom God wants to call? When these disappointed parents, however, begin turning their anger and blame outside themselves, consensual crimes are born. *(Finally* we get back to consensual crimes.)

Some may point their finger and say, "Pornography (prostitution, gambling, homosexuality, drugs, or any of the other consensual crimes) sets a *bad example* for my children. They may yield to the *temptation of Satan* and fall!" Without religion—the *specific* religion followed by the family—the child will become a hopeless, helpless, heinous subhuman. In other words, *immoral.*

Of course the devil is going to tempt: that's his *job.* (Those who don't believe in the devil can re-interpret that last sentence, *"Of course* your children are going to be tempted; that's Madison Avenue's *job,"* or *"Of course* your children are going to be challenged, that's *life.")* To the degree that parents are able to raise strong children, the children will, to quote Nancy Reagan, "Just say no."

At one of President Clinton's first town meetings, a little girl got up and properly recited a question her parents had obviously rehearsed her to ask: "Mr. President, what are you doing to make it safe for me to walk to school without people offering to sell me drugs?" The audience burst into applause. Clinton (alas) gave a by-rote answer about the importance of the War on Drugs. If *I* were president, *I* would have handled it this way:

PRESIDENT McWILLIAMS: Can I ask *you* a question?

LITTLE GIRL: Yes.

PRESIDENT McWILLIAMS: If someone offered to sell *you* drugs, would you buy them?

LITTLE GIRL: No!

PRESIDENT McWILLIAMS: Very good! (Lead the audience in a round of applause for the little girl's big answer.) That's because your parents taught you to say no to drugs! Let's hear it for your parents! (Lead the audience in another round of applause. Have parents stand. Let them think President McWilliams is *absolutely wonderful,* even though President McWilliams is saying that their daughter's original question is fraught with irresponsibility and is based on an entirely unworkable premise.)

If all children said no, drug sellers would stop trying to sell drugs to children. That's what we need in this country: more parents who'll teach more children how to be strong, how to say no to temptation. Yes, we can pray, "lead us not into temptation," but when temptation finds its way to us, let us be strong enough to say no!

(Thunderous applause. "The Battle Hymn of the Republic" or "Don't Stop Thinkin' about Tomorrow" [whichever is cued up] plays triumphantly in the background. Alternate shots of the girl and her parents tearfully embracing as President McWilliams bites his lower lip and accepts his triumph with sincere humility—which he knows how to fake so well.)

Of course the next question was about some foreign leader I had never heard of before, and Clinton knew everything about him. I would have been forced to give the standard presidential response, "We're in delicate negotiations about that matter, and we'll be making an announcement about it within the next few weeks. For the sake of national security, allow me to defer this question until that time."

Making *all children* strong against *all* temptation is not possible. That's the point of this chapter. Some children are going to be genetically predisposed to do certain things. If a child is genetically predisposed toward self-destructive behavior, for example, he or she will self-destruct. *What* he or she uses for that self-destruction is up for grabs: the choices are nearly endless, even in the most repressive and totalitarian societies. That he or she *will* eventually self-destruct is a given. As anyone who has battled an addiction in someone who doesn't want to be rid of the addiction can tell you, it's hopeless. (In fact, trying to remove an addiction from an unwilling addict is, in itself, self-destructive, addictive behav-

> *I mean, folks are going to come back to the good solid husband, like George Bush, sooner or later—I believe that— or the good solid lady, whichever.*
>
> PAT ROBERTSON
> August 17, 1992

ior.)*

Anyone who has tried to get an overeater to modify eating, a smoker to stop smoking, or a person in an abusive relationship to get out of it, knows that at a certain point one can only conclude, "This person must be getting something out of this," and give up trying to help. It's not easy to watch people—especially loved ones—destroy themselves. They are, however, adults, and they are consenting to their choice. Apple trees make apples, lemon trees make lemons, and people with self-destructive tendencies make bad choices.

> *I could be the poster boy for bad judgment.*
>
> ROB LOWE

Of course, many of the choices are only bad *in the eye of the beholder.* For the person partaking of it, it may be a simple lifestyle choice. For the person observing it on the sidelines, it's appalling. Why do we have so much trouble accepting that different people have different desires and fulfill those desires in different ways?

⚖ ⚖ ⚖

If a tree is attacked by insects or choked by weeds, a good gardener goes in and gets rid of them. Those who demand laws against consensual activities, however, say, "There shouldn't *be* any bugs. There shouldn't *be* any weeds." They then want to start multibillion dollar bug-and-weed eradication programs which (a) are ineffective and (b) do more harm than good. Yes, by spraying the proper pesticides almost everywhere, one may be able to wipe out a harmful insect species. But what about all the species of beneficial insects (and the birds that eat them) that get eliminated at the same time? "That's the price we have to pay for keeping our trees safe!" the eradicators huff. The irony is that, although the beneficial species are completely wiped out, the harmful species often adapts to the poison, and continues being harmful as usual.**

---

*In the world of addiction and recovery, this is known as a *savior complex.* Trying to save the unsavable can destroy the savior. Some unsavable people have gone through ten or twelve saviors in their gradual but rocky road to ruin. (Then there are those who self-destruct by trying to save the saviors, and those who try to save those trying to save the saviors—as I say, if you're on a self-destructive path, there are many methods of self-destruction.)

**The number of DDT-resistant insects is legion. And did you ever have roaches that seemed to *thrive* on Raid? I had mice in my apartment in New York that *loved* D-Con. I think they took it to open-air mouse markets and sold it to other mice. They couldn't have *eaten* that much. They *thrived* on the stuff. If I put a piece of cheese next to the D-Con; they would eat the cheese only after all the D-Con was gone. I think Mickey Mouse took some of his Disneyland royalties and started the D-Con company as a clever way of feeding his fellow mice. It's probably the most nutritionally superior mouse food in the world. I bet it even contains little mouse vitamins. Giant advertising campaigns have jerks like me buying D-Con by the barrel and shoveling it into mouse holes. The mice

Everything is good for something. Children, when they're grown, may make choices that will disappoint their parents. (Count on it.) Those caterpillars that seem to be attacking the tree could be sold five for $29.95 and shipped UPS (along with a little pesto sauce) to teach a sheltered writer the miracle of genetics.*

say grace, "Thanks, Mickey!" and chow down.

*The pipe cleaners and pesto sauce are available from Insect Lore Products, P.O. Box 1535, Shafter, CA 93263. I do *not* get a royalty. I will *not* be making an infomercial for them. I'll leave that to Cher. (They should hire Butterfly McQueen.)

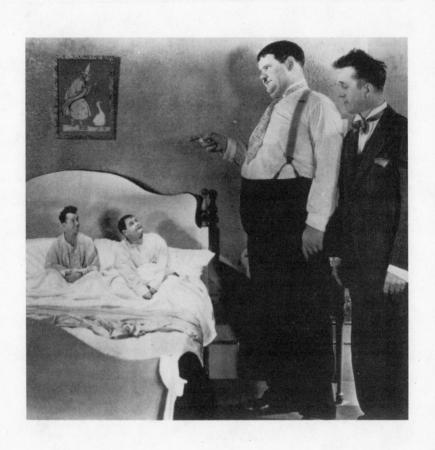

The Family

> *Whatever trouble he's in, his family has the right to share it with him. It's our duty to help him if we can and it's his duty to let us and he doesn't have the privilege to change that.*
>
> JARROD BARKLEY
> *"The Big Valley"*

THOSE OF US WHO grew up in the 1950s got an image of the American family that was not, shall we say, *accurate*. "Father Knows Best," "Leave It to Beaver"* and "Ozzie and Harriet"** were, we were told, not just the way things were *supposed to be;* it was the way things *were*. Things were not that way.

It's probably a good thing life *wasn't* like the television shows in the '50s—we wouldn't have many women now. Take a look at the ratio of boys to girls on the most popular family shows. "Ozzie and Harriet" had two boys, no girls. "Leave It

---

*Why did they call it "Leave It to Beaver?" No one ever left *anything* to Beaver. They were always taking things away from him. Especially Eddie Haskell. Eddie was *supposed* to be the sleazy character in the show, the example of what *not* to do. He was, however, just about everybody's favorite. Rumor had it for a while that Eddie grew up to become a porn star. Not true. Eddie became a member of the Los Angeles Police Department. It fits. Truth is stranger than rumor.

**"Ozzie and Harriet" was—and still is—my favorite. The popular conception is that "Ozzie and Harriet" was the blandest show of the '50s. Hardly. The Nelsons were role models for rebellion. Ozzie never worked. (He was a retired band leader.) He spent all his time getting into one misadventure after another. Harriet was smarter than Ozzie; she knew it, he knew it—she never had to flaunt it. She'd go along with Ozzie's schemes with a bemused smile, warn Ozzie he was wrong, always be right, and make it all better in the end. The only reason she spent so much time in the kitchen was that their sponsor for the first few seasons was Hotpoint, and they had to show off the sponsor's products. Ricky was smarter than David, and had the heart of an entrepreneur. ("I don't mess around, boy.") Ricky became a rock 'n' roll star back when rock 'n' roll had about as good an image as cocaine does today. If Bart Simpson became a drug dealer, he would cause less furor than Ricky did by singing rock 'n' roll. But, every week he had a song, and parents eventually decided that Ricky's singing was okay. (As long as he kept up his studies, which he did.) The first rock video ever was created by Ozzie Nelson. He added some stock travelogue footage to Ricky's rendition of "Travelin' Man" and anticipated MTV by twenty years.

to Beaver" had two boys, no girls. "Rifle-man" had one boy, one rifle, no girls. "Las-sie" had one boy, one dog (supposedly a girl dog, but played by a boy dog) and no girls. "My Three Sons" had, well, that one's obvi-ous. "Bonanza" had three grown-up boys. Although Lucille Ball and Desi Arnaz in real life had one boy and one girl, on "I Love Lucy" they only had one boy. (Little Ricky was television's first baby. Lucy's pregnancy was considered scandalous. They were not even permitted to use the word *pregnant* on the show. My, how things change.) The only shows with daughters were "The Donna Reed Show" (one boy, one girl) and that lighthouse to womanhood—de-spite its title—"Father Knows Best" (one boy, *two* girls). Grown to maturity, that's fifteen men to three women, or a late 1960s dating population of 83.3% men and 16.7% women.

All the households were mamma-papa-kiddies: the nuclear family. (The excep-tions were "My Three Sons" and "Bonanza": Steve Douglas [Fred MacMurray] and Ben Cartwright were widowers.) There were no prior marriages, no children from prior relationships, no threat or even thought of divorce, and the closest thing we saw to physical abuse was Ralph Kramden's, "One of these days, Alice, one of these days . . . to the moon!" There were no infidelities, no drinking prob-lems, no drugs (not even prescription tranquilizers), no racism (How could there be? With the exception of Hop Sing and Ricky Ricardo, there was only one race; even the Hispanic gardener on "Father Knows Best" was named Frank Smith). There was no dropping out of school, no political differences (there were no political discussions), no unemployment (except for Ozzie's early retirement, but everyone who *wanted* a job *had* a job), no severe economic problems (except for a crop failure on "Lassie," when they had to sell off all the livestock, including Lassie; but just before being carted off, Lassie pawed the ground for a while and struck oil, and everything was okay again). The father was the breadwinner; the mother was the bread maker (the only mother who came close to working was Lucy, with her occasionally successful attempts at crashing showbiz and that after-noon at the candy factory). There was no fear of the bomb (which is what we kids were *terrified* about back in the '50s), and no severe disobedience (although white lies, mischief, and misunderstandings were needed for laughs). Life was all wholesome, wholesome, wholesome.*

*As much as those on the religious right like to point to this 1950s sitcom wholesomeness as the Ideal American Family, these shows had a remarkable lack of religion. Ben Cartwright prayed more than everybody else put together. What religion *were* all these people? They certainly weren't Jew-ish. And, other than possibly Ricky Ricardo, probably none of them was Catholic. They were all probably, safely, mainline Presbyterians. But that was the name of the game on these shows: play it

AIN'T NOBODY'S BUSINESS IF YOU DO

That life doesn't exist anymore. But then, it never did.

In her book, *The Way We Never Were,* Stephanie Coontz explains,

> Pessimists argue that the family is collapsing; optimists counter that it is merely diversifying. Too often, both camps begin with an ahistorical, static notion of what "the" family was like before the contemporary period. Thus we have one set of best sellers urging us to reaffirm traditional family values in an era of "family collapse" and another promising to set us free from traditional family traps if we can only turn off "old tapes" and break out of old ruts. . . . The actual complexity of our history—even of our own personal experience—gets buried under the weight of an idealized image.
>
> Families have always been in flux and often in crisis; they have never lived up to nostalgic notions about "the way things used to be."

> *The ultimate result of shielding men from the effects of folly is to fill the world with fools.*
>
> HERBERT SPENCER

Here are some random facts about "the good old days":

- In 1960, one in three children lived in poverty.

- Fewer than half the students who entered high school in the late 1940s ever finished.

- The United States has had the highest homicide rate in the industrial world for almost 150 years. (Think there'll be some sort of celebration on the 150th consecutive year of holding the record?)

- From 1950 to 1959, 257,455 cases of polio were reported, mostly in children; 11,957 people died of the disease.

- In 1940, one American child in ten did not live with either parent. (Today the figure is one in twenty-five.)

- More couples reported their marriage "happy" in 1977 than did in 1957. (The "happy marriage" index dropped slightly by the late 1980s, but still remained higher than it was in 1957.)

- A woman over thirty-five has a better chance of marrying today than she did in the 1950s.

- In the mid-1950s, 25% of the population lived below the poverty line. (And this was in the days before food stamps and housing programs.)

safe. In playing it safe, there was less mention of God and religion on these shows than probably actually took place in American families in the '50s.

- In 1958, 60% of the population over sixty-five had incomes below $1,000.

- In the 1950s, one-third of the white, native-born families could not get by with the income of only one working parent.

- The '50s were not a good time for racial minorities: 50% of black families lived below the poverty line; migrant workers suffered appalling working and living conditions; racism was deeply institutionalized, and people of color were not permitted to take part in "The American Dream."

- In 1952, there were 2,000,000 more wives working outside the home than there were at the peak of wartime production.

- Women who failed to conform to the June Cleaver/Margaret Anderson role of housewife and mother were severely criticized. A 1947 best seller, *The Modern Woman,* called feminism a "deep illness," labeled the idea of an independent woman a "contradiction in terms," and explained that women who wanted equal pay and equal educational opportunities were engaged in a "ritualistic castration" of men.

- Women were often denied the right to serve on juries, convey property, make contracts (including leases on apartments), establish credit in their own name (including mortgages and credit cards).

- Men who failed to marry were considered immature, selfish, or homosexual. A man without a wife found it difficult getting promoted or even finding work.

- Unmarried men and women were routinely paid less than married men and women because, it was believed, their needs were less.

- The witch hunts against communists extended to homosexuals and other political and social "deviants." During the 1950s, 2,611 civil servants were fired as "security risks," and 4,315 resigned while being investigated.

- In her book, *Private Lives: Men and Women of the 50s,* Benita Eisler quotes film producer Joel Schumacher: "No one told the truth. People pretended they weren't unfaithful. They pretended they weren't homosexual. They pretended they weren't horrible." The uniformity we sense about the '50s, with everyone happily "fitting in," was, in fact, a great number of frightened people *pretending* to fit in—and pretending to enjoy it.

- A "sure cure" for homosexuality for either men or women was marriage. This myth was propagated not just by maiden aunts, but by psychologists and psychiatrists. When marriage failed to work, as it always did, having a child would surely take care of the problem. When that didn't work, a second child was "prescribed." When that didn't work, well, the least you could do is *pretend* to be heterosexual and do your duty.

10,000 Negroes work at the Ford plant in nearby Dearborn, [but] not one Negro can live in Dearborn itself.

LIFE MAGAZINE
1957

- Congress discussed nearly two hundred bills to deal with the problem of "juvenile delinquency" in 1955 (the year *Rebel Without a Cause* was released).

- Marilyn Van Derbur, Miss America of 1958, revealed in 1991 that her wealthy, respectable father had regularly sexually violated her from age five until she was eighteen.

- Alcoholism soared in the 1950s.

- Wife-beating was not really considered a crime. Many psychologists explained that battered wives were masochists who provoked their husbands into beating them.

- Husbands raping their wives was not considered a crime at all, but a sign that the woman was deficient in fulfilling her marital duties.

- One half of the marriages that began in the 1950s eventually ended in divorce.

- During the 1950s, more than 2,000,000 legally married people lived separately.

- "Staying together for the children" surpassed baseball as the national pastime.

- Far from Beaver and Wally telling Ward and June carefully edited versions of their daily adventures over the dinner table, more often "the evening meal" was a TV dinner on a TV tray in front of the TV.

- What the TV couldn't numb, tranquilizers could. A *New Yorker* cartoon from that period showed a 1950s couple, floating down the river in a gondola, surrounded by beautiful flowers, singing birds, and playful butterflies. The husband asks the wife, "What was the name of that tranquilizer we took?" In 1958, 462,000 pounds of tranquilizers were consumed in the United States. A year later, consumption had more than doubled to 1.5 million pounds.

- By the end of the 1950s, when *Redbook* asked readers to supply examples for an upcoming article, "Why Young Mothers Feel Trapped," 24,000 young mothers replied.

- The number of pregnant brides more than doubled in the 1950s.

- Teenage birth rates had never been so high. In 1957, there were more than twice as many births to girls aged fifteen to nineteen than in 1983.

- The number of illegitimate babies put up for adoption rose 80% from 1944 to 1955.

Ms. Coontz concludes, "The historical record is clear on one point: Although there are many things to draw on in our past, there is no one family form that has ever protected people from poverty or social disruption, and no traditional arrangement that provides a workable model for how we might organize family relations in the modern world."

၁၅ ၁၅ ၁၅

It is, of course, television's job to entertain. No one seriously believes, for example, that there is an American family—black or white—that even remotely resembles the Huxtables. A full-time working lawyer and doctor with an immaculate house full of children and no household help? Come on. How could anyone walk the line between warmth and cynicism (without twelve writers and a week of rehearsal) as does Cosby? And how could he afford—even on a doctor's income—five new designer sweaters every week? (His lawyer-wife must have bought them for him.) No, we don't see "The Cosby Show"—or any other contemporary sitcom—as a reflection of reality. Then why do we consider "Leave It to Beaver," "Ozzie and Harriet," "Father Knows Best," and all the '50s sitcoms as an accurate reflection? Two reasons.

First, they were made a long time ago. We tend to minimize the bad and enhance the good from the past. It's a form of mental illness known as *nostalgia*. (The '50s infected us with it; it was a side effect of the Salk vaccine.) Second, all these shows are in black and white. Somehow, we think of them as *documentaries*. It was *real life* filmed with hidden cameras. I think we should send all of these episodes to Ted Turner and have them colorized. Then we wouldn't believe them at all.

> *So four men and four women*
> *have sealed themselves off*
> *inside Biosphere 2. No contraceptives*
> *are allowed and if a woman gets*
> *pregnant she's expelled.*
> *This is progress?*
> *Sounds more like high school*
> *in the 1950s.*
>
> CHRISTOPHER BLINDEN

⚖ ⚖ ⚖

The 1950s were the high point of the "nuclear family," which flourished during an unprecedented economic boom in the United States that had never happened before and, almost certainly, will never happen again. The United States was almost the only country untouched economically by World War II. All the international competition lay in ruins, whereas the United States was ready to switch immediately from wartime production to peacetime production. It didn't matter *what* we made—it sold. The gas-guzzler—one of the most inefficient objects made by humans—is an icon of that era. (By the late 1950s, Germany was already challenging the American automotive vise-hold with its Volkswagen. Japan had attacked with its transistor radio. American industry would never be that fat and sassy again.)

There had been nothing like the American nuclear family before, and there has been nothing like it since. Depending on whose statistics you read, today the traditional nuclear family represents anywhere from 6% to less than 50% of the American population. One can fiddle with the statistics endlessly. Should the household have only the male as the breadwinner? Should there be no one living in the household except the mother, father and children? Should the household be in a single-family house, or will an apartment do? Does a couple living alone without children count? What if there's a two-car garage and it's not attached, but there's a breezeway connecting it to the house? Whether we fiddle with these questions or not, the point is clear: even taking the most conservative estimate, more than half the country lives today outside anything remotely resembling a nuclear family.

Are we saying these more-than-50% who do *not* live in a "traditional American family" are condemned to lives of quiet desperation? Of course not.

We must understand that the family is not the basic building block of society, the *individual* is.

The people who want us to return to "traditional family values" are the ones

> *Jesus was a bachelor.*
>
> DON HEROLD

who had it *good* in the 1950s: specifically, white, male, Christian heterosexuals. The '50s were a bad time for women, minorities, homosexuals, political dissidents, and anyone who was in any way "different." Each of these groups is—and has been since the 1950s—demanding what they are rightfully due as citizens of the United States. Life will never go back "the way it was," and some people are *very* unhappy about it.

Take, for example, this rather simple statement: "Equality of rights under the law shall not be denied or abridged by the United States or by any State on account of sex."*

Straightforward. Clear. Fair. And yet, here's what Pat Robertson had to say about it:

> It is about a socialist, anti-family political movement that encourages women to leave their husbands, kill their children, practice witchcraft, destroy capitalism and become lesbians.

The prejudice is obvious, but can we also detect a little fear there? Pat Robertson wants to marry June Cleaver, not Murphy Brown. He would find it more *comfortable* that way. (In fact, he *has* married June Cleaver.)

What those who demand "traditional family values" want, then, cannot be had. We will never have the economic domination of the world we had in the 1950s, nor will the white, male, Christian heterosexual be able to dominate again the women, blacks, Jews, Hispanics, gays, and the rest. There's no going back— nor *should* there be a going back. It never should have happened in the first place.

⚖️ ⚖️ ⚖️

Families are important because the infant human being requires more time and attention than any other animal before it can function independently. Human infants require—at an absolute *minimum*—three years before they can manage without the help of an adult. (If three years seems young to be without parental care, it is far from unheard of in third world countries, or in countries torn by war or natural disaster.) Adults, then, need to feed and protect the infant for at least three years in order for the human species to survive. But who says the child needs more than one adult? And who says the adult needs to be a birth parent? Only tradition. Long before the nuclear family, *tribes* raised children collectively— a system that continues in many parts of the world to this day.

Our modern concept of two people raising their children under one roof grew out of feudal necessity. The absolute *minimum* number of people necessary

*The Equal Rights Amendment fell three states short of the thirty-eight it needed for ratification.

to maintain a plot of land during the Middle Ages was two. As the lord of the manor wanted his serfs to "be fruitful and multiply" (thus multiplying the wealth of the lord), it was also necessary that one of the two people be a man and the other a woman. Serfs were paired until death did them part. Love had nothing to do with it. (The only people who had time for such luxuries as love were those at court—hence the term *courtship.*) That the serfs had loveless marriages didn't seem to bother them (although, frankly, the opinions of feudal serfs have not exactly survived in history). They spent very little time together. The man tended the land all his waking hours, and the woman tended the house, livestock, and children. Even if a husband and wife hated each other, all they had to do was wait a little while: what with disease, war, childbirth, and a life span far shorter than our own, the average marriage lasted less than five years. The departed partner was immediately replaced, and the system continued.

> *Human beings are not animals, and I do not want to see sex and sexual differences treated as casually and amorally as dogs and other beasts treat them. I believe this could happen under the ERA.*
>
> RONALD REAGAN

It wasn't continued because the serfs necessarily *liked* this system, but because it was *economically viable* to the aristocracy. Two people made one economic unit that produced crops, livestock, and children. Three would be too many; one was not enough.

The system worked so well, and the aristocracy was so happy with it, that they got the church involved. A marvelous theology developed (marvelously useful to the landowners): work hard in this life (which is but a blink in the eye of eternity), serve your lord (who represented the Lord), and you will have paradise for all eternity—and that's a long, long time. Rebel against the lord (Lord), and you will spend all eternity (which is a long, etc.) in hell. Be true to your spouse (*not* being true to your spouse would take valuable time away from essential serf stuff), work hard, and eternal paradise will be yours.

Today, of course, the idea that two people are one economic unit is no longer true. With labor-saving devices, reduced work hours, and prepackaged everything, one person can raise a child perfectly well. So can twenty. Personally, I always wanted a greater variety of adult input than I got from my two parents. Looking back on my childhood, I think I spent more time with my friends' parents than I did with my friends.*

So what are these "family values" we want to maintain?

In a 1989 *Newsweek* survey, only 22% of the respondents believed that family

---

*From twelve on—at my own insistence—I began spending weekends at my grandmother's house. It was a large house, and she rented out rooms. There were college students, working people, and retirees, along with an endless parade of their visitors, relatives, and friends. I loved it.

was directly tied to blood lines, marriage, children, and adoption. A whopping 74% declared that a family is any group whose members love and care for one another. It's too bad former Vice-President Quayle didn't read this poll before he accused Murphy Brown of destroying traditional family values by having a child without the formality of marriage.

As Diane English said when accepting her Emmy for creating "Murphy Brown,"

To all you mothers out there who are raising your children alone either by choice or necessity, don't let anyone tell you you're not a family.

America's "traditional family values" are love, support, tolerance, caring, nurturing, and—if you don't mind my adding my favorite—a sense of humor.*

Isn't that what the situation comedy is all about? We find ourselves in a situation (life) and are faced with the fundamental question: do we laugh or do we cry? The choice is up to us—choice being a traditional American value, too.

---

*As one of my "family" members, John-Roger, puts it: "If it's going to be funny later, it's funny now. Relax: this is funny."

Season's Greetings

and best wishes for 1955

THE McWILLIAMS

Mac, Mary, Peter, Michael

What Is the Age of Consent?

> *Do what you want.*
> *You're over twenty-one.*
> *(Tramp!)*
>
> WOODY ALLEN

AT WHAT AGE do we become consenting adults? At what age are. we—not our parents—responsible for our actions? For the purpose of discussing the ideas in this book, let's assume the age of consent to be twenty-one.

But let's consider for a moment the age of consent and what it means. In this country, the laws and customs that determine the age of consent are glaringly inconsistent. Since 1971, by constitutional amendment—ratified faster than any constitutional amendment in history—eighteen-year-olds have been entitled to vote. During wartime, eighteen-year-olds can be drafted to fight and possibly die for their country. Eighteen-year-olds can get married without parental approval. In every court of law in the land, eighteen-year-olds are considered adults. They are tried as adults and pay adult penalties for their misdeeds.

If a group can elect officials, be forced to die for their country, get married, and stand trial as adults, *surely* they are adults.

Not so.

In order to receive federal highway funds, each state must maintain the drinking age at twenty-one. Every state, of course, succumbs. The government points with pride to the number of lives that have been saved by keeping teenaged drunk drivers off the road. However, look at the number of eighteen-, nineteen- and twenty-year-olds who died for their country (often against their will). We trust teenagers to elect a president, get married and raise a family, but do not trust them with the choice of whether to drink or not. And has anyone explored how many teenagers turn to drugs rather than alcohol as recreational chemicals because drugs, for young people, are considerably more available?

> *The time not to become a father
> is eighteen years before a war.*
>
> E. B. WHITE

Some children mature more quickly than others, taking on more and more adult responsibility. Other children rebel more, grabbing more and more responsibility until, one day, they have it all. Either way, it seems only reasonable that a system for transferring the responsibility of adulthood from the parent to child (the new adult) should be established.

Here's my suggestion: Whenever both the parent and child agree (by whatever method they come to agreement) that the rights and responsibilities of adulthood should be passed from the parent to the child, they fill out and sign a standard form, which is then filed with the state. This would give the new adult all the privileges of adulthood, but all the responsibilities of adulthood, too. He or she would have reached the age of consent (might not be a bad name for it: the Age of Consent Form, and one would be issued an Age of Consent Card, rather like a driver's license) and would be entitled to enter into any consensual activities.

If the would-be new adults mess up, however, they do not get to hide behind their youth, inexperience, or innocence. They got the name (adult) and now they can play the game (adult court).

Some children may reach maturity in some consensual areas faster than in other areas. Just as a driver's license may have restrictions (corrective lenses, daylight only, commercial vehicles), so, too, could the Age of Consent certificate. A child may, for example, be able to handle sex* before being able to handle alcohol—or vice versa. Some children may be "old" enough to gamble, but not old enough for X-rated movies.

If you have the idea that an early age of consent corrupts children, consider the state that has an age of consent—except for cohabitation and alcohol—of thirteen. I'm talking about New Mexico. Not exactly sin center. In Maine and Iowa—not exactly sin *anything*—the age of consent is fourteen. The truly wicked state of California, on the other hand, has a strictly enforced age of consent at eighteen. What kids do and how moral they grow up to be seems to depend on variables other than the law.

All right, back to the book. Please return to the idea that a consenting adult is someone over twenty-one. This chapter is here to provoke a little thought and discussion, not to reach any conclusions about the age of consent.

---

*Pretending that children wait until they're eighteen, much less twenty-one, before experimenting with you-know-what, is one of our sillier cultural myths. Whether they *should* wait or not is an entirely different question. The fact is, most don't, and parents waste a lot of emotional energy getting upset about their children doing something they did themselves (or certainly would have done if they'd had the opportunity).

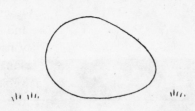

Hemp for Victory

> America has an opportunity to,
> once and for all, say farewell
> to the Exxon Valdez,
> Saddam Hussein,
> and a prohibitively expensive
> brinkmanship in the
> desert sands of Saudi Arabia.
>
> HUGH DOWNS
> *ABC Radio*

YOU MAY FIND the information in this chapter astonishing, unlikely, fascinating, unbelievable, amazing, and too good to be true. That, at least, was my first reaction. What amazed me even more was that I first heard this information not from an underground newspaper, but on the ABC Radio Network, presented by someone who ranks right up there with Walter Cronkite as a trustworthy journalist, Hugh Downs:

The reasons the pro-marijuana lobby wants marijuana legal have little to do with getting high, and a great deal to do with fighting oil giants like Saddam Hussein, Exxon and Iran. The pro-marijuana groups claim that hemp is such a versatile raw material that its products not only compete with petroleum, but with coal, natural gas, nuclear energy, pharmaceutical, timber and textile companies. It is estimated that methane and methanol production alone from hemp grown as bio-mass could replace 90% of the world's energy needs. If they're right, this is *not* good news for oil interests, and could account for the continuation of marijuana prohibition.

As we explored in the chapter, "Recreational Use of Drugs," marijuana is the hemp plant *(Cannabis sativa)*, and was one of the primary agricultural products in this country for more than 250 years. We explored how the DuPont Corporation and William Randolph Hearst, working with Federal Bureau of Narcotics Director Harry Anslinger, succeeded in having marijuana prohibited nationally in 1937. On his ABC Radio broadcast, Hugh Downs explored possible reasons why marjuana is still illegal today:

When Rudolph Diesel produced his famous engine in 1896, he assumed that the diesel engine would be powered by a variety of fuels, especially vegetable and seed oils. Rudolph Diesel, like most engineers then, believed vegetable fuels were superior to petroleum. Hemp is the most efficient vegetable.

In the 1930s, the Ford Motor Company also saw a future in biomass fuels. Ford operated a successful biomass conversion plant that included hemp at their Iron Mountain facility in Michigan. Ford engineers extracted methanol, charcoal fuel, tar, pitch, ethyl acetate, and creosote—all fundamental ingredients for modern industry, and now supplied by oil-related industries.

> *They've outlawed the number one vegetable on the planet.*
>
> TIMOTHY LEARY

The difference is that the vegetable source is renewable, cheap and clean, and the petroleum or coal sources are limited, expensive and dirty. By volume, 30% of the hemp seed contains oil suitable for high-grade diesel fuel, as well as aircraft engine and precision machine oil. Henry Ford's experiments with methanol promised cheap, readily-renewable fuel. And, if you think methanol means compromise, you should know that many modern race cars run on methanol.

If we could domestically produce the necessary fuel for automobiles, generating electricity, heating, and all other petroleum uses, imagine the number of businesses that would harm. A short list would include the big oil companies, nuclear power plants, coal mining, and the Pentagon (without the oil-based friction* in the Middle East, where are our enemies?). A powerful list. But in addition to oil, let's explore some of the other things the hemp plant could be used to manufacture. In addition to being excited about the potential, also be aware of the powerful industries the full cultivation of hemp would either significantly alter or eliminate.

⚖ ⚖ ⚖

Jack Herer's book, *The Emperor Wears No Clothes,* is the bible on industrial uses for marijuana. The subtitle of the book is *The Authoritative Historical Record of the Cannabis Plant, Marijuana Prohibition, and How Hemp Can Still Save the World.* This is an ambitious subtitle—especially for a book that looks more like the *Whole Earth Catalog* than a scholarly tome. For the most part, however, Herer succeeds in his quest. He may become a little *too* enthusiastic about the industrial uses of hemp at times, but even if 10% of his information is accurate (and certainly more than that is), marijuana could prove a major boon to the economy, the environment, and humanity.

In addition to oil and fuel, here are some of the industrial uses for the hemp plant:

*"Oil-based friction": now *there's* a term.

- **Paper.** Whereas trees—currently our primary source of paper—take twenty years to grow, hemp can grow to be twenty feet tall in a single season. Warm climates can produce three hemp harvests per year. This, obviously, makes hemp a far more efficient plant for producing paper than trees. In addition, making paper from hemp—unlike wood pulp—doesn't require acid, so all hemp paper is "acid free" and thus lasts for hundreds of years. Hemp could supply virtually all of our paper, cardboard, and other packaging needs. (Half the paper used in America is for packaging.)

> *It takes an entire forest— over 500,000 trees— to supply Americans with their Sunday newspapers every week.*
>
> *Over one billion trees are used to make disposable diapers every year.*

- **Textiles and Fabrics.** The hemp fiber is very similar to flax—in fact, much of the linen produced prior to the 1930s (including fine Irish linen) was made from hemp, not flax. The hemp plant, then, is an excellent source for textiles. Prior to the invention of the cotton gin, most clothing in the United States was made from the hemp plant. The hemp fiber is stronger, softer, warmer, and longer lasting than cotton.

- **Food.** The hemp seed is an excellent source of protein. It can be ground, baked into breads, sprouted, and turned into a tofu-like food. In addition, hemp seed makes an excellent oil similar to flaxseed oil. You cannot "get high" eating marijuana seeds or their oil. ("Hash oil," which is highly intoxicating, does not come from the seeds.)

- **Medicine.** Marijuana (yes, the part that gets you high) is the best medicine for reducing nausea in people being treated with chemotherapy.* Marijuana is also an excellent treatment for glaucoma, which is responsible for 14% of all blindness in America and affects 2.5 million people.** Marijuana has also been proven effective in treating asthma, epilepsy, MS, back pain and muscle spasms, arthritis,

---

*Some states allow the psychoactive chemical, THC, to be sold in pill form as a treatment for nausea. These states, however, do not allow the smokeable form of marijuana to be sold, even to cancer or AIDS patients. The absurdity of this is immediately evident: if one is nauseated, he or she would be unable to keep down the pill form of THC long enough for it to be absorbed into the system. The smokeable form of marijuana, however, acts much more quickly than the pill form and can be taken even on an upset stomach.

**Some doctors hint strongly that glaucoma patients obtain marijuana illicitly to use in their glaucoma treatments.

cystic fibrosis, rheumatism, emphysema, migraines, reducing tumors, and—as should come as a surprise to no one who has ever smoked marijuana—in promoting an appetite.

- **Building Materials.** The hemp plant can be pressed into fiberboard which is fire resistant and has excellent thermal- and sound-insulating qualities.

- **Other Products.** The hemp plant is rich in cellulose. Cellulose can be used for making more than 150,000 plastic products, many of which are made from petroleum today. Hemp can also be used to make paint, varnish, and even dynamite.

⚖ ⚖ ⚖

Here are some fascinating hemp facts, taken directly from *The Emperor Wears No Clothes:*

- HEMPstead, Long Island; HEMPstead County, Arkansas; HEMPstead, Texas; HEMPhill, North Carolina; HEMPfield, Pennsylvania; among others, were named after cannabis growing regions, or after family names derived from hemp growing.

- Cannabis hemp was legal tender (money) in most of the Americas from 1631 until the early 1800s. You could pay your taxes with cannabis hemp throughout America for over 200 years.

- You could even be jailed in America for not growing cannabis during several periods of shortage, e.g., in Virginia between 1763 and 1767.

- George Washington and Thomas Jefferson grew cannabis on their plantations. Jefferson, while envoy to France, went to great expense—and even considerable risk to himself and his secret agents—to procure particularly good hemp seeds smuggled illegally into Turkey from China. The Chinese Mandarins (political rulers) so valued their hemp seeds that they made their exportation a capital offense.

- Benjamin Franklin started one of America's first paper mills with cannabis. This allowed America to have a free colonial press without having to beg or justify paper and books from England.

- The United States Census of 1850 counted 8,327 hemp "plantations" (minimum 2,000 acre farms) growing cannabis hemp for cloth, canvas and even the cordage used for baling cotton. (This figure does not include the tens of thousands of smaller farms growing cannabis, nor the hundreds of thousands—if not millions—of family hemp patches in America.)

- In 1942, after the Japanese invasion of the Philippines cut off the supply of manila (Abaca) hemp, the U.S. government distributed 400,000 pounds of cannabis seeds to American farmers from Wisconsin to Kentucky, who produced 42,000 tons of hemp fiber annually for the war effort until 1946. In 1942–43 farmers were made to attend showings of the USDA film *Hemp for Victory*, sign that they had seen the film and read a hemp cultivation booklet. Farmers from 1942 through 1945 who agreed to grow hemp were waived from serving in the military, along with their sons; that's how vitally important hemp was to America during World War II.

> *Can we have rope without dope?*
> *A Jekyll-and-Hyde plant, hemp*
> *provides twine and rope urgently*
> *needed for military purposes.*
> *But it also yields marijuana,*
> *a drug that makes depraved*
> *creatures of its addicts.*
>
> **POPULAR SCIENCE**
> **1943**

- The paintings of Rembrandt, Van Gogh, Gainsborough, etc., were primarily painted on hemp canvas, as were practically all canvas paintings.

One of the most beneficial aspects of using hemp (or other plants) for fuel is that, as plants grow, they take carbon dioxide out of the atmosphere and replace it with oxygen. This helps solve one of our primary environmental problems: too much carbon dioxide in the atmosphere. When a portion of the hemp plant is burned for fuel, it has already "earned" the oxygen it uses by having placed that oxygen in the atmosphere while it grew. Fossil fuels (oil, gas, or coal), on the other hand, come from plant and animal sources that died millions of years ago—whatever carbon dioxide they took or oxygen they left (the beneficial effects) happened millions of years ago. Burning fossil fuels, then, only adds to carbon dioxide and reduces the amount of oxygen in the atmosphere.

Without even *mentioning* its recreational uses, the hemp plant has remarkable potential for agriculture, manufacturing, energy, and the environment. And yet, due to the prohibitions on marijuana flowers (the intoxicating portion—and, not coincidentally, the sex organs of the plant), cultivating, using, or even possessing hemp can get you mandatory life imprisonment.

As with most consensual crimes, this prohibition of hemp is both silly and sinister. As Portland, Oregon, physician Dr. Fred Oerther asked,

> Should we believe self-serving, ever-growing drug enforcement/drug treatment bureaucrats, whose pay and advancement depends on finding more and more people to arrest and "treat"?

> More Americans die in just one day in prisons, penitentiaries, jails and stockades than have ever died from marijuana throughout history. Who are they protecting? From what?

PART VII

WHAT TO DO?

Why Consensual Crimes
Have So Few Advocates

> *I believe we are on an*
> *irreversible trend toward*
> *more freedom and democracy.*
> *But that could change.*
>
> VICE-PRESIDENT
> DAN QUAYLE

ALTHOUGH CONSENSUAL "criminals" make up the vast majority of our society (almost everyone, at one time or another, has taken part in an illegal consensual activity), there is no single organization—or coalition of organizations—fighting for their (our?) rights. This is because most consensual criminals identify more strongly with at least one other group than their (our?) fellow consensual criminals. All the groups that have political, economic, or persuasive power in the United States seem opposed to decriminalizing consensual acts.

Let's take a look at the various moving-and-shaking organizations and see why none of them protects our right to do with our person and property whatever we choose as long as we do not physically harm the person or property of another.

Religions

You name the religion and it's against one (often all) of the consensual crimes. Religious leaders—and fundamentalists in particular—don't seem to grasp the fundamental notion that keeping the government from criminalizing consensual acts between adults *protects religion*. If a government establishes its authority to control what people can and cannot do with their person and property, either "for their own good" or "for the good of society," that same government can later begin dictating how much of one's person and property should or can be devoted to the discovery of, communication with, and worship of God. The essence of almost all religions is that one must choose, with one's free will, to worship God: a prayer said at the point of a gun is not a prayer. Likewise, the government has no business restricting how much of ourselves or our property we devote to religion. (It's already happening, of course, in the governmental suppression of "cults.")

> *And will not God bring about*
> *justice for his chosen ones,*
> *who cry out to him day and night?*
> *Will he keep putting them off?*
> *I tell you, he will see that*
> *they get justice, and quickly.*
>
> JESUS OF NAZARETH
> *Luke 18:7–8*

For the sake of religion itself, then, religious leaders should support the concept that consensual activities should not be illegal. I support someone's freedom of speech to say something I don't like, to protect my freedom to say what I like. In this case, the issue is *freedom of speech*. The concept of freedom of speech is a platform even diametrically opposed speakers can agree upon.

So, too, should be the freedom for people to do with their person or property whatever they choose as long as they don't physically harm the person or property of another; it is one of the platforms on which all our other freedoms rest—including the freedom of religion.

In order for people to use their person and property to go to heaven in their own way, they must also protect the right of others to use their person and property to go wherever they want, including hell, in their own way.

It's clear, however, that the religions with any clout in the United States—all of them Christian denominations—will not be the ones leading the battle for the repeal of prohibitive laws.

Although Christian religions disagree strongly on their interpretations of what Jesus said and what it means to us today, they generally agree that taking part in currently illegal consensual activities is not a good idea and should remain illegal. One can only pray that the revivalists are revived again, the Protestants start protesting, and the Catholics become more catholic.

Lawyers

Lawyers have sometimes been the ones to come out in favor of social reform. After all, they're on the front lines of the injustice and inhumanity perpetrated by unjust laws. When it comes to consensual crimes, however, the lawyers' social conscience has not been too active. At least not yet. They may make occasional rumblings about one or two of the consensual crimes, but the wholesale repeal of all consensual crimes would, frankly, be bad for business. Half their workload—that is, financial opportunity—would disappear overnight. They can't afford to recommend that.

The United States has more lawyers than all other countries in the world combined; 70% of the world's lawyers are American. The United States has 299 lawyers per 100,000 people. Compare this with England, 82 per 100,000, and Japan, a mere 11 per 100,000. Remember, it's the lawyers who make up all of the prosecutors, all of the judges, and the majority of legislators. Intuitively, I have difficulty accepting that, in exchange for job security, people would keep laws on the books that destroy the lives of millions each year. But then, I have to remind myself: these are *lawyers*. Lawyers have held an unsavory reputation in the United States for some time. Even Dan Quayle (a lawyer) had to wonder:

> Does America really need 70 percent of the world's lawyers? There is one lawyer for every 335 people in the U.S., as opposed to one for every 9,000 people in Japan.

Although his words make sense, and his question is a valid one, his sense of politics was typically misguided: he made the comment in his speech before the annual meeting of the American Bar Association.

*If the laws could speak
for themselves,
they would complain
of the lawyers in the first place.*

LORD HALIFAX
1633–1695

And let's keep in mind, we're not talking about lawyers *getting by;* we're talking about lawyers *getting rich.* Here's a fanciful fee negotiation from the television show, "Perry Mason":

PERRY MASON: My fee? Well, what do you think is fair?

LITTLE OLD LADY CLIENT: Well, I paid you $5 the first day. It was high, but it was worth it.

PERRY: What do you think now?

CLIENT: Well, I want to do the right thing. After all, I could have gone to prison—or even worse. Would $25 be all right?

PERRY: Just exactly the figure I had in mind.

CLIENT: Well, good. I've got it right here.

Liberals

One would think all the demonstrable human pain and suffering (the oft-quoted arrest, probation, parole, and incarceration rates), not to mention the ongoing violations of the Constitution, would have liberal hearts bleeding enough to fill the needs of both the Red Cross and Count Dracula for years to come. That's not happening. The liberals seem to be taken in by the propaganda of the religious right that connects human suffering to drug use, prostitution, gambling, and all the rest. When will the liberals wake up, acknowledge that they've been duped, and get on the bandwagon? I do not know.

The irony is that most of the middle-aged liberals smoked pot and did a pharmacological cornucopia of other drugs during college, and they all seemed to come out of it just fine. Don't they remember who ended Prohibition? The liberal icon of the twentieth century: Franklin Delano Roosevelt.

When talking to some liberals about the evils of laws against consensual activities, I feel like Churchill talking about the evils of Nazism to the British in 1934—they just don't get it. Maybe I'll write a book; one of the Pulitzer Prize–

winning epics with a title such as *While Liberals Slept*. Perhaps I'll go after the Nobel Prize, too, and call it *Whilst Liberals Slept*. At any rate, it doesn't look as though I'll be able to write the history of liberal slumber anytime soon: a history requires a beginning, a middle, and an end, and the end is not in sight: most liberals are still snoozing away. In discussing sleeping giants, one is always tempted to quote Churchill, a temptation to which I now happily succumb. Here is Sir Winston in 1942:

Now this is not the end. It is not even the beginning of the end. But it is, perhaps, the end of the beginning.

Three years after making this statement, he won. *(Then* he went on to write a book about World War II and won the Nobel prize.)

Conservatives

Why did I always have the belief that conservatives wanted to *conserve* all that was good in America: the Declaration of Independence, the Constitution, the Bill of Rights, individual responsibility, free enterprise, and liberty? Whatever gave me the impression that conservatives saw big government as an enemy to freedom? Why did I ever think (just because Ronald Reagan said it at least 4,000 times) that a primary goal of conservatism was "to get the government off our backs"? Well, if the conservatives *do* believe in these ideas, when it comes to consensual crimes, the conservatives have been sleeping right alongside the liberals.*

Fundamental religious leaders' seductive influence (and the political power they wield), combined with, for the most part, genuine personal religious convictions, caused the right to fuse with the fundamentalist religions sometime in the late 1970s and form the religious right. It helped to elect any number of Republican officials—not the least of whom was Ronald Reagan—but in embracing religion, the right lost a goodly portion of its soul. That's okay. They're politicians. It's to be expected. Now that the conservatives have embraced too many of the fundamental religious doctrines, however, mainstream right-wing America is displeased (at last!). Political pundits on the right are advising conservatives to distance themselves from the fundamentalists as quickly as they embraced them.

Oh, it would still be fine to have Billy Graham (or someone like him) lead the Republican convention in an opening prayer, and there's no problem thanking and invoking God at nearly every opportunity, but let's back off all this *intolerance*. That is at least the message the conservatives are being given, and they seem to be

---

*Interesting image: Ted Kennedy snoozing next to Rush Limbaugh in a *very* crowded bed.

listening. The vitriolic messages of hatred delivered in the name of God at the 1992 Republican Convention shocked and appalled far more viewers than they encouraged or converted. Pat Robertson tested the political winds, beat a path back to his Christian Broadcasting Network, and nary, nary a conservative pleaded for his return. They are not likely to again in the future. If there is a God.

> *I simply refuse to give up the party of Lincoln to the bigots.*
>
> LEONARD MATLOVICH
> *American Air Force Sergeant discharged for being gay*

Politicians

Time was when we looked to politicians for leadership: Jefferson and Washington led us into a free country; Lincoln led us from slavery; Roosevelt led us from the Depression; Kennedy led us from racial discrimination. Clinton, however, took a leadership position in giving gays an equal chance to serve in the military and he was crucified. (Not that Washington, Jefferson, Lincoln, Roosevelt, and Kennedy weren't—literally murdered, in the cases of Lincoln and Kennedy.) With this intolerance being the state of the nation (and the state of most states), don't look for much political leadership in the way of decriminalizing consensual crime.

Politicians today tend to follow popular beliefs (even if those beliefs are based on prejudice, inaccuracies, and myths), repeat the popular beliefs back to the populace (thus enforcing the prejudices, inaccuracies, and myths), and make laws to support the popular beliefs (thus institutionalizing the prejudices, inaccuracies, and myths). Some say it's democracy. Actually, it's cowardice. Our elected officials are elected so that, theoretically, they can devote full time studying all sides of a situation, gathering the facts, and educating their constituents as to the truth. It is also their job to educate their constituents about the supreme law of the land (the Constitution), what it says, and what rights it gives minorities, no matter how unhappy the actions of those minorities may make the majority.

Politicians aren't doing their jobs; they are only concerned with keeping them. As soon as there's a groundswell of popular opinion that currently illegal consensual activities have no business being crimes, watch the politicians—from every side of the political fence—become leaders of the pack.

A politician's attitude on consensual crimes also affects the votes he or she receives. Politicians who come out in favor of personal freedom are generally attacked by their opponents as being "soft on drugs," "soft on vice," "soft on pornography"* and just basically soft. This costs votes. Conversely, promising to "crack down," "get tough," and "draw a hard line" against any of the consensual crimes is sure—in our current climate—to win votes. So, whether a politician

*I'm not saying a word.

> *Under democracy one party always devotes its chief energies to trying to prove that the other party is unfit to rule—and both commonly succeed, and are right.*
>
> H. L. MENCKEN

believes that certain consensual activities should be illegal or not, doing what's expedient to get in or stay in office often takes precedence. That little matter of the oath of office, by which they swear to preserve, protect, and defend the Constitution of the United States, is conveniently set aside.

Law Enforcement

Other than congenitally not enjoying changes in the status quo, law enforcement has four primary reasons it isn't interested in removing the laws against consensual activities.

First, consensual crimes provide easy arrests. This is helpful when either an individual officer's monthly minimum has not yet been met, or when a certain division of law enforcement has to look as though they are "getting tough on crime."

Second, those who are in law enforcement for the macho thrills and chills certainly don't want to give up their drug busts. Police work, for the most part, is paperwork. The average police officer has to draw his or her gun twice *in an entire career.* This is far too boring a lifestyle for those who think the police force is the blue version of the Green Berets. Besides, only a violent drug bust is *guaranteed* to get them on "COPS!"

Third, arresting people (or threatening to arrest people) for consensual crimes is often used as a way of getting information about other crimes. Police are not eager to give up this source of easy information.

Fourth, when police make a drug bust, they get to keep everything. Everything. Police get to take the house, land, car, and all money they can find anywhere. (This is not the case with *real* crime such as murder or robbery.) Where does this money go? To the law enforcement agency. Assets forfeiture is the largest single source of new funding law enforcement has found in the past five years. Why would they want to give that up?

I'm not quite as cynical about the police as I am about lawyers. I believe that there are good cops who want to do a good job. It should be painfully clear to law enforcement officials that enforcing consensual crimes is bogging them down, and that, if consensual crimes were no longer crimes, police could do a much better job protecting us all from real crime. People would respect law enforcement more, cooperate more, and the officers could do a much better job. However, law enforcement officers have at least four strong motivations that keep them from acting on that reasoning.

The Media

Why on earth would the media want to let go of all those hot news stories?

Of the top ten news stories in any year, the majority deal in some way with consensual crime. The headlines, covers, and teasers that make the most sales or get the most viewership often involve consensual crimes. ("TOPLESS BAR RAIDED. FILM AT ELEVEN.") Besides, printing something other than what is officially dispensed in political press conferences and press releases takes time, work, and, frankly, is risky. (You can't *appear* to be making a mistake if you follow the official "party line"—it's what everyone's reporting.)

> *It is part of the social mission of every great newspaper to provide a refuge and a home for the largest possible number of salaried eccentrics.*
>
> LORD THOMSON OF FLEET

A decision was made by the media in the mid-to-late 1980s to self-censor any comedy related to drugs or any pro-drug dramatic shows. Dean Martin, Foster Brooks, and W. C. Fields can make a living playing drunks and getting lots of laughs, but can anyone play being stoned for laughs? Nope to dope. What *are* the media afraid of? At Simon and Garfunkel's 1993 reunion concert, Steve Martin asked them to play "Feelin' Groovy" because it brought back so many memories of his getting high in the '60s. As Simon and Garfunkel played the song, Martin set up a card table, pulled from a cardboard box a large colander and began straining his pot. He rolled a joint, smoked it, and immediately began feelin' groovy. The audience (most of whom probably hadn't done drugs of any kind in years) loved it. They were obviously starved for drug comedy. One is almost tempted to pull out some old Cheech and Chong albums. Almost.

I wish the media would realize that if drugs became cheap and legal, people currently *stealing* TVs to pay for drugs would stay home and *watch* TV. This would bring crime down, the ratings up, and everyone would be happier.

When writing for the media, it's easier to work in stereotypes than to create flesh-and-blood characters. Need a quick laugh? Throw in an effeminate gay. And make him a hairdresser. Sort of a transvestite. Ha ha. Need someone to die of a drug overdose? Make it a prostitute. Need to show someone completely down and out with no hope of redemption? What else? A drug addict. Using stereotypes is a form of shorthand communication: the screenwriter doesn't have to work; the audience doesn't have to think. Hollywood was *very* unhappy when social pressure demanded that blacks no longer automatically be portrayed as lazy and shiftless, women no longer be automatically weak and helpless, and Jews no longer stingy and conniving. The film and television industry now has a new set of shorthand—mostly involving consensual crimes—and it has no desire to lose it.

If they take too strong a position on removing laws against consensual activities, the media fears a boycott from the right. A dentist in Texas, for example, has taken it upon himself to see that "Donahue" does not get a sponsor. This dentist

> *Freedom of the press is perhaps the freedom that has suffered the most from the gradual degradation of the idea of liberty.*
>
> ALBERT CAMUS

(based on his fundamental religious beliefs) considers "Donahue" too "immoral" and writes each sponsor a letter expressing his displeasure and threatening boycotts. More than 190 companies have dropped their sponsorship in the dentist's local market. Jerry Falwell went on the air suggesting that other "good Christians" do the same in their local areas.* Fundamentalists know the power of an economic boycott. They boycott for almost any reason at all. A boycott was threatened against Proctor and Gamble because its symbol (a moon with stars around it) is considered a Satanic symbol. Some groups boycotted Bantam Books because their offices were located at 666 Fifth Avenue, and 666, fundamentalists believe, is "the mark of the beast (the devil)."

The Reverend Donald Wildmon of the American Family Association in Tupelo, Mississippi, has a monthly newsletter he sends out to "concerned Christians" listing the shows with objectionable content (the list of consensual crimes, basically), the sponsors of those shows, along with the sponsors' addresses and phone numbers.

Objectionable shows listed in the July 1993 issue of the *Journal of the American Family Association* included "Seinfeld" ("at least six uses of God's name in vain"), "Saturday Night Live Mother's Day Special" ("explicit bestiality and other illicit jokes galore"),** the mini-series "Wild Palms" ("bizarre situations"), "Melrose Place" ("promiscuity, homosexual themes"), "Married . . . with Children" ("remains true to the series theme of sleaze and illicit sex"), "Golden Palace" ("teen sex and booze"), and "Designing Women" ("cross-dressers").

Any disparaging mention of religion or the clergy is singled out as objectionable by Reverend Wildmon. Among the offenders whose sponsors should be contacted: "Matlock: The Final Affair" ("crooked Christians"), "Martin" ("charlatan preacher"), and "Seinfeld" *[again,* Mr. Seinfeld: tsk, tsk] ("Elaine [series heroine] is a laughingstock because she's dating a religious man").

Reverend Wildmon not only attacks the sponsors of shows that have already aired; he threatens boycotts of shows *yet* to air. If he hears (and he seems to have

---

*"Donahue" is a syndicated show—individual stations buy the show and then sell commercial time locally.

**"Explicit bestiality"? On "Saturday Night Live"? "The Mother's Day Special" no less? The "explicit bestiality" turns out to be a satire of a TV commercial "in which a man and a dog have simulated sex. The dog swims across a swimming pool to be lifted out by the man; the man and dog embrace, nuzzle, and kiss (mouth-to-mouth)." That's it. That's "explicit bestiality" according to Reverend Wildmon. If you think I'm unfairly focusing on some obscure reference, the headline of the article reads, "Ford, PM/General Foods lead advertisers in Mother's Day bestiality."

more informants than the *National Enquirer, People,* and "Entertainment Tonight" combined) about a program that discusses anything that "a good Christian" might find offensive (again, any of the consensual crimes), he will contact all *potential* sponsors and threaten them with economic sanctions. Many sponsors simply take the route of least resistance and sponsor another program. Networks begin to self-censor in order not to lose sponsors, and producers begin to self-censor in order not to lose networks.

> *I find television very educational. Every time someone switches it on I go into another room and read a good book.*
>
> GROUCHO MARX

Let's remember it's not called show *business* for nothing. The Christian right has learned that if it upsets the business end of the show, the show folk will change. And they have. And they continue to. (Can you imagine how many boycotts a show based upon this book would gather?)

Speaking of books: perhaps I'm *terribly* jaded, but I think of Waldenbooks stores as rather *wholesome* places. When I think of "pornography," I don't think of Waldenbooks. When I am possessed by Satan and simply *must* get some pornography *right now,* my local Waldenbooks is not the first place I consider; in fact, it's not a place I would consider *at all.* Nonetheless, the American Family Association is calling for a boycott not only of Waldenbooks, but of Waldenbooks' parent company, K-Mart.* A "sample resolution" for "Christian denominations and groups" to endorse reads:

> We wish to express our concern to Kmart *sic* regarding the pornography sold in their Waldenbooks stores. We believe that pornography is detrimental to the moral fabric of our society. We are especially distressed that Kmart, through their Waldenbooks stores, is one of the largest retailers of pornography in America.
>
> We call upon Kmart to discontinue the sale of pornography and return the company to its historic image of a family-oriented business.
>
> Until Kmart takes such positive action in disassociating itself with pornography, we urge concerned individuals, churches and businesses to discontinue doing business with the Kmart Corporation including Kmart stores, American Fare Stores, Basset Book Shops, Borders Bookstores, Brentanos Bookstores, Coles Bookstores, CopperSmith Bookstores, Pay Less and Pay N Save Drug Stores (located in the northwestern states), Bargain Harold's, Builders Square home supply stores, Office Max, Sports Authority and PACE Membership Warehouse stores.
>
> AFA also urges calls to Kmart customer service. The number is 1-800-63

---

*Yes, Waldenbooks is owned by K-Mart; also: Haagen-Dazs is owned by Pillsbury, and Godiva Chocolates is owned by Campbell's Soups.

Kmart. Please be polite when you call.

> *A man's library is a sort of harem.*
>
> EMERSON

Gee, I wonder why the American Family Association must urge its members to "be polite." Could it be that some Christians have been *less* than polite in the past? God forbid!

And what *is* the "pornography"? Just the usual books carried by all mainstream bookstores—Danielle Steel, Mapplethorpe anthologies, Madonna's *Sex.* ("Pornography" is not just sexually explicit material; it is *anything* the religious right finds "objectionable.")

If you think the American Family Association is a small minority of kooks, consider that the circulation of its 24-page *Journal* is 1,040,045. Consider, too, this front-page story (June 1993):

> ### Southern Baptists pull millions as Kmart refuses to get out of pornography business
>
> The Southern Baptist Annuity Board has voted to sell all of their 221,200 shares of Kmart stock because Kmart refuses to stop selling pornography in their Waldenbooks stores.
>
> "Kmart's refusal to get out of the pornography business is beginning to hurt them big time," said Donald E. Wildmon, president of AFA.
>
> The action by the Southern Baptist group follows similar action taken by the United Methodist General Board of Pensions only weeks ago. The two groups are the largest Protestant denominations in America. The Southern Baptist Convention has approximately 15,000,000 members and the United Methodist Church has nearly 9,000,000.
>
> "Kmart is being hurt by the boycott. Other denominations will divest their holding in Kmart as more Americans hold corporations which profit from pornography responsible. The 24,000,000 members of these two denominations will hear the message their pension groups are sending and many of them will join the boycott of Kmart. It is amazing to me that Kmart is willing to lose millions of dollars in order to stay in the pornography business. They are losing life-long customers simply because they arrogantly refuse to get out of the pornography business," Wildmon said.*

The 24,000,000 members of those two denominations alone represent more than 12% of the U.S. adult population—far from insignificant numbers. While such pressure is not exactly causing the publishing industry to quiver and quake, it does tend to have its effect. Take Marianne Williamson's book, *A Woman's Worth,*

---

*"Arrogant" is one of Wildmon's favorite descriptions of advertisers and media that refuse to do precisely what Wildmon thinks best. If this is not a *clinical* case of projection, I don't know what is.

for example. Although a #1 *New York Times* bestseller and about as pornographic as Dale Carnegie's *How to Win Friends and Influence People*, Williamson's book was nevertheless banned at several retail outlets because the cover showed "too much breast." The cover photograph is an artsy profile of a nude woman whose arm is covering most of her one exposed breast. Publishers hear of this book banning and ridicule it, but the next time they're choosing a cover and they want the sales of the stores that censor, the previous book banning does have an effect.

> *Without books*
> *God is silent.*
>
> DR. THOMAS BARTHOLIN
> (1616–1680)

In choosing the front and back covers of this book, I *intentionally* chose "pornographic" images. Female nudity! Bestiality! (What is she doing with that bird??!) Pornography! (The full frontal nudity of one cherub.) Homosexuality! (The man's hand on Socrates' thigh on the back cover.) Assisted suicide! Both paintings (*The Toilet of Venus* and *The Death of Socrates*) are, of course, masterpieces of the Enlightenment. They were painted at the time the Constitution was written. Both hang in the Metropolitan Museum of Art in New York. That anyone would object to such classic beauty is a sign of how far the religious right has gone. Sure enough, the cover alone has caused this book to be banned in one book chain. Several "Christian" bookstores—based on the cover alone—have *demanded* that they be removed from Prelude Press's mailing list.*

Although I haven't been in a K-Mart store *in years* (all right: call me a snob), ever since reading of the American Family Association boycott, I've had an overwhelming desire to *buy* something there. (Maybe I'll stock up on antifreeze.) Somehow I long to hear those musical words, "Attention K-Mart Shoppers." I also feel like writing the sponsors of "pornographic" shows such as "Seinfeld" and "Designing Women," thanking them for bringing smut into my home, thus saving me a trip to Waldenbooks. (If you, too, feel similarly inclined, write the American Family Association, Post Office Drawer 2440, Tupelo, Mississippi 38803, and ask to be put on its mailing list. If nothing else, the *Journal of the American Family Association* will give you a good preview of upcoming explicit bestiality on "Saturday Night Live.")

Organized Crime

Often, organized crime puts its money, influence, and persuasive abilities behind lessening the penalties for certain real crimes. If beating people up to teach

---

*Absurd censorship is not just a right-wing thing: a "liberal" bookstore also insisted on being removed from Prelude Press's mailing list because we sold *Playboy* the right to print a portion of this book in its September 1993 issue. *All* Prelude Press books are then tainted. What *is* this world coming to?

them a lesson can be seen as merely "altercations," so much the better for organized crime. With consensual crimes, however, their illegality not only keeps them within the sphere of organized crime; it also keeps them profitable. Organized crime would not be *at all* happy if consensual crimes became legal and organized crime had to compete with other organizations.

The Medical Establishment

Why on earth would doctors want to give up any of their God-like control of the American population? Doctors don't tell the truth (at least not very loudly) about drugs proven to be extremely life-threatening. (Doctors know tobacco is far more addictive than cocaine, for example, but that's not the popular perception, and doctors do little to correct this.) Doctors make money by writing prescriptions. What if consumers were able to self-prescribe drugs? Doctors, naturally, don't like this.

Further, accepting the alternative forms of healing—Eastern, Western, or native—means sharing some of the "power to heal" with foreigners, inventors, or savages. The traditional medical community can't let that happen. Also, doctors believe they know all there is to know about healing. They don't want to learn a whole new system of healing, any more than the rest of us want to learn a whole new language. The status quo is *just fine* with the medical establishment, and even though the laws against certain consensual activities are doing more physical and mental harm than the activities themselves, the medical profession is remarkably silent about this.

Pharmaceutical companies, of course, don't want some herb or some public domain compound competing with their patented and profitable drugs. The pharmaceutical companies exist to make money, and they don't make as much money by manufacturing and popularizing drugs that other companies can also manufacture.

The medical profession is a very large and profitable boat, and it has no intention of rocking itself.

⚖ ⚖ ⚖

About the only champion of First Amendment rights is the American Civil Liberties Union (ACLU). It has taken a firm stand against censorship and firmly supports gay rights; however, it has yet to take as firm a stance on many other consensual crimes. What about the civil liberty of gamblers to bet, prostitutes to sell, and drug users to narcotize? While the ACLU is as close as consensual criminals have to a champion, it fights some battles far more aggressively than others. It seems as though the ACLU hasn't quite made the connection between the First

Amendment's guarantee of freedom of and from religion and the laws against consensual crimes, even though it *has* seen the connection between any form of censorship and the First Amendment guarantees of a free press. My guess is this lack of focus on other consensual crimes has more to do with limited funding than a limitation in its philosophy.

⚖ ⚖ ⚖

If all the leaders of our society have a vested interest in keeping consensual crimes crimes, what does that mean?

Don't get mad; get busy.

> *"Do you pray for the Senators, Dr. Hale?"* someone asked the chaplain.
>
> *No, I look at the Senators and pray for the country.*
>
> EDWARD EVERETT HALE

We Must All Hang Together

SIGNING THE Declaration of Independence was a dangerous act. To call the King of England a tyrant—especially in such a public and eloquent way—was high treason, punishable by death. Although the signers of the Declaration of Independence had different reasons for doing so, were very different individuals, and had radically different political points of view, the executioner's rope could be equally effective for one and all. John Hancock was bold. He signed his name first and large. "There," he said; "King George should be able to read that without his spectacles." When Benjamin Franklin signed, he was expected to say something witty, pithy, and to the point; he was, after all, the greatest aphorist of his day. Franklin did not disappoint. "We must all hang together," he said, "or, most assuredly, we shall all hang separately."

The most popular American flag (prior to Betsy Ross getting her hands on it) showed a snake divided in thirteen parts, each part representing one of the thirteen colonies. The slogan was: UNITE OR DIE. That is precisely the situation that all of us consensual criminals find ourselves in today:* we must unite or die. Another popular early flag showed the snake united, with the warning:

DON'T TREAD ON ME.

⚖ ⚖ ⚖

*Forgive me for assuming that you have taken part in one of the consensual crimes at some point in your life. (Yes, that time you were nineteen and very drunk counts.) If this statement does not apply to you, please forgive my presumption—but please join with the rest of us criminals in supporting our constitutional rights.

Another way of stressing the need for unity came from Martin Niemoeller:

In Germany they came first for the Communists, and I didn't speak up because I wasn't a Communist. Then they came for the Jews, and I didn't speak up because I wasn't a Jew. Then they came for the trade unionists, and I didn't speak up because I wasn't a trade unionist. Then they came for the Catholics, and I didn't speak up because I was a Protestant. Then they came for me, and by that time no one was left to speak up.

> To preserve the freedom of the
> human mind then
> and freedom of the press,
> every spirit should be ready
> to devote itself to martyrdom.
>
> THOMAS JEFFERSON
> June 18, 1799

As I explained when discussing the pecking order, those who take part in consensual activities often end up like chickens in a farmer's yard: they turn against, criticize, ridicule, and pick on other consensual criminals. One bold example of this came from NORML (National Organization for the Reform of Marijuana Laws). I was listening to a tape of its national convention. One of the speakers suggested that the U.S. government would never be able to convince foreign countries to stop growing coca for cocaine because it was a major cash crop. If those countries were encouraged to grow marijuana, however, on the same land, it would be just as profitable. This would wipe out the "cocaine problem" and provide some high-quality marijuana for importation. The suggestion received an enthusiastic and lengthy round of applause. I looked at my tape player with disbelief. "Don't these people realize that pot smokers and cocaine users are two chickens in the same farmer's yard?"

The people who oppose drug use altogether for health reasons must realize that the *same* people who regulate recreational drugs now are working on regulating vitamins, too. Prostitutes, gays, adulterers, sodomites, and heterosexuals who have sex outside of marriage all violate the *same* sexual taboo. (If you live in a state where sex outside of marriage, adultery, oral intercourse, or even homosexual acts are legal, be assured that there are forces of the religious right who are working diligently to correct that legal and moral oversight.) The law that makes adults wear seat belts springs from the same paternalism—and political compromise—that would if it could (and apparently it can) regulate every other aspect of your life; for your own good, of course.

We are all chickens in the same farmer's yard. What would happen if the chickens all got mad at the farmer instead of pecking each other? Well, remember Alfred Hitchcock's movie, *The Birds?* There is a reason falcons, lions, and tigers are not raised for their eggs, milk, and meat: chickens, cows, and sheep are far more docile; they don't complain when their eggs are taken, readily cooperate in being milked, and are easily led to slaughter.

There is, of course, the rare animal that does act up. It's branded a renegade, and quickly eliminated. If the entire group of animals—that is, the entire *species*—is known for acting up when tread upon, however, they are, for the most part, left alone. If consensual criminals stood up not only for their own rights, but the rights of each other, the group would have the power to keep the government from treading upon it.

Well, I've made as stirring a speech on the subject as I can make. Allow me to quote the comments of other famous stirrers, agitators, and renegades.

> *It's time for us
> to turn to each other,
> not on each other.*
>
> JESSE JACKSON

He that would make his own liberty secure must guard even his enemy from oppression.—*Thomas Paine 1795*

When bad men combine, the good must associate; else they fall, one by one, an unpitied sacrifice in a contemptible struggle.—*Edmund Burke*

The Politics of Change

THIS IS A CHAPTER ON THE specifics of what to do if you'd like to see the laws against consensual activities changed.

The single most effective form of change is one-on-one interaction with the people you come into contact with day-by-day. The next time someone condemns a consensual activity in your presence, for example, you can ask the simple question, "Well, isn't that their own business?" Asking this, of course, may be like hitting a beehive with a baseball bat, and it may *seem*—after the commotion (and emotion) has died down—that attitudes have not changed. If a beehive is hit often enough, however, the bees move somewhere else. Of course, you don't have to hit the same hive every time. If all the people who agree that it ain't the government's business what people do, as long as they're not physically harming the person or property of another, would go around whacking (or at least firmly tapping) every beehive that presented itself, the bees would buzz less often.

> *The only thing necessary*
> *for the triumph of evil is*
> *for good men to do nothing.*
>
> EDMUND BURKE
> 1770

Also, some people actually *do* start to think when they are asked a question such as, "Shouldn't people be allowed to do with their own person and property whatever they choose as long as they do not physically harm the person or property of another?" Granted, these people are few and far between, but they do exist and, perhaps, some of the people you know or meet may have never been asked that question. It is not a very popular question.

A good follow-up question: "Is it worth putting people in jail for doing these things?" Other possibilities: "Isn't it up to God to punish violations of God's laws?" "Who decides what is and is not 'right'?" "Don't we have more important things to worry about?" "Have *you* ever committed a consensual crime?" If "yes": "Do you think you might feel differently about laws against consensual activities

> *The job of a citizen
> is to keep his mouth open.*
>
> GUNTER GRASS

if you had gone to jail for your crime?" If the answer is "no," the person is (a) lying or (b) truly dull. In either case, move on to another person (preferably) or another topic of conversation (if trapped).

Although it may not seem so, asking such questions and challenging people's misconceptions is a *very* political act. This personal contact is, in fact, the *essence* of politics. Change begins with individuals, and individuals communicating with individuals is the way attitudes are most often changed. If any of your thoughts or beliefs changed as you read this book, that's because we've been communicating one-on-one. I'm sure I didn't address all of your concerns or answer all of your questions, but perhaps I asked enough questions and provided enough information for a process of change to begin within you. When I write a book, I write to *one person.* It is the sort of letter I might write a friend (although, obviously, considerably longer).

In television, radio, and lectures, the most effective communicators are those who speak directly to individuals, not to a group. People like Larry King and Oprah Winfrey, and even Ross Perot, are effective communicators because they speak to *people,* not *masses.*

Changing one mind by talking *to* one person is more valuable than lecturing *at* one million people who walk away indifferent. You can make a change; you can make a difference in the thinking of the people with whom you naturally come into contact. When you write to elected officials, you represent a vote. When you write or speak to friends, you're a *person.*

⚔ ⚔ ⚔

The second most effective area of influence any individual has is with the media, because here, too, we can make personal statements. Writing letters to the editor, calling talk shows, asking questions from a studio audience gets your message out to thousands, tens of thousands, hundreds of thousands, even millions of people. A certain percentage of those people are going to personally relate to *you,* what *you* have to say, and the way *you* say it. You will probably never know who these people are, but—even if you seem to lose the argument with the commentator or guest on the show or even if the editor of the newspaper prints your letter with the comment, "Get a load of what the kooks out there are writing these days!"—a certain number of people will accept what you have to say, and a change will be put in motion.

And then there's traditional politics.

Government is organized at three levels: local, state, and national (or federal). Any action you take on any of these levels counts. The simplest action is to write

AIN'T NOBODY'S BUSINESS IF YOU DO

a letter or make a phone call. Here, of course, one must know whom to call or write.

At the national level, the four most important people to contact are (a) your two senators (every state has two), (b) the member of the House of Representatives who represents your congressional district (everyone has one of those), and (c) the president of the United States (we all share just one). While technically senators are there to serve *all* the people of the United

> *Washington is a city of Southern efficiency and Northern charm.*
>
> JOHN F. KENNEDY

States, their "special interest group" is made up of the citizens (and more particularly the *voters*) of their own state. Similarly, every member of the House of Representatives is there to serve all the people of the United States, and all the citizens of his or her home state, but representatives have a special interest in the needs and opinions of the voters of their congressional districts.

When the mail comes in to a congressional office, it is sorted into two piles: "Constituents" and "Everybody Else." The "Constituent" pile gets preferential treatment. This is not unfair—in fact, it's the way the system was designed: each citizen of the United States has the same number of representatives in Congress (two senators and one member of the House) who consider that citizen a constituent. Members of the House of Representatives usually divide the "Everybody Else" pile into "My State" and "Those Other States." A member of Congress, then, will pay attention to, in order, (1) the voters within his or her own congressional district, (2) the citizens of his or her home state outside of his or her congressional district (who knows, he or she may run for senator one day, and need the vote of everyone in the state), and (3) everyone else (he or she may run for president one day). The next group of people to write to, then, on the national level, are all the members of the House of Representatives from your state.

State governments are set up with variations, but generally there is a house of representatives or an assembly and a senate. Here, you also have elected representatives who consider you their constituents, and these are the people to write first (in addition, of course, to the governor). Start with the state senator and representative from your own senatorial and house (or assembly) districts.

Local government is a hodge-podge of city and county elected and appointed officials. To make change on a local level, however, it's worth your time to find out who runs the show. You might not be able to *fight* city hall, but you can quite often influence it, and a call to city hall will give you the names and addresses of those in power (our "public servants," tee-hee-hee).

When writing a public servant, there's no need to be elaborate or eloquent. Usually, your letter will not be read: it will be scanned and summarized. If you're writing about a particular issue in the public debate, your letter will become part of a statistic. ("Today's mail: 673 letters in favor of [the topic]; 2,476 letters opposed.") The same is true of phone calls, post cards, telegrams, or any form in which you care to communicate. Even though you're just a number, you are a very important number.

The religious right is well organized and can produce massive mailings (millions of pieces) on key issues within a few days. You can bet that, for the most part, they are going to favor enacting more laws against consensual activities, strict enforcement of the laws we already have, and, in the name of the Prince of Peace, *violently* oppose repealing or eliminating *any* oppressive law. No similar network exists for those who favor eliminating laws against consensual crimes, and the legislators know this. Each letter, then, that comes in supporting a position *not* endorsed by the religious right is given special attention—and extra weight—by most legislators. As the religious right can "out-letter" its opposition by a ratio that is sometimes 10 to 1, one letter in favor of our freedom to do with our person and property whatever we choose as long as we do not physically harm the person or property of another can count for as many as *ten* letters written by those who think our laws should be dictated by their moral code—so *write*. It's not the size of the letter, but what it says—and that you sent it at all—that counts.

A copy of this book was sent to all members of the United States Senate and House of Representatives, as well as to the legislators and governors of all fifty states, and to the mayors of the top 100 cities (those who held office as of September 1993). If you generally agree with the idea of this book, please write your elected representatives: "Have you read the book, *Ain't Nobody's Business If You Do?* If not, I certainly recommend it. After you read the book, I would appreciate your thoughts on it."

An amazing number of consensual crimes can be repealed on the local level. In fact, most consensual crimes are enforced on the state and local level, not the federal level. Generally, something becomes a "federal offense" when (a) it threatens the national defense (that's why declaring "wars" is necessary), or (b) it involves an activity or product that crosses state lines. A cartoon in *The Realist* depicted a man sitting behind an enormous desk, telling someone on the other end of the phone, "I'm sorry, but the FBI can only get involved in a case of oral-genital intimacy if it obstructs interstate commerce."

People working at the state and local levels to dismantle the laws against consensual activities—and to keep new ones from being put on the books—could give us a free country in a short period of time. *(Could* is the operative word in that sentence. I am not overly optimistic. I am, in fact, something of a realistic pessimist.) For a look at what is and is not a crime in your state, please see the next chapter, "A State-by-State Look at Consensual Crime."

At the other end of the spectrum, perhaps the thing to do is to propose a constitutional amendment that restates what is already in the Constitution. The amendment might read:

> No citizen of the United States, or the several States, shall be subject to criminal prosecution unless he or she physically harms the person or property of a nonconsenting other.

I am being frank about myself in this book. I tell of my first mistake on page 850.

HENRY KISSINGER

That would lay it out clearly, I think; the "or the several States" part insures that state governments don't pass their own restrictive codes in the name of "states' rights." Limiting the government's *criminal* enforcement allows for the government to take *civil* action when appropriate. (Not in enforcing consensual crimes, of course, but in the course of governmental business—fulfilling contracts, collecting money, etc.) Proposing a constitutional amendment would stir a national debate on the subject, as well as directly counter the religious right's desire to introduce a constitutional amendment declaring the United States a "Christian nation."

Obviously, a lot of work needs to be done. The religious right is well financed, well organized, and *big.* They are involved in politics as an *act of religious faith.* Those who do not believe that religion and politics should be one and the same don't seem to have the same fervor when it comes to political action. The religious right has also co-opted every phrase and symbol that those who *fought* religious oppression once rallied around. *Freedom, liberty* (Jerry Falwell's institute of higher political learning is called Liberty University), the American flag, the Liberty Bell—even the word *American.**

Because there is such formidable opposition, those of us who believe that the laws against consensual activities should be repealed have our work cut out for us. Saying that people should be permitted to do with their person and property what they choose as long as they don't physically harm the person or property of another is not perceived by the religious right as a political statement, but as *an attack upon God.* Those who are not willing to take the heat of the emotional outburst that will inevitably follow will soon leave the kitchen. We do, however, have something quite nice on our side: the United States Constitution and its Bill of Rights.

*That the religious right *completely* took over the word *Christian* is a given. At one time, phrases such as *Christian charity* and *Christian tolerance* were used to denote kindness and compassion. To perform a "Christian" act meant an act of giving, of acceptance, of toleration. Now, *Christian* is invariably linked to right-wing conservative political thought—*Christian nation, Christian morality, Christian family.*

> *The human being who*
> *would not harm you on an*
> *individual, face-to-face basis,*
> *who is charitable, civic-minded,*
> *loving and devout,*
> *will wound or kill you*
> *from behind the corporate veil.*
>
> MORTON MINTZ

Then there are those who want to keep the laws against consensual activities in place due to greed. As we explored in the chapter, "Why Consensual Crimes Have So Few Advocates," lots of people are making lots of money because certain consensual activities are illegal. Naturally, they do not want to lose any meal tickets.

Those who want personal freedom in this country, then, have such interesting and diverse opponents as organized crime on one hand, and law enforcement on the other. Organized crime would practically go out of business if all consensual activities were legal. The politicians and media organized crime already own (or have a few favors coming from) will be opposed to legalizing consensual activities—but oppose it with the "highest" moral, legal, social, and even scientific justifications. Law enforcement would (a) lose funding (the tens of billions being thrown at it to fight the War on Drugs plus all that assets forfeiture money), and (b) have to catch *real* criminals (who have *guns*). The big businesses that currently make a fortune on *legal* (including prescription) drugs don't want any of the currently *illegal* drugs cluttering up the marketplace. This is a spectrum that has tobacco and alcohol companies at one end and the AMA and pharmaceutical companies at the other.

Yes, consensual crimes make strange bedfellows: organized crime and law enforcement; cigarette companies and the AMA. Not surprisingly, none of them wants to get out of bed. If you're working to repeal the laws against consensual activities, allow me to state an obvious reality: people can be as passionate about *money* as they can about *God* (if not more so).

⚖ ⚖ ⚖

One can neither point to the Democratic nor Republican party and say, "Here, join this party; they support this cause." *Neither* political party supports this cause; nor do, necessarily, either liberals or conservatives. Take a guess, for example, at the political orientation of the author of the following piece, published in a letters to the editor column of *American Heritage* magazine, May/June 1993:

> Would you want your son or daughter or spouse to spend their [sic] days smoking crack, or injecting heroin, or hallucinating on LSD? . . .
>
> I remain convinced that the drugs we outlaw today must remain illegal, because I have personally witnessed the effects of drugs too often and too painfully. I have seen crack babies, trembling, their minds and bodies damaged by their mothers' drug abuse. . . . I have seen innocent victims maimed and murdered by drug addicts. . . .

Candidly, no society has ever or will ever succeed in abolishing the use of all mind-altering drugs, just as no society in the foreseeable future will succeed in abolishing all cancer. But that doesn't mean we can simply throw up our hands and say we won't even defend ourselves against these plagues. While the cost of prohibiting drugs is high, the cost of legalizing them would be much, much higher.

Drugs are cancer. Trembling crack babies. Sound like some of George Bush's comments? Pat Robertson's? Pat Buchanan? Rush Limbaugh? No, these words come from a person some liberals consider to be the prototypical liberal, Governor Mario Cuomo of New York. There is no guarantee that a liberal's bleeding heart is going to bleed for the cause of repealing the laws against consensual crimes. (What about all the *prisoners,* Mario? What about the prisoner's *families?*)

1992 presidential candidate Dave Barry had these astute observations:

> The Democrats seem to be basically nicer people, but they have demonstrated time and time again that they have the management skills of celery. They're the kind of people who'd stop to help you change a flat, but would somehow manage to set your car on fire. I would be reluctant to entrust them with a Cuisinart, let alone the economy. The Republicans, on the other hand, would know how to fix your tire, but they wouldn't bother to stop because they'd want to be on time for Ugly Pants Night at the country club.

Removing the prohibitions from consensual activities will probably take place due to popular opinion within *both* political parties. When Prohibition was enacted in 1920, both parties strongly favored it. By 1924, the Republicans still strongly favored it, and the Democrats were vacillating. By 1928, the Democrats opposed it, but the Republicans still favored it. By the election of 1932, both parties opposed Prohibition. That's the politics of change.

In the 1992 election, Ross Perot introduced the urgency of reducing the national debt and, due to the immediate popular support of this idea, it was quickly adopted by both parties. The idea of eliminating the laws against consensual activities will probably gain acceptance along the same lines. (And, I pray, as quickly.)

The political party that supports this concept—in fact, seems to be based on it—is the Libertarian party. Although its political philosophy is interesting and its information educational, I doubt if the majority of the American people are going to switch party affiliations in order to support this one issue. When the idea of eliminating consensual crimes becomes popular enough, one of the major

> *That the "conservatives" think they are winning proves very little. Conservatives always think they are winning. That the "liberals" think they are losing proves even less. Liberals always think they are losing.*
>
> ANDREW M. GREELEY

> *Tyranny is always better
> organised than freedom.*
>
> CHARLES PÉGUY
> (1873–1914)

political parties will adopt it, thus removing whatever wind the Libertarian sails might have captured. This, however, is just a political prediction on my part. People may be so fed up with both the Democratic and the Republican parties that they'll switch to Libertarianism just for the hell of it.

The people most motivated to change the laws against consensual activities, of course, are those who have been arrested for them, and the "criminals'" friends and family. That includes the 350,000 people currently in jail, the 1,500,000 currently on parole or probation, the 4,000,000 arrested each year, as well as their loved ones. These are people who know, from personal experience, the absurdity of consensual crimes. They also know the arbitrary and often cruel ways in which these laws are enforced. One can only quote Woody Guthrie's advice to union organizers: "Take it easy, but take it." So often, people trapped in the legal system alternate between rage and resignation. Neither emotion will help repeal the laws against consensual activities. A middle ground in which the rage is channeled into constructive action not only provides an effective outlet for one's justifiable frustration; it gives one the satisfaction of, day-by- day, doing his or her part to change an unfair system.

⚖ ⚖ ⚖

And let's not forget the value of *money.* Donate some to organizations that defend personal freedom. Whether that be those with more general goals such as the American Civil Liberties Union and People for the American Way, or single-cause organizations such as NORML (National Organization for the Reform of Marijuana Laws); C.O.Y.O.T.E. (Call Off Your Old Tired Ethics), which seeks to legalize prostitution; Lambda Defense Fund, which defends gay rights; or one of the many others. If you have no money to send, drop them a note and say, "I don't have any money to send you, but I support what you're doing. Keep up the good work." Every bit of encouragement helps.

⚖ ⚖ ⚖

Politically, these are interesting times. The idea that the government should leave people alone unless they are physically harming the person or property of others is catching on quickly, and from many directions. Simultaneously, the forces that want more government intervention in our lives are gathering political momentum as well. Yes, these are interesting times. The Chinese have an ancient saying, "May you live in interesting times." Unfortunately, the Chinese use it as a curse.

For inspiration, then, and blessings, here is what some others have had to say about the politics of change:

Half of the American people never read a newspaper. Half never vote for President. One hopes it is the same half.—*Gore Vidal*

For those who say I can't impose my morality on others, I say just watch me.—*Joseph Scheidler, Executive Director, Pro-Life Action League*

> *You should never wear your best trousers when you go out to fight for freedom and truth.*
>
> HENRIK IBSEN

Our wretched species is so made that those who walk on the well-trodden path always throw stones at those who are showing a new road.—*Voltaire*

When I was in third grade, there was a kid running for office. His slogan was: "Vote for me and I'll show you my wee-wee." He won by a landslide.—*Dorothy*, The Golden Girls

Until you've lost your reputation, you never realize what a burden it was or what freedom really is.—*Margaret Mitchell*

The politicians were talking themselves red, white, and blue in the face.—*Clare Boothe Luce*

Freedom is not a luxury that we can indulge in when at last we have security and prosperity and enlightenment; it is, rather, antecedent to all of these, for without it we can have neither security nor prosperity nor enlightenment.—*Henry Steele Commager*

When a man says he approves of something in principle, it means he hasn't the slightest intention of putting it into practice.—*Bismarck*

If a politician found he had cannibals among his constituents, he would promise them missionaries for dinner.—*H. L. Mencken*

The basic guarantees of our Constitution are warrants for the here and now, and unless there is an overwhelmingly compelling reason, they are to be promptly fulfilled.—*Arthur J. Goldberg*

Many politicians are in the habit of laying it down as a self-evident proposition that no people ought to be free till they are fit to use their freedom. The maxim is worthy of the fool in the old story who resolved not to go into the water till he had learned to swim.—*Thomas Babington Macaulay*

It's not a pay raise; it's a pay equalization.—*Senator Ted Stevens on the $23,200 raise in Senate salaries*

At least 250 current or former members of the House owed more than $300,000 for meals and catering services from Capitol restaurants. More than $47,000 of the bills dated back as far as 1986, and more than 50 congressmen owed $1,000 or more.—*Newsweek, 1992*

> *Liberty does not consist*
> *in mere declarations*
> *of the rights of man.*
> *It consists in the translation*
> *of those declarations*
> *into definite action.*
>
> WOODROW WILSON

The most eloquent prayer is the prayer through hands that heal and bless. The highest form of worship unselfish Christian service. The greatest form of praise is the sound of consecrated feet seeking out the lost and helpless.—*Billy Graham*

Evil is near. Sometimes late at night the air grows strongly clammy and cold around me. I feel it brushing me. All that the Devil asks is acquiescence . . . not struggle, not conflict. Acquiescence.—*Suzanne Massie*

A brave world, sir, full of religion, knavery, and change: we shall shortly see better days.—*Aphra Behn (1677)*

The jury system has worked. What's needed now is calm, respect for the law.—*President George Bush, after the FIRST Rodney King verdict*

As long as the world shall last there will be wrongs and if no man objected and if no man rebelled, those wrongs would last forever.—*Clarence Darrow*

Let my people go.—*Exodus 5:1*

Liberty, when it begins to take root, is a plant of rapid growth.—*George Washington*

Liberty trains for liberty. Responsibility is the first step in responsibility.—*W. E. B. DuBois*

We know that the road to freedom has always been stalked by death.—*Angela Davis*

A man is either free or not. There cannot be any apprenticeship for freedom.—*Imamu Amiri Baraka*

The spirit of resistance to government is so valuable on certain occasions that I wish it to be always kept alive.—*Thomas Jefferson*

Honest statesmanship is the wise employment of individual meanness for the public good.—*Abraham Lincoln*

Whatever must happen ultimately should happen immediately.—*Henry A. Kissinger*

If there's anything a public servant hates to do it's something for the public.—*Elbert Hubbard*

History teaches us that men and nations behave wisely once they have exhausted all other alternatives.—*Abba Eban*

When good people in any country cease their vigilance and struggle, then evil men prevail.—*Pearl S. Buck*

The moments of freedom, they can't be given to you. You have to take them.—*Robert Frost*

Freedom is not something that anybody can be given; freedom is something people take and people are as free as they want to be.—*James Baldwin*

Freedom is never voluntarily given by the oppressor; it must be demanded by the oppressed.—*Martin Luther King, Jr.*

America was born of revolt, flourished on dissent, became great through experimentation.—*Henry Steele Commager (1947)*

We have to pursue this subject of fun very seriously if we want to stay competitive in the twenty-first century.—*Singapore Minister of State*

> *The natural progress of things is for liberty to yield and governments to gain ground.*
>
> THOMAS JEFFERSON

But how shall we educate men to goodness, to a sense of one another, to a love of truth? And more urgently, how shall we do this in a bad time?—*Daniel Berrigan*

Democracy is a device that ensures we shall be governed no better than we deserve.—*George Bernard Shaw*

He who tells the truth must have one foot in the stirrup.—*Old Armenian proverb*

The war for freedom will never really be won because the price of freedom is constant vigilance over ourselves and over our government.—*Eleanor Roosevelt*

Pray as if everything depended on God, and work as if everything depended upon man.—*Cardinal Francis J. Spellman*

I would remind you that extremism in the defense of liberty is no vice. And let me remind you also that moderation in the pursuit of justice is no virtue.—*Barry M. Goldwater*

If a man is right, he can't be too radical; if he is wrong, he can't be too conservative.—*Josh Billings*

The solar system has no anxiety about its reputation.—*Ralph Waldo Emerson*

I dislike arguments of any kind. They are always vulgar, and often convincing.—*Oscar Wilde*

If you make people think they're thinking, they'll love you; but if you really make them think, they'll hate you.—*Don Marquis (1878–1937)*

I belong to no organized party—I'm a Democrat.—*Will Rogers*

Liar: one who tells an unpleasant truth.—*Oliver Herford*

Pandemonium did not reign; it poured.—*John Kendrick Bangs*

Nature intended me for the tranquil pursuits of science, by rendering

> It's better to debate a question
> without settling it
> than to settle a question
> without debating it.
>
> JOSEPH JOUBERT

them my supreme delight. But the enormities of the times in which I have lived have forced me to commit myself on the boisterous ocean of political passions.—*Thomas Jefferson*

A man does not have to be an angel in order to be a saint.—*Albert Schweitzer*

The mode by which the inevitable is reached is effort.—*Justice Felix Frankfurter*

I arise in the morning torn between a desire to improve (or save) the world and a desire to enjoy (or savor) the world. This makes it hard to plan the day.—*E. B. White*

Some mornings it just doesn't seem worth it to gnaw through the leather straps.—*Emo Philips*

Get in my way when I really want to accomplish something, I can be a mean monster.—*Dick Clark*

The idea of political leadership means inspiring people, persuading people, saying, "Look, listen to me, I've got the right idea. Come with me and we can do this." And that's performance.—*Actor Charlton Heston*

I haven't voted since 1964, when I voted for Lyndon Johnson, the peace candidate.—*Gore Vidal*

I am a man of fixed and unbending principles, the first of which is to be flexible at all times.—*Senator Everett Dirksen*

Be polite; write diplomatically; even in a declaration of war one observes the rules of politeness.—*Otto Von Bismarck*

Never hate your enemies, it affects your judgment.—*Michael Corleone*

For my own part I consider it as nothing less than a question of freedom or slavery. . . . If we wish to be free, if we mean to preserve inviolate those inestimable privileges for which we have been so long contending, we must fight!—*Patrick Henry, March 23, 1775*

My advice to the women's clubs of America is to raise more hell and fewer dahlias.—*William Allen White*

Bad officials are elected by good citizens who do not vote.—*George Jean Nathan*

You've got to rattle your cage door. You've got to let them know that you're in there, and that you want out. Make noise. Cause trouble. You may not win right away, but you'll sure have a lot more fun.—*Florynce Kennedy*

As a girl my temper often got out of bounds. But one day when I became angry at a friend over some trivial matter, my mother said to me, "Elizabeth, anyone who angers you conquers you."—*Sister Elizabeth Kenny*

Perseverance and audacity generally win.—*Dorothee DeLuzy*

We criticize and separate ourselves from the process. We've got to jump right in there with both feet.—*Dolores Huerta*

The pursuit of truth shall set you free—even if you never catch up with it.—*Clarence Darrow*

It is useless for the sheep to pass resolutions in favor of vegetarianism while the wolf remains of a different opinion.—*William Ralph Inge*

> *The hottest places in hell are reserved for those who in a period of moral crisis maintain their neutrality.*
>
> DANTE

The highest patriotism is not a blind acceptance of official policy, but a love of one's country deep enough to call her to a higher standard.—*George McGovern*

Justice is: JUST US.—*Richard Pryor*

Those who profess to favor freedom, and yet depreciate agitation are men who want rain without thunder and lightning.—*Frederick Douglass*

This government is ours whether it be local, country, State, or Federal. It doesn't belong to anybody but the people of America. Don't treat it as an impersonal thing; don't treat it as something to sneer at; treat it as something that belongs to you.—*Harry L. Hopkins*

There comes a time in the affairs of men when they must prepare to defend, not their homes alone, but the tenets . . . on which their governments and their very civilization are founded.—*Franklin Delano Roosevelt*

A man does what he must—in spite of personal consequences, in spite of obstacles and dangers and pressures—and that is the basis of all human morality.—*John F. Kennedy*

Those who won our independence by revolution were not cowards. They did not fear political change.—*Louis Brandeis*

The boisterous sea of liberty is never without a wave.—*Thomas Jefferson*

The good that Martin Luther King, Jr. did remains undiminished. He was great precisely because, like other heroes, he did not allow human weakness to deter him from doing great works.—*Carl McClendon*

"They say that freedom is a constant struggle," goes the old song. It is. It is also more than that. Freedom is *the* struggle. It is never achieved except in the effort to reach it.—*Wallace Roberts*

When liberty is taken away by force it can be restored by force. When it is relinquished voluntarily by default it can never be recovered.—*Dorothy Thompson*

Liberty has never come from the government. Liberty has always come

> *People come to Washington*
> *believing it's the center of power.*
> *I know I did.*
> *It was only much later that*
> *I learned that Washington*
> *is a steering wheel*
> *that's not connected to the engine.*
>
> RICHARD GOODWIN

from the subjects of it. The history of liberty is a history of resistance. The history of liberty is a history of limitations of governmental power, not the increase of it.—*Woodrow Wilson*

In a certain town there was a judge who neither feared God nor cared about men. And there was a widow in that town who kept coming to him with the plea, "Grant me justice against my adversary." For some time he refused. But finally he said to himself, "Even though I don't fear God or care about men, yet because the widow keeps bothering me, I will see that she gets justice, so that she won't eventually wear me out with her coming!"—*Jesus of Nazareth (Luke 18:2–5)*

You give a hundred percent in the first half of the game, and if it isn't enough, in the second half you give what's left.—*Casey Stengel*

Whatever you think it's gonna take, double it.—*Richard A. Courtese*

Th' hand that rocks th' cradle is just as liable to rock the country.—*Kin Hubbard*

It is better to be making the news than taking it; to be an actor rather than a critic.—*Sir Winston Churchill*

The voice of protest, of warning, of appeal is never more needed than when the clamor of fife and drum, echoed by the press and too often by the pulpit, is bidding all men fall in and keep step and obey in silence the tyran-nous word of command. Then, more than ever, it is the duty of the good citizen not to be silent.—*Charles Eliot Norton*

My kind of loyalty was to one's country, not to its institutions or its office-holders. The country is the real thing, the substantial thing, the eternal thing; it is the thing to watch over, and care for, and be loyal to; institutions are extraneous, they are its mere clothing, and clothing can wear out, become ragged, cease to be comfortable, cease to protect the body from winter, disease, and death.—*Mark Twain*

Common sense is the knack of seeing things as they are, and doing things as they ought to be done.—*Josh Billings*

Tell a man whose house is on fire to give a moderate alarm; tell him to moderately rescue his wife from the hands of the ravisher; tell the mother to gradually extricate her babe from the fire into which it has fallen; but urge me not to use moderation in a case like the present.—*W. L. Garrison*

A really good diplomat does not go in for victories, even when he wins them.—*Walter Lippmann*

I have a most peaceable disposition. My desires are for a modest hut, a thatched roof, but a good bed, good food, very fresh milk and butter, flowers in front of my window and a few pretty trees by my door. And should the good Lord wish to make me really happy, he will allow me the pleasure of seeing about six or seven of my enemies hanged upon those trees.—*Heinrich Heine*

Appeasers believe that if you keep on throwing steaks to a tiger, the tiger will turn vegetarian.—*Heywood Brown*

> *How wonderful it is that nobody need wait a single moment before starting to improve the world.*
>
> ANNE FRANK

One day I sat thinking, almost in despair; a hand fell on my shoulder and a voice said reassuringly: "Cheer up, things could get worse." So I cheered up and, sure enough, things got worse.—*James Hagerty*

Mama exhorted her children at every opportunity to "jump at de sun." We might not land on the sun, but at least we would get off the ground.—*Zora Neale Hurston*

It is a tragedy when the mind, soul and heart are in slavery in a way of life which refuses to recognize that people have rights before God. Not to resist would make one an accomplice to crime. Resistance was part of the program of Jesus. We must resist oppression and tyranny. We have to end it no matter what it costs.—*Joseph R. Sizoo. D. D.*

He who passively accepts evil is as much involved in it as he who helps to perpetrate it.—*Martin Luther King, Jr.*

Now the 21st Century approaches and with it the inevitability of change. We must wonder if the American people will find renewal and rejuvenation within themselves, will discover again their capacity for innovation and adaptation. If not, alas, the nation's future will be shaped by sightless forces of history over which Americans will have no control.—*John Chancellor*

When we got into office, the thing that surprised me most was to find that things were just as bad as we'd been saying they were.—*John F. Kennedy*

The moment the slave resolves that he will no longer be a slave, his fetters fall. He frees himself and shows the way to others. Freedom and slavery are mental states.—*Mohandas Gandhi*

To keep a lamp burning we have to keep putting oil in it.—*Mother Teresa*

Freedom does not always win. This is one of the bitterest lessons of history.—*A. J. P. Taylor*

It was involuntary. They sank my boat.—*John Kennedy, on how he became a war hero*

> *They said it couldn't be done,*
> *but sometimes*
> *it doesn't work out that way.*
>
> CASEY STENGEL

I love my country—I fear my government.—*Bumper sticker*

There's something contagious about demanding freedom.—*Robin Morgan*

The ultimate measure of a man is not where he stands in moments of comfort and convenience, but where he stands at times of challenge and controversy.—*Martin Luther King, Jr.*

My hates have always occupied my mind much more actively and have given greater spiritual satisfaction than my friendships.—*Westbrook Pegler.*

Character consists of what you do on the third and fourth tries.—*James A. Michener*

I do the very best I know how; the very best I can; and I mean to keep doing so until the end. If the end brings me out all right, what is said against me won't amount to anything. If the end brings me out wrong, ten angels swearing I was right would make no difference.—*Abraham Lincoln*

Character is determined by what you accomplish when the excitement is gone.—*Anonymous*

Apathy is one of America's greatest problems—but who cares?—*Anonymous*

If the claims of Individuality are ever to be asserted, the time is now, while much is still wanting to complete the enforced assimilation. It is only in the earlier stages that any stand can be successfully made against the encroachment. The demand that all other people shall resemble ourselves grows by what it feeds on. If resistance waits till life is reduced *nearly* to one uniform type, all deviations from that type will come to be considered impious, immoral, even monstrous and contrary to nature. Mankind speedily become unable to conceive diversity, when they have been for some time unaccustomed to see it.—*John Stuart Mill*, On Liberty, *1859*

There is as much chance of repealing the 18th Amendment as there is for a humming-bird to fly to the planet Mars with the Washington Monument tied to its tail.—*Morris Sheppard*

I believe in getting into hot water; it keeps you clean.—*G. K. Chesterton*

Great spirits have always encountered violent opposition from mediocre minds.—*Albert Einstein*

We are not to expect to be translated from despotism to liberty in a featherbed.—*Thomas Jefferson*

I'm a political person. It excites me to be a political person. But I want to have fun while I'm doing it.—*Madonna*

I've always been behind musically but ahead politically.—*Joan Baez*

God doesn't require us to succeed; he only requires that you try.

MOTHER TERESA

A State-By-State Look At
Consensual Crime

IT HAS ALWAYS STRUCK ME as the height of absurdity that a consensual act should be legal in one state and illegal in another. What is it about an action that, stepping over the imaginary line that divides state from state, you move from being a criminal to a noncriminal or from being illegal to legal?

Imagine a bed in a motel room. The state line divides the bed precisely in two: on one side of the bed you are in one state, on the other side of the bed you're in another. You and your consenting adult partner, lying on either side of the bed, could be committing the same activity, and one of you would be a criminal and the other would not.

If you were on the Connecticut–Rhode Island border, for example, you could be involved in an act of oral sex (either heterosexual or homosexual) and the partner on the Rhode Island side would be breaking the law while the partner on the Connecticut side would not.

On the New York–New Jersey border, if one of you happens to be married to another, you are guilty of adultery on the New York side of the bed, but not guilty of adultery (in the legal sense) on the New Jersey side.

Perhaps the most stunning example of this would be anal sex (again, either homosexual or heterosexual) if you were on the Idaho-Wyoming border. The partner on the Wyoming side of the bed would be committing no crime at all; the partner on the Idaho side of the bed would be subject to life imprisonment.

Drug use* and unconventional medical practices, thanks to the Drug Enforce-

---

*Several states make it a minor crime to use and possess small amounts of marijuana. These same states, however, do not permit marijuana to either be purchased or grown. When it comes time to

ment Agency and the Food and Drug Administration, are illegal everywhere.

Unpopular political beliefs are likely to be investigated by the Federal Bureau of Investigation, and somehow the Bureau of Alcohol, Tobacco, and Firearms has taken it upon itself to investigate unconventional religious beliefs. "Cults" are also suppressed nationally by the Internal Revenue Service (Reverend Moon was put away for tax evasion) and the Immigration and Naturalization Service (Rajneesh was deported).

Full-scale gambling is legal only in Nevada and Atlantic City. Limited forms of gambling (race tracks, card clubs, off-track betting) are usually determined at the local (not state) level, thus too ambitious for our humble chart. If your state has a state-run lottery, you'll know: lotteries tend to advertise more than Coca-Cola.

Every state has a seat belt law, thanks to federal pressure. Change for this must take place at the federal level first, then the state level. Motorcycle laws are, as of this writing, entirely state regulations (although the feds are leaning in this direction).

This leaves us with a state-by-state chart that deals mostly with sex and assisted suicide. What a combination. The "Age of Consent" column applies to sex only, not alcohol—due to federal pressure, alcohol is limited to persons twenty-one and older. Lowering that age must start at the federal level, then go to the states.

The chart is as accurate as we could make it as of September 1993. The fastest growing category, in terms of illegality, seems to be assisted suicide. This chart is provided as a starting point for political change. Before you take part in any activity within any state, please check with local authorities. End of disclaimer; let's move on to the chart. (Information provided by Thomas Coleman, Spectrum Institute, P.O. Box 65756, Los Angeles, California 90065.)

obtain marijuana, then, it's a serious crime. Because of this, and the federal laws against marijuana, I consider marijuana illegal in all fifty states.

	HETERO ORAL SEX	HETERO ANAL SEX	GAY ORAL SEX	GAY ANAL SEX	ADULTERY	PROSTITUTION	FORNICATION	COHABITATION	PORNOGRAPHY	AGE OF CONSENT	ASSISTED SUICIDE
ALABAMA	☹	☹	☹	☹	☹	☹				16	
ALASKA						☹				18	☹
ARIZONA	☹	☹	☹	☹	☹	☹		☹		18	☹
ARKANSAS			☹	☹		☹			☹	16	☹
CALIFORNIA						☹				18	☹
COLORADO					☹	☹			☹	18	☹
CONNECTICUT						☹			☹	15	☹
DELAWARE						☹				16	☹
D.C.						☹	☹			16	
FLORIDA	☹	☹	☹	☹	☹	☹		☹		18	☹
GEORGIA	☹	☹	☹	☹	☹	☹	☹		☹	16	
HAWAII						☹			☹	14	
IDAHO	☹	☹	☹	☹	☹	☹	☹	☹	☹	16	
ILLINOIS					☹	☹	☹			16	
INDIANA						☹				16	☹
IOWA						☹			☹	14	
KANSAS			☹	☹	☹	☹				16	☹
KENTUCKY						☹				16	
LOUISIANA	☹	☹	☹	☹		☹			☹	17	
MAINE						☹			☹	14	☹
MARYLAND		☹	☹	☹	☹	☹				16	

☹ = INDICATES LAWS PASSED
(or severe constipation, or both)

	HETERO ORAL SEX	HETERO ANAL SEX	GAY ORAL SEX	GAY ANAL SEX	ADULTERY	PROSTITUTION	FORNICATION	COHABITATION	PORNOGRAPHY	AGE OF CONSENT	ASSISTED SUICIDE
MASSACHUSETTS		☹		☹	☹	☹	☹			16	
MICHIGAN	☹	☹	☹	☹	☹	☹		☹	☹	16	☹
MINNESOTA	☹	☹	☹	☹	☹	☹	☹		☹	16	☹
MISSISSIPPI	☹	☹	☹	☹	☹	☹		☹		14	☹
MISSOURI			☹	☹		☹			☹	17	☹
MONTANA			☹	☹		☹			☹	16	☹
NEBRASKA					☹	☹			☹	17	☹
NEVADA						☹			☹	16	
NEW HAMPSHIRE					☹	☹				18	☹
NEW JERSEY						☹			☹	18	☹
NEW MEXICO						☹		☹		13	☹
NEW YORK					☹	☹				17	☹
NORTH CAROLINA	☹	☹	☹	☹	☹	☹		☹		16	
NORTH DAKOTA					☹	☹		☹	☹	16	☹
OHIO						☹			☹	16	
OKLAHOMA			☹	☹	☹	☹			☹	16	☹
OREGON						☹			☹	18	☹
PENNSYLVANIA						☹				16	☹
RHODE ISLAND	☹	☹	☹	☹	☹	☹			☹	16	
SOUTH CAROLINA	☹	☹	☹	☹	☹	☹	☹			16	
SOUTH DAKOTA						☹			☹	16	☹
TENNESSEE			☹	☹	☹	☹				18	☹
TEXAS						☹			☹	17	☹
UTAH	☹	☹	☹	☹	☹	☹	☹			18	
VERMONT						☹				16	
VIRGINIA	☹	☹	☹	☹	☹	☹	☹	☹	☹	15	
WASHINGTON						☹			☹	18	☹
WEST VIRGINIA					☹	☹	☹	☹	☹	16	
WISCONSIN					☹	☹			☹	18	☹
WYOMING						☹			☹	19	

AIN'T NOBODY'S BUSINESS IF YOU DO

Epilogue

> *The best way*
> *to become aquainted with a subject*
> *is to write a book about it.*
>
> BENJAMIN DISRAELI

I had no idea this book would be so long. I feel like the woman who set out to write a short story about a Southern girl named Pansy O'Hara. One Civil War and one thousand pages later, Pansy had become Scarlett and the short story had become a doorstop.* I have never written so much in my life. I honestly believe that my previous thirty-something books *combined* have fewer words than this one. I thought a simple book about a single subject which fits within a parentheses (You should be able to do with your person and property whatever you please, as long as you don't physically harm the person or property of another) within a not–very–long sentence would be a relatively short book.

I was wrong.

At each turn in this journey, I found something either (a) needed explaining, or (b) was too fascinating not to pass along. This for me was less a book and more of a *process*. Time and again, something I thought was true turned out to be false, and what I feared might be true turned out to be truer than I feared. I am, as they say, older and wiser. I have lost more of my innocence; in fact, I discovered innocence I didn't even know I had—*then* I lost it. I feel inspired and resigned, confident and terrified, optimistic and curmudgeonly.

Thank you for joining me on my journey.

---

*That book, of course, was Gone With the Wind; and, yes, Scarlett's original name was Pansy O'Hara.

Your book is dictated
by the soundest reason.
You had better get out of France
as quickly as you can.

VOLTAIRE
1758

ABOUT THE AUTHOR

PETER McWILLIAMS has been writing about his passions since 1967. In that year, he became passionate about what most seventeen-year-olds are passionate about—love—and wrote *Come Love With Me & Be My Life*. This began a series of poetry books which have sold nearly four million copies.

Along with love, of course, comes loss, so Peter became passionate about emotional survival. In 1971 he wrote *Surviving the Loss of a Love*, which was expanded in 1976 and again in 1991 (with co-authors Melba Colgrove, Ph.D., and Harold Bloomfield, M.D.) into *How to Survive the Loss of a Love*. It has sold more than two million copies.

He also became interested in meditation, and a book he wrote on meditation was a *New York Times* bestseller, knocking the impregnable *Joy of Sex* off the #1 spot. As one newspaper headline proclaimed, MEDITATION MORE POPULAR THAN SEX AT THE *NEW YORK TIMES*.

His passion for computers (or more accurately, for what computers could do) led to *The Personal Computer Book*, which *TIME* proclaimed "a beacon of simplicity, sanity and humor," and the *Wall Street Journal* called "genuinely funny." (Now, really, how many people has the *Wall Street Journal* called "genuinely funny"?)

His passion for personal growth continues in the ongoing LIFE 101 Series with co-author John-Roger. Thus far, the books in this series include *You Can't Afford the Luxury of a Negative Thought: A Book for People with Any Life-Threatening Illness—Including Life*; *LIFE 101: Everything We Wish We Had Learned About Life In School—But Didn't* (a *New York Times* bestseller in both hardcover and paperback); *DO IT! Let's Get Off Our Buts* (a #1 *New York Times* hardcover bestseller); and *WEALTH 101: Wealth Is Much More Than Money*.

His passion for visual beauty led him to publish, in 1992, his first book of photography, *PORTRAITS*, a twenty-two-year anthology of his photographic work.

All of the above-mentioned books were self-published and are still in print.

Peter McWilliams has appeared on "The Oprah Winfrey Show," "Larry King" (both radio and television), "Donahue," "Sally Jessy Raphael," and, a long time ago, on the "Regis Philbin Show" (before Regis met Kathie Lee—probably before Kathie Lee was *born*).

Personal freedom, individual expression, and the right to live one's own life, as long as one does not harm the person or property of another, have long been his passions. Now, he writes about them.

Author photograph: Christopher McMullen

Acknowledgments

I WOULD LIKE TO THANK those who read portions of this manuscript prior to publication and were kind enough to offer their comments, especially my brother Michael McWilliams, Heide Mintzer-Banks-Smith, Christopher McMullen, William F. Buckley, Jr., Lee Baumel, Rick Edelstein, and Laren Bright.

> *I stand by all the misstatements.*
>
> VICE-PRESIDENT DAN QUAYLE

I would like to thank those who contributed ideas, articles, recommended books, sent videotapes, and in other ways supplied support and essential information. These include my mother Mary McWilliams; Norma Jean Almodovar; David Anderson; Bertrand Babinet; Adam Blossom; Matthew Childs; Ted Conley; Stuart Elliott; Gene GeRue; Professor Lawrence Kaplan; Dr. Bryan McMullan; Jimmie McWilliams; John Morton; Kristin Onuf; Dr. Pei; Susan Post; Lake Puett; Diane Reverand; Dr. Richard Rockwell; Dr. I. Nelson Rose; Pauli Sanderson; Professor Edwin Schur; Peter Scott; Peter Sepp; Michael Snell; Cinder Stanton; Dr. Ed Wagner; Andrew Weil, M.D.; and Roy Tuckman of KPFK's "Something's Happening."

Thanks to the people at Prelude Press: Shawn Abrahams, Zac Cook, Chris GeRue, Lorraine Harrell, Stephanie Horsley, Perry Segal, Janet Stoakley, Carol Taylor, Simon Taylor, and Paurvi Trivedi.

The Bible research probably could not have been done (at least not completed in this century) without my trusty computer and the Bible-text programs Biblesoft (The PC Study Bible), QuickVerse, and the Bible Library.

While riding around in my car, I especially enjoyed listening to the tapes on Thomas Paine's *Common Sense* and Thomas Jefferson's Declaration of Independence, by Knowledge Products, Nashville, Tennessee.

For copy editing, I would like to thank Debbie Sidell; for much of the desktop publishing, Victoria Marine, who made thousands of picky little comments, with-

> *Without freedom,*
> *no one really has a name.*
>
> MILTON ACORDA

out which this book would be a far worse one.

For invaluable editorial comments as well as indexing, my gratitude and appreciation goes to Jean Sedillos. For research, transcription, and taking the project over when others abandoned it, my thanks to Chris GeRue (who must transcribe even this, so if she's added words such as *ever-faithful, brilliant,* or *overworked,* this would be accurate, but she added them on her own). Without the support of these two women in particular, this book could not have taken place.

Thanks to Paurvi Trivedi, who rearranged schedules with the printers six times while I discovered one invaluable bit of information after another that simply had to be in the book. Thanks as well to the printer of this book, Bertelsmann, for making the six scheduling changes.

I would like to thank my friends—particularly Christopher McMullen and Heide Mintzer-Banks-Smith—who didn't see or hear from me for long periods of time as my obsession (I like to call it "dedication") with this book grew and my personal life shrank. (Come to think of it, they never complained. Maybe they didn't notice I was not around. Hmmmm.)

Thanks to Bessie Smith, a black, drug-using, bisexual whose 1923 recording of "T'aint Nobody's Biz-ness If I Do" inspired the whole book.

And, finally, I'd like to thank Pat Robertson and Jerry ("Jer") Falwell, without whom this book not have been inevitable.

AIN'T NOBODY'S BUSINESS IF YOU DO

Bibliography

Adams, Abby, comp. *An Uncommon Scold*. New York: Simon & Schuster, 1989.

Adams, Edie, and Robert Windeler. *Sing A Pretty Song. . . : The "Offbeat" Life of Edie Adams, Including the Ernie Kovacs Years*. New York: Morrow, 1990.

Alley, Robert S., ed. *James Madison on Religious Liberty*. Buffalo: Prometheus Books, 1985.

Almodovar, Norma Jean. *Cop to Call Girl: Why I Left the LAPD to Make An Honest Living as a Beverly Hills Prostitute*. New York: Simon & Schuster, 1993.

Anderson, Patrick. *High in America: The True Story Behind NORML and the Politics of Marijuana*. New York: Viking, 1981.

Andrew, Christopher. *The First World War: Causes and Consequences*. New York: Paul Hamlyn, 1969.

Andrist, Ralph K., ed. *The American Heritage History of the 20's & 30's*. New York: American Heritage Publishing Co., 1970.

Appleby, Amy, ed. *Quentin Crisp's Book of Quotations*. New York: MacMillan, 1989.

Bailyn, Bernard. *The Ideological Origins of the American Revolution*. Enlarged Edition. Cambridge, MA: Harvard University, Belknap Press, 1992.

Barrett, Marvin. *A Dramatic View of the Twenties and Thirties*. Boston: Little, Brown and Company, 1962.

Barry, Dave. *Dave Barry's Greatest Hits*. New York: Fawcett Columbine, 1988.

_____. *Dave Barry Slept Here: A Sort of History of the United States*. New York: Fawcett Columbine, 1989.

Barth, Alan. *The Rights of Free Men: An Essential Guide to Civil Liberties*. New York: Knopf, 1984.

Bazelon, David L. *Questioning Authority: Justice and Criminal Law*. New York: Knopf, 1988.

Bergland, David. *Libertarianism In One Lesson*. Costa Mesa, CA: Orpheus Publications, 1984.

Blumenfeld, Warren J., ed. *Homophobia: How We All Pay the Price*. Boston: Beacon, 1992.

Boatner, Mark M. III. *The Encyclopedia of the American Revolution*. New York: McKay, 1966.

Booth, Father Leo. *When God Becomes a Drug: Breaking the Chains of Religious Addiction & Abuse*. Los Angeles: Tarcher, 1991.

Boswell, John. *Christianity, Social Tolerance, and Homosexuality: Gay People in Western Europe from the Beginning of the Christian Era to the Fourteenth Century*. Chicago: University of Chicago Press, 1980.

Bowen, Catherine Drinker. *The Most Dangerous Man in America: Scenes from the Life of Benjamin Franklin*. Boston: Little, Brown and Company, Atlantic Monthly Press, 1974.

Bowen, Ezra, ed. *This Fabulous Century, Sixty Years of American Life*. Volume II: 1910–1920. New York: Time-Life Books, 1969.

_____, ed. *This Fabulous Century*. Volume III: 1920-1930. New York: Time-Life Books, 1969.

Brecher, Edward M. *Licit and Illicit Drugs: The Consumers Union Report on Narcotics, Stimulants,*

Depressants, Inhalants, Hallucinogens, and Marijuana—Including Caffeine, Nicotine, and Alcohol. Boston: Little, Brown and Company, 1972.

Buckley, William F., Jr. *Right Reason.* "A Collection Selected by Richard Brookhiser." Garden City, NY: Doubleday, 1985.

Calkins, Carrol C., ed. *The Story of America.* Pleasantville, NY: The Reader's Digest Association, Inc., 1975.

Carmen, Arlene, and Howard Moody. *Working Women: The Subterranean World of Street Prostitution.* New York: Harper & Row, 1985.

Carson, Gerald. *The Social History of Bourbon: An Unhurried Account of Our Star-Spangled American Drink.* New York: Dodd, Mead, 1963.

Cerf, Christopher, and Victor Navasky. *The Experts Speak: The Definitive Compendium of Authoritative Misinformatior* New York: Pantheon Books, 1984.

Chancellor, John. *Peril and Promise: A Commentary on America.* New York: Harper & Row, 1990.

Church, F. Forrester. *God and Other Famous Liberals: Reclaiming the Politics of America.* New York: Simon & Schuster, 1991.

Coontz, Stephanie. *The Way We Never Were: American Families and the Nostalgia Trap.* New York: HarperCollins, Basic Books, 1992.

Coote, Colin, and Denzil Batchelor. *Winston S. Churchill's Maxims and Reflections.* New York: Barnes & Noble, 1992.

Cowan, Thomas. *Gay Men & Women Who Enriched the World.* New Canaan, CT: Mulvey, 1988.

Currie, Elliott. *Reckoning: Drugs, the Cities, and the American Future.* New York: Farrar, Straus and Giroux, Hill and Wang, 1993.

Davis, Burke. *George Washington and the American Revolution.* New York: Random House, 1975.

Dover, K. J. *Greek Homosexuality.* New York: Random House, Vintage, 1978.

Duster, Troy. *The Legislation of Morality: Law, Drugs, and Moral Judgement.* New York: The Free Press, 1970.

Dynes, Wayne R., ed. *Encyclopedia of Homosexuality,* Vols. 1 and 2. New York: Garland, 1990.

Earley, Pete. *The Hot House: Life Inside Leavenworth Prison.* New York: Bantam, 1992.

Earth Works Group. *50 Simple Things You Can Do To Save the Earth.* Berkeley: Earthworks Press, 1989.

Ellman, Richard. *Oscar Wilde.* New York: Knopf, 1988.

Federal Bureau of Investigation. *Uniform Crime Reports for the United States 1991.* Washington, 1992.

Feinberg, Joel. *The Moral Limits of the Criminal Law: Vol. 3, Harm to Self.* New York: Oxford, 1986.

_____. *The Moral Limits of the Criminal Law: Vol. 4, Harmless Wrongdoing.* New York: Oxford, 1988.

Ferris, Robert G., ed. *Signers of the Constitution.* Washington: U.S. Department of the Interior, 1976.

_____, ed. *Signers of the Declaration.* Washington: U.S. Department of the Interior, 1975.

Flanagan, Timothy J., and Kathleen Maguire, eds. *Bureau of Justice Statistics Sourcebook of Criminal Justice Statistics—1991.* Washington: U.S. Government Printing Office, 1992.

Foner, Eric, and John A. Garraty, eds. *The Reader's Companion to American History.* Boston: Houghton Mifflin Company, 1991.

Fromm, Erich. *Escape From Freedom.* New York: Avon Books, 1969.

Geis, Gilbert. *Not The Law's Business? An Examination of Homosexuality, Abortion, Prostitution, Narcotics and Gambling in the United States.* Rockville, MD: National Institute of Mental Health, 1972.

Gerberg, Mort. *The U.S. Constitution for Everyone.* New York: Putnam, Perigee Books, 1987.

Gilfoyle, Timothy J. *City of Eros: New York City, Prostitution, and the Commercialization of Sex, 1790—1920.* New York: Norton, 1992.

Green, Mark, ed. *Changing America: Blueprints for the New Administration.* "A Citizens Transition Project." New York: Newmarket Press, 1992.

Grinspoon, Lester. *Marihuana Reconsidered.* Cambridge: Harvard University Press, 1971.

Gross, K. Hawkeye. *Drug Smuggling: The Forbidden Book.* Boulder: Paladin Press, 1992.

Grun, Bernard. *The Timetables of History of People and Events.* New, Updated Edition. "Based on Werner Stein's *Kulturfahrplan."* New York: Simon & Schuster, 1979.

Hadden, Briton, and Henry R. Luce, eds. *TIME Capsule/1923: A History of the Year Condensed From the Pages of TIME.* New York: TIME Incorporated, 1967.

Hamowy, Ronald, ed. *Dealing With Drugs: Consequences of Government Control.* San Francisco: Pacific Research Institute for Public Policy, 1987.

Harris, Richard. *The Fear of Crime.* New York: Praeger, 1969.

Herer, Jack. *The Emperor Wears No Clothes: Hemp & The Marijuana Conspiracy.* Revised Edition. Van Nuys, CA: HEMP Publishing, 1992.

Heward, Edward Vincent. *St. Nicotine of the Peace Pipe.* London: George Routledge & Sons, 1909.

Higginbotham, Don. *The War of American Independence.* New York: MacMillan, 1971.

Hilton, Bruce. *Can Homophobia Be Cured? Wrestling with Questions That Challenge the Church.* Nashville: Abingdon Press, 1992.

Hodges, Andrew. *Alan Turing: The Enigma.* New York: Simon & Schuster, 1983.

Hoffman, Frederick J. *The Twenties: American Writing in the Postwar Decade.* Rev. Ed. New York: MacMillan, The Free Press, 1962.

Hoffman, Mark S., ed. *The World Almanac and Book of Facts 1993.* New York: Pharos Books, 1992.

Hofstadter, Richard. *The Paranoid Style and American Politics.* New York: Knopf, 1965.

Hoover, J. Edgar. *Masters of Deceit: The Story of Communism and How to Fight It.* New York: Henry Holt, 1958.

Hunter, Nan D., Sherryl E. Michaelson, and Thomas B. Stoddard. *The Rights of Lesbians and Gay Men: The Basic ACLU Guide to a Gay Person's Rights.* Carbondale, IL: Southern Illinois University Press, 1992.

Hutchens, John K., ed. *The American Twenties: A Literary Panorama.* Philadelphia: J.B. Lippincott Company, 1952.

International Association of Chiefs of Police. *Building Integrity and Reducing Drug Corruption in Police Departments.* Monograph NJC 120652, September 1989. Washington: U.S. Department of Justice, 1992.

Janus, Samuel S., and Cynthia L. Janus. *The Janus Report on Sexual Behavior.* New York: John Wiley & Sons, 1993.

Jensen, Merrill. *The Making of the American Constitution.* Malabar, FL: Robert E. Krieger, 1958. Reprint 1979.

Johnson, Otto, ed. *Information Please Almanac Atlas & Yearbook 1993.* Boston: Houghton Mifflin, 1993.

Johnson, Paul. *A History of Christianity.* New York: Atheneum, 1976.

Kaltenborn, H. V. *It Seems Like Yesterday.* New York: G.P. Putnam's Sons, 1956.

Karnow, Stanley. *Vietnam: A History.* New York: Viking, 1983.

Katz, Jonathan Ned. *Gay American History.* New York: Harper & Row, 1985.

_____. *Gay/Lesbian Almanac: A New Documentary.* New York: Harper & Row, 1983.

Kettelhack, Guy, comp. *The Wit and Wisdom of Quentin Crisp.* New York: Harper & Row, 1984.

King, Coretta Scott, ed. *The Martin Luther King, Jr., Companion: Quotations from the Speeches, Essays, and Books of Martin Luther King, Jr.* New York: St. Martin's Press, 1993.

Krassner, Paul, ed. *Best of The Realist.* Philadelphia: Running Press, 1984.

Larzelere, Bob. *The Harmony of Love.* San Francisco: Context Publications, 1982.

Leary, Timothy. *High Priest.* New York: World Publishing Company, 1968.

Lett, AlexSandra. *Natural Living: From Stress to Rest.* Raleigh, NC: ALL Communications, 1984.

Levy, Leonard W. *The Establishment Clause: Religion and the First Amendment.* New York: MacMillan, 1986.

Leyland, Winston, ed. *Gay Sunshine Interviews, Vol. 1.* San Francisco: Gay Sunshine Press, 1978.

Locke, John. *A Letter Concerning Toleration.* Edited by Charles L. Sherman. Chicago: Encyclopaedia Britannica, 1952.

Logan, Joshua. *Movie Stars, Real People, and Me.* New York: Delacorte Press, 1978.

Ludlam, Charles. *The Complete Plays of Charles Ludlam.* New York: Harper & Row, 1989.

Maggio, Rosalie, comp. *The Beacon Book of Quotations by Women.* Boston: Beacon, 1992.

Mannix, Daniel P. *The History of Torture.* New York: Dorset, 1986.

Marsh, Dave. *50 Ways to Fight Censorship and Important Facts to Know About the Censors.* New York: Thunder's Mouth Press, 1991.

McKenna, George, and Stanley Feingold, eds. *Taking Sides: Clashing Views on Controversial Political Issues,* 7th Edition. Guilford, CT: Dushkin Publishing Group, 1991.

McKenna, Terence. *Food of the Gods: The Search for the Original Tree of Knowledge: A Radical History of Plants, Drugs, and Human Evolution.* New York: Bantam, 1992.

Mitford, Jessica. *Kind and Usual Punishment: The Prison Business.* New York: Knopf, 1973.

Montgomery Ward & Co. *Catalogue and Buyer's Guide No. 57, Spring and Summer 1895.* "An unabridged reprint of the original edition with a new introduction by Boris Emmet." New York: Dover Publications, Inc., 1969.

National Narcotics Intelligence Consumers Committee. *The NNICC Report 1991: The Supply of Illicit Drugs to the United States.* Washington: Drug Enforcement Administration, 1992.

New York Public Library. *The New York Public Library Desk Reference.* "A Stonesong Press Book." New York: Webster's New World, 1989.

Noble, William. *Bookbanning In America: Who Bans Books?—And Why.* Middlebury, VT: Eriksson, 1990.

Office of National Drug Control Policy. *National Drug Control Strategy: A Nation Responds to Drug Use: Budget Summary, January 1992.* Washington: The White House, 1992.

Osborne, David, and Ted Gaebler. *Reinventing Government: How the Entrepreneurial Spirit is Transforming the Public Sector.* New York: Penguin, 1993.

Packer, Herbert L. *The Limits of the Criminal Sanction.* Stanford: Stanford University Press, 1968.

Paine, Thomas. *Common Sense.* Audiotape version. Nashville: Knowledge Products

Paxton, John, and Sheila Fairfield. *Calendar of Creative Man.* New York: Facts on File, 1979.

Petras, Ross, and Kathryn Petras. *The 776 Stupidest Things Ever Said.* New York: Doubleday, 1993.

Qualls-Corbett, Nancy. *The Sacred Prostitute: Eternal Aspect of the Feminine.* Toronto: Inner City Books, 1988.

QuickVerse for Windows Version 1.0G. Hiawatha, IA: Parsons Technology, Inc.

Radcliff, Peter, ed. *Limits of Liberty: Studies of Mill's "On Liberty."* Belmont, CA: Wadsworth Publishing Company, 1966.

Reiterman, Tim, with John Jacobs. *Raven: The Untold Story of the Rev. Jim Jones and His People.* New York: Dutton, 1982.

Robertson, Pat. *The New Millennium: 10 Trends That Will Impact You and Your Family by the Year*

2000. Dallas: Word Publishing, 1990.

Rogers, Agnes, comp. *I Remember Distinctly: A Family Album of the American People 1918-1941.* New York: Harper & Brothers, 1947.

Sann, Paul. *The Lawless Decade: A Pictorial History of a Great American Transition: From the World War I Armistice and Prohibition to Repeal and the New Deal.* New York: Crown, 1957.

Scanzoni, Letha, and Virginia Ramey Mollenkott. *Is the Homosexual My Neighbor? Another Christian View.* San Francisco: Harper San Francisco, 1978.

Schur, Edwin M. *The Americanization of Sex.* Philadelphia: Temple University Press, 1988.

_____. *Crimes Without Victims: Deviant Behavior and Public Policy.* Englewood Cliffs, NJ: Prentice-Hall, 1965.

_____, and Hugo Adam Bedau.*Victimless Crimes: Two Sides of a Controversy.* Englewood Cliffs, NJ: Prentice-Hall, 1974.

Scott, George Ryley. *Curious Customs of Sex and Marriage.* London: Torchstream Books, 1953.

Scott, Peter Dale, and Jonathan Marshall. *Cocaine Politics: Drugs, Armies, and the CIA in Central America.* Berkeley: University of California Press, 1991.

Shaw, George Bernard. *Plays by George Bernard Shaw.* New York: Penquin, Signet Classic, 1960.

Sheehy, Gail. *Hustling: Prostitution in Our Wide-Open Society.* New York: Delacorte Press, 1973.

Shenkman, Richard. *"I Love Paul Revere, Whether He Rode or Not."* New York: HarperCollins, HarperPerennial, 1992.

_____. *Legends, Lies & Cherished Myths of American History.* New York: Harper & Row, 1988.

Shepherd, Chuck, John J. Kohut, and Roland Sweet. *More News of the Weird.* New York: Penguin, Plume, 1990.

Shipley, Joseph T. *Dictionary of Word Origins.* New York: The Philosophical Library, 1945.

Silberman, Charles E. *Criminal Violence, Criminal Justice.* New York: Random, 1978.

Sloan, Irving J. *Our Violent Past: An American Chronicle.* New York: Random House, 1970.

Smith, Jane S. *Patenting the Sun: Polio and the Salk Vaccine.* New York: William Morrow, 1990.

Smith, Malcolm E. *With Love, From Dad: Why Haven't Marijuana Smokers Been Told These Facts?* Smithtown, NY: Suffolk House, n.d.

Sowle, Claude R., ed. *Police Power and Individual Freedom.* Chicago: Aldine, 1962.

Spiegelman, Art, and Bob Schneider, eds. *Whole Grains: A Book of Quotations.* New York: Douglas Links, 1973.

Spoto, Donald. *Lawrence Olivier: A Biography.* New York: HarperCollins, 1992.

Sprong, John Shelby. *Rescuing the Bible from Fundamentalism: A Bishop Rethinks the Meaning of Scripture.* San Francisco: Harper San Francisco, 1991.

Stevenson, Elizabeth. *Babbitts and Bohemians: The American 1920s.* New York: MacMillan, 1967.

Stone, Oliver, and Zachary Sklar. *JFK: The Book of the Film.* "The Documented Screenplay." New York: Applause Books, 1992.

Swezey, Stuart, and Brian King, eds. *AMOK: Fourth Dispatch.* Los Angeles: AMOK, 1991.

Sykes, Charles J. *A Nation of Victims: The Decay of the American Character.* New York: St. Martin's Press, 1992.

Szasz, Thomas. *Ceremonial Chemistry: The Ritual Persecution of Drugs, Addicts, and Pushers.* Revised edition. Holmes Beach, FL: Learning Publications, 1985.

_____. *Our Right to Drugs: The Case for a Free Market.* New York: Praeger, 1992.

Toklas, Alice B. *The Alice B. Toklas Cook Book.* New York: Harper & Row, 1954.

Trager, James. *The People's Chronology: A Year-by-Year Record of Human Events from Prehistory to the Present.* Rev. Ed. New York: Henry Holt and Co., 1992.

Trebach, Arnold S. *The Heroin Solution.* New Haven: Yale University Press, 1982.

U.S. Department of Commerce. *Historical Statistics of the United States: Colonial Times to 1970*, Part 1. Bicentennial Edition. Washington, 1975.

U.S. Department of Commerce. *Historical Statistics of the United States: Colonial Times to 1970*, Part 2. White Plains, NY: Kraus International Publications, 1989.

U.S. Department of Commerce. *Statistical Abstract of the United States 1992.* 112th Edition. Washington, 1992.

U.S. Department of Justice. *Bureau of Justice Statistics, National Corrections Reporting Program, 1988.* Washington, 1989.

U.S. Department of Justice. *Census of Local Jails, 1988.* Vol. I. Selected Findings; Methodology and Summary Tables. Washington, 1989.

U.S. Department of Justice. *Correctional Populations in the United States, 1988.* Washington, 1989.

U.S. Department of Justice. *Data Collections Available From the National Archive of Criminal Justice Data.* Update: Summer 1992. Washington: National Archive of Criminal Justice Data, 1992.

U.S. Department of Justice. *Drugs and Crime Facts, 1991.* Washington, 1992.

U.S. Department of Justice. *Drugs, Crime, and the Justice System: A National Report from the Bureau of Justice Statistics,* December 1992, NJC-133652. Washington, 1992.

U.S. Department of State. *International Narcotics Control Strategy Report, March, 1992.* Washington, 1992.

U.S. Department of the Treasury. *Protecting America: The Effectiveness of the Federal Armed Career Criminal Statute. An Assessment Conducted by the Bureau of Alcohol, Tobacco and Firearms, March, 1992.* Washington, 1992.

U.S. Sentencing Commission. *Annual Report 1991.* Washington, 1992.

Vergon, Vertner. *Abuse of Privilege: How to Deal With Lawyers.* Los Angeles: Exeter, 1986.

Vidal, Gore. *United States: Essays 1952–1992.* New York: Random House, 1993.

Wasserman, Harvey. *America Born & Reborn.* New York: MacMillan, Collier, 1983.

Watts, Alan. *The Book on the Taboo Against Knowing Who You Are.* New York: Random House, Vintage Books, 1989.

White, Larry C. *Merchants of Death: The American Tobacco Industry.* New York: William Morrow, Beech Tree Books, 1988.

Winokur, Jon, ed. *A Curmudgeon's Garden of Love.* New York: Penguin, New American Library, 1989.

_____, ed. *The Portable Curmudgeon.* New York: Penguin, New American Library, 1987.

_____, ed. The Portable Curmudgion Redux. New York: Penguin, Dutton, 1992.

_____, ed. *True Confessions.* New York: Penguin, Dutton, 1992.

Wright, John W., ed. *The Universal Almanac 1993.* Kansas City: Andrews and McMeel, 1992.

Wyly, James. *The Phallic Quest: Priapus and Masculine Inflation.* Toronto: Inner City Books, 1989.

Zahniser, J.D., comp. *And Then She Said . . .Quotations by Women for Every Occasion.* Second Ed. St. Paul, MN: Caillech Press, 1990.

_____, comp. *And Then She Said . . . More Quotations by Women for Every Occasion.* St. Paul, MN: Caillech Press, 1990.

Zall, P.M., ed. *Ben Franklin Laughing: Anecdotes from Original Sources by and about Benjamin Franklin. Berkeley: University of California* Press, 1980.

Index

A

T

U

V

W

Y

Z

I have suffered
from being misunderstood
but I would have suffered
a hell of a lot more
if I had been understood.

CLARENCE DARROW